# Protect Your Digital Privacy

*Survival Skills for the Information Age*

Glee Harrah Cady
Pat McGregor

# Protect Your Digital Privacy: Survival Skills for the Information Age

International Standard Book Number: 0-7897-2604-1

Library of Congress Catalog Card Number: 2001094302

Printed in the United States of America

First Printing: December 2001

04      03      02                    4   3   2

## Trademarks

## Warning and Disclaimer

**ASSOCIATE PUBLISHER**
Dean Miller

**ACQUISITIONS EDITOR**
Lloyd Black

**DEVELOPMENT EDITOR**
Sean Dixon
Gayle Johnson

**TECHNICAL EDITOR**
Deborah Claudio
Chuck Marson

**MANAGING EDITOR**
Thomas F. Hayes

**PROJECT EDITOR**
Karen S. Shields

**COPY EDITOR**
Candice Hightower

**INDEXER**
Mandie Frank

**PROOFREADER**
Harvey Stanbrough

**TEAM COORDINATOR**
Cindy Teeters

**INTERIOR DESIGNER**
Anne Jones

**COVER DESIGNER**
Alan Clements

**PAGE LAYOUT**
Brad Lenser
Heather Stephenson

# Contents at a Glance

# Appendixes

# Table of Contents

## 11 How to Secure Your Internet Transactions 285

## 12 What Can I Do If My Privacy Is Compromised? 323

# Dedication

This book is for my children, Kevin and Brian, because I am so proud of them and strive to be worthy of their respect as well as their love.

*-Glee*

This book is dedicated to my children, Jen and Duncan, because they think I'm cool even knowing about my clay feet, and because I care about their futures.

*-Pat*

# ACKNOWLEDGEMENTS

Brad Templeton of the EFF wrote the foreword for us, putting into words the reasons we care about this issue, and want you to be well educated about it.

Jo Beverley, award-winning writer of fabulous stories that entertain, make the heart sing, and illustrate the human condition, as well as an early user of the Internet to reach out to her audience, wrote the thoughtful introduction to our book. We are big fans of her work and are thrilled that she accepted our invitation.

The sidebars and essays in this book were created by the following wonderful people: Carl Ellison, Chuck Marson, Cindy Cohn, Declan McCullagh, Ed Vielmetti, Elton Wildermuth, Ron Plesser, Milo Cividanes, Jason Catlett, Marty Abrams, Ross Stapleton-Gray, and Timothy Casey.

Molly Ivins and Angela Gunn graciously gave us permission to reprint their articles that we thought were relevant and interesting. Bill Holbrook, creator of the online comic *Kevin and Kell* (www.herdthinners.com), gave us permission to reprint one of our favorite strips from that series.

Judi Clark, Tess Koleczek, Jerzy Rub, and John Stracke created chapter material for us, or gave us permission to use material they had already created as the basis for chapters.

You can read more about all these people and why we thought you would be interested in their opinions in Appendix D, "Our Co-Conspirators."

Any errors in fact or interpretation can be attributed to our error, not at any of our contributors.

This book would not have been possible without the folks at Que Publishing. Lloyd Black, our acquisitions editor, was very patient about elastic deadlines. Gayle Johnson, Karen Shields, and Sean Dixon shepherded us through the edit and rewrite process and gave us lots of new thoughts to chew on. Deborah Claudio was our tech editor, who reminded us of other viewpoints, and Candice Hightower dealt with our highly idiosyncratic grammatical styles. As with the others, the improvements we owe to them, and the mistakes are entirely our own.

## Glee

I hesitate to even try to list all the people who have helped me learn about personal privacy, the law, and the digital world. I have been blessed to be able to work with and around some of the very best people who try very hard to solve complex policy problems.

Some of my best friends are attorneys <grin>. These are a few of the really good ones who've helped me understand the issues.

- Ron Plesser and Jim Halpert of the Piper Marbury Rudnick and Wolfe office in Washington, D.C.
- Marc Pearl now of Shaw Pittman in Washington, D.C.
- Bob Butler, Bruce Joseph, and John Kamp of Wiley Rein & Fielding in Washington, D.C.
- Christine Varney of Hogan Hartson in Washington, D.C.
- J. Beckwith (Becky) Burr of Wilmer Cutler & Pickering, Washington, D.C.
- Stewart Baker of Steptoe & Johnson in Washington, D.C.
- Chris Kuner of Morrison & Foerster in Brussels, Belgium
- Deirdre Mulligan of the Samuelson Law, Technology and Public Policy Clinic, Boalt Hall, UC Berkeley
- Marc Jacobson of Marc Jacobson, PC, Woodbury, NY

I've been privileged to work with good people in trade associations that represented companies I work for. I want to thank them, too.

- Emily Hackett of the Internet Alliance
- Barbara Dooley and Eric H.M. Lee of the Commercial Internet eXchange Association
- Marc Uncapher of ITAA
- Lauren Hall, Mark Bohannon, and Ted Karle of SIIA

Thanks also go to

- Eric Olson, former NETCOM colleague, who went east to help out Congresswoman Anna Eshoo and the Senate Democrats and who continually helped me out with understanding how to effectively work with our legislature.
- Three special Democratic women who work in Congress for us all: Anna Eshoo, California 14th; Jane Harman, California 36th; and Zoe Lofgren, California 16th
- My fellow policy workers: Maura Colleton, Mark Stechbart, and the many others who attend all those meetings, hearings, discussions, and gab sessions as we try to make good policy.
- Jerry Berman, Paula Bruening, Ari Schwartz, Alan Davidson, and Jim Dempsey of the Center for Democracy and Technology were always there, encouraging and helpful.
- Dorothy Dunnett, admirable writer of wonderful stories that teach the importance of personal documents, contributed an electronic fan club whose worldwide members include Jo Beverley, Pamela Belle, and myself. Without her writings, our lives would be less.

Finally, I'd like to thank my super support team: Barbara Bellissimo, Gail Bronson, Blas and JoAnn Cabrera, Rich and Frances Monroe, Susan Estrada and Don McLaughlin, Joe Stockhus, and Bob Callan. They've listened, read, criticized, and laughed their way through my struggles.

## Pat

First I must thank the people at Intel who have taught me, worked with me, and nurtured me.

- The Virtual Privacy Team (Rob Gratchner, David Hoffman, Jeff Nicol, Jim Sleezer, Stuart Tyler, and their predecessors Lee Hirsch, Kelly Block, Steve Ellis, and Michael Moropoulis). They help make Intel a Great Place To Work for all its employees.

- Hong Li, Senior Information Security Architect, who is one of the most valuable assets we have, and who kept the home fires burning while her boss was distracted by this project.

- The Information Security staff worldwide, who had to figure out how to protect "stuff" after we figured out what private information we needed to protect. They are about the most dedicated, knowledgeable, and supportive folks with whom I've ever worked. *(Safe passage, Kai. May you be granted the accomplishment of your true Will.)*

- David Aucsmith, Chief Security Architect and John Richardson and Carl Ellison of the Intel Architecture Group, for all the information I needed whenever I needed it.

- The Government Relations team, in particular David Rose and Melika Carroll, who kept me straight on what was happening in legislatures around the world and had patience while I struggled to understand legal issues.

- Mel Kowardy, Cary Dougherty, Buzz Cutting, Maureen Glynn, and David Mills. Managers who have helped me be a better manager to my own staff, and who coped along with me as we learned to do this thing.

- Dave Ahluwalia, Kathy Sieber, Tim Casey, Jim Hobbs, Grant Fraser, Eddie Balthasar, and Carl Davenport for passion about doing the right things and really terrible jokes right when I needed them.

- Barbara Burgham, Nancy Erlichman, Lisa Malatesta, Pam Lankford, Debbie Miller, and all the other Admins. We know you really run the place. I couldn't do without you.

- Jane and Dave Hartley and their son Trevor, who are wonderful co-workers, have also been good friends to me and to Duncan when I needed some place to send him while I worked.

- Finally, perhaps most of all, Doug Busch and Louis Burns, who despite being vice presidents of big corporations, (or perhaps because of that), gave me my head and a safety net when I needed it. They have taught me more than I thought I'd ever need to know about pragmatism, negotiation and influence, and saw things in me I didn't see in myself (and kicked me into the deep end so I'd learn to use those things).

Also, the folks at the Electronic Frontier Foundation (`http://www.eff.org`). They accept that I might be a good guy even though I'm part of a big corporation. Most especially among these folk is John Gilmore, not the least because he is my friend and lets me trade on that shamelessly.

John Stracke, who contributed the Macintosh sections of Chapter 10, "Guarding Your Privacy When Online," has been more than patient in answering technical questions about products he's no longer responsible for or even works for the company any more.

Sydney Thornton, who seems to have been born fighting for women's rights, has saved my...dignity...more times than I care to remember in far too many ways, but especially by keeping my various computers up and running.

Clifton Brown and Glenn McGregor, my ex-husbands, have been and continue to be excellent sources of technical information, as well as great fathers.

Dr. Helen Heineman, President of Framingham State College, was the first woman I ever met who had written a book and lived to tell the tale. She refused to let me laze my way through college and threw me off the cliff into British and American literature with no mercy. I may even someday learn to call her by her first name comfortably and without visions of blue books dancing in my head.

And, last, because they are the basic foundation, my children, Jen Brown and Duncan McGregor. My biological sisters, Barbara Kuekes, Peggy Thomas, Linda Moore, and their families. Doug, Cindy, Robert, Catherine, and David who stayed family when they didn't have to. Cynthia and Crystal, who taught me more than I can ever teach them. Rusty, who carries my honor. My family of choice, Caitlin, Leigh Ann, and Elton. Family is why we do this stuff, and where we get recharged when life just seems like too much to cope with. I love you all.

# Tell Us What You Think!

As the reader of this book, *you* are our most important critic and commentator. We value your opinion and want to know what we're doing right, what we could do better, what areas you'd like to see us publish in, and any other words of wisdom you're willing to pass our way.

As an associate publisher for Que, I welcome your comments. You can fax, e-mail, or write me directly to let me know what you did or didn't like about this book—as well as what we can do to make our books stronger.

Please note that I cannot help you with technical problems related to the topic of this book, and that due to the high volume of mail I receive, I might not be able to reply to every message.

When you write, please be sure to include this book's title and author as well as your name and phone or fax number. I will carefully review your comments and share them with the author and editors who worked on the book.

Fax:      317-581-5831

E-mail:   feedback@quepublishing.com

Mail:     Dean Miller
          Que
          201 West 103rd Street
          Indianapolis, IN 46290 USA

# FOREWORD

One of the most important and misunderstood issues about the need for privacy is that the real harm of lost privacy comes in lost freedom. The truth is that a few extra pieces of junk mail may be bothersome, but it's not enough to spend a lot of effort to stop it.

The real danger comes because when we feel we are under surveillance by the government, by strangers, by our neighbours, or by faceless databases we feel less free. We censor our activities and utterances, with a fear that somehow they might come back to haunt us. Even though they may never do so.

The fringes of society need their privacy so that their own explorations, so vital to society, are not crushed by the disapproval of the small-minded. If we are watched, we don't feel free, and as such we aren't free.

*Brad Templeton*
*Electronic Frontier Foundation*
*June 2001*

## A School For Heroes

Now, what is a writer of popular fiction doing here? When I told my husband I was doing an introduction to this book he practically choked. I am not, I assure you, a technical sort of person, and in his mind I'm a gothic heroine (see below) when it comes to the Internet.

We popular fiction authors know all about danger, seduction, and deception. They're the basis of all good stories. However, we also know about courage, intelligence, and resourcefulness. They form the heroes that make good stories popular. Popular fiction is all about winning at life, even when life is perilous—especially when life is perilous——and that's what this book is about, too.

A few decades ago, gothic romances were popular. They were usually set in Victorian times in which a heroine made vulnerable by isolation and poverty would find herself in the power of a mysterious, threatening man. *Jane Eyre* is the classical origin of the gothic romance.

Such books fell out of fashion because too often the heroine was TSTL (too stupid to live). She was the one who, when she heard screams from the attic at midnight, grasped her candlestick and went up alone to investigate (usually in her flimsy nightgown).

Romance novels today usually give the heroine better survival skills, especially knowledge and awareness of her dangers. In a recent novel of mine, *The Devil's Heiress*, the heroine is, I think, a lot like a modern Internet user.

Due to a freakish circumstance, Clarissa Greystone is about to inherit a lot of wealth. She is, therefore, unprepared for this, as many of us are or have been unprepared for the riches of the Internet. However, like us, she recognizes that riches can give her the interesting, fulfilling, rewarding life she wants. The consequences are sometimes overwhelming, but she's not stupid enough to wish to be poor and helpless again. How many Internet users truly wish to do without it?

However, Clarissa also knows that her wealth thrusts her into danger, which is a step many Internet users miss. The most significant danger Clarissa faces is the men who want to capture her to own her wealth. They are fortune hunters. In Regency England a husband had total control over a wife's property unless she was protected by clever legal arrangements, and even then he would have the use of most of it. I'm sure you all know that the Internet is full of people who want to capture our wealth.

Clarissa has friends and allies, but she knows that most people are driven by self-interest, so she is wary. In time she learns, as expected, that some people are not what they seem.

As always, however, it is what you don't know and what you don't watch out for that gets you. Clarissa suspects that Major George Hawkinville is a fortune hunter and she progresses in that belief to the point where she decides that the benefits of marrying him are greater than the loss of her independence. She does not suspect—how could she?—that he is not after her hand in marriage, but wants to prove her to be a murderer and a thief so that his father can claim the money. Very often on the Internet, as did Clarissa, you think you are taking all due precautions, but in fact are still stepping into danger.

So, when it comes to the Internet, are you a male or female gothic protagonist wandering cluelessly into danger? Or are you a modern protagonist, aware, informed, and armed? And if the latter, do you realize that there are and always will be dangers that you haven't seen yet?

If romance analogies don't work for you, let's look at the second most popular form of popular fiction, mystery.

In a mystery you usually have the most heinous sin, murder, and a cast of suspects. The sleuth, with intelligence, courage, and resourcefulness must decide which are the honest people, and which are the snakes. Sometimes the sleuth must do this before the snake strikes again and often the murderer turns out to be the least likely suspect, the one who seems incapable of taking life.

You have to be your own sleuths, and you have to be especially wary of the people and sites that seem most innocuous.

In a fantasy novel, on the other hand, the evil is generally clear and the main problem is that the protagonist seems unlikely to be able to win a fight against it. Often the protagonist is an ordinary person without the background and skills necessary for the battle, such as King Arthur, the child who shocked everyone by pulling the sword Excalibur from the stone. Or Frodo, the ordinary hobbit. Or Harry Potter, the youth who didn't even know about the world of magic until summoned to Hogwarts School or that he was the foe that the evil Voldemort most feared.

So, welcome to hero training school. Here you learn the way the magical world of the Internet works, and how to recognize the dangers, even in disguise. You learn how to assess benefit and risk, how to tell heroes from villains, and what to do about them once you know. You are taught the skills, given a sword anda book of secrets. You will have, in other words, all you need to enjoy your good fortune, and your own heroically happy ending.

—*Jo Beverley*

# PART I

## SETTING THE STAGE: PRIVACY IN THE INFORMATION AGE

# 1

# PROTECTING YOUR PRIVACY IN THE 21ST CENTURY

Once upon a time, most of us perceived privacy as whether or not the neighbors could see in our blinds at night, see what prescriptions we bought at the drug store, or if Mom could hear our phone calls to our boyfriend. As we were taught about privacy most of us were concerned with simple things like closing the bathroom door or not showing off our pretty new underpants to everyone. However, with the rise of the connected world, digital privacy—and the protection of ones' personally valuable information —has become a topic of concern even for folks who still leave their doors unlocked because their small hamlets are so safe.

## How Perceptions of Privacy Have Changed Since the Rise of the Internet

Ensuring privacy has been a concern long before the Internet became a viable means of popular communication. However, now that the Internet is a communication medium used by large numbers of people throughout the world, and personal information is both circulating through and stored by computers to an unprecedented degree, digital privacy has become one of the principal concerns of the information age. Once large quantities of information started being collected and stored, our right to privacy was being threatened at places like our local grocery stores, whether we recognized that or not. Those collections were not being made by the neighbors we trust, but by faceless and nameless people somewhere else.

In neighborhood pharmacies, the source of prescription drugs for most U.S. customers, our local pharmacist was likely to be able to warn us about mixing drugs because he had records of what we had been prescribed previously. We trusted our pharmacist not to share the information inappropriately—particularly, we did not want him to discuss our prescriptions with our neighbors or our relatives. Confidentiality was something we expected and received in our transactions.

However, once it became common in the United States to have medical insurance, we began to sign forms that released information from our medical records before the doctor's bill would be paid. Once insurance companies started gathering all your medical records together, including prescription records, it became possible for a clerk at that insurance company to put together a pretty good idea of your lifestyle, income, interests, and so on.

For example, consider your local grocery store. Once scanners became popular, the grocery store could link your identity (if you paid with a check that required an accompanying card that was also scanned) to the kinds of things you bought at the store. Just think what could three or four months of recording your grocery purchases say about you and your family? An astute marketer could tell that you had a pet, or two, and what kind—dog, cat, budgie, or snake? He may also be able to discover something about your nutritional habits. Whether you liked fast food or all prepared fresh from natural ingredients? Lots of ice cream, or lots of carrots? Cigarettes, cigars, or chewing tobacco? The marketer may also be able to gather that your family included a baby, a pregnant or menopausal woman, or an incontinent adult. A survey of your purchases could tell something of your reading tastes (do you buy romance novels or fitness magazines or adult magazines?); your sexual practices (for example, how often do you replenish your supply of prophylactics?); your relationship with your family (do you buy a lot of greeting cards?); and so on.

There are lots of examples of large collections of information on individuals that have been accumulating over the past half-century. For instance, in the mid-1980's most magazines began using a subscription service based in Colorado. The owner of that database, a direct marketing organization, could now chart *all* your reading habits, your payment habits, and correlate it against your geographic and demographic data, including census data.

By themselves, these collections of information were not dangerously likely to infringe on your privacy. As long as the insurance database, the grocery store database, and the direct marketing database stayed separate, your insurance information and your lifestyle information were not connected to one another, so inferences couldn't be drawn between them. For example, your insurance company might know that you had asthma, but they likely might not know that someone in your house consumed three cartons of cigarettes a week, which could exacerbate your symptoms.

But once the ability to combine and correlate that information became available—once large databases could be searched, indexed, and connected over a network—then a new use of these large collections of data became visible. The ability to gather information from more than one source, correlate it to form a picture of you and your family, and use that information in ways you never expected became a reality. Businesses that produce products you might like could get your grocery shopping habits and ply you with offers for competing dog food, coupons for the brands you most often buy, or enticements from competing stores. Potentially, your insurance company could refuse your claim for treatment because your grocery habits showed that your symptoms existed before you were covered by their policy. The grocery store—or the food companies—could access your magazine purchasing record and put advertisements in the magazines you read, custom designed for your tastes and delivered with your mailing label on the front.

**NOTE**

Magazine publishers have been able to custom bind the magazines we read for almost 20 years. Compare your copy of the national news magazine you subscribe to with the same magazine delivered to your neighbor or your family member or friend who lives in a different geographical area of the country. If you are an older person and your neighbors are a young family, you may be surprised to see different ad pages in the two copies of the magazine. If you live in Northern California you will see different advertisements than if you live in Northern Virginia.

As the Internet grew and became the worldwide communications connection it is today, the opportunity to gather, sift, correlate, and use information from a wide variety of sources grew as well. Instead of having to buy a tape of a grocery store's records, and having to subscribe to updates every month, a food company possibly could get real-time access to the records.

**NOTE**

We don't actually know of anyone currently offering this sort of service. The privacy policies of the individual stores and Web sites at which you shop may well prohibit the sharing of this type of data with organizations that are not actually part of the company. See, for example, the privacy policy of Safeway Stores at `http://www.safeway.com/privacy_page.asp` or the privacy statement of Meijer at `http://www.meijer.com/privacy/privacy.html`.

Magazine publishers perhaps could obtain information from online retailers about your browsing and purchasing habits, and target advertising—online or offline—to your tastes or needs. Or the combined data could possibly be offered to other marketing organizations, retailers, or even governments.

Interestingly enough, journalists (whose work was published by those very same people trying to sell you things) began pointing out to us the dangers inherent in information gathering. Reporting depends on finding out information about people and organizations. Whether a story gets published usually depends upon an audience that is willing to be educated on this topic, and an efficient distribution mechanism for sharing the information. The Internet itself has provided the means to gather and distribute information about more people to more people more efficiently than anyone could have predicted.

Cries of privacy invasion and the potential for misuse of information became louder and louder as use of the Internet has penetrated into the far corners of the globe. Among the folks who have raised the cry were parents, support groups for illnesses such as AIDS or Cystic Fibrosis, associations for ethnic or lifestyle support, civil libertarians, and human rights organizations. The collection and correlation of data, once largely invisible to most people, has become a looming threat to any user of the Net. Because Internet users are becoming sensitized to privacy issues, companies who collect and correlate data may find those practices a potential pitfall for any company that does business on the Net.

# Why Do Other People Care About Your Privacy?

Privacy advocates, and their organizations, care about your privacy for many of the same reasons you do. Some of their concern is fear—for themselves and for others. If one individual's privacy can be compromised by shady or damaging information practices, chances are that other people's information is at risk as well. These advocates are also motivated by a strong sense of responsibility toward others. They understand that many people won't even know that damage is being done to them before it's too late.

One could argue (and many will) that concerns for others can be intrusive, arrogant, and just plain meddling. Others point out that, as individuals, we can't effectively monitor everything that can happen in our world. Just as we need newsgathering and reporting organizations to keep us up to date about the events in our world, we need organizations whose staffs analyze those events and say how those events might affect each of us. We understand, for example, how a sports analyst tries to assess the skills and abilities of a basketball team's members individually and collectively and compares them to those of an opposing team to help estimate which team might win a game.

In a similar way, advocates analyze and help us understand possible risks and benefits to ourselves and to others—risks and benefits that we wouldn't necessarily see on our own. Just as the sports analyst can forecast a picture of how two teams interact, advocacy groups build a picture from a pattern of practices and can see the potential danger to individual liberties. Advocates are especially sensitized to particular issues because of their experience and training. For example, the groups that specialize in protecting children online have been trained in how children interact with online personalities. They may collect information from teenagers on whether they meet people they interact with online down at the local mall. They are especially sensitive to practices that are particularly attractive or dangerous to children. Because they know the data on both the threats and the way to protect children, they can help you see potential problems. This enables you to take informed action to protect yourself and your loved ones from unanticipated consequences.

# Why Are People Collecting This Information Anyway?

The answer to this question is very simple: Without a delivery address, the merchant can't ship you his merchandise; without some payment information, the merchant can't be paid for the merchandise; and without your account number and password, your bank won't authorize the display of information about your account.

Let's imagine that there is a merchant who maintains and operates an online store that provides information about fishing and sells fishing equipment. This merchant also provides a paper catalog of merchandise distributed to people who are interested in fishing equipment.

Our imaginary merchant is one that reads books and articles about how to produce attractive and useful Web sites and tries to implement the ideas that seem appropriate. So, having read about how people like (and return to) sites that provide items of specific interest, that are interactive, and make information easy to obtain, our merchant adds a personalized component to the Web site called "My Fishing Trip." Each visitor to the site can create a calendar and a trip itinerary; make a list of camping and fishing gear that would be appropriate to this trip; order the gear and have it shipped to home, office, or hotel near a trailhead; extend invitations to friends to join the expedition; and even get a new credit card to pay for it all.

This sounds great, doesn't it? You are offered a convenient, one-stop way to plan a trip. But think about all the information you need to provide to get this convenient service:

- A user name to store information separate from other user's information.
- Some sort of password to improve the likelihood that the person accessing this information is, in fact, the person who stored it.
- The dates and locations where the people involved will be—noting that they will be away from their homes and places of work.
- The product names and identification numbers of items that the user would like to or has purchased. (By inference, the items the user already possesses—boat, shotgun, camping stove?)
- Some sort of payment method: debit card, credit card, and so on, with account numbers and amounts authorized by the payment institution.

- A shipping address for the gear.
- Mailing addresses and possibly names of other people that might be going on this trip.
- And, for the credit card application, sufficient financial information for the credit granting institution to make a decision on granting credit.

Each piece of information that comes from the user is needed by the merchant in order to provide a desired service for the user. And each piece of information could possibly be misused.

It's all about trust, isn't it? As a user, you must choose which merchants and information providers to trust with your personal information. As a merchant, you must prove yourself worthy of that trust. Both parties should be able to make a deliberate choice.

# Profiling

*Profiling* can be a deceptively innocent word. To some, it means nothing more than someone gathering enough data about you to draw a picture. For example, when you give your medical history at the hospital, the doctor is building a profile that helps her figure out your problem. Your child's teacher gives a series of tests at the beginning of the year to build a profile that helps him know what reading group best fits your child. However, for some people—who have lived under a repressive government— the word *profiling* is very frightening.

To those people, this powerful word conjures up images of secret police or private investigators covertly following them around, making secret lists of where they go and who they see, and filing that information where those who we don't know can access it. For example, the German government used the census figures from the 1930's and 40's to develop profiles that helped them find folks who might be Jewish. Stalin's government kept profiles of "criminals against the state." Because of this history, there very few common uses of the word don't make us feel ambivalent about the practice. One use that most of you can approve of is how the FBI uses profiling to help catch dangerous criminals. That's how Clarice Starling catches the killer in *The Silence of the Lambs*. That's how they found the Son of Sam. You like the good guys to catch the bad guys. But profiling doesn't always ensure the person who fits the profile is a bad guy.

In 1999, the FAA approved the official use of "profiles" to help security staff at airports locate people who might be hijackers or drug smugglers. That sounds Okay, unless you happen to fit some or most of the characteristics in these profiles. Pat is one of those people who do; almost every flight she makes, she gets stopped and her carry-on luggage is checked for drugs or guns or some other contraband. Doesn't matter if she's wearing a business suit or blue jeans and a T-shirt, traveling with her kids or a boyfriend or alone. And because those profiles are classified, she can't find out what it is about her that trips the security guards' awareness. Pat doesn't have a drug record, an arrest record, or even a lot of unpaid parking tickets. What she does know is that security guards make the assumption that she could be dangerous in advance of any evidence to support it.

**NOTE**    You can use assumptions about those profiles to your advantage. If you, for example, come through an international airport when entering the United States, the entire customs and immigration processes are likely to take much less time if you are wearing formal business attire. Pat's experience notwithstanding.

You may have read in the past year or so about local police departments being charged with of giving more traffic tickets to black people than white people. These police departments have been accused of a discriminatory practice called "racial profiling." If the police are using profiling, they have a set of criteria they use to stop violators. If the charges are true, then those criteria target individuals solely on the basis of color or ethnicity. This is where the stories of "driving while black" come from. People from black communities sometimes feel that they were stopped simply because they were black and driving in a largely white neighborhood, rather than for a real infraction. Some believe they are stopped for driving a nice car in a largely white neighborhood. This is similar to "redlining," a practice where banks refused mortgages to individuals in neighborhoods largely populated by members of one ethnic group or another.

Because of these malign uses, profiling is a practice that many advocacy groups warn against. They fear that the information gathered about you without your knowledge enables assumptions to be made about you that might not be true. For example, the assumption that Pat could be a hijacker. That's why the use of profiling on the Web rings alarm bells.

At its simplest, a Web site can build a profile of pages you have seen and combine it with the profiles of other users so that patterns of many users can be reviewed to find out which pages users like and which they don't. That's sort of okay; you like good content and the Web sites want you to come back and stay interested. However, what if that information isn't just used by that site? Special sites that support advertising networks keep track of what ads you have seen and where you have seen them. They try to keep you from seeing the same ads over and over again. This way they can report to the people buying the ads about the effectiveness of those ads. This tracking is more frightening: You don't particularly mind that a particular site can track what you do, but you aren't that comfortable with people knowing about all the places you might go on the net.

## The Fear of Profiling

Consumers, advocates, and businesses are concerned about the potential for abuse when personal information is collected from unwilling or unwitting sources. Consumers and advocates worry that, in the wrong hands, personal information can be used against the individual. Businesses are more and more aware of the costs of not protecting consumer privacy.

Complicating the issue for all concerned is the fact that definitions of privacy are individual. They depend on factors such as gender, culture, nationality, age, and personal comfort with technology.

## Profiling and Personal Preferences

Despite the worry, profiling in the form of personalization can provide highly desirable benefits for consumers. Here are the personal profiles of Glee's college-age son and herself, who shared a house and computer during the summer of 2000.

### Mother

*Northern California resident, parent of two children, and widow of cancer patient. I own a home. I'm an employee and a technologist. I'm a fan of the Oakland Raiders, San Francisco Giants, and Stanford Cardinal baseball. A UC Berkeley alumna, I read Dorothy Dunnett, science fiction, and mysteries. My preferences run to single-malt scotch and good red wine, and Mozart over Metallica. I am a frequent flyer, drive an SUV, shop at Safeway, and buy goods from Coldwater Creek and Amazon.com.*

### Son

*Likes Gangsta rap, gambling in Las Vegas, beer, and World Championship
Wrestling. A student at UNLV, he reads James Patterson, Robert Jordan, and
Stephen King. He drives a 1972 Oldsmobile Cutlass Supreme with a trunk
full of stereo speakers, and shops at Vons, sporting goods stores, and car-
accessory stores.*

Both of us receive mail at our home and the catalogs that come addressed
to him are different than the ones addressed to me. I don't buy auto parts
and he doesn't buy dishes. We both buy flowers and books. Online, we
face the same issue.

Without personalization, mother and son are faced with more information
than they each want or can use. We must sort the mail.

Sorting the information we do want from the information we don't want
can be nice. I really don't want any more information about hip-hop artists.
I don't like hip-hop. I am a fuddy-duddy that way. My son doesn't mind
some science fiction; after all, he does read the Jordan fantasy series,
but he is not fond of historical novels. He'd rather read history. I'd rather
read about people. The personalization provided by Amazon.com, for
example, serves us well. I get recommendations for things I am more
likely to be interested in. He gets his own recommendations.

Online profiling as personalization separates the preferences for my son
and myself so that neither has to see items the other finds interesting and
we find boring or repulsive. At the same time, the information collected
through profiling can move into more potentially revealing territory, such
as health history. Such realms that could cost an Internet user a job or
the ability to buy an insurance policy.

In the Amazon.com instance, our preferences are noted based on our
behavior after we sign in. Librarians and booksellers have long protected
the lists of people's reading habits from third parties, particularly representatives of governments who might have used the information in ways
that are injurious. We, based on our experience and knowledge, trust
that this information will not be released to our detriment.

When we see banner advertisements, it's not necessary for us to sign in
to be profiled. The advertisements we are shown can be based on past
sites we have visited or which ads we have seen most recently. This is

not as comfortable a case for us. We generally don't even pay attention to the possibility that our meanderings through the Web can be traced, measured, and ultimately become valuable information to someone. Reputable online advertising networks give Internet users notice and perhaps control of the collection of information about them. As Internet users, we need to find a way to allow personalization when we want it, and to block the transfer of personal information when we don't trust it. We need to feel assured that our personal information is under our own control.

# We Need Healthy Skepticism and Informed Consent

As you can see from the examples above, the chance of your personal information being gathered and used by people you don't even know is high. Frequently, the choice of how that information is used is not under your control. The *misuse* of that information, or the use of it in ways that you do not believe benefits you, is more possible than ever before. And as more of our businesses go digital (whether they are connected to the Internet or not), the amount of information available to be harvested about you and your family increases every day.

We believe that personal information is very powerful. It can be used in ways that are very helpful to you or in ways that can injure you. But the choice of whom may gather information about you and the control of how that information is used should be yours. (Do you complete and return postal questionnaires about your personal preferences? Do you stop in the street and answer canvassers' questions? Do you want to do the same on the Internet?) As you see in this book, you have the right to make that choice. Certain information practices take that choice away from you, so you must learn to have a healthy skepticism when you are asked to fill out forms, for example. Likewise, you need to ask how the information you give at, say, a home show is used. Once information about you is in someone else's possession and control, you cannot easily recover it.

Because many of our habits were developed in an era where we mostly dealt with people we knew, learning to question the use of information is not a habit we've actively developed. We are used to trusting those we deal with. But in today's increasingly connected world, more and more we are dealing with strangers and those with whom those strangers do business.

If we want to protect the way our personally identifiable information is used, we need to develop a sense of caution about the information practices of the organizations we deal with. This is analogous to the practice of informed consent that has become commonplace in dealing with medical practices. We need to ask why information is requested, and what will be done with it. And if we don't like the answers, we can weigh the consequences of not giving the information. Ask yourself if the benefit is worth the risk?

Today, choice must be active. People who wish to choose to whom they will give information need information about tools, practices, and laws that will help them protect themselves. This book tries to lay out how information about you and your activities can be gathered, so that you can protect your right to privacy.

There's a saying that has been circulating on the Internet for the last decade, and it is as true today as it was the first time we heard it in 1989:

> *That's how freedom will end: not with a bang, but with a rustle of file folders.*
> *If you love any of your rights, defend all of them!*

> **Joe Chew, on the Net**

# WHAT *IS* PRIVACY IN A DIGITAL WORLD?

Before discussing how to protect your privacy, we need to agree on what privacy means. Let's look at several commonly accepted definitions and see what they say about privacy in this digital, wired world.

## The Right to Be Left Alone...

*"[Privacy is] the right to be left alone—the most comprehensive of rights, and the right most valued by a free people."*

**Justice Louis Brandeis,
Olmstead v. United States (1928)**

Justice Brandeis' definition has for many years been the classic definition. It is one many of us can relate to. Especially when we receive unwanted commercial e-mail, or coupons for a product related to a medical condition that we only shared with our pharmacist. It is the basis for the general understanding of privacy in modern life. Most people, when asked to define privacy, give an answer much like Brandeis'. This is a definition that includes more than just freedom, however. It describes the right to benefit from life and the fruits of one's life, without interference from others. Justice Brandeis outlined this basic right as

> *"...the right to enjoy life—the right to be let alone; the right to liberty [that] secures the exercise of extensive civil privileges; [where] the term 'property' has grown to comprise every form of possession—intangible, as well as tangible."*

> **Harvard Law Review, December 1890**

In today's interconnected world, where we have phones, cable TV, Internet service, newspapers, magazines, and regular mail delivery, being left alone is probably different than Justice Brandeis considered it in 1928. Unless your household goes off the grid, abandoning electric, telephone, water, and other public utilities, cancels all subscriptions to publications, buys only with cash, and sends only paper mail, there will be interactions with the outside world. Brandeis' definition doesn't expect that, however. It means that people have the right to limit interactions with others, and to limit the nuisance or even the affect that other people and institutions have on our lives.

In the same *Harvard Law Review* article, Justice Brandeis and Samuel Warren wrote of how these precious intangibles of life have come to be protected by law.

> *"This development of the law was inevitable. The intense intellectual and emotional life, and the heightening of sensations, which came with the advance of civilization, made it clear to men that only a part of the pain, pleasure, and profit of life lay in physical things. Thoughts, emotions, and sensations demanded legal recognition, and the beautiful capacity for growth which characterizes the common law enabled the judges to afford the requisite protection, without the interposition of the legislature."*

> **Samuel D. Warren, Louis D. Brandeis, HLR, Vol. IV, December 15, 1890, No. 5**

Just as at the turn of the century, we see now a change in how the law recognizes and enforces the right to privacy. With the expanded possibility for interference that the Internet and our connected world gives us, we need to expand the protections currently offered by legal precedence and make sure that we are able to exist free from interference from others.

# Information About Us Is Not Acquired by Others

*"...privacy is the condition which obtains to the degree that new information about one's self is not acquired by others."*

**Shaun MacNeill, The Dalhousie Review, V. 78 No. 3, "A Philosophical Definition of Privacy"**

Everywhere we turn these days, there is a form to be filled out. If we want a discount card at the grocery store, register our children in sports, buy a CD from a small record company, or get a new kitchen appliance, we also end up disclosing more information about ourselves by filling out the "required" forms.

What many people don't know is that they don't have to give all this information out unless they see a benefit from it. Privacy advocates are working to make those sort of warnings happen right up front. Whether online or on a paper form advocates want to make people aware of their choices.

MacNeill describes in his article the slippery slope he sees us on with regard to privacy rights. He believes if consumers are not educated about the choices they have, they will not make intelligent choices. And this problem extends into the work-a-day world. Employers now have tools that allow them to monitor keystrokes while their employees work, or scan and filter their e-mail. While appropriate use policies at most companies allow these practices, many experts believe this is a symptom of the erosion of trust in employees, and a decrease in the right to privacy which even employees have. MacNeill describes it this way:

*"...these social and technological threats present a formidable challenge to the preservation of privacy, a challenge which must be engaged now before privacy erodes intolerably." (ibid.)*

# The Protection Given to Information

*Privacy: 1. In a communications system or network, the protection given to information to conceal it from persons having access to the system or network. 2. In a communications system, protection given to unclassified information, such as radio transmissions of law enforcement personnel, that requires safeguarding from unauthorized persons. 3. In a communications system, the protection given to prevent unauthorized disclosure of the information in the system. (188) Note 1: The required protection may be accomplished by various means, such as by communications security meas-ures and by directives to operating personnel. Note 2: The limited protection given certain voice and data transmissions by commercial crypto-equipment is sufficient to deter a casual listener, but cannot withstand a competent crypt-analytic attack.*

**National Telecommunications and Information Administration (NTIA), a part of the U.S. Department of Commerce (DOC),** `http://www.its.bldrdoc.gov/fs-1037/ dir-028/_4148.htm`

Many people understand privacy only in relation to the protection their information has, or which they assume it has. They think of privacy of information much as they believe that a locked door or closed drapes protect their privacy at home. This is a misconception. As more and more information is gathered together, and analysis made of an individual's behavior, lifestyle, or other traits as a result of that data, the right to pri-vacy is eroded. We have relied on security technology to protect our rights. However, policy, laws, and ethical standards protect the individ-ual's right to privacy while security technology can only protect the infor-mation itself, and be an enabler to protect your right to chose when to disclose it.

The regulatory climate is different for citizens in countries around the world and so is the right to privacy. This has always been true, but the Internet has made that even more apparent. Citizens in the European Union have more privacy rights defined in law than we do in the United States, while some nations have even fewer protections. And since a con-sumer of information is not always located in the same country as the provider of information, it is hard to sort out what laws or regulations apply to the use of that information. Legislators and courts around the world are struggling to determine whose laws prevail when. The Europeans, for example, have decreed that no matter where their citi-zen's information is collected and used, physically, the laws in the EU apply. This means, for example, that North American countries that have customers in Germany must protect the rights of that individual as if they were doing business in Germany.

Europeans are more sensitized to the collection of personal data than Americans for many reasons. They have had more experience with the harm that can be done to private citizens by the secret collection of information. For that reason the European Union has taken steps to stop more damage before it can get even more uncontrolled, and have mandated data protection laws. The tension, of course, is between the government mandating what behavior private companies must take, and those companies acting responsibly to regulate themselves. (As individuals, Pat and Glee admire that the government has recognized the potential danger; we fear the chilling effect that too much government regulation can have on private industry.)

# The Ability to Protect Ourselves from Being Judged Out of Context

*"...the ability to protect ourselves from being judged out of context by controlling the conditions under which we reveal personal information to others...protection of privacy from eyes of state authority is only one aspect, and maybe not the most important."*

**Jeffrey Rosen, E-mail, Internet and Privacy [presentation].** `http://www1.union.edu/~condryi/ctech/ppt/` `L25-E-mail/sld001.htm`

Many people have described the problem of privacy protection by comparing our current situation to the book *1984* by George Orwell. In that novel, even ordinary citizens are always under surveillance. Nothing they do is secret from the government. Rosen, in the passage quoted earlier, describes a situation that he fears is already reality—that our privacy is already so compromised that we cannot recapture it.

Carl Kaplan, in his article "Kafkaesque? Big Brother? Finding the Right Literary Metaphor for Net Privacy," published in the 2 Feb 2001 *Cyber Law Journal*, believes that the danger is not just the observation and collection of our lives and information. He believes that it is the assumptions that can be made about us that are the danger, especially when those assumptions are made by governments, or, perhaps, insurance companies or large corporations. He compares the danger to the book *The Trial* by Franz Kafka.

In the novel, the main character is awakened one morning by government officials who announce that he is under arrest. However, they don't take him to jail, or otherwise imprison him. He doesn't find out what he is charged with or to whom he must answer. At the end of the book, having discovered that there is, in fact, a Court that has gathered evidence, judged him, and convicted him, he is taken out and executed. During the whole proceeding, he has no information on what is known about him nor anyone to appeal his sentence to.

Kaplan says that the real danger is this judgement that bears no resemblance to any other process we are subject to.

> *"Understanding the problem as surveillance fails to account for the majority of our activities in the world and web," he wrote. "A large portion of our personal information involves facts that we are not embarrassed about: our financial information, race, marital status, hobbies, occupation and the like. Most people surf the web without wandering into its dark corners. The vast majority of information collected about us concerns relatively innocuous details. The surveillance model does not explain why the recording of this non-taboo information poses a problem.*

> *...The hallmarks of The Trial are impotence, anger and anxiety—a character's sense that an unseen bureaucracy has information about him and that he has no control over the use of that information. That's pretty close to the average person's nagging sense of loss of privacy at the hands of some computerized databases."*

## The Right Not to Be Surprised

> *"The right to privacy is the right not to be surprised."*

> **Seth Goldin, The Executive Forum, Washington, DC,**
> **January 2001**

Goldin takes the tack that we don't have a problem with privacy, but that we have a problem with information overload. He says people should use market forces and their power as consumers to correct the problem of losing control of one's data. That power will help consumers avoid unexpected results from information you didn't even know was coming. For example, if a gay person was not "out" in his or her public life, but began receiving information from manufacturers of HIV-preventing medicines, it could be a very unpleasant surprise. Goldin suggests that we give our brand loyalty to companies that don't assault your sense of confidentiality, and let that lesson be visible to their competitors.

Martin Abrams is an anthropologist as well as a thinker about privacy and database issues. He has long worked in the field, frequently representing the point of view of the owners and builders of databases. He speaks on privacy issues and if you are attending a conference where he is speaking, we highly recommend going to hear him. Marty has contributed the following for us to ponder.

## PRIVACY'S THREE BASIC CONSTITUENT PARTS

April 15, 2001—Managing information in a data rich world is a complex endeavor, but our lack of precision in how we talk about privacy makes it even more complex. To most Americans, privacy is the collection of fears related to the use of information and includes identity theft, telemarketing calls during dinner, credit decisions we don't like, and frustration when the shirt we ordered doesn't fit. The fact is privacy is important and becomes even more so as technology allows us to collect additional information, communicate it more quickly, and enhance productivity from its use. But managing privacy requires us to do so in a manner that allows us to deal with the actual interests at play individually, rather than as a whole.

### The Three Privacy Components

Structurally one can break privacy into three components. The first is security—the individual's interest in information being ranked based on its sensitivity, access to information being properly limited, and files being protected from inappropriate changes.

Protection against harmful use is the second data subject interest. Harmful use includes situations like using inaccurate data for decision-making where the outcome might harm the data subject.

The third and by far the most difficult component to manage is autonomy assuring that the data flows pertaining to an individual are not solely being used to judge him or her, but instead are acting as part of the defining framework. My ability to walk into a meeting and define myself by use of language, the clothing I wear, and how I carry myself, instead of being characterized by the biography generated through an Internet search, is an example of autonomy. Further illustrations might be helpful is seeing the differences between security, harmful use and autonomy.

### Security

Identity theft is an issue which concerns American consumers. Identity theft is the process by which individuals pass themselves off as other people, and leave behind a data trail that cripples the victim with a negative credit history. The bad guys gain *access* (a security violation) to enough information about their prey to convince others that they are the victim. They then change the victim's file (another security violation) either explicitly by giving credit grantors new addresses or other identifying information, or implicitly by not paying the new debts accumulated under the victim's good name. These changes effect the *integrity* of the file.

As you can see, identity theft is a classic security breach. The bad guy has stolen information, used it to cause harm, and then corrupted the integrity of the data files. The access breach takes place in many different places and media. The perpetrators rummage through garbage, steal mail out of mailboxes, and even to a limited extent hack into data files. If one confronts identity theft as either an autonomy or harmful use issue, one might be tempted to restrict data flows, which it turn takes much of the immediacy out of retail markets.

Confronting identity theft in this manner would be like stopping drunk driving by equipping all cars with a sensor that prevents them from exceeding 25 mph.

The better solution would be operational improvements and user education that would reduce access breaches on the front end, and consumer friendly processes to restore integrity to the file on the back end. That is exactly the approach the credit reporting and lending industries are taking to address identity theft.

### Harmful Use

Many privacy advocates raise questions about "frequent shopper cards" at grocery stores because of the concern that information about your food purchases will be sold by the store, or some intermediary, to an insurance company, which might either deny you coverage or raise your rates because you eat too much red meat. This would absolutely be a harmful use of information collected to make marketing processes work more effectively.

The quantifiable harm is the denial of insurance, while the data issue is that information about our grocery purchases is being collected and used for a purpose not anticipated by the consumer. In this case, there is both a defined harm and a direct relationship with a data use not connected to the collection purpose or disclosed to the consumer.

It was just this scenario with similar facts that led to the granddaddy of privacy laws, the Fair Credit Reporting Act. In fact, the Fair Credit Reporting Act probably covers this set of facts, since the act covers insurance underwriting. The point is where a harmful use can be defined, we can craft specific rules to cover the it.

In Australia, policy makers went in a different direction. They restricted the types of data that could be collected from credit grantors and used in decision-making, and the societal cost is fewer creditworthy citizens get credit. In fact, if the

Australian rules were applied to the United States, 19 percent of creditworthy consumers would not get it.

### Autonomy

Not all things that happen when information is collected and used is harmful in the sense that we can measure the affect. There is a definitive relationship between information flows in the direct marketing industry and the mail that I receive at my house. Some of the mail is interesting and brings me opportunities with value, others are a complete waste of my time; however, none of those advertisements is harmful to me. My wallet isn't less full and my body bears no bruises. Data flows do not inconvenience or embarrass me; although I might want to reinvent myself and the data flows could make that more difficult. Nonetheless, this is not the type of harm that has been recognized by our legal system.

What we have is a matter of autonomy. We all have an interest in preserving a space where we may define ourselves. That is increasingly difficult in a world where another party has the ability to do an immediate search and define us based on our data flows.

The policy debate often confuses these three concepts. Advocates desire greater autonomy, and employ hypothetical harmful uses to justify restrictions on data collection. Rather than proposing a solution to the hypothetical that fits the situation, they propose solutions that take data out of play.

Autonomy is a real issue. Civilized societies give all individuals a place where they can be a stranger. Increasingly that has become difficult because of the ease in collecting and using data. But rather than letting myths define policy, let's address autonomy with honesty. Let's have a national (or global) debate where we define how much space will be protected by law.

---

*Marty Abrams, Executive Director, Center for Information Policy Leadership at Hunton & Williams,*
`mabrams@hunton.com`

# Finally, It Comes Down to Control

*"...individuals, groups, or institutions have the right to control, edit, manage, and delete information about themselves and decide when, how, and to extent that information is communicated to others."*

**Dr. Alan Westin, Privacy & Freedom**

Dr. Westin's definition of privacy is the one that many online businesses, privacy advocacy groups, and governments have used when deciding on fair information practices. Westin takes Brandeis' description and applies it to the life of the average person who interacts with business or online sites, by describing exactly what management of one's own information means. In the next section of this chapter, "Fair Information Practices Protect Your Rights," those fair information practices are described.

In the March 2001 *Atlantic Monthly* Toby Lester says that loss of control is why privacy has become so important to a majority of consumers in the past few years.

> *"What is unsettling to a lot of people is the idea that personal data—in this case, one's very life signs—might be converted into information that could be exchanged, bought, or sold for secondary use without one's knowledge or consent."*

# Fair Information Practices Protect Your Rights

Combining all these nuances together and attempting to form a legal and regulatory framework around the right to privacy is not easy. However, the legal experts and the privacy advocates have been able to work out the definition of fair information practices. These are the ways in which information is gathered and handled so that you have the chance to say what happens to data about you.

Law in some countries, such as in Europe and Canada defines fair information practices. Canada's new Federal law, for example, gives consumers explicit rights in choice, access, and challenges to inaccurate information, although the law is applied differently in the various provinces. In other countries, like in the United States, fair information practices generally are defined by administrative regulation, and companies comply with them voluntarily. The United States Federal Trade commission is the regulatory body that defines fair information practices in the commercial setting. The FTC, however, has no power over Securities regulation or health practices. (In the case of children's information, actual law regulates fair practices.)

Generally, a fair information practice policy has five components to: a definition of personally identifiable information, and then notice, choice, access, and security in how that information is handled. The number varies from instance to instance, but those form the basis for the principles. In Europe, there is a fifth component. The European Data Protection directives mandate that companies must practice *minimalization* of data collected. That is, they must collect only the information needed to perform the task and *no more*.

## Personally Identifiable Information

Personally Identifiable Information, or PII, is any data that can be linked to a single individual. Sometimes it is defined as data that could help someone identify or locate an individual. Some examples of PII are

- Your name
- Your street address
- Your ZIP+Four code in the United States
- Your social security number or government issued identification number
- Your fingerprint
- Your retinal scan, iris print, or voiceprint
- Your phone number
- Your credit card number
- Your medical records
- A photograph of you
- Your driver license number
- Your passport number

and so on.

Demographic data is data which can be collected about you but which would not help the person collecting the data to find you. Demographic data is information such as

- Your age
- Your gender
- Your racial self-description
- Your eye color

- Your marital status
- Your employment status
- Your occupation
- Your job function
- What kind of company you work in
- Whether you have children, how many, and their ages
- Whether you have pets and their type
- What kind of car, bicycle, or truck you own
- Your favorite color
- The town you live in (and or your ZIP code, as long as you don't include the +4 extension)
- Your yearly income
- What kind of books or magazines you read
- What kind of activities you enjoy

Demographic data gets tricky under two conditions. The first is when that data is linked to a unique identifier, such as the examples of PII above. In that case, where the demographic profile is linked to you, the possibility exists to infer or discover other information or characteristics about you. As we discussed earlier, implications made about you based on demographic data gathered about you can either help you or be harmful to you. The second instance is where the collection of demographic data, taken as a whole, is enough to uniquely identify you. For example, knowing that Pat is white, 45, a divorced mother of two, a computer specialist, owns a Honda, reads science fiction, and who has six cats is probably not enough to identify her uniquely in, say, San Francisco. But in a small town of four or five hundred people, that profile would probably enable many people to identify her, just from that description.

Now that we've defined PII, we must describe the practices used to handle that information.

## Notice

First, anyone who wants to collect your information must tell you what they want to collect, how they want to use it, how long they will keep it, with whom they will share it, and any other uses they intend for the information. They must also notify you if they want to make a change in how the information is used. This is a "notice" in the legal sense.

If they are collecting the information for use by someone else, or will give it to other people, they have to tell you. This is called a *third party transfer*, and companies that are treating your information appropriately don't transfer your information without informing you first and getting your permission.

Figures 2.1 through 2.4 are from several different Web sites, showing how they handle notice.

The Amazon.com privacy notice, shown in Figure 2.1, tells you about the information it gathers.

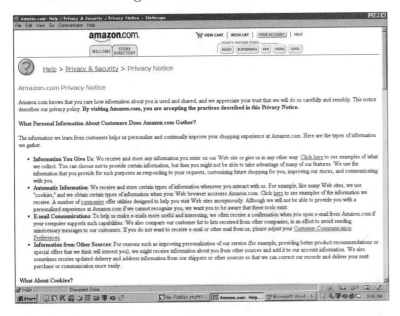

**FIGURE 2.1**

*The Amazon.com privacy notice.*

Bank of America's privacy notice, shown in Figure 2.2, discusses marketing practices.

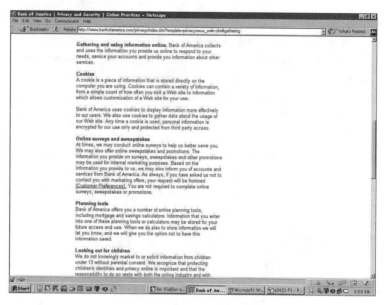

**FIGURE 2.2**

*Bank of America's privacy notice.*

Nerve, a site for adults only, describes their privacy practices in their Terms of Service, as shown in Figure 2.3.

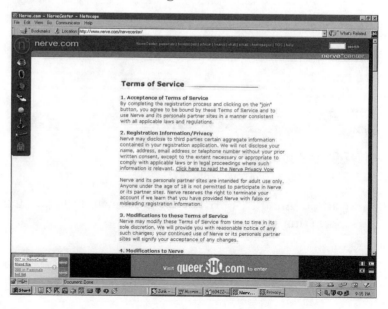

**FIGURE 2.3**

*The Nerve site.*

Nerve also has a "privacy vow" that describes their information practices in more detail, as shown in Figure 2.4.

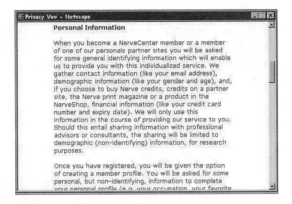

**FIGURE 2.4**

*Nerve's "privacy vow."*

# Choice

Next, you must be given the choice of whether you want this information to be collected or not. In some cases, what kind of relationship you have with the information collector, be it a Web site, grocery store, or employer, is dictated by what you will allow them to collect and how you allow them to use the info.

For example, on many Web stores, you can't buy anything unless you have a registered account with the vendor. On others, you can just give them your billing and shipping information, and not establish any kind of long-term relationship with the store. There are benefits to having a relationship with a store you shop at often, as long as you trust the way they protect your information and that they are not going to lie to you about how they use what they collect.

See Part III, "Taking Control: Privacy Survival Skills," for more informa-tion for information on how to decide whether to trust a company.

Some privacy advocates and lawyers feel that sometimes you really have no choice about giving up personal information. For example, if you are required to give medical info before you can get insurance coverage, do you really have a choice? If you can't pay with cash, but must pay with a credit card or a check, are you really anonymous? If you are forced to use a government-issued ID to receive discounts, were you really free to make the choice? The jury is still out on this issue, but some regulations and policies now specify that you must be given a chance to receive benefits or services without having to give up your personal information in the bargain.

Choice also means you have the right to change your mind. If at any time you decide you do not want the company or organization to be in possession of your data, you should be able to ask them to delete it from their records, and then get proof that they have done so.

Choice is sometimes tricky. The two main ways that sites offer you a choice are called *opt in* or *opt out.*

Opting in means that unless you take an action, no information about you will be saved. Opt in is the method required by the European Data Protection Directives for European Economic Community countries. Figure 2.5 shows an example of opting in. The box where you ask for more information is *not* checked by default.

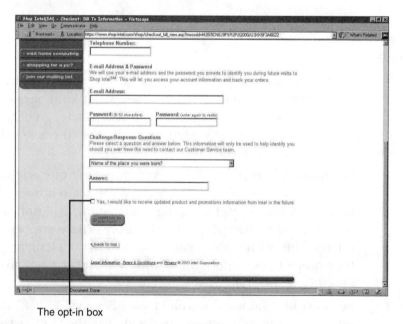

The opt-in box

**FIGURE 2.5**

*Opting in.*

Opting out means that unless you actively tell the site not to send you information, they will use your information by default. Figure 2.6 shows a registration form using opt out. To opt out of the free e-mail, you must *uncheck* the box. Otherwise, you are signed up by default.

Opting out is legal in most countries, although most consumer advocacy groups, and government agencies such as the Federal Trade Commission, recommend the use of opt in. Users are used to the idea that they must *do* something to allow people to send them e-mail or use their information. Frequently users do not realize they have signed up for something on sites with opt out, and this can lead to misunderstandings and anger on the part of the user.

## Access

After you give your personal information, you must be able to get access to it, to see what is being held about you. Companies do not have to provide you immediate, online access to your data (although many do). Giving you an address to which you can write is good enough to satisfy most legal requirements.

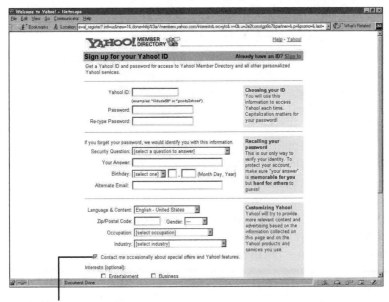

Uncheck this box to opt out.

**FIGURE 2.6**

*Opting out.*

Companies also don't have to show you everything they have. For example, if they have collected clickstream information on your browsing habits on their site, they do not have to show you that information. Clickstream data is the information provided by your browser to the Web page server that is saved in logs on the server. All transactions to Web sites are logged. In general, Web server operators maintain this data only long enough to process it for statistical information.

Access requirements are generally stated in terms of financial transactions, and the requirements are consumer protection laws or rules. A company must be able to tell you what you bought, for example, and what you paid for it. However, demographic data and clickstream data, in general, are not required to be available for you to see.

Which jurisdiction's rules apply is an issue for matters of access, too. Some states, such as California, have extensive consumer protection laws. Those laws may conflict with the laws of, England, for example. An international treaty conference called "The Hague Conference on Private International Law" (after its location and held every four years since 1893) continues to try to iron out the methods of choosing which laws apply in what instances. So far, the Hague Conference has been devisive and has reached no conclusions that can be supported by all.

Access also means you must be able to challenge, change, or modify information that is being held about you. The idea is that you should be able to have inaccurate information corrected. Some sites, such as Travelocity.com (see Figure 2.7), let you edit your profile online. However, companies that hold information about you don't have to let you make these modifications online in real time. If you see an error in your bank statement, for example, you would probably send a letter or a fax. Letting you change the profile data that shapes your experience online is sensible. However, it is less clear that it is a good idea to allow you to update your financial records online. The normal checks and balances that take place to protect the integrity of the record still need to be observed and a credible authentication and authorization process are needed. Unauthorized persons cannot change important records.

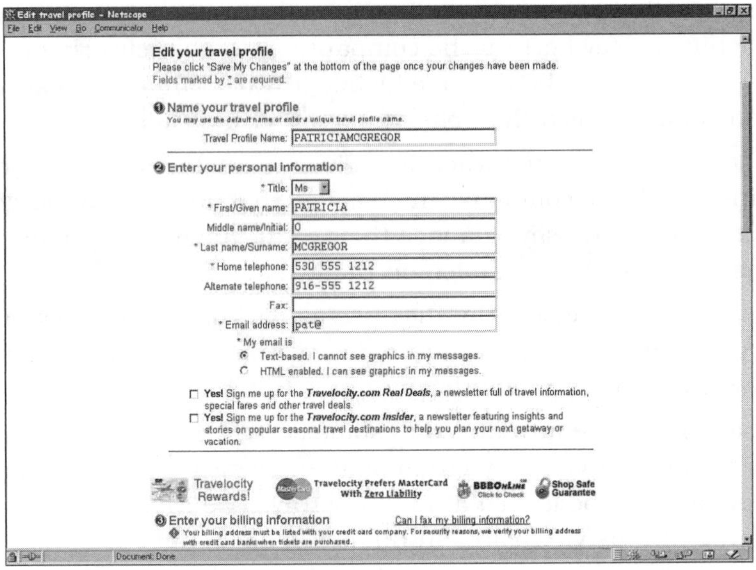

**FIGURE 2.7**

*Travelocity.com lets you edit your profile online.*

# Security

Security is the protection a company provides for your information. When companies promise that they will not share your information with anyone else, use it, or let it be used for anything that they do not have your permission for, it means they must protect that information from access by other people. Those other people include staff at their company, hackers, and other potentially hostile users.

There are several ways that companies protect your information. One way is to protect it *in transit*, which means they protect it as it travels between you and them. On paper, this might mean giving you a sealed envelope to send your information to them, rather than a postcard. On line, this generally means using some sort of protected link between you and them. The most common link protection is called SSL, or Secure Sockets Layer. SSL encrypts your data at your end and doesn't decrypt it until it reaches the company's computer. We'll talk more about SSL and other forms of protection in Chapter 4.

In transit also means that the information is protected while it travels around the organization's network. For example, the machine that sits on the Internet that receives your data usually passes it to a more protected machine somewhere on the company's internal network, or *Intranet.* The data must be protected while it travels from the machine on the net (sometimes called the *front end*) to other machines.

Data must also be protected when it is given to another company to use. This means that if the company which collected your information gives it to another company to, say, manage their catalogue list, they must protect it from being hacked or stolen on the way.

Many sites describe the security they use as part of their privacy policy. Wells Fargo, for example, has a guarantee against loss if their customers use browsers and precautions they describe (see Figure 2.8).

In this chapter you are introduced to some of our friends and their viewpoints on privacy. As you may guess by the varieties of definitions in this chapter, privacy can be looked at in many ways. We can't hope to expose you to all the various viewpoints in this short book, but we do hope that by letting our friends describe some of the issues that they care about, we can help you get a handle on the complexities of the privacy debate. In Appendix D, "Our Co-Conspirators," you find more information on our guest essayists and why we invited them to tell you their stories.

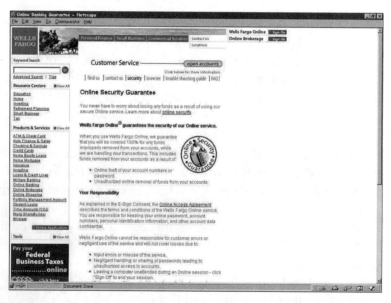

**FIGURE 2.8**

*Wells Fargo's security page describes their guarantee and the user's responsibilities.*

## PRIVACY IS NOT A TECH PROBLEM

*"Small Town (def): A place where you don't have to use your turn signals because everyone knows where you're going. "* *[caption on a T-shirt]*

To get some privacy, one could move to a big city and get lost in the crowd. With the global Internet, there is an even larger crowd to get lost in but then one often worries about spies eavesdropping on net communication. To counter that worry, we have encryption of messages and connections (PGP, SSL, TLS, S/MIME, …).

Unfortunately, that is neither the real threat nor the real solution.

Privacy threats come from data aggregation. If someone knows you exist, that is no substantial privacy problem. If someone knows that there is someone who is HIV positive, that is no privacy problem. If someone knows you are HIV positive, that is a significant privacy problem.

In the 1960's, people recognized that computers would permit the data aggregation that would lead to privacy threats but incorrectly assumed the governments would be the culprit. After all, a computer capable of holding a database about the whole US population, much less the world population, would be a mainframe with many magnetic tape drives and a vault of tapes. There would need to be rooms full of clerks entering data on punched cards. So, the solution was obviously to legislate against government abuse of personal data.

Today, a computer capable of searching a database of the world's population costs under $1000 while that database need no longer be on magnetic tape. It can be on rapidly accessed random access disks. The disk farm would cost a few thousand dollars (depending on the amount of data per person). Information is supplied by the individual himself or herself, via web forms. So, most individuals in the US could set up such data aggregation computers. Thanks to the global Internet, individual data aggregators could share their information with each other. All of this can happen peer-to-peer, without a central server to legislate against.

Is there no hope? As Scott McNealy is reputed to have said, "You have no privacy. Get over it."

The good news is that we know how to prevent most data aggregation, through technical means. That is, we know how to do very strong access control, so that a person can hold her own data and release it only to others of her own choosing. We also know how to anonymize data by presenting only average characteristics over a large enough population that no individual characteristics can be deduced from the processed output. We can pseudonymize data effectively even with manual methods (e.g., with a deck of cards).

The bad news is that privacy isn't a technical problem. It's a policy problem. A patient in the US does not legally own his own medical data. The US worked to keep US companies free from European privacy laws.

Unfortunately, there are no technical solutions to the problem of getting policy changed.

—*Carl Ellison*

# Understanding What Privacy Means to You

Once you understand what personally identifiable information is, and how to find out what that information will be used for, you can make a judgement on whether the benefit you receive by offering that information is worth it.

Seth Grodin told us that the right to privacy is the right not to be surprised; not by the places your information ends up nor by the uses to which it is put. Clearly, that means that you must pay attention to how your information is used, and make conscious decisions about that use. Privacy doesn't mean the absolute guarantee of anonymity—in some ways it's almost impossible to be truly anonymous in a wired world. However, exercising the use of your data—getting the maximum benefit and the minimum harm from the use of it—is a choice you should make with all the information you need at your disposal.

# PART II

## BECOMING AWARE: PRIVACY AND THE INDIVIDUAL

*"The technotronic era involves the gradual appearance of a more controlled society. Such a society would be dominated by an elite, unrestrained by traditional values. ... [T]he capacity to assert social and political control over the individual will vastly increase. It will soon be possible to assert almost continuous surveillance over every citizen and to maintain up-to-date, complete files, containing even most personal information about the health or personal behavior of the citizen in addition to more customary data. These files will be subject to instantaneous retrieval by the authorities."*

Zbigniew Brzezinski (protégé of David Rockefeller, cofounder of the Trilateral Commission, and National Security Advisor to Jimmy Carter), *Between Two Ages*, 1971

*"Consumer privacy issues are a red herring. You have zero privacy anyway."*

Scott McNealy
CEO, Sun Microsystems
*Wired Magazine*
Jan. 26, 1999

# WHO WANTS TO KNOW WHAT ABOUT WHOM?

We've talked some now about the types of information that might be collected about you and the things you might want to be worried about. Now let's talk about what is really happening, what kinds of data collection is actually going on, who is using the data, and maybe why.

In this chapter, we discuss the evolution of information gathering. We start by talking about how people are curious about other people, especially celebrities, and how far our culture thinks that curiosity can go, appropriately or not. We'll move on to talk about news reporting—other people gathering information for us that we couldn't likely gather ourselves. From there has evolved the idea of open government information, easily obtainable these days via the Internet. And then we're going to get personal with you and talk about information gathering about *you*, your preferences, purchases, and activities online and off. Different kinds of information gathering and the motivations behind them are discussed a lot in this chapter. We want you to understand the pros and cons, from all sides, so that you can make intelligent choices in your own situations.

First, let's consider our own culture and how and what we like to know about ourselves and others.

# We All Want to Know about Other People

We do? Yes, we do; just look at our behavior.

As human beings we are extremely interested in other human beings and how we relate to one another.

We want to know about movie stars, music performers, actors, elected officials and other types of people with celebrity. These people are "public" people and even if we think they are entitled to a modicum of privacy, we don't really grant it. We avidly read articles about the homes they own, the businesses in which they invest, the people they marry, and the activities of their children. We call it news. Of course, it's news about entertaining people, so it's also entertainment.

Some of us cheer when people we think we "like" do well. We do that for San Francisco Giant Barry Bonds' terrific home run pace this 2001 spring baseball season, for example. Other times we take morbid pleasure in the downfall of a celebrity. For example, Robert Downey, Jr. having another bit of trouble with his drug treatment program. We cheer or boo Mr. Bonds, depending on our feelings about the San Francisco Giants or congratulate ourselves that we don't have the sort of drug dependency, like Mr. Downey, that keeps us in and out of drug treatment centers. We sigh through the sagas of celebrity divorces, choosing sides just exactly as though we really know the people involved. We are angry on behalf of one of the couple and frantically defend their actions, just as if we knew what we were talking about.

Before September 11, 2001, most days the top news stories on many of the online news outlets included stories about famous or important people. Even now, stories about people get a lot of notice. Just look most days at the top news. Netscape's Netcenter (www.netscape.com) is shown as an example in Figure 3.1, but almost any other news source would be the same. The lead articles typically are not only about the President's proposed tax program, but also about the activities of the President's daughters. The sports articles contain descriptions of yesterday's contests and a number of articles about the off-field activities (both good and bad) of some sports personages. Human interest? Of course it is.

Clearly, the publishers of these pages and other pages and printed materials know we're interested and that is what they provide.

**FIGURE 3.1**

*Netscape's NetCenter.*

We all want to know about the activities of our friends and neighbors, too. We want to know where they are going, what they are doing, what they just admired at the store, and what sports contest they are interested in. We never think of this as prying or invasive. Some of us have nosy neighbors who we find a pain. Some of us *are* the nosy neighbors.

Our interest in celebrities is an extension of that curiosity about the world we are in. We learn to emulate people we admire, and in many ways we learn who to admire by seeing who other people are interested in. We make celebrities of the people who create art we admire, and we learn to appreciate some art because people we admire like it. We learn what athletic feats are marvelous from stories about sports stars, and we admire athletes because they perform marvelous feats. We make celebrities of people who act the way we should or wish we could act, and in turn we try to act like them.

In general, our culture seems to accept the idea that reporting on the activities of celebrities is acceptable as long as the activities happen in public. We have even created an industry of celebrity watching. We have special television programs and channels devoted to it. We have sections of news-oriented Web publications such as the Living Section of MSNBC.COM shown in Figure 3.2. We subscribe to magazines that are devoted to it. We turn to pages in our daily newspapers for

entertainment about entertainers. We can't seem to get enough information about our celebrities. We want to know everything about them, public or not. We don't like to think that our interest might be invasive.

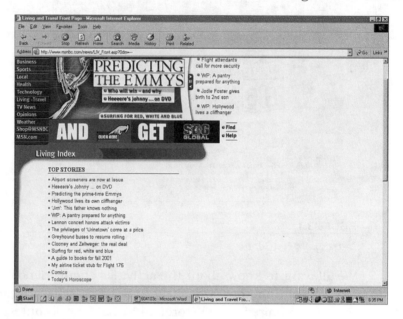

**FIGURE 3.2**

*A typical page from the MSNBC.COM Web site, Living section.*

It can be, though. Intense public interest might have contributed to the
death of Diana, the former Princess of Wales. Certainly, some celebrities
go to great lengths to keep their weddings private—or at least to make
certain that the photographs that are released are the official ones,
rather than ones stolen via telephoto lenses. And two baseball players
originally from Japan, now playing with the Seattle Mariners, have
recently refused to speak with the Japanese media anymore. One player
was unable to get in his car and drive to work at the ballpark because
there were so many photographers and reporters in his driveway. Clearly
he felt that public interest in his celebrity had gone too far.

# Celebrities Can Educate, Too

Most of us think of Michael J. Fox as Marty McFly from *Back to the
Future*, reworking history so that his parents are happy and successful,
or as the not-quite sleazy mayor's aide in *Spin City*. Yet, when he

announced that he was quitting the show because he suffered from Parkinson's Disease, we were shocked. In the interviews and specials which followed, we learned a great deal about the disease and how it affects families, famous or not. Figure 3.3 shows the Web site for the Michael J. Fox foundation, where you can find lots of information on Parkinson's, current research, and resources.

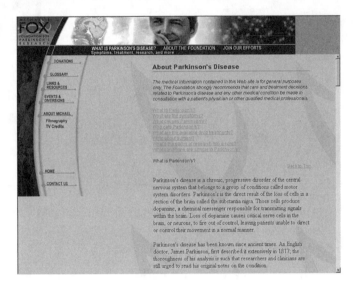

**FIGURE 3.3**

*Information on Parkinson's Disease.*

It's very likely that many of us would not have given much thought to Parkinson's Disease, unless we had a family member who suffered from it. However, we have adopted celebrities into a kind of pseudo-family, and so Michael's struggles and successes felt personal.

Many other celebrities have causes they champion. Dick Ward, TV's Robin in *Batman*, champions neglected Great Danes. Destiny's Child, a popular music group, supports a youth center in Houston, Texas. Daisy Fuentes wants pregnant moms to make sure they get enough folic acid. Ron Silverman, a well-known actor, has started a foundation called "The Creative Coalition," to help celebrities find out how to help their favorite causes. Celebrity Web pages help us find out what causes entertainers and other popular figures are involved in. Figure 3.4 shows one such page, on About.com.

**FIGURE 3.4**

*About.com's celebrity causes index.*

# Freedom *of* or Freedom *from* the Press

In this discussion we've located two broad types of interest in information about specific people: entertainment and education.

We have another type of interest in certain kinds of public persons. We want to make sure that they are executing their public duties with care for the trust placed in them. Scandalous behavior in the Congress, the White House, or the Governor's mansion has always interested us. Some argue that people who act badly in one area of their lives shouldn't be trusted with our interests or allowed to control the spending of our tax dollars. Others argue that just because a person acts badly toward a family member, for instance, doesn't mean we shouldn't trust them with our army and navy. The two types of activities are not the same. We are pretty sure that we don't want convicted embezzlers having control of public funds. We are pretty sure that people who cheat in counting votes shouldn't represent us. We are not as sure if people who lie about matters of sexual preference or matters of their health should be elected. Cultural stigmas might matter more than we would like to think.

In any case, because these people are public people, the news media watches them and reports their activities so that we easily can obtain information about them. The theory is that informed voters make better decisions. And voters should be informed about all aspects of a person who aspires to or holds the trust of the public, even if the people who are being reported on believe the articles invade their privacy.

For example, does it matter if your mayor has a girlfriend? Is our answer different if the official story is that the mayor is happily married? Is it different still if the girlfriend is on the city's payroll? What if all them are on the payroll? What if the mayor's office provides no salary? The people of New York have been debating these questions about New York's Mayor Giuliani all through 2001.

Do the answers to these questions about the mayor's personal life affect how he performs his duties? They certainly affect the people involved. Does the mayor's wife deserve more hurt because her husband is a public person? If the people involved were important people in the company we work for, the triangle would definitely be office water-cooler discussion fodder. We might be upset if the girlfriend seemed to be rewarded or receive benefits that seemed to be unrelated to her professional contribution to the company. We might like and want to protect the errant company officer. However, these matters usually don't make the front page of the local newspaper.

Of course, if the activity moves across the line from the merely unwise to the criminal—if money disappears from corporate coffers and turns up in the pockets of the corporate officer—that's a different matter.

Likewise, our opinion changes if the mayor's girlfriend is on the payroll for other than her professional expertise. Most likely she is forced to leave her job, even if she is thought to have been doing a good job. The fact that her competence is now questioned makes it impossible for her to perform her job.

We generally believe that the reporting of the mayor's indiscretions is a good thing. His behavior does affect whether or not we trust him.

For our elected and appointed officials, we want to know about automobile accidents, drunk driving arrests, hospital treatments for depression or drug rehabilitation. We want to know who owns what—who might receive a benefit from a public purchase. We have learned that not all people who say they want to serve the public are actually serving the public.

So we have investigative reporting. We do want and deserve to know. And, largely because of the efforts of the press, we have laws requiring open access to much of our government-collected data. That data can be very interesting and can provide us with a better picture of areas we care about.

## REMEMBER: AS YOU VIEW OUR SURVEILLANCE OVERVIEW, THE SURVEILLANCE OVERVIEWS YOU

IT'S YOUR PRIVACY, after all, and maybe you're more determined than the average soul in protecting it. If you don't cross an international border, don't go online, don't travel on commercial airlines? If you don't use credit cards, don't use a cell phone, don't use a phone at all. If you don't register to vote? If you don't go outside?

Nope, sorry. Your privacy's already compromised, and you didn't feel a thing.

As the privacy debate matures and expands, people who initially screamed for their absolute right to absolute privacy have by and large moderated that stance, seeking a comfortable middle ground between a mythical total anonymity (which hasn't existed since humans started inhabiting adjacent caves) and the Orwellian all-seeing, all-processing eye—we kick at banks selling our data to telemarketers but keep our phone numbers listed, for instance—and are happy in the main with the tradeoffs between privacy and convenience, privacy and security, or simply privacy and not worrying about privacy when there's a whole world of other stuff to fret about.

To invoke the spirit of Summer 2000 Past once more, we've come to the conclusion that even though we're not able to create for ourselves a retreat into Pulau Tiga-level isolation, we also aren't subject to Survivor-style ubiquitous monitoring either, unless we want to be. Fine, if the playing field is really so level as that. But it's not.

Whatever precautions you choose to take—even if you choose not to tangle with the Net and its privacy issues—there are some technological invasions that you just can't barricade yourself against. The following are technologies that do, or have the capacity to, significantly infringe on the privacy of even the most wary citizens. Lest we send our more nervous readers scurrying for their lead-lined headgear and Y2K-era survival bunkers, we reiterate: There's not a thing you can do about it. Add one more item to the list that includes death and taxes.

SOMEWHERE OVER OUR heads, hundreds of miles up, whirl the satellites. A great number of them act as sophisticated phone and cable antennas, moving human communications and broadcasts from Point A to Point B; a great number more float overhead in death, long since decommissioned but cheaper to leave in orbit than to recycle. There are the weather satellites, kicking butt and saving lives.

And there are the ones that can spot the box of cereal in your bag as you walk through the grocery-store parking lot.

News earlier this month that the general public can now get high-res satellite photos is pretty cool for those of us who like to see the lay of the land—real-estate agents, for instance, or folks tracking weather—or agriculture-related situations. But a wise rule of thumb states that if X technology is widely available, next-level versions of that technology are available to those with the money to buy them. The advent of "Keyhole"-class visible-light satellites with resolutions of 5 to 6 inches—a satellite that can count how many pieces of luggage you're taking to the airport, or how many people have gathered for your anti-WTO demonstration— has already been reported in the mainstream media. Tighter resolution takes us to facial-feature-recognition level—something done currently by on-the-ground surveillance equipment such as traffic cameras, used to great effect in apprehending British demonstrators recently. And combining multiple images is not beyond the reach of fast computers, as seen in Bosnia recently where UN officials showed stunningly detailed 3-D maps of the Serb-held countryside to demonstrate that negotiations were in Serbia's best interest. Those images were a blend of satellite images and recon photos. Other tools in the über-surveillance arsenal include infrared/ ultraviolet photography (is your home energy-efficient?) and radar-imaging technology (what have you got buried in your backyard?).

BACK ON EARTH, the great specter of ubiquitous surveillance has traveled in privacy circles under the name of ECHELON, the vast Anglophone transmission monitoring system that has received increased attention in the past year. Meanwhile, while the Europeans ponder ECHELON's implications and Americans inquire into the FBI's proposed Carnivore monitoring system, the British government has passed the Regulation of Investigatory Powers (RIP) Bill, which provides nearly unprecedented powers to monitor Net transmissions and punish people who, say, forget a password the government would like to know. (Yes, I mean jail time— check it out at www.uk.internet.com/Article/100347.) And the Israelis are currently floating a proposal that would allow their GSS (General Security Service) to listen to e-mail, Net, and satellite links.

Meanwhile, if you're still worried about the satellite spying on your cereal purchasing patterns, be it known that you've got a lot less to worry about from the eye in the sky than from the eye in the ceiling. Supermarket monitoring of shoppers is nigh-ubiquitous—to cut down on shrinkage, sure, but primarily to figure out how to build a better mousetrap. When you picked up that box of Wheaties, did you pace past the whole cereal shelf? Did you compare prices? Did you have a problem finding the brand or the aisle? All of that's data for designers trying to improve store traffic flow and profits. And though you're not likely to miss the surveillance notices in places that want you to be aware of the cameras (in crime-prone shops, for instance), in your average grocery store they're not likely to risk unnerving the shoppers by mentioning the monitoring.

YOU'D HAVE TO BE an idiot not to expect it, just as you expect to pass through a mildly annoying security check at an airport on your way to the gate. Procedures vary widely—X-rays, handheld metal detectors, the occasional switching on of a notebook or PDA (and don't get me started on the Sea-Tac miss who demanded I take a sip of my latte in front of her to prove it wasn't...hell, I don't know what her deal was), the occasional swab test for explosives residue, but the common thread among all these procedures is that you're aware of them.

The good news for very impatient travelers is that such things could infringe on their IPO-addled consciousnesses somewhat less somewhat soon. The bad news, well...

Holographic body-searching (no, it's not some kinky Princess Leia-Star Wars thing) uses waves in about the 30GHz range to generate a 360-degree full-body image of what's under one's clothes. Leaving aside the health implications of that zap of radiation, one wonders where the inevitable security tapes of such scans would be stored—and how much the black market will offer for the archives when Natalie Portman (for instance) passes through the security checkpoint. (And if you think that's nasty, imagine the uproar over those images when kids pass through the scanners. Patrick Naughton, phone your office! )

Even weirder, you might one day be insta-searched not for what's on your person but for what's in it and where it's been. A Penn State chemist has been developing a metal-detector device that reads what he calls the human thermal plume—the little cloud of airborne particles that envelopes every human body. Where your cat registers body warmth and you notice that the person sitting next to you has been eating garlic, Gary Settles' chemical analyzer reads and analyzes, through a process called schlieren photography, the little bits of skin and chemicals and dust and fabric fibers and whatnot that float off us. If you've been handling gunpowder or smack, for instance, a quick scan might tip the authorities.

How long do you have to clean up your act? A Massachusetts company called Ion Track estimates its reader, which will take about 10 seconds to perform such a scan, is approximately a year from market. On the up side, a major audit of US airport security last year revealed that between airport operators and the FAA, airport security's a mess, so don't expect much soon. Positive uses for such technology might include less invasive tests for disorders such as diabetes; negative uses...well, say goodbye to the relatively occasional company drug piss-test.

WHAT GOOD DOES it do to worry about these things? Lobbying your Congressperson isn't likely to cut down on the number of telemarketers interrupting your supper; is there anything that can be done about large-scale, noninvasive surveillance capabilities? Because it's in your best interests to know. It must be. After all, many other folk have invested a lot of money to know about us; it's only polite to return the favor.

—*Angela Gunn*

*Source: http://www.seattleweekly.com/features/0035/tech-gunn.shtml*

*Reprinted with permission.*

## Some Government Data Usable as News Sources

The following is a list we selected to show some of the information that can be obtained from federal government registration and compiled data. You can see that a good reason for collecting the information exists. You can also see that, if you were cheating or trying to hide your activities, some of this information could be embarrassing.

Much more information is available, of course. More information about these databases and others can be found on the Investigative Reporters and Editors, Inc. Web site at `http://www.ire.org`. And the Federal government is not the only source of information. States and counties have lots of information, much of it easily accessible via the Internet. For example, the County of El Dorado, California, has a Web site that makes searching for information about individuals and property fairly easy. See it at `http://www.co.el-dorado.ca.us/countyclerk/`. Others don't necessarily have all the information online, but make it easy to request that information from official records (see the following list):

- **Air Transportation** (see the complete list of databases at `http://www.faa.gov/safety2.htm`)

  *FAA Enforcements:* A database of FAA enforcement actions against airlines, pilots, mechanics, and designees.

  *FAA Service Difficulty Reports*: A database of maintenance incidents collected by the FAA for the purpose of tracking repair problems with commercial, private, and military aircraft, and aircraft components.

- **Road Transportation**

  *DOT Fatal Accidents*: A nation-wide database of fatal road-vehicle accidents. (http://www-fars.nhtsa.dot.gov/)

  *NHTSA Vehicle Recalls and Complaints*: A database of vehicle complaints, recalls, service bulletins, and inspections. (http://www.dot.gov/affairs/nhtsa99.htm)

- **Waterways**

  *Boat Registration:* The database contains information on registered recreational and commercial boats.

- **Federal**

  *FEC Campaign Contributions*: A database of all individual and political action group (PAC) contributions to federal election campaigns. (http://www.fec.gov/finance/finmenu.htm)

- **Health**

  *National Practitioner Databank*: This database contains information about doctors and other health care practitioners who have had medical malpractice suits filed or adverse action taken against them. Although names are not included, some news organizations have been able to use this database with other public records to determine the identity of individual practitioners. (http://www.npdb.com/)

- **Business**

  *Home Mortgage Disclosure Act Data:* A database of home mortgage loan requests, information about the requesters as well as the financial institutions. (http://www.ffiec.gov/hmda/)

## When Data Collection Focuses on You

Public persons are private persons, too. Balancing the public's need to know with the individual's right to privacy is something that editors and publishers do every day.

And while the editorial staff at your local paper does the privacy balancing act with the articles, the advertising staff is doing a very different balancing act. They are responsible for making sure that the advertising is bringing in sufficient revenue so the paper stays afloat. They also ensure that the amount of advertising is appropriate for the editorial content and that they reach the audience that is most receptive to the advertising message. To do that, they have to know something about their readers.

# Learning to Like New Things

The advertising community knows that we are interested in the likes and dislikes of celebrities and they use that knowledge to try to convince us that we enjoy a new movie, a new athletic shoe, or a new cosmetic. We know that buying a Kobe Bryant branded basketball shoe does not give us the extraordinary abilities of Kobe Bryant, but we buy the shoes with the hope that this time, despite past experience, the magic will happen and we will make that fabulous shot.

We also know that buying Martha Stewart paint colors and re-painting the dining room does not make our home eligible to be used in a magazine photograph, but a lot can be said for the feeling of accomplishment we get from executing such a plan. And the paint manufacturer is pleased that we choose his brand of paint from that store rather than some other brand of paint from some other store or no brand at all because it would not otherwise have occurred to us to paint the dining room.

We accept the practice of the Kobe Bryant billboard or the Martha Stewart advertising insert in the Sunday newspaper. However, what if the advertiser knew more about what you are interested in? What if instead of seeing a broadcast commercial with Tiger Woods suggesting that a Buick is the new car for you, you could get information about the exact kind of car you wanted to know more about? Or in your mailbox you found a brochure describing a book you really wanted, complete with ordering form? And your neighbor didn't get that brochure, but instead received a brochure describing a new gardening tool that she really wanted.

That's *target marketing*. If you are a businessperson who is trying to sell something, you can see how enticing it would be.

# Knowing Your Customer

In business, the idea is to provide a service or a product to the people who want it at more than it costs to provide the service or produce the product. We do this to provide for the sustenance of our families and ourselves. Ever since we gathered together in living units larger than the family and developed a method of measuring the value of people's contributions to society (that is, money), this is what we all strive toward. We want to make sure that our families are well cared for, that we have athletic shoes and clothing for school, books to read, whatever is important for each of our living situations.

When the society that people participated in seemed smaller (like a village or small town), and when the products were bread from the local baker or milk from the local dairy farmer, exchanging money for products was relatively simple. The baker or the dairy farmer was well known in his or her market area. People liked the product and purchased it or the baker or the dairy farmer changed the product or went out of business. In a smaller-scale society, people could band together to support one another in hard times. If the baker's supplies were affected by drought (or overabundance), people would know and could change their purchasing patterns to help. They would accept higher prices or buy less bread, so there would be enough to go around. And the community—the baker's market—would want to do this because everyone understood that if the baker went out of business, there would be no baker now or even when things got good again.

The market was not a concept that was discussed much. And it probably wasn't studied too much, either. It just was. The market was a geographical place where people gathered to buy and sell necessities. You could tell what was for sale and who was selling it, just by being there. Because you knew your neighbor, you could decide if the quality of his product was good enough to pay the asking price. Perhaps you negotiated a lower price. Perhaps you traded your product for his product. If you didn't like the product, you could speak to your neighbor about it. Perhaps he would make some arrangement with you to keep you happy. Perhaps he didn't care if you were happy. But you had the power of word of mouth to defend your point of view. You could tell others your story. If the seller felt cheated, he could tell his side. The market would know of the dispute and people could act accordingly.

Society didn't stay static, though. It grew. When it grew so that the market was larger than we could see, it was no longer necessary or even possible to take some of the products and services to a central geographical location. Then people could no longer touch and feel the products and decide if they wanted them. When it became difficult to gather and discuss the product offerings on Market Day, we discovered new kinds of marketing.

We got advertising. Advertising informs you about the availability of a product: who made it, where you can get it, and what it might cost. We can imagine that the first advertiser probably painted something on a cloth to hang over a booth in a marketplace. As more and more banners were hung (figuratively, of course), the size, shape, color, and so on of the cloth banners changed. Each new idea escalating the concept, until a cacophony of banners was reached and you could no longer tell what products were available where.

At that time businesspeople employed barkers to shout about their wares or drummers to attract attention. Business people have always been concerned about attracting attention to the availability of a product.

Finding people who are interested in chocolate chip cookies is easier if you are selling them right from the oven in a shopping mall than it is if you are trying to sell them across the Internet. Buyers in a shopping mall are tempted by the wonderful odor of warm cookies and know that, for a relatively small amount of money, they can instantly gratify their desire for a warm cookie. Buyers over the Internet have to plan ahead, find a source of cookies, fill-out forms, pay, and wait for shipping and delivery. Clearly some kinds of products are a bit easier to sell in person. The potential marketplace of the Internet is much larger than the shopping mall, however. And that makes it a desirable marketplace for an expanding business.

The Internet is also a good marketplace for products that are entirely digital, like music recordings or images. Because they aren't tangible (until perhaps, after delivery) the place that sells them needn't be tangible either.

But among the millions of people who can be connected to the Internet, how do you find your potential customers? You have to know enough about those customers to tell them the story that sells—that describes your product as exactly the right match for their needs. You have to collect and analyze data. How do you do that?

Many business people feel that the processes collectively known as personalization are the answer.

## What is Personalization?

*Personalization* is the automated process that tries to predict what the user wants next and presents it. The perfect implementation would be presenting the right content at the right time, every time.

Businesses use a number of techniques to try to produce that perfect implementation. Some of the techniques are simple ideas in complex implementations: keep track of what the customer did in previous visits and make guesses about what the customer does next. That's what Amazon.com's Recommendations process does.

Some sites use intricate processing that reviews the actions you have just performed on the Web site and tries to present what you find most pleasing. The successful business uses a number of tools to engage in interactions with the user. The following list presents 10 reasons businesses might want to engage in personalization:

1. Provides the customer with convenience and save his or her time.

2. Allows the vendor to become a trusted source, building loyalty, customer retention and sales.

3. Enables a comprehensive, integrated, and intelligent customer communication strategy.

4. Allows the vendor to proactively present the customer with contextually relevant offers creating the potential to transact with each and every customer.

5. Provides a 360-degree view of the customer relationship, helping to better understand customer needs and habits.

6. Allows the vendor to focus on retention rather than acquisition, which is much more cost effective and dramatically increases customer lifetime value.

7. Offers faster and more accurate response rates to measure future sales.

8. Provides up-sell and cross-sell opportunities, driving additional revenue.

9. Creates a competitive advantage, building barriers of entry for new businesses.

10. Allows a more cost-effective way of doing business, improving sales and customer satisfaction.

*Source: Software and Information Industry Association eBusiness Division Whitepaper: Connect with your Customers*

Electronic and Internet tools are among the important tools being sought to help businesses solve their problems. These include tools that help keep track of customer interactions (generally called *eCRM* or *Customer Relationship Management* tools). Also included are tools known as *ERP* or *Enterprise Resource Planning* tools. Additionally, tools that help manage relationships among partners and affiliated organizations are much sought after. All these tools are data-based. This means that people collect the information, organize it so that it can be manipulated, and many uses can be made of it.

An eCRM system, for example, makes it possible for your Airline mileage club to keep track of your miles for you. Using the telephone number you are calling from makes it possible for the person answering your technical support call to have a screen in front of them with all the relevant information about you and your purchase in front of them when they answer the phone.

Now, if you are a member of a mileage program, you know that it is a loyalty marketing program. Because you are a continuing customer, you get the reward. The reward the airline gets is your continued patronage *and* a lot of information about your travel preferences. These travel preferences help them plan, so they can provide better service where it is needed.

The technical support person can do a better job of answering your questions if she has information about the make and model of your computer and the program you are trying to run. If she doesn't have this information at the beginning of the call, she has to take the time to ask you about it and you need to supply it. It is more convenient for both of you if she has access to information you have already provided to the company.

The following are two reasons for personalization from the individual's point of view:

1. Saves me time by going directly to what I want to see, making it easier for me to find things.
2. Helps me communicate with the business because all my information is in one place.

That's really it. Convenience.

How much are you willing to pay for convenience?

Businesses are willing to pay quite a lot to try to provide convenience for you because it is much less expensive to keep you as a current customer than it is to find a new customer. If you are not pleased with your service, if you find the Web site hard to use, or even just awkward, you do not go back.

The personalized relationship between you and a business is based upon knowledge and trust. When we shopped at local pharmacies, we knew the pharmacist and expected that he would do the best possible job of fulfilling our prescriptions. We could count on a warning about not mixing this drug with some other drug the pharmacist knew we were taking. We relied on the pharmacist not to talk about our prescriptions to anyone else.

Our local drugstore maintained records in our name that included our address and telephone number, the doctors who prescribed our medicine, the types of medicine and the quantities, how many refills were allowed, and so on. We felt safe with those records stored there because we trusted the people and the process. Later, medical insurance providers and other organizations had to be extended our trust so that we could receive insurance benefits.

Now we need to decide if we can further extend that trust to online pharmacies, to online bookstores, or to online shoe stores. Because the currency of personalized convenience is the sharing of information about ourselves.

### FINDING THAT IMPORTANT BOOK

Most of you are familiar with the online store, Amazon.com, and the various features that are intended to make it easier for you to find and purchase what you want.

The recommendations feature, for example, is based upon what was purchased before by the currently signed in online identity. So, if you bought a book published in 1901 about equitation (the art of riding horses in specific ways) and some Romance novels by Jo Beverley and some technical books about database programming, you are likely to get a rather wide array of recommended material. This will be especially true if you purchased music as a present for someone else as well as your mother's favorite movies to send her a gift.

The search feature is one you may not have employed. If you are looking for a specific item, say a no longer stocked novel by Lynn Kerstan, you might be disappointed because no one is offering it for sale, new or used. But at Amazon.com you can put in a request and store it for the pre-order service. This service compares the stored requests to the new arrivals among the many dealers in the Amazon.com affiliated network. If the book you want is offered for sale by one of the dealers, Amazon.com will forward your order and the dealer can charge your credit card and ship you the book.

This service requires that you trust Amazon.com with your credit card number, shipping information, and the title of the book you want to buy. You must also trust that Amazon.com will not charge you for the item before it is available—or charge to your card without your authorization. (As part of the request process, you supply the amount of money you are willing to pay for your desired item.) You also trust that Amazon.Com will not give that information to someone other than the merchant/dealer who offers your item for sale. That's a lot of trust.

But it's worth it!

Just read this story. Glee's friend Bill was seeking the book, *On Thermonuclear War*, by Herman Kahn. Greenwood Press published the second edition of this book in 1978, and the book really is difficult to find now. Our friend had been looking for a long time because he wanted to read the book and because he had a personal connection to the work: his mother had helped Herman Kahn in preparing the original manuscript. The book itself is difficult to read and it can't have been a popular book. It is a scholarly study of the scenarios of nuclear war, and it probably wasn't going to turn up in the 'normal' used book channels.

But it is listed in Amazon.Com's database. So, Bill filled out the form and forgot about it.

Fortunately, a dealer offered the book for sale, and Bill is now the proud owner of the book his mother worked on. Since the dealer operated far away from Bill's residence, Bill was really, really pleased with the personalized service. He would never have been able to find that copy without it.

*"Our vision is that if we have 20 million customers, we should have 20 million stores."*

*—Jeff Bezos, CEO, Amazon.com*

---

Unless a business knows that you are a current customer, it cannot provide you with information based on your previous transactions. Unless a business knows you prefer classical music, it might show you gangsta rap.

Consider the difference in the information you can receive from a financial institution's Web site if you are a current customer or a prospective one. If you have an account with a bank, you can probably sign on through a process like the one shown in Figure 3.5 and you can check your account balance. You can probably ask your bank to make an electronic payment to a creditor. If you don't have an account at that bank, you are only shown information about services you might want to use, like those shown in Figure 3.6. And this is appropriate. We don't want to have our account information shown to unauthorized people.

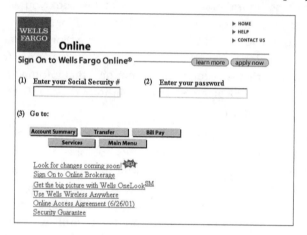

**FIGURE 3.5**

*The Sign-on screen for Wells Fargo Electronic Banking Customers.*

The importance of identification and authorization are apparent to you when we discuss financial transactions. In personalized interactions, the same process must take place, although in many instances the sign-in process isn't as secure or as formal. The recognition process might be as simple as reading a cookie-file written to your disk from a previous visit. Or it might involve a sign-on process that "connects you" to the profile you built during one or more visits to a Web site. See the difference between the opening screen for Amazon.com if you don't have the cookie-file stored on your computer (see Figure 3.7) and the one you see after you've signed in (see Figure 3.8).

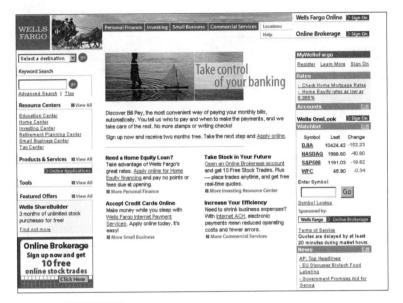

**FIGURE 3.6**

*The general Wells Fargo page.*

Some people complain about their recommendations from Amazon.com. If you bought a book on equitation for a friend and you never intend to buy another one, receiving information about new books on riding horses will annoy you. You can actually control this by going to your recommendations page and "grading" the choices. You can remove certain kinds of recommendations from your list without making the list useless. Or, of course, you can just ignore them.

Amazon.com personalized recommendations really enlist our cooperation. We can look at each item on our recommendation list and rate its relevance to our preferences. We can even tell Amazon.com that we own material that we didn't buy from them. This is truly cooperation between merchant and customer.

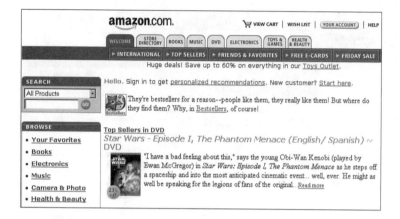

**FIGURE 3.7**

*The general opening page for Amazon.com.*

**FIGURE 3.8**

*Glee's recommendations in early July 2001.*

# Providing You with Personal Service

Anytime you set up an account or sign-on name with a Web site, you are giving the Web site the capability to track what you do, at least on that site, and helping them provide you information based on preference that you give them. You may give the information explicitly by filling in a form or implicitly by providing a sign-on name that enables them to correlate any movement on that site to your sign-on name.

If you provide information to receive a service, you should assume that that information is saved and that it is used by itself or in combination with other information to try to provide you with information you want.

For example, if you visit the Excite home page at `http://www.excite.com` (see Figure 3.9) you see several places where you can supply information to change your experience. For instance, if you want a horoscope, you need to supply a date of birth. If you want to know about your local weather, you need to supply the zip code. You have now trusted the Web site with your zip code and your birth date.

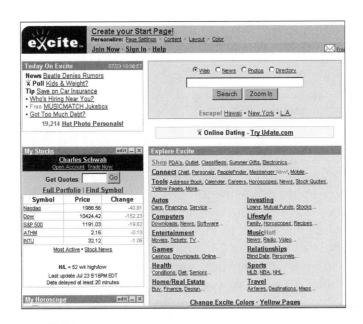

**FIGURE 3.9**

*The Excite home page.*

Furthermore, if you want to change the appearance of the Excite page when you visit, you can set preferences that are remembered and used each time you sign-in. In Figure 3.10 you can see the information that is collected when you set the preferences.

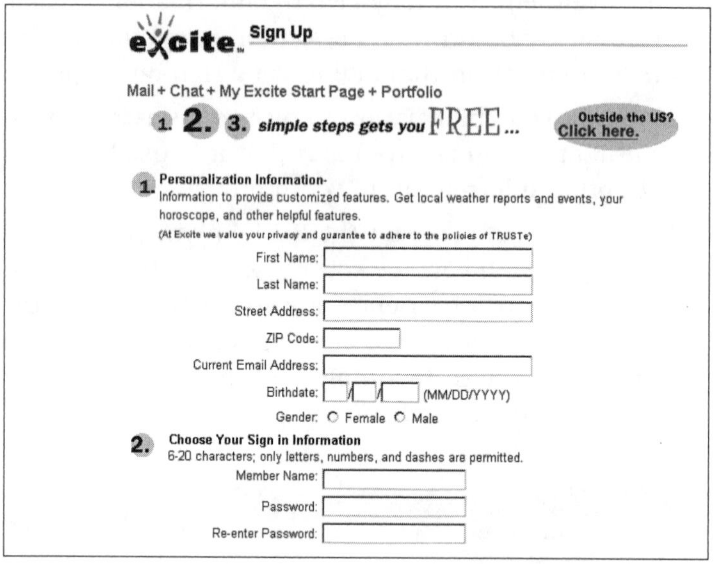

**FIGURE 3.10**

*The Excite Preferences page.*

With this information, it would be possible for Excite to combine the information you gave them with the information about what you looked at on their Web site and produce a very detailed profile about you. The Excite Privacy Policy explicitly outlines the information Excite collects and what they do with that information. This Privacy Policy, the beginning of which is illustrated in Figure 3.11, is a good one to read to understand possible uses of personal information. This policy gives you the chance to make up your own mind if the benefit you receive from disclosing information about yourself actually is worth the cost to you.

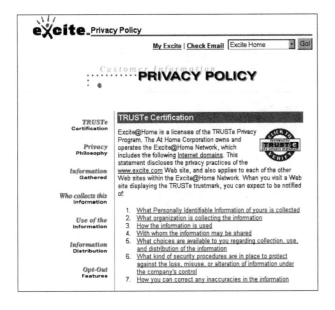

**FIGURE 3.11**

*The Excite Privacy Policy page.*

# It's All About Trust

You must decide if the Web sites can be trusted with your information. The businesses all have tools. You need some, too. In this book we give you a selection, the ones we think will help you most.

# THREATS TO YOUR CHILDREN'S PRIVACY

We feel we should give you a warning about this chapter. We are parents; we have kids who are grown and kids who are teenagers, and we have strong feelings about parenting. Luckily for us, those feelings are pretty similar; it's one of the things that has kept us friends for so long. However, we couldn't write this chapter without some of those kid-raising philosophies creeping in. We figured we should tell you that up front.

## Are Your Kids in Danger on the Net?

Different people have different answers to this question. For some, the biggest risk is that their kid finds material that offends their philosophical or religious beliefs. For some, there is risk that the kid meets up with people who are a bad influence on the kid, whether a "bad influence" is defined as someone who will hurt them physically, or just expose them to new and different ideas.

Just as in any other venue where our kids interact, there is both truth and fable about the dangers to kids on the Internet. Some people on the Net are not nice. There is material that would probably be offensive to many of us. There are temptations and lures. At the same time, there is an overwhelmingly high number of really good things for kids to use, play with, study, and enjoy on the Net. As with any other venue, the risk to your kids lies largely in how you and they use it.

Your kids are most at risk when their exploration of the Net goes unsupervised and undiscussed. Just as it is important for you to be involved in your kids' schooling, their religious or philosophical education, and their friends and after-school activities, it is important that you be involved in how your kids use the Internet. If you actively discuss the Internet—and the hazards that may wait there—your kids are better prepared to evaluate what they are finding, and less likely to get into trouble. Some of this chapter sounds much like any other book on being a good parent. As parents, we know that there is no way to totally protect your kids from all the dangers in the world. We can, however, give you some tried and true methods to at least stay engaged with your kid's life.

Does this mean that your kid will never look at pornography, download a file with a virus, or meet questionable people? No. Kids being kids, they will be tempted and they will likely experiment. With luck, coupled with a clear parental presence and interest, most kids don't stay interested in the "iffy" material for very long.

First, let's talk about the real risks on the Internet. Not all of them are directly privacy-related, but they are important for you to know about. Next, we'll give some tips for parents, and then talk about the role of companies and governments. This chapter simply touches on parental concerns and possible actions. It's important to remember that there are many good resources on the Net that point you to additional information.

# What Are the Risks?

When evaluating risks on the Internet, it is important to keep a sense of balance and reality. Although we hear horrible stories about kids being lured to meet molesters, or being used for kid pornography, it's important to remember that those kinds of events are rare. Your kid is more likely to have an online encounter with rude or nasty people; receive e-mail from someone trying to sell something or promoting some sort of "get rich quick" scheme; or view pornography or get manipulated into downloading a game or program that doesn't live up to the advertising.

However, there *are* real dangers out there. We consulted with Parry Aftab, Executive Director of Cyberangels (`http://www.cyberangels.com/`). She is also the author of *The Parent's Guide to Protecting Your Children in Cyberspace*, and helped the FTC write many of the guidelines about children's privacy protection.

In the past  few years, there have been many surveys trying to determine how many children are actually using the Internet. As best we (and they) can tell, there are something in excess of 26 million children online. Many of them are under the age of 7.

Parry's research indicates that these children, the young ones, are not in great danger of being molested or kidnapped or hurt as the result of their online involvement. There are no published, validated results of a small child being attacked as a result of online involvement. They don't have a lot of unsupervised time, and are usually not interacting with other people online. They don't generally spend their time in chat rooms or use instant messages.

On the other hand, children over 17 are not likely to be enticed or fooled by a sexual predator because they're learning to be more cynical.

According to Parry, it's the critical 11 to 16 year-old age group that is most vulnerable to real physical assault. These young people are at an age where they have more unsupervised hours outside of the home. Combining their new freedom with the fact that online predators frequently approach these kids leads to potentially dangerous situations that parents need to monitor closely.

## Meeting Online Can Lead to Meeting Offline

Cyberangels works with middle-school and high-school students regularly. They talk to more than 1,000 teens a month, and get some good information about what these kids encounter online. Parry reports that if these kids are surveyed *without their parents or teachers in the room,* 65% of the girls and 45% of the boys report having had a physical meeting with someone they met online.

There are 4,500 to 6,000 reported cases of sexual predation on teens as a result of Internet contact in 2000, out of that estimated 26 million kids who are online. We don't know if this is because there is no box for "Internet" on most crime forms, or because the crime itself is underreported. Cyberangels reports that there were only seven kids reported missing as a result of online contact as of August, 2001.

These kids are meeting people in chat rooms, over instant messaging, and in other online environments where kids talk freely. The teens are signing up for services, building profiles, using provocative names, putting their pictures on their personal Web sites, and talking to anyone who will talk to them. The problem, of course, is that you don't really know who's typing on the other end of the line. It might be another 14 year old—or it might be a 35 year old who likes to "date young,"[1] and finds new potential partners online. It's hard to tell the difference between an adult posing as a teen and a real teenager, says Aftab. The adults study the kids' slang, sentence structures, and other mannerisms. They are good at imitation, and there are a lot of them out there.

CBS News in June 2001 reported that almost every day police or federal agents arrest what they call a "traveler," a sexual predator who uses the Web not just to ask an underage child for sex, but who also arranges a meeting, even if they must travel to get there (http://www.kyw.com/now/story/0,1597,198189-406,00.shtml). FBI agents pretending to be children go to chat rooms where they suspect child predators are waiting, based on reports from other children and other successful investigations.

CBS News correspondent Wyatt Andrews interviewed FBI Special Agent Pete Gullotta, spokesman for the FBI's "Innocent Images" operation. Gullotta says that it doesn't take long to be approached for sex. "Our agents go online into predicated chat rooms...using the identity of a young boy or a young girl,...and in a very, very short period of time they are contacted by an adult, generally an adult male who thinks that we are children.

Parry says that the conversation soon turns to sex, a point with which the FBI experience agrees. Of 10,800 teens surveyed in 2000 by Cyberangels, 60% admitted to having cybersex with strangers they meet online. Soon after that, the online "friend" suggests a meeting.

And a significant number of these kids go willingly, alone, to meet this stranger. Why? Parry says that there are several reasons. One of them is that the parental warning "not to talk to strangers" doesn't apply to other kids. After all, we take kids to the playground and insist they play with the other kids. We encourage them to make new friends at school, church,

---

[1] *Many individuals who have engaged in real-world meetings and sexual relationships with teenagers do not think of themselves as sexual predators. Rather, they see that their dating preferences are for "very young" partners and these people object to statutory rape laws and other regulations regarding the age of the partners.*

and other places they gather. Online, when the person they're meeting is projecting the identity of another child, the warning flags *do not go up.*

When the meeting occurs, of course, the child may find that this person is really an adult, and sometimes an adult from another city. In the CBS interviews quoted above, Agent Gullotta reported that these adult "travelers" will drive up to 500 miles to meet a new child.

Parry says that the adult takes advantage of the confusion, shock, shame, and disconnect from reality that happens when the child finds that their online romance is an adult. "These kids can't separate the online persona, who professes to love them and cherish them, understand them in ways that others don't, from the real-world adult person standing in front of them." The adult reminds the child of the things they've shared, of the trust that is built. It works, says Aftab, in a disturbing number of cases. Fourteen percent of the teens worldwide who admit to having met a stranger offline further acknowledge having had sex with them. "Boys sometimes think experimentation in homosexuality is cool. Girls have been promised love, romance, and frequently marriage, and they believe it."

The good news is that police are getting better at catching these predators. The bad news, of course, is that so many kids don't report these events, and thus there's no hope of catching the adult behind it.

Of course, not every person your child meets online is going to be a sexual predator. More likely, it's another kid, and many really long-term and important relationships have been started online. The point is that you and your child can work together to weed out the bad guys from the good guys.

## What Can I Do?

This is very frightening to parents everywhere. It might make you want to unplug the computer permanently. As parental experience for thousands of years shows us, forbidding something only makes it sweeter. The best idea is to be a participative parent in your children's computing lives. If you have a pre-teen or teen in the danger zone of 12–16, you need to be particularly aware.

Parry says that these things happen right under the parents' noses because "the parents are too busy to understand what they read online, and clueless about the technology. Most parents have no idea what instant messaging is, much less how to set it up."

Clearly, the only hope you have as a parent is to pay attention. The following sidebar, *Guidelines for Parents*, summarizes in a useful format good habits for you to use in helping your kids to be safe online. It is used with permission of Larry Magid and SafeKids.org. You might consider photocopying it and keeping it near your computer for later reference.

## GUIDELINES FOR PARENTS

By taking responsibility for your children's online computer use, parents can greatly minimize any potential risks of being online. Make it a family rule to

- Never give out identifying information—home address, school name, or telephone number—in a public message such as chat or bulletin boards, and be sure you're dealing with someone that both you and your child know and trust before giving it out via e-mail. Think carefully before revealing any personal information such as age, marital status, or financial information. Consider using a pseudonym or unlisting your child's name if your service allows it.

- Get to know the services your child uses. If you don't know how to log on, get your child to show you. Find out what types of information it offers and whether there are ways for parents to block out objectionable material.

- Never allow a child to arrange a face-to-face meeting with another computer user without parental permission. If a meeting is arranged, make the first one in a public spot, and be sure to accompany your child.

- Never respond to messages or bulletin board items that are suggestive, obscene, belligerent, threatening, or make you feel uncomfortable. Encourage your children to tell you if they encounter such messages. If you or your child receives a message that is harassing, of a sexual nature, or threatening, forward a copy of the message to your service provider and ask for their assistance.

- Should you become aware of the transmission, use, or viewing of child pornography while online, immediately report this to the National Center for Missing and Exploited Children by calling 1-800-843-5678 or visiting the CyberTipLine (http://www.cybertipline.com) online. You should also notify your online service.

- Remember that people online may not be who they seem. Because you can't see or even hear the person, it would be easy for someone to misrepresent him- or herself. Thus, someone indicating that "she" is a "12-year-old girl" could in reality be a 40-year-old man.

- Remember that everything you read online may not be true. Any offer that's "too good to be true" probably is. Be very careful about any offers that involve your coming to a meeting or having someone visit your house.

- Set reasonable rules and guidelines for computer use by your children (see the "Kids' Rules for Online Safety" sidebar later in this chapter). Discuss these rules and post them near the computer as a reminder. Remember to monitor their compliance with these rules, especially when it comes to the amount of time your children spend on the computer. A child or teenager's excessive use of online services or bulletin boards, especially late at night, may be a clue that there is a potential problem. Remember that personal computers and online services should not be used as electronic babysitters.

- Be sure, to make this a family activity. Consider keeping the computer in a family room rather than the child's bedroom. Get to know their "online friends" just as you get to know all their other friends.

# Your Tone Sets the Stage

It's also true, that your response when your kid has these encounters can set the tone for the rest of their experience on the Net. If you get outraged or punish them, you may set up a "forbidden fruit" scenario that leads to more trouble. If you can talk reasonably and calmly about the incident, discuss why you think the site is inappropriate or ill-advised. You're more likely to keep your kid's confidence and that's the key to keeping kids from getting into too much trouble in any venue.

It's really important that you encourage your kid to come to you when he encounters *anything* online (or not) that makes him uncomfortable. If you can talk about your kid's experience, explain to your kid about the material or activity, and help your kid to understand how to deal with their discomfort, you have gone a long way in providing your kid with adequate protection. Obviously, explanations and discussions need to be appropriate for the age and understanding of your kid. Long philosophical discussions are usually not appropriate, but concise, factual responses to your kid's questions do not only help your kid with the material in question, but also give your kid armor for the next encounter. Unfortunately, recognizing danger is something we have to teach our kids because we can't be with them and protect them all the time.

So, let's look at what else is realistically lurking on the Net.

## Objectionable or Inappropriate Material

No kid surfs the Net for long without running into material that is inappropriate for their age, education, or your family beliefs. Searching for things on the Net occasionally has unexpected results. A word that means one thing to you may have a specifically different meaning in another community, for example. The Internet is one of the most powerful aids to free expression ever created, and that, of course, means that people who are sexual predators, hateful, bigoted, violent, or involved with unlawful activities use it, too. You will also find Web sites espousing every possible political viewpoint, some of which you may not agree with.

A quick way to see this is to choose a search engine you like and put in the word "Flag." As you would expect, your results include links to a page about world flags, links to pages about the U.S. flag, and links to pages for companies who sell flags. You might not have expected a link to "The Flag Burning Page" though. Many people do not find flag burning to be a legitimate form of protest and would not want their kids to study this site. What do *you* want your kids to do when they encounter a site like this?

Think how you respond to information and material that makes you uncomfortable or angry or sad. Now think about your kids and how you'd like them to be prepared to respond. You need to have your kids understand what you want them to do when they encounter these materials. For example, some erotica sites start new browser teaser windows when the first page displays. Your kid may need help shutting down all the windows.

Internet software developers have designed filtering and blocking software that attempts to block out material inappropriate for kids. These programs, or settings within your already installed browser, restrict the viewer by not showing sites that meet specific criteria. Instead of taking the blocking approach, the American Library Association, among many other developers, tries the positive list approach by maintaining a large list of excellent and appropriate sites for young people. Another approach is to use kid-friendly browsers or online services where the browser or the service does the blocking and filtering for you. There are even kid-friendly search engines that guard against the unexpected search result.

One of the best search engines, which has good kid controls, is Google. They are at http://www.google.com, and the page that lets you set up filters for your kids is in Figure 4.1.

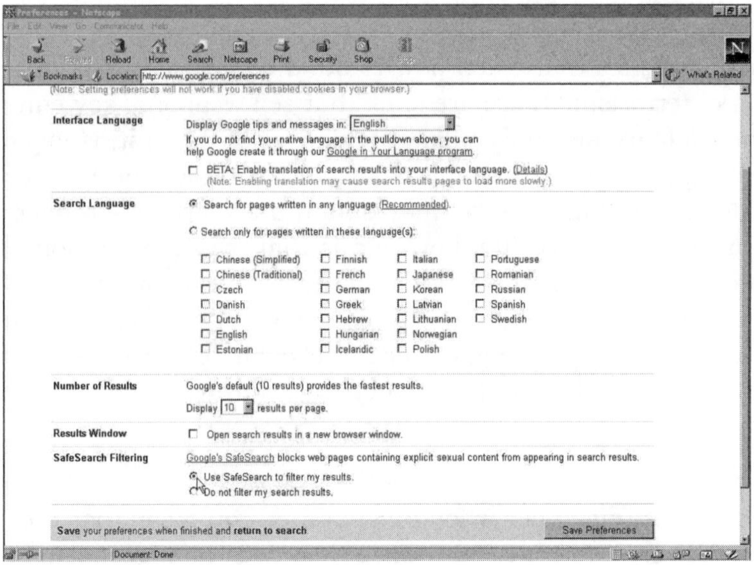

**FIGURE 4.1**

*The Google SafeSearch configuration page.*

## Drugs, Alcohol, and Tobacco

Your kid can encounter drugs, alcohol, or tobacco on the Internet in two ways. The most common is information about them, advocating their use or misuse. The other is information about how to purchase these items.

Many sites on the Internet discuss the wide variety of drugs available, from those mostly used for medicinal purposes to those mostly used for "recreational" purposes. Some of these sites advocate that drug use is harmless; other organizations, such as the DARE (Drug Abuse Resistance Education) and MADD (Mothers Against Drunk Driving), seek to educate kids about the dangers of drug and alcohol abuse. In searching for those that educate about the risks of drugs, an Internet search is bound to find the advocacy sites, too.

Then there are sites that sell alcohol, tobacco, and pharmaceutical products. Many of these sites only ask for a credit-card number, expiration date, and the billing address—information that is easy for your kid to obtain. Besides all the other indicators that your kid may be using or selling these substances, it doesn't hurt to be particularly vigilant in reading your credit card and bank statements.

## Weapons and Warfare

There are sites that teach how to build bombs, fire weapons, and commit acts of terrorism. There are sites that sell weapons, spy equipment, and other military paraphernalia. The danger of the first, is, of course, the knowledge of how to commit violence. The danger of the second, less obviously, is that your kid may obtain these articles by spending your or their money. The reality, however, is that the Internet alone has never been the sole reason why a young person has committed violent acts. If a young person is going to use a pipe bomb at school, or use an automatic weapon to start shooting his or her classmates, there is usually much more going on than just too much Web surfing.

## Free Spending

Some of us remember when our parents would say that they knew we wouldn't get into trouble because there was no place for us to go—or refuse to give us an allowance because there was no place to spend it. The Internet has changed all that. Anyone with a valid credit card and some simply obtained information, as we mentioned earlier, can buy and buy and buy. Before 2000, the only solution to this was a two-part strategy: Teach your kids about money at an early age (including the fact that credit cards really are money, not just Monopoly money) and keep track of the expenditures on your charge cards.

In 2000, several financial institutions recognized that teens, in particular, might benefit from stored value cards. These cards are not credit cards, but prepaid cards that work like a prepaid long-distance telephone service card. Parents choose an amount to prepay into the card account and the user of the card chooses where the money is spent. It's an interesting way of implementing an allowance and is a good solution to the "how to get money to the kid away at college" problem. The idea is that the young people learn how to spend money appropriately (and what happens when the money is gone). Money can be added to these cards relatively simply, and the tracking that adults expect with monthly credit card statements can be accomplished. Some cards block spending at certain kinds of merchants. Others flag the expenditures in their reports. As of this writing, the cards available are The Cobaltcard from American Express (see Figure 4.2) `http://www.cobaltcard.com`; Visa Buxx from several financial institutions including Capital One, Bank of America, National City, and U.S. Bank (see Figure 4.3) `http://www.visabuxx.com`; and the M2Card from PointpathBank.com `http://www.m2card.com`. The financial information site Bankrate.Com `http://www.bankrate.com` can provide additional information and comparison of these stored value cards (see Figure 4.4).

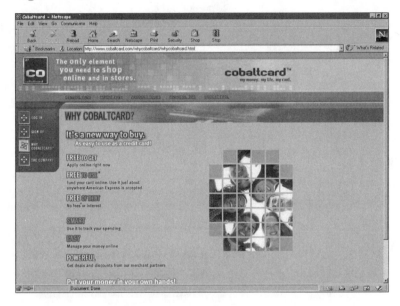

**FIGURE 4.2**

*American Express's Cobaltcard Web site.*

Another approach is to use sites specially geared for teens: DoughNet (`http://www.doughnet.com/`); iCanBuy (`http://www.icanbuy.com`); and RocketCash (`http://www.rocketcash.com`) (see Figure 4.5) responded to the concerns of parents that their kids would spend foolishly by setting up virtual malls with stores appropriate for teens. Rather than funding a card that can be used anywhere, parents set up prepaid accounts for their kids with these sites.

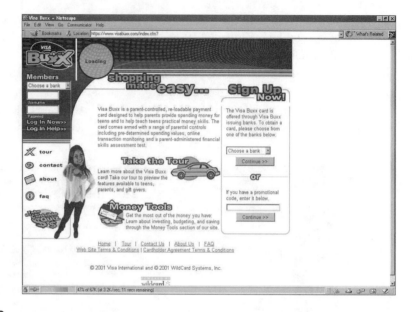

**FIGURE 4.3**

*The Visa Buxx Web site.*

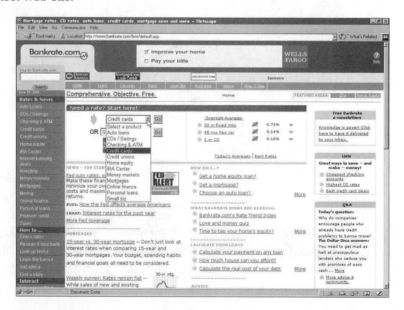

**FIGURE 4.4**

*Bankrate lets you compare stored value cards.*

**FIGURE 4.5**

*RocketCash lets parents set up accounts with specific stores online.*

## Harassment

A kid might encounter e-mail, chat, or bulletin board messages that are harassing, demeaning, or belligerent. This risk may not be life threatening, but it could affect a kid's self esteem and, frankly, it's pretty likely to occur for any kid who engages in chat rooms or exchanges messages on bulletin boards. Figure 4.6 shows a chat room on the Nickelodeon Web site.

Of course, this is not unlike the playground or schoolroom experience of most kids. Kids can be very cruel to their classmates, picking on perceived differences in very hurtful ways. There is little that parents can do to protect kids from receiving this kind of treatment. If it happens, it's good to discuss your kid's feelings and console their hurts. It's also wise to understand that your kid could be harassing others. A frank discussion of how hurtful what we say to and about others can be is good for all parents to have with their kids, whether or not the conversation is specifically about online activities.

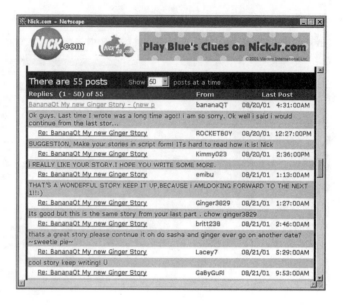

**FIGURE 4.6**

*A chat room at Nickelodeon.*

## Legal and Financial

There is also the risk that a kid could do something that has negative legal or financial consequences, such as giving out a parent's credit card or doing something that violates another person's rights. Legal issues aside, kids should be taught good "netiquette" and to behave online as they would in public and to avoid being rude, mean, or inconsiderate.

## Social Engineering

Social engineering is when someone uses people, not technology, to get information. For example, someone might call and say that they are your bank, working on a computer problem, and ask for the PIN for your ATM card. Kids are especially susceptible to social engineering because they are so trusting. We hate having to make them suspicious, but it's a necessary evil in this world, just as we have to teach them not to go with strangers.

Kids should be cautioned to never give out their Internet or AOL password to anyone, even if the person claims to work for AOL or an Internet service provider. When in doubt, kids should ask their parents and parents should know their provider's policy regarding passwords (AOL staff, for example, will never ask a member for their password).

## Extraction of Personal Information

Kids have a claim to privacy. Everything about them—their name, age, and what school they go—is their business and the business of their families. No one, including reputable companies, have a right to extract this information from kids without first checking with the kid's parents.

## Gambling and Other Inappropriate Behaviors

There are sites that enable people to gamble with real money or just "for fun." In some cases these sites may be operating legally in the jurisdiction where they are physically located, but it is generally illegal (and inappropriate) for minors to gamble, regardless of where they are. Most online gambling sites require a person to use a credit card or write a check to transfer funds. Speaking of gambling, it's also possible to buy and sell stocks and securities over the Internet. If your kid has access to your Web browser or AOL account and your brokerage password, it is possible that he might be able to conduct such a transaction. Keep an eye on this. Either prevent your kid from doing it or watch closely, so you can learn something.

# What More Can You Do?

Before we start talking about specific cases, we want to discuss talking to your kids. Especially in this age, there are so many difficult choices and decisions. Setting some ground rules for your interactions with your kids can be the key to the whole family successfully negotiating these tricky waters.

## Always Be Truthful with Your Kids

This doesn't mean overwhelming them with facts. Or telling them things they can't really comprehend yet. However, tell them the truth as you know it and be honest when you don't know an answer.

Let's take an example relevant to this book. Let's suppose your 10-year-old asks why you have kid-protection controls enabled on your browser.

The best answer, probably, is that there are a lot of materials out there that aren't appropriate for 10-year-olds. You have to be prepared for the follow-up, which is probably going to be, "Like what?" Keep that list simple, too, without going into a flood of detail on everything you think is scary out there. However, be sure to tell the truth.

The trick to this is simple. Only answer the question your kid asked. She didn't ask, "Why don't you want me to see material on birth control?" or "What *is* pedophilia?" So, don't answer those questions until they actually get asked.

Is this duplicitous? Certainly not when your kid is little. Frequently, if the kid can't articulate the question, he isn't ready for the answer. When holding back on information feels like cheating, it probably is. You'll know it when you feel it.

## Don't Pretend to Be Something You're Not

As parents, we aren't omnipotent. We're not omniscient. There are things we aren't experts at. However, that's okay. In fact, it's better than okay. It's critical that your kids not think you're perfect, because when you fail to live up to that expectation, it's an awful shock. There are lots of famous stories—novels, even—about kids finding out that their moms or dads have clay feet. If you don't set them up with that expectation, from the very beginning, they grow up thinking you are human. Why is that important? Because it gives *them* permission to be human, too. If you give yourself permission to be less than perfect, to try and fail and try again, or to color outside the lines once in awhile, they can fail without beating themselves up. That gives them space to get up and try again.

An important result comes from this realization that directly affects how your kids and you work out the rules for the Internet. If your kids know you are human, not superhuman or perfect, they are more comfortable working out issues with you. It builds trust. That means they are likely to come and say, as Pat's 12-year-old is prone to do, "Mom, I think this Web site isn't what I'm supposed to be looking at."

In addition, your children find that they can teach you things. Do you know how wonderful it feels when your kid discovers there is something he can teach you? One of the things that helps kids and parents stay friends, when they are growing and grown, is sharing things. If a kid knows he can do something for you, something that's special, he has a firm foundation to stand on, something to help build his confidence.

# Kids Need to Know That There's Reality Out There

Do you remember (well, maybe you don't) when Walter Cronkite introduced us to day-by-day pictures of war during Vietnam, something we'd never seen before? Pat was just a few years older than her son is now when she first saw soldiers sitting in the mud with bloody clothing and bandages. Her parents were horrified at the thought of her seeing real warfare. Today, more horrific things are on every newscast, and as parents, we want to protect our kids from horrific things that are beyond their understanding. Kids understand things a lot earlier than we think, however, and more and more information is available to them than was available to us when we were kids. There are more news programs, the Internet, and so on—a lot of ways that kids hear about what's going on. We guard them better by exposing them to the truth than we do by shielding them. This is sort of like allergy therapy—a little exposure every week helps prevent massive allergy attacks later on.

Our kids need to know about a lot of things, and they need to hear the straight answers to questions at home. Glee and I discovered that one of the things this does is give our boys armor against schoolyard jibes and taunts, and a willingness to shelter younger kids from schoolyard harassment. Knowledge is power; it's never smart to withhold the facts of life from kids, because it leaves them naked and alone when life smacks them in the face. Your job is to prepare them for life; don't leave them unequipped.

One tool that can help is the following sidebar, a kid's list of safe practices online. We suggest that you photocopy it and discuss it with your kids, and give the copy to them so they'll have it at home and at school.

## KIDS' RULES FOR ONLINE SAFETY

1. I will not give out personal information such as my address, telephone number, parents' work address/telephone number, or the name and location of my school without my parents' permission.

2. I will tell my parents right away if I come across any information that makes me feel uncomfortable.

3. I will never agree to get together with someone I "meet" online without first checking with my parents. If my parents agree to the meeting, I will be sure that it is in a public place and bring my mother or father along.

4. I will never send a person my picture or anything else without first checking with my parents.

5. I will not respond to any messages that are mean or in any way make me feel uncomfortable. It is not my fault if I get a message like that. If I do I will tell my parents right away so that they can contact the service provider.

6. I will talk with my parents so that we can set up rules for going online. We will decide upon the time of day that I can be online, the length of time I can be online, and appropriate areas for me to visit. I will not access other areas or break these rules without their permission.

7. I will not give out my Internet password to anyone (even my best friends) other than my parents.

8. I will be a good online citizen and not do anything that hurts other people or is against the law.

Rules one through six are adapted from the brochure, "Child Safety on the Information Highway," by SafeKids.Com founder Lawrence J. Magid. Printed copies are available free by calling 800 843-5678.

---

## Don't Lie to Yourself

It doesn't help anyone. If your kid acts like he's hiding drugs or cigarettes or *Playboy* magazines in his room, he probably is. If you ignore it, are you helping him? If she's going to class stoned, it's not the teacher's fault she's flunking algebra, and making excuses for her doesn't help her develop strength of character or pass the class. If the calendar (or the mirror) tells you your kid was born 15 or 16 years ago, he is probably going through the same kind of angst, carbonated hormones, and confusion that you did at the same age. He's worthy of the respect due someone who in many other cultures is already taking on adult responsibilities. Don't treat him like a six-year-old. That includes being realistic about what's going on.

## Discover Your Resources and Options

There are a lot of resources out there to help you. Specific laws regulate what information can be collected from kids, and you have recourse for complaints. Of course, the best way is to not have problems in the first place, and that means finding out what to look out for. First, let's talk about some sites that give you general information and help educate your kids.

# SafeKids, by Nickelodeon and Larry Magid

As you can see from Figure 4.7, SafeKids (`http://www.safekids.com/`) is a very good site for kids to cruise by themselves. The Nickelodeon people have used their skill at making things bright and interesting to kids of many ages. One of the best things for kids is an interactive quiz about online behavior. You can see it in Figure 4.8. The questions and answers are not complex, but kids learn a lot, and many of the answers point kids to have conversations with their parents about the issues. The quiz helps kids understand how seemingly innocent actions can affect their safety online. There is also an excellent list of rules to help kids protect themselves online.

**FIGURE 4.7**

*The SafeKids home page.*

SafeKids also features Larry Magid, who was one of the first to write about kids online, and has an excellent set of guidelines for parents. He also has a technology column for parents to help explain about some of the new and bewildering features that come out on the Web.

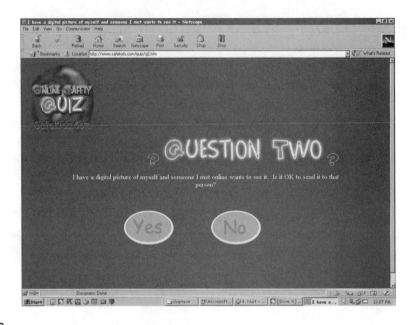

**FIGURE 4.8**

*The SafeKids Online Safety Quiz.*

## KidzPrivacy, by the U.S. Federal Trade Commission

The FTC Web site (`http://www.ftc.gov/bcp/conline/edcams/kidzprivacy/biz.htm`), as shown in Figure 4.9, has great, clear explanations of the laws regarding privacy, and also good resources for teachers and media people. The teacher's page, especially, spells out what teachers can and cannot do when helping kids negotiate the Web.

The site is one of the best places to find links to all the U.S. Government documents related to kids' privacy issues. It also contains a very clear explanation of the rules Web sites must follow when handling kids' information.

**FIGURE 4.9**

*The FTC site has information for parents and kids.*

# The Center for Media Education

The Center for Media Education maintains a page called KidsPrivacy.org (http://www.kidsprivacy.org/). The CME published a report in 1996, called *Web of Deception*, which helped kick off the campaign to make laws about kids' privacy online. One of the nicer features of their Web site is a concise glossary of basic terms to help parents and kids understand Internet privacy and issues. The glossary is shown in Figure 4.10.

The Center's Web site has a very nice explanation of the Kids' Online Privacy Protection Act (COPPA), which was one of the results of that 1996 campaign.

In the following sidebar, we have reprinted a report from Ron Plesser and Milo Cividanes of Piper, Marbury, Ruddnick & Wolfe LLP, Washington, D.C., dated April 24, 2001, on the effectiveness of COPPA after it was in effect for more than a year.

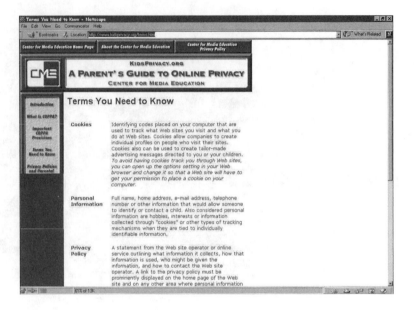

**FIGURE 4.10**

*The Center for Media Education's Glossary of Online Privacy Terms is a good intro-
duction to kids' privacy protection.*

## YEAR 1: COPPA AND THE FTC

Marking the first anniversary of the effective date of the Children's Online Privacy
Protection Act ("COPPA"), the Federal Trade Commission ("FTC") recently
announced settlements with three Web site operators for violations of the COPPA
Rule. The prosecutions centered on the Girlslife.com Web site and several sites that
partnered with it. The Girlslife.com Web site is the online counterpart to a magazine that has been published for more than six years; the magazine has a circula-
tion of about three million readers. In fact, the Girls' Life Web site was recently
named one of the top sites on the Web for children by *U.S. News and World
Report*.

The FTC accused Girls' Life and several of its partner sites of illegally collecting
names, addresses, telephone numbers, and other personal information from children under 13 years of age without parental consent. Working together, these
three companies offered children access to free e-mail, message boards, advice
columns, and other online activities. These companies have agreed to pay a total
of $100,000 in fines to settle the charges brought against them that they violated
COPPA. In addition, settlement of these cases requires each of them to delete all
personal information collected online from children since COPPA became effective.

These settlements indicate that the FTC is actively pursuing Web site operators for violations of COPPA. These operators ran afoul of COPPA not because they engaged in marketing, but rather because the approaches they took resulted in their illegally collecting personal information from children. The practices of these Web sites were particularly problematic because these sites allowed children to disclose personal information to others on message boards and via an e-mail account absent the very reliable method of consent that COPPA requires because of the dangers these activities pose to children.

Below is an overview of the operator practices the FTC focused upon in its COPPA enforcement actions. We also provide additional information about the three companies.

### A. Practices that Ran Afoul of COPPA

1. *General audience Web sites that do not comply with COPPA in those areas of the site that are directed to children and in other areas where they obtain actual knowledge that specific visitors are children*

   These cases underscore that general audience Web sites with message boards or content that is directed to children in certain areas of the site need to comply with COPPA's requirements for those children's areas. Moreover, collecting year-of-birth information results in sites acquiring the "actual knowledge" that triggers COPPA's requirements.

   For example, the Looksmart case illustrates that a general audience Web site, providing free messaging board services directed at children through a seamless portal from the Girls' Life Web site, is responsible for complying with COPPA's requirements for those areas of the site directed to children, such as its "kids message board areas." Moreover, asking for age at registration also obligates a site to comply with COPPA.

2. *Web sites directed at children that seek to avoid COPPA's requirements by "outsourcing" features to other Web sites*

   The FTC will enforce COPPA against companies that "outsource" a particular data collection feature to another Web site (*i.e.*, although advertised as a feature on a children's Web site, the message board or e-mail service actually takes place at another Web site, which could be a site directed to general audiences), even if the sponsoring sites do not themselves collect the personal information from children.

   The FTC charged that Girlslife.com—a site directed at children—offered certain features with other Web site operators, including a bulletin board service with Looksmart Ltd. and free e-mail accounts in conjunction with BigMailbox.com. The FTC held Girls' Life equally responsible for the failures of these other companies to obtain verifiable consent.

3. **Web sites that do not undertake reasonable efforts to determine whether registrants referred from children's sites are children**

   The FTC charged that despite the company's actual knowledge that Web sites such as Girlslife.com are directed to children, BigMailbox did not make reasonable efforts to determine whether registrants referred from such Web sites are children, and to notify and obtain consent from their parents.

4. **Web sites that merely state on a registration page that visitors must be 13 years of age or obtain parental consent**

   Prior to COPPA, most sites' entire efforts to protect children's privacy centered on statements both in their privacy notices and on the Web site advising children to consult with their parents or to obtain parental permission. BigMailbox continued this practice after COPPA's effective date. The BigMailbox case underscores that simply instructing visitors on a registration page that they "must be 13 years old or obtain their parent's permission" is not sufficient either to avoid triggering COPPA or to comply with its notice and consent requirements.

5. **Web sites that collect more personal information than reasonably necessary for a child to participate in the Web site's activity**

   These cases all stand for the proposition that the FTC is highly concerned with sites collecting more personal information from children than reasonably necessary for them to participate in the site's activity. For example, the FTC charged that a Web site operator does not need to collect information about a child's interests, gender, and occupation to enable a child to sign up for e-mail accounts. Similarly, the FTC charged that collecting full names and e-mail addresses of both the electronic card sender and recipient was more personal information than necessary to participate in the activity.

6. **Privacy notices that do not accurately reflect the Web site's practices and activities, or fail to contain all of the required COPPA disclosures**

   The FTC alleged that BigMailbox's privacy policy did not clearly and understandably or completely disclose its information collection, use, and disclosure practices, and contained false or misleading statements that amount to deceptive practices. For example, contrary to its practices, the BigMailbox site indicated in its privacy notice that it does not structure any part of its services to attract anyone under 13, and that it requires persons under 13 to obtain their parent's consent before allowing them to register for a BigMailbox account.

   These three cases also illustrate the importance of ensuring that all of the required statements appear in the privacy notice, and that the notice be posted at both the home page of the Web site and in close proximity to all points at which children are asked to provide personal information.

### B. Additional Background on the Defendants

The FTC reached settlements with three companies. The **Girlslife.com Web site** targets girls aged 9 to 14, offering such activities and services as bulletin boards, online articles, advice columns, contests, pen-pal opportunities, and free e-mail accounts.

Through a co-branding type of arrangement, the Girlslife.com Web site referred visitors to the **BigMailbox.com** Web site for free e-mail account service—"Girl's Life Mail"—where registrants also were asked for their age. BigMailbox.com also operated the "Smurfs.com eMail" service, which offered free e-mail accounts to visitors to the smurfs.com Web site.

The third defendant was **Looksmart**—operator of the insidetheweb.com Web site—which offers free message board services through its own Web site and through numerous other Web sites. This Web site posted the e-mail addresses and full names of participants. Although labeled a general audience Web site, insidetheweb.com contained areas directed to children, such as its "kids" message board area, where participants are required to provide their age.

Through a co-branding type of arrangement, Looksmart operated six message boards that used the Girls' Life name in their titles and to which Girlslife.com's visitors could post directly.

*For further information, contact Ron Plesser (202/861-3969) or Milo Cividanes (202/861-3911).*

# TRUSTe Kids' Privacy Seal Program

TRUSTe (http://www.truste.org/programs/pub_kid.html) is a *seal organization.* They run a program to certify that Web sites have good privacy policies, and the site is following the information practices in that policy. TRUSTe also has a separate kids' seal program (see Figure 4.11), which educates parents and kids on the information practices used by a Web site that subscribes to the seal program. According to the TRUSTe site, the charter of this program is:

Parents and kids who visit sites that post the Kids' Seal will know the site has complied with TRUSTe's Kids' Program, TRUSTe is providing ongoing review to ensure the site is not violating its privacy statement, and that a formal complaint and resolution process exists if consumers perceive that the site may not be in compliance with the TRUSTe program.

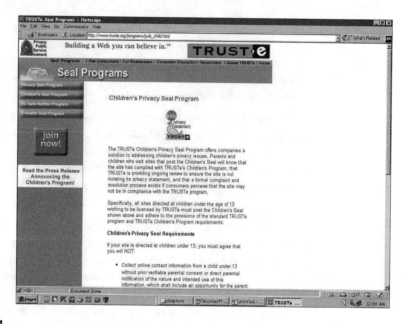

**FIGURE 4.11**

*The TRUSTe Kids' Seal Program helps parents find out how their kids' information is handled.*

## CDT's Kids' Privacy Page

The Center for Democracy and Technology (CDT) has some excellent information for parents about the laws regarding kids' privacy (see Figure 4.12). It is mostly directed at parents and professionals rather than for kids themselves. You can find their kids' privacy page at
`http://www.cdt.org/privacy/children/`.

## Keeping Kids in Safe Spaces While Searching Online

One of the most worrisome aspects of kids surfing the Net is that they go to a search engine, enter what seems like an innocent question, and come up with inappropriate results. SafeKids, as mentioned earlier, has an index site for a lot of search engines that are either configured to prevent this sort of accident, or have a controlled list of sites that they search on. You can find this site at `http://www.safekids.com/search.htm`.

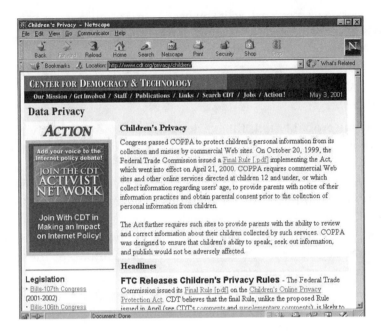

**FIGURE 4.12**

*The CDT's Web site is aimed at parents and professionals.*

SafeKids also has a good index to other sites with general education about kids and the Web, at `http://www.safekids.com/other_sites.html`.

# What Help do Parents Have in Protecting Their Kids?

Two things do the most good: getting the family into the habit of good communication about online computing, and teaching us the laws that companies must abide by. We've talked a lot about what parents should do in terms of strengthening the communication with their kids. Now we discuss what legal protections we have and how to use them effectively.

At the end of this chapter are three important tools for your use, written by Larry Magid, one of the first people to write about children online. Those tools are the kids' privacy checklist, the parent's privacy checklist, and the family computing contract.

CAUTION

We should say again: We are not lawyers, nor are we licensed to practice law. We are not giving legal advice, and we are not allowed to advise you on specific problems. The information here is subject to change, and you should check with your own lawyer or legal aid if you need help. The privacy advocacy organizations listed in Chapter 14, "Canaries in the Coal Mine," or the Seal organizations in Chapter 15, "Self-Regulation and Privacy," may also be able to help you.

## What the Law Says

As you can probably tell, this varies a lot depending on where you live. If you live in Europe, the European Union (EU) data protection statutes cover kids' privacy along with regular issues, with no particular attention paid to kids. In the United States, where protection of kids from harmful content on the Internet has sometimes reached fever pitch, there is a special law for kids' privacy protection, called the Children's Online Privacy Act (COPA). Its partner regulations, the Children's Online Privacy Protection Regulations (COPPR), outline how companies must act to be in line with the law's provisions.

COPPR applies to "personally identifiable information" for kids under the age of 13. If you remember back in Chapter 2, "What *Is* Privacy in a Digital World?," where we defined fair information practices, personally identifiable information (PII) is defined as data that can be used to identify, contact, or locate someone. Examples include name, address, phone number, and e-mail address. Demographic information (for example, gender, hobbies, and favorite color) is not considered "personally identifiable" unless it has been linked to PII (such as a kids' name).

Throughout this chapter, we have used the word "permission" when talking about the rules Web sites must follow. The actual laws and regulations discuss "parental consent," which is defined by law, including who is considered a parent.

## What Companies Must Do

U.S. companies who deal with children online are required by law to do the following:

- **Post their privacy policy**—Web sites directed at kids or that know they plan to collect information from kids under 13 must post a notice of their information collection practices that includes

   Types of PII they collect from kids. For example, name, home address, e-mail address, or hobbies.

How the site will use the information. For example, to market to the kid who supplied the information, to notify contest winners, or to make the information available through a kid's participation in a chat room.

Whether PII is forwarded to advertisers or other third parties.

A contact at the site.

- **Get parental permission**—In many cases, a site must obtain permission from the parent(s) before collecting, using, or disclosing PII about a kid. Permission is not required when a site is collecting an e-mail address to
  - Respond to a one-time request from the kid.
  - Provide notice to the parent.
  - Ensure the safety of the kid or the site.
  - Send a newsletter or other information on a regular basis as long as the site notifies a parent and gives them a chance to say no to the arrangement.

How the company gets parental permission is an interesting question. It depends on what they intend to do with the information.

## Kid's Info Must Be For Internal Use Only

If the information is for *internal use only*, that is, they do not pass it along to any other person or company, the COPPA rule is:

Web sites may use *e-mail* to get parental permission for internal use of PII, such as marketing back to a kid based on his or her preferences or communicating promotional updates about site content.

The company must, however, show that they have taken some care to be sure the person replying to the e-mail is really the parent. They can, for example, use a delayed e-mail (they send a note to the parent's address, and the parent must confirm before information is collected). Or, they can send an e-mail and ask the parent to call back before they start collection.

## Get a Permission Slip to Share Info with Others

Sometimes companies want to share a kid's personal information to third parties. For example, imagine that a kids' shoe company wanted to run a contest with a Web site that featured a kids' TV show, and collect the kids' names, addresses, and schools. The TV show's Web site would collect the information and then turn it over to the shoe company. (The purpose for a contest run by a commercial company is, we hope you know, to collect info on all the entrants. The price of the prize is much smaller than the cost of getting all that information from a survey company, for example.) Usually, when there is one of these joint contests, the site that runs the contest gets to use the information, too. That makes the information collected twice as useful.

Sometimes a company wants to make kids' info publicly available. For example, if they run a chat room or message board, they might want to offer a way for kids to find other kids interested in the same things. They might have a hobbies search, or a city search. Or, they just might want to have the information about a member of the chat room show up during the chat, to help the kids feel more like a community. If they want to display this info publicly, they *must* use a more reliable method of confirming they really have the permission of a real parent or guardian. Some of those methods might be

- Getting a signed form from the parent via postal mail or fax
- Accepting and verifying a credit card number in connection with a transaction
- Taking calls from parents, through a toll-free telephone number staffed by trained personnel
- Sending e-mail signed with a digital signature

However, in the case of a monitored chat room, if all PII is stripped from postings before it is made public—and the information is deleted from the Web site's records—the Web site operator does not have to ask the parents in advance.

One special note about credit cards as proof of age or that the person is a parent: This may not be as good a method as you might think. In June 2000, Mark MacCarthy, Senior Vice President for Public Policy, VISA U.S.A., testified before the commission that was working on the COPA regulations. He said:

*"Access to a credit card or debit card is not a good proxy for age. The mere fact a person uses a credit card or debit card in connection with a transaction does not mean the person is an adult.*

*Many individuals under the age of 17 have legitimate access to, and regular use of, credit cards and debit cards. ...In addition, many children under the age of 17 have their own deposit accounts and may have access to a debit card that accesses such accounts."*

**(Source: Mark MacCarthy, COPA commission testimony,**
`http://www.copacommission.org/meetings/hearing1/agenda.shtml`**)**

When a parent agrees to the collection and use of their kid's personal information, the operator may release that information to others who use it solely to provide support for the internal operations of the Web site or service, including technical support and order fulfillment.

## But There Are Always Exceptions

The regulations include several instances that enable Web sites to collect a kid's e-mail address without getting the parent's permission in advance. These exceptions cover many popular online activities for kids, including *contests*, *online newsletters*, *homework help*, and *electronic postcards*.

Prior parental permission is not required when

- A Web site collects a kid's or parent's e-mail address to provide notice and get their permission for more information collection.

- A Web site collects an e-mail address to respond to a *one-time* request from a kid and then deletes it.

- A Web site collects an e-mail address to respond *more than once to a specific* request—for a subscription to a newsletter. In this case, the operator must notify the parent that it is communicating regularly with the kid and give the parent the opportunity to stop the communication *before* sending or delivering a *second* communication to a kid.

- A Web site collects a kid's name or online contact information to protect the safety of a kid who is participating on the site. In this case, the Web site must notify the parent and give him the opportunity to prevent further use of the information.

- A Web site collects a kid's name or online contact information to protect the security or liability of the site or to respond to law enforcement, if necessary, and does not use it for any other purpose.

## They Must Ask Again if They Want to do Something New

The COPPA regulations say that Web site operators need to notify parents and get permission again if they plan to change the kinds of information they collect, change how they use the information, or offer the information to new and different third parties. For example, new parental permission would be required if the Web site decides to

- Send information from kids to marketers of diet pills instead of only marketers of stuffed animals, as covered in the original permission.
- Give a kid access to a chat room if the parent's original permission covered only sending a newsletter.

## Parents Should Have Access to the PII

- **Allow parents to review personal information collected from their kids**—To do this, Web site operators must verify the identity of the parent who has made the request, and may use a variety of ways to do that.
- **Allow parents to revoke their permission, and delete information collected from their kids at the parents' request**—Parents can revoke their permission and ask that information about their kids be deleted from the site's database. When a parent revokes permission, the Web site must stop collecting, using, or disclosing information from that kid. You need to know, however, that the site stops letting a kid participate in an activity if the information it collected was necessary for participation in the activity.

 **NOTE**    If you own a business and want to be in compliance with the law, the best place to start learning how is at the FTC's KidzPrivacy site. The business rules are at http://www.ftc.gov/bcp/conline/pubs/buspubs/coppa.htm.

## What Parents Should Do

As parents, we can protect our children by making a habit of the following practices.

- **Look for the privacy policy on any Web site directed to kids, and read it**—The policy must be available through a link on the

Web site's homepage. It must also show up anywhere PII is collected from kids. Web sites for general audiences that have a kids' section must post the notice on the home pages of the section for kids.

Read the policy closely to find out what kinds of PII will be collected, how it will be used, and whether it will be passed on to other companies. (Other companies are called "third parties" in the regulations.) If you find a Web site that doesn't post basic protections for kids' personal information, ask for details about their information collection practices.

Some sites are collection agencies for other companies. For example, a manufacturer of kids' shoes might run a survey or contest on a site for a kids' TV show. If the site is not using the info themselves, but is collecting it to pass along, they must tell you in advance.

- **Decide whether to give consent**—Giving consent authorizes the Web site to collect personal information from your kid. You can give consent and still say no to having your kids' information passed along to a third party.

  Your consent isn't necessary if the Web site is collecting your kids' e-mail address simply to respond to a one-time request for information.

- **Decide whether to approve information collection from your kids based on new uses for the information**—Web site operators will let you know about the need for new consent by sending you a new notice and request. They will do this when they are changing the terms of use of the information in a "material" or significant way.

- **Ask to see the information your kid has submitted**—The site will ask you to verify your identity to ensure that your kids' information isn't given out improperly.

- **Understand that you may revoke your consent at any time and have your kids' information deleted**—To stop a Web site from collecting additional information from your kid, you can revoke your consent. You also may ask a site to delete any personal information it has already collected from your kid.

# What Parents *and* Kids Should Do

Together, parents and children can make and sign a contract, each to help the other, making everyone responsible and aware of the potential harm.

As with other contracts with your children, whether they be explicit or implied, it is important to determine in advance what punishment might be given for breaking a contract.

### FAMILY CONTRACT FOR ONLINE SAFETY

Parents' Pledge

1. I will get to know the services and Web sites my child uses. If I don't know how to use them, I'll get my child to show me how.

2. I will set reasonable rules and guidelines for computer use by my children and will discuss these rules and post them near the computer as a reminder. I'll remember to monitor their compliance with these rules, especially when it comes to the amount of time they spend on the computer.

3. I will not overreact if my child tells me about a problem he or she is having on the Internet. Instead, we'll work together to try to solve the problem and prevent it from happening again.

4. I promise not to use a PC or the Internet as an electronic baby-sitter.

5. I will help make the Internet a family activity and ask my child to help plan family events using the Internet.

6. I will try get to know my child's "online friends" just as I try get to know his or her other friends.

I agree to the above

_____

Parent(s) sign here

I understand that my parent(s) has agreed to these rules and agree to help my parent(s) explore the Internet with me.

_____

Child sign here

Kids' Pledge

1. I will not give out personal information such as my address, telephone number, parents' work address/telephone number, or the name and location of my school without my parents' permission

2. I will tell my parents right away if I come across any information that makes me feel uncomfortable.

3. I will never agree to get together with someone I "meet" online without first checking with my parents. If my parents agree to the meeting, I will be sure that it is in a public place and bring my mother or father along.

4. I will never send a person my picture or anything else without first checking with my parents.

5. I will not respond to any messages that are mean or in any way make me feel uncomfortable. It is not my fault if I get a message like that. If I do I will tell my parents right away so that they can contact the service provider.

6. I will talk with my parents so that we can set up rules for going online. We will decide upon the time of day that I can be online, the length of time I can be online, and appropriate areas for me to visit. I will not access other areas or break these rules without their permission.

7. I will not give out my Internet password to anyone (even my best friends) other than my parents.

8. I will be a good online citizen and not do anything that hurts other people or is against the law.

I agree to the above

_____

Child sign here

I will help my child follow this agreement and will allow reasonable use of the Internet as long as these rules and other family rules are followed.

_____

Parent(s) sign here

©2000 SafeKids.Com

## Now You Have All the Tools

In this chapter you have learned about the dangers to kids online, and some ways to protect them. You have also learned how to evaluate when it's safe to let your kids give away personally identifiable information, and when to restrict that information. In this chapter, we have given you checklists for both parents and kids, and a family contract to help everyone feel good about the computing habits of your family. We encourage you to photocopy them and put them in the places where your kids do computing. You might even put a copy in your kids' notebooks if they are using the computer at someone else's house. If you are a teacher, you might want to send these home with the students, or use them to create your own. (Please give Larry Magid credit if you do use, them, however!)

# 5

# ONLINE DISCLOSURES AND THAT BARN DOOR

A digital copy is a perfect copy every time. A digital copy is very easily transmitted, stored, and retransmitted, again and again. This is an advantage if you want to preserve something. If the information in digital form is information about you that you didn't realize was floating around in cyberspace without your permission, it's a distinct disadvantage.

We're all familiar with the old saying about closing the barn door after the horses are gone. Some things you think about doing to help yourself are too little, as well as too late. Closing the barn door to keep the horses from escaping before the horses discover they can leave is better.

We expect horses to wander off if they are not carefully closed into a corral or barn. We know that the horses have minds of their own and that their agendas don't necessarily match ours. Our expectations of horse behavior are an important part governing the actions we take around horses.

On the Internet, users have expectations, too. These expectations govern our behavior.

Something is interesting in our interactions with and on the Net. In a previous book, we speculated that the fact that a blank screen reflects our own images probably affects the way we act in ways that we don't explicitly think about. We tend to see others as we are ourselves, rather than as they are.

Because most of us are honest, we really do expect that others are honest, too. Of course, most people are honest. However, like the horses, some folks' agendas may not match ours, even if they are honest. So, it's important to know about the territory we are in, as well as know about the barn doors.

# Defensive Internet Travels

When we drive a car on the highway, we are supposed to have a driver's license, issued by our state government. This process assures us that those who are steering potentially lethal vehicles have a minimum level of competence that was measured and certified. The places where we refuel are carefully inspected to make sure they are safe and that the fuel we purchase is the appropriate grade and measured fairly. The public roads are designed and built according to safe standards. Our governments change the standards as more information becomes available about improving the engineering of roads and bridges. Where we live in California, many of the state's overpasses and bridges have been structurally improved based on the feedback from what was and was not successful engineering for earthquake country.

Over time, our driver's license has come to be used to identify us. It has taken the place of the identity card used by other governments. When we travel by air these days, we are used to producing some sort of government-issued identity document for the airline personnel. Usually the document is a driver's license or a passport. This simple security measure helps to make sure that those who are traveling are those for whom the ticket was purchased.

There is no driver's license, identity check, or security check before you get on the Internet—for you, or for anyone else. This means that people on the Internet haven't been tested for minimum competence or understanding of the rules. The rules aren't always clear, either. Later in this book, we discuss some of the different privacy laws that can affect the passage of information from one place to another. Who you are and where you are matter a lot in determining which rules you must follow. Remembering that not everyone needs to play by the rules that you think are in force is important. The law is not the same in every place.

Because of the ease with which one can set up a service on the Internet, it is possible that some of the service operators are not what they seem. If you are driving, you can see other drivers in cars near you. If you see someone doing unsafe things, you can try to avoid that driver. This is called driving defensively. For your own safety it's good practice. If you are shopping downtown, you can see the type of surroundings and gauge whether you are physically safe. You can choose not to go to unsafe places. When people ask you questions, you can choose what you want to tell them about yourself, based on your feelings about the environment.

On the Internet, unlike when you are driving or shopping downtown, you can't see the other people. That means that you always have to act defensively. We think that's the hardest thing to keep in mind when you are on the Internet. You need to keep your guard up, and release information about yourself with caution because you can't see to whom you are giving it.

## Information You Share on Purpose

We are all familiar with the mechanics of the magazine subscription. You fill out a form with your mailing address. You promise to pay the bill for the subscription. The magazines come in the postal mail.

Some of us learned to subscribe with fake names, or "interesting" middle initials not actually our own, to see what mailing lists we ended up on. For example, when Pat subscribed to *Vanity Fair,* she put her middle initial as *V.* From the mailings, which came to Pat V. McGregor, she could tell when *Vanity Fair* had sold her name. Most of us were amused by the trail our names left, because we wanted to read the original magazine and usually didn't mind receiving the direct marketing materials. After all, we could easily toss them into the trash if we didn't want to read them. They might have been irritating, but we didn't see them as invasive.

Many online services are similar to magazine subscriptions, whether they are shopping rating services, personal relationship services, such as sites that match interested singles, or places to get today's horoscope. You fill out a registration form and you receive a service. Advertising may support the service or it may require a fee, or both—not unlike magazine subscriptions.

The important point is that any information the service gains about you, you have given them. The registration/signup process is an explicit one. Figure 5.1 shows the initial part of the signup page for the BizRate.com shopping service. BizRate.com is a shopping service that maintains ratings about the various merchants who offer their wares through this program.

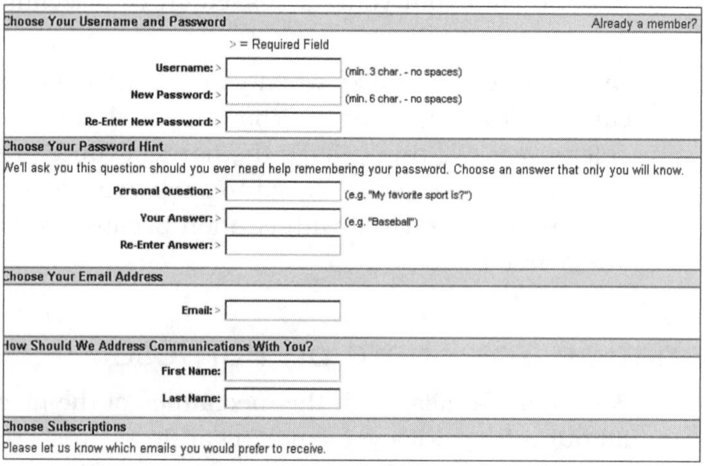
Choose Your Username and Password
Already a member?
> = Required Field
Username: > (min. 3 char. - no spaces)
New Password: > (min. 6 char. - no spaces)
Re-Enter New Password: >
Choose Your Password Hint
We'll ask you this question should you ever need help remembering your password. Choose an answer that only you will know.
Personal Question: > (e.g. "My favorite sport is?")
Your Answer: > (e.g. "Baseball")
Re-Enter Answer: >
Choose Your Email Address
Email: >
How Should We Address Communications With You?
First Name:
Last Name:
Choose Subscriptions
Please let us know which emails you would prefer to receive.

**FIGURE 5.1**

*The beginning of the BizRate.com signup page.*

Information about customers and what they think definitely helps businesses. Any good business would want to know what its customers think so that it could fix things that are problems and understand the things that make customers happy. Additionally, if a business can understand what makes people under 25 respond or what women customers prefer or any of a number other demographic-based sets of responses, that is valuable, too. So, signup pages such as BizRate.com also ask for demographic information a user is willing to share. Figure

5.2 shows the last part of the signup page. You can see that if the merchants correlated the demographic information with the ratings responses, the merchants would have excellent information about their customers.

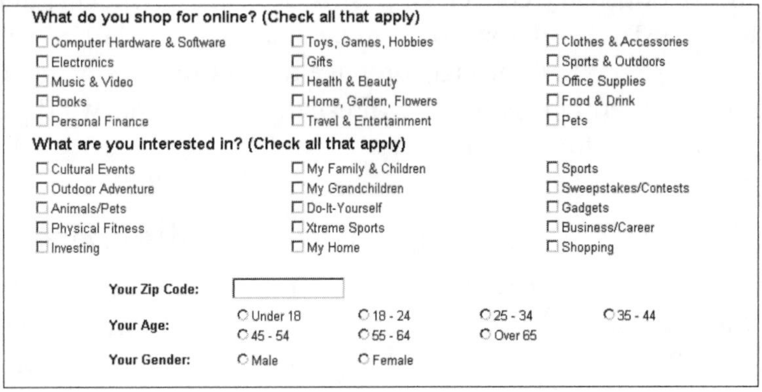

**What do you shop for online? (Check all that apply)**

| | | |
|---|---|---|
| ☐ Computer Hardware & Software | ☐ Toys, Games, Hobbies | ☐ Clothes & Accessories |
| ☐ Electronics | ☐ Gifts | ☐ Sports & Outdoors |
| ☐ Music & Video | ☐ Health & Beauty | ☐ Office Supplies |
| ☐ Books | ☐ Home, Garden, Flowers | ☐ Food & Drink |
| ☐ Personal Finance | ☐ Travel & Entertainment | ☐ Pets |

**What are you interested in? (Check all that apply)**

| | | |
|---|---|---|
| ☐ Cultural Events | ☐ My Family & Children | ☐ Sports |
| ☐ Outdoor Adventure | ☐ My Grandchildren | ☐ Sweepstakes/Contests |
| ☐ Animals/Pets | ☐ Do-It-Yourself | ☐ Gadgets |
| ☐ Physical Fitness | ☐ Xtreme Sports | ☐ Business/Career |
| ☐ Investing | ☐ My Home | ☐ Shopping |

**Your Zip Code:** [            ]

**Your Age:** ○ Under 18　○ 18 - 24　○ 25 - 34　○ 35 - 44　○ 45 - 54　○ 55 - 64　○ Over 65

**Your Gender:** ○ Male　○ Female

**FIGURE 5.2**

*The last of the BizRate.com signup page.*

The entire service is based on a bargain made between the user and the merchant with the BizRate.com service as the facilitator. The merchant provides reduced purchase price for desired items because the customer identified that he was interested in the "deal" and was willing to trade information to receive that benefit.

This is a fair trade in the marketplace. Each party knows the value of the other party's contribution to the transaction. If you do participate, you receive notification about sales and discounts that you yourself identified as being of interest to you. If you do not trust the BizRate.com site, you need not participate.

If you only "sort of" trust the BizRate.com site, you can still participate. You can give them information that does not identify you.

You are able to choose your own username. You choose the e-mail address to which the e-mail is sent, and you choose the way the e-mail is to be addressed. If you carefully choose a non-identifying e-mail address, give a zip code other than your own, and don't answer the gender and age questions, you most likely are not identifiable.

Although you were taught not to lie, keeping yourself private in this way can be wise, particularly if it makes you feel safer online. Because you sign in to their program each time you use it, they are able to gather information and build a profile associated with your username. This helps them provide information to their merchant partners without necessarily identifying you specifically. The BizRate.com people, by the way, are aware of privacy concerns, post a clear privacy policy, and participate in the TRUSTe Web-trust program (see more about TRUSTe in Chapter 15). We were using their sign-up page as an example of the kind of pages that are frequently seen on the Internet, not because we think they might misuse information.

# E-mail and Chat Can be Information Collectors, Too

Web sites aren't the only Internet activities where you can choose to give out information, but just the places where you are most likely to be asked to fill out forms. Information can be sought using other Internet programs, too.

If you get an unsolicited e-mail asking for credit card information, along with your name, address, phone number, or any other information that could be used to defraud you, it would be wise to just delete it. It is hard to think of a good reason to send anyone this information this way. No matter how enticing the merchandise offered, there is little you can do to check out the *bona fides* of an unsolicited e-mail.

The market fraud experts at the Federal Trade Commission continually remind us that if a deal sounds too good to be true, it probably is. Don't let yourself be cheated by being greedy.

The same cautions should apply to requests in chat rooms, communications within bulletin board systems or message boards, or requests sent via instant messenger programs. You cannot really "know" the other participants in a chat room, unless you obtain identifying information about their usernames outside of the chat room. Even if the username is familiar to you because you have corresponded or chatted with that user before, you can't be sure who is on the receiving end. Don't be taken in by requests for help with money problems, no matter how deserving the requester seems. Don't share your real name or physical address with someone unless you are sure who they are. Don't offer to lend them money. Don't bite on offers of fabulous merchandise at very low prices.

People who seem friendly over the Net are no different from people who seem friendly if you spoke to them on the public street. You can't tell much about new acquaintances right away. Walk softly and guard your personal information carefully. Many people are good. Some aren't. Don't let yourself be taken.

## Love Online: A Special Case for Privacy

Most of us who are not part of a couple are fascinated by personal advertisements. Whether they are online or in the local newspaper, they attract and repel us at the same time. We read the ads of those seeking us and of those like us who are seeking. We read the former to see if someone wants us. We read the latter to see if we can get ideas for our potential ad, or we read them with the superior knowledge that we would never, ever resort to meeting people this way.

Whether we seek or are seeking, it is important to remember that giving out unnecessarily identifying information to people we "meet" this way is a really bad idea. Use a fake name. Do not give out your phone number. If you choose to meet someone in person that you first met online, be sure it is in a public place and that someone knows where you are and when you should be back.

There is a reason why people have run background checks on possible scoundrels who seek to marry their daughters.  Some people really are scoundrels. The scoundrels can be of either sex. People seeking love and companionship are particularly vulnerable. If you want to play, play carefully. Many happy couples have met this way. Be one of those, not one of the ones who are very sorry that they chose to participate.

## Urban Legends and "Hi, I'm from Nigeria and..."

Like computer viruses that travel the Internet in e-mail, so do false stories and requests for help. Not all of them have a "send money" message, so you might not suspect that the story is false. Probably the most famous of these is the "Craig Shergold" chain letter hoax. It asks you to send get well cards or business cards to a seven-year-old diagnosed with brain cancer who seeks to break the Guinness Book of Records count of cards. Some of this story is true; however, it all happened a long, long time ago (Craig Shergold was born in 1979). Don't believe stories such as this without checking them out, whether or not they ask for money. If they ask for money, don't send it. If the Web site or e-mail asks you to add your name to the bottom of the list and send $1 to each of the people at the top of the list, you are participating in a chain letter. Chain letters are against the law in the United States.

The following are excellent sites that offer additional information about urban legends and hoaxes:

- **The AFU and Urban Legends Archive site**—http://www.urbanlegends.com/

- **The TruthorFiction.com site**—http://www.truthorfiction.com

- **The Urban Legends and Folklore site within About.com**—http://urbanlegends.miningco.com/cs/urbanlegends/index.htm

- **The Urban Legends Reference pages**—http://www.snopes.com and Glee's personal favorite:

- **The NetSquirrel Urban Legend Combat Kit**—http://netsquirrel.com/combatkit/

# Safety Tips for Giving Out information About Yourself

The following are some simple things that help protect your privacy when you are giving information about yourself:

- **Look for privacy policies on the Web**—That should always be the first thing you do. Look and read the Web site's privacy statement. If it doesn't match your own preferences, consider going elsewhere. If you have a browser or other tools that easily lets you know about a site's privacy, remember to watch for the privacy information.

- **Get a separate e-mail account**—With the numerous and excellent Web-based e-mail sites, you can get a separate account for each of many activities. Your true challenge may end up being keeping all your accounts and passwords straight.

- **Remember: Giving out personal information online means giving it to strangers**—If the privacy policies and other information found in the "About us" sections of the Web site seems suspicious, don't send any private information.

- **Be sure that online forms are secure**—Look for the little lock in the bottom of your browser window, as shown in Figure 5.3. It's very small but you can still see if it is open or shut. If it isn't shut, don't send information that needs to go to a secure spot, like any numbers that identify you or an account that is yours.

**FIGURE 5.3**

*If the small lock displayed in the browser status bar is closed, the connection is secured using the SSL protocol.*

# Information You Might Not Know You Are Sharing

So far we have written about the active choices you can make about sharing your information. Now we'll discuss information you share without necessarily knowing that you did so.

## How Web Pages Work

We need to start this discussion by talking a little bit about how the World Wide Web works. The Web is a co-operative endeavor. The browser program on your computer (called the *client*) reads instructions sent to it by a computer called a *server*.

A client program is usually responsible for

- Providing the user interface (what you see and how you interact with the program)
- Processing the commands the user gives and sending them to the appropriate server program
- Opening and maintaining connections to the appropriate server programs (which may be on the same computer system or on some system connected somewhere on the Internet)
- Receiving any information from the server program and delivering it as an appropriate display on your screen

The server program performs the commands given to it by the client program and sends the data (images, sounds, and information) back to the client for display. Usually, this is done without special or particular knowledge of your online/Internet service provider. Client/server program interaction may be logged/archived at either end, depending on the construction of the client/server architecture. Server programs interact with the commands given to them by approved clients without much knowledge about the user who caused the commands to be issued. Clients and servers are connected by the network infrastructure built and maintained by the online/Internet service providers.

The Web page instructions tell the browser what color the page should be and in what size and font the letters should be displayed. Included in the page are instructions for the images and ads, which are fetched separately from the instructions. Different parts of a Web page may come from different sources. The final product is displayed on the user's computer screen (or telephone display) as a single entity. The simple illustration shown in Figure 5.4 shows what we mean. A simple text Web page from Server A is displayed for the user, with a banner from Server B and a star from Server C. Notice that the banner and the star come from different server computers, but the entire page appears as a single entity to the person who views the page.

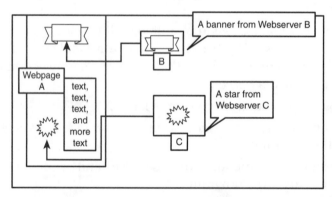

**FIGURE 5.4**

*A Web page can be displayed from several different computers.*

The instructions that told the browser what to display in our simple illustration were written in a standard language and sent to the user's computer using a standard protocol. A *protocol* is a set of rules understood by both the user's program and the server computer so that each knows what its part is. For Web pages the protocol is called the *Hypertext Transport Protocol*, or HTTP. You have no doubt noticed that

Web page addresses start with the letters http. This tells the receiving computer that the information that follows is a Web page address that should be sent to the requesting computer.

## Information Sent to the Web Server

A request to a Web server contains a lot of information about your computer and your browser program so that your requested page can be sent in a form that can be displayed to you. For example, there is a difference in how pages display on a computer screen or the way it would appear on a WebTV or wireless telephone display. The request also includes the IP (Internet Protocol) address where your computer is connected to the Internet. Otherwise, it would be like ordering a pizza to be delivered and not giving the driver the address. The request also includes the languages that your browser is capable of displaying. This is useful if your browser only displays English language characters and you request a page that is in a Cyrillic alphabet. You receive a message asking if you want to download the appropriate alphabet or if you prefer to see an incomplete page.

Programs called *scripts* running on the server use this information (called *environmental variables*) in a number of ways, usually to try and provide you with a better user experience. The scripts may take the information about the browser you are using and send information that your browser can handle. The script doesn't send that information to the other browsers that can't use the information.

The environmental variables also include a variable called HTTP_REFERER that contains the name of the page that you last visited. (If you directly typed in the address or clicked on the address in your bookmark file, this variable is blank.) This is useful to the people who operate the Web server because it shows them what site you were visiting before you came to visit their site. It also enables them to trace the path you took through their site.

Most Web sites maintain logs of the transactions that they provide. The information in the logs is saved from the HTTP request and its associated environmental variables. There is an entry in the log for each page or image requested, the time and date stamp of the request, the IP address, the name of the host computer (if available), and the information about browser type, operating system, and so on. This can provide interesting information for site operators. How many people visited? Where did they come from? What operating systems did they use? How long did they stay on each page? Which pages were more popular than others? How did people find the page? Which search engines are more popular with the people who find the site? You can see that this information is very helpful to someone who is trying to make the site more useful.

Most of us don't object to the idea of a Web site logging our activities. We chose to visit the site and the environmental variables, by themselves, are not usually enough to identify us. It is prudent to note, however, that IP addresses can identify individual computers. For always-on Internet connections like those of cable modems or DSL connections, the IP address can be traced to a specific location by combining the information gained in explicit information sharing (like an order for a product) with the information in a Web log. Although it would be difficult to say exactly who was using the computer at 11:30 p.m. on July 27, 2001, it would be relatively easy for someone to find out who lived at the residence connected at that IP address. This is why a site's privacy policies and practices are so important. Companies need to have responsible policies to guard the information that has been entrusted to them by their customers. If a company doesn't post such a policy, you should ask them to, and consider refusing to visit their site until they do.

Most Web servers collect and save logs of their visitor traffic. Those logs are processed by programs to obtain information about the visits. Software companies have designed products that perform this analysis and present reports that people can easily read. Figure 5.5 shows part of an example from the product NetTracker 5.0. Further processing of the data on visitors can produce a graph like the one shown in Figure 5.6. This information comes from counting the number of visitors coming to the site from a particular host computer. Most of the ones shown here are computers that are gateways onto particular networks such as America Online.

The report and the graph show the types of information that Webmasters need to maintain their sites. The logs show errors that need to be fixed, pages that are most popular, and ones that never get visited. Webmasters use this kind of information to incorporate improvements to their sites.

Most of the reports generated by tools such as NetTracker provide summary data, not data on individual connections.

```
                       Kendall Whaling Museum
                        Executive Summary
                           All Months

        Starting date: June 1, 2000              Ending date: Aug. 31, 2000

  Totals:                           Averages:

  Number of hits: 309041            Number of pages viewed per day: 440
  Number of megabytes transferred: 1707.80   Number of pages viewed per visit: 4
  Number of pages viewed: 40464     Length of visit: 3 minutes, 31 seconds
  Number of estimated visits: 11471  Number of visits per day: 125
  Number of unique visitors: 8086   Number of visits per week: 873
  Number of new visitors: 7405      Number of visits per month: 3824
  Number of repeat visitors: 1264   Number of unique visitors per day: 88
  Number of unique hosts: 7422      Number of new visitors per day: 80
  Number of unique pages: 448       Number of repeat visitors per day: 14
  Number of error hits: 1187        Visitor repeat rate: 15.6%
  Number of unique errors: 176
```

**FIGURE 5.5**

*A simple report from a Web log.*

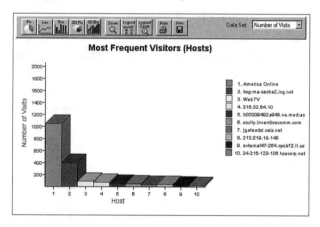

**FIGURE 5.6**

*A graph from a processed Web log.*

# Polly Wants a Cookie

The HTTP protocol is one that is called *stateless* when computing people describe it. Stateless means that each transaction is treated separately, without any knowledge of any other transaction. Without additional help, a Web server doesn't know that you have made any previous requests of it, even if the request is on the same "page" as far as the user is concerned.

This is a good thing because it means that requests to Web servers don't need to arrive in a specific order for the page to display properly. It is a bad thing if you are trying to fill a "shopping cart" on behalf of a user. Web servers need some method of recognizing that the request being processed is related to a series of requests that result in a complete transaction (from the user's point of view).

To solve this problem, the programmers at Netscape invented a small file that could be written by the browser to the user's disk. The server would check to see whether the file were present, and act accordingly. The programmers called the file a *cookie*, a computing term that describes an opaque piece of data held by an intermediary. In Web usage, your computer is the *intermediary*. The data is *opaque* because you cannot determine by inspection exactly how it is used, even if it were unencrypted and you could read the information. Your computer hands the cookie back to the Web server with an HTTP request.

The cookie itself is a text string. Cookies are used to save passwords. Cookies are used to hold *transaction numbers* so that data collected on the shopping cart server can be displayed to the right customer. Some Web servers assign a transaction number to you when they set a cookie on your machine. When you visit this or another page within the site, the transaction number tells the server to recognize your visit.  Cookies can be used for whatever a programmer thinks needs to be stored on a user's computer. The Cookie FAQ at `http://www.cookiecentral.com` describes the cookie as a laundry ticket. When your browser client visits a server, it is given a ticket. When you return with your claim check, you are given your "Vlaundry"—whatever the server was asked to remember about the transaction.

This is how it works. The Web server sends a page at your request. Included in the header might be the following additional information: `Content-type: text/html. Set-Cookie: bird=blue; path=/; expires Mon, 05-Nov-2001 13:00:00 GMT.`

The set-cookie instruction causes your browser to write a cookie called `bird` with the value `blue` that can be used by this entire Web server until Monday, November 5, 2001 at 1 p.m. Greenwich time.

The next time your browser sends a request to this Web server, it includes `Content-type: text/html Cookie: bird=blue` in the request. The

Web server then processes your request *and* does any additional processing triggered by the value `blue` for the cookie named `bird`. If the value of the cookie `bird` were `finch` instead of `blue`, the actions would most likely be different.

Cookies are stored on your computer in specific places. If you use Microsoft's Internet Explorer browser, you can find them in the \WINDOWS\Temporary Internet Files\ folder. They are text files whose names begin with "Cookie:". Some of the many cookies saved here on Glee's computer are shown in Figure 5.7. You can see that Glee's username is stored at the beginning of the cookie. This enables different users to have different values for cookies at sites. Otherwise, a single computer couldn't be shared among several users and used to visit a site that appears differently for each user.

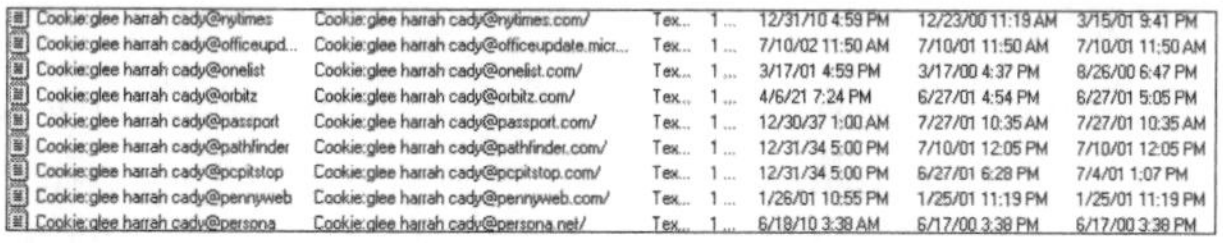

| | | | | | | |
|---|---|---|---|---|---|---|
| Cookie:glee harrah cady@nytimes | Cookie:glee harrah cady@nytimes.com/ | Tex... | 1 ... | 12/31/10 4:59 PM | 12/23/00 11:19 AM | 3/15/01 9:41 PM |
| Cookie:glee harrah cady@officeupd... | Cookie:glee harrah cady@officeupdate.micr... | Tex... | 1 ... | 7/10/02 11:50 AM | 7/10/01 11:50 AM | 7/10/01 11:50 AM |
| Cookie:glee harrah cady@onelist | Cookie:glee harrah cady@onelist.com/ | Tex... | 1 ... | 3/17/01 4:59 PM | 3/17/00 4:37 PM | 8/26/00 6:47 PM |
| Cookie:glee harrah cady@orbitz | Cookie:glee harrah cady@orbitz.com/ | Tex... | 1 ... | 4/6/21 7:24 PM | 6/27/01 4:54 PM | 6/27/01 5:05 PM |
| Cookie:glee harrah cady@passport | Cookie:glee harrah cady@passport.com/ | Tex... | 1 ... | 12/30/37 1:00 AM | 7/27/01 10:35 AM | 7/27/01 10:35 AM |
| Cookie:glee harrah cady@pathfinder | Cookie:glee harrah cady@pathfinder.com/ | Tex... | 1 ... | 12/31/34 5:00 PM | 7/10/01 12:05 PM | 7/10/01 12:05 PM |
| Cookie:glee harrah cady@pcpitstop | Cookie:glee harrah cady@pcpitstop.com/ | Tex... | 1 ... | 12/31/34 5:00 PM | 6/27/01 6:28 PM | 7/4/01 1:07 PM |
| Cookie:glee harrah cady@pennyweb | Cookie:glee harrah cady@pennyweb.com/ | Tex... | 1 ... | 1/26/01 10:55 PM | 1/25/01 11:19 PM | 1/25/01 11:19 PM |
| Cookie:glee harrah cady@persona | Cookie:glee harrah cady@persona.net/ | Tex... | 1 ... | 6/18/10 3:38 AM | 6/17/00 3:38 PM | 6/17/00 3:38 PM |

**FIGURE 5.7**

*These are some of the cookies stored in the Temporary Internet Files portion of Glee's hard disk.*

Netscape Communicator users find their cookies all in one file, stored in the \Program Files\Netscape\Users\<username> folder.

The major browser programs—Internet Explorer, Netscape Communicator, and Opera—all give control over your ability to accept cookies. Check in their privacy and preference settings for the appropriate instructions. Each version of these programs has improved the ability of the user to have better control in the interaction between our browser clients and the Web servers.

You can erase cookie files in Internet Explorer 6 by choosing Tools, Internet Options, General, Temporary Internet Files, Delete Cookies. In Netscape 6.1, Netscape has provided a Cookie Manager. To use it, go to the Tasks menu, choose Privacy and Security, and then choose Cookie Manager. Choose View Stored Cookies from the submenu. The Cookie Manager presents a list of all the cookies stored on your computer. You then can select one or more cookies and remove them, or you can select

Remove All Cookies. A nice feature is that you can also choose to prevent the removed cookies from being re-accepted later. In Opera 5.5, from the File Menu, choose Delete Private Data to remove session cookies. Use File, Preferences, Privacy to control other cookie preferences in Opera.

Be warned, however, that in removing cookies from your computer you will delete information that affects how you interact with the Web sites. If you asked to have your password saved, for example, it is likely saved in a cookie.

To determine whether you have removed the cookies you meant to remove, you can use your favorite method of listing files on your computer. In Opera 5.1, the files are in C:\Program Files\Opera\ Cookies4.dat. In Netscape 6.1, they are in C:\Application Data\Mozilla\Profiles\<yourusername>\. In Internet Explorer 6, they are in C:\Windows\Cookies.

Cookies can only be set and read by servers within the same Internet domain. Thus, one site cannot set a cookie to be read by another. Cookie information is contained. Cookies are also only text files. They cannot read other files on your computer. They cannot write other files on your computer. They are not dangerous by themselves.

# This Site Brought to You By...

The advertising community recognized early on that the Web presented an excellent marketing platform. In combination with easily recognizable domain names, one can create remarkable Web experiences that subtly (or not so subtly) advertise a product. See the marvelous Harry Potter Web site done by Warner Brothers studios at `http://www.harrypotter.com` for an excellent example of a site that entertains while it advertises. (What House did you get sorted into? Have you chosen a wand yet?)

Many informational sites were wondering, however, how to support the costs of providing information on the Web. As in broadcast and print media, the interests of the advertising community and the publishing community soon arrived at the notion of providing advertising space on Web sites. Ta-da! The Web banner ad business was born. Figure 5.8 shows a banner ad that advertises banner ads on the Web site of 24/7 Media, one of the large ad networks.

**FIGURE 5.8**

*An advertisement for banner ads.*

Now we come to the "interesting" part. The ads placed on Web sites need not come from the same server as the remainder of the information. Services were created that served ads to numerous Web sites. This enabled businesses to advertise easily on more than one Web site and the ad serving company was able to produce good reports about which Web sites were the most effective for particular kinds of ads.

Placing advertising effectively is difficult. People who buy ad space try hard to get the right ad in the right venue. Travel ads are in places where people who want to go places see them. Ads for face makeup need to be placed where more women than men see them. Television ads for the new National Football League season need to be placed where people who might want to watch those programs see them. If you are not interested in a product being advertised, your eye just glides right over the ad and you don't see it. The business that purchased that space doesn't want that to happen. So everyone works hard to attempt to get an ad in front of you that you want to see.

So far, so good. People had space. Other people wanted to place ads in the space. The Web enabled a single ad-serving network to serve many different pages. Businesses who advertised wanted reports about effectiveness. That's where things started to get a little sticky.

The ad server logs are the same as any other Web servers. The IP address, the host name, the referrer URL, the time and date stamp, and so on are all reported. Cookies were set by the ad servers to prevent showing the same ad over and over. Those cookies enabled the ad server to recognize a returning user, even if the user was visiting a different Web site than the one being visited when the initial cookie was set.

Web users didn't seem to understand that the ads they were seeing were not from the same place as the other information on the page. Cookies like those set by ad servers are now called *third-party cookies* because the server that sets them is not an explicit part of the Web page request and service transaction. And the most popular browsers (IE 6, Netscape 6.1, and Opera 5.1) now enable you to record your preferences about the setting of third-party cookies.

In IE 6, you can control the types of cookies you accept by selecting Tools, Internet Options, Privacy and then moving the slider bar to your preferred choice. In Opera 5.1, from the File menu, choose Preference, then Privacy to record your choices. In Netscape 6.1, use the Cookie Manager.

The "dangerous" part of third-party cookies is that now an advertising company with a large network of ad space sites would be able to track your progress across the Web. If you are served an ad on a page about cars and another ad on a page about urban legends and another ad on a page about local weather, the urban legend page people might know about the car page. The local weather page might know about the urban legend page visit. However, the ad network knows about all three of them.

If you found out about the local weather via your ZIP code into a search box, the ad server might have that information. Your ZIP code could end up as part of the address of the Web page that displayed the weather forecast. If they combined that information with your IP address, it might be possible to trace where you are.

An additional worry about correlating information comes from the potential to combine information gathered online with the information that exists in the offline world. DoubleClick advertising caused much consternation with an announcement that they intended to buy Abacus Direct, a company that owned databases of information about people, and combine the sets of data. This announcement and the subsequent uproar led to the formation of the Network Advertising Initiative, which is discussed in Chapter 15, "Self-Regulation and Privacy."

## Tracking Your Invisibly

Another weapon in the arsenal of those who want to know more about what we are doing is the small image from a third-party server that is embedded in a page in a way we aren't intended to notice. These little files are called variously Web-bugs, Web-beacons, 1-pixel-gifs, clear-gifs, or traffic-log cookies.

These very little files can carry the same information to a Web log that a full Web page does. Web transmissions need not be large to have cookies attached to them. So these unnoticeable files can track us across the Web without our knowledge. Again, combined with information from the Web logs, it might be possible for determined people to identify who we are and where we live.

With e-mail sent in HTML format, Web-bugs can be introduced into e-mail. This means that a bug can transmit a Web log entry and any associated cookie when an e-mail is opened. This would enable tracking of the forwarding of an e-mail, for example. Normally, no third party would be able to "spy" on the opening of a particular e-mail message.

A Web-bug within an e-mail message can also be used to associate a particular e-mail address with cookie data. That might well enable the otherwise anonymous unique ID that a site assigns to a Web visitor to be associated with an individual's e-mail address. If you use an HTML-capable client to read newsgroups, it would be possible for you to have your newsgroup participation tracked. Opening a bugged HTML posting to a newsgroup would send Web log information to the bug server, set and read cookie data on your computer, and perhaps identify the username under which you post to newsgroups.

We do not begrudge people gathering information about us, but we strongly believe that this technique is cheating. You are not notified that people are using this technique. You cannot use cookie-filtering programs to stop it, although if you refuse cookies or choose to not accept third-party cookies you gain some protection. You can, however, watch for them, and complain to the people who do it.

## Stamping Out Bugs and Shutting Off Beacons

The tool you need is one that works with Microsoft's Internet Explorer 5.0 and higher. This is called Bugnosis and it comes from the University of Denver-based Privacy Foundation. Because it uses programs that only work with IE, it's not available for other browser clients.

You can download it at the Bugnosis Web site: `http://www.bugnosis.com`. Figure 5.9 illustrates a part of a bugged page with the "default" bug design used. The bug was imbedded in the far right side of a page about one-third of the way down. There would have been no way to know it was present without the Bugnosis program.

**FIGURE 5.9**

*A bug found by Bugnosis.*

Figure 5.10 shows the top part of the DoubleClick Web page and the Bugnosis report about the bug located in the upper-left corner of the page. In the report, you can see the reasons why Bugnosis believed that the image was a bug. In addition, you can see the small icons in the Bugnosis report that tell you the home page of the site placing the Web bug (in this case, DoubleClick itself) and a link which opens an e-mail to the Webmaster of that site. This feature makes it easier for you to complain to the Web beacon owner, should you want to do so.

**FIGURE 5.10**

*A Bugnosis report on the DoubleClick Web site.*

If you have Bugnosis running, you can also see explicitly when no hidden bugs were found. Figure 5.11 shows the Center for Democracy and

Technology Web site and the Bugnosis report declaring that no bugs were found. Sometimes Bugnosis reports a Web beacon and you look at the report and you can say to yourself, okay, I understand what they are doing here and it doesn't bother me. Glee felt that way about the beacon report for the CNN Web page that is shown in Figure 5.12. The top line of the screen has a very small toolbar that directs you to the Netscape Web site in another window. This is really an ad. The Netscape folks probably are counting how many times the toolbar was seen and comparing that number to the number of times someone clicked on the toolbar. The advertising toolbar does, though, set cookies for each of the little choices. You have to decide if you think their use of Web beacons here is legitimate.

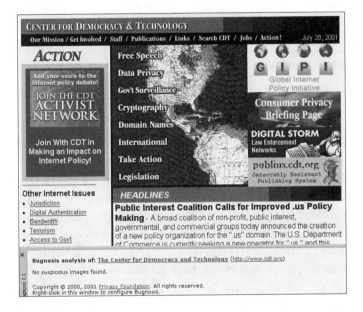

**FIGURE 5.11**

*No bugs found on the CDT Web site.*

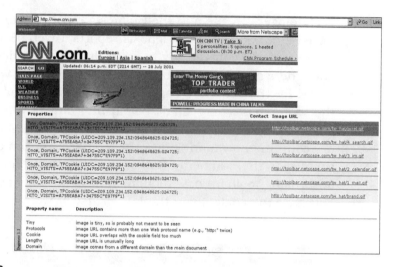

**FIGURE 5.12**

*Netscape's advertising toolbar on the CNN Web site.*

# What If I Don't Understand the Privacy Policies?

Privacy policies can be hard to read. They can be very complex, especially for those sites that have many different ways of interacting with users. Skipping the policy is easy because it is too long or covers too many different cases, many of which is not relevant to you and everyone knows that. Some people think that sites that want to obscure their activities concoct needlessly complicated policies to discourage our understanding of their practices. There needs to be a better way to get this information, so we can make better choices.

The World Wide Web Consortium (http://www.w3c.org) has facilitated a team of people who have been working on the Platform for Privacy Preferences (P3P) specification for nearly five years. The specification has a release candidate now, which means that the group is seeking implementations to find out whether the specification is close to meeting the stated goals or if it has to go back for more work. By the way, W3C is also the home of the specifications for the Web languages themselves (HTML, XML, and so on). A visit to their Web pages is interesting indeed for those of us fascinated by Internet technology.

P3P doesn't solve every privacy problem on the Internet. In fact, there are plenty of critics of P3P as it exists today. (For a particularly well-stated argument, see Karen Coyle's discussion of it prepared for a Department of Commerce policy workshop in September 2000. You'll find her discussion at `http://www.kcoyle.net/ntia91900.html`.) It provides a shared vocabulary so that everyone can be talking about the same thing. It is now intended to accurately describe information practices so that programs can "read" the controlled vocabulary and display the results for users. Additionally, the specification enables for a "compact" privacy policy statement describing the use of the cookie files, which the compact statement accompanies. Compact policy statements enable browsers or similar programs to compare user preferences to the site's practice and act accordingly. So, if a site's information practice doesn't match your preferences, the browser can refuse to accept information from the Web site.

Microsoft's Internet Explorer 6 for Microsoft Windows-based computers, in an early implementation of a P3P browser client, includes a feature that visually displays a Web site's P3P settings, based on the compact privacy policy. P3P is an encoding scheme that enables computer programs to display a more succinct version of a privacy policy. If a site does not have a P3P policy, a small warning signal is displayed in the status line in the bottom row of the IE 6 browser. Figure 5.13 shows the small, but noticeable warning that is displayed when IE 6 is not able to detect a satisfactory compact privacy policy. (Unfortunately, the newest version of IE for the Macintosh does not have the P3P features in it.)

**FIGURE 5.13**

*This warning is displayed when a site does not have a satisfactory compact privacy policy detectable by IE 6.*

To help with information about privacy policies, IE 6 has a new item in its View menu, as shown in Figure 5.14. Near the bottom of the menu there is a choice to view the privacy report for the currently displayed Web site. Figure 5.15 shows the result of that menu choice. You can see that the first few of all the Web server requests for the main Amazon.com Web page are listed and the main URL (uniform resource locator or address) is highlighted. Figure 5.16 shows the site's privacy summary in July 2001. (Of course, the Web, and privacy policies, changes all the time. It may well be that Amazon.com has implemented a P3P-enabled policy by the time you read this section.)

**FIGURE 5.14**

*The IE 6 View menu has an option you can choose to view the privacy policy for a Web site displayed in your browser window.*

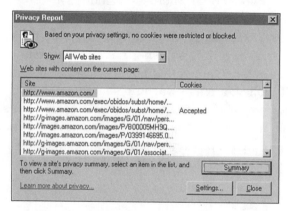

**FIGURE 5.15**

*IE 6 displays the first section of the Amazon.com privacy report in July 2001.*

The real problem for us all right now is that very few Web sites have P3P-readable policies available. A site must take its privacy policy and translate it into the P3P vocabulary, and then install the policy in a standard location on the appropriate Web site. Webmasters can use policy generation and conversion programs to create their P3P-enabled policies. Pointers to these conversion programs are on the W3C Web site. Once again, we are caught in the distributed nature of the Web. Because there is no central location for information or no forced registration, there is no easy way to let everyone know they should participate. There is certainly no way to force people to participate. The best thing we can all do is request that our favorite sites make their privacy policies available in P3P form. Send e-mail to the Webmaster and tell them you care about this.

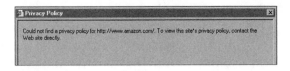

**FIGURE 5.16**

*The IE 6 privacy summary for Amazon.com in July 2001.*

# Watching You at Home and Work

The first part of this chapter has assumed that the people who are watching you do not have access to the actual computer you are using. If you share your computer with someone else, trusted family member or not, or if you are using your employer's computer on your employer's network, it is possible for someone to have a pretty good idea of what you have been doing on the Internet—and on the computer.

First, on your employer's computer network, it is likely that your Internet transmissions are going through some sort of packet-filtering, firewall, or proxy-server configuration. The most common reason for configuring a network this way is to protect the network from intrusions from outside the company. However, it is relatively easy for a network administrator to configure some of these protection tools to monitor network activity and to narrow the monitoring down to a specific computer via a specific IP address.

It is legal, generally, for an employer to monitor your work. It is legal, generally, for an employer to monitor the use of the employer's equipment. (Remember, we can't give legal advice, so if you want to monitor your employees, it would be good to get competent legal advice relevant to your jurisdiction.) It is courteous of your employer to inform you that you are being monitored, but it isn't generally required. If you are a concerned employee, ask your employer. If you are a concerned employer, we recommend you inform your employees. If you are an employee, it is best to assume that someone can see everything you do at work.

## Cleaning up After Yourself

If you aren't ashamed of what you are doing, but just generally feel like you don't want someone looking over your shoulder, take advantage of the *Internet File Cleaning* processes. Delete your cookie files; clear out your history files; don't save sites in the bookmark area; erase all your sent e-mail; delete trash on exit from the program; and so on. You could encrypt your e-mail, which means only you and your recipient could read it, but remember your recipient can forward it or it can be printed without your specific approval. (Some products make this difficult, but when your e-mail arrives and is seen by the person you sent it to, you are no longer in control.) You could try to use an anonymizing process for your Web traffic, but remember if it is a server-based program, you are not anonymous between your computer and the server.

Your Internet traffic can still most likely be seen when it leaves the corporate network and goes out onto the Internet, but it's less likely to be noticed particularly unless your connection is being specifically monitored.

If you must do something on the Net that you don't want your employer to see, don't use your employer's connection. The safest thing to do in this instance is to go to a public Internet connection in a library or Internet café, sign on using a fake username, and leave fewer traces. Remember that if you use a fake username and visit a site where you sign in using an already registered name, it might be possible for someone to correlate the new fake name with the already registered name and, in turn, with your real identity.

## Traces at Home

If you share your home with another person, chances are that other person has access to the computer you use to access the Internet from there. You can, of course, put a password on the computer itself, but few of us do that. If another person has access to your computer, they can easily find out things.

First let's look at the simple stuff. Your browser client keeps history files. Originally, browsers kept track of where they'd been because programmers found that people wanted to go back to where they came from. The only way it would be possible to implement a Back or Forward button would be to maintain a list of URLs that had been visited. This is another "feature" of the statelessness of the HTTP protocol. Then, as newer versions were developed and more people used the programs, the developers found that people liked to go to "that nice Web site about Hawaii that I visited last Thursday." This led to keeping more information about where you have been with your browser. The next three figures show parts of the History files on Glee's home computer, using all three major browsers. Figure 5.17 shows a part of the History files list from Netscape 4.7 for Windows. Figure 5.18 shows a part of the History files list from Opera 5.1 on a Windows computer. Figure 5.19 shows a part of the History files list from Microsoft Internet Explorer 6.

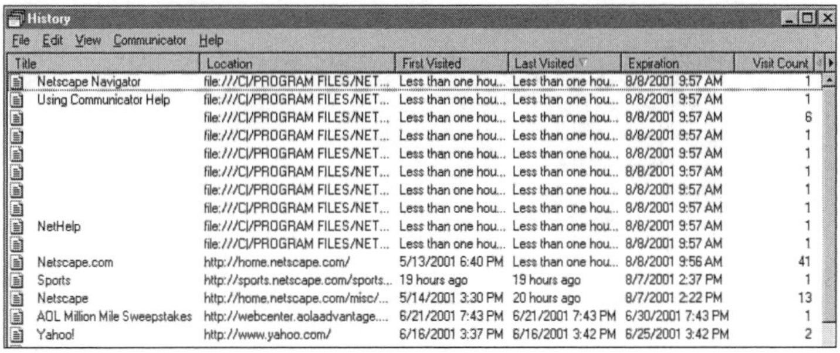

**FIGURE 5.17**

*History files in Netscape 4.7.*

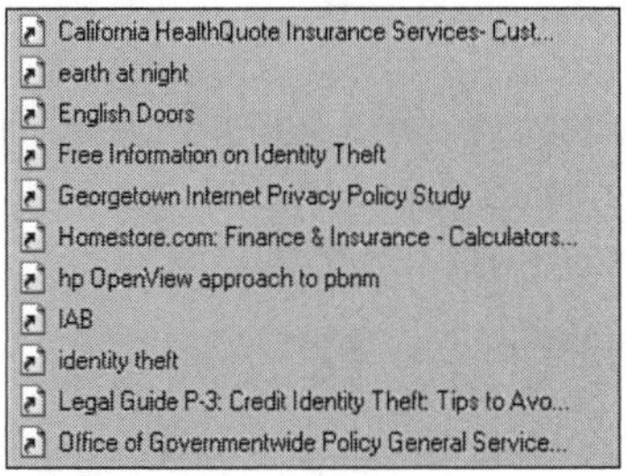

**FIGURE 5.18**

*History files in Opera 5.1.*

You can control the amount of history that your browser saves. Look in the Tools and Preferences menus for the appropriate settings. The more you save, the more disk space you use doing this and the easier it is for someone to retrace your steps—whether it's you or someone else. Some browser clients enable you multiple user profiles. Usually, this means that history files are kept separate for each user and each user can control when the files are erased, and so on.

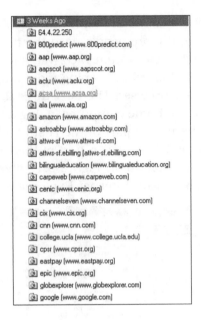

**FIGURE 5.19**

*History files in Internet Explorer 6.*

E-mail clients generally keep track of what you sent and to whom. Usually a copy of your e-mail messages is kept in a Sent Mail folder, like that shown in Figure 5.20. This is great if you need to reconstruct a message to remember what you said. It is not so great if you don't want to share what you are sending with others who have access to your computer. You do have options, however, and just what those options are depends on the e-mail client you are using.

| ! | D | ▽ | 0 | To | Subject | Sent ▽ | Size |
|---|---|---|---|----|---------|--------|------|
| | | | | 'Ed Vielmetti'; 'Pat... | RE: future of privacy (2d draft) | Mon 7/30/01 9:27 AM | 9 KB |
| | | | | 'Pat McGregor' | RE: Chapter 8 on other devices | Mon 7/30/01 9:25 AM | 2 KB |
| | | | | 'Pat McGregor' | RE: Facial Recognition graphics | Mon 7/30/01 9:16 AM | 2 KB |
| | | | | 'Amy.Neidlinger@... | RE: Introduction by ... | Mon 7/30/01 9:03 AM | 4 KB |
| | | | | 'Lloyd.Black@pea... | Introduction by ... | Sun 7/29/01 1:01 PM | 3 KB |
| | | | 0 | 'Pat McGregor' | RE: Front Matter | Sun 7/29/01 11:43 AM | 48 KB |
| | | | 0 | 'Pat McGregor' | RE: Chapter start quotes | Sun 7/29/01 11:03 AM | 45 KB |
| | | | | 'Pat McGregor' | RE: Chapter start quotes | Sun 7/29/01 11:03 AM | 2 KB |

**FIGURE 5.20**

*Sent mail folder.*

Microsoft Outlook XP, for example, lets you put passwords on the files that store your e-mail. That's *all* your e-mail: that you sent, that you received, that which is still in draft, and so on. The feature covers your calendar and address book data, too. Eudora gives you the option of saving a copy of all your outgoing e-mail, saving only the current e-mail message, or saving none of them. Other e-mail clients still have other options. It is a good idea for you to look through the options your preferred client program offers, read the Help files that explain how the options work, and set the options to your particular preference or need.

## So, You Always Wanted to Live in a Spy Novel

If you are the one doing the investigating, perhaps looking at history files and sent e-mail aren't enough for you. A lot of products are available to monitor the use of your computer. Some are used by parents to keep an eye on their kids' activities on the Internet. Others are used by non-trusting spouses to watch their partners. Many of them can work without the knowledge of the person being watched. What's the easiest way to find these products? Use your favorite Internet search utility. We entered "PC monitoring surveillance" into Google (at www.google.com) and turned up the category "Computers; Security; Products and Tools; Keyloggers and Spyware" in the Open Directory. There were 30 products listed in late July 2001.

Of course, some of these products can be used by hackers as well as by non-trusting spouses. For current protection mechanisms against hackers—more current than can be in a printed book—consult the Web. We like the AdvICE section of the Network Ice Internet Security Systems Web page at http://advice.networkice.com/advice.

## What If the Police and Courts Get Involved?

Law enforcement agencies know all the things about history files and sent e-mail that we've just mentioned. Did you follow the story of the search for Ms. Chandra Levy, the young woman who disappeared in Washington, D.C.? The Associated Press news agency has widely reported (http://www.washingtonpost.com/wp-dyn/metro/specials/missing/levy/A29167-2001Jul20.html) the list of Web sites that Ms. Levy visited. We suspect that they were gathered from her browser's history files. The following is a quote from a July 16, 2001, *Washington Post* article:

"For more than three hours starting about 9:30 a.m. May 1, Levy was on her computer, looking up the Rock Creek site and other locations as well as Web pages for airline and train tickets to California, where she planned to attend her graduation ceremony at the University of Southern California, Executive Assistant Police Chief Terrance W. Gainer said."

This statement probably combines the information available in the history files, information from her telephone records, and possibly information from her Internet or online service provider. The history files would show what Web sites she visited. Her e-mail client probably had copies of any e-mail she received or sent. Her telephone records, available under certain legal measures (see Chapter 13 for more about privacy law), would have shown a connection to her Internet access or online service provider's modem bank. With instructions from a judge, the Internet access or online service provider could reveal information about duration of connection. It is possible to link the IP address assigned when a computer connects via modem to a specific user account. Because service providers have billing information associated with that user account, it is possible to connect a sign-on name with the person to whom the account is billed.

The service provider has other information, too, although the information available most likely wouldn't add all that much to the picture because so much information was available on Ms. Levy's computer. Service providers keep logs of activity on their networks. Some of the information is kept so that you can be billed properly. That information would include the number you called and the length of time you were connected. IP addresses and user accounts are the entry point to gain useful information from the network logs. Usually, these logs are kept to trace back problems with the network itself, not to trace individual user behavior. Occasionally, however, service provider information has been helpful in tracking people. Because the network logs are overwritten on a regular basis, it's not usually possible for a service provider to go back very far in time. Official requests need to come quickly so that the material can be preserved.

Finally, you should know that civil courts can play a part in linking individuals with specific online behavior. These are usually bulletin-board posting cases. Let's say you were part of a discussion on a Web site that provided a message board to discuss stocks. You pick a username that is intended to mask your real identity. Using your online persona, you say something that someone else doesn't like. Perhaps you reveal some special knowledge about a specific stock and that posting affects how others act in the stock market. Perhaps your posting has caused the value of the stock to change dramatically.

Whether the dramatic change was positive or negative, someone is unhappy. They want to find out who you are. If you are an "insider" you might have broken securities law and your employer would very much like to find out who you are. Or your former employer would like to find you if you are a disgruntled former employee. In any case, the people whose holdings you affected with your remark are going to want to know who you are. So the company sues, even though you are anonymous.

They can sue for defamation, for example, forcing the message board operator to disclose your identity as part of the legal evidence discovery process. Or they can just sue to disclose your identity. The Medinex case against 14 John Does tried this. The article about this case on the Electronic Frontier Foundation (EFF) Web site can be found at `http://www.eff.org/Legal/Cases/Medinex_v._Awe2bad4mdnx/20010522_eff_dismiss_pr.html`. EFF believed that the suit was only to identify the posters, not to actually recover damages. Documents in the case are located at `http://www.eff.org/Legal/Cases/Medinex_v._Awe2bad4mdnx/`. In the United States, the First Amendment, guaranteeing free speech, has been used to defend one's right to speak anonymously. Remember, though, that the Internet is a global place. Not all services are within the United States. Be aware of your rights, but also be aware of possible consequences.

Speak responsibly and truthfully and protect your identity when necessary. If you are going to blow a whistle and need to do so anonymously, do it in a way that is difficult to trace. Don't use your home or employer's Net connections; use a username that can't be traced to you. Remember what we said in the beginning of this chapter: Digital information is perfect every time, and it can be used to find you.

# 6

# BROADBAND: ALWAYS ON, ALWAYS CONNECTED, ALWAYS EXPOSED

Broadband offers the promise and convenience of blazing speed and a continuous ("always-on") connection to millions of home computers. This connection is not unnoticed by opportunistic and malicious forces. By the very nature of your *DSL* (*Digital Subscriber Lines*) or cable Internet connection, you are at increased risk for security problems. However, you can take steps to decrease that risk. In this chapter we discuss the nature of broadband and some common vulnerabilities. In Chapter 10, "The Least You Should Do to Guard Your Privacy When Online," we talk about tools to use to protect yourself and your computer.

Why are security problems related to privacy? Think back to Chapter 2, "What *Is* Privacy in a Digital World?," where we discussed Fair Information Practices. Companies and organizations that hold your information are required to take security precautions to protect that information from uses you don't authorize. In the same way, much of your private information is on your home computer, and you need to be aware that when that machine is connected to a network, you run the risk of that information being read, stolen, or corrupted by outsiders.

According to an article in *The Industry Standard* in May 2001 (`http://www.thestandard.com/article/0,1902,23975,00.html`), only 10% of American households currently have high-speed Internet access. However, in the same special section, *The Standard* says that although only 9 million people—just 9 percent of those who use the Net at home— have high-speed access now, they predict that number will grow by 2005 to a whopping 59 million. Figure 6.1 shows the rise in homes with broadband access compared to all other methods of Internet access.

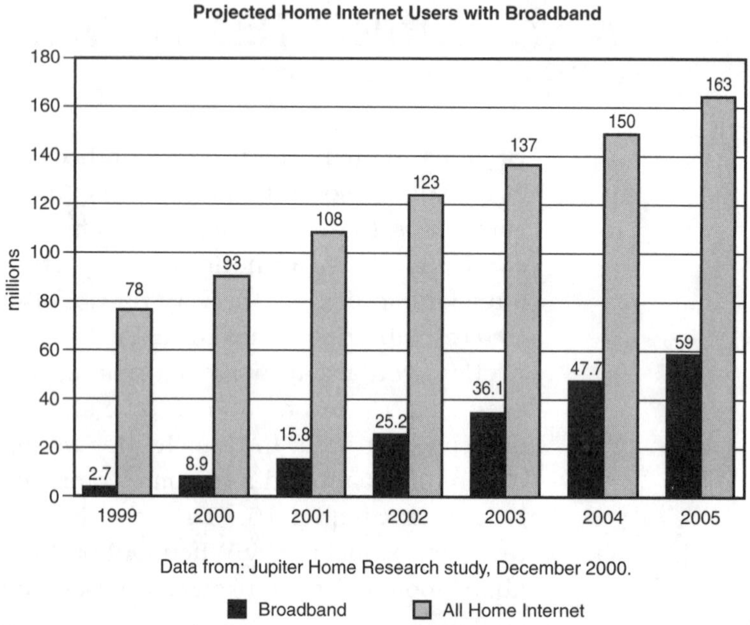

**Projected Home Internet Users with Broadband**

Data from: Jupiter Home Research study, December 2000.

■ Broadband      ☐ All Home Internet

**FIGURE 6.1**

*Broadband subscribers are rising quickly compared to dialup.*

The promise of broadband, of course, is that you are able to get bigger, better, faster, and more extensive content that takes advantage of, or even requires, this expanded bandwidth. The marketplace for expanded and enriched goods and services is poised for explosive growth. However, consumers and network operators are increasingly aware of the perils, as well as the rewards, characteristic of this technology-based future.

# Once Connected, Always Connected

Your modem and your Internet Service Provider (ISP) link your personal computer to the Internet. Traditionally, your ISP has provided you with a dial-up account. Using a regular dial-up modem and your phone line enables you to do the following:

- Call your ISP
- Log in to their server
- Use their Internet services (e-mail, the Web, and more)

More recently, ISPs began offering high-speed broadband service as an alternative to dial-up. One of the greatest conveniences of broadband service is that you're ready to surf or get your e-mail at any time. Broadband access is available whenever your computer and modem are turned on.

Most people who have DSL or cable modems leave them on all the time, rather than shutting them down when they are not using the connection. Some do this because they are using the connection to make their machine a Web server to enable friends, family, or customers get to material on the home computer. However, most just leave it on because it's easy.

# If You're Always Connected, You're Easy to Find

All traffic on the Internet is routed according to a common protocol called *IP numbers* or *IP addresses*. Your Internet service provider assigns an IP number to your computer whenever you're connected to the Internet. This number identifies the route to and from your machine.

 **NOTE** An IP address is a nine-digit number that identifies the sender and receiver of information on the Internet. Your IP number corresponds to your domain name, if you have one. IP, or *Internet Protocol*, is part of TCP/IP, the communication language of the Internet. More information on IP addresses and other technical topics can be found at http://whatis.techtarget.com/.

Many service providers assign one fixed IP number to each subscriber; some assign different IP numbers each time a subscriber connects. If you have a fixed IP number, your computer has a dependable "location" in cyberspace. Given your ISP's permission, your fixed IP number enables you to run a home server with Web, e-mail, and other applications. However, if your machine is running a server, you also provide a dependable target for mischief. You are a target because of how the Internet was designed and built, and how the operating systems that run on your home computer were built.

## The Internet Is Open

What we know today as the "Internet" was just an experiment back in the early 1960s. At that time, the people who were developing the Internet believed in sharing information on the technologies and protocols. They used a public review process for scrubbing problems and errors out of the technologies, and because of this, the Internet is a pretty robust network. Because of that belief, they developed the technologies, hardware and software, in what we call an *open architecture*.

Much of the development and innovation that happens today relies on this open architecture and the knowledge of how things work. The Internet's open architecture enables anyone, anywhere in the world to make significant contributions to our body of information, software, and abilities.

---

**NOTE**  To learn more about the origins of the Internet, see "A Brief History of the Internet," by Barry M. Leiner, Vinton G. Cerf, David D. Clark, Robert E. Kahn, Leonard Kleinrock, Daniel C. Lynch, Jon Postel, Larry G. Roberts, and Stephen Wolff: http://www.isoc.org/internet-history/brief.html.

---

What makes the Internet revolutionary is also the very thing that makes it vulnerable. The Internet's open architecture offers potential for big headaches. Our computers can be infiltrated by others to cause us, and others, problems. The trouble might include:

- Eavesdropping
- Theft of information
- Alteration or corruption of our information
- Copying and plagiarism
- Denial of service attacks (keeping us, or others, from using our system)
- Consumption of our system resources (making our system unusable or using it to do the hacker's work)
- Spoofing, masquerading, or impersonating

## Operating Systems Are Closed

The development of the personal computer (PC) enabled a single person to conveniently use applications such as spreadsheets, word processing, e-mail, Web browsers, and computer games. These applications ran on top of a PC operating system that was designed to facilitate file sharing among other PCs. In the design of operating systems, little regard was paid to security.

During the recent antitrust case concerning Microsoft, the findings of fact tell us that Microsoft's consumer operating systems, Windows 98 and Windows NT, are the most commonly used on the planet. The document says "Microsoft possesses a dominant, persistent, and increasing share of the world-wide market for Intel-compatible PC operating systems. Every year for the last decade, Microsoft's share of the market for Intel-compatible PC operating systems has stood above ninety percent. For the last couple of years the figure has been at least ninety-five percent, and analysts project that the share climbs even higher over the next few years. Even if Apple's Mac OS were included in the relevant market, Microsoft's share would still stand well above eighty percent." (http://www.usdoj.gov/atr/cases/f3800/msjudgex.htm#iiia).

Operating systems created by Microsoft and Apple are proprietary, or closed. Most of us can't tell what's going on inside our own machines. These systems were not designed so that we would need to know. They were designed to easily run programs and to facilitate file sharing.

**NOTE** A few operating systems such as Linux and FreeBSD have an *open architecture*. They are often referred to as *open source*. With these systems, you can tell what's going on inside your machine. However, these operating systems are complicated—beyond the understanding of most computer users. For more on Open Source software, see NetAction's archives: http://netaction.org/opensrc/ or the Open Group's site at http://www.opengroup.org/.

Microsoft's operating systems, by far the most widely used, were not originally designed to support the kind of interdependent access as is provided now by the Internet. Nor was it designed to tell us about its internal problems. The applications have become more tightly integrated with the operating system, enabling programs and tools (including malicious code) to move through our files and applications without our knowledge or consent. In a twist of unintended consequences, most people are now dependent on Microsoft operating systems, which to provide the features designed are vulnerable to attack.

The good news is that Microsoft has responded to users' concerns about security. A comprehensive security site is on their Web site at `http://www.microsoft.com/security/default.asp`. Figure 6.2 shows the various topics on the Microsoft security page.

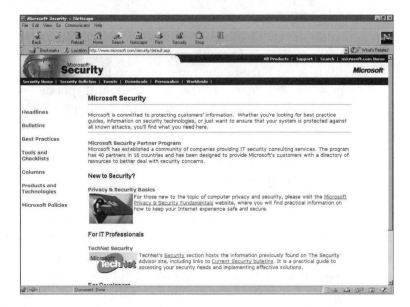

**FIGURE 6.2**

*The Microsoft security page has sections for home users and technical folk.*

# What is Broadband?

In general, *broadband* means a communications network in which a frequency range is divided into multiple independent channels for simultaneous transmission of signals (such as voice, data, or video). Because a wide band of frequencies is available, information can be *multiplexed* and sent on many different frequencies or channels within the band at the same time. This allows more information to be transmitted in a given amount of time (such as more lanes on a highway enable more cars to travel on it at the same time).

Various definers of broadband have assigned a minimum data rate to the term. These are a few:

- Newton's Telecom Dictionary: "...greater than a voice grade line of 3 KHz...some say [it should be at least] 20 KHz."
- Jupiter Communications: at least 256Kbps.
- IBM Dictionary of Computing: A broadband channel is "6 MHz wide."

Cable modems and residential DSL are two of several high-speed Internet technologies grouped under the term *broadband services.* Although the whole of broadband services can be either one-way or two-way, and wired or wireless, this chapter primarily discusses two-way, consumer-oriented services predominated by cable modems and residential DSL.

Why would someone want broadband services? Convenient, high-speed delivery. Broadband services are desirable for the following reasons:

- Faster and graphically enhanced Internet content
- Streaming audio, video, and other multimedia productions
- Digital TV
- Improved resolution for traditional TV (HDTV)
- Added interactivity when TV is used with your Internet connection
- More capability on one line than traditional one-use lines

Broadband services can provide multiple channels of data over a single communications medium, such as a telephone or cable TV line. This means you can use one line for multiple services such as voice (telephone) or other (fax) analog signals, and data (digital movies or your computer) at the same time. Depending on the condition and age of your house's present phone lines, rewiring or additional phone or cable lines are often unnecessary.

Broadband offers an affordable alternative to regular dial-up modems: subscription dial-up services. A modem is required for this type of dial-up service. You need to dial up and log on each time you want to access the Internet. In addition, if you want to use your telephone and your computer at the same time, you more than likely need a separate phone line.

Broadband services don't need to go through a lengthy connection process. Instead, they offer a continuous or *persistent* connection to the Internet, sometimes referred to as "always on." Broadband services mean you're connected to the Internet whenever your computer is turned on.

# Cable

The cable system was designed to carry television programming to subscribers' homes. Lots of the bandwidth (or capacity) of the cable network was unused, and technologists wanted to find a way to use that excess capacity and enable many more homes to have high-speed Internet connections. With the addition of a cable modem, cable services can now offer broadband access to Internet services.

## How Does It Work?

A cable modem is a device that enables you to hook up your PC to a local cable TV line and receive data at about 1.5Mbps. This data rate far exceeds that of the most common telephone or dial-up modems, which tend to run at 28.8Kbps and 56Kbps. If you have Integrated Services Digital Network (ISDN), you may be able to have speeds of up to 128Kbps. This is similar to the data speeds available to subscribers of Digital Subscriber Line (DSL) telephone service. A cable modem can be added to or integrated with a *set-top box* that provides your TV set with channels for Internet access. In most cases, cable modems are furnished as part of the cable access service. Subscribers rarely buy the modems themselves.

All the cable modems attached to a cable TV company coaxial cable line communicate with a Cable Modem Termination System (CMTS) back at the local cable TV company office. All cable modems can only receive from and send signals to the CMTS, but not directly to other cable modems on the line.

Most cable modem connections can receive data faster than they can send it. This is because for most of us, we get bigger chunks of data coming to us than we send out. For example, if we are listening to MP3 files or looking at an online concert, the files coming down to us are very large. We want a very fast line to bring them down. The actual bandwidth for Internet service over a cable TV line is up to 27Mbps on the download path to the subscriber. Theoretically, you can usually get about 2.5Mbps of bandwidth for interactive responses in the other direction. However, because your local cable company may not be connected to the Internet on a line faster than 1.5Mpbs, a more likely data rate is close to 1.5Mpbs.

With cable, all homes within the network's community share available bandwidth. Each local cable controller serves up to 2,000 subscribers, and there may be more than one controller, or "headend" at your cable office.

The cable network is shared by all homes that are active at any moment in time. (Subscribers are considered "active" whenever they request or receive information. They are not active, with regard to network usage, while reading or composing e-mail, scanning a Web page, or if their computer is turned off.) For example, if many homes are actively using the Internet at 8 p.m., service is divided among all active requests at that moment. This results in slowed services. Fewer people are active at the same time at  4 a.m., for example, and the system is much faster then. This is why some people feel their cable modems do not actually give the advertised services.

**NOTE**  For more info on how cable Internet works, see
`http://www.howstuffworks.com/cable-modem.htm`.

## Digital Subscriber Lines (DSL)

DSL is a newer technology that may enable an ordinary phone line to be "split" into two parts: the traditional voice/fax (analog) services and a new digital data line. These two parts can be used simultaneously.

DSL services connect the subscriber's home directly to the local telephone company's Central Office (CO). This point-to-point connection cannot exceed 18,000 feet, limiting DSL's effective range. Internet Service Providers (ISPs) offer DSL Internet access accounts using telephone company lines. Figure 6.3 shows a page from DSLReports on how the DSL signal gets to your house.

With the addition of a DSL modem, home (and "small business") subscribers can now get broadband access to Internet services over their existing phone lines.

**NOTE**  Not all kinds of DSL use a single telephone line. Depending on the age of your home's phone wires and other factors, you may require an additional phone line to your house. You can find more information about DSL technologies is found at `http://whatis.techtarget.com/wsearchResults/1,290214,sid9,00.html?query=DSL`, which is an index to search results about DSL.

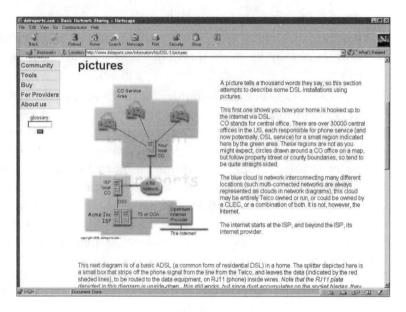

**FIGURE 6.3**

*A picture of how DSL gets to you.*

## How Does It Work?

Traditional phone service (or *POTS* for "plain old telephone service") connects your home to a telephone company office over copper wires that are wound around each other and called *twisted pair*. Traditional phone service was created to enable you to talk to other phone users, but when it was created using the phone lines for anything other than conversation was not imaginable. The kind of signal used for voice is called an analog signal. Your normal telephone set takes the sound of your voice, which is an acoustic signal. Acoustic signals are natural analog signals. The telephone handset converts that analog signal into an electrical equivalent in terms of volume (signal amplitude) and pitch (frequency of wave change).

To make your computer talk to your ISP over a telephone line, the signals the computer sends out have to be converted into an analog signal. That's why your computer has to have a modem. A modem is a device that takes the computer's digital signal, strings of 1s and 0s, converts them into an analog signal, and sends it over the phone line. At the other end, a modem takes the signal and converts it back into digital signals for the computer at the other end.

Telephone wires are measured in the amount of information that can be sent over them. Because analog transmission, either normal conversations or information converted by a modem, only uses a small portion of the available amount of information that could be transmitted over copper wires, the maximum amount of data that you can receive using ordinary modems is about 56Kbps (thousands of bits per second). The capability of your computer to receive information is constrained by the fact that the information comes cross-country in the telephone system as digital data, and then the telephone company has to change it back into analog form for your telephone line. Your modem then has to translate it back into digital signals that your computer is able to use. In other words, the analog transmission between your home or business and the phone company is a bandwidth bottleneck.

DSL is a technology that takes advantage of the fact that digital data does not require change into analog form and back before the computer can use it. Digital data is transmitted to your computer directly as digital data and this enables the phone company to use a much wider bandwidth for transmitting it to you. Meanwhile, if you choose, the signal can be separated so that some of the bandwidth is used to transmit an analog signal so that you can use your telephone and computer on the same line and at the same time. DSL comes in several forms. xDSL is a generic term referring to any of these forms. ADSL, or Asymmetric DSL, offers higher speed (bandwidth) usually coming into a home than the speed of signals going out. SDSL, or Symmetric DSL, offers equal bandwidth coming and going.

A good resource on DSL is http://www.dslreports.com/, where you can find out if DSL is available in your neighborhood and get some idea of prices in your area. Figure 6.4 shows the form at DSLReports to find out if DSL is available where you live.

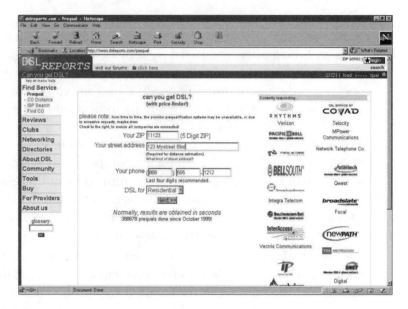

**FIGURE 6.4**

*Filling out the form at DSLReports.*

# Broadband: Connecting the World

Many promises and perils of a networked world are still to be realized. As thousands of new subscribers sign up every day, the complexity and diversity of our world increases. New opportunities for good also bring risks.

In particular, being connected to a high-speed connection that is up all the time, even when you're not online, opens you up to some specific dangers.

- Hackers have plenty of time when you're not watching to probe your system for vulnerabilities and then exploit them.
- Hackers can leave stolen software on your machine for others to come and download from you.
- Hackers can use your machine as a launch point for viruses, worms, and other malicious attacks to disguise where they are really working from.

The following sections discuss some of these dangers in more detail. See Chapter 10 for more information on how to protect your computer and ward off most common attacks.

## The LoveBug, Trojan Horses, and Other Mischief

Malicious software comes in several types. The most common of these are

- **Viruses**—A virus is a piece of code or small program, usually disguised as something else, that causes some unexpected and, for the victim, usually undesirable effect. Viruses are frequently designed so that it automatically spreads to other computers and users. Viruses can be transmitted by sending them as attachments to an e-mail note, by downloading infected programming from other sites, or they may be present on a floppy disk or CD you receive. Unfortunately, the person who sent you the e-mail note, file to be downloaded, or floppy disk you've received is often unaware that the virus is lurking there. Some viruses wreak their effect as soon as their code is executed; other viruses lie dormant until circumstances cause them to be executed by the computer. For example, some viruses wait until the clock in the operating system reads a certain date. Or until a certain sequence of keys are pressed. Some viruses are playful in intent and effect ("Happy Birthday, Ludwig!") and some can be quite harmful, erasing data or causing your hard disk to require reformatting. Many viruses these days can replicate or make perfect copies of themselves and send them off to other users on other computers, using a network connection or e-mail address book. The LoveBug was an example of an e-mail virus.

- **Macro viruses**—A macro virus is a computer virus that infects an application that enables little automated programs to be run within itself. In Microsoft Word and Microsoft Excel, for example, macros help with complex formatting, indexing, or calculations. A macro virus runs in Word or a similar application and causes a sequence of actions to be performed automatically when the application is started or some other event triggers it. Macro viruses have so far tended to be surprising, but relatively harmless. A typical effect is the undesired insertion of some comic text at certain points when writing a line or to cause a dialog box with an offensive comment to pop up. A macro virus is often spread as an e-mail virus. A well-known example in March, 1999 was the Melissa virus.

- **Hostile applets**—Hostile applets are little applications (hence the term *applet*) which generally get loaded onto your system through your browser or one of its advanced features or its plugins, such as Java, JavaScript, or ActiveX. Hostile applets can work just like any other program on your system, sending information out to a parent company or a hacker doing damage, or simply creating an access point that a hacker can then use to take over your machine.

- **Trojan horses**—Like the horse in the story, a Trojan horse is a program which slips into your computer disguised as something else and then works behind the scenes to do harm to your computer and your information. Two particularly bad Trojans, which people on broadband connections need to protect against, are Back Orifice and Netbus. Both of these run like a server on your system (a "back door" is opened on an infected PC to make access from outside possible), and with a client they can be accessed by other people, who can then do virtually anything on your system, including deleting files.

**NOTE**   Want to get the canonical scoop, the real word on what virus alerts are real and which are not? Before you believe that "virus alert" e-mail you just got (and especially before you forward it to 150 of your closest friends), go to the Snopes urban legend site at `http://www.snopes.com/inboxer`.

One of the reasons that broadband users have to be particularly aware of these potential attacks is that "always connected" aspect of use. This is convenient for you and for the hackers. Unlike dial-up connections, a broadband connection that is up 24/7 gives a hacker plenty of time to probe your system for vulnerabilities and exploit them.

This is one of the reasons that software manufacturers get so much grief when vulnerability is exposed in their products. They walk a fine line between being responsible for the unsecured nature of their software and creating transparency by design (and vulnerability without intention).

For example, the Love Letter worm is a malicious program written in Microsoft Visual Basic. Visual Basic, a scripting language, runs on Microsoft Windows, and also on Microsoft Internet Explorer (MSIE) (by default, Windows and MSIE come with scripting enabled). People generally don't change software defaults, so the Love Letter worm (virus) runs on most MSIE systems. Microsoft, a leader in adding new features, has been, and continues to be, plagued by their own vulnerabilities.

To be fair, all systems on the Internet can be compromised. CERT/CC, a major reporting center for Internet security problems, documents Trojan horses as an "apparently useful program containing hidden functions that can exploit the privileges of the user [running the program], with a resulting security threat. A Trojan horse does things that the program user did not intend." The CERT/CC is the Computer Emergency Response Team Coordinating Center, located at the Software Engineering Institute, a federally-funded research and development center operated by Carnegie Mellon University. You can find more about CERT at http://www.cert.org.

Trojan horses can affect any system. Given that the Internet is open, software was created to share and execute files, and operating systems (which are already vulnerable and evolve, therefore introducing new vulnerabilities), we have a computing environment characterized by continuous and evolving risk. It makes sense then to put products and monitoring processes in place to help you be aware of and active about managing your risk.

# The Big Question Is Not "What Do I Have to Hide?"— It's "Who's in Control?"

Having a computer connected to the Net is a potential resource for outsiders. Without your knowledge or consent, your computer can be used as:

- A staging area for exchanging pornographic files
- A mail relay for unsolicited commercial e-mail
- A participant in a distributed denial of service attack

...and more.

When a malicious person gets access to your home computer, you lose control of it. You may not know. You may never know until something goes wrong and the police come knocking on your door.

Even if you install antivirus software or a firewall (special security hardware and/or software that sits between your computer and the Internet), it's not safe to assume you never need to worry about security again.

Noted security expert Bruce Schneier points out:

> "Security is a process, not a product. Products provide some protection, but the only way to effectively do business in an insecure world is to put processes in place that recognize the inherent insecurity in the products. The trick is to reduce our risk of exposure regardless of the products or patches"

**(Source: *Crypto-Gram* newsletter, May 15, 2000,**
`http://www.counterpane.com/`
`crypto-gram-0005.html#ComputerSecurityWillWeEverLearn`**)**

Toward this end, NetAction has developed a guideline called The Five "A"s of Security. For more information on how to protect your home computer see Chapter 10, where we include this checklist.

# Some Questions to Ask Your (Potential) Broadband Provider

To help you evaluate broadband offerings, the following are questions you can use. You have to evaluate whether to sign up with them after you get the answers, but we hope this chapter and its resources help.

**Availability:**

- Can I get service at my home address? (You need to be within a certain distance from your local CO, and need to have "twisted pair" phone lines, not old copper lines, in your house.)
- Do they mainly serve businesses or residences? For instance, most DSL companies in the San Francisco Bay Area are for business and are not family-friendly in prices or service orientation.

**Pricing:**

- What's the monthly charge? Who bills me for this? Are there any separate phone line charges? Does it include ISP charges as well as line charges? Is this a flat rate charge, or is it based on my usage of network services?

**Technical Support:**

- What kind of computer do I need/do you support? If I have a computer which you do not support, do you have pointers to other sources of information that might be helpful?

- What kind of technical support do you offer? Is it available 24 hours a day, seven days a week, or during the ISP's business hours only?

### Installation:

- What are the installation charges? Is there an equipment charge? (Typically a modem, possibly a telephone line splitter) What's the labor or installation charge?
- Who will do the installation? How long will it take before they will do the installation? How long will the installation take? If there are unexpected problems, how long might it take to resolve?
- Are you offering any specials on installation or monthly service?

### Network Services:

- How many network providers do they have? What kind of connections does your ISP have to each of these providers?

---

**NOTE**  For example, if your ISP is MCI, and MCI is its own provider, and MCI goes down (which it does sometimes), you are out of luck. Another example is if your ISP has only a couple of smaller incoming network lines (two or three T-1 lines), will that (3Mbps to 4.5Mbps) be enough to serve the thousands of subscribers that they have? (Not if they're promising you 1.5Mbps in at least one direction.)

---

### Service Profile:

- How many e-mail boxes do you get? Are extra e-mail boxes available? How much will extra boxes cost for other family members?
- Do they include a dial-up account, so you can get your e-mail when you're travelling out of town?
- Do they give you any storage space on their server? You may want to put up your own Web page with the baby pictures or other information.
- How many IP addresses? Multi-PC households are becoming very common. Does your ISP charge more for having more than one IP address? If only one IP address, do they support multiple PCs in the home, or do they forbid it? Do they permit it, but leave you to figure out the details of your own home network? This includes how to set up a firewall, a hub, network address translation, setting up your own proxy server, and the like. If you've never heard these terms before, the task of setting it all up may be a challenge.)

- If they support additional home networked computers, is there an additional cost of supporting more than one PC?

- Do they provide shell access? Does the person answering the phone know what shell access is? Shell access is a Unix term for an interactive user interface that enables a user to execute commands. Shell access is similar to the DOS C:\> prompt. You may not need shell access, but it's a bad sign if your ISP doesn't know what it is. In a December 1999 survey, a Flashcom technical support person answering the phone didn't know what it was.

**Security Services:**

- Do they offer any spam or Unsolicited Commercial E-mail (UCE) filtering service?

- Do they offer firewall or monitoring services for your PC?

- What security precautions/monitoring do they take for their own network? Do they do routine intrusion detection or security monitoring?

# Keep Your Eyes Open; Keep Your Guard Up

We don't want you to leave this chapter feeling scared of getting a cable modem or DSL. The advantages are huge if your family wants to use multimedia, online role-playing games, or be a server for family pictures. You need to remember, however, that a slow dial-up connection has less risk. If you are going to leave your connection on all the time, *be sure* to read Chapter 10 and take precautions to protect your information.

---

**NOTE**

This chapter is based on information available from NetAction.org, written by Judi Clarke. NetAction has graciously allowed us to use their essay as the foundation of this chapter.

---

# 7

# PRIVACY OVER THE AIRWAVES

"Beam me up, Scotty." (Don't you just wish?)

How did Captain Kirk do that?! As much as we all think it would be cool to beam ourselves to and from work to avoid brutal commuting, we are far from it. However, we've also come a very long way since Samuel Morse's telegraph in 1837, Alexander Graham Bell's first working telephone in 1876, and Nicolai Tesla's venture into wireless with the invention of the radio in the 1880's. In this chapter we introduce wireless communications and address how these communications present complications in our desire to remain private.

## Understanding Cellular Technology

You've probably seen movies about earlier (but still modern) wars in which the communications officer carried a huge hunk of radio gear on his back. That stuff must have been very heavy and hard to lug around. Those were early mobile radios that enabled dispersed groups of soldiers to communicate with their commanding officers and to get information to the troops faster. This was a big improvement over earlier attempts to do the same thing. Mobile communications changed warfare. Officers could instruct troops much more quickly, moving them from one point to another. Sometimes, of course, the communications were "overheard." Protecting against eavesdroppers caused the communications to be "encrypted." In the United States military the encryption was done by the Navaho code talkers who spoke their complex language over the radio waves. Enemy troops overhearing the transmissions were unable to break the code and the allied troops were able to communicate safely.

**NOTE**    For more info on the Navaho Code Talkers, see the following links:

- The Navaho Nation's description of the Code Talkers:
  `http://www.navajo.org/nnhistory/codetalk.html`
- Bibliography of books about Code Talkers:
  `http://www.history.navy.mil/faqs/faq12-1.htm`
- Code Talkers' Dictionary:
  `http://www.history.navy.mil/faqs/faq61-4.htm`
- Code Talkers' Fact Sheet:
  `http://www.history.navy.mil/faqs/faq61-2.htm`

It was in 1973 that Dr. Martin Cooper from Motorola filed a patent on a "radio telephone system" for what was to become the first handheld personal cellular telephone. This was the great-grandfather of today's compact and versatile devices that make up the multi-billion dollar wireless industry. The first mobile phone was really just a radio telephone that people carried in their cars to fill their need for mobile communications. This device required one large antenna and a powerful transmitter in the phone.

Each geographic area, much as cellular telephony works today, contained a low-power radio transmitter with a range approximately equal to the size of the area. The service areas fit together, sort of like the sections in a chicken wire fence. Each telephone call would use a channel (like dedicating a channel on a radio or television to the call). The radio transmitters on the telephone itself enabled channel reuse in the adjacent areas. Each call would take a channel in the cell where the telephone was. A telephone call might use a different channel as the transmissions moved from area to area as the telephone did. Those early devices had a very short battery life, long recharging times, and a limited number of channels available for each radio antenna, meaning not many people could use their telephones at one time. The resources were just too limited for widespread use. Of course, widespread use was also discouraged by the cost to the telephone user for the instruments and for the airtime.

To solve the problem of limited channel resources, a cellular system was developed. A geographic area was divided into multiple cells within one large grid.. Each cell, about 10 square miles, contained its own tower with radio equipment. The cellular carrier then was able to reuse frequencies in separate cells. This enabled simultaneous usage. For instance, a telephone call in one cell is assigned a frequency for that particular call so that call both transmits and receives that radio telephone call from the antenna in that cell. Each cell has an antenna with a base station that connects calls to the mobile switching center. From there, calls are transferred to regular telephone land lines to complete the call to either a wired phone, or repeats the process of cellular connection if the other party is also using a cellular phone. Now we have many cells and many cell towers placed in strategic locations all over the world as shown in the simple diagram of cells and towers in Figure 7.1.

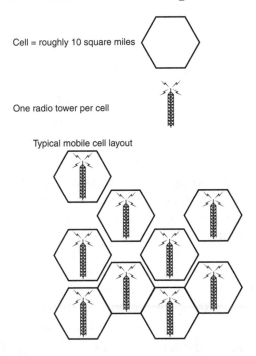

Cell = roughly 10 square miles

One radio tower per cell

Typical mobile cell layout

**FIGURE 7.1**

*Cells and towers.*

Understand that cellular phones are radios, not telephones like you think of a telephone. In a telephone connection there is a physical connection through the telephony system of one caller directly to another. In Internet telephony, where the Internet serves as the physical carrier of the call, the connection is through the Internet packet system to another caller. Cellular telephones are radio broadcast transmitters and receivers.

Each cellular telephone has an associated profile. The telephone service provider, called a carrier (Cingular, VoiceStream, AT&T, and so on), gathers your personal information for the unique account when the account is created. In addition, each account is assigned an electronic serial number (ESN) that is programmed into the phone (SIM card) when it is built by the manufacturer (Nokia, Motorola, and so on). A telephone also has a mobile identification number (MIN) that is your phone number, and a five digit system identification code (SID) that identifies the "home carrier" for the phone's account. Your home telephone carrier is the one with whom you have an account.

When you turn on your cellular phone, it broadcasts its system identifier and looks for an antenna to pick up the signal. If the phone reads "No Signal" that simply means that the phone is not within range of any antenna. If an antenna picks up the phone's signal, the signal strength is typically shown on the phone screen. If your home carrier operates from that antenna, your phone displays the name of the home carrier. Multiple carriers can have equipment attached to a single antenna. When your home carrier doesn't operate from that antenna, the phone displays either the name of the carrier receiving the signal, or simply the word "ROAM," indicating "roaming service."

When you make a call in roaming mode, the carrier that is handling the call identifies the phone's home carrier using the system identifier (SID). As part of setting up the call, the carrier contacts your home carrier with the phone's mobile ID number (MIN), and gets a profile of your preferences, and then completes the call. Preferences received by the carrier include your mobile phone number and any capabilities that the account has, such as numeric paging, voice messaging, and Web access. The home carrier, in turn, receives the information that the user is in "ROAM" mode and your specific location so your account is charged appropriately.

Radio frequencies that carry cellular phone calls are part of the electro-magnetic spectrum, which is simply the range of electromagnetic radiation that carries everything from visible light to the radio waves that we tune in on our radios. Although this spectrum is considered a publicly owned natural resource, allocation of frequencies of the spectrum is managed by the government. In the United States, the Federal Communications Commission (FCC) grants licenses to companies to use specific portions of the spectrum in certain geographic areas.

# The Wireless Spectrum

Certain frequencies best accommodate certain uses. Ranges of frequencies and some ways they are used are shown in Figure 7.2. For instance, broadcast television stations generally use the 54 MHz–216 MHz range for VHF channels. If the television is attached to an antenna, it captures waves that are broadcast at this frequency and receives the programs that are shown on your television screen. When you change the channel, it means that you have tuned the television to pick up a wave of a slightly different frequency. Wireless telephones are no different, except they transmit and receive signals that are broadcast at a different frequency than television signals.

Cordless phones differ from cellular phones in that the range is limited to a few hundred yards, with the phone consisting of the base and handset. The telephone base acts as the actual telephone, plugging into the land lines just like an ordinary telephone. When you receive a call, the base receives an electronic signal and rings the handset. The base then translates that electronic signal into a radio signal and transmits it to the handset using an FM radio frequency. The handset, in turn, converts that FM signal back to an electronic signal, which then is changed to the voice signal heard through the handset speaker. The process is reversed when your voice is sent back through the handset to the caller on the other end of the line.

Privacy can be an issue when using the simple radio transmissions of a cordless telephone. Because of the simple technology and use of FM frequencies in early manufactured and low-end cordless phones, a common radio scanner can pick up and listen in on your conversations. To combat this invasion, cordless phones were developed that use Digital Spread Spectrum (DSS) technology. This technology uses multiple frequencies to transmit signals, essentially scrambling the calls, somewhat encrypting them to make interception very difficult.

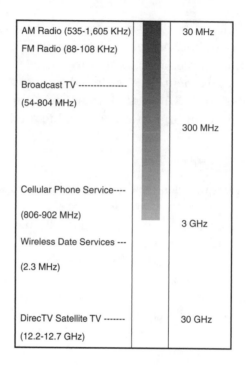

**FIGURE 7.2**

*Wavelengths measured in Hertz (Hz).*

Cellular systems relied on the standard of AMPS (Advanced Mobile Phone System) that used a range of frequencies for analog communications. With analog, up to 56 people can use their cell phones at any one time within a cell. As cell phones became more popular and inexpensive, it is easy to see how this number would be inadequate in most urban settings. Soon digital phones were developed to convert data —in this case voices— into binary information (0s and 1s) that could be easily compressed. This enabled a greater number of calls per channel than the analog system.

By switching to digital format for wireless communications, cellular devices were no longer limited to handling only voices. Traditional industry players in the telecommunications sector were joined in the market by developers of digital technology. Processors became smaller and faster, and cellular devices became smaller with added features such as e-mail and text messaging capabilities.

Although features are added to cellular telephones with each new release, the internal workings of a cell phone remain somewhat consistent (see Figure 7.3).

**FIGURE 7.3**

*The internals of a Nokia phone.*

In this typical Nokia phone, the components are the obvious external pieces: liquid crystal display screen, touch pad, and battery. The internal pieces look more complicated, but consist of the microprocessor (including the maze-like circuit board, antenna, microphone and speaker).

Today the mobile communications industry is divided into several inter-dependent players: end users, equipment vendors, service providers, network operators, and regulators. End users (or individuals) buy telephones manufactured by Equipment Vendors (Ericsson or Nokia, for example), who package their product for compatibility with Service Providers (AT&T or Nokia, for example), who then partner with various Network Operators (AT&T or VoiceStream, for example) to provide service to the individual. Regulators (FCC or Industry Canada, for example) supply the radio license to the Network Operators who, along with Service Providers, must abide by the regulations applicable to the issuance of that license.

Typically, mobile operators such as AT&T and SBC provide an end-to-end vertically integrated service to customers. They get a license from the applicable regulator, buy infrastructure from a vendor, design and build a network, and market and sell devices and services directly to customers. For instance, AT&T, Sprint, and Cingular all have retail stores in which a customer can do one-stop shopping for both telephones and services.

The emerging model in mobile communications is breaking away from the traditional wireline world, in which large telecommunications companies ruled the phone lines. Now these companies have been mostly relegated to a mere carriage role. Internet services, running on digital technology, are a new logical addition to cell phone features. We see mobile portals starting to emerge to cater to the capabilities of mobile devices. However, mobile operators hold licenses to the airwaves and therefore control the precious resource of access to the user.

By the year 2003 an estimated 1.2 billion mobile phones will be dotted across the planet. Close to half of these are Web-enabled phones, meaning more cellular devices are connected to the Internet than personal computers. Figure 7.4 shows today's version of a Web-connected cellular phone. Billions of dollars are spent worldwide using these devices, as m-Commerce (that's mobile commerce) creeps up on e-Commerce. Technologies such as Bluetooth (a technology standard that uses short-range radio links in place of cumbersome and range-limiting cables to connect devices) and 3G associations (a third generation wireless service that enables carriers to offer capabilities such as high-speed data transfers) turn mobile phones and devices into a form of universal remote control, or a trusted personal device through which users buy goods and services, activate appliances remotely, use as security passcards or keys, and maybe even someday to vote. However, to accomplish this multitude of information transmission through wireless channels, authentication, security, and privacy must be ensured.

**FIGURE 7.4**

*Motorola cell phone with Web browser.*

# There's Gold in Those Profiles

Mobile operators can predict future revenue streams in several forms: transport (minutes of device use and packets of airtime), m-commerce (mobile commerce), mobile advertising, financial transactions, and sale of customer profile information. It is incredibly valuable for mobile operators to know who is using the telephones, how they use them, where they use them, and so on. As in other forms of electronic communications marketing discussed in earlier chapters, the more detailed the profile of the user, the more valuable the information is to potential mobile service providers, wireless advertisers, and content providers. Everyone is worried that all the mentioned revenue streams could be jeopardized by a demonstrated or perceived breach of security and privacy, spamming or unauthorized 'pushing' of content to devices, or even location and usage surveillance.

Security of mobile phone conversations was more of a concern when analog systems were the standard, rather than the more frequently used digital telephones of today. Without much difficulty, radio scanners could monitor the appropriate radio frequencies and pick up and listen to mobile calls because the networks were unencrypted. This might have been a privacy invasion, and it might have been embarrassing, but it wasn't necessarily illegal.

We generally trust telephone companies who sell us airtime minutes and mobile calling plans. With a few exceptions best illustrated by analog interceptions, mobile operators and telecommunications companies have traditionally fallen within our trusted domain. On the other hand, we are generally skeptical of Internet services such as portals or Web sites, and how personal information is collected and used. As more mobile devices become Web-enabled and Internet services start to invade the screens of mobile devices, the traditional level of trust associated with using the device may erode.

## Is The Convenience Worth the Risk?

As your cell phone becomes the ultimate Web-enabled hub of your personal communications and transactions, it also carries with it a significant risk to your privacy. The possible invasions of your privacy are found in a combination of the typical Internet threats, location-based mobility threats, and m-commerce threats.

Information about you gleaned from your activity when you use wireless devices includes, but is not limited to the following profile information:

- Where your telephone is now geographically and where it has been
- Which sites you visit on the Web, how you get there, and how long you stay

- What you are buying over the wireless Web and how your money is flowing; What accounts you maintain, and so on
- Demographic information that you may choose to give out and which is kept associated with your account information, either by your cellular telephone service provider or by the Internet services you use
- Who you call and who calls you, including time and date and length of call

Ownership and access to the information profiles that can be built about your mobile device use has significant value for obvious players such as marketers, providers of Internet services, and content providers. It also has significant value to less obvious parties such as insurance companies, employers, and law enforcement bodies. Without privacy protections, users may shy away from utilizing the full capabilities of mobile devices for fear of their information falling into the hands of unauthorized parties.

## Location, Location, Location

In a series of administrative actions since 1996 the FCC has dictated that cellular telephones should be able to provide location information with enough detail to enable 911 emergency operators to determine location in cases of emergency. By October of 2001, the FCC requirement for enhanced 911 services (e911) is to be able to isolate the location of cellular telephone to within 150 meters. Incorporating this solution into cellular telephones is not easy—or cheap—for manufacturers or the networks that service them. Given that it's not the habit of corporations to act in a purely benevolent manner, what's in it for them? The answer is *location*, which they perceive as a goldmine.

Thus, a number of high profile companies are getting onboard. AOL, for example, is going wireless. Recently announced deals with VoiceStream and DoCoMo incorporate instant messaging and e-mail into wireless products and services. High-end automobiles from General Motors, Toyota, Honda, Subaru, and Audi are offering OnStar, an in-vehicle communications service that enables drivers to contact a 24 hour call center to get information based on their current location. Directions, traffic reports, hotel and restaurant information, as well as emergency services are just the beginning of this push-of-a-button location-based service.

Features being added to wireless devices enable users to be less dependent on bulky and immobile desktop computers. E-mail, stock quotes, sports scores, and weather reports can all be delivered to a cellular telephone handset. In the future, coupons, sale alerts, and retail special offerings might delivered as well. However, the convenience of these services come at a price to the consumer in addition to any subscription or service costs. Location-based marketing is able to target individuals based not only on their personal profiles, but on their actual physical location. Age, gender, and home address profile information is complemented by average geographic location at any time of day. Even trips outside the user's home range could be documented for future marketing reference.

The options to ensure privacy in mobile devices are a jigsaw puzzle of jurisdiction, regulation, and technical capabilities. The United States currently handles most consumer privacy through industry self-regulation. (For more about self-regulation see Chapter 15, "Self-Regulation and Privacy") Aside from a few specific sectors, such as financial services and health care, where legislation addressing privacy exists, companies and industries set their own standards for the handling and use of personally identifiable information. Enforcement of stated policies is difficult, and accountability is hard to come by. Many of the EU countries and Canada have legislation addressing the collection and use of personal information. However, the mobility that is the essence of wireless devices poses problems that are very difficult to solve under a multi-regulatory scheme, and even more difficult to enforce.

# Technology to the Rescue?

Considering the puzzle of problems inherent in policy, privacy addressed through technology may just be the best solution when it comes to mobile devices. Privacy enhancing technology is being developed by a few companies that want to provide multi-jurisdictional compatibility aimed at solving regulatory problems for mobile operators and service providers who cater to a global market. In the near future look to see privacy enhancements for e-cash, m-commerce, location-based services, public key-based encryption, and privacy protection for those of us who use wireless Internet services and receive wireless advertising. Technological solutions go a long way toward maintaining and enhancing the level of trust between users and mobile operators. The result is a more successful and diverse market for wireless products and services. Who knows, in the not-to-distant future wireless technology may just enable you to beam yourself home from the office!

# 8

# DO THE WALLS HAVE EARS? OTHER DEVICES THAT CAN AFFECT PRIVACY

*"No matter where you go, there you are."*

**Peter Weller, *The Adventures of
Buckaroo Banzai Across the
Eighth Dimension*, 1984**

The question, of course, is not whether *you* know where you are, but whether anyone else does. In general, the right to disappear is taken for granted. Some people turn off their cell phones to enjoy their ride in privacy when they are on the way to a vacation spot, knowing no one knows precisely where they are. While everyone has run into someone we know in unexpected places, in general we assume we can go where we want without anyone tracking our movements or recording where we are.

That assumption may not be true anymore. More and more, convenience or safety features in our cars, our phones, even our televisions are wired and can send reports about us to some central location. Beyond that, our movements and actions are traceable and may even be collated.

Consider these excerpts from recent news stories:

*Strolling along Centro Ybor\*, the young woman stopped to browse at a shop window. Unbeknownst to her, she was presenting her back to a camera monitoring her progress.*

*"Turn around," coached the man watching her on a video monitor tucked within a building several yards away, even though she could not hear him.*

*The man, David Watkins of Advanced Biometric Imaging, was trying to compare the woman's face with thousands of images stored in a database of wanted criminals and sex offenders.*

**(Source: St. Petersburg Times, 30 June 2001,**
`http://www.sptimes.com/News/063001/TampaBay/`
`Ybor_police_cameras_g.shtml`**)**

\*(pronounced "EEE-bo" by natives)

*So beloved is TiVo, a service that lets you watch any TV program anytime you choose, that subscribers use the brand name as a verb, as in: "Honey, let's TiVo The Sopranos." But a report to be released this week says the system is even more active than that. While you're watching TiVo, it's watching you back.*

*TiVo's manual assures its 150,000 subscribers that "all personal viewing information stays on the receiver and does not get transmitted to TiVo without your consent." But the nonprofit Privacy Foundation found that the system sends back potentially valuable data, including which shows a viewer tunes in to and when, along with the subscriber's TiVo serial number. Matthew Zinn, TiVo's chief privacy officer, says that the data are processed to be anonymous. "We don't spy on you. We could, but we don't and won't."*

*"They're playing language games," responds the Privacy Foundation's Richard Smith. "TiVo should make it clear that every day it's phoning home the shows you watch."*

**(Source: US News and World Report, 2 April 2001,**
`http://www.usnews.com/usnews/issue/010402/nycu/`
`estrogen.brf.htm#tech.`
**Note: This is an archive of paid articles.**
**TiVo's response is at**
`http://www.tivo.com/privacy_response.html.`**)**

*Imagine that you carried a miniature homing device in your wallet. As you dropped the kids off at school, drove to work, met with a friend for lunch, and visited the doctor's office, it would send out a signal identifying your exact location. This transmitter would enable anybody to track you down at any time—or to figure out where you had been at a particular point in the past. It would also give marketing companies the ability to build a detailed profile of your travel patterns. That valuable data could then be sold to local restaurants, dry cleaners, clothing stores, collection agencies, or anybody else who wanted it.*

*Guess what? You may very well be carrying such a device—or its functional equivalent—one day soon. Thanks to the government's decision to open up the Global Positioning System (GPS) to the general public, as well as lightning-fast advances in wireless technology, it is now cheaper and easier than ever to figure out where somebody is. As a result, sophisticated location-tracking technology is rapidly finding its way into cell phones, personal digital assistants, cars, trucks, and boats. One Long Island (NY) company, Digital Angel, even wants to put it into a tiny chip that can be implanted into people's bodies.*

***(Source: Business Week, 25 Septemeber 2000)***

*Karla Guiterrez drowned in February, pleading for help over her mobile phone. For three horrifying minutes, she tried to identify her exact location to 911 operators after her car skidded off the Florida Turnpike into a canal. The Guiterrez case received national coverage, but it was far from the first incident where tracking technology might have saved a life. This year in Orlando, a man collapsed on a jogging trail after suffering from a heart attack. Though a bystander called 911, she got confused about her exact location and by the time rescuers located her, the man had died. In Santa Fe, NM, a woman who was brutally attacked by her boyfriend called 911, but was too upset to say where she was. Her boyfriend returned in the middle of the call and the phone went dead.*

*The Federal Communications Commission (FCC) has mandated that technology that pinpoints the location of mobile callers be in place across the country by Oct. 1. Controversy already surrounds the program, called e-911. Privacy advocates worry that technology designed to track victims like Guiterrez can also track everybody, everywhere they go. That would make it easy for say, Starbucks, to send an e-coupon to a customer approaching one of its stores. (And let's face it, how often is anyone very far from a Starbucks?)*

***(Source: Business Week, 21 June 2001,*** `http://www.`
`businessweek.com/bwdaily/dnflash/jun2001/`
`nf20010621_803.htm?c=bwtechjun22&n=link11&t=email`***)***

*A SECURITY BREACH on the E-ZPass electronic toll system for the New Jersey Turnpike has led to a suspension of the application pending repairs, although no customer payment information was accessed, according to a spokesman for the Turnpike Authority.*

*The application is based on an e-mail-based account information system. A programmer and user of the E-ZPass system, Christopher Reagoso, who lives in Pennsylvania, brought the security glitch to the attention of a local Philadelphia television station last week. Although Reagoso was not able to access home addresses, telephone numbers, or checking information, turnpike officials acknowledged that he was able to view account information such as the turnpike usage and names of the users in the e-mail billing system of the largest electronic toll collection system in the United States...*

*(Source: InfoWorld, 25 October 2000,*
`http://iwsun4.infoworld.com/articles/hn/xml/00/10/25/`
`001025hnezpass.xml`*)*

### SAN FRANCISCO—*Big Brother wore khakis.*

*Either that, or he'll be watching you buy yours at the new flagship Levi's Store, opening here Tuesday.*

*At the lavish, frenetic, 24,000-square-foot, four-story complex, you are invited to deliver the most intimate details about you and your body in exchange for a dazzling entertainment experience and a perfect pair of jeans.*

*The corporate take is slightly different, of course.*

*"It's the intersection of technology and the best a brand has to offer," said Gary Magnus, content and development director for Levi's Global Retailing.*

*The store of the future is aimed at teenagers who have grown up plugged into big-screen video, electronic art, digital audio, and high-speed Net connections.*

*It is also a digital nerve center wired with more than 40 miles of cable, hundreds of speakers, and video routers, all pumping video and MP3.*

*Customers can take a dip in a hot tub for true shrink-to-fit jeans, and then stand in a human-size blow dryer while watching experimental films. Store visitors can also spy on other customers with remote operated videocam "periscopes" that tilt, pan, and zoom. They peer into tourist nexus Union Square across the street, but not into the fitting rooms.*

*The store is engineered for fun. It's also orchestrated to learn as much as possible about its customers, right down to their very fingertips and bust sizes. The resulting profiles are uploaded at the end of each business day to a Levi's corporate data warehouse.*

**(Source: Wired news, 16 August 1999)**

Many technologies can track you and your activities. As Table 8.1 shows, these technologies have both beneficial and potentially hostile uses.

**TABLE 8.1   BENEFICIAL VERSUS HOSTILE USES FOR TRACKING MECHANISMS**

| Use | Pro | Con |
| --- | --- | --- |
| Government | Emergency crews are able to locate you if you're in a car accident or the victim of a crime | Could be misused to pinpoint all the attendees of say, a certain political rally, or monitor movements of political dissidents |
| Safety | Direct you out of an unfamiliar neighborhood or away from a traffic jam | Could be used by stalkers to track down celebrities or estranged spouses |
| Marketing | Consumers receive timely offers from nearby shops | Constant interruptions and time-wasting wireless SPAM (Sometimes called *WAM*) |

*(Source: Business Week Magazine, 25 September 2000)*

To better understand the environment, let's take the technologies and practices one by one, and look at both the pros and cons.

# We Can Pick You Out in a Crowd of Strangers

Can you really get lost in a crowd anymore? You'd like to think so, but the combination of technology that can scan and identify faces and cameras that can focus on single faces in crowds is changing that assumption quickly. The Florida town in the earlier story example is not the only place where this is happening. This year's Super Bowl XXV (called the 'Snooper Bowl' in media reports), was one of the first American examples of massive scanning of faces in a crowd to look for known criminals and terrorists. Law enforcement officials captured the images of everyone who attended the game in Raymond James Stadium. They then compared the captured images with a database of criminals' faces. Civil liberties experts say that this massive example of video surveillance coupled with facial recognition technology was an invasive waste. The system was designed to discover terrorists and other criminals, but only a few pickpockets and ticket scalpers got caught.

In the East London borough of Newham, a surveillance network of more than 200 cameras have been keeping watch over this small town for more than two years by scanning pedestrians and passersby. It employs a facial-recognition system that alerts local authorities if it recognizes known criminals. The civil liberties groups have opposed this system, too. Privacy International, a human-rights group, gave the borough council a "Big Brother" award last year on the 50th anniversary of the publication of George Orwell's famous novel.

Residents of Newham, according to a Scientific American article published in December 1999, overwhelmingly support the program. They are, according to reports, more concerned about crime than about government intrusions. One of Newham's other major supporters is the U.S. Department of Defense. The DOD is watching the results of the Newham project as well as those of other, related biometric technologies. They hope that some combination of biometrics and surveillance technologies vastly improve its ability to protect its facilities worldwide.

The most commonly used facial recognition software in use now is *FaceIt*.

## How Does It Work?

According to the manufacturer, Visionics (`http://www.visionics.com/faceit/tech/verif.html`), "FaceIt can find human faces anywhere in the field of view and at any distance, and it can continuously track them and crop them out of the scene, matching the face against a watch list. Totally hands off, continuously and in real-time." They also claim that FaceIt can compress a face print into 84 bytes for use in smart cards, bar codes readers, and other limited size storage devices.

At its simplest, facial recognition software takes a human face, converts it to a series of equations and measurements, coming up with a unique pattern, or signature, for that face. That's only the beginning, though. Next the software compares the unique signature against a database of patterns that have each been linked to a person's identity. If the software finds a match, it notifies the operators that the captured face belongs to someone it knows. Figure 8.1 shows a simple example of how this works.

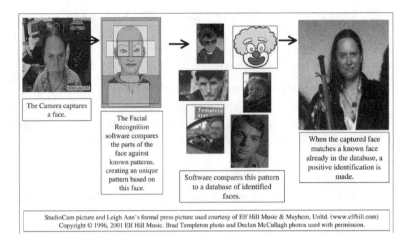

The Camera captures a face.

The Facial Recognition software compares the parts of the face against known patterns, creating an unique pattern based on this face.

Software compares this pattern to a database of identified faces.

When the captured face matches a known face already in the database, a positive identification is made.

StudioCam picture and Leigh Ann's formal press picture used courtesy of Elf Hill Music & Mayhem, Unltd. (www.elfhill.com)
Copyright © 1996, 2001 Elf Hill Music. Brad Templeton photo and Declan McCullagh photos used with permission.

**FIGURE 8.1**

*Facial Recognition software comparing a captured image to a database of identities.*

In the past few years, facial recognition software has gotten much more reliable. The false positive rate (the rate at which the software mistakenly identifies an image as someone already in its database) is now very low, as is the false negative rate (the rate at which the software fails to accurately identify an image as someone currently in its database). This is critical—you don't want to be stopped at a football game because the security system says you're a terrorist wanted across four continents, but you don't want to miss criminals, either. Many civil libertarians say that they are willing to miss a few crooks to keep from falsely branding innocent citizens as criminals. The following sidebar by Declan McCullagh of *Wired* magazine explores the problem of avoiding surveillance cameras and the equally complex legal issues around the practice.

## AVOIDING SURVEILLANCE

When tens of thousands of football fans packed into a Florida stadium for Super Bowl XXXV, they weren't merely watching the game: They were also being watched. Face-recognition software surreptitiously scanned everyone passing through turnstiles and flashed probable matches with the mugs of known criminals on the screens of a police control room.

The response from privacy advocates was fast, furious, and predictable: The American Civil Liberties Union condemned the Super Bowl system—provided free by its manufacturers—as the Snooper Bowl and asked the mayor and city council of Tampa, Fla. to hold public hearings on the topic. The ACLU argued that the public did not agree to be subjected to a computerized police lineup as a condition of admission.

It didn't work. Instead of backing down, city officials moved forward with plans to station cameras outfitted with Advanced Biometric Imaging's FaceIt™ software on city streets. Faces are matched on a scale of 1 to 10, with police computers emitting an audible "whoop whoop!" alarm for scores of 8.5 and higher. Tampa is the first U.S. city to use such a system.

This practice, which is growing in popularity among law enforcement, is set to become the greatest privacy threat of the next decade. Forget much-ballyhooed cases involving Microsoft and Amazon's purported privacy misdeeds: It's easy enough to avoid those companies by running MacOS or Linux and shopping at barnesandnoble.com. Worried about Carnivore? Use encryption. Avoiding omnipresent police cameras that have the ability to track your movements at all times, on the other hand, will be far more difficult. As cameras become ubiquitous, as face-recognition technology becomes more accurate, and as databases of known faces grow, everyone from direct marketers to the FBI will be able to track your movements and compile detailed dossiers on your life.

Worse yet, there may be only weak legal arguments against face-recognition cameras. In its letter to Tampa, the ACLU said "this activity raises serious concerns about the Fourth Amendment right of all citizens to be free of unreasonable searches and seizures." That's a phrase borrowed from the Fourth Amendment to the U.S. Constitution, which explicitly outlaws "unreasonable searches and seizures"—and implicitly allows reasonable ones. The Fourth Amendment, like much of the rest of the Constitution, only restricts the actions of government officials. It doesn't prohibit private firms such as banks or stores from face-scanning, although smarter companies may pledge to limit the practice to reassure their customers.

But does the Fourth Amendment permit governments to point cameras at us anywhere, anytime, and scan our faces for matches? Can the word "search" in the Bill of Rights stretch to include matching facial characteristics against a database? The answer, sadly, may be no. Many legal experts say there's no Fourth Amendment problem if the government is simply observing—or even recording—what goes on in public. For constitutional purposes, that's just not a "search," because there's no legitimate expectation of privacy. In fact, police have long used high-powered binoculars to monitor crowds at sporting events. And nobody says a cop shouldn't scan the crowd to try to recognize someone on the FBI's most-wanted list.

Yet if public outcry grows, perhaps courts can be convinced to side with privacy over police. So far, there's scant independent review of the systems to ensure they're working in the way their backers claim. Cameras, after all, do make a practical difference: They allow cops to monitor the public in ways they never had the manpower to do before. If we're not careful, the only place we'll have privacy is when we're sitting in our living rooms.

*—Declan McCullagh*

Richard Jewell, the security guard from Atlanta's bombed Centennial Olympic Park, knows that as well as anyone in America. For 88 days he was investigated and held up to public ridicule before being cleared as a suspect in the fatal bombing at the 1996 Atlanta Olympic Games.

## Webcams: Their Eyes Are on You

Wondering if facial recognition technology is something you might need to worry about? Maybe. Many cities now have live "citycams" in place to get traffic reports, or simply to show potential tourists how delightful it is in their city. Figure 8.2 shows the live WebCam in Trafalgar Square, in England, which is part of a tourist information site about London. Webcams are being used to check the parking at the ballpark to help us decide whether to drive or take the subway.

We even use Web cameras to watch for Nessie, the fabled beast of Loch Ness! Figure 8.3 shows one of the "NessieCams" at the Loch Ness Visitor Center.

**FIGURE 8.2**

*Trafalgar Square's early morning traffic via WebCam. Source:*
`http://www.camvista.com/england/london/trafsq.php3`.

**FIGURE 8.3**

*Will Nessie appear on the NessieCam at Urqhardt Castle in Scotland? Source:* `http://www.lochness.scotland.net/webcam.htm.`

Web cameras are just about everywhere on the Net—the picture shown in Figure 8.1 was taken with the "StudioCam" at Elfhill Music and Mayhem (`www.elfhill.com`). But surveillance cameras—used for security, traffic control, and voyeuristic activities—are just as common. When a community decides to add facial recognition capability to its downtown security cameras, citizens of that community may not even know. The only way you can tell why you're being watched is to pay attention to your local community government notices.

# By Air, by Land, or by Sea—GPS Isn't Just for Planes and Fish Anymore

We've discussed the pros and cons of video surveillance. Now let's take a look at another technology, one which lets people track you even if they can't see you.

GPS, or Global Positioning Satellite service, was developed by the U.S. government as a mechanism for accurately deploying troops and weapons even in nighttime or bad weather. Commercial aviation used it for a long time to help airplanes find the airports and land even in heavy fog. Commercial and sport fisherman adopted it to help them find the big schools of fish and then find a way back to port safely. Many "gadget freaks" had them in their cars, or even hooked to their laptop map database, just so they'd always know where they were.

More or less, that is. GPS wasn't as accurate for non-military use as we might have wanted. The government kept the readings we could get just slightly off, to prevent the technology being used effectively against the United States. In 2000 the Clinton Administration gave the executive order to turn off the system that kept the readings inaccurate. When that happened, the commercial use of GPS exploded.

Trimble Marine, one of the larger fishing and boating supply companies in the United States, has an excellent Web site, and on it is a very good explanation of GPS. Their definition reads:

> The Global Positioning System (GPS) is a worldwide radio-navigation system formed from a constellation of 24 satellites and their ground stations. GPS uses these "man-made stars" as reference points to calculate positions accurate to a matter of meters. In fact, with advanced forms of GPS you can make measurements to better than a centimeter!
>
> In a sense it's like giving every square meter on the planet a unique address. GPS receivers have been miniaturized to just a few integrated circuits and so are becoming very economical. And that makes the technology accessible to virtually everyone.
>
> These days GPS is finding its way into cars, boats, planes, construction equipment, movie making gear, farm machinery, even laptop computers.

If you want to know more, Trimble Marine has a great tutorial about GPS at http://www.trimble.com/gps/. Figure 8.4 shows a simplified diagram of how GPS satellites help locate vehicles (and the people operating them) on land, sea, and in the air.

In the next few sections, we'll talk about some new uses of GPS technology in ways that might have privacy consequences.

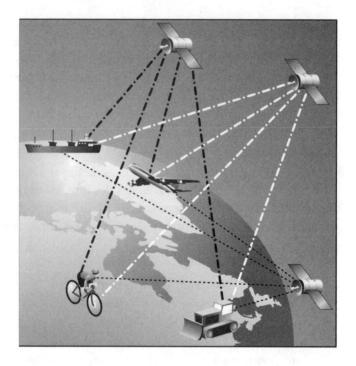

**FIGURE 8.4**

*GPS units help identify an object's precise location.*

## OnStar, Car.Net, LoJack, and Their Cousins

One of the most amusing commercials in the past year shows a man trekking up from the beach ahead of his family to open up the car. He's locked his keys inside the car. His family, loaded down with beach balls, picnic baskets, and other paraphernalia of a day at the shore, is catching up to him. What does he do? He gets out his cell phone, and calls his OnStar help desk. The nice lady unlocks the car for him, seemingly almost by magic, just before his family troops up. Had he had a flat tire, the help desk could have used the GPS unit in the car to dispatch a local tow truck. Figure 8.5 is a page from the OnStar Web site, showing services they offer.

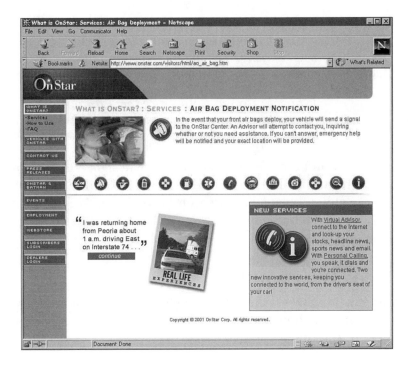

**FIGURE 8.5**

*OnStar can even tell if your airbags have deployed.*

OnStar is just one of several similar services available in modern cars. This is not just good for opening the door to your car (although that's a nice convenience). According to Edmunds Automotive, one of the oldest automobile news publications in the United States, OnStar means that you never have to be alone or lost again.

*"Pushing one of the three OnStar buttons grouped on the instrument panel, rearview mirror, or overhead controls—sends a signal, via satellite, to the main OnStar headquarters in Troy, Mich. Once a signal is received, a connection is made by a live OnStar "Advisor" via cellular technology and a small speaker/mic in the vehicle. The OnStar staff is trained to answer any number of questions, from the important—Emergency Medical Services calls—to the ridiculous—the words to the "Banana Boat Song." If necessary, they can pinpoint your location using GPS (global positioning system) satellite technology and give that information to you or the ambulance racing your way.*

*If asked, they will stay connected and give you explicit directions to the local hospital or get you back on the main highway. If your car stalls, they can run*

*an electronic diagnostic on it and tell you to head to the nearest dealer or
wait for a tow truck. They'll even give you a call if your airbag deploys,
checking to make sure everyone's OK and reminding you that an emergency
vehicle is on its way to you at that very moment."*

**(Source: Gonzo Schexnayder, Edmunds.com,**
`http://www.edmunds.com/news/innovations/articles/43031/`
`article.html`**)**

LoJack, Car.Net, and other similar services are designed to cut down on
car theft—or, rather, to improve the recovery of stolen vehicles. When you
report the car stolen, they start a search for the car's GPS ID. In the
movie *Fair Game*, the bad guy found the runaway couple through his
theft-prevention GPS service.

# Can Your Cell Phone Call Home?

Okay, you say. I make sure my car doesn't talk to anyone, but I want to
take my cell phone, so people can call me if they need me. Or if I need to
call for help out in the boonies.

## 911 Wants to Know Where You Are

Until 2001, you would have probably been safe from easy location,
depending on what kind of phone you had. But remember the example
from the beginning of the chapter, about the woman who drowned
because she couldn't tell the 911 operator where she was? The U.S.
Congress decided that this sort of thing had to stop and passed a law
requiring that all cell phone companies find a way to locate their subscribers within 100 feet.

As you might guess, the civil liberties and privacy advocates aren't happy
about this law. Yes, it can help save lives—perhaps hundreds of lives—
every year. But what about the millions of other people who could now
be tracked and traced all the time? Since their cell phones will be broadcasting their location in the clear any time the phone is on, anyone can
track them down. We'll talk about some potential abuses.

According to an opinion column written by the Gartner Group, a
research and consulting company, the cellular providers aren't finding
this law easy to comply with, especially with the consumer advocates trying to preserve some vestiges of anonymity for cellular customers.

Sprint PCS is planning to put GPS chips inside its handsets, which require it to persuade as many consumers as possible to buy new phones. Cingular Wireless, the company being created out of BellSouth and SBC Communications, uses a similar technology for part of its footprint, but uses a "network based" approach for the rest.

Verizon Wireless says it, too, uses one of several network approaches, which involves judging a person's location from such data as signal strength and simple triangulation. AT&T says it needs more time to decide.

For more information on how cellular providers are struggling to comply, see CNET.com at `http://news.cnet.com/news/0-1004-200-3624256.html?tag=st.ne.ni.gartnercomm.ni.`

## They Know You're in the Neighborhood

GPS combined with cell phones isn't just for safety. Marketers have decided that they want to reach out and touch you, just so you don't miss a special offer that you might be about to pass by. Or, perhaps you might like to subscribe to a service that lets you know when you are near a Chinese restaurant so that you can have your favorite Crab Rangoon even when you're traveling in a strange town.

If you live or shop in West Nyack, NY, you might be able to experience this right now. According to *Forbes* magazine, the Palisades Center mall started a program in October 2000 to beam electronic advertisements to consumer's cell phones when they get in range of the mall. According to the article, the "wireless promotions, which is sent only to consumers who've registered through the mall's Web site, can be directed to all cell phone users, regardless of whether the units are Internet-enabled. Cell phones that cannot display e-mail messages receive an audio advertisement, says Salim Samaha, director of business development for GeePS.com, the Cranbury, NJ, company supplying the technology to Palisades Center." (Source: `http://www.forbes.com/2000/08/23/feat2.html`.) Figure 8.6 shows the signup page at the Palisades' Web site.

**FIGURE 8.6**

*The Palisades Center GPS program signup page.*

This technique is part of a new marketing system called "location-sensitive marketing." In the past, most people who subscribed to this system had to first tell the phone company where they were, by giving a ZIP code or a street address. As soon as they did, they started to receive local business directories, to help find the nearest automatic teller machine, gas station, or theatre. Some received text advertisements that are billed as electronic coupons.

After October 2001, though, the customer doesn't have to tell the cellular service where he is. The built-in GPS, or other locating scheme, does that for him. GPS enables merchants to target consumers carrying cell phones or handheld computers as they approach a store.

## Your Rental Car May Rat You Out

When a movie character tosses off a comment about a ding in a car, "It's only a rental!" rental company employees must cringe. There are Web pages that recount, with pictures, the abuse heaped on rental cars.

So it's no surprise that rental car companies used services such as LoJack to help find their lost or stolen cars. But in October 2000, a new twist was added to the story.

Acme Rent-a-Car of Connecticut charged a customer named Turner $450 for speeding in one of their rentals. Turner was understandably upset, and took the company to small claims court. According to ZDNet news, Acme felt Turner was adequately warned. "On its contracts, the company noted: Drivers of 'vehicles driven in excess of posted speed limit is charged a $150 fee per occurrence. All our vehicles are GPS equipped.' Turner, and many other customers, didn't connect the two statements, and paid for it later.

> *"Turner apparently drove greater than 77 mph at least three times, not knowing that the car's GPS receiver was giving him away. Without providing him any warning apart from the contract, the rental company went ahead and charged Turner $150 for each incident."*
>
> **(Source: Robert Lemos, ZDNet News, 2 July 2001,**
> `http://www.zdnet.com/zdnn/stories/news/0,4586,5093616,00.html`**)**

In July 2001, the Connecticut Department of Consumer Protection agreed with Turner that Acme was out of line and ordered the company to cease this practice. They also have to make restitution to the two dozen or more customers who have been previously fined for speeding.

Cars that come equipped with instant map services, such as Hertz's NeverLost, are equipped with a GPS to make the mapping gadget work. If you rent a car with such a device, you might want to check to see what else the company is tracking.

## Your Insurance Agent Is Watching

Most of us are glad our insurance companies don't see what we're doing all the time, especially if we accidentally go the wrong way on a one-way street or make an illegal U-turn when we get lost in a bad neighborhood. But one insurance company is offering their drivers a reward for being tracked.

> *In April 2000, The IEEE journal, Spectrum reported this: "The real future of GPS, however, may lie in business applications not yet dreamt of, as well as*

*in applications just beginning development. For example, The Progressive Insurance Co., an automobile insurer based in Mayfield Village, Ohio, is testing Autograph, a GPS-equipped computer that tracks driving habits, such as time spent in high-traffic areas. The hope is to lower premiums."*

**(Source: Spectrum, IEEE, April 2000,** http://www. spectrum.ieee.org/pubs/spectrum/0400/gps.html**)**

Since 1998, Progressive has been selling metered insurance based on actual driving practices to customers in Texas. Here's how it works: The company installs a special device, including a standard GPS receiver, a cellular modem, a computer chip, and 256Kb of memory. Every time the car's ignition is turned on, the system, called Autograph, logs the date, time, latitude, and longitude. Every six minutes, until the car is turned off, it logs the same information. That counts as one trip.

Every month, the central office computer calls the Autograph device, using the built-in cell phone. The device sends its log, which Progressive then uses to generate a bill. In each bill has a basic fee, covering the car's comprehensive insurance for damage or theft when it is not in use, plus fees based on how much the car was driven, where, and at what time of day or night. Figure 8.7 shows a portion of an Autograph bill, with usage divided into risk zones and driving patterns.

"A mile driven at midnight," said Bob McMillan, the company's former business development leader, "is 10 times more dangerous than one driven at 8 a.m. Commute miles, in fact, are the lowest cost miles of the day—people are alert, know the route, and traffic is moving slowly."

At a Washington, D.C. speech in January 2001, McMillan reported that participating drivers save 25%–50% more than conventional billing methods. Those methods use historical data based on a driver's age, gender, marital status, residence, and driving record to estimate driving habits. For the new program, Progressive has targeted people who they think would save money because of their driving habits. It expects GPS-based billing to move its customers from traditional insurance programs.

| Minutes and usage premium by risk zone, time of day for the 1996 Toyota Corolla DX | | | | |
|---|---|---|---|---|
| Risk zone<br>Time of day | 1 | 2 | 3 | Unidentified |
| 5:00–11:59 a.m. | 16 min/$0.08 | 33 min/$0.14 | 0 | 16 min/$0.04 |
| 12:00–7:59 p.m. | 16 min/$0.11 | 176 min/$0.97 | 50 min/$0.24 | 13 min/$0.04 |
| 8:00–10:59 p.m. | 0 | 18 min/$0.13 | 0 | 1 min/$0.00 |
| 11:00 p.m.–4:59 a.m. | 0 | 1 min/$0.02 | 0 | 0 |

**FIGURE 8.7**

*A portion of a Progressive "Autograph" bill.*

McMillan also reported that the company is very concerned about the privacy of its subscribers. For that reason, they only keep the actual driving data linked to the individual driver for 90 days (the length of time records must be retained in case of bill challenges). After that, they discard the personally identifiable linkage and just keep aggregate data.

Progressive's customers are happy both with their savings and with the company's concerns for their privacy, said McMillan.

# Digital Angels or Digital Snoops?

It started with "Help, I've fallen and I can't get up!" and a radio transmitter Grandma could push to summon help. Today's devices are more sophisticated. A company called "Digital Angel" provides products for children, the elderly, people with chronic diseases, and others who might need help because of chronic or severe illness, or because they live alone.

Digital Angel's first products, shown in Figure 8.8, are watches, which run on a standard watch batter, or a pager, which comes with a rechargeable battery. Both kinds have a 911 alert button that calls for emergency help as well as contacting the parents or caregivers. In other words, a wandering child or senior can call 911 from anywhere.

Digital Angel also offers a service for pets, with a collar device. That way, if Fido gets lost, they can track him just the same way they track kids.

## "Where Are You?" Plus "How Are You?"

According to the Digital Angel Web site, their devices report the wearer's physical condition, as well as the location. "Miniature sensors make a world of difference. The patient's pulse rate is just one proprietary

Digital Angel sensor technology. Other sensors for monitoring body temperature and blood oxygen levels will also be available in the first generation Digital Angel." The next addition they plan to add is electrocardiogram (EKG) and brain wave monitoring (EEG).

**FIGURE 8.8**

*Digital Angel's products (http://www.digitalangel.net/da/index.htm).*

This is how it works: Let's say your parent, who lives with you, has Alzheimer's, and you subscribe to the service. Grandma wears the watch all the time. One day she wanders away from the house while you are shopping. When you discover she is missing, the Digital Angel Web site says, you log onto the Web site. The signal from Grandma's watch or pager is always transmitting location and medical condition information. When you log in, the information is displayed on a map. It can also be displayed on a PDA or cell phone. Figure 8.9 shows a sample display. The address is printed as well as displayed on a map.

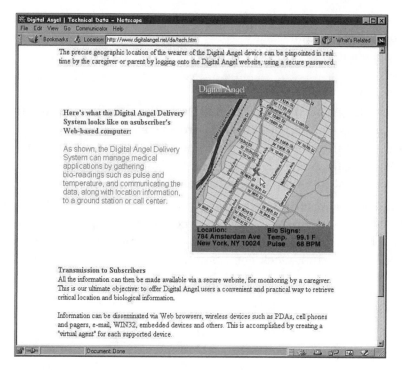

**FIGURE 8.9**

*Grandma's location is displayed on a Digital Angel map.*

Digital Angel has taken precautions to keep other people from checking on Grandma. Location information is displayed over a secure link (SSL), and you must have an account and password to log in. Digital Angel says they are using the most modern digital cell phone technology, which is encrypted. Unfortunately, hackers have broken that encryption. Although you have no guarantee that someone listens in, you also have no guarantee that someone isn't.

Digital Angel also sells services for children so that you know where your child is. Parents of active toddlers can see the benefits in this, as well as parents of older children. But since the encryption has been hacked, people who want to find that child—let's say the other parent in a custody battle—can zero in on the child precisely. It's then an easy matter to take him or her away during a walk home from school or during playtime in the park.

The Digital Angel technical information says that you can turn off the signal to keep from transmitting when you don't want to, but the base stations can turn it on if there is an inquiry. As long as you can take the watch or pager off, that's okay. However, the next generation of the device has some new and troublesome ramifications.

## Getting Under Your Skin

In April 2000 , Applied Digital Signal (ADS, the parent company for Digital Angel) bought a company, Destron Fearing, which had patented a miniature digital transceiver that can be placed just underneath a person's skin. Digital Angel plans to track the signal from the chip anywhere in the world just like they can track wearable devices.

The announcement of this technology purchase caused great concerns in the civil liberties and privacy advocacy community. Even hardcore techies got concerned. The following is an excerpt from an editorial on the online tech forum, Geek.com. Sam Evans, Chief Editor, says:

> [C]heck out the description of the Digital Angel's potential use in "Identification:"
>
> "Digital Angel could constitute an important security measure. It can carry personal identification information and transmit this information via wireless communication with personal computers. Requiring this ID for logon would prevent unauthorized access to those computers.
>
> It's tough to get more obviously Big Brother than that one. Remember, even it its current modeling configuration, although you can turn it off the base stations can turn it on....
>
> What I find interesting about this whole thing is that some products can do what the Digital Angel does. The integration of the monitoring, broadcasting, receiving, and location functions into such a small unit just gets me nervous. After all, the first thing I think most of us think of when we read this is the way people on house arrest or parolees are sometimes given location devices to wear (ADS lists that sort of thing as one of the Digital Angel's uses). So why does this technology, which DOES have some legitimate, good uses, make me so nervous? I just don't like the fact that maybe in 15 years (or less!) my children will be forced by the government to have a chip implanted to monitor them for safety reasons...and that that chip will know who they are, what they're doing, where they are, etc....AND that that info will be broadcast to receiving stations."

**(Source:** `http://www.geek.com/news/geeknews/oct2000/`
`gee20001030002749.htm`**)**

Sam's fear might seem like wild speculation, but permanent, non-removable identity mechanisms are being proposed by the U.S. Government in the wake of the events of September 11, 2001 for anyone residing or visiting in the United States who is not a U.S. citizen. And, implantable chips are already in use, to help us identify our pets when they go astray or are stolen.

## Pet Chips

For at least five years, an implantable radio transponder has been available through veterinarians. A transponder is a radio or radar set that does not transmit continuously. When it receives a signal from its partner transmitter, it emits a radio signal of its own. Transponders are used all around us. Proximity badges that unlock doors when you get close, the tags on clothes that spray ink or set off an alarm if you go out the door with it still attached, all are transponders.

Like Digital Angel, this too is a subscription service, called HomeAgain. The American Kennel Club Companion Animal Recovery program, partnered with Schering-Plough Animal Health, offers it. The chip is injected just under the skin between the pet's shoulder blades. According to the literature, this device provides "positive, permanent identification for the life of the animal."

According to the manufacturer, this is how it works:

> *"The transponder's electronic circuitry is energized by a low-power radio beam sent by a compatible reading device. The transponder sends the identification number as a radio signal back to the reader, which then encodes the number and displays it on a small screen similar to that on an electronic calculator. And, the transponder contains no batteries to replace."*

> **(Source:** http://www.spah.com/usa/products/
> fulldescr.cfm?prodid=273&sID=1**)**

Part of the reason for Sam's fears is that the HomeAgain chip is made by Destron Fearing, the same company that Digital Angel bought to make their human-tracking chips. However, the big difference between Digital Angel's proposed products and HomeAgain is this: The microchip in your pet can't be located by GPS (yet). If your pet is found by a pound, kennel, or vet with the proper equipment, they can scan the pooch for a microchip, and it responds with your pet's unique ID number. The kennel then calls the AKC, who calls you to come and get your pet. Future products are proposed to let you track your pooch on his wanderings, just like you track Grandma.

It's not enough that businesses will be able to send you ads by tracking your location over a cell phone. New technology will let you simply get *close* to a check-out terminal to pay. As we'll see in the next section, there are some dangers of theft and fraud, as well as privacy and tracking issues, in these technologies.

# No More Waiting in Line—We'll Bill You

A few years ago, gas stations started offering to make your refill even faster, by putting credit card or ATM stations right on the gas pump. Technology is offering even more convenience, developing systems that enable you to pay without even having cash or your credit card with you—in some instances you can just drive by and pay.

## Drive-By Toll Pay

Almost every state in the United States now has some kind of easy-pay toll system. These offer regular commuters the opportunity to just drive through the tollbooth, instead of having to stop and fumble for coins or cash. As your car goes through the gate, a radio transmitter in the booth sends a signal. One of those transponders discussed earlier, mounted on your car, responds with your unique identifier, and the toll system charges you the right amount. In most instances, driving through causes a charge to be made against an account you've already set up with the state. In some, when that account gets low, you can authorize the state to charge your credit card to fill it up again.

These systems go by many names: TollPass, EZPass, FasTrak, and so on. As a kind of technology, they are called ITS, or Intelligent Transportation Systems. Figure 8.10 shows the Massachusetts Fast Lane Web page, including how to fasten the transponder unit onto your car.

These systems are really convenient. According to facts from the Massachusetts system, shown in Table 8.2, they are rugged and durable, lasting for up to five years, and can even withstand Massachusetts blizzards and travel across California's Death Valley. In most areas, you find at least one dedicated fast pay toll lane, and some have several combination traditional and radio-equipped booths, as well. You can whiz ahead in line and slide through the booth without even having to stop (although you do need to slow down to 5–10 mph for the system to work). At the end of the month, you get a statement showing all your trips and how much was charged to your account. Some states offer discounted tolls if you use their systems, making the use of them good for your budget.

**FIGURE 8.10**

*The Massachusetts Fast Lane Web page.*

## TABLE 8.2   SYSTEM SPECIFICATIONS FOR MASSACHUSETTS TOLL PAY SYSTEM

| System Specifications | FAST LANE |
| --- | --- |
| Throughput | 2,000 vehicles/hr/lane |
| Transponder Density | One FAST LANE transponder per vehicle. |
| Accuracy | 99.9 percent |
| Security | Tag-to-tag reader communications use error checking. |
| Operating Frequency Band | 912.750 to 918.750 megahertz. |
| Transponder Battery Life | 5 years |
| Transponder Operating Temperature | -40 degrees F to 158 degrees F |

*(Source: Massachusetts Department of Transportation)*

Privacy advocates see a problem with that billing statement and the corresponding records.

To have a statement, someone is keeping a record of your trips and everyone else's trips through the toll booths. While this opens up a whole new world of interesting plot twists for murder mystery writers ("Honest, officer, I couldn't have murdered her. See, here on this statement it says I was crossing the Tappan Zee Bridge at the time."), it also means that someone can check where you go and when.

Simson Garfinkel, author of the book *PGP: Pretty Good Privacy*, wrote as early as 1995 that the potential for abuse with this system is high. He said,

> *"Phil Agre, who teaches communications at the University of California, Los Angeles, and closely follows privacy issues, warns that there might be other unintended consequences of the widespread use of ITS systems. Auto insurance companies already offer discounts to drivers who don't live in areas of high auto theft or accidents; in the future, says Agree, they might offer discounts to drivers who can prove that they haven't driven onto the wrong side of the tracks. The data could also be sold illegally by insiders. Information about a person's movements might be a key fact in forcing an out-of-court settlement in a divorce or worker's compensation case. Private investigators would have a big incentive to bribe low-paid clerical workers for a photocopy of somebody's toll-crossing bill."*

**(*Source:* http://www.alts.net/ns1625/electoll.html)**

Just as in the Richard Jewell case, the chances for someone to be mistakenly branded a liar or arrested for a crime are high. In fact, it has already happened. Phil Agre reported in 1996 that such an event had already taken place, in France.

Jacques Mellick, mayor of the northern French town of Bethune and former cabinet minister, provided an alibi in the trial of politician and businessman Bernard Tapie on charges of trying to bribe a football coach to throw a match. He claimed that he and Tapie had met at Tapie's offices in Paris between 2:30p.m. and 3:30pm on the date when the offence had supposedly taken place. Doubts soon arose about Mellick's story. A photo claimed to have been taken 2:00pm that day placed Mellick at a ceremony in Bethune. And, says the story, "the motorway toll booths between Paris and Bethune had no record of Mellick's car on the road that day." Mellick claimed that he had paid the toll himself because he had been travelling to Paris on private business. The article does not explain who had checked the records or who had made the information about them public. (Source: `http://dlis.gseis.ucla.edu/people/pagre/`)

Keeping this convenience while preserving privacy is possible. If the ITS implementers would accept digital cash, commuters could make a choice between having logs kept on them or not. True digital cash is a system where you can put money into an account, and the financial institution issues some sort of payment chit, either a smart card or a stored value card. See Chapter 4, "Threats to Your Children's Privacy," for a longer discussion of stored value cards.

That payment chip would have no identifier on it that names you. It simply points back at the financial institution, which guarantees payment, something like an electronic money order or International Mailing Coupon. The financial institution does have a record of the purchase and the purchaser, but those records would not be linked to the toll records. New financial privacy laws make it harder to get those account records. See Chapter 13, "Privacy and the Law: 2001," for a more complete discussion of financial privacy laws.

Unfortunately, digital cash is not catching on as fast as its inventors, and privacy mavens, would like. The technology is not simple, and because it's new and unfamiliar, hasn't caught on in the public imagination. For an excellent article on why digital cash isn't more widely used, see Declan McCullagh's excellent article in *Wired* magazine, 14 June 2001. (Source: `http://www.wired.com/news/ebiz/0,1272,44507,00.html`).

# Just Wave Your Fob at the Register

An even greater convenience than drive-through toll systems are fob payment systems. These systems put the transponder in a small key fob, like those shown in Figure 8.11. When the fobs are waved near a radio equipped payment screen, such as on a vending machine, gas pump, or cash register, payment is recorded. You can have your fob account deduct money from a checking account, charge card, or stored value account.

Two such systems are FreedomPay and Mobil's SpeedPass.

**FIGURE 8.11**

*Key fobs for the Freedoms payment system.*

## Freedom to Pay

Freedom Pay offers two ways to pay—using a key fob, or using a PIN (personal identification number) and passcode. Figure 8.12 shows the FreedomPay Web site. On the right side are pictures of vending machine units and key fobs.

The *Philadelphia Business Journal* describes FreedomPay like this:

> "FreedomPay operates somewhat like a debit card without the card. Customers signing up with the company provide a Visa, MasterCard, American Express, or checking account; money is deducted directly from there. Signing up is free.
>
> On vending machines, customers enter a PIN and a password, which deducts the purchase from their account. At establishments with a cash register, they merely wave a keychain-like wand called a Radio Frequency Identification and the purchase is subtracted, again through the magic of computers and the Internet.
>
> FreedomPay equipment works best in places that don't often accept credit cards or debit cards, Pons said. That might include vending machines, fast-food restaurants and convenience stores.
>
> The company, which is funded by Nokia Venture Partners, Sun America/AIG and Kellett Investments, makes money with licensing fees."

**(Source: *Philadelphia Business Journal*, 27 April 2001,**
`http://philadelphia.bcentral.com/philadelphia/`
`stories/2001/04/30/newscolumn7.html`**)**

**FIGURE 8.12**

*The FreedomPay terms and conditions page.*

FreedomPay, or systems like it, would work really well for places where you have to use cash (street vendors, independent musician concerts, and so on). Because the fees to the licensing merchant are lower than with credit cards, merchants may like this system better.

FreedomPay's Web site says that if your wand/fob gets stolen, you should call them immediately and they suspend the account and send you a new fob that you initialize just like a credit card.

## SpeedPass

SpeedPass is a similar system, owned and managed by Exxon Mobil. Figure 8.13 shows how SpeedPass works at a cash register, according to the Web site. SpeedPass is accepted at Mobil and Exxon. It can also be used at McDonald's in the Chicago area.

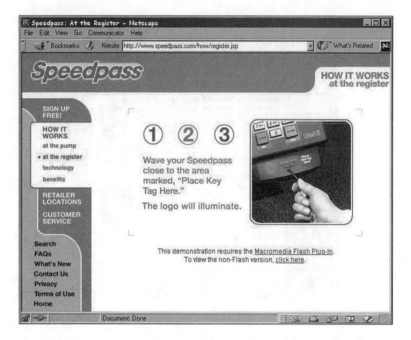

**FIGURE 8.13**

*How Mobil's SpeedPass works at the register (*`http://www.speedpass.com/how/register.jsp`*).*

SpeedPass was featured in a story from *Popular Science* that appeared in May 2001. It talks about the McDonald's partnership with Mobil to experiment with fast pay systems:

> ### BOISE, Idaho—McDonald's wants to make fast food even faster.
>
> *The Oak Brook, Ill.-based restaurant chain is monitoring closely a marketing test that lets its patrons use a tiny, gray plastic wand to pay for meals, instead of cash. The concept, while novel, is by no means new, but McDonald's, which is testing it in 26 locations in Boise, thinks it might be a good idea.*
>
> *More than 2,000 people have signed up for the program, which, essentially, gives them the convenience of waving the wand in front of an electronic sensor to pay for a meal. No more fumbling for loose change or looking for smaller bills.*
>
> *"Fast food is not fast anymore," says Jerry McVety, the president of McVety & Associates, a Farmington Hills, Mich.-based food service consulting group.*

> *...The McDonald's trial electronic payment program in Chicago, which McVety says has proven popular, works with Speedpass, a system developed three years ago by Mobil for use at its gas pumps and which the company is now offering other businesses.*
>
> *Participants wave a tiny, barrel-shaped Speedpass transponder at the cash register, or at a drive-through window. Each Speedpass then charges a purchase to a credit or debit account.*
>
> **(Source: PopSciWire, 27 May 2001,**
> `http://www.popsci.com/news/05272001_epayment.html`**)**

As of August 2001, more than 400 McDonalds' in the Chicago/Boise area now accept SpeedPass.

Along with the fob system, SpeedPass also offers a Car Tag, which fits in the rear window of your car on the same side as your filler cap. When you drive up to a Mobil gas pump, the Car Tag activates the pump and authorizes your purchase. You have to align the car with the pump and get pretty close, which takes a little practice. If your filler cap is in the back, or under your license plate, you can center the Car Tag in the bottom of the rear window and pull up to the pump on either side of your car. Or, you can locate the Car Tag in your rear window on either one side or another, and always pull that side of your car next to the pump. If your fuel door is located in the front, you must locate the Car Tag in the bottom of your front window.

We don't know if McDonald's accepts the Car Tag at their drive-up window yet.

## Pros and Cons for Fobs

The good news about fobs is that your credit card number never gets transmitted on the air. Like with the digital cash devices discussed earlier, what actually gets transmitted is a unique identifier for you and your account. Payment happens elsewhere, on a secured system.

Key fob payment systems have two problems. The first is theft. Because you don't have to enter a PIN to confirm that you're really the one who owns the fob with most of the systems, anyone who has it can charge on your account.

The second problem is forgery. If someone copies your fob, it's just like having the original. They can pay anywhere your fob is accepted. Currently, no key fobs have been duplicated, although speculations about how to go about it do exist. Like digital cellular, however, it's just a matter of time.

# Check Yourself Out

The popularity of Costco, Pak'n'Save, Food Source, and other warehouse shopping stores demonstrate that customers are willing to do a lot of the work themselves to save money. The bottleneck, of course, comes at the checkout. The lines get long, and if you have a slow cashier, much of the productivity you've saved gets eaten up in waiting.

Some conventional stores are now offering a system where you do some of the work yourself by scanning items as you put them in the cart. When you get to the checkout, you return the scanner to a docking port, go to an express pay station, and you're done. (Of course, no one has solved the problem of self-packing or self-unloading groceries yet.)

The grocery inventory, all the items and prices, are stored in the handset so that when you scan the barcode the price is retrieved from local storage. The handset runs a local total, so you can figure out how much you've bought as you go.

While more widely used in Europe, the system is being introduced in the United States. Chains using the method include Finast (United States), Safeway (United Kingdom), Tenglemann (Germany), and Albert Heijn (The Netherlands).

## Scanners Do Not Live in Vain...

Pat tried out this system when she was in Scotland a couple of years ago, and it was pretty easy. When you enter the store, you plug a smart card into a rack of bar code scanners. The dispenser rack unlocks and gives you a scanner, which is registered to you when you insert your card. As you push your cart along the rows, you scan the items as you select them. If you change your mind, you press a "minus" (-) key and deduct that item.

Getting used to scanning items isn't easy, but it's not terribly hard, either. After a few rows, you get as good as the average checkout person.

When you get done, you plug the scanner back into the storage rack.

Your total is added up, a receipt pops out of the bottom of the rack. While a bagger puts your groceries in sacks, you go to a special aisle and pay for your order. Figure 8.14 shows a British shopper using the handset system.

**FIGURE 8.14**

*A shopper using the handset system.*

B&M Coupon News, a grocery retailer publication, introduced the technology to American grocers in the mid 1990s. They described the advantages to the store.

> *"The scanner provides numerous benefits to both the retailer and the shopper besides the obvious timesaving element. Shoppers on a budget appreciate the scanner's capability to total their purchases, so they know when they reach their limit. They may even end up purchasing more than usual because customers often tend to overestimate their order amount. Retailers benefit from the image of cutting-edge customer service and the use of the technology that help them track purchases, customer and price data through the store's computer system. While some have expressed reservations about the security of the system, this is not expected to pose a problem. Where similar systems have been in use throughout Europe, shrinkage has even decreased. In addition to having shoppers who register for the system provide information that allows a detailed background check, the bar coded ticket that customers present to the cashier includes an analysis of the order and highlights any potential scanning problems. The order can then be rescanned to verify the purchase. While the system is still in the process of being tested, it is the most innovative attempt at improving customer service in some time. Though time tells how successful it is, it promised to be something to watch in coming months."*

**(Source:** http://www.bmpro.com/bmprocessing/v10i2.htm #avoid**)**

Privacy-related problems exist beyond the theft of the ID card that links your credit or debit account to the scanner. A simple PIN would help fix that problem. Other questions to ask are: Is the memory for the scanner wiped every time, or is my purchase record available after I'm gone? Could someone replay the order and charge my account? And, again, the question of linking your identity to the food you purchase comes in. This is another place where digital cash would help significantly.

Let's not forget the problem of hackers. When a grocery store has all your information, including your grocery preferences and your credit card information, in a central database, that database is a tempting target. Because a hacker could capture hundreds or thousands of valid accounts in one place, the reward for hacking the system would be high.

## Moving to Wireless

As convenient as the system is, many stores now have an inventory and prices far too large to be easily stored in a handheld scanner. And, each scanner has to be reprogrammed when prices change.

The next logical development in the technology is to go to a wireless LAN. Symbol Technology, developer of the Portable Shopper system, introduced a wireless system in the spring of 2001:

> *"Symbol's new RF Portable Shopper runs on Symbol's Spectrum24 wireless local area network and is designed for stores with a huge inventory of many items sold at many different prices. Storing that amount of information in a handheld scanners' memory would add unnecessary cost and download time, so the network allows the Portable Shopper instant access to a server which can hold even the largest price file."*

**(Source: Computer Telephony Magazine, 7 May 2001,**
`http://www.computertelephony.com/article/CTM20010425S0004/6`**)**

For information on how wireless communications work, and related security and privacy issues, see Chapter 7, "Privacy Over the Airwaves."

When the customer scans an item, the handset queries the network for price information. A running total is kept in the handset. All the problems inherent in wireless communications apply to this system, too. For more information, see Symbol Technology's company Web site at `http://www.symbol.com/solutions/retail/retail_pssbrochure.html`.

## Re-Order Is in the Palm of Your Hand

Some people, and some families, buy the same grocery order every week so that the family shopper could reuse the shopping list if they hadn't written notes all over it. Not surprisingly, retailers have figured out a way to make shopping more convenient for those folks, too, and for those who hate the act of shopping itself. Many European, and some American stores now have online ordering, where you can go to a Web site and make an order, and then pick it up (or have it delivered) the next day. You do, however, have to have the empty item (or the last one in the cupboard) on hand to enter the barcode or item number on some systems. On others you can only buy the brands offered through the online catalog.

Safeway in the United Kingdom (owned by Wal-Mart, not the U.S. Safeway Grocery chain) were the first to try the personal scanning system. More than 160 stores now have that convenience. Safeway, partnered with IBM, developed a method to order what you want without having to remember what you just threw away, using Personal Digital Assistants (PDAs). Figure 8.15 shows the IBM Web page about the project, including one of the Palms used. Safeway piloted the system in 1999, enabling PalmPilot users to speed up their shopping. *Time* magazine reports that all the customer has to do is go shopping once; from then on, it can be done over the phone (or using a wireless modem, in the case of newer models):

> *"...[I]n a trial program at the chain's superstore in Basingstoke, shoppers receive a customized PalmPilot (free of charge) that they bring to the store each time they drop by. Everything they purchase during the visit is stored on the device at checkout. The next time they go shopping, they simply use the Pilot to check off items they want to buy again, and then hook the organizer up to a phone line to transmit their order online. They can pick up their purchases the next day. Each time they place an order, notices on special discounts will appear onscreen. Up to 10 more Safeways will try the program later this year."*

**(Source: Time Magazine, March 8, 1999,**
http://www.time.com/time/digital/magazine/
articles/0,4753,37719,00.html**)**

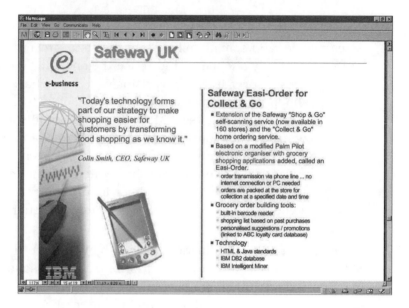

**FIGURE 8.15**

*IBM partnered with Safeway to develop this system.*

According to the Retail Technology news story on the topic, the specially-equipped PalmPilots, called "Easi-Orders" also have a built-in bar code reader customers can use at home to scan any items they would like to include in an upcoming order.

# Stop or We'll Shoot (Your Picture, That Is)

The concept is simple enough: instead of having a policeman watch intersections where a lot of folks run red lights, use a sensor system with a camera. Take a picture of the license plate, and possibly of the offending driver as well, and send a ticket along with the picture to the registered owner of the car.

As you might guess, the system has its champions and its opponents. Local governments and law enforcement love them. An August 1, 2001 film story on Sacramento's local news station, Fox40 News, said that red light violations were down significantly—perhaps as much as 15%—since the red-light camera system was installed. Sacramento fines for red-light violations are in excess of $245. Signs such as the one shown in Figure 8.16 are prominently posted around the intersection.

**FIGURE 8.16**

*A red-light camera warning sign.*

Sacramento is not the only community to use this enforcement method. As of July 2001, the U.S. Department of Transportation says:

> *"Currently, twenty-one known states and one territory have considered camera technology for enforcement and have passed legislation or are considering legislation to enforce red light running with camera technology. These are Arizona, California, Colorado, Delaware, Florida, Georgia, Illinois, Iowa, Kansas, Nebraska, North Carolina, Oklahoma, South Carolina, New York, Massachusetts, Maryland, Michigan, Minnesota, Texas, Virginia, Washington State, the District of Columbia and Puerto Rico. As well, some local communities are utilizing red light camera technologies based on the passage of local ordinances."*

> *(**Source:** http://safety.fhwa.dot.gov/ fourthlevel/srlr/overview.htm)*

In an early test case on the legality of the red light cameras, a San Diego, CA Superior Court judge dismissed many of the cases from cameras at three intersections because the police discovered that Lockheed Martin Corp. employees (the manufacturers of the camera) had adjusted the underground electromagnetic sensors at the three intersections in ways that might have affected their accuracy. According to the San Diego Union Tribune article of July 3, 2001, the city is now considering hiring an engineering firm to make sure the cameras are operating properly.

The sidebar "Red Light Facts from the US DOT" (presented later in this chapter) has other facts about stoplight violations and safety programs around the United States.

The cameras are used in Europe, as well, and similar systems are also used to catch speeders on the M and A highways in the United Kingdom.

Although manufacturers and form factors vary, most camera systems look something like the one in Figure 8.17.

**FIGURE 8.17**

*A typical red-light camera system in California.*

## Red Light District?

From the beginning, police departments have taken steps to preserve the privacy of people caught in the pictures. In some jurisdictions, for example, anyone in the passenger side of the car is blurred out, as the identity of the passenger isn't relevant to the driver's identity. (It hasn't stopped a few irate spouses from wondering who their sweetie was with when he or she was supposed to be at work.) The pictures are mailed only to the address where the car is registered; if the driver isn't the owner, the owner has to prove otherwise. (In some cities, the owner has to bring the driver in with him or her to the police department.)

The Insurance Institute for Highway safety says this in their online brochure when asked if red light cameras violate motorists' privacy:

> *"No. Driving is a regulated activity on public roads. By obtaining a license, motorists agree to abide by certain rules—to obey traffic signals, for example. Neither the law nor common sense suggests drivers shouldn't be observed on the road or have their violations documented. In addition, red light camera systems can be designed to photograph only a vehicle's rear license plate— not vehicle occupants, depending on local law."*

> *(Source:* `http://www.hwysafety.org/ safety_facts/qanda/rlc.htm#9`*)*

The following sidebar presents some facts about accidents at red lights and the attitudes we have about them, gathered by the United States Department of Transportation.

## RED-LIGHT FACTS FROM THE U.S. DOT

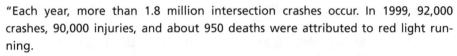

"Each year, more than 1.8 million intersection crashes occur. In 1999, 92,000 crashes, 90,000 injuries, and about 950 deaths were attributed to red light running.

In 1998, there were 89,000 red light running crashes that resulted in 80,000 injuries and 986 deaths.

Overall, 55.8% of Americans admit to running red lights. Yet ninety-six percent of drivers fear they will get hit by a red light runner when they enter an intersection.

This campaign's safety message is clear to everyone: red light running is the leading cause of urban crashes today. Phase I of Red Light Running significantly decreased these crashes in 28 of 31 participating communities. During the most recent years of the campaign, we have seen nearly a 10% decline in red light running crashes and fatalities.

One in three people claim they personally know someone who has been injured or killed in a red-light-running crash—similar to the percentage of people who know someone who was killed or injured by a drunk driver.

About 21% said they felt that drunk driving incidents are decreasing, but only six percent felt that red light running incidents were decreasing.

Although social scientists might hypothesize that 'frustration' and 'road rage' would represent what most people perceived as the cause of red light running, the results proved otherwise. Only 15.8% of respondents cited those reasons, while nearly half (47.8) admitted to being prompted by nothing more complicated than being in a hurry.

Red light runners do not conform to a set demographic —the dangerous practice reaches across drivers of all age, economic groups and gender. The perpetrators are everyday people; professionals, blue-collar workers, unemployed, homemakers, parents, and young adults."

*(Source: US Department of Transportation, Federal Highway Administration*
`http://safety.fhwa.dot.gov/fourthlevel/pro_res_srlr_facts.htm`*)*

Republican Governor James S. Gilmore III of Virginia, who is at odds with many liberals for his positions on the War between the States, is, nonetheless, one of the strongest voices opposing stoplight camera systems. In May, 2000, he was quoted in the *Washington Post*, where columnist Courtland Milloy said of the governor's position, "As insensitive as Gilmore's support of Confederate History Month may seem, his opposition to such surveillance shows that he has a deep understanding of the real threats to our liberty." Gilmore vetoed bills in May 2000 that would have expanded the technology in Virginia.

Gilmore said, "The slippery slope we travel down when we pass laws that enable the government to record our actions is the gradual loss of our freedom as citizens to conduct our lives without looking over our shoulder. We should not require our citizens to become accustomed to being watched by government authorities through electronic means."

## How Does It Work?

In general, when a set of sensors buried in the pavement sense that a car is going too fast to stop for a light that is going to turn red, it turns on the camera system. The camera takes two photos of offending drivers: one near the limit line and another about 0.5 seconds later.

Figure 8.18 shows a typical intersection picture captured by a stoplight camera, from the Oxnard, CA, police department Web site.

**FIGURE 8.18**

*A typical intersection picture*

On every intersection picture a data block helps the police department decide if the camera really caught a violator or not. Figure 8.19 shows a blow-up of a sample data block, courtesy of the Oxnard PD.

**FIGURE 8.19**

*A data block from Figure 8.18.*

The data block on this picture is described on the Oxnard Web site:

*"On every photo is a 'Camera Data Block.' This block can tell us many things about the violation. This picture was taken on July 7, 1997 at 5:50 p.m. and was the eighth photo citation of the day at this intersection. This is the second of two photos taken of this car. The first photo was exposed 0.5 seconds prior to this shot. At the time of this photo, the light had been red for 0.9 seconds and the speed of the car is 58 miles per hour."*

**(Source:** http://www.oxnardpd.org/redlite.htm**)**

The Oxnard PD does the math for us, to explain why the system works:

*"So what does all this data mean? First off, neither photo would have been shot if the vehicle had not crossed into the intersection on the red. Given that, we know that the red Chevy was traveling at 58 miles per hour (mph). That translates into 85 feet per second (fps) [5280 feet in one mile/3600 seconds in one hour × 58 mph = 85.066 fps]. The light for the Chevy was red for 0.9 seconds at the time of the exposure, so the light actually turned red for this vehicle some 76 feet back, which is well before the limit line [85.066 fps × 0.9 seconds = 76.559 feet]. Never mind the speed limit on this street is 45 mph. This equation does not take into consideration the braking time and distance required to stop at this speed. With an average coefficient of friction on a dry roadway (0.8), it would take about 135 feet and 3.2 seconds to stop this Chevy sports utility vehicle. Then the driver's reaction time must be taken into consideration. The point is that running red lights combined with excessive speed can lead to tragedy."*

**(Source:** http://www.oxnardpd.org/redlite.htm**)**

If your community is installing red light systems, you should contact the city to find out what the details of the system are. If your city has a Web site, urge them to put the details of the system online, as the Oxnard police have done. This helps everyone understand the system better, and helps encourage open debate about such surveillance systems.

# Glitches Mean Tickets Tossed Out

Most computer-operated systems have bugs from time to time, and the stoplight camera systems are no different. One recent story illustrates the problem.

In May, 2001, the San Diego police dismissed more than 5,000 tickets issued through the red light system. The reason? The sensors buried in the pavement that help activate the system and measure the vehicle's speed had been moved, but the cameras hadn't been reprogrammed. That meant that all the tickets issued were suspect, because the math (see the explanation above) wouldn't work out the same way. It would be impossible to tell who had really run a red and who had not (Source: http://www.sacbee.com/news/news/old/local04_20010609.html).

Similar problems have cropped up in Washington, D.C., Sacramento, and communities across the United States. Civil liberties activists all over the country are becoming more and more vocal as more glitches in the system are found.

# A Movie Rather Than a Still?

Pleasanton, CA, is trying a different approach. In April 2001 the city staff proposed installing digital video cameras to record red light violations instead of still cameras. The system uses sensors to predict which cars are not going to stop for a red light. Then the cameras begin recording, capturing images of the front and rear license plates and the driver. The video images are sent to a central processing facility and forwarded to the Police Department to be reviewed by an officer. If the answer is that a violation occurred, a citation is issued to the registration holder on record with the California Department of Motor Vehicles. Drivers who are cited under the system have the right to see the video of the incident. If the driver isn't the owner, the owner must bring the driver in to protest the ticket.

An additional safety feature, according to the Pleasanton Weekly city council report appealed to all the council members. When the system predicts a red-light runner, along with starting the camera, it delays the traffic signal in the other direction from turning green, keeping traffic from entering the intersection and having a collision with the violator (Source: `http://www.pleasantonweekly.com/morgue/2001_04_20.council20.html`).

Some privacy advocates think the video system would be less invasive of privacy than the still picture, because the context of the violation is included. However, most still oppose routine monitoring of the public. Proponents of the system argue that because the system doesn't start until a sensor determines that someone approaching a red light isn't stopping, these systems are not routine monitoring.

# What Happens When You Add It All Up?

Taken by themselves, these new technologies clearly have benefits as well as potential privacy threatening uses. Consumers and online users can probably deal with individual companies and their privacy policies, even though managing those many separate agreements is a hassle. However, it's the combination of services and technologies that are most worrisome.

One of Pat's colleague's recently characterized the privacy climate as being much like the story of the frog in the cooking pot. That story says that if you put a frog in a pot of cool water and gradually raise the temperature to boiling, you can cook the frog before it even notices the temperature change, because the change is so gradual. If you toss a frog into a pot of boiling water, however, it thrashes around because it definitely notices the temperature. "It's like that with privacy," this colleague said. "We hardly noticed the temperature going up, because all these things happened so slowly and so subtly, but now we're definitely in hot water. If we don't take some action to take control of our own information, and the intrusions in our lives, we're sunk."

# PART III

## TAKING CONTROL

*The precautions you choose to take really depend on how much privacy you require. In all likelihood, you could surf and post freely your whole life without dire consequences—but why take the chance? A few simple measures can put you in control of what people know about you and what they don't.*

> Elliot Zaret & Scholle Sawyer
> Protect Yourself Online
> Macworld, July 2000

*Ever watch one of those TV lawyers skillfully chip away at a guilty defendant's Big Lie?*

*The same thing is happening to the Big Lie about Internet privacy. The lie is that privacy safeguards are working. Truth is, you're more vulnerable than ever. And unless we take action to defend ourselves—soon—our private information will be exposed to anyone who wants it.*

> Jesse Berst, Editorial Director
> ZDNet Anchor Desk
> The Big Privacy Lie (And Why You Must Protect Yourself)
> http://www.zdnet.com/anchordesk/story/story_3970.html

# 9

# TAKING AN INVENTORY OF YOUR PERSONAL INFORMATION

Before you can make good choices about what information you might want to disclose, you need to know what of your information is available.

In Chapter 5, we discussed how you can disclose information about yourself inadvertently. When that information is combined with other information, it can be very revealing. This chapter is concerned with the information about you that may exist in relatively public places so you can see what others might be able to find out about you without too much effort or expense.

If you have a listed telephone number, own property, maintain a license from a government to pilot an airplane or a boat, for example, you are relatively findable. Unless you decide that you will forgo property ownership, unlist all your telephones, and refrain from activities that require some sort of certification, you will find it difficult, if not impossible, to disappear completely. This is not new with the Internet. What is new is the relative ease and the small expense with which almost anyone can find this information.

We considered a number of different methods of illustrating personal information collection and storage. However, using searches about Glee made the most sense because it's really impossible to show you the types of information about a person without using and disclosing personal information. The people we are most likely to get permission from to do this are ourselves.

We go into quite a bit of detail about how to find people. We find the "how to" interesting and useful, but that's not the point of this book. The point is to show you how much (or how little) is known about you, to help you make decisions about the information that's there, and help you figure out how to control the information about you.

# Where Are Youuuu? Whooo Are Youuu?

Like the Caterpillar's question to Alice in her trip to Wonderland, questions like these probably are sent through Internet search engines millions of times each day. The following are some personal anecdotes about the Internet and searching for us:

> A long time friend of Glee's who'd been out of contact for many years recently got a new laptop computer and an Internet account. She wondered aloud about how to use the Net to find out what Glee was up to these days. An acquaintance of hers said "Why don't you just Google her?" She did and found Glee quite quickly.
>
> A high school buddy of Pat's found a mention of Pat's current professional activities in a news article. He was able to trace her to her place of employment by using various search engines.
>
> Glee was approached by a recruiting director. He'd seen her name on the program of a conference, noted it, did a search for her on the Net, and called asking if she'd be interested in interviewing for a position in his company.

These stories have nice endings. We hope all the stories about tracing people through the Net do, even though we know they don't. Just look, though, at how easy it is to find out a lot about us.

## I'm Searching, Searching...

Searching on the Internet can be a "miss"-ing proposition as much as it can result in hits. Web pages can change frequently. Web sites come and go. Sometimes the content and the site have been archived by one of the Web-crawling spiders. Sometimes they haven't. Some archives are much larger than other archives. There is not a good way to predict what will be preserved and what won't, what will be indexed or what won't. It is not even possible to know how many pages exist or how to find them all. Some pages are excluded from being searched because they aren't "findable" via one of the Web crawlers, or because their administrators specifically ask that they be excluded.

In general, pages that are "private" because they are behind firewalls, pages that are "secure" because they required the HTTPS protocol, and pages that are filled-in forms are not included in archives of Web sites. All other pages may be found in some archive, but not necessarily all archives, because the archives are built at different times under different conditions.

Web crawlers, spiders, or robots work by visiting a page and taking a copy of it. Then the program goes, in succession, to each page that is linked to the first page. Each of those successive pages is copied and all the pages that are linked to them are then visited, and so on. This is why the results might be different when you search different archives.

In addition, the searches themselves work differently. And the different results are presented differently. The possibilities seem endless. (If you are interested in more information about Web crawlers, we suggest the Robot FAQ at `http://www.robotstxt.org/wc/faq.html`.)

Now that you are prepared, look at the charts of searches for Glee shown in Tables 9.1 and 9.2. The results vary widely. When you are searching for something, you might want two distinct kinds of results. The first is a "Give me exactly what I want and nothing else" search. The second is more like browsing the "I don't know exactly what I want, so show me lots of things to choose among" search.

If you have the first kind of request, an exact phrase search is best. That request is "Show me pages with these exact words in this exact order." Next best is a Boolean search with "Show me pages with both of these words," termed "AND." Sometimes the Boolean operators include "AND NOT," "NEAR," and "FOLLOWED BY." Each of these operators is applied to the "search terms" and cause a smaller result set.

If you want a very large search result, a search with a Boolean "OR" is just the ticket. A Boolean "OR" search says "Show me pages with any of these words."

Most of the searches found the same pages. The searches that allowed for exact phrase searching returned fewer results than the ones that didn't. However, some searches found pages that others didn't. All in all, this was an interesting exercise, and most informative. A really good explanation of how Internet searching works can be found online on the How Stuff Works Web site at `http://www.howstuffworks.com/ search-engine.htm`.

### TABLE 9.1    SEARCHING FOR GLEE—USING SEARCH SITES

| Search sites | glee cady | Glee harrah cady | "glee cady" | "glee harrah cady" |
|---|---|---|---|---|
| about.com (www.about.com) | 203 Web documents | 58 Web documents | 31 Web documents | 49 Web documents |
| altavista.com (www.altavista.com) | 238,153 results | 238,153 results | 38 results | 97 results |
| Ask Jeeves /findwhat (www.aj.com) (www.findwhat.com). | Note: Found Glee's Bio page, but mostly found a lot of pages about Elizabeth Cady Stanton and a large number of interesting, but totally irrelevant pages | These search engines ignore quotation marks | | |
| Excite/Webcrawler (www.excite.com)/ (www.webcrawler.com) | 6,875 Web sites | 235,007 Web sites | 91 Web sites | 108 Web sites |
| FAST search (www.alltheweb.com) | 614 pages | 190 pages | 84 pages | 159 pages |
| Infoseek/GoTo/Snap (www.go.com) | Engine does not present totals | | | |
| Google (www.google.com) | 770 results | 250 results | 130 results | 222 results |
| Hotbot (www.hotbot.com) | More than 900 matches | 97 matches | Fewer than 200 | |
| Looksmart (www.looksmart.com) | 106 results | | | |
| Find articles selection | 834 articles relating to | 2,122 articles relating to… | no articles | 5 articles relating to… |
| Lycos (www.lycos.com) | 605 articles | 188 articles | 94 articles | 159 articles |

**TABLE 9.1   CONTINUED**

| Search sites | glee cady | Glee harrah cady | "glee cady" | "glee harrah cady" |
|---|---|---|---|---|
| Northern Light (www.northernlight.com) Note: Tries to organize results into folders | 589 items in 464 sources | 187 items in 117 sources | 95 items in 58 sources | 166 items in 98 sources |
| Yahoo! | 336 Web pages | 118 Web pages | 65 Web pages | 102 Web pages |

**TABLE 9.2   SEARCHING FOR GLEE—USING METASEARCH SITES**

| Metasearch sites | glee cady | Glee harrah cady | "glee cady" | "glee harrah cady" |
|---|---|---|---|---|
| Intelliseek/ProFusion (www.Profusion.com) | 30 items | 29 items | | |
| Mamma (www.mamma.com) | 27 pages | 25 pages | 27 pages | 25 pages |
| Search.com (www.search.com) | 12 pages | 18 pages | Quotation marks ignored | |
| ixquick.com (www.ixquick.com) | 46 unique top 10 pages in 13,1718 results | 45 unique top 10 pages in 238,153 results | 36 unique in at least 108 matching results | 33 unique top 10 pages in at least 159 matching results |

---

**NOTE**   Another interesting note is that we started the search process by checking for third-party reviews of searching on the Internet. A good overview and set of reviews is at http://www.zdnet.com/products/stories/reviews/0,4161,2327819,00.html. This site lists the Editor's Choice search sites from *PC Magazine*, September 9, 1999. Many of those sites are now gone. They've been acquired and/or merged into other companies or gone the way of old Web sites.

Finally, speaking of old Web sites, some of the pages you can find by searching on Glee's name do not exist any more. So you see versions of the pages that existed at one point in time. This is another illustration of the Internet Time Machine: Sometimes digital impressions just don't go away, even when the company that created them does.

If you chose to run the searches yourself, you may get different results, depending on whether Glee does anything sufficiently interesting to show up on new Web pages between the time we wrote this chapter and the time you tried the searches. The results that mention Glee include

- Pages Glee made at various times (some quite old)
- News releases from the companies for which she worked
- News articles about speeches she made or Congressional testimony she gave
- Quotes in news articles on topics about which she was considered expert
- Transcripts from television and/or radio programs on which she appeared
- Book reviews or mentions of the books Pat and Glee have done previously
- Notes from Internet Engineering Task Force events or publications
- Her name among others in attendance at some meeting being reported
- Acknowledgements of her help in other people's work.

If you choose to run your own name through the search engines, your results are based on whether or not you, your family, your friends, and/or your employer have mentioned your name on pages in the Web or on whether or not you have posted to newsgroups or someone has posted to newsgroups about you. If you or your activities have been reported in any news media, there will be more.

The other thing that affects your search results is the common-ness of your name. If you are named Robert Smith, there will likely be many direct hits on your name, but perhaps the results are not necessarily about you. For example, in late July 2001, the search "robert smith" returned 17,800 results in Google. A cursory glance at the first results shows you that the references are not all to the same people. Exact phrase searching with more words rewards you with a smaller, more concise result. Of course, if you are simply "Charles Olson" like the famous twentieth-century poet, it is difficult for you to add more words to achieve a smaller result.

The good part about having a more common name, of course, is that information about you is obscured by the size of the larger result.

A final point about putting information on the Web: In the "good old days" before search engines and Web crawlers, if you didn't share the URL of your Web page with someone, it was very hard to find. Thus, you could publish pages with relatively personal information on them, like your birthdate or your home address, and not feel vulnerable. You could publish pages that stood alone, without a link to other pages, and expect them to not be searchable. This is no longer true. With improved Web searching, even through the millions of pages available, it is easier to find the pages concerning a single person, specifically you. If your pages have been on the Web for a long time, you might want to review them. Look for information you no longer feel comfortable with publishing so widely. Check your online resume. Do you want it to contain your home address and telephone number? Perhaps an e-mail address would do instead? However, be careful with that, too. If you use one of your "anonymizing" e-mail addresses and have it on the same page with your name, anyone reading your resume could connect the two.

# Finding You at Home

Let's say you wanted to find a buddy from long ago, like Glee's friend in the anecdote earlier in the chapter. However, the Web-based searches produced too much noise; that is, too many pages that you didn't want to crawl through to find what you needed. You just wished you could look in the telephone book.

However, you don't know in what city your friend lives now and all your traditional sources don't work: their parents have moved on; your parents don't remember this person (maybe you weren't supposed to know them); or you can't ask your best friend because they didn't like this person. Whatever.

Before the Internet, you would have had a big problem. Telephone books were available in public libraries across the country, but you still needed to have some idea of which one to look in. Now we have consolidation of telephone providers and consolidation of telephone white pages. (Yellow pages are readily accessible, too, but we are assuming that you are looking for a person, not a business.)

It's good to be able to look up the name of a business someplace far away. For example, Pat recently went looking for an estate cleaning service in North Dakota, because a friend's mother had a stroke and needed to be moved to South Florida. While the friend coped with finding health care, Pat helped find services back in North Dakota. That was a good use. But what if you were trying to avoid a pesky former spouse? You might not be so happy if you were easy to find.

With that cautionary note, let's look for Glee again. Look at our results:

- **WhoWhere** (http://www.whowhere.com)—Note that we are running the Bugnosis program and at this time, the WhoWhere site is carrying a Web beacon (see Figure 9.1).

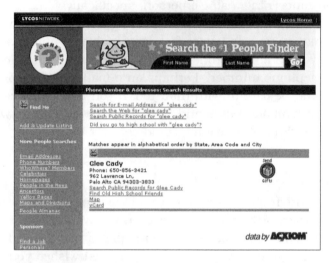

**FIGURE 9.1**

*Searching for Glee—the WhoWhere result.*

- **Yahoo People Search** (http://people.yahoo.com)—This one lists Glee's son Brian as well, but in a strange manner. If you didn't know that from reading one of her Web pages, it would be hard to tell that, though (see Figure 9.2).

- **Switchboard.com** (http://www.switchboard.com)—This one is clearly based on telephone directory data because it shows the additional listing for the apartment that Glee had in Washington, D.C., during 2000. Note that you can link to a map showing where geographically the telephone is located (see Figure 9.3).

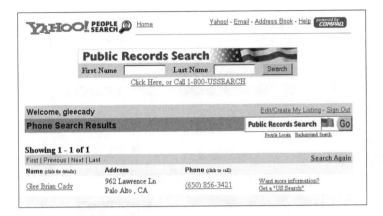

**FIGURE 9.2**

*Searching for Glee—The Yahoo People Finder result.*

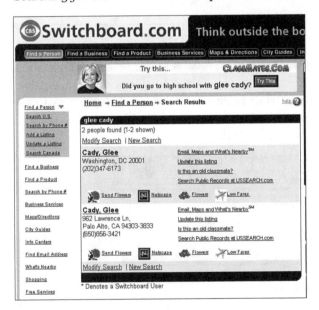

**FIGURE 9.3**

*Searching for Glee—the Switchboard.com result.*

- **AnyWho** (http://www.anywho.com)—This site from AT&T requires you to choose what state you search in. We chose Washington, D.C. Get a map to where Glee used to live (see Figure 9.4).

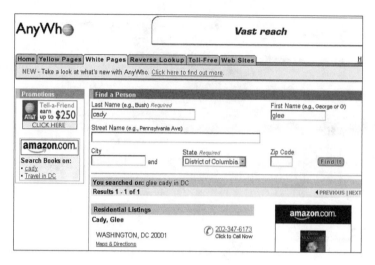

**FIGURE 9.4**

*Searching for Glee—the AnyWho result.*

- **WhitePages.com** (http://www.whitepages.com)—This one shows the listing as it exists in the Palo Alto telephone book. Glee is listed with her son Brian because both use this phone number. Clicking "more information" gets you a page that allows you to map the address (see Figure 9.5).

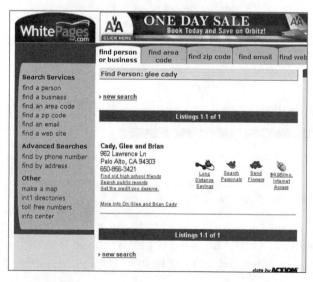

**FIGURE 9.5**

*Searching for Glee—the WhitePages.com result.*

- **AOL White Pages** (http://www.aol.com/netfind/whitepages.adp)—AOL's service includes a white pages. Bugnosis reported that this page, too, carried a Web beacon. AOL's White Pages service is based on InfoSpace. Maps, directions, and city guides are easily linked in (see Figure 9.6).

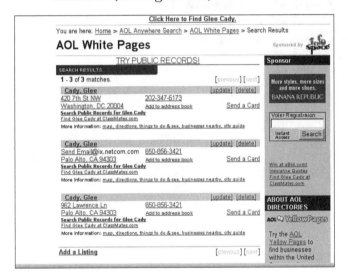

**FIGURE 9.6**

*Searching for Glee—the AOL White Pages result.*

- **InfoUSA.com** (http://www.infousa.com)—This site enables you to input incomplete last names. It does require a state to be selected (see Figure 9.7).

**FIGURE 9.7**

*Searching for Glee—the InfoUSA result.*

- **WorldPages.com** (http://www.worldpages.com)—This site produces a single listing result and links that to additional information with maps and directions (see Figure 9.8).

**FIGURE 9.8**

*Searching for Glee—the WorldPages result.*

- **Verizon's SuperPages.com** (http://www.superpages.com)—This is the one with the option that makes us feel really weird. If you click the "Find Neighbors" link, the search returns the name, address, and phone number of (in this case) 31 people who live near the address given. These people include folks from several streets away that we wouldn't even normally consider neighbors except in the larger sense that they all live in the same general neighborhood (see Figure 9.9).

- **SmartPages.com** (http://www.smartpages.com)—From Pacific Bell, this site lists 3 entries. Clicking the one with the Lawrence Lane address offers a similar "Find Neighbors" choice that returns 12 names. These entries are actually all within several houses of the address listed because the search was limited to listings on Lawrence Lane (see Figure 9.10).

**FIGURE 9.9**

*Searching for Glee—the SuperPages result.*

**FIGURE 9.10**

*Searching for Glee—the SmartPages result.*

There are all these different ways to find Glee. They appear to be information gathered from telephone listings combined with maps to more precisely locate her. With so many choices, how do you know which one to use when you want to find someone? The appropriate answer to that question depends on how much information you have to begin with. With more information, the search can be more precise. If you only know your sought after person is in the United States, choose a search that doesn't demand preciseness. If you know your search object can be found in Arizona, use that information in your search. If you don't want to choose, use the search site that helps you search many databases using the Ultimate White Pages. You'll find that at `http://www.theultimates.com/ white/` (see Figure 9.11). This page points you to many people finding sites. Another site, Freeality.Com (`www.freeality.com`) lists a number of different search sites, too, but when we visited it in early August of 2001, it carried many Web beacons.

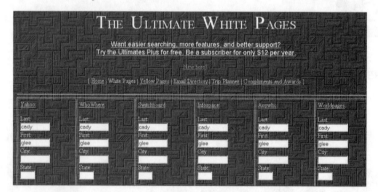

**FIGURE 9.11**

*Searching for Glee—the Ultimate White Pages search.*

If you want to find a person's e-mail address, the best way to do that remains asking them directly. Otherwise, if the address cannot be found on the Web using the searches listed previously, you might try Internet Address Finder at `http://www.iaf.net` (see Figure 9.12). The data in this database goes back a long way, so the addresses may not be current. A search for Glee, for example turns up some e-mail addresses that she hasn't used since 1993.

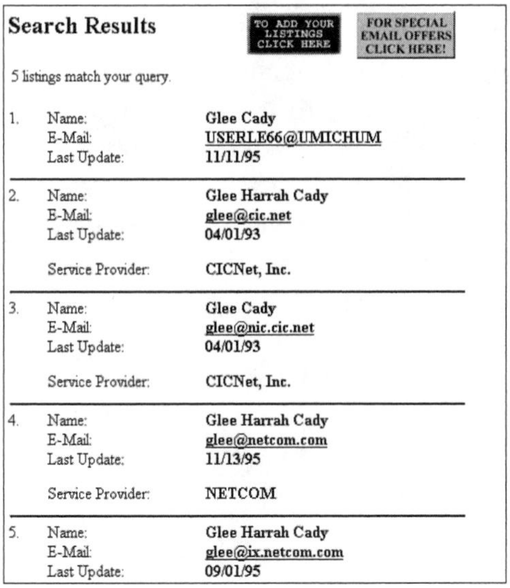

**Search Results**

TO ADD YOUR LISTINGS CLICK HERE    FOR SPECIAL EMAIL OFFERS CLICK HERE!

5 listings match your query.

| 1. | Name: | Glee Cady |
| | E-Mail: | USERLE66@UMICHUM |
| | Last Update: | 11/11/95 |

| 2. | Name: | Glee Harrah Cady |
| | E-Mail: | glee@cic.net |
| | Last Update: | 04/01/93 |
| | Service Provider: | CICNet, Inc. |

| 3. | Name: | Glee Cady |
| | E-Mail: | glee@nic.cic.net |
| | Last Update: | 04/01/93 |
| | Service Provider: | CICNet, Inc. |

| 4. | Name: | Glee Harrah Cady |
| | E-Mail: | glee@netcom.com |
| | Last Update: | 11/13/95 |
| | Service Provider: | NETCOM |

| 5. | Name: | Glee Harrah Cady |
| | E-Mail: | glee@ix.netcom.com |
| | Last Update: | 09/01/95 |

**FIGURE 9.12**

*Searching for Glee—the Internet Address Finder result.*

# What's the Point?

Okay, up to here we've taught you several ways to find an old friend from high school, or a phone number in a distant city. You may be wondering why we are concentrating on this in a privacy book.

The only way we can show you all the information available about a person using the Internet is to actually lead you through those searches. If you follow the steps we outline here, using yourself as an example, you'll find that there's probably more out there than you expected—things you may not have expected to pop up again. For fun, we recently ran a search on a friend who is now a director of technical engineering at a software firm. This person has a PhD, many published papers, testimony in front of congress, charitable activities, and so on. We didn't expect to find papers he wrote more than 20 years ago transcribed onto the Web as the archives for a local chapter of the radical political group he belonged to in college—and neither did he.

And so, we'll go a little further on our quest for information on Glee—so you can find out what is out there about you. The rest of the book will help you decide how you want to respond to what you find.

# Where Am I From?

One of the wonderful things that the Internet has facilitated is genealogical research. Many of us are now able to trace our ancestry using tools and information available via the Net. This chapter on inventorying your personal information is not really about that topic, but if you are interested, you might start with the following sites: Geneaology.Com (www.geneaology.com), the Roots and the Ancestry sites (www.rootsweb.com and www.ancestry.com), and perhaps the FamilySearch site of the Church of Jesus Christ of Latter Day Saints (www.familysearch.org). An annotated list of genealogy Web sites, known as Cyndi's List, is maintained by Cyndi Howell at http://www.cyndislist.com/. If you haven't tried finding your family before, this is a good place to start.

# Uncle Sam (and His Younger Cousins) Lists You!

People who are "off the grid"—those who really don't participate by using telephones and electricity, those who are part of the cash economy, and so on—are probably the only people who have a chance to remain truly hidden in our society. Because United States Federal law required all people, even children who are not yet part of the work force, to have a Social Security Number, it has become harder and harder to not be listed somewhere in some government record.

All infants born are registered, with their names, the names of their parents, including the mother's maiden name. Those registers are increasingly available online. All deaths are recorded, and sites such as Geneaology.Com provide access to the Social Security Death Index. Figure 9.13 shows the listing for Glee's father, Glenn Harrah.

You still have the general problem of not knowing exactly how the name is listed. For example, Glee's mother: Clarice Duffy "Dee" Harrah was born in 1909 and died in 1973. She certainly had a Social Security number. However, we can't find her via the online searches. We have all these problems with a person whose name, address, birth and death dates are known to us. Sometimes technology doesn't do what we want it to do.

More and more public records are being moved to places where they can be relatively easily searched by casual users like ourselves. A good list of these sources is maintained by BRB Publications at http://www.brbpub.com/pubrecsites.asp, shown in Figure 9.14. This page is updated as more information is made available. You find sources of information such as your mother's maiden name (found in birth records); the value of your property (found in county assessor records); and so on. You can trace business transactions and court verdicts, probate records, and civil court records. Unimaginable wealth in information is kept at your fingertips.

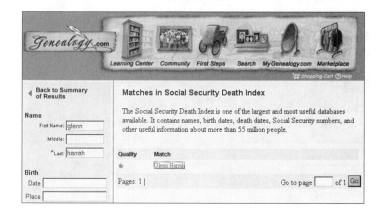

**FIGURE 9.13**

*Searching for Glee's father Glenn.*

**FIGURE 9.14**

*Searching for government information online.*

Again, the biggest problem is knowing how to search. Public information has been gathered over time and compiled in ways that make it easy for the public agency to do their jobs. It wasn't gathered with the idea that it would be widely and easily available to casual users. Thus, to really "mine" the information, you need to have experience with searching and with processing the information you find.

Naturally, companies are happy to do this for you for a fee. You have probably received unsolicited commercial e-mail promoting one of these services—something like the message shown in Figure 9.15.

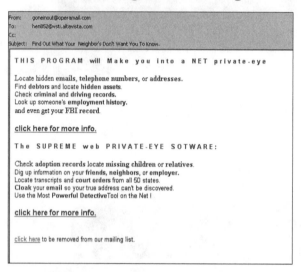

**FIGURE 9.15**

*E-mail soliciting your search business.*

Or you saw an advertisement on one of the many search pages mentioned earlier in this chapter. That's how we chose USSearch.com, shown in Figure 9.16. We clicked a link on a search result page. It probably said something like "For more information…". We wanted to be able to show you what kinds of information can be found. These are our results.

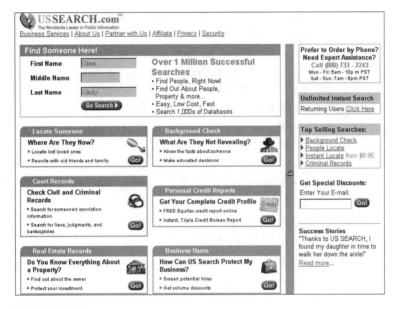

**FIGURE 9.16**

*USSearch.com initial search.*

We used the following search criteria:

Name: Glee Harrah Cady
Address: 962 Lawrence Lane, Palo Alto, California 94303
Birthdate: mm/dd/yyyy

These were the results:

- Reported current address as given, but added that it is in San Mateo County, California. This is incorrect. The result was influenced by the ZIP code information. 94303 spans the county line between San Mateo and Santa Clara counties.

- Reported the listed telephone number correctly; missed the fax/modem line.

- Reported the ownership of the property correctly. Included site address, owner address, telephone number, APN (?), and assessed valuation correctly.

- Individuals reported at this address:

    - Son #1 at current address; missed the Coronado Naval Amphibious Base and the apartment he lived in while stationed there; address after college; this address; address of residential college fraternity; missed the dormitory year.

- Son #2 at first-year dormitory address; this address; missed dormitory address #2.
- Deceased husband at this address (he never lived there); previous address, recorded twice—once called Stanford and once called Palo Alto (he never lived there); address in Michigan; Palo Alto address before that.
- Eight addresses for one woman and 10 addresses for another who lived at this address just previous to Glee. No mention of the owner. Some addresses repeated with variant spellings.
- Two addresses for one of the couple who owned the home two owners ago.
- Four addresses for the other of the couples who owned the home two owners ago.
- Possible relatives at this address:
  - Reported two sons and deceased husband with same addresses listed in previous category.
- Possible neighbors:
  - Both names of couple who used to live two houses away.
  - Both names of couple who currently live two houses away.
  - Both names of couple who live three houses away.

  Note: these were only properties that changed owners in the last 10 years. All other properties don't get listed because the owners have not changed.

- Address History associated with your search (up to 10 years):
  - Glee's previous address with friends on the Stanford campus (correct):
    - No telephone listed in this part of the report (see later).
    - No property ownership listed.
    - Individuals listed
      - Previous owner
      - Son #3 at this address, no college
      - Son #2 at this address with two college addresses
      - Mother of current resident—not actually a resident at this address
      - Son #2 listed again, same addresses

- Glee's deceased husband, same addresses as in previous listing
- Son #2, different spelling of name, with two variant spellings of this address and four college addresses
- One of the current couples, listing business address as well as previous address, missing a five-month temporary address
- The other current couple, listing two variant spellings of this address, their previous address, plus the address of the university, again missing the temporary address
- Missing: Glee's sons
- Missing: Son #1

- Glee's possible relatives at this address:
  - Glee's deceased husband with all addresses, listed twice
- Possible neighbors of this address:
  - None on file
- Glee's previous address in Michigan (correct):
  - Listed phone number at this address (presumably correct)
  - Property ownership not on file
  - Individuals reported at this address:
  - One individual with two other addresses
  - Individual in whose name the phone is listed and seven other addresses (some spelling variants)
  - One of the couples who owned previous to Glee's ownership, reported only at this address
  - The other couple, reported eight addresses, some spelling variants
  - Variant spellings of first individual listed with three addresses
  - Glee's deceased husband, same addresses as listed previously
    - Glee, listed at this address, variant spelling
  - One of the previous owner couples, variant spelling of name, with four addresses
- Possible relatives at this address:
  - Glee's deceased husband (who did live here)
  - Glee, listed with a variant spelling

- Glee's sons not listed
- Possible neighbors:
  - •None listed
- Glee's previous address in Palo Alto, before the move to Michigan:
  - Listed phone numbers: listings for current residents
  - Property ownership: current resident, owner address, current assessed valuation
  - Individuals reported at this address:
    - Current owner and three previous addresses
    - Wife of current owner and two previous addresses
    - Another resident (unknown if current) and four other addresses
    - Another resident, only this address listed
  - Glee's deceased husband (who did live here) at the same addresses previously listed:
    - Another resident, with one other address
    - Glee's sons not listed
  - Possible relatives at this address:
    - Glee's deceased husband, listed twice
    - Glee's sons not listed
  - •Possible neighbors:
    - Three names of residents in house next door
    - Seven names (four variants of one name) of residents in house across the street
  - A variation of Glee's address when she lived with friends on the Stanford campus, with the street name misspelled:
    - Correct telephone numbers for this address
    - Correct property ownership: site address, owner address, assessed valuation
    - Individuals reported at this address:
    - Same information as reported previously, still missing one son of this family and both of Glee's sons

- Possible relatives:
  - Glee's deceased husband, listed twice
- Possible neighbors: none
- The following databases were searched but yielded no results:
  - Bankruptcies, tax liens, and civil judgments
  - National Death Index
  - Drug Enforcement Agency
  - FAA Airmen
  - FAA Aircraft
  - National Coast Guard Merchant Vessels
  - Marriage Index
  - Divorce Index

It is puzzling that the records of Glee's marriage and her husband's death were not found as they are certainly recorded. The marriage took place in Santa Clara County, California. The death was recorded in Washtenaw County, Michigan.

Indeed, this report has many mysteries. Why are some name variations reported and not others? Why are some people reported and not others?

## Sources for the Reported Information

The report says that it searched:

- State licensing and registration information
- Self-reported addresses in proprietary databases based on publicly-available, public record, and non-public information

## Type of Information Available

The information about the report says it includes the following types of information:

- Addresses associated with the name for the last 10 years
- Available listed telephone numbers for the addresses
- Property ownership (purchase date/description) limited to 38 states
- Property value (limited to 38 states)

- Deed transfers
- Bankruptcies
- Tax liens and judgments (limited to 31 states)
- FAA pilots licenses
- FAA aircraft registrations (limited to 44 states)
- National DEA controlled substance licenses
- USCG documented vessels
- California, Texas, and Nevada marriage and divorce records
- Relatives: individuals associated by last name and physical address
- Others who used the same address
- Neighbors, including listed telephone numbers

Again, comparing what we know about Glee to the information in the report, we find much missing. The variations in spellings of names and addresses create confusion rather than clarity. The report definitely raised more questions than it answered.

The price for this service was $59.95.

## Our Conclusions?

A lot of information is floating around that can be obtained by almost anyone on almost any pretext for not very much money. Some of it might even be accurate. More information is undoubtedly available to the licensed private investigator and to law enforcement agents and other government personnel. You don't have to be contemplating subversive or illegal activities to wonder whether there isn't too much information about you too widely available. You may want to keep information about yourself more closely guarded, but if you own property, keep credit accounts, or list a telephone number, it seems difficult to completely disappear.

For the most part, most of us don't want to disappear. Our public personas—the things that are known about us in the world—help us do business and interact with organizations and companies. What we need to do is learn how to control what goes out about us, and what to do if it does. Keep reading.

# 10

# THE LEAST YOU SHOULD DO TO GUARD YOUR PRIVACY WHEN ONLINE

By now you may think that going online may not be worth the threat to your privacy. However, you can do things to address these threats, and make the time you spend on the Internet safer. Those actions start by protecting your home computer. If the machine is protected before you even connect to a network, your risks from network-based attacks are much lower.

What steps you take depend on your preferences for privacy (or your paranoia). This chapter gives you some precautions and alternatives. Usually they involve a trade-off between disclosure and convenience (or even service). Keep in mind that complete non-disclosure of any personal information probably is not practical in this age. Anonymity versus privacy is discussed in Chapter 18, "Can You Really Be Anonymous."

Remember this simple maxim: If you really want to keep information private, don't put it on a computer that's connected to anyone's network, even your own.

This chapter also discusses PC and Macintosh protection. The section on the Macintosh builds on the concepts explained in the preceding sections, which discuss how to secure PCs running Windows, so you need to read both if you have a Mac. Unix is beyond the scope of this book and is not discussed specifically. However, there are many sites available that discuss detailed protection for Unix-based computers.

# Keeping Your Data Private

Let's start with your home computer. If you are like most people, you probably keep a good deal of personal information on your machine. Perhaps most of that information is useful only to you. However, you might also store information that pertains to your finances, health, or other aspects of your life that you do not want to share with others.

The information on your machine can reside in a variety of places and forms. Some of these are plain files (and directories), or passwords, encryption keys, cookies, e-mail address books, Web favorites or bookmarks, and browsing history. We describe some of the more criticalitems and also the controls you can use to protect them. The section "Some Key Concepts" has some basic definitions of terms used in this chapter. A more complete list of definitions is in Appendix A, "Glossary."

# Some Key Concepts

The following list of terms and concepts are important for you to understand if you want to make good decisions about protecting yourself and your computer. Some of them build on one another and are important to this chapter. Some you will also encounter in privacy policies or discussions.

## Access Control

Access control is the practice of limiting access to those people you want to have the ability to see the information, and keeping others out. In non-computer terms, the locks on your house would be access control mechanisms. Only those with a key could come in. Some systems divide data into several classification levels, with differing access controls on each level. Simple access control mechanisms are passwords or Personal Identification Numbers (PINs).

## Plain Text

Plain text is unformatted, unencrypted, or un-enhanced text that can be stored in files or sent in e-mail messages. Information stored in plain text is easily read by others.

## Encryption

At its simplest, encryption is scrambling information to make it difficult for anyone who doesn't know the secret to read the information. The "Jumbles" puzzles in the daily newspaper are simple encryption methods. More complex encryption (and decryption) methods are made possible by computers because computers can handle thousands of complex calculations in a matter of minutes.

## Steganography

Pronounced STEHG-uh-NAH-gruhf-ee, from Greek *steganos*, or "covered," and *graphie*, or "writing," this method of protecting data involves hiding a secret message within an ordinary message and extracting it at its destination. Steganography takes cryptography a step farther by hiding an encrypted message so that no one suspects it exists. Ideally, anyone scanning your data doesn't know it contains encrypted data.

## Password

A password is a secret word or phrase assigned to an individual's account. A password is designed to help prove the person with the account name or number is actually the authorized user. However, most passwords are easily guessed or stolen. Keep your password safe by never writing it down.

## Sniffing

Stealing data off a computer connection by capturing all the characters that come over the connection is called *sniffing*. This requires that the hacker have physical access to the network you are on. To capture useful information such as credit card numbers or site passwords, a sniffer would probably be connected to the part of a network that a Web site is on rather than the part of the network your home PC is on.

## Compromise

If someone has broken into your PC, or has taken it over to use for their own purposes, your machine has been *compromised.* Simple attacks are intended to capture information such as credit card numbers or other information which would let the attacker pretend to be you to buy something on the Net or even to use your identity to get credit, and so on.

## Port Scan or Port Probe

If you install firewall software and watch the kinds of attacks that hit your machine, you will see that port scans or port probes are the most common intrusion detected on the Internet. They are common because hackers do frequent widespread scans looking for one specific weakness they can exploit to break into systems. The typical hacker probes thousands or millions of machines in a typical scan. In most cases, the hacker isn't targeting you personally. In particular, if your personal firewall program or other monitoring program detects this event, it has already failed, so you don't need to worry. Probes like this result from "script-kiddies", new hackers who are not particularly skillful and do not write their own hacking programs. They download attack programs (called "scripts") from various sites on the Net and run them against millions of machines. Thousands of script-kiddies are out there, so if you have an always-on connection (cable-modem, DSL, or if you leave your modem line up all the time), you can expect one to ten of these scans per day. For a detailed list of attacks (sometimes called intrusions) that might be made on your machine, see Network Ice company's database at `http://advice.networkice.com/advice/Intrusions/default.htm`.

## Operating System (OS) Fingerprinting

An attack that sends an unusual series of probes against your machine to determine what OS is running on it is called *fingerprinting.* The responses your computer makes to each request a hacker sends tells the hacker how to further attack the system. For a detailed description of this attack from the hacker's point of view, see `http://www.insecure.org/nmap/nmap-fingerprinting-article.html`.

## Applet

An applet is a little application. Prior to the World Wide Web, the built-in writing and drawing programs that came with Windows or Macintosh OS were sometimes called "applets." On the Web, using Java, JavaScript, or ActiveX, an applet is a small program that can be sent along with a Web page to a user. Applets run on the user's computer by default if the user has not set up the browser to prohibit it. They can perform interactive animations, immediate calculations, or other simple tasks without having to send a user request back to the server. They have the potential to be used for hostile attacks.

## Java

Java is a programming language expressly designed for use in the distributed environment of the Internet. Java can be used to create complete applications that may run on a single computer or be distributed among servers and clients in a network. It can also be used to build a small application module or applet for use as part of a Web page. Applets make it possible for a Web page user to interact with the page. Java applets run on the user's computer by default if the user has not set up the browser to prohibit it. Java applets can perform interactive animations, immediate calculations, or other simple tasks without having to send a user request back to the server. They have the potential to be used for hostile attacks. Java applets run on almost any operating system without requiring recompilation.

## JavaScript

JavaScript is an interpreted programming or script language from Netscape. It is somewhat similar in capability to Microsoft's Visual Basic, Sun's Tool Command Language (TCL), the UNIX-derived Practical Extraction and Reporting Language (PERL), and IBM's Restructured Extended Executor (REXX). In general, script languages are easier and faster to code in than the more structured compiler languages such as C and C++. Script languages generally take longer to process than compiled languages, but are very useful for shorter programs. JavaScript is used in Web site development to do such things as:

- Automatically change a formatted date on a Web page
- Cause a linked-to page to appear in a popup window
- Cause text or a graphic image to change during a mouse rollover

## ActiveX Controls

ActiveX is a method invented by Microsoft to run programs, called scripts, either on the server or on the user's Windows-based computer, as a response to accessing a Web site. Because ActiveX scripts can easily be run on the user's computer, they also can be easily used by those with malicious intent. ActiveX scripts can be used to deliver viruses, hostile programs, or to simply acquire information that has been stored on your computer such as your e-mail address, or other profile information. They can also discover information about your connection, such as what kind of machine or programs you are using.

## Files

Files are the basic unit of information on your machine. Most everything is stored in a file of one kind or another. Some files are human-readable, and some are computer-readable. Files can have access control permissions set on them, or the folders they reside in.

Figure 10.1 shows a typical file directory on a Windows machine. Which items are files and which are folders are distinguished by icons.

If you share your PC with others—and you want to keep some information private from them—you have a few options:

- If you are using Windows 98 system (or 95 or Me), you cannot rely on the operating system to provide you with effective access controls so that only you can access your information. Instead you need to use something that hides your data. The most common method is encryption. Encryption takes "plain text" information and transforms it into an unreadable stream of bits. To decrypt it you need a decryption key, which, like a password, you need to keep very private. Some of the more popular encryption tools are PGP (Pretty Good Privacy), available free for non-commercial use from http://www.pgpi.org, and Network Associates PGP (commercial version, relatively inexpensive), available at http://www.nai.com. Entire disk encryption (which protects all files automatically, even temporary ones) comes in SecureDoc commercial software available from `http://www.winmagic.com`. Scramdisk, a less robust but free tool, is available from `http://www.scramdisk.clara.net`.

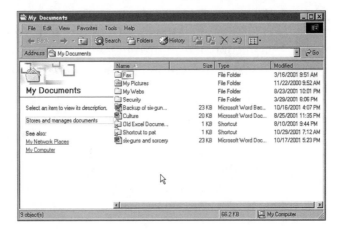

**FIGURE 10.1**

*A typical file directory.*

An alternative to encryption is steganography—a technique that hides information within another set of information. For example, through steganography you could hide your password in a file containing a picture you took. Unless someone knows that a message is within a picture and has the right tool to extract it, that someone just sees the picture. Several free, shareware, and commercial steganography tools are available on the Web. Two steganography tool sites are: `http://www.ise.gmu.edu/~njohnson/Security/stegtools.htm`, maintained by Neil Johnson at George Mason University and PCWorld's Steganography download archive at `http://www.pcworld.com/downloads/file_description/0,fid,4699,00.asp`.

- In Windows 2000 (or NT), you can set up separate accounts for each person to use when they login to the PC. By using built-in file system file permissions you can set access on the private files so that no one or only the people you designate can access those files. Figure 10.2 shows a typical home computer user account setup. Figure 10.3 shows how to change file permissions on a particular file to prevent sharing with other users. If you choose to use separate accounts, just keep the following points in mind:

- This method is relatively effective when you (but not someone else) control the special Administrator account on the PC.

- This method stops most people, but is not bulletproof against someone determined to gain access to the files.

- If you want a much higher confidence that your files stay private, you should encrypt them.

- In Windows 2000 (or NT) if you cannot gain control over the Administrator account, you need to resort to encrypting your private files. Be warned, however, that because you are sharing the PC with others, your private information is exposed to a greater level of risk than if you had exclusive use of the PC. For example, someone else that shares the PC with you could install a hidden, keystroke-grabbing program on the PC. With that program they could capture your secret decryption password and use it to gain access to your private information.

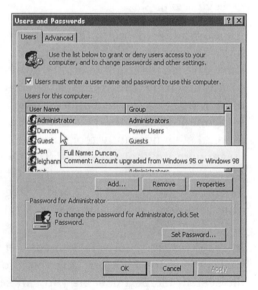

**FIGURE 10.2**

*A Windows 2000 system with several users.*

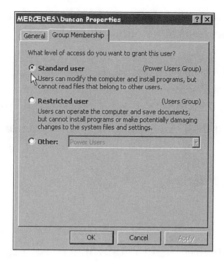

**FIGURE 10.3**

*Setting sharing permissions on a file.*

Now let's look at the measures available to you when you are the only user of your PC:

- If you are running Windows 98 (or 95 or Me), you may choose to rely on physical access to your PC as sufficient. However, if you have significant private information on the PC and your PC is connected to the Web or the PC can fall into the wrong hands (for example, a laptop you travel with), you should rely on encryption to protect that information.

- If you are running Windows 2000 or NT, you can still use the any of the access control options we have listed previously for Windows 2000, but if you want higher confidence that your files stay private, encrypt them.

- To go a step further, you can turn on a password your PC requires to start up (before the PC boots the operating system). This can be effective in preventing your PC from working for the wrong person (for example, a thief). Just beware that there often are ways to defeat this protection mechanism. To turn this feature on you need to review the hardware documentation that came with your PC. (This is not a feature in Windows. If your computer manufacturer does not offer it as part of the base configuration, you can download utilities to do this from either the manufacturer's site or download sites such as PC World.)

- The most private option is encrypting the entire hard drive or drives of your PC. With this method you effectively lock up the information on your PC from others. Even if your PC is stolen, the thief is unable to retrieve any information you have stored on it.

Two disk encryption products mentioned previously—SecureDoc and Scramdisk—offer this level of privacy. SecureDoc is more thorough especially in protecting information in temporary files and system files.

## Passwords

Passwords are used to control access to the computer, to various applications and to Web sites. They are the computing equivalent to your house or car keys. Keeping them private is important.

The following are some tips for making up good passwords:

- **Use passwords with at least eight characters.** If your operating system has more specific rules, they are in the documentation.

- **Never use the word "password."** (This sounds silly, but this is the most commonly used password on most systems.) Similarly, don't use the abbreviation "PW," the words "girlfriend," "system," or your initials.

- **Never use public knowledge about you as your password.** For example, don't use your birthday, your mother's name, your pet's name, your address, or anything else that could be discovered about you in public records or an Internet search on your name.

- **Use the first letters of the first line of a favorite song.** For example, if your favorite song is "The Crown" by the band Nuit, the first line is "I know where a wond'rous city rises from a shining plain". Your password would be *Ikwawcrfasp.* This is pretty unguessable and hard to break.

- **Use numbers, capitals, and special characters in your password.** For example, a password that would be very hard to break, but is pretty easy to remember is Bos+on75. This is formed by taking the word Boston, and the year Pat first lived there. Substitute the + (plus) symbol for the "t" in Boston, and you have a very strong password.

- **Don't use "master keys".** In other words, don't use the same password for every system. At the least, have three—one for the machine itself, one for your dialup or network access, and one for online Web sites.

As a general rule, you should make all your passwords difficult to guess, you should never write them down (at least, not in a plain format) and you should store them away from the PC they are used to protect. (For example, don't tape the password to the bottom of the keyboard or put a sticky-note on the monitor.)

This last part, about not storing passwords on the computer they protect, is very important. One of the ramifications of this rule applies to letting various applications "remember" your passwords. This is because in most cases this "remembering" takes the form of recording the password somewhere on your computer. Because it is recorded in a file somewhere on the computer, anyone else who takes possession of your computer is able to use those applications without knowing your password.

You should be cautious about letting your dialup program remember the password for your Internet account. This lets anyone who has physical access to your machine dial up your Internet provider, use your e-mail, and potentially launch attacks from your machine. If you have children whose use of the Internet you want to control or monitor, you especially want to make sure they have to type the password to start a dialup connection. You want to keep that password secret from them. Figure 10.4 shows a typical dialup dialog box for an ISP. Notice that the Save Password box is not checked.

**FIGURE 10.4**

*A dialup dialog without password saving turned on.*

Computer account passwords, such as those used to logon to the computer in Windows 2000 or NT, are stored on the PC in a security database located in \WinNT\System32\Config\SAM. Only the account called SYSTEM (which is an internal Windows account) and the user belonging to the Administrators group should have access to this database. You can protect this database using the same file access controls as for other files. Take care to protect the Repair directory that often contains a copy of the security database. If other people can access that copy, they can try to brute-force crack passwords.

For application passwords we can give you only general guidance because specifics vary from application to application. The general rule is the same as with the account passwords: if you know where the application stores passwords, protect those files. If you don't know, don't enable the application to remember your passwords.

For Web site passwords, the same rules apply. In addition, Web sites typically store passwords in their site-specific cookies. Cookies are kept on your PC as files in a cookies file or cookies directory (more on this in the "Cookies" section later in this chapter). As a first rule, for sensitive sites (such as your bank account, credit card account, or health care account) do not enable the site to remember your passwords. For other sites, where your privacy is less of a concern, you can enable those sites to remember your passwords as a matter of convenience. Some Web sites do a better job of protecting passwords they have stored in their users' cookies. In fact, they encrypt the cookies or the passwords in them. However, in general, users often have no way of knowing how the password is protected in the cookie, thus our general rule is to avoid having passwords stored in them.

An added protection measure for passwords is encrypting them as part of the entire disk. However, do not rely on this measure alone because when you are using your PC the entire disk is available to you. If you fall victim to running some untrusted code (a Trojan horse downloaded from the Internet), you still want your passwords to be encrypted at the file level and accessible only with a manually entered decryption pass phrase.

# Encryption Keys

By now you probably have figured out that if encryption is a key method to protect your privacy, safekeeping encryption keys is of great importance. In particular, it is very important to safeguard the password (or pass phrase) used to decrypt information. Those passwords (or pass phrases) should never be recorded anywhere. You should use long passwords to protect your encryption keys—at least 20 characters that include letters, numbers, and other special characters. Pick a good pass phrase and commit it to memory (it helps if you use the pass phrase often). And don't ever forget it, as trying to recover a forgotten pass phrase is usually an impossible task.

With PGP, yours and other people's keys are stored on *key rings*. These key rings are usually kept in separate files in a PGP directory called PGP Keyrings. You should set file permissions such that only you have access to that directory. Figure 10.5 shows a directory with several keyrings in it.

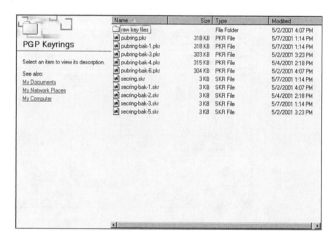

**FIGURE 10.5**

*Public and secret keyrings.*

An added protection measure for encryption keys is encrypting them as part of the entire disk. However, as with passwords, do not rely on this measure alone because when you are using your PC the entire disk is available to you. If you fall victim to running some untrusted code (a Trojan horse downloaded form the Internet), you still want your encryption keys to be encrypted at the file level and accessible only with a manually entered decryption pass phrase.

# Cookies

To improve your Web browsing experience, Web browsers and servers use cookies. Cookies are character strings that store all kinds of information such as your account name (and password), your address, your preferences, and, unfortunately, whatever else the Web site chooses to put in them.

If you use Netscape, your cookies are in a file called *cookies* in the directory for your browser profile. If you use Microsoft Internet Explorer, they are usually kept in a directory called Cookies on your PC. You can look for that directory and examine the cookie files stored there. Some of these files have fairly intelligible contents, others don't. Figure 10.6 shows a fairly typical cookie file for a Netscape user. Some of it, such as the names of the Web sites that set the cookie, is pretty clear. Much of it is unintelligible to us humans.

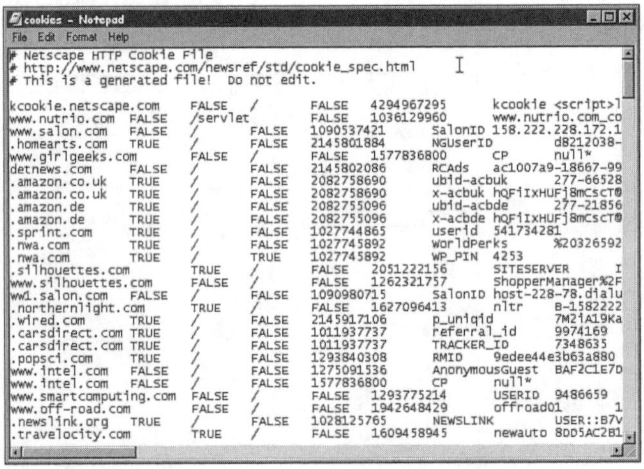

**FIGURE 10.6**

*A Netscape cookie file.*

On your PC you should make sure that only you can access your cookies. This is easily done on Windows 2000 or NT by setting appropriate file permissions on the Cookies directory. Unfortunately, under Windows 98 (or 95 or Me), your choice is limited to removing the Cookie files when you are done using the PC. A couple of problems with that are that you might end up deleting someone else's cookies, too, and you have to remember to delete the cookies every time you are done using the PC. Because of this, if your privacy concerns are paramount, you should use a PC that you do not share with anyone you don't trust or you should use a disk-level encryption tool (such as SecureDoc or Scramdisk) to hide cookies from others.

A final note on cookies—while they present a venue through which your private information may leak, disabling cookies and deleting them from your PC is usually not a realistic option because of the amount of convenience and access to the Web you lose. A better idea is to set your permissions on your browser to only accept cookies that are being returned to the site that you are visiting. This reduces the number of sites and companies your information is shared with. Figure 10.7 shows how you configure a Netscape browser to accept the cookies you are willing to use. Versions of Internet Explorer after version 5 do not let you completely disable cookies.

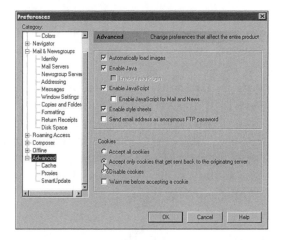

**FIGURE 10.7**

*Telling your Netscape browser how to handle cookies.*

# E-mail Messages, Files, and Address Books

Your e-mail program's address book can tell others who you correspond with. If that's something you want to keep private, you need to protect the address book (and all the e-mail directories such as Inbox, Sent, Deleted) using file permissions in Windows 2000 or NT. In Windows 98

(95 and ME), you don't have an option. If you choose to encrypt these files, you cannot use them with your e-mail program until you decrypt them. That's a tedious process each time you use your computer. A better measure is to use a disk-level encryption tool (such as SecureDoc or Scramdisk) to protect the address book and other e-mail files from others.

**CAUTION**    As with passwords, if you fall victim to running some untrusted code (an e-mail attachment with a virus in it or a Trojan horse downloaded from the Internet), your e-mail address book and files may become accessible to the perpetrator. Microsoft Outlook is particularly susceptible to e-mail macro viruses that read your address book, and then send copies of itself to the people you regularly correspond with. Of course, they open it, because it's from you, and the virus goes on its merry way, flooding the network in an ever-expanding scope.

Keep the following two rules in mind when using e-mail:

- **Rule 1: Never open a file attachment on a message from someone you don't know.** Save it to disk and enable your antivirus software to check it. (Pat says she deletes the whole thing unread. The risk is too high.)

- **Rule 2: Don't blindly open attachments from people you know.** Save it to disk or enable your antivirus software to scan it in place. Even if your friends say they are running antivirus software on their machines, you can't control how recently they have gotten virus signatures, whether their antivirus software monitors their system continuously or just at start-up, or how careful they are about scanning things.

## Browser Bookmarks or Favorites

Remembering the URLs for all your favorite Web sites is a pain, so browser developers have developed a mechanism where the browser remembers them for you. If you use Internet Explorer, that list is called "Favorites." If you use Netscape, they are called "Bookmarks." This is a handy feature, but it can also let others know which sites you have visited. Your bookmarks list or favorites folder holds information in plain text on where you have visited and what you liked well enough to want to come back. If, for example, you are a leather fetishist and have a lot of support and shopping sites bookmarked, you might not want anyone else to see that you've been visiting those sites. Even if you do *not* have any unusual characteristics or hobbies, you may not want to share all your browsing interests with others.

Figure 10.8 shows how a folder of favorites generated by Internet Explorer looks.

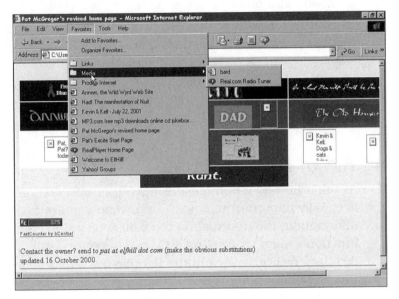

**FIGURE 10.8**

*Favorites for an Internet Explorer users.*

Like other files and folders, favorites and bookmarks can be protected using file permissions in Windows 2000 and NT so that only those you authorize can see their content.

Under Windows 98 (or 95 or Me) you don't have that option. To keep that information private you have to resort to a disk-level encryption tool. (See the section, "Files," for a list of file protection methods.)

## Web Browsing History

Browsing history is a convenience tool that let's you quickly revisit Web sites. You can program your browser to remember some number of days' worth of history or you can use the browser to clear it. If you don't want others to see where you have been, set history to 0 and clear it before you exit your browser.

This is especially important if you use Internet Kiosks, cafes, or public Internet access sites. Clear out the history before you leave. You can't rely on the machine owner to do it. The paranoid among us think the amount of information left behind on public Internet machines would be worth a lot to someone who is working on stealing identities, credit card numbers, and other personal data.

As with Web favorites, you can also resort to encrypting information at the disk-level (See the section, "Files," for a list of file protection methods.)

A new product, Window Washer, cleans up caches, cookies, bookmarks, and other files when you sign off. For more information, see `http://www.lpwebroot.com`.

# Getting Rid of Files and Data

As important as it is to ensure privacy of information while it's in use, it is equally important to ensure that when you are finally getting rid of information, the information truly disappears. Keep in mind that typical functions, such as deleting a file or a directory still make that file or directory recoverable from the Recycle Bin. Even if you empty the Recycle Bin, the information is still there, recorded byte by byte on your PC's hard drive. It is no longer available as a file, but chances are good that someone determined to get it can recover it.

To prevent this kind of recovery, you need to truly get rid of the information. For everyday use, you should use a tool that overwrites information in files (as they are being deleted), in file slackspace (which is usually created as a result of how file space is allocated on disk), and in swap files. Eraser from `http://www.tolvanen.com` works well with Windows 2000 and NT, and it's free. It works equally as well with Windows 98 and 95, except that in those systems it cannot erase the content of the system swap file automatically; you must do that as a separate step. After Erase is done deleting data, chances are good that no one is able to retrieve the information except perhaps a well-funded government laboratory using special equipment and examining disk platters under an electron microscope.

## Minimum Controls to Keep Your Information Private

Table 10.1 is a concise list of items you should protect and the mechanisms you can use to protect them.

**TABLE 10.1   ITEMS YOU SHOULD PROTECT TO ENSURE YOUR PRIVACY**

| Places to Protect | Win98,95,Me | Win2000, NT* |
| --- | --- | --- |
| Files and directories | Encryption | |
| Steganography | File permissions | |
| Passwords | Encrypt | File permissions |
| Encryption keys | Encrypt | File permissions |
| Cookies | Erase, Encrypt | File permissions |
| Address book | Encrypt | File permissions |
| Favorites | Encrypt | File permissions |
| Browsing history | Erase, Encrypt | File permissions |

 **NOTE**   For Windows 2000 and NT, file permission is a minimum control available. Information encryption and erasure add significant strength and should be considered.

# Summary for the Most Privacy Conscious

To enhance the level of privacy of information on the PC that you use, do the following:

- On your PC, keep only private information that you are willing to disclose to others.
- Share your PC with no one, or with no one you don't trust.
- Use disk-level encryption to protect the entire PC.
- Use Windows 2000 or NT (instead of Windows 98, 95, or Me).
- Use file-level encryption to protect passwords, encryption keys, and most sensitive files.
- Keep your Web site history short.
- Regularly erase unneeded information using tools that truly overwrite information.

# Online Session Privacy

After you have protected your private information on your PC, you can move on to working online. The scenarios examined in the following sections include Web sessions and listening to music using Windows Media Player or RealPlayer.

## Web Sessions

Let's start with the obvious: you can control what information you voluntarily share or don't share. In many instances, when you visit a Web site, you may be asked to provide some information about yourself. You may also be asked to participate in a survey, to join a mailing list and to be automatically opted-in (included) on mailing lists and having information shared about you.

Figure 10.9 shows a signon page for a personalized account at Nutrio.com, a health and nutrition site. As you can see, you are asked to give a lot of personal information. The figure shows one way to give inaccurate personally identifiable information while still giving the site enough info to design a weight-loss plan for you.

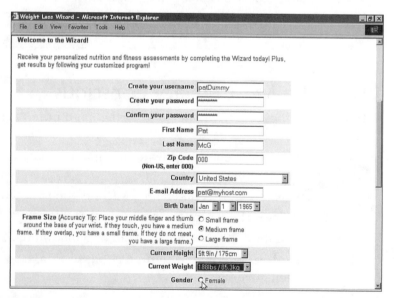

**FIGURE 10.9**

*Filling in a form with fake data.*

If you are concerned about giving out detailed or even any information about yourself, don't do it. If the Web site insists that you provide that information, consider providing only some information (that may or may not be all that accurate). For example, you can give a fake e-mail address that has the right format but isn't a real address, such as "`test@test.gov`" or "`root@localhost.com`". You can also create an alias that you use with that site.

If you are very privacy-conscious, you may want to generate a public persona for yourself that hides the real you. If you do that, you probably want to make a record of it to keep it consistent.

This approach can also provide you with an interesting lesson on how much information about you spreads and how it's used. For example, if you register online as Johnny True or J. B. True instead of John True, see how much SPAM and even paper junk mail comes to that name. That gives you good evidence about how those sites use your info or to whom they give it.

## Anonymous Surfing

A way to automate hiding your identity when surfing the Web is to use so-called Web *anonymizers.* Those are Web sites that take your Web surfing requests and re-package them on your behalf so that the ultimate destination can only tell that the request came in from an anonymizer site, not from you. Two examples of such anonymizer sites are `http://www.anonymizer.com` and `http://www.idzap.com`. The `http://www.anonymizer.com` site also has a program that tells you what any Web site can learn about you when you visit them.

Figure 10.10 shows what you see when you click anonymizer.com's free trial button to visit USA Today. Figure 10.11 shows what USAToday looks like when visited through the anonymizer. The fact that one of the ads on the anonymized version promises no more pop-up ads, but a pop-up ad for privacy services *did* pop up was amusing. This is apparently the behavior you see until you buy the service (see Figure 10.10).

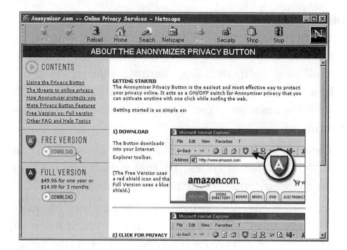

**FIGURE 10.10**

*The anonymizer.com technology initializing on your browser.*

**FIGURE 10.11**

*USAToday through the anonymizer.*

Surfing anonymously is a personal preference. You can use it for Web sites that are more invasive, like those that want to harvest more information about you. This can include sites you do regular business with.

You should also surf anonymously when you don't want to leave tracks. Just beware that although the anonymizer sites attempts to protect your privacy, they can be forced to reveal your identity and logs about where you have visited. Most Web anonymizers are proxy systems. They place themselves in between you and the Internet at large, acting on your behalf. They need to keep some transitory information to connect your session to the incoming information that you requested and then to pass it back to you. So, logging of anonymizing systems could trace your activity if the logs are kept. Because the point of an anonymizing system is to help you hide your activity, most anonymizers will not maintain extensive logs. Check the site's privacy policy to confirm the practice of an individual site.

## Dealing with Cookies

Most Web sites send cookies to your PC. While you can set your browser to always block them, you often discover that doing so limits how much information you can gather from the site or even whether you can effectively browse the site. In fact, most shopping cart applications must have cookies to enable shopping, because the Web wasn't originally designed to enable that kind of interaction. The Web was designed so that every click through a browser was a separate interaction (something called a *sessionless* connection). To make a shopping cart remember what you've chosen and who you are, the Web server has to use something to remind it—and cookies are the mechanism that was invented to do it.

You do have options. You may consider being prompted by your browser every time a cookie is sent to your PC. Figure 10.12 shows the dialog box that pops up when you have asked your browser to consult with you for every cookie. For the record, four more dialog boxes for four *additional* cookies popped up before you actually get to Amazon. Because some sites set so many cookies, it's likely that you shortly decide that the level of interaction with most Web sites is simply too high to practically work with this setting. Figure 10.7 shows the other options you have in Netscape to deal with cookies.

The newest Internet Explorer 6, gives you an additional option by letting you choose among privacy settings in your acceptance of cookies. You will find the privacy settings by choosing Tools, Internet Options, Privacy.

The lowest setting accepts all cookies. The low setting checks to see if the site maintains a *compact privacy policy* that is part of the Platform for Privacy Preferences (P3P). P3P is a system that enables a Web site to state its privacy policy in a machine-readable language which can be read by a client program. A compact policy is a privacy policy that expresses in a few codes the privacy policy for the site. The codes are read by a program, in this case IE6, and acted upon, usually based on settings configured by the user. At the lowest setting for IE6, if the compact policy is missing for third party cookies, those cookies are restricted. Third party cookies that use personal information without your consent are also restricted.

A third-party cookie is one set by a domain that is different from the domain from which the page comes. Cookies set by advertising networks, for example, are third party cookies. They come from the computer serving the advertising page rather than from the computer serving the page requested by the user.

The medium setting blocks third party cookies without a compact privacy policy  and those that use personally identifiable information without your implicit consent. IThis setting also restricts first party cookies that use personally identifiable information without your implicit consent.

The medium high setting blocks third party cookies without a compact privacy policy and those that use personally identifiable information without your explicit consent. This setting also restricts first party cookies that use personally identifiable information without your implicit consent. This is the default setting.

The high setting blocks third party cookies without a compact privacy policy in addition to those that use personally identifiable information without your explicit consent.

The highest setting blocks all cookies.

Regularly delete persistent cookies from your PC. Most cookie files can be edited with NotePad or another text editor. You get a warning dialog box if you try to delete cookie files for a Microsoft Internet Explorer, but you can ignore it. For per-session cookies (they are not stored on your PC), practicality says that you should enable them. For situations in which you want to hide your identity, use an anonymizer (where cookies are usually disabled).

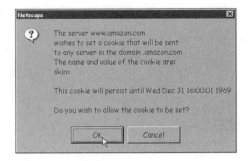

**FIGURE 10.12**

*A dialog box for dealing with cookies.*

## Dealing with Temporary Files

In the course of surfing the Web, most people download some files from it to their PC. These files often reside in a "cache" or "temporary" directory on your PC. However, unless you explicitly instruct your Web browser to delete them, nothing is temporary about those files. You can view the files and objects through your Internet Explorer browser. And you can delete them using that browser.

Regularly review and delete all these temporary files. You enhance your privacy (and you often improve the performance of your PC, too).

Figure 10.13 shows how to delete the cache on a Netscape browser. There are two kinds of cache: cache in memory and cache in actual files. To reach the menu shown in Figure 10.13, click the Edit menu in the browser and go to the preferences menu item. Figure 10.14 shows how to do the same thing on a Microsoft Internet Explorer. To reach this menu, click the Tools menu and choose the Internet Options menu item.

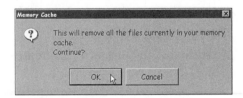

**FIGURE 10.13**

*Deleting the cache on Netscape browsers.*

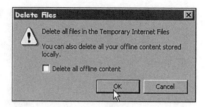

**FIGURE 10.14**

*Deleting temporary files in MSIE.*

# Protecting Against Malicious Attacks

As a general rule, you should visit only those Web sites you trust. This is because while surfing the Web you may subject your PC to an attack from a malicious Web site. This can happen when that site sends your browser instructions to execute in a form of ActiveX controls and JavaScripts.

However, it would be no fun to always visit the sites you know, and never try something new. Kids and others might also use your machine and go to places you hadn't considered. For that reason, you should configure your browser to help protect your machine against malicious attacks. We recommend the following settings for your Microsoft Internet Explorer:

- Prompt for downloading signed ActiveX controls.
- Disable unsigned ActiveX controls.
- Disable ActiveX controls not marked as safe.
- Enable running ActiveX controls and plug-ins.
- Enable ActiveX controls marked as safe for scripting.
- Set Java permissions on high safety.
- Disable script debugging.
- Warn about invalid site certificates.

The custom security section in the Internet Options menu has all these settings available (see Figure 10.15).

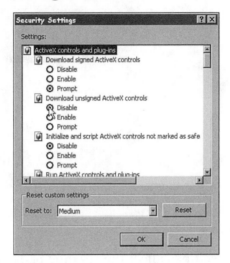

**FIGURE 10.15**

*Setting up security on Microsoft Internet Explorer.*

The following are Netscape settings. They are similar to the settings for Microsoft Internet Explorer, but are not as detailed:

- Do not enable Java applets.
- Enable JavaScript, but do not enable JavaScript for e-mail and news.

These settings are in the advanced menu in Figure 10.7.

If you enable SmartUpdate, which lets Netscape install updates to your machine automatically, make sure it prompts you for each install. Figure 10.16 shows this setting, which is in the Advanced menu under SmartUpdate.

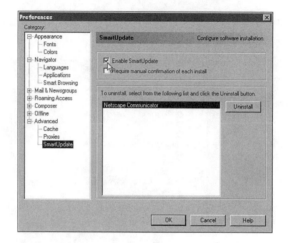

**FIGURE 10.16**

*Setting up SmartUpdate in Netscape.*

Additional settings affect the running of Java applets and browser
Security settings. You should experiment with them until you find a combination that best fits your browsing habits.

# Firewalls

When going online with your PC, you are making your PC visible to
everyone on the Internet. This also means that your PC can become a
target of someone's attack, someone that may want to retrieve information from your PC. To protect yourself against this possibility, you should
install and always use a personal firewall. You have several choices. For
example, ZoneAlarm, which is free from http://www.zonelabs.com for non-
commercial use and BlackICE Defender, commercial software from
http://www.networkice.com, which is an alternative.

Earlier in this chapter, in the "Key Concepts" section, some of the attacks
a personal firewall might help detect were discussed. Chapter 6,
"Broadband: Always On, Always Connected, Always Exposed" discusses
how vulnerable PCs connected to the Internet by Cable modem or DSL
are. However, dialup users are also vulnerable. Figure 10.17 shows a

month or two of attacks on Pat's machine, detected by BlackICE. Before DSL was available in her area, Pat used a dialup provider, and she still got hit by script kiddies trying port probes and other kinds of attacks. For that reason, every computer in her house has personal firewall software installed.

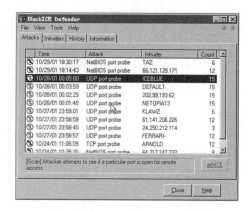

**FIGURE 10.17**

*Attacks on Pat's machine May to July.*

Figure 10.18 shows what BlackICE has been able to detect about a certain attacker, by reading the information in the packets (information bits) used in the attack. This information could be spoofed and point at someone who is innocent, but it may also be real evidence that would help an ISP track down an attacker. Most personal firewall software enables the collection of information about attacks that ISP providers and law enforcement officials can use.

In Figure 10.18, the darker dot shows the most dangerous attacks. Most personal firewall software helps you determine which attacks are most dangerous, and most have an auto-blocking feature that stops known attackers from getting in when the attack is recognized. To facilitate this, you need to get upgrades from the software manufacturers that detect known attacks. (This is like updating virus signatures. Do that regularly, too!)

**FIGURE 10.18**

*Information about an attacker captured by BlackICE.*

## Antivirus

Some of us get pretty nervous about doing without our antivirus software. Cartoonist Bill Holbrook shows just how that twitchiness feels. Figure 10.19 is a recent "Kevin and Kell" cartoon.

**FIGURE 10.19**

*Feeling naked without antivirus protection. Copyright © 2001 Bill Holbrook. Used with permission.* http://www.herdthinners.com.

Last but not least, you need to protect your PC from malicious software, which usually takes the form of viruses or Trojan horses. As with personal firewalls, several options are available and among them is Norton AntiVirus from `http://www.symantec.com` and McAfee VirusScan from `http://www.nai.com`.

 **TIP**

You probably know this, but there have been some people who have been confused about computer viruses and human viruses such as that which causes the common cold. One U.S. Congressman reputedly believed for a while that you could get pregnant from online sex. Rest assured. Computer viruses are not contagious to people. If you should happen to get an e-mail warning you about a virus that people can catch, you know it's a joke. The best site to check on email hoaxes and other email stories is the Urban Legends site at `http://www.snopes.com`.

You should install and always use antivirus software on your PC. Most antivirus software has options that scan e-mail messages, attachments, and Web programs and applets as you first encounter them. For example, if you get a message with an attachment, and the attachment has a virus, your antivirus software detects the virus, isolates it to keep it from running, and warns you.

Figure 10.20 shows how to configure Norton AntiVirus to scan files as you work.

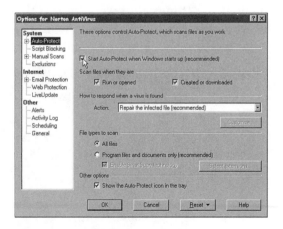

**FIGURE 10.20**

*Configuring Norton AntiVirus.*

Figure 10.21 shows how to configure Norton to protect your e-mail and attachments. From this menu you can enable auto protection for your browser, whether Internet Explorer or Netscape, as well.

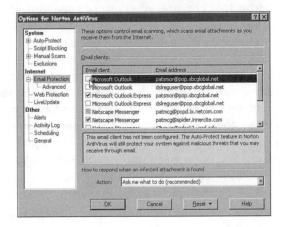

**FIGURE 10.21**

*Protecting your e-mail.*

Just as with the firewall software, it's critical that you make sure you keep the virus signature file up to date. Folks who develop viruses and other malicious software work all the time, and release viruses constantly. If you don't keep your signatures up to date, you are protected only against the things that were known the day you got and installed the software. Figure 10.22 shows how to use Norton's LiveUpdate feature to get the latest virus signatures and antivirus engines from the vendor.

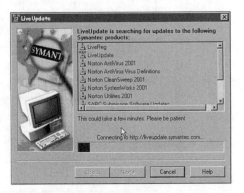

**FIGURE 10.22**

*Getting the latest updates from the vendor.*

## Media Players

Next to the Web, various media players are probably the most common applications used over the Internet. As with the Web, some of these applications ask for personal information and want to subject you to surveys. Your response should be the same as with the Web applications: you can avoid deliberately disclosing personal information. If you must answer personal or survey questions, consider developing a unique persona just for that, record your answers and stick to it.

Some media players use your established Internet connection to send information about your use of the applications (for example, what songs you are playing). Some players enable you to configure this behavior; others do not even disclose it. You should use a firewall tool that intercepts outgoing Internet connections from your PC and gives you a choice about permitting them or stopping them. ZoneAlarm software is particularly good at catching these attempts.

# E-mail Privacy

Using e-mail on the Internet has two principal privacy issues: keeping your identity anonymous and keeping the content of your messages private.

## Keeping Your Identity Anonymous

At times it is advantageous to keep your identity anonymous. For example, to avoid repercussions, people sometimes don't want to have their name associated with a particular piece of information or critique. In a country governed by an oppressive government, anonymity helps to give people some freedom of expression. Using a pseudo-anonymous account, or one where you can get the information but it doesn't point directly at you, can help with managing spamming.

A few tools are available on the Internet to provide this kind of anonymity. Anonymous remailers are e-mail services that accept your e-mail, sending it through a series of remailers before routing the e-mail to its ultimate destination. The remailing process not only makes the backtracking process very difficult, but also removes information identifying you as the source of the message. One such well-known remailing service is available at `http://www.gilc.org/speech/anonymous/remailer.html`.

Figure 10.23 shows how to type mail in at the remailer at GILC.com. After you have used the remailer, you are directed to a page where you can download anonymizing software to use on locally on your PC. That page warns you that it may take a long time for the recipient to get the message, because it goes through what's called the "mixmaster" network. In this experiment, it took more than an hour for the message to get back to Pat.

**FIGURE 10.23**

*Using an anonymizing remailer form online.*

## Keeping the Content of Your Messages Private

To keep the e-mail message content private, you have several choices. You can combine the anonymity with content privacy by using Internet services that eliminate your identity and encrypt your message. Some also delete their internal records of the message as coming from you. Some services use remailers in several foreign countries to make the trail reconstruction much more difficult if not nearly impossible. This also let's them truthfully answer legal requirements by saying they have no knowledge of who sent the message, where it was going, and what it contained. Some examples of such services include SafeMessage provided commercially by http://www.safemessage.com and HushMail offered at no cost by http://www.hushmail.com.

If anonymity is not a requirement for you and all you want to do is send a private message, you can use file encryption tools such as PGP to encrypt the text before including it in an e-mail message. PGP is available free for non-commercial use from http://www.pgpi.org and Network Associates PGP (commercial version, relatively inexpensive) is available at http://www.nai.com. PGP has plug-ins that enable you to use it with Eudora and Outlook to enable smooth, one-button encryption. These plug-ins enable you to click the "encrypt" option, and the mailer automatically finds the keys for the recipient, encrypts it for them, and also encrypts a copy for you.

One other option is to use a service that encrypts and decrypts messages for you. Some businesses use either WorldSecure (now a part of Tumbleweed systems) at http://www.tumbleweed.com/worldtalk.html (or Omniva Policy Systems (formerly Disappearing, Inc.), at http://www.omniva.com/. If run a small business working out of your home, you might want to consider either of these products. Tumbleweed provides an encrypting gateway that protects e-mail from your gateway to the Internet to the other end. Omniva enables you to send mail where the message is encrypted at your client and decrypted by the other client, but they also offer a retention option. This lets you decide how long the decryption key is good. After that date, the message becomes permanently scrambled and unreadable, even when stored on other people's mail servers.

# What About Macs?

The general principles for protecting your home computer are outlined previously. This section discusses applying those principles to your Macintosh.

**NOTE**     In this section, we will assume that you have read the previous section.

## Privacy Considerations for Macintosh

Most of the information from the previous section on Windows privacy tools applies to the Macintosh as well. The basic considerations remain the same; only the details change. For example, MacOS 9 includes file permissions similar, but not identical, to those of Windows NT.

## Files

In MacOS 9, you can set up separate accounts for each person to use when they log in to the Mac, via the Multiple Users Control Panel. By using built-in file system permissions, you can set access on the private files so that no one, or only the people you designate, can access those files. This protection also lets you control which applications people can run. Just keep the following in mind:

- This method is effective only if you (and no one else) have access to the special owner account (the one created when the Mac was first set up).

- This method stops casual snoops, but is relatively easy for a determined attacker to foil; all they need to do is boot from a floppy or CD.

- As always, if you need truly effective protection, you should encrypt your files. PGP is available for Macintosh, as is PGPdisk, which provides disk-level encryption.

In MacOS X, the story is much the same: file permissions exist, but the first account created is an administrator, which can ignore them; and a determined attacker can bypass the permissions.

Again, truly sensitive files require encryption. PGP is available for MacOS X. PGPdisk, as of this writing, is not; however, because MacOS X is based on a free version of Unix, one or another of the disk-level encryption systems from the free-Unix world may eventually become available. As with any disk-level encryption system, any program you run, including untrusted code such as viruses, can access your files.

In both cases, if more than one person uses the computer, it is advisable to use the file permission system. Even if you have absolute trust in the other user, you may prefer to protect your information, not from them, but from software they run. If they install a program from an unscrupulous company that starts searching their files, file permissions protect your files.

## How to Set Up Multiple Users

First, open the Multiple Users control panel (found under Control Panels, on the Apple Menu). If you have not set up multiple users before, see Figure 10.24. The single user shown is the owner, whose name (in this case John Doe) was probably set when you first set up your Macintosh. To create another user, click New User. Figure 10.24 shows the Multiple Users control panel, with John Doe as the owner.

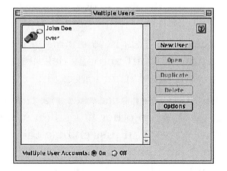

**FIGURE 10.24**

*The Multiple Users control panel.*

This is the dialog you get when you create or edit a user; you can set their name, password, and overall level of access. If you need to set more details, you can click Show Setup Details. Figure 10.25 shows the creation of new user "Richard Roe."

**FIGURE 10.25**

*Adding in Richard Roe as a user.*

In this panel, you can set some basic properties of the new user:

The picture for them is shown on the login screen. You can click the up or down arrows to pick a different picture, or drag a picture onto the frame (see Figure 10.26). In this case, an image from a Web page (open in Netscape) was dragged into the frame. Some of the properties you can configure for individual users include:

- **Changing their own password.** They almost always should be able to. That way, if they accidentally tell it to someone, they can change it to stop that person from using their account.

- **Logging in.** This is to enable you to block them from using their account, without actually deleting it. For example, if you want to stop your child from logging in until their homework is done.

- **Managing user accounts via the Multiple Users panel.** If they can do this, no other blocks on what they can do make sense, because they can just change their own account. This is useful for a family computer where each family member has their own account; each parent can have the ability to manage the children's accounts.

- **Enabling other users to read and/or write their documents.** (The owner can read and write all files on the system, of course.)

**FIGURE 10.26**

*Setting basic properties for a new user, including a picture from their Web site.*

If you choose to make the user a Limited user, you can restrict the set of applications they can use. Figure 10.27 shows the control panel to restrict applications for this user. "Richard" has permissions to run a Acrobat Reader 4.0, Adobe PhotoShop LE, Norton AntiVirus scan, NCSA Telnet, and Netscape versions 4.74 and 6.

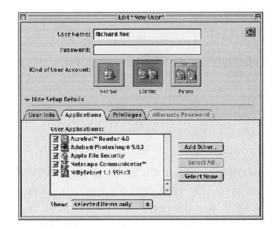

**FIGURE 10.27**

*Restricting applications for a new user.*

**FIGURE 10.28**

*What the restricted user sees.*

When Richard logs in, he gets a desktop with only a few icons, including one for a folder containing his available applications. Figure 10.28 shows this folder.

If Richard logs in, and tries to open an application he is not enabled to use, he gets the message shown in Figure 10.29.

**FIGURE 10.29**

*Stop! You don't have permission to do this.*

You can also use the Privileges tab to further restrict a Limited user. The user shown in Figure 10.30 (Richard Roe) cannot use CD-ROMs, DVD-ROMs, or any other removable media (for example, floppies and Zip disks), and cannot get at shared folders, resources on an AppleTalk network, control panels, or anything else under the Apple Menu. He can print, though.

This user has extremely limited use of the system. He can't do anything except use a few applications you've set up for them. This might be a good way to set up profiles for children on your Macintosh. However, the user also can't save his work to a floppy, which could become a problem if he wants to do backups. The system does not currently provide a way to enable a user to save to floppy without permitting him to use whatever removable media (except CD and DVD) he wants. You have to decide which is more important for your situation: letting the user back up his work, or keeping the user from using removable media. Of course, if you enable him to use a Web browser, he can already bring any files he wants in and out of the system, though it might be slow.

If you don't have a floppy drive (as so many Macs don't these days), you might prefer not to make the decision; but be aware that someone could plug in an external drive via USB or FireWire. Again, how likely that is depends on your situation. If you're just trying to keep your 6-year-old from, accidentally reading your files, you don't need to worry about it (they're probably not going to go out and buy their own USB drive). If you're trying to protect a computer containing corporate secrets, you should be more careful.

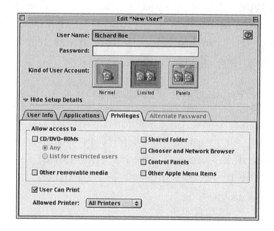

**FIGURE 10.30**

*This user cannot use removable media.*

## Passwords

The story on passwords on the Mac is much the same as on Windows. One interesting wrinkle is that MacOS 9's Multiple Users system permits users to establish voiceprint passwords, meaning that someone who knows the password still can't use it unless their voice matches yours. This feature may have pitfalls of its own, though. The following is a list of these possible pitfalls:

- If you have to speak your password aloud, you may be overheard. Someone may be able to imitate your voice well enough to fool the computer. Even if they can't, if you use the same password elsewhere, they may be able to type it in there.

- As with any voice-input system, if there is too much noise, the system may not respond.

- If your voice changes (due to laryngitis, for example), you may not be able to log in.

Another tool to consider is Web Confidential, which stores your various passwords in one encrypted file. To get them, you just have to remember the Web Confidential password. (A similar feature is included in Netscape 6.) The upside is that this makes it easier to use a different password at each Web site (so that Site A doesn't know your password to Site B). The downside is that anybody who can decrypt the password file now has all your passwords.

## Web Browsing History

If you use Netscape 4 for Mac, you do not need to worry about browser history. Although it has a History window, it does not store long-term history data. Instead, the information in the History window is the same as in the browser window's Back button; it is lost when the browser window is closed.

If you use another browser, or if you want to obliterate stored cookies, you may be interested in NetShred (`http://www.mireth.com/NS.html`), which uses ShredIt (see the following section) to securely delete browser history and similar information.

## Getting Rid of Files and Data

To securely remove files, you can use ShredIt (`http://www.mireth.com/SI.html`), similar to the Eraser program for Windows.

## Anonymous Surfing

Both `http://www.anonymizer.com` and `http://www.idzap.com` work with Mac browsers, though some of their ancillary software is Windows-only.

## Firewalls

Two personal firewall products for Mac are Norton Personal Firewall and PGP Corporate Desktop (which also includes a VPN client and the PGP encryption software). Both include Internet Protocol firewall and intrusion detection features; Norton Personal Firewall also warns you if you go online with AppleTalk active (which could expose your shared files or printers, if any, if you use cable or DSL).

MacOS X has firewall capabilities built in. As of this writing, they are not made available via a control panel, but instructions are available online at `http://wopr.norad.org/articles/firewall/ipfw.html`.

## Antivirus Software

Both Norton AntiVirus and McAfee VirusScan are available for Mac.

## E-mail: Protecting the Content

SafeMessage and HushMail are not currently available for Mac; PGP is.

# Putting It All Together

If you've followed this chapter and set up your protections to match how you feel about protecting your computer and your privacy, you're well on your way to surfing more confidently and with greater awareness of potential threats.

The following is a checklist from NetAction on the "The Five A's of Personal Computing Security." They are *Awareness, Authentication, Authorization, Access Control,* and *Auditing.*

# The Five A's of Personal Computing Security

*"Security is a process, not a product. Products provide some protection, but the only way to effectively do business in an insecure world is to put processes in place that recognize the inherent insecurity in the products. The trick is to reduce our risk of exposure regardless of the products or patches."*

**Bruce Schneier, Crypto-Gram newsletter, May 15, 2000,**
`http://www.counterpane.com/`
`crypto-gram-0005.html#ComputerSecurityWillWeEverLearn`

Toward this end, NetAction (`http://www.netaction.org/`) has developed a guideline called The Five "A"s of Security:

- **Awareness**—Your computer is part of a bigger picture now
- **Authentication**—Set log-ins and passwords to verify users
- **Authorization**—Should this user be permitted access to your computer?
- **Access Control**—Set permissions to limit access to certain resources
- **Auditing**—Check your logs, and your monitoring and scan tools

## Awareness

Your computer is one among millions of other computers networked together. As a broadband subscriber, your computer is (generally) reliably connected to the Internet, and your connection is quickly responsive. You have physical control over your machine, and can take informed action to protect your resources and files.

## Authentication and Authorization

If you don't want to enable global access to your files, you may need to set logins and passwords to limit your computer's users. Authentication means verifying the user. Authorization is allowing that user access to your system. Verifying users of your machine can help you track the activity in files and resources.

## Access Control

To further limit access to your resources, you may want to set permissions on individual files. For instance, you may have a text file that anyone can read. This is called global access. Another file may only be read by anyone in a special group that you design. This is group access. A third file may only be readable by you—individual access.

## Auditing

Your computer may generate logs which can be important diagnostic tools. For instance, your Web server keeps track of machines that have requested your Web pages:

- Machine and domain name or IP#
- Time and date of request
- Page or file requested
- Success or error code
- Number of bytes transferred, and so on

If you run an FTP server, you also have logs of who moved files in or out. Your security products also produce information logs that can inform you about traffic, system users, and more. In combination with active security products, logs can be a powerful tool to mitigate your security risks.

In reality, these five "A"s are somewhat intertwined. For example, it doesn't make sense to have Authentication without Authorization. Access control doesn't happen without Authentication and Authorization, and none of these make sense without Awareness.

Let's take a look at the first of these Five "A"s in practice:

## Your Computerized Self

The first step is awareness about your computerized self.

Most people keep stored computer files that reflect their lives. Generally, the "ordinary life" is not of interest to malicious hackers and crackers—unless they have easy access to your financial persona: transactions, credit card numbers, mother's maiden name, and so on.

- Do you store this or other important information on your always-connected computer?

- Do you use your home computer for work? Do you ever store trade or other company secrets on your home computer?
- Do you back up your files regularly? How would your life be affected if all your computer files were to suddenly disappear? If your computer were to become dysfunctional? If your computer were to be used by an outside force for illegal activities?

## Your System

The second step is awareness about your system.

Many of your system's vulnerabilities are known and described on public security sites. In some cases, fixes (often called patches) are also published for your use.

What you can do to reduce your system's security risks:

- Turn off your computers and/or modem when not in use.
- Keep your operating system software up to date. This does not necessarily mean you should buy the latest version. Rather, it means you should make sure you've installed all available patches for your system.
- Use a hard-to-guess password to access your computer. Good passwords have mixed upper- and lower-case letters, numbers, and characters, and are not obvious. Do not use names or birthdates of family members, or common English words such as "password" or "guess."
- Back up your files regularly.
- Run virus scanning software, and keep your virus definition profiles up to date by visiting software manufacturer's sites and downloading their virus update files (updated monthly).

If you only have one computer:

- Turn off file and print sharing; you don't need them.

If you have a home network with more than one computer:

- Set up passwords to shared computers on your network.
- If you run file/printer sharing, make sure you set a password on all shared devices. (See Appendix 1 for more on this)

### Your Network

The third step is awareness about your network.

- Don't open e-mail attachments from strangers. Confirm attachments from friends. Be especially wary of unexpected files ending in .vbs or .exe

- Do not volunteer more info to Web sites or strangers than is absolutely necessary. You already leave plenty of information behind in the logs of sites you've visited.

- Use encrypted e-mail services and programs when possible. Encryption is a process by which plain text (what you type on the screen) is "scrambled" into a code that can't be read without a special "key" that unscrambles that code. Encryption programs such as PGP have plug-ins that enable them to work with common e-mail programs. Encryption isn't very easy to use yet, but many developers are working on this problem.

- Do not run public servers without adequate protections. Many vulnerabilities are known and published on the Net; many fixes and system patches are also available.

- Look at your logs and run security scans periodically. Your logs and tools can provide a picture of what's going on.

## Some General Security Resources

**Bugtraq**—http://www.securityfocus.com/

**Secure-Me (automated security testing)**—http://www.secure-me.net/ and their related project: DSL Reports—http://www.dslreports.com/

**DSL Reports Security page**—http://www.dslreports.com/information/ rated/security

**PGP Freeware**—http://web.mit.edu/network/pgp.html

**(MIT distributes PGP Freeware without cost for personal, noncommercial use**—http://www.pgp.com/ for commercial use.

**z**—ftp://ftp.cerias.purdue.edu/pub/ tools/

**Purdue's Computer System and Network Security**—http:// rvl4.ecn.purdue.edu/~cromwell/lt/468.html

**Interesting, recent article on ZDnet called "Home is where the hack is" (Apr 10, 2000)**—http://www.zdnet.com/enterprise/stories/main/ 0,10228,2524160,00.htm

**Internet Sharing from cable-modems.org**—http://www.cable-modems.org/articles/internet_sharing/

## For Macintosh Operating Systems

**Macintosh Security**—http://securemac.com/

**DoShelp.com's Protection Tools For Macs**—http://www.doshelp.com/mprotection.htm

**A useful document on Macintosh file sharing: AppleShare IP 6.3: About Sharing, Share Points, and Access Privileges**—
http://til.info.apple.com/techinfo.nsf/artnum/n60612

## Regarding Microsoft Security

**NT security info**—http://www.disastercenter.com/ntos.htm

**Security Recommendations for Windows Desktop Computers from Virginia Commonwealth University (Revised 01/00)**—http://views.vcu.edu/ucsmcv/faq_pages/WinSecurity.html

**A Few Microsoft security pages: "For Starters: #8. How to Feel Secure"**—http://msdn.microsoft.com/workshop/essentials/forstarters/starts0709.asp

**(How annoying. I need to have scripting turned on to access some of the relevant content on)** Microsoft's Windows Security page—
http://www.microsoft.com/technet/security/windows.asp

Two articles on Outlook Mail Attachments:

**OL97: Mail Attachment Security Add-in Available on Web**—
http://support.microsoft.com/support/kb/articles/q165/1/16.asp

**Outlook E-mail Attachment Security Update**—
http://support.microsoft.com/support/kb/articles/q235/3/09.asp

## Learn What the Hackers Think

http://www.l0pht.com/

http://packetstorm.securify.com/index.shtml

http://www.rootshell.com/

http://www.anticode.com/

# HOW TO SECURE YOUR INTERNET TRANSACTIONS

If only using common sense protected your privacy while you are shopping online or hard and fast rules guaranteed protection. Unfortunately, they don't. This chapter offers some guidelines and suggestions on how to shop online with more confidence and also on how to make privacy decisions based on law and experience. It educates you on how to respond if a problem arises, what your rights and recourse are, in addition to telling you where to go to get the latest information on technology, laws, and risks.

So let's start with shopping online.

## Can You Let Your Fingers Do the Shopping?

As more and more busy people are discovering, you can shop for and buy almost anything online. In the past year, friends of Pat and Glee have purchased the following, among other things:

- A Ford Explorer
- A Honda Civic

- Books on every conceivable topic, including textbooks, religious writings, legal references, romance, foreign language books, and erotica
- Clothing
- Shoes
- Lawn furniture, including hammocks and yard lanterns
- Photoelectric cell outdoor lighting
- Art objects, such as statuary and glass
- Paintings, art prints, framed prints, and posters
- Major appliances, including refrigerator, washer, dryer, and dishwasher
- Prescription medications
- Over the counter medications
- Plants and bulbs
- Tools, including a lawnmower, gardening tools such as trowels and dibbles, pruning shears, chainsaw, leaf blower, band saw, sledgehammers, and other woodworking tools
- Medieval pavilion(s), poles, ropes, and stakes
- Camping equipment including backpacking tents, sleeping bags, ground pads, lanterns, braziers, and canopies
- A Canoe
- Winter Coats
- A mortgage and a home equity loan
- Flowers, chocolate, gift certificates, balloons, and stuffed toys
- Strip-o-grams to be delivered in other cities
- Airplane tickets to England, Germany, Australia, China, and Israel
- Passport renewal services
- Rental car reservations

And the list keeps getting longer.

As the number of things that can be bought online multiplies every day, so does the number of things that can go wrong. There can be simple errors (people who don't realize they have clicked on the button that says, "Yes, I want to buy this!") If you buy things online, you might be surprised by this. Pat attended a seminar in the summer of 2001 at which she stated that many Web merchants have as much as 55% of their sales returned because the customer said they didn't actually want to buy the item or didn't know they were buying the item. There are also instances of actual fraud, such as a merchant who sets up a site and collects money, then never delivers the goods. Just being an online sales site doesn't guarantee good customer service, kid-glove delivery services, or an easy return mechanism.

Some of the following recommendations are common sense. The same rules apply to online shopping that apply to shopping at the mall.

## If in Doubt, Don't

Use your good judgement about the site, just as you would if you were walking into a store for the first time. Is the site tidy and well maintained? Does it have spelling or grammar errors? Are there lots of broken links? Are there messages that are days, months, or even years old? This is the same as walking into a store with outdated goods, notices of sales that are long gone by, or where the store is dirty or unpleasant. If it makes you feel uncomfortable, go look for another vendor. These days, very few things can't be bought someplace else.

Web sites have other warning signs and characteristics that should make you think twice before ordering. Does the company have a telephone number, so you can reach them for inquiries, customer service issues, or other information? Do they have a street address, or just a post office box? If you call the number, does the person who answers sound professional? While these aren't absolutes, they are things you should keep in mind.

## Do Business with Folks You Know

Discovering a new store or a new place to shop is something you all love. However, it's no fun to discover a new store is a rip-off. Some people do not treat you fairly when you walk in—it's the same online. For your first forays into online shopping, go with companies you already know. When you're feeling more adventurous and go with a company that is unfamiliar, do some homework before buying their products. To be really cautious, start out with an inexpensive order to learn if the company is reliable.

## Use a Credit Card

In the United States you are protected by a federal statute protecting the use of credit cards. The law is the Fair Credit Billing Act.

Under the FCBA, you have the right to dispute charges on your credit card, and you can withhold payments while the credit card issuer investigates. If it turns out that your charge card or credit card was used without authorization, you are only responsible for the first $50 in charges, and you are seldom even asked to pay that. The rules for credit cards are spelled out in the following sidebar.

### HOW DOES THE U.S. FAIR CREDIT BILLING ACT PROTECT YOU?

The Fair Credit Billing Act outlines a process for handling some problems you may encounter when you buy something with a credit card or charge card. The law says that if you feel a charge is in error, you can dispute that charge. You can also temporarily withhold payment while the credit card company investigates the problem. You can do this if

- The charge listed on your bill is in error.

- The charge listed on the bill was not made by you, or by someone you authorized to use the card.

- The charge is for goods or services that you or someone you designated rejected on reasonable grounds. For example, you can dispute the charge if the item didn't meet the terms of sale. (For advice on whether to accept the item outright, or to accept it and then challenge the company for a refund, speak to your charge card issuer.)

- The charge is for goods or services not delivered to you, or to someone you designate, as agreed in the terms of sale. For example, if you paid extra shipping to get 2nd day shipping, but was delivered more than a week late, different from what you ordered, or the wrong number of items were delivered.

You can dispute your bill because of other conditions related to the condition of the goods or the contract. Contact your credit card issuer or go to the following URL for more information.

> The Fair Credit Billing Act *does* apply to overseas purchases made on a card issued from a U.S. bank. This is one reason to always consider paying by credit card instead of cash or check when you are outside of the United States. For more information on overseas use of credit cards, see the U.S. Government's Consumer Information Guides at `http://www.pueblo.gsa.gov/cic_text/travel/overseas/overseas.txt`.
>
> To dispute a charge under the Fair Credit Billing Act, you must write to your credit card issuer within 60 days of the postmark date of the bill on which the charge appeared. Phone calls and e-mail do not count. Instructions on how to dispute a charge can be found on the back of your charge bill.

Almost every privacy and consumer advocacy group recommends that you have one credit card that you use only online. This helps you keep track of your online purchases, and helps you spot problems more quickly.

The old adage from physical shopping that it's safer to pay with a check is not true in the online world. Shopping online and then sending the merchant a check leaves you vulnerable to bank fraud. It gives a potential crook all the routing information they would need to empty your checking account. And sending a cashier's check or money order doesn't give you any protection should something go wrong.

Many online advocacy and consumer's rights Web sites advise you to only use a true charge card or credit card, and not an ATM or debit card. Up until recently, depending on the rules with your bank, a debit card could expose your bank account to would-be thieves just like a check would. Your checking account could be wiped out in minutes.

However, the Electronic Funds Transfer Act (EFTA) protects s debit cards just like charge and credit cards. According to the Federal Trade Commission's Web site (`http://www.ftc.gov/bcp/conline/pubs/online/payments.htm`) these are the rules:

> *The EFTA applies to electronic fund transfers—transactions involving automated teller machines (ATMs), debit cards and other point-of-sale debit transactions, and other electronic banking transactions that can result in the withdrawal of cash from your bank account.*
>
> *Under the EFTA, if a mistake or unauthorized withdrawal is made from your bank account through the use of a debit card (an electronic fund transfer), you must notify your financial institution of the problem or error within 60*

*days after the statement containing the problem or error was sent. For retail purchases, your financial institution has up to 20 business days to investigate after receiving notice of the error. The financial institution must tell you the results of its investigation within three business days of completing the investigation. The error must be corrected within one business day after determining the error has occurred. If the institution needs more time, it may take up to 90 days to complete the investigation—but only if it returns the money in dispute to your account within 20 business days after receiving notice of the error.*

*If someone uses your debit card without your permission, you can lose from $50 to $500, depending on when you report the loss or theft. But if you do not report an unauthorized transfer or withdrawal within 60 days after your statement is sent to you, you risk unlimited loss. Some financial institutions voluntarily cap your liability at $50, regardless of when you report the loss or theft. Ask your financial institution about its liability limits.*

Chapter 5, "Online Disclosures and That Barn Door," discusses children's privacy protection and the use of stored value cards for online payments. The FTC pamphlet also discusses them. The risk of loss and the protections are not as clear as with credit or debit cards:

*The FCBA and the EFTA may not cover stored-value cards or transactions involving them, so you may not be covered for loss or misuse of the card. However, you might want to use stored-value cards for micropayments and other purchases online, because they can be convenient and—in some cases—offer anonymity. Before you buy a stored-value card or other form of electronic money, ask the issuer for written information about the product's features. Find out the card's dollar limit, whether it is reloadable or disposable, if it has an expiration date and any fees to use, reload, or redeem (return it for a refund) the product. At the same time, ask about your rights and responsibilities: does the issuer offer any protection in the case of a lost, stolen, misused, or malfunctioning card; and who do you call if you have a question or problem with the card.*

## Shop at Secure Sites

What makes a site secure, and how do you tell? First, a site that is concerned about your security uses encryption to protect your information while it travels from your keyboard to the online system. This encryption is implemented in a browser protocol called SSL, or Secure Sockets Layer. The strongest encryption available for browsers uses 128-bit encryption.

As described in Chapter 10, encryption scrambles the information you send to prevent anyone unauthorized from obtaining it off the network. The only people who can unscramble the information are the people at the other end who have the right key to unlock the code.

SSL is an industry standard. If a Web site is not using it, you should be very cautious about buying from them or giving them your information.

You can tell if the Web site is using protection. First, look at the URL (Web address) at the top of the screen. If you don't have a toolbar showing that displays the location, you can open it. On both the Netscape and Microsoft Internet Explorer browsers, go to the View menu. On Netscape Communicator, as shown in Figure 11.1, select Show, Location Toolbar. In Microsoft IE, as shown in Figure 11.2, start by selecting the View menu, Toolbars, Address Bar.

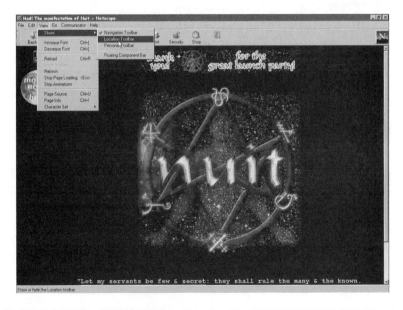

**FIGURE 11.1**

*Displaying the URL with Netscape Communicator.*

**FIGURE 11.2**

*Displaying the URL with Microsoft Internet Explorer.*

If a site is using cryptography to protect your information, you should see a URL that starts with `https://` instead of `http://`. The "s" stands for "secure." Often, you do not see the "s" until you actually move to the order page on the Web site. Figure 11.3 shows the Sign On page for Wells Fargo's online banking service. You can see the "`https`" notation in the location toolbar.

Another way to determine if a Web site is secure is to look for a padlock displayed at the bottom of your screen. If that lock is open, you should assume it is not a secure site. Figure 11.4 shows an unlocked lock symbol on a Netscape Communicator browser. If the lock is closed (and sometimes it glows yellow or gold), your information is being encrypted. Figure 11.5 shows a locked padlock.

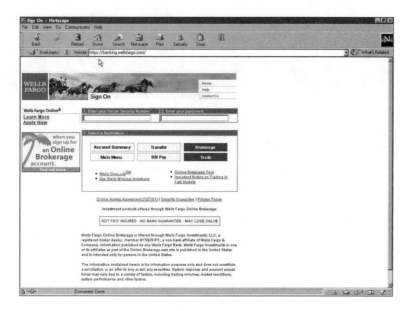

**FIGURE 11.3**

*The Wells Fargo banking site uses encryption to protect your information.*

**FIGURE 11.4**

*An unlocked lock means no protection.*

**FIGURE 11.5**

*A locked lock means encryption is active.*

You can also check the protection on a Web site by explicitly asking your browser to display the security being used to the site. For example, on Microsoft Internet Explorer, you can see this by looking in the Properties item. To get there, as shown in Figure 11.6, go to the File menu and select Properties.

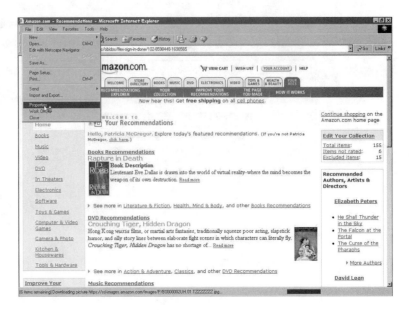

**FIGURE 11.6**

*Finding the Properties item in the File Menu.*

When the Properties dialog box opens, you can see that the site is using the Hypertext Transfer Protocol with Privacy (https) , and that it is using SSL Version 3.0 with strong encryption. These are shown in Figure 11.7.

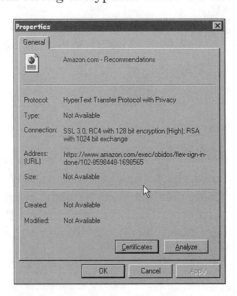

**FIGURE 11.7**

*Browser properties show protection is enabled.*

Some sites help you figure out if your browser is compatible with their security. Figure 11.8 shows the Wachovia Bank Web site's browser test page. As you can see in the figure, the browser has 128-bit encryption capability, which is strong.

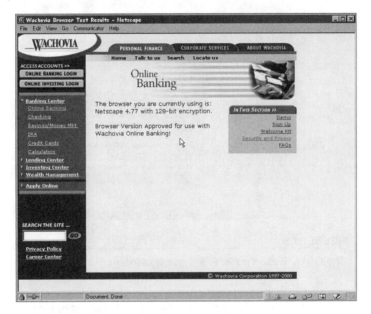

**FIGURE 11.8**

*Wachovia helps you test to see how secure your browser is.*

Of course, transmitting your data via secure channels doesn't help if the merchant doesn't take precautions to protect it at their end. If the merchant doesn't use appropriate protections, their site is a fat target for hackers because of all the information conveniently stored in the same place. If the site you're thinking of buying from doesn't have any information online about how they protect your data, you may want to find another place to buy. That information should be in their privacy and security policies.

Figure 11.9 shows The Great Western Bank's online security and privacy policy. They describe that they use encryption, Internet firewalls, and strict access control to protect the information they hold.

**FIGURE 11.9**

*The Great Western Bank's security statement.*


## ENCRYPTION: THE BATTLE FOR THE TOOL OF PRIVACY

No discussion of privacy in the digital age would be complete without a discussion of cryptography. This once obscure area of applied mathematics, with a racy past filled with spies, counter spies and enigmas, has emerged as one of the essential building blocks of the Internet.

But it was not always clear that this would be the case. Encryption scrambles data and when properly implemented, allows only the intended recipients to have access to the unscrambled text. In that way messages and information can be sent over computer networks in a form unreadable by third-party interlopers. Applications for encryption range from protecting doctor-patient communications, allowing competitive bidding, facilitating online purchasing and protecting stored data, just to name a few.

The U.S. Government, raising concerns of terrorist and criminal uses of encryption, attempted to prevent the introduction of strong encryption into digital networks. The battle to free encryption took well over 8 years and engaged individuals from Bill Gates to Phyllis Schafley to John Perry Barlow. Even now, while encryption is much freer than it was, the science remains subject to complex regulations that can easily change with the political winds.

## BACKGROUND

Prior to December 1998, encryption was subject to a licensing scheme under the control of the United States Department of State. Licensed as part of the general regulations controlling the export of military items, "software with the capability of maintaining secrecy" was subject to the same basic controls as tanks, missiles and landmines. In 1998, a combination of political and legal pressures led the Clinton Administration to shift primary licensing control from the State Department to the Commerce Department. When it became clear that this shift did not actually change the stringent level of regulation, complaints continued and the government issued a series of retrenchments over the next two years that slowly reduced their control over portions of the technology. Yet they refused to eliminate the general requirement that any encryption computer program in electronic form must be submitted to the licensing agency for broadly discretionary, case-by-case licensing prior to export or publication.

Political pressure to change the regulations included a series of proposed laws that would have lessened governmental control over the technology. Other pressure came from three separate lawsuits, each charging that the regulations were unconstitutional prior restraints on speech because they prevented cryptographers from publishing their work. Still more pressure came from public education and grassroots organizing, arising in part from the grand jury investigation of Phil Zimmermann, creator of a computer program that allowed non-technical individuals access to "pretty good" privacy.

Over the years one of the widest coalitions ever arising from a technology issue arose to battle the encryption regulations. Business rivals such as Sun Microsystems and Microsoft, political rivals such as the Eagle Forum and the American Civil Liberties Union and persons as diverse as mathematicians, CEOs and computer security professionals all joined in the call to free encryption technology from government control.

In April, 1999, the 9th Circuit Court of Appeals ruled that the encryption regulations violated the prior restraint doctrine of the First Amendment. The lawsuit was titled *Bernstein v. Department of Justice* and was sponsored by the Electronic Frontier Foundation. At the same time, the list of co-sponsors to the proposed legislation grew and Silicon Valley voters and donors indicated that encryption liberalization was one of their key issues.

## THE JANUARY 2000 REGULATIONS

As a result of these efforts, in September, 1999, the Clinton Administration announced a major change in the licensing scheme. The new regulations were released in January 2000. Responding to the 9th Circuit, the new regulations largely eliminated the prior restraint contained in the previous regulations for publicly available non-commercial encryption software. The regulations replaced that process with a simultaneous government notification requirement that allows general publication of publicly available noncommercial encryption software.

Even as to commercial software the regulations allow export of a broad category of encryption software if the government fails to act to prevent the export within thirty days. They also eliminate the reporting requirements applicable to anonymous downloads of some encryption software; the remaining reporting requirements for other encryption software have also been streamlined.

## REMAINING ISSUES

With these regulations came great and well deserved celebrations among those who had fought to release encryption from the government's grip. And while those celebrations are in order, the current regulatory scheme is not perfect.

First, the regulations are even more complex than they were before. Even before the recent changes the encryption regulations were so Byzantine that a company or an individual dare not enter without an experienced attorney as a guide. Now they are even more difficult to navigate. While this may not be a major obstacle to a big corporation that regularly relies on export counsel, academics, freelance cryptographers and small businesses are also required to understand the regulations and this poses a significant burden and risk of discretionary application.

Next, the regulations still contain a prior restraint on the sharing of much non-public encryption software and create a strange regulatory distinction between code that is sold and code that is given away. Additionally, the regulations prevent "knowing" export to a list of denied persons and denied countries. What constitutes "knowing" export is not particularly clear, creating possible dangers for individuals and discretion in the agency. Moreover, the regulations require those who wish to export to continually check the relevant lists, posing a burden not placed on speakers on any other topic.

The regulations also maintain wide discretion in the agency to prevent "export" of commercial encryption software. Simply by issuing a letter within the thirty-day period, the agency can prevent export of much commercial software. Once such a letter has been issued, the agency has no further requirement to make a quick decision, a fair decision or any decision at all.

Finally, the new regulations are subject to change at any time. Between 1998 and 2000, the government issued over 6 different changes to the encryption regulations. While the current regulations are a step forward, nothing about them is per-

manent. Due to their roots in national security concerns, the encryption regulations are not subject to the normal deliberative processes and limits on regulatory
changes applicable to most other regulations, so changes to the regulations are
not particularly difficult or burdensome for the administration to implement.

In fact, representatives from the FBI recently testified before a Congressional committee that the new regulations are causing them difficulty. Given the history of
this area, it seems unlikely that the FBI or the NSA has surrendered this issue. The
next national emergency or terrorist act may well serve as a platform from which
they will insist upon renewed encryption controls.

## CONCLUSION

In the meantime, however, the loosening of government controls and the expiration of several key patents have led to the blooming of thousands of applications
for encryption. The science is flourishing and the international discussion continues. Consumers and businesses are using encryption seamlessly, often without even
knowing that they are doing so, which is how it should be. Hopefully, all of this
will solidify encryption's place in the digital world, making recontrol of the technology impossible or, better yet, unthinkable.

*—Cindy Cohn*
*Legal Director, Electronic Frontier Foundation*

# Look For and Read the Privacy and Security Policies

Any merchant or service vendor online with whom you'd like to do business offers you information about how they go about providing fair information practices (see Chapter 2), and what security practices they use to
protect your information. In general, you can find these under the head-
ings "Privacy," "Privacy Policy," or "Privacy and Security."

Reading these policies is important. A good privacy policy tells you
explicitly what information is gathered, what is done with it, and who
gets to see it. The components of fair information practices, as discussed
in Chapter 2, are Notice, Choice, Security, and Access. Security and how
to find out what security protects your information was discussed earlier
in this chapter, so the following is how you can evaluate a site's privacy
policy given the other three components:

- **Notice**—Their privacy policy should tell you exactly what they are
  collecting and how they collect it. It should also tell you to what
  use the data is put and with whom they share it.

Figure 11.10 shows a privacy policy, for Elf Hill Music and Mayhem, which is much less formal than the bank's, but still meets the Fair Practices test. It tells you what information they collect and what they do with it.

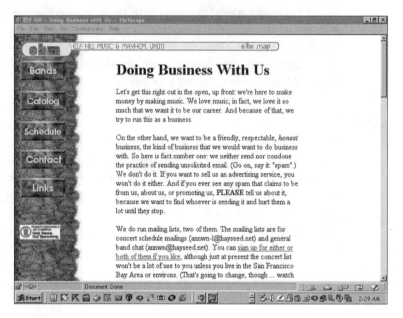

**FIGURE 11.10**

*Notice of information collection.*

- **Choice**—A good policy gives you the chance to share or not share your information with them. It also tells you the consequences if you do not share this information with them. Sometimes this information is in the Privacy Policy or on the signup screen.

Figure 11.11 shows the Harryanddavid.com privacy policy. It tells you that you can order from them without registering, but that your options for order tracking, order history, and other services are limited if you don't register. The policy also states that they occasionally partner to provide special offers to their clients, but that they do not give your personally identifiable information (PII) to the other parties beyond what is needed to actually provide you with the special offer.

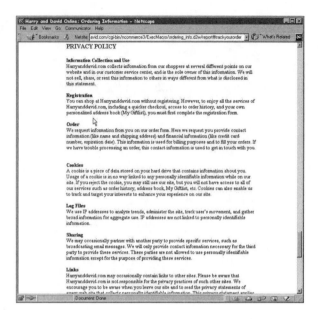

**FIGURE 11.11**

*Harryanddavid.com tells you what to expect if you opt-out.*

- **Access**—If a merchant gathers information from you, they are required to give you permission to see the personally identifiable information (PII) they have about you. You can also make corrections or ask them to remove any PII about you from their databases. (They should tell you what the consequences are if you are removed, however.)

Figure 11.12 shows the Eddie Bauer Online Store privacy policy, which tells what information they show you and how to get access to it.

- **Security**—Security is the technology and practices that protect your PII while it is in the possession of the vendor. The site you are dealing with should tell you what security precautions it uses. Banks and other financial institutions are required by law to meet strict security standards to protect your data.

**FIGURE 11.12**

*Eddie Bauer tells you how to get access to your information.*

# Seal Organizations

Remember the "Good Housekeeping Seal of Approval"? It was a seal given by Good Housekeeping Magazine to give consumers an extra degree of quality assurance about the products they purchase. The Better Business Bureau is another such organization—if something has the Better Business Seal, they meet minimum standards of business practice to get the seal. Similar organizations exist for online merchants, such as TRUSTe (www.truste.org) and BBBonline (www.bbbonline.org).

## TRUSTe's Trustmark

TRUSTe awards their seal of approval only to sites that follow privacy principles as established by the U.S. Department of Commerce. The sites must also agree to comply with ongoing TRUSTe oversight and consumer resolution procedures, which includes filling out a rigorous questionnaire several times a year. When you see the TRUSTe seal, as shown in Figure 11.13, you know that the Web site tells you the following things in its privacy policy:

- What personal information is being gathered about you
- How the information is used
- Who the information is shared with, if anyone
- Choices available to you regarding how collected information is used
- Safeguards in place to protect your information from loss, misuse, or alteration
- How you can update or correct inaccuracies in your information

**FIGURE 11.13**

*The TRUSTe Trustmark.*

You can also file a complaint with TRUSTe if you feel one of their seal members has violated the stated privacy policy. The TRUSTe Web site has a complaint form at `http://www.truste.org/users/users_watchdog_reports.html`.

Figure 11.14 shows a TRUSTe Watchdog report for June 2001. While the report doesn't show individual companies, it does show what issues were raised and how they were resolved.

## Better Business Bureau Online

The BBB's slogan for online privacy is "Say what you do, do what you say and have it verified." They do what the Better Business Bureau Council has done for many years for bricks and mortar businesses. The BBB has significant experience in self-regulation (see Chapter 15) and dispute resolution, and the Privacy Program uses verification, monitoring and review, consumer dispute resolution, a compliance privacy seal (see Figure 11.15), enforcement mechanisms, and an educational component to help protect consumer privacy online. You can find the BBB online complaint forms, for more than just online issues, at `http://www.bbbonline.org/consumer/complaint.asp`.

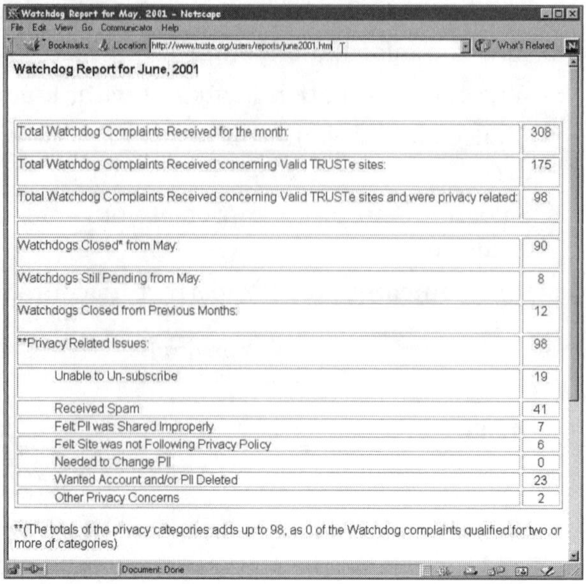

| Watchdog Report for June, 2001 | |
| --- | --- |
| Total Watchdog Complaints Received for the month: | 308 |
| Total Watchdog Complaints Received concerning Valid TRUSTe sites: | 175 |
| Total Watchdog Complaints Received concerning Valid TRUSTe sites and were privacy related: | 98 |
| Watchdogs Closed* from May: | 90 |
| Watchdogs Still Pending from May: | 8 |
| Watchdogs Closed from Previous Months: | 12 |
| **Privacy Related Issues: | 98 |
|     Unable to Un-subscribe | 19 |
|     Received Spam | 41 |
|     Felt PII was Shared Improperly | 7 |
|     Felt Site was not Following Privacy Policy | 6 |
|     Needed to Change PII | 0 |
|     Wanted Account and/or PII Deleted | 23 |
|     Other Privacy Concerns | 2 |

**(The totals of the privacy categories adds up to 98, as 0 of the Watchdog complaints qualified for two or more of categories)

**FIGURE 11.14**

*A TRUSTe Watchdog Report.*

**FIGURE 11.15**

*The BBBOnline Privacy Seal.*

One of the aspects of the BBBOnline privacy program is that it has some global influence. BBBOnline participants, if they meet the requirements for the seal, are by default eligible to apply for the European Safe Harbor program. (For more information on the European Union's (EU) privacy regulations see Chapter 13.) Any company collecting and transferring personally identifiable information from European consumers, or its own European employees, to the United States via their Web site, must meet EU Data Directive requirements. The agreement between the United States and the European Union is called a Safe Harbor agreement.

BBBOnline also has a partnership with a similar Japanese organization. Their notice says

> The Privacy Program has also extended itself internationally in a first of its kind, partnership with the Japanese Privacy Seal authority (JIPDEC.) This partnership enables BBBOnLine Privacy Program participants to participate in the Japanese privacy seal program and vice versa. The partnership seal combines the BBBOnLine and JIPDEC seals to form a combined seal that is highly recognized in both countries.

Figure 11.16 shows the two corresponding seals for Japan and the United States.

**FIGURE 11.16**

*The BBBOnline and JIPDEC seals.*

## Is a Seal Enough?

While seals are good indicators that a merchant tells you what they do with your information, things can change. Companies that had a strong privacy policy and membership in a Web seal program can change their practices for several reasons. For example, the company might file for bankruptcy and sell its customer database. Another company might purchase the Web merchant, and that company might have a weak privacy policy. Don't forget law enforcement investigations; a company's data can be subpoenaed either for criminal or civil cases.

Recently, Amazon.com changed their privacy policy, and now tell you in advance that they might sell or give your information away in certain circumstances. The revised privacy policy is shown in Figure 11.17. Amazon.com sent a letter to all their customers when they changed their policy, and it raised a great deal of debate. Some people felt that Amazon.com, having promised in the past to use different practices, should be bound to those promises forever. Others felt that, like any other business, it could make changes in its business model if it so chose. Nonetheless, the fact that Amazon.com notified everyone whose information it held about the change, and in a clear, understandable way was well received.

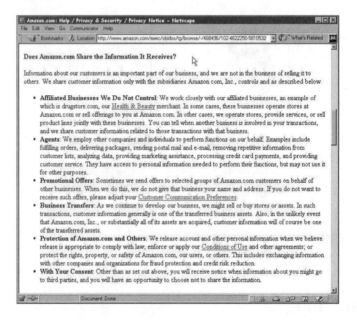

**FIGURE 11.17**

*When Amazon.com gives away your information.*

The bottom line is you have little control over the disposition of your customer data in these instances. Because of the uncertainties, you want to think about the sensitivity of the data that is being compiled about you when you shop online. Using the information in this book, and the privacy checklist in Appendix B, you can make your own decision about what is sensitive and what isn't.

# Practice Safe Shopping

You can take some action to prevent rip offs, identity theft, and annoying surprises. The following sections discuss some of these methods in addition to some pointers to further information.

## Never Give Out Your Social Security Number

An online merchant *does not* have a valid reason to have your Social Security number (SSN) for you to make a purchase. Some financial institutions may have valid reasons; research before you type that number in. Giving out your Social Security number is one of the easiest ways to help someone steal your identity. For more information on identity theft and others kinds of privacy compromise, see Chapter 12.

## Disclose Only the Bare Facts When You Order

At bare minimum, when placing an order, you need to give the merchant a shipping address, a credit card number, and enough billing information for them to verify that the name you are using is the name on the credit card. That's about it. Other questions, such as how much your household earns in a year, what kind of pets you have, or any other information, is used to target you for marketing—either spam, pop-up windows or banner advertising, or paper junk mail.

You don't have to answer any question not required to process your order. Often, the Web site marks which questions need to be answered with an asterisk (*). You can decide to leave the others blank. However, if a company says they "require" information you are not comfortable sharing, leave the site and go somewhere else. (You may also want to go and get rid of the cookies from that site, as discussed in Chapter 10.)

## Keep Your Password Private

If a Web site gives you the option of coming back and viewing orders or checking on shipping, they probably ask you to create an account on that system. This is a good idea. It keeps other people from seeing your information or stealing your payment info. Many times they enable you to select your own username and password. Pick a different password for your online Web site accounts than you use for your work computer or network login, or your home ISP account. The account sign-up process should also ask you for a question that should be answered to reset your password.

Although many guides advise against it, it's probably Okay to use the same password at several online sites, as long as you take care of that password. Face it, most people don't want to remember 10 to 20 passwords online, even if they can remember that many. To be extra careful, you might consider having one password for places that enable you to spend money, and another for sites where you just get personalized info or news.

The rules for an online password are the same as discussed in Chapter 10:

- Pick a complex password, not something in a dictionary.
- Never give your password to anyone.
- When selecting a password, do not use publicly known information, such as your address, birth date, dog's name, mother's maiden name, or your driver's license or Social Security Number.
- If this is your banking or brokerage account, you should not reuse the same password for other sites.

## Make Sure You Know Where You Are

If you have your browser configured to show it, a small window at the top of the screen has the Web site address (also called the URL, or Uniform Resource Locator). Figure 11.18 points out the address or location window. You should make sure you have that window showing. Check the address to see that you're on the Web site you think you are. Hackers may have gotten to the site, diverting you from the real site when you click the shopping link. Or, someone may have created a Web site that looks very much like the Web sites of well-known companies. When shoppers order on such a site, the crooks capture their credit card numbers and use them, either to buy things or to commit identity theft.

## Check the Return and Exchange Policies

Pat shops a lot with Plow and Hearth, both from the paper catalog and online. They are a reliable, reasonable company. However, despite the good relationship Pat and the company have, a glider she ordered this summer came with a cracked part. Even under the best of circumstances, occasionally you want to return something or get a replacement. *Before you buy,* look for the cancellation and return policies. Among these are

- Is there a time limit for returns?
- Who pays for shipping the item back?
- Is there a time limit on returns or cancellations?
- Is there a restocking fee if you return it?
- If you return it, do you get credit against other items in the catalog? If so, is there a time limit on the credit?
- If you ordered with a charge card, does the company refund that card or send you a check?
- How long does the refund take?

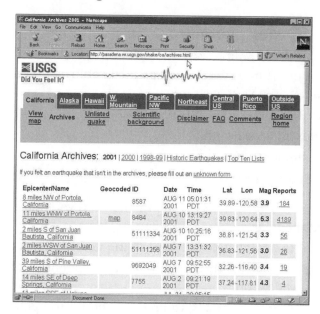

**FIGURE 11.18**

*The location window in a browser.*

## Find Out How to Get It Fixed or Serviced

In a physical store, you can stand at the returns counter and get eye-to-eye with the returns clerk or manager. You may overhear customer interactions. While you don't have that option for an online store, it doesn't mean you have no chance of good customer service. In an era where online companies are going out of business, one with good customer service has an edge over one whose customers are unhappy. Word of mouth works for online stores just as it does for physical stores.

Find out what the customer service mechanisms are—a hotline, e-mail, or a form? If you order some item that may need to be cleaned or serviced, this is really important (and you should have checked on it before you purchased). Other questions you should know the answer to are

- Is there local service for the item?
- Is there a warranty on the product, and who honors that guarantee?
- What are the limits, and under what circumstances can you exercise your warranty rights?

## Print Copies of Your Order *Every Time*

After placing an order online, you should receive a confirmation page that reviews your entire order. Like a printed confirmation at a physical store, it should at the very least show

- The items you ordered and their costs
- Any shipping fees or other fees
- Your customer information
- A confirmation number

Print this page out. If it's a new company for you, you should also consider printing the following:

- A copy of the catalog description of the item you ordered
- The contact page for the company—name, phone, physical address, and so on
- Any legal terms, including the return and refund policy

You should keep this information for at last the period covered by the return or the warranty on the item.

Frequently you get e-mail confirming the purchase. Save this message (print it out and file it with the pages listed earlier). If you have any other e-mail correspondence with the company, save and/or print that too.

**TIP** If you use Hotmail or Yahoo! Mail for your e-mail, save the e-mail to your local computer or print out a copy. Don't rely on saving it online at these mailers.

## Shop with Companies Located in the United States

In the United States, state and federal consumer laws cover you. Other countries may not have the same protection. For your strongest protection, only purchase online from companies located in the United States.

Buyers in other countries are protected by the U.S. laws, but find out if you can have the item shipped to you.

## When Will It Be Shipped?

Under U.S. law, a company must ship your order within the time stated in its ad or catalog. If they don't tell you when it ships, the merchant must ship the product within 30 days. If it is taking longer, or backordered, they must give you an "Option Notice." This gives you the choice of canceling the order and getting your money back promptly, or you can agree to the delay.

Your card should not be actually charged until the order is shipped. However, the money is reserved by the finance companies to verify funds are available. Partial orders means partial charges.

You should know these things about shipping before you order:

- Do you have choices for shipping?
- What are the shipping and handling fees, and are they reasonable?
- Who pays shipping?
- Are there restrictions on delivery based on geography, weight, or other considerations?
- Can you get shipping insurance?

## Don't Let Anyone Steal Your Good Name

Identity theft is what it sounds like—someone using your identity to get credit, get a job, or use your credentials. The easiest ways for thieves to get your identifying information are low-tech (dumpster diving, mail theft, or workplace access to SSNs, for example), but increasingly they can use the Web. For more information on identity theft see Chapter 12, "What Can I Do if My Privacy Is Compromised?"

# Safe Surfing

While shopping online, you might reveal or give away information in other places as well. The following sections discuss some rules for dealing with this.

## There Are No Free Lunches: Watch Out for Sites That Offer Rewards or Prizes if You Give Them Information

If you give away this information, you're probably giving it away not only to one promotion, but to a bunch of other marketing groups, as well. If the site has a privacy policy, it may well be so worded to promise nothing. If you're tempted to enter a sweepstakes or contest, think twice. The odds of you winning are terrible, and the real winners are the marketing folk who have your info.

## Configure Your Browser to Manage Cookies the Way You Want

Remember from Chapter 10 that most cookies are useful and innocuous. They may contain your passwords and user IDs, to make it more convenient for you (you won't have to keep retyping them every time you load a new page at the site.) Internet Explorer has a cookie management interface in addition to Netscape-like features. You can selectively enable or disable cookies on a site-by-site basis. You can even allow cookies for a site, but delete a specific cookie you are suspicious about. Figure 11.19 shows the control panel for cookies (select Tools, Internet Options, Security menu).

## Cookie Management Software

You can also use cookie management software and services. One example is the Internet Junkbuster Proxy (http://www.junkbusters.com/ht/en/ijb.html). It runs on Win95/98/NT and Unix (no Mac version), and can selectively block cookies and banner ads for you. According to the site's FAQs (Frequently Asked Questions), their product

> *"...is free privacy-enhancing software that can be run on your PC or by your ISP or company. It blocks requests for URLs (typically banner ads) that match its blockfile. It also deletes unauthorized cookies and other unwanted identi-*

*fying header information that is exchanged between Web servers and browsers. These headers are not normally accessible to users (even though they may contain information that's important to your privacy), but with the Internet Junkbuster you can see almost anything you want and control every-thing you're likely to need. **You** decide what's junk. Many people publish their blockfiles to help others get started. Guidescope maintains a proprietary central database available to users of its service."*

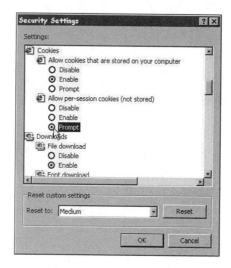

**FIGURE 11.19**

*Configuring Internet Explorer for cookies.*

Configuring the Junkbuster Proxy takes some understanding of how your computer works. Figure 11.20 shows the detailed instructions from Junkbusters on how to configure your browser (http://www.junkbusters.com/ht/en/ijbfaq.html#browser).

## Use a Mediator

Yet another option is to use an *infomediary* (some are home-use software products, others may be network-based services), such as SeigeSoft's SiegeSurfer (http://www.siegesurfer.com/).

SiegeSurfer takes control of your interaction with Internet sites to dis-guise who you are. According to their site, after you type the URL of the Web site you want to visit in the SiegeSurfer address box their software does the following:

1. The URL is scrambled (user controlled option) and sent out to the SiegeSurfer server. This scrambling masks your final surfing destination from your employer and/or ISP.

2. The SiegeSurfer server contacts the Web site you want to visit.

3. Data transfer between the Web site and the SiegeSurfer server begins.

4. Cookies, scripts, and so on are filtered out (user controlled option) by the SiegeSurfer server.

5. Cleansed data is encrypted so that it cannot be intercepted during transit.

6. This encrypted data is sent to your computer from the SiegeSurfer server.

7. In your browser, the data from the SiegeSurfer server is decrypted.

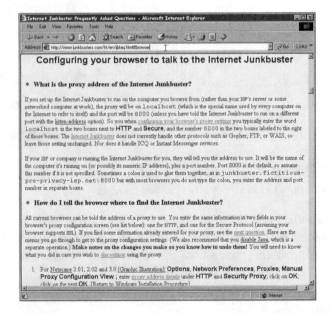

**FIGURE 11.20**

*Configuring a browser to use the Junkbuster Proxy.*

Zero Knowledge Systems' Freedom (http://www.freedom.net) system lets you create *nyms* or alternate identities under which to browse. Figure 11.21 shows a demo from the product Web site on how the product works.

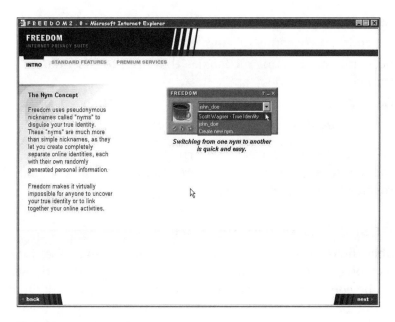

**FIGURE 11.21**

*The first step of the Freedom proxy.*

## Anonymizer

An Anonymizer hides your identity from the site you are visiting. Using the online anonymizer at http://www.anonymizer.com is discussed in Chapter 10.

Interestingly, in the wake of September 11, 2001, more anonymizing services are online. As of September 25, 2001, 37 anonymizing remailers were operating. Remailers are services which strip off all the identifying information from email messages and then send them to the recipient.

The Anonymizer service offered an anonymous gateway to the FBI's tip site for people with information concerning the attacks In addition, the remailer network was considered to be a safe vehicle for informants to provide information to the authorities.

## The Best Is Yet to Come...Unfortunately

The technology to manage cookies as much as you would like isn't here yet. The best would be fully configurable cookie management abilities built into browsers. Some useful configurations would be

- Accepting or rejecting cookies on a entire domain basis
- Accepting or rejecting all third-party cookies by default
- Accepting or rejecting all cookies that are not essential for the transaction at hand
- Getting a notice of exactly what a cookie is intended for
- Configuring default behaviors and cookie handling

As browsers evolve and privacy concerns become more apparent to the site owners and browser manufacturers, more improvements like those in Microsoft's IE 6 can be expected.

## Don't Let Personal Information Slip Out

Remember the discussion in Chapter 10 about knowing what information was stored on your machine and could be accessed by browsers? That can be controlled. One way is by creating a false identity to surf the Web. Figure 11.22 shows how to make up a new identity in Microsoft's Internet Explorer. (Under the Tools menu, choose Internet Options, Content. Under Personal Information choose My Profile.)

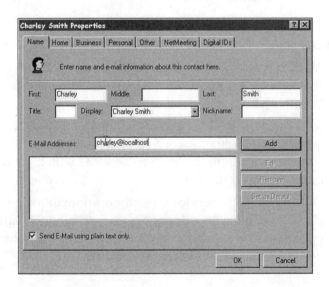

**FIGURE 11.22**

*Making up an online personality.*

However, let's take a close look at what else your browser stores and is willing to tell about you. The other tabs across this section are Home, Business, Personal, Other, Netmeeting, and Digital IDs. For example, under Business, you can put your place of business, Web site, phone number, and so on. Figure 11.23 shows one of Pat's business identities, as a partner in a music production company. Figure 11.24 shows some of what can be stored in the personal area.

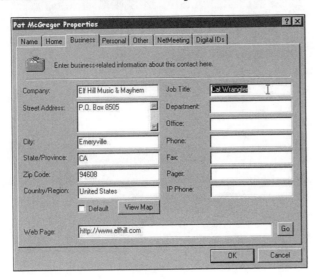

**FIGURE 11.23**

*The business profile in a browser*

Why would you want to have false information stored in your browser? To keep hostile scripts from getting it, of course. If you are at a site you trust, you can give them whatever info you choose by filling out a form—you don't need your browser to make those decisions for you.

# Using E-mail and Chatting Online Safely

In addition to the practices you can follow to protect yourself while surfing online, you can also do things to protect yourself when you use e-mail or chat online.

## Keep a "Clean" E-mail Address

If you've received spam or unwanted mail at your e-mail account, you understand why it might be nice to have an e-mail address that isn't a target for those things. To accomplish this, keep one side e-mail (one of the free e-mail addresses from Hotmail, Yahoo! or the like) to use on newsgroups, chat rooms, surveys, and other public spaces on the Net. If you have a Web page that mentions your e-mail address, use that side address on your page.

**FIGURE 11.24**

*Personal information stored in a browser*

Use your main or preferred address only on small, members-only lists and with known, trusted individuals. Your friends, boss, and so on know your "real" address. Use a "real" ISP or business e-mail for your main account, but be sure to check out their privacy policies and terms of service.

You may find it works best to use an e-mail package on your home machine (such as Eudora, Netscape, or Outlook) that enables you to create several personalities or user IDs and addresses. This makes it easier for you to manage e-mail even if you have several e-mail boxes.

Remember that e-mail addresses that are posted in public spaces can be easily discovered by automated collection agents and "harvested" by Spammers. E-mail addresses harvested in this way are not only used by the collector, but can be (and frequently are) sold to other prospective Spammers. If your public "throw away" address gets enough spam that it is useless, you can kill it off, and start a new one.

## Don't Be a Blabbermouth Until You Know to Whom You're Talking

Internet relationships develop like wildfire in most instances. Just a few conversations, and most people feel like the person on the other end of the line is a bosom buddy. But remember that you don't really know who the person on the other end is. You might think it's a fellow 18 year old, or another mom interested in home schooling, but it might be someone impersonating that identity.

Until you really know to whom you're talking, you might not want to reveal any of the following:

- Your full name
- Address
- Phone number
- Place of employment
- Credit card numbers
- Children's names, schools, and so on

If you have a personal Web site, you shouldn't put this information on it, either.

Be leery about face-to-face meetings. If you just can't wait to meet your online buddy, do it in a public place and take a friend. It might be perfectly harmless, but it might not.

Even if you are willing to share personal information with a Net friend, remember that if you share it on, say, a chat room or in a newsgroup, more than just your friend sees it. Remember that electrons are forever. The famous mandate for e-mail, which is pertinent in all forms of Internet interaction, is this: *If you don't want to see it on the front page of the Wall Street Journal (or on the community bulletin board at the local market), don't put it in e-mail!*

## Don't Reply to Spammers

Almost everybody is already tired of spam, or unsolicited commercial e-mail. According to BrightMail (`http://www.brightmail.com/index.html`), a spam prevention company, most spam attacks involve hundreds of thousands of e-mail addresses. Many of those addresses are bought from address harvesters or generated from e-mail-guessing programs. You've probably already gotten spam offering a million e-mail addresses on a CD for $59.95. A large number of these addresses are old, outdated, or just made up.

If you reply to the spam message, you are validating your e-mail address, which makes it worth a hundred times more than those random addresses on those lists. Generally no human reads them, even if they do say you can remove yourself from the list.

For this reason, too, you should also turn off your mailer's automatic honoring of return receipt requests, if any. (Look in the preferences or options). If your ISP is very responsive, you may be able to forward copies of spam to them and they send a complaint to the ISP of the spammer. For more info on fighting junk e-mail, see the Junkbusters Web site at `http://www.junkbusters.com/junkemail.html`. Figure 11.24 shows the Junkbuster's main anti-junkmail page.

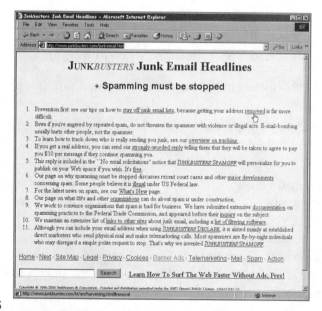

**FIGURE 11.25**

*Junkbusters tell you how to fight spam.*

# Remember: You Can Stay in Control

This section of the book is all about how to stay in control of your personal information. If you make educated choices about what information you want to share, you can navigate the Internet and take advantage of its resources with only a little bit of paranoia to protect you.

# WHAT CAN I DO IF MY PRIVACY IS COMPROMISED?

In this chapter, we discuss things that can be done to improve your personal privacy, even if information about you has already escaped your control. None of these techniques is perfect. Performing these actions *after* you are already annoyed or hurt is much less effective than taking the actions mentioned in Chapter 11, "How to Secure Your Internet Transactions," *before* you are injured.

We start with simple privacy invasions, more like nuisances, and go on to more critical instances of compromising your privacy. Our aim is to make you aware of some simple steps you can take to protect yourself.

## Telephone and Similar Listings

Received too many telemarketing calls and unsolicited e-mail messages? Sometimes you can prevent these calls by unlisting yourself. You probably know that you can get an unlisted telephone number. Some local telephone service providers charge an extra fee for this service. Consider changing your number and having the new one be not listed in public directories.

Remember that you need to tell your friends and colleagues your new number. If you still use printed checks (rather than using online banking, PayPal (www.paypal.com), debit or smart card transactions, and so on), you might consider not reprinting your checks with your new number on them. Of course, if you don't tell the people with whom you do business how to get hold of you, they may not be able to reach you with information you want to know.

Change your information in the publicly available people directories available online. Many of the services we cited in Chapter 9, "Taking an Inventory of Your Personal Information," enable you to update your information. You can choose to delete some or all the information available. Unfortunately, you have to seek out each occurrence of your information because there is not a central directory or even a central directory of directories.

Currency, as well as accuracy, in these sites can be a problem, too. Many of the online directories don't provide information about their update cycles in a place where you can easily find it. In some cases, the information displayed is based on the update cycles of the printed telephone directories, which are only changed once a year. This is why, when we searched for information about Glee online, we could find her address and telephone number in Washington, D.C., even though she no longer maintains that telephone number and address.

The following are some of the more popular people search sites where you can control the information presented about you:

- Switchboard (http://www.switchboard.com)
- WhitePages.com (http://www.whitepages.com)
- AOL White Pages (http://www.aol.com/netfind/whitepages.adp)
- Verizon's SuperPages.com (http://www.superpages.com)
- Smartpages.com (http://www.smartpages.com)

These are the ones that don't provide an update link:

- AnyWho (http://www.anywho.com)
- Infousa.com (http://www.infousa.com)
- WhoWhere (http://www.whowhere.com)
- WorldPages (http://www.worldpages.com/whitepages)
- Yahoo People Search (http://people.yahoo.com)

# Toss the Spam

E-mail marketing can be a very effective means to grow and maintain a business. Building a mailing list of customers and using that list to inform them of special opportunities is relatively inexpensive and provides good return.

Unfortunately, some marketers don't want to wait for you to give them your e-mail address and they find it some other way. Then you get e-mail from them with a message suggesting that you invest in their idea, buy their product, or something. Sometimes you can't even tell what the e-mail is about. That's *spam*, a name used to describe unsolicited commercial e-mail, even though it's a respected trademark of Hormel, the meat packing people. Actually, the e-mail could be noncommercial, too, but usually it's from someone who wants to help you spend your money. As a result, your mailbox gets filled with e-mail like the one shown in Figure 12.1.

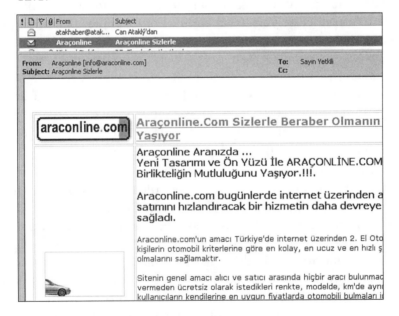

**FIGURE 12.1**

*Spam (we think) in Turkish.*

When your e-mail address is on a mailing list, that list is sold or traded and the use of your address spreads. So, what do you do?

The first rule of spam-handling is *do not reply*. Resist the temptation to "Remove your name from our list." Avoid sending them a nasty-gram. Replying confirms to the sender that the address used is a viable e-mail address. You don't want to do that because you are just sent more unsolicited e-mail.

The second rule of spam-handling is *do not buy* the product. No matter how good the deal seems, your purchase not only moves money from you to the sender, it encourages them. Now they know that sending spam works, and that sending spam to you works really well. They have information about what you like and where you are and what your e-mail address is. You have become a customer. You get more and more e-mail. If people receiving unsolicited e-mail never replied or bought any of the offered deals, the senders would stop because there would be no reason to send it.

Consult the information presented by your Internet access or service provider. Their services might include one that tosses e-mail from known mass-mailers before you download it. For example, Earthlink provides the Spaminator, shown in Figure 12.2, and AT&T WorldNet provides a service called E-mail Screener. The Web-based e-mail service Hotmail (www.hotmail.com) provides a junk mail screener also. AT&T's E-mail Screener program from Brightmail (www.brightmail.com) analyzes the e-mail and filters out known spam as well as viruses transmitted via e-mail. If your provider offers such a system, turn it on and you receive fewer unwanted e-mails.

If your service provider doesn't operate a mail filtering service, you might consider using your mail client's filter rules to set a filter up for yourself. Figure 12.3 shows a simple filter setup in Eudora 5.1. This filter moves all e-mail not directly addressed to Glee's account to the trash folder. If you use this type of filter, you need to remember to run it *after* you run filters that move e-mail addresses to mailing lists to other folders. Otherwise, your mailing list e-mail is tossed out. Messages moved to trash should be checked before you exit the program until you learn whether the filter is working the way you want it to.

**FIGURE 12.2**

*The log-in screen to Earthlink's Spaminator service.*

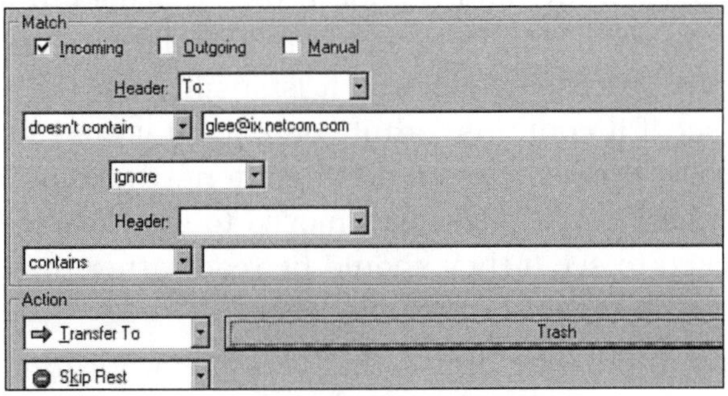

**FIGURE 12.3**

*Filter in Eudora 5.1.*

Figure 12.4 shows a similar filter set up in Netscape 6.1's e-mail client. This one moves all e-mail where the "To:" field does not contain bhcady and moves it to the local folder called trash. The name of the filter is "junk." Again, if you run this filter, all e-mail sent to mailing lists is moved to the trash folder, so you want to make a filter to handle those e-mail messages before this filter is run. Messages moved to the trash should be checked before you exit the program until you learn whether the filter is working the way you want it to.

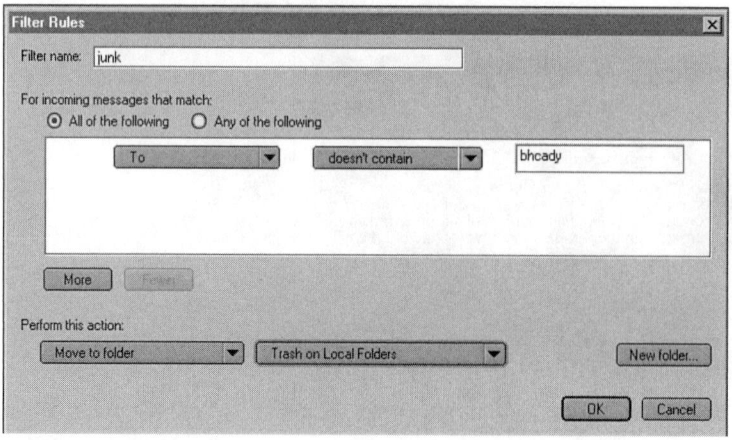

**FIGURE 12.4**

*Filter in Netscape 6.1 e-mail.*

Figure 12.5 shows a more complex filter set up in Outlook 2002. This one first checks to see if my name is not in the "To:" field. If it isn't, the e-mail is checked to see if it is from suspected senders of junk. If it is not suspicious, the rule processing stops. If it is suspicious, the e-mail is then checked to see if it contains "adult content." If it does not, rule processing is stopped. If it does contain adult content, the e-mail is moved to a folder called "junk mail." Messages moved to the junk mail folder can later be checked to see if they should be read rather than deleted. Or you can just delete them without reading them.

Eudora 5.1 has an interesting option that you may want to investigate: *MoodWatch*. Figure 12.6 shows the settings dialog box for this feature. Turning it on enables a scan of message content for "offensive" material. If a message contains a word deemed offensive, an appropriate number of hot chili peppers appear in the message detail menu, warning you before you open the message. In testing this feature, we found that mild expletives are not warned against, but the usual ones in English that denote excrement and sexual activities seem to be caught. As we have configured it here in this illustration, Eudora also warns you if you attempt to send a message with potentially offensive material in it. This might be handy if you are inclined to send messages before thinking. <grin>

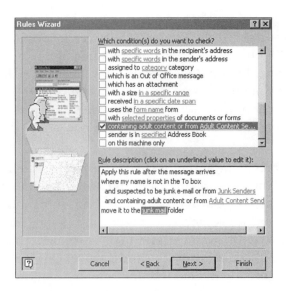

**FIGURE 12.5**

*A complex filter in Outlook 2002.*

**FIGURE 12.6**

*Eudora 5.1's MoodWatch setting.*

# But Don't Toss the Privacy Notices

By July of 2001, the financial institutions with which you do business were required by U.S. Federal law (see Chapter 18, "Can You Really Be

Anonymous?") to send you a notice about your privacy rights and choices. The Congress passed the Financial Services Modernization Act, giving banks the ability to diversify (own more kinds of businesses) than was previously possible. In addition, because the Congress believed that financial privacy is an important shared value in the United States, and that it deserves protection, they addressed the sharing of personal financial information among these companies that are now enabled to work together.

The law gave the enforcement of the privacy protection to the Federal Trade Commission, which then made rules that now apply. One part of the rule said that financial institutions (now defined as organizations that lend, safeguard, exchange, manage, and insure money for consumers or their representatives) must give their customers the ability to say "Do not share my information" with third parties. Of course, there are exceptions to this broad statement of the rule, but mainly banks and their affiliates—credit card companies, insurance companies, mortgage lenders—now need to send you a privacy notice and tell you how to communicate your wishes to them.

The financial organizations also must now tell us what type of protection they are providing for our information and our assets. This enables us to make better decisions about which organizations to trust with our financial transactions.

The good news is that there are now rules. The bad news is that we have to tell the organizations, one by one, for each account, what we want. Even more bad news comes from the fact that the privacy rules don't really apply if you are moving information from one part of an organization to another. That type of information movement is permitted without your choice.

In the United States, any time you get a complex rule, you get complex responses, and many of us were lazy and didn't read the long notices sent to us. Thus, information about us is probably now being exchanged among people we don't know.

We can stop *some* of the information trading. If you want to do so, you need to send a notice to the organizations with whom you have accounts. If you have more than one account with a single institution, you can notify them of your choice with only one notice. If you share an account, you probably want to provide a notice from each person on the account.

You have to use the organization's specified procedure and send the notice to a specific address.

If you haven't already notified your financial institutions of your wishes, they have probably already shared your personal financial information. There is no specific time for you to notify them of your wishes. You can wait until the next year's annual notice and follow the instructions then, or you can take action now. However, after information has been shared (like your name and address being added to a mailing list), that information cannot be recalled.

To notify your financial institutions now, you need to gather information about each of your accounts. If you tossed your privacy notice, visit http://www.junkbusters.com/optout.html, the Junkbuster's Opt Out page. Here you may find the appropriate address for your financial institutions and a letter that you can modify and print out and mail. The letter instructs the institution to not release information about you to third parties. You can, of course, write your own letter. However, look at the letter prepared (and copyrighted) by Junkbusters with additional credit to the Privacy Rights Clearinghouse. The letter covers the points necessary under the appropriate laws and extends them to information sharing not covered by Gramm-Leach-Bliley. It probably doesn't hurt to ask. An alternative to the Junkbusters page is a well-organized page at the Privacy Rights Clearinghouse site: http://www.privacyrights.org/fs/ fs24a-OptOutAddresses.htm. Here you can not only find the addresses of your financial institutions, but the Clearinghouse tells you which organizations provide additional choices other than those required by the Gramm-Leach-Bliley law.

As we have mentioned elsewhere, credit reporting agencies maintain financial histories about your payment histories and so on. When your credit is "checked," it is with these agencies. Your credit report is a picture of when you pay (on time, in full, slow, partial) for all the accounts that you hold. Although the agencies are not enabled to sell information from the credit histories themselves, they do develop information products that include name, address, Social Security Number, previous addresses, telephone numbers, and birth date. This *directory* or *credit header* information is frequently used for direct marketing. You can call 1-888-5-OPT-OUT (888-567-8688) to tell all three of the credit reporting agencies that you do not want to have your information appear on any of their lists. The result should be that you no longer receive "pre-approved" offers of credit.

# Buying Items that Don't Exist and Similar Mistakes

We all like bargains. We've heard that there are great bargains on the Internet. So, we go looking for those bargains. Sometimes we find them; other times we don't. When the product isn't delivered or doesn't match the specifications, and we can't get our money back, we've joined the victims of fraud.

Technology helps the defrauders as much as it helps legitimate businesses. It can make it easy for the fraudulent to separate us from our money. Fraudulent businesses can look like legitimate businesses quite easily. The National Fraud Information Center (NFIC), a project of the National Consumers League, reports that in the year 2000, 82% of the reported Internet fraud came from contacts initiated through Web sites. This means that people visited a Web site and were taken in by the information presented there. It also means that, according to these reported statistics, most of the fraud was not initiated by an invasion of privacy.

Table 12.1 shows the Internet Fraud Statistics from the NFIC.

### TABLE 12.1   INTERNET FRAUD STATISTICS

| Top 10 Frauds in 1999 | Top 10 Frauds in 2000 |
| --- | --- |
| Online Auctions 87% | Online Auctions 78% |
| General Merchandise Sales 7% | General Merchandise Sales 10% |
| Internet Access Services 2% | Internet Access Services 3% |
| Computer Equipment/Soft. 1% | Work-At-Home 3% |
| Work-At-Home 1% | Advance Fee Loans 2% |
| Advance Fee Loans .2% | Computer Equipment/Soft. 1% |
| Magazine Sales .2% | Nigerian Money Offers 1% |
| Information Adult Services .2% | Information Adult Services 1% |
| Travel/Vacations .1% | Credit Card Offers .5% |
| Multilevel Market/Pyramid .1% | Travel/Vacations .5% |

*(Source: National Fraud Information Center* http://www.fraud.org*)*

You can see that online auctions remain the largest troublemakers. The large online auction "houses" such as eBay and Amazon.com Auctions provide guarantees that make purchasing via their services safer. These organizations have procedures to follow when you believe you have been defrauded. The procedures start with communicating with the seller. Perhaps there has been a misunderstanding. If you can't resolve your dispute with the seller, you can file claims against the seller. The first part of the eBay Fraud Reporting Form is shown in Figure 12.7. The first part of the Amazon.com A-to-Z Guarantee Claim Form is shown in Figure 12.8. Both of these forms provide help and expertise in resolving disputes.

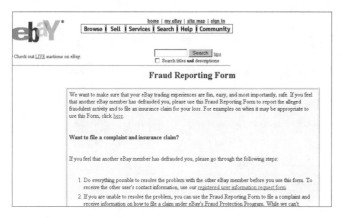

**FIGURE 12.7**

*The eBay Fraud Reporting Form.*

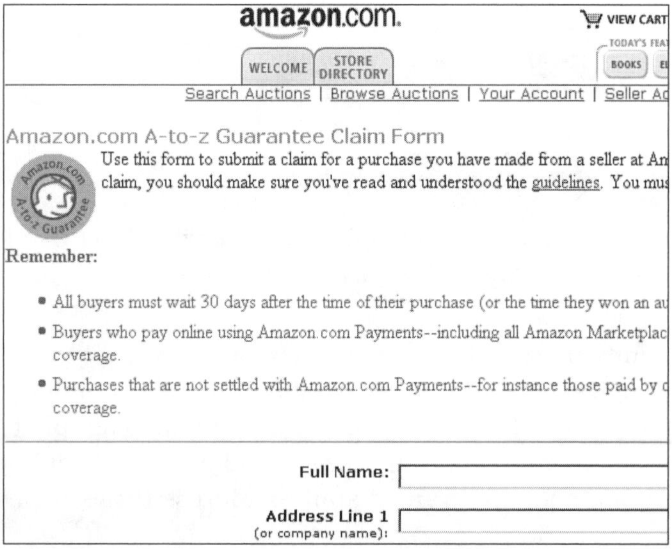

**FIGURE 12.8**

*The Amazon.com A-to-Z Guarantee Claim Form.*

Similar statistics are available from the Internet Fraud Complaint Center, a joint operation of the U.S. Federal Bureau of Investigation (FBI) and the National White Collar Crime Center, at `http://www.ifccfbi.gov/strategy/statistics.asp`. Their Web site is illustrated in Figure 12.9. The statistics reported there show that the highest dollar amounts of fraud are in securities fraud, the largest number of frauds are perpetrated in auctions, and the largest number of fraud perpetrators are individuals rather than businesses.

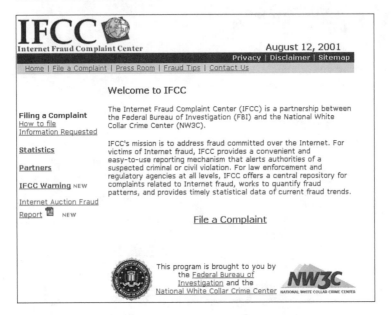

**FIGURE 12.9**

*The Internet Fraud Complaint Center Web site.*

Sellers, too, need to be protected from people who don't pay for the merchandise received. eBay and Amazon.com also provide protections for sellers.

The community marketplace is one where all parties need to feel and be safe for the marketplace to be successful. Moreover, auction houses fight against other kinds of auction fraud: people bidding simply to raise the bid, people selling items that are illegal, and so on. The online marketplaces maintain specially trained staff to address these issues.

## Dealing with Fraud

If you have been defrauded, the following are some steps you should take to try to set the matter right.

- **Contact the other party**—First, try to resolve your dispute directly.
- **Contact the service provider**—If the transaction took place in a supported marketplace, such as Amazon.com or eBay, follow the dispute resolution processes posted on their Web sites. The support personnel of these sites help you.
- **Report the fraud to the National Fraud Information Center**—You can report via telephone to 1-800-876-7060. You can also fill out the Online Incident Report Form shown in Figure 12.10 at `http://www.fraud.org`.

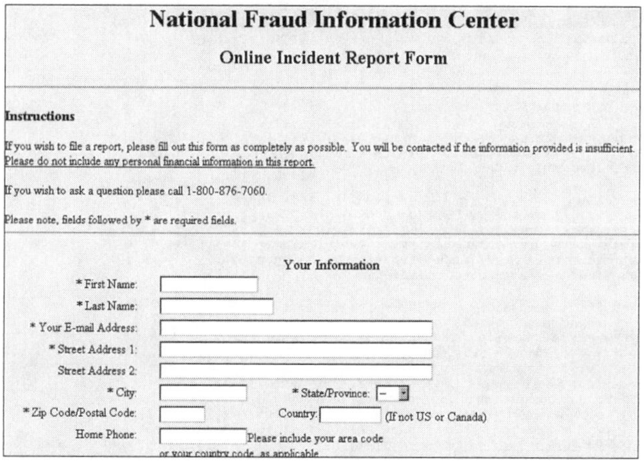
National Fraud Information Center

Online Incident Report Form

**Instructions**

If you wish to file a report, please fill out this form as completely as possible. You will be contacted if the information provided is insufficient. Please do not include any personal financial information in this report.

If you wish to ask a question please call 1-800-876-7060.

Please note, fields followed by * are required fields.

Your Information

* First Name:
* Last Name:
* Your E-mail Address:
* Street Address 1:
Street Address 2:
* City: * State/Province: --
* Zip Code/Postal Code: Country: (If not US or Canada)
Home Phone: Please include your area code or your country code, as applicable

**FIGURE 12.10**

*The NFIC Fraud Report Form page.*

- **Report the fraud to the Federal Trade Commission (FTC)**—The Consumer Response Center can be reached at 1-877-FTC-HELP (382-4357) or via their Consumer Complaint Form shown in Figure 12.11. The FTC collects the information into a secure database that law enforcement may access. Fraud investigations may lead to law enforcement actions, but the FTC does not resolve individual consumer disputes.

**FIGURE 12.11**

*The FTC Consumer Complaint Form page.*

- **Report the fraud to the Internet Fraud Complaint Center (IFCC) at** `http://www.ifccfbi.gov/cf1.asp`—Figure 12.12 shows the IFCC Complaint Center page.

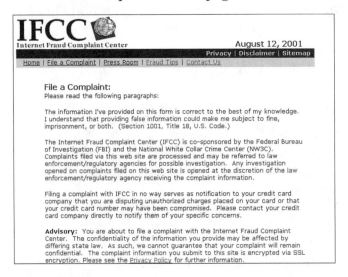

**FIGURE 12.12**

*The IFCC Complaint Center page.*

- **Report the activities of the person or business that you believe defrauded you to the appropriate authorities in their state of operation**—If you can determine the location of the defrauder), you can check for Consumer Affairs and similar offices in the appropriate state. If the perpetrator is operating outside the United States, you may have had a learning experience. Cross-border fraud is difficult to combat.

# Other Types of Cybercrime

The United States Department of Justice provides a Cybercrime Web site at `http://cybercrime.gov`. It includes the lists of crimes and agencies to which they should be reported, as shown in Table 12.2. Many of these crimes are more likely to be perpetrated against businesses than they are against individual consumers, but the information remains useful.

The legal term *nexus* is used to describe the causal connection between two actions, events, or people; that is, a particular action caused a particular result. In taxation discussions, you may hear it used to describe whether an agency can tax a particular company or transaction. This has led people to use the term when they are really trying to describe which law enforcement agency, court, or government has jurisdiction for a specific instance. Legal jurisdiction for crimes committed via the Internet remains an issue not yet consistently settled in the courts, but certain agencies have developed expertise in dealing with certain types of crimes. This table reflects that expertise.

## TABLE 12.2 CRIMES AND WHERE TO REPORT THEM

| Type of Crime | Appropriate Federal Investigative Law Enforcement Agencies |
| --- | --- |
| Computer intrusion (or hacking) | FBI local office; NIPC (202-323-3205); U.S. Secret Service local office |
| Password trafficking | FBI local office; NIPC (202-323-3205); U.S. Secret Service local office |
| Copyright (software, movie, sound recording) piracy | FBI local office; if imported, U.S. Customs Service local office (800-BE-ALERT, or 800-232-2538) |
| Theft of trade secrets | FBI local office |
| Trademark counterfeiting | FBI local office; if imported, U.S. Customs Service local office (800-BE-ALERT, or 800-232-2538) |
| Counterfeiting of currency | U.S. Secret Service local office; FBI local office |
| Child Pornography or Exploitation | FBI local office; if imported, U.S. Customs Service local office (800-BE-ALERT, or 800-232-2538) |
| Child Exploitation and Internet Fraud matters that have a mail nexus | U.S. Postal Inspection local office |

**TABLE 12.2    CONTINUED**

| Type of Crime | Appropriate Federal Investigative Law Enforcement Agencies |
| --- | --- |
| Internet fraud | The Internet Fraud Complaint Center; FBI local office; U.S. Secret Service local office; Federal Trade Commission; if securities fraud, Securities and Exchange Commission |
| Internet harassment | FBI local office |
| Internet bomb threats | FBI local office; ATF local office |
| Trafficking in explosive or incendiary devices or firearms over the Internet | FBI local office; ATF local office |

(*Source:* http://www.cybercrime.gov/reporting.htm)

# Stalking

Someone watching where you go online is a form of stalking. In cases where the goal is to discover your likes and dislikes so that you can be shown advertisements more relevant to your preferences, watching where you go might (if we really stretch) be considered service.

Enabling the tracking of people's activities in the physical world, however, is really scary. Sometimes information that was gained online has been used in the physical world to cause real harm. Amy Boyer was one such case. She was stalked and killed by an obsessive admirer who had been openly following her for two and a half years. We say openly because he had published a Web site that detailed his thoughts and his obsession. He used one of the for-fee information services to trace her Social Security number and her place of work. (Although we don't believe a direct relationship between having that information and his actions has been established. He had definitely been waiting outside her home and following her for some time. Following her likely provided the information about her place of work. Certainly, however, the ease with which he obtained the information is scary.) He waited for her after work. He shot and killed her. He shot himself.

The crime and the perpetrator were clear. The connection between the perpetrator and the victim was not so clear. Why Amy? Why this young man? Why had no one reported the site? And the question for us all: What part did the Internet play in this crime?

A young man with a gun killed Amy Boyer, not the Internet. However, just as the car he drove to the murder site was a tool, so was the information he found. New Hampshire Senator Judd Gregg introduced a controversial bill forbidding the sale of Social Security numbers over the Internet. It was defeated. The law, according to those who opposed it, would have protected information brokers without protecting privacy. Given that Amy Boyer's death was tragic, why would anyone oppose such a law? A coalition of organizations who strongly believe in individual privacy did just that. The coalition of the American Civil Liberties Union, Consumer Action, Consumer Federation of America, Consumers Union, Electronic Privacy Information Center, Identity Theft Resource Center, National Consumers League, Privacy Journal, Privacy Times, The Named, and the U.S. Public Interest Research Group opposed the law because it was "riddled with loopholes." You can read their letter urging the bill's defeat on the Web at `http://www.pirg.org/consumer/greggssn3.htm`.

Each state has an anti-stalking law, prompted by the California law enacted after an actress was a stalking and murder victim. In California there are both civil and criminal penalties for stalking. This means that, as a stalking victim, you can sue your stalker, as well as have the stalker prosecuted criminally. You can also ask that your motor vehicle registration and license information not be released except to a short list of specific functionaries. Stalking victims need to be especially careful of releasing personal information. Following the suggestions here, the ones at the National Center for Victims of Crimes' Stalking Resource Center at `http://www.ncvc.org/SRC.htm`, and telling others not to release information about you are the minimum steps you need to take to protect yourself.

There are many legitimate uses of information concerning you: making sure you are credit worthy, checking to make sure you are who you say, and so on. So far, those legitimate uses are still deemed more of a benefit than the detriment of providing information to the wrong person. Mistakes can be costly. In Amy Boyer's case, information to the wrong person may have cost her life.

# I Am Not Me: Identity Theft

Other than the physical danger that can come from stalking, the most danger we can encounter in cyberspace is people using our credentials: identity theft.

Identity theft is a silent crime. You don't know it's happening to you. A thief obtains your Social Security number, your checking account number, a credit card number, and/or your driver's license. He uses that information to open a new account or changes the address on a current account and then adds charges to the accounts and does not pay the bills. It may take you some time to find out what has happened.

Your first clue may be when a store at which you've shopped for years refuses to take your check. You may find that checks for which you knew there was money in your checking account are returned. You may get calls from credit agencies with whom you didn't know you had an account.

Not all identity theft takes place with information obtained online. Thieves can take advantage of our trust in a lot of ways. Perhaps you lost your wallet. Perhaps your handbag was stolen. Those instances would make you wary. You could expect that unusual activities might show up on your records and you'd be looking for them.

In one case we know of, the victim wasn't so lucky. He had no warning that his identity had been stolen. He mailed his mortgage statement along with a check for the payment. The envelope was stolen before it was picked up by the postal carrier. The checking account number and the name and account number on the mortgage statement were more than enough information for the thief to open new accounts in the victim's name, but with an entirely different address, a fake address located in another state. Several of the new accounts were checking accounts and the thief was able to write checks from one credit card account to deposit in a checking account, writing a check on that account to deposit in another, creating the appearance of money where there was none.

It wasn't until the wildly unusual activity was noticed by one of the credit card issuers, that the victim was aware that anything at all was wrong. It took some time to trace what had happened. The victim's credit record is now trashed; full of asterisks noting which accounts were real and which were not. It takes a long time to find and erase all the fraudulent accounts. It takes even longer for the victim to begin to feel safe again.

Other people have not found out they've been victimized until they applied for a mortgage or were turned down for a job. Obviously, you can't fix something that you don't know has happened. So, the following are some hints to protect yourself, courtesy of the United States Federal Trade Commission:

1. Understand why your personal information is needed and how it will be used before you release it. Ask if you can keep it confidential.

2. Be wary of late or missing bills from your financial services providers. A missing bill could mean that someone has re-routed your bills to another address.

3. Guard your mail: Use only post office collection boxes. Don't leave your mail in your mailbox for others to find. Ask the postal service to hold your mail if you are going to be away.

4. Put passwords on your accounts. Choose non-guessable combinations of letters and numbers.

5. Don't carry more identification and credit cards than you need.

6. Don't give out personal information on the phone, over the Internet, or through the mail unless you have initiated the contact. Thieves plausibly pose as trusted officers in order to get your information. No legitimate organization will ask for your personal information to be sent unless you initiate the transaction.

7. Take care with your information, even at home. Shred account information you don't need. Password protect information on your computer.

8. Understand how your personal information is protected in your place of employment. Verify that your records are secure.

9. Give out your Social Security number only when absolutely necessary. Don't carry it with you; keep it in a secure place.

10. Check your credit report annually with each of the three major credit agencies. Make sure the reports are accurate and include what you expect. You legally may be charged up to $8.50 for a copy of your report, but many financial services providers will offer you a report as part of your business with them.

# But I Really Didn't Do That

If you are a victim of identity theft, you need to do several things to regain your good record. Remember, it isn't possible to do this quickly. These instructions come from the Federal Trade Commission and Privacy Rights Clearinghouse, both excellent sources of information. Check their Web sites for additional instructions. See `http://www.consumer.gov/idtheft/victim.htm` and `http://www.privacyrights.org`.

1. At the fraud departments of each of the three major credit bureaus, ask that a "fraud alert" be placed in your file. Have them add a statement asking that creditors call you before opening any new accounts or changing your existing ones.

| *Credit Bureaus* | *Equifax* | *Experian* | *Trans Union* |
|---|---|---|---|
| *Address* | P.O. Box 740241 Atlanta, GA 30374-0241 | P.O. Box 2104 Allen, TX 75013 | 760 Sproul Road P.O. Box 390 Springfield, PA 19064-0390 |
| *Order Credit Report* | 1-800-685-1111 | 1-888-EXPERIAN (397-3742) | 1-800-916-8800 |
| *Report Fraud* | 1-800-525-6285 | 1-888-EXPERIAN | 1-800-680-7289 |
| *Web Address* | `http://www.equifax.com` | `http://www.experian.com` | `http://www.tuc.com` |

Carefully review copies of your credit reports and follow up with a letter detailing the information you believe is inaccurate. Ask for the deletion of "inquiries" from the company or companies where fraudulent accounts were opened. Check the credit reports again in a few months to see if the appropriate corrections were made and that no additional fraudulent accounts have been opened.

2. Contact your financial service providers to cancel any accounts that have been tampered with or opened fraudulently. If appropriate, open new ones with passwords and new personal identification numbers (PINs). Speak to someone in the security or fraud department and have them note on your records that you have been a victim of fraud. Then, to safeguard your rights as specified by law (the Fair Credit Billing Act), follow up with a letter explaining the situation.

3. File a report with the local police or the police in the community where the identity theft took place. Get a case number and record it. Keep a copy for your files.

4. If an identity thief has stolen information from your mail or falsi-fied change-of-address forms, file a report with your local postal inspector.

5. Notify your bank. Stop payment on stolen or misused checks. Either call the major check verification companies or have your bank notify the one they use.
   - National Check Fraud Service: 1-843-571-2143
   - SCAN: 1-800-262-7771
   - TeleCheck: 1-800-710-9898 or 927-0188
   - CrossCheck: 1-707-586-0551
   - Equifax Check Systems: 1-800-437-5120
   - International Check Services: 1-800-526-5380

   If your ATM card has been lost, stolen, or otherwise compromised, cancel the card as soon as you can and get another with a new PIN.

6. If you believe that an identity thief has tampered with your securi-ties investments or a brokerage account, immediately report it to your broker or account manager and to the Securities and Exchange Commission.

7. If an identity thief has established new phone service in your name; is making unauthorized calls that seem to come from—and are billed to—your cellular phone; or is using your calling card and PIN, contact your service provider immediately to cancel the account and/or calling card. Open new accounts and choose new PINs.

8. If you are having trouble getting fraudulent phone charges removed from your account, contact your state Public Utility Commission for local service providers or the Federal Communications Commission for long-distance service providers and cellular providers at `http://www.fcc.gov/cib/ccformpage.html` or 1-888-CALL-FCC.

9. If you believe someone is using your Social Security Number to apply for a job or to work, that's a crime. Report it to the Social Security Administration's Fraud Hotline at 1-800-269-0271. Also call Administration at 1-800-772-1213 to verify the accuracy of the earnings reported on your Social Security number, and to request a copy of your Social Security statement. Follow up your calls in writing.

10. If you suspect that your name or Social Security Number is being used by an identity thief to get a driver's license or a non-driver's ID card, contact your Department of Motor Vehicles. If your state uses your Social Security number as your driver's license number, ask to substitute another number.

11. If you believe someone has filed for bankruptcy using your name, write to the U.S. Trustee in the region where the bankruptcy was filed. A listing of the U.S. Trustee Program's regions can be found at `http://www.usdoj.gov/ust`, or look in the blue pages of your phone book under U.S. Government—Bankruptcy Administration.

    Your letter should describe the situation and provide proof of your identity. The U.S. Trustee, if appropriate, will make a referral to criminal law enforcement authorities if you provide appropriate documentation to substantiate your claim. You also may want to file a complaint with the U.S. Attorney and/or the FBI in the city where the bankruptcy was filed.

12. An identity thief may create a criminal record under your name. For example, your imposter may give your name when being arrested. If this happens to you, you may need to hire an attorney to help resolve the problem. The procedures for clearing your name vary by jurisdiction. Ask the court, the police, or the FBI what you should do to clear your name.

    If a civil judgment has been entered against your name being used by an imposter, contact the court where the judgment was entered and tell the court that you are the victim of identity theft.

13. Notify the United States Passport Office that someone might try to obtain a passport in your name.

## Invasions Can Be Harmful to Your Health

Be aware that Identity theft, although not physically harmful, is a very invasive crime. As is the case with a criminal invasion of your home or office, victims rightly feel violated. If you are a victim, make sure you get the kind of support you need to take effective action. Unfortunately, when thieves take your identity, you are the one who must cope.

It is much easier to prevent identity theft than it is to recover from it. Follow the previous outline to best protect you, your family, and your identity.

- Be vigilant
- Keep control of your information
- Check your credit reports and monthly bills
- Take action promptly if you suspect a problem

## Personally Identifiable Information

What information am I being asked to give?

- Name
- Street address
- ZIP+four code in the United States
- Social Security number or other government-issued identification number
- Phone number
- Credit card number

What demographic data is being gathered?

- Age
- Gender
- Marital status
- Employment status
- Occupation
- Job function
- Children, how many, and their ages
- Yearly income for me, my spouse, and/or my household

## Notice

- Does this site have a privacy policy?
- Does the privacy policy tell me how they will use my information?
- Does it tell me what my options are if I do not give them my information?
- Will my information be shared with anyone else?
- Will my information be kept forever, or will it be discarded at some point?

## Choice

- Do I have a choice about sharing my information?
- Does the privacy policy or instruction for the site tell me what will happen if I do *not* share my information?
- Does the privacy policy tell me how to communicate with the site owners if I change my mind?

## Access

- Does the privacy policy or instruction tell me how to see what information is being held about me?
- Does the policy tell me how to make changes to that information?

## Security

- Does this site have a page explaining how they protect my information?
- If I am filling out a form with personally identifiable information, does SSL or other security protect that page? (Is the key or lock symbol glowing or dark, or is the lock icon open or closed?)
- When I display my profile or billing information, is my entire credit card number printed out, or just the last four or five digits (better)?
- Do I have to re-enter my billing information every time, or is it stored away?
- If I forget my password, how do I get back in?

# PART IV

## WHAT YOU NEED TO KNOW ABOUT LEGAL PROTECTIONS FOR PRIVACY

*Global computer-based communications cut across territorial borders, creating a new realm of human activity and undermining the feasibility—and legitimacy—of applying laws based on geographic boundaries. While these electronic communications play havoc with geographic boundaries, a new boundary, made up of the screens and passwords that separate the virtual world from the "real world" of atoms, emerges. This new boundary defines a distinct Cyberspace that needs and can create new law and legal institutions of its own.*

*Territorially-based law-making and law-enforcing authorities find this new environment deeply threatening. But established territorial authorities may yet learn to defer to the self-regulatory efforts of Cyberspace participants who care most deeply about this new digital trade in ideas, information, and services. Separated from doctrine tied to territorial jurisdictions, new rules will emerge, in a variety of online spaces, to govern a wide range of new phenomena that have no clear parallel in the nonvirtual world. These new rules will play the role of law by defining legal personhood and property, resolving disputes, and crystallizing a collective conversation about core values.*

*David R. Johnson and David G. Post*
*Law And Borders—The Rise of Law in Cyberspace*
*48 Stanford Law Review 1367 (1996)*
http://www.cli.org/X0025_LBFIN.html

# 13

# PRIVACY AND THE LAW: 2001

The first and most obvious point we need to make is an important and traditional disclaimer: Neither of us is an attorney, we are not admitted to the bar to practice law, and nothing that we say here should be considered to be legal advice. That's important information. However, we do know a lot about the practices of businesses and consumers and which laws might be important to think about. We hope that sharing that information with you makes you a more informed person. However, what we say is only our own opinion, no matter how well informed we might be.

This book is not primarily a book about the philosophy of privacy, the philosophy of the law, or even our own personal philosophies, although our personal philosophies are bound to creep in. It is, however, difficult to discuss privacy and the law without a bit of philosophical discussion.

## What Is the Law?

The law is about drawing lines. On one side of the line, activities are legal. On the other side, they are not legal. It's really that simple. "Hah!" you say, "What about all those attorneys and courts and appeals courts and so on?" The practice of law is about arguing on which side of the line your client's actions reside. Lawyers represent their clients and make their arguments with that motivation. So, a good attorney tries to define the location of the line so that the client is best protected. In court cases, one attorney tries to define the line so that his or her client in a civil proceeding, or the state in a criminal proceeding, is the party that is protected. The opposing attorney does the same for the party he or she represents. The judge tries to make sure that all the attorneys are playing by the rules and presenting those rules to the jury deciding the case, or the judge decides the case based on his own interpretation of the rules. In cases in which someone disagrees with the judge's ruling, the case may be appealed to a higher court.

When your attorney is preparing a sales contract for your home, your attorney is drawing a line for you between things that are your responsibility and those that are the responsibility of the other party, whether buyer or seller. When both parties sign the contract, the contract becomes part of the set of rules that govern the sale. Contracts have a huge body of law and previous decisions included in them already. People have learned over time what kinds of legal problems occur in sales transactions and the previous resolution of those problems has become part of contract law. Many laws address privacy and security concerns also, but in the digital arena that body of law is neither so large nor so well understood as in the contract law example.

The law itself comes from a number of sources. Some of it is written as part of constitutions that set out rules by which we are governed. Some of it is *legislated.* That means passed by a legislative body. In the U.S. system, those bodies include the U.S. Congress, the state legislatures, the county boards of supervisors or the city councils, and so on. Some of the law comes through *adjudication* or decisions of the courts.

Each legislated law goes "on to the books" and then is enforced (or not). Some laws contain sections that call for immediate judicial review. The controversial Communications Decency Amendment to the Telecommunications Act of 1996 was one such law. Because the legislators were aware that a constitutional challenge would be made to the law, and because they wanted to be certain that the review would happen promptly, the amendment included provisions for an accelerated review. After passage, several advocacy organizations sued the United States to cause the review in a three-judge district court. That court's decision was promptly appealed to the U. S. Supreme Court, where the law was held to be unconstitutional. Unconstitutional laws cannot be enforced.

Laws are reviewed by the courts when necessary as part of a specific dispute. The courts make their decisions based on the law as both written and interpreted in past decisions. The interpretation part can be interesting. That's how a case ends up in the Supreme Court: Advocates challenge the law as written or interpreted through the system until a final ruling is made in the highest court. The judicial system—as a whole of course, because not all within the system maintain pure motives at all times—is based upon advocate representation of differing views with the adjudicator representing the law itself.

Laws differ from place to place. In fact, the term for the place where the law applies is *jurisdiction*. Just look at the parts of the word—part law (juris) and part speaking (diction). A jurisdiction is the place where the law speaks. Well, perhaps that is stretching the definition a bit, but the law is usually tied to a specific political region. As a country built from the traditions of several different cultures and jurisdictions, the United States has laws that derive from those cultures. In particular, in the United States we have many laws that derive from English Common Law. Some western states have laws that derive from Spanish law because the states were settled by people who brought that law with them.

The differences that come from these two traditions are illustrative of differing approaches to law. To take an example (which we are making simplistic) from laws governing property and marriage, some states have laws based on the concept called *community property*, where the property that comes to a married couple after the date of their marriage belongs equally to each person in the marriage. Other states use a law based on *dower rights* where, should the marriage be dissolved, the wife is entitled to a fixed percentage of the property.

These different laws are based on solving different problems. In the dower right states, emphasis is placed on protecting rights to property brought to the marriage by the wife, on making sure she would have some assets of her own. Many of the western states were settled by "outlaws." Hence, this was a method of trying to keep family property from acquisition by unscrupulous men via marriage into a propertied family. The idea conjures up brave young women trying to protect their family ranch from unprincipled ruffians, and so on. We have all seen wonderful movies based on this story. And we've seen other entrancing movies based on the agony that can be caused in fairly developing the list of community property, or rather based on unfairly developing the list so that one partner receives less than his fair share in dissolutions.

It's interesting that these laws are such a part of us that we base movie and reading entertainment upon their premise. It's also interesting that although the films may be shown in various parts of the world, the premise upon which they are based may not translate (or dub) well so that the premise is equally understood by all viewers. The regions of the world have very diverse, deeply imbedded cultural differences in developing the laws that govern them. For instance, we Americans believe in addressing problems as they develop. In Europe, a much more "top-down" culture, they believe in regulating against future harm.

A very real problem then is that jurisdiction has been constrained to political boundaries while the cyberworld is not bound in the same way. Therefore, when there are disputes or malfeasant behavior it is not always clear which is the jurisdiction that is used. As we write this in the spring of 2001, international treaty conferences are being held in which diplomats are trying to agree upon the rules to decide jurisdiction. In consumer protection cases, some argue that jurisdiction should be in the country of the buyer. Thus, the buyer would always know what his rights are. Sounds great if you are the buyer. The contrary point of view is that if you were the seller, how could you, sitting in California in the United States of America, know the consumer protection laws of the United Arab Emirates or Singapore, for example. It should be enough to be responsible for knowing and abiding by the laws of the jurisdiction in which we do business because, on the Internet, we can't necessarily know the legal jurisdiction of each potential buyer.

Obviously, there are multiple good arguments on each side as well as the embedded cultural viewpoints, the long traditions, and diverse current law that need to be clarified for a worldwide economy. It can no longer be assumed that the marketplace of goods and ideas is geographically and legally local. It is not a small problem and it no doubt will take years of discussions to arrive at a regime that is generally accepted.

It is in this environment that we place our discussion of current privacy law.

# Is Privacy a Right?

As usual in a discussion of the law, the answer is: "It depends." It depends on who you are, where you are, and what you are doing, among the many variables.

Many people have pointed out that no strict right of privacy is written into the United States Constitution, even in the Bill of Rights. However, the right to free speech and assembly (the First Amendment); the forbidding of unreasonable search and seizure (the Fourth Amendment); and the right to a fair trial with due process (the Fifth Amendment) have all been cited in court cases to protect people from being inappropriately interfered with or observed.

In discussing Griswold versus Connecticut, a 1965 U.S. Supreme Court case, Mr. Justice Douglas for the court majority stated:

> *"Various guarantees create zones of privacy. The right of association contained in the penumbra of the First Amendment is one, as we have seen. The Third Amendment in its prohibition against the quartering of soldiers "in any house" in time of peace without the consent of the owner is another facet of that privacy. The Fourth Amendment explicitly affirms the "right of the people to be secure in their persons, houses, papers, and effects, against unreasonable searches and seizures." The Fifth Amendment in its Self-Incrimination Clause enables the citizen to create a zone of privacy which government may not force him to surrender to his detriment...."*

The Court held in Griswold that there is a right to privacy between married couples that may not be intruded into by the state. Other controversial cases have been decided based on rights to expect privacy in one's own home, cases overturning sodomy laws, and so on.

The First Amendment enables you to have and state opinions that may not be popular to teach about them, to gather others, and to try to influence them.

The Fourth Amendment engenders the expectation of privacy in terms of requiring probable cause for activities such as blood tests and fingerprinting. The citizenry has a right to expect search warrants to be applied for, permission to be sought for entry, and that governmental intrusion be reasonable. As a minimum standard, probable cause is needed before agents of the government can enter or search your home, require you to enable your car to be searched, and so on. Many interesting cases have discussed the expectation that driver's actions are private.

Basically, these cases revolved around law enforcement roadblocks intended to identify drunken drivers and so on. Those cases well illustrate the tension between the personal right to privacy and the public good: not having impaired people operating lethal equipment on a public thoroughfare.

The Fifth Amendment is designed to keep you from being required to violate your own privacy when it would not be in your own best interest. We usually describe it in terms of self-incrimination.

### *The Bill of Rights, United States Constitution*

### *Amendment I*

*Congress shall make no law respecting an establishment of religion, or prohibiting the free exercise thereof; or abridging the freedom of speech, or of the press; or the right of the people peaceably to assemble, and to petition the government for a redress of grievances.*

### *Amendment IV*

*The right of the people to be secure in their persons, houses, papers, and effects, against unreasonable searches and seizures, shall not be violated, and no warrants shall issue, but upon probable cause, supported by oath or affirmation, and particularly describing the place to be searched, and the persons or things to be seized.*

### *Amendment V*

*No person shall be held to answer for a capital, or otherwise infamous crime, unless on a presentment or indictment of a grand jury, except in cases arising in the land or naval forces, or in the militia, when in actual service in time of war or public danger; nor shall any person be subject for the same offense to be twice put in jeopardy of life or limb; nor shall be compelled in any criminal case to be a witness against himself, nor be deprived of life, liberty, or property, without due process of law; nor shall private property be taken for public use, without just compensation.*

# What U.S. Federal Law Applies

Many United States Federal laws are designed to protect individual privacy. Some are (or will be) applicable in the digital environment. Some won't. The following are some for you to think about.

# Cable Communications Policy Act (1984)

This law (47 USC 551) provides cable services subscribers with the right to be informed about the collection of personal data. This is an Opt-in law, requiring prior consent of the subscriber to the collection of data. The cable service provider may not share or disclose any data collected. The government may obtain a copy of the data about a subscriber with a court order.

The nature of the information would be what programs or information are transmitted to the subscriber. If the law is broken, a court may award actual damages of $100 per day for each day of the violation or $1,000, whichever is greater. Punitive damages and attorney's fees and other litigation costs may also be awarded. There are no criminal penalties.

# Census Confidentiality Act

This law (13 USC 9) restricts the Census Bureau from using the information it collects for anything other than its intended statistical purpose. A government employee who shares information from the Census faces a fine of up to $5,000 or imprisonment of up to 5 years or both.

# Children's Online Privacy Protection Act (COPPA) (2000)

COPPA (15 USC 6502) regulates unfair and deceptive acts in connection with collecting information from children on the Internet. It forbids Web site or online service providers directed to children (or any operator who has actual knowledge that it is collecting information from a child under 13) from collecting that information without disclosure and, more importantly, requires verifiable parental consent. Operators may satisfy the requirements by participating in self-regulatory programs intended to protect children.

This law specifically addresses the notion that children are unable to determine the wisdom of trading information about themselves and their families to play games, enter contests, or to receive some other small remuneration with which their parents may not agree.

People who violate the law are subject to Federal Trade Commission action for unfair or deceptive trade practice. In addition, state Attorneys General may bring a civil action against a person who violates a regulation of the Federal Trade Commission.

## Communications Assistance for Law Enforcement Act (CALEA)

You might not think of a law about law enforcement's interception of communications as a privacy-related act. However, CALEA (47 USC 1001 ss) is about keeping interceptions narrowly focused and yet possible, given ever expanding new technologies. Congress balanced the societal need to be able to trace bad guys with the reasonable expectation that we all have for privacy within our telephone conversations.

CALEA is a framework that enables law enforcement to expect and receive help in tracing the communications of suspected criminals. It requires that wire and telephony providers enable a tap into the communications of specific subscribers, at the time of the communications. It requires call-identifying information to be given to law enforcement, and all this activity must take place under court order.

Section 1002 a3a requires that this be done with "the privacy and security of communications and call-identifying information not authorized to be intercepted" giving protection to people who are *not* suspected and for whom the court order was given. Additional protections are given to the carriers and a fund that pays them back for their efforts is authorized.

Under CALEA the Federal Communications Commission has the duty to enact regulations implementing the law. The FCC has struggled for over five years to do so, and recently the District of Columbia Circuit Court rejected most of the proposed regulations on the ground that they gave insufficient protection to privacy and were not authorized by CALEA. The FCC is now writing new regulations.

## Customer Proprietary Network Information

This law (47 USC 222) forbids the disclosure of certain kinds of information about the customers of telecommunications services to others unless the customer approves. The following information is protected:

"Information that relates to the quantity, technical configuration, type, destination, location, and amount of use of a telecommunications service subscribed to by any customer of a telecommunications carrier, and that is made available to the carrier by the customer solely by virtue of the carrier-customer relationship; and information contained in the bills pertaining to telephone exchange service or telephone toll service received by a customer of a carrier."

Of course, it explicitly enables some kinds of disclosures, too—those that enable the construction of directories of users, for example. It also enables billing information to be gathered and sent to you so you can pay your bill.

## Driver's Privacy Protection Act (1994)

This statute (18 USC 2721) forbids employees of motor vehicle departments from releasing vehicle registration information except to a government representative in conjunction with theft recovery, motor vehicle emissions queries, and so on. Representatives of manufacturers and dealers may obtain information to send information about recalls. Businesses may use the records to verify the accuracy of information submitted by the individual. Information may be released to carry out court proceedings and information may be summarized for statistical reports.

The civil penalty for a person who discloses or uses personal information from such a record may be a court-awarded actual damage amount of up to $2,500. Punitive damages may also be assessed if the court determines that the law was willfully or recklessly disregarded. Court costs and other relief may also be awarded. Knowing that you are in violation of the law may also be subject to criminal fine.

## Electronic Communications Privacy Act (ECPA) (1986)

ECPA (18 USC 2701-2711, 3121-3127) updated and clarified surveillance laws to cover electronic information transmission as well as voice communications. Because ECPA long predated today's widely deployed Internet, its provisions no longer map precisely to the technologies and practices that underlie today's electronic transfer of information. This law is, however, the one governing *government electronic surveillance* within the United States.

The act addresses two types of information: that gathered in real time (or tapping into communications as they are transmitted) and historical information. It also distinguishes between the *content* of the communication and what is called *other records*, which means information about the transaction or about the subscriber.

Consider an e-mail message. If one of us sends an e-mail to the other, the following information would exist:

- The content of the e-mail
- The e-mail address from which the message was sent
- The e-mail address to which the message was sent
- A date/time stamp
- The number of bytes in the e-mail, and so on

Most e-mail client programs store a copy of the message and header information on the sender's computer. The sender's outgoing mail server has a copy of the message until the recipient mail server signals that it has received the message. The recipient's mail server stores a copy of the message and the header information until told to erase it. In general, the instruction to erase the message is transmitted by the recipient's e-mail client program at the time the message is downloaded from the mail server. Most e-mail client programs enable you, the user, to decide whether you want the messages erased when you download them or whether you want to control their retention by individual message.

As long as a message remains on the server, it can be obtained by law enforcement under the specific conditions outlined in this law. Remember, too, that responsible providers keep backup copies of the data residing on their servers so that it can be restored in the event of hardware failure.

 **NOTE**    Remember, if you are using Web-based e-mail readers, you must actively delete the messages you no longer want to save. Your messages remain on the server until you delete them. Again, responsible providers have backup copies that may be searched.

ISPs we use have information about each of our access accounts and about each connection we make to the Internet, at which IP address we were connected, the time of day, date, and length of time connected. Our providers also have whatever registration information we gave at the time we signed up for the service. Because we use commercial Internet service providers and pay for this service, the provider also has financial transaction information. In our case, each of our providers has credit card information because we signed up to pay automatically. This information is called customer records.

Now that we know what and where the information is, let's look at who can request it.

ISPs are usually forbidden from disclosing the content of any electronic communication. Customer records, however, are not similarly protected by the law. ISPs are not forbidden from disclosing records *about* a customer to any entity other than a government body. Of course, the ISP, like other companies, must do what their privacy policy states or the Federal Trade Commission may act against it and the Cable Act may protect the information if the subscriber uses a cable connection. The Federal Government has generally taken the position that ECPA applies to cable-based ISPs rather than the Cable Act.

In general, an ISP may only disclose customer records to a government agency in response to two things: a warrant or "specific and articulable fact" court order or the subscriber's consent to such disclosure. "Specific and articulable facts" is a lower legal standard than "probable cause." Remember that, unless its privacy policy forbids it, it would be possible for an ISP to share information with advertisers, for example, and yet not be able to share the same information with a law enforcement agency.

Basic subscriber information (name and billing address, for example) may be released to a government agency when requested with a subpoena. Account logs, transaction patterns (URLs of visited Web sites), and e-mail addresses of correspondents can only be obtained with a warrant or court order.

A law enforcement agency may request that an ISP preserve information about a specific user while the court order is being obtained. The information may not be turned over without the court order, but the ISP is required to save it.

In the telephonic world, it is possible to record what numbers are being called and the length of each call. These transaction records are recorded via pen register or trap and trace devices. The Justice Department has taken the position that the list of IP addresses that are reached from the user's IP address or from which the user receives information is the same thing. This assertion led to the development of the FBI's infamous Carnivore System, which has been improved and renamed DCS 1000. The courts haven't yet ruled on a case based upon Justice's assertion.

Exceptions to ECPA enable an ISP to detect hacking, bill its customers, and otherwise perform its functions. However, the general case remains that law enforcement is required to convince a judge to enable them access to the information.

Stored electronic communications are generally protected from disclosure whether that storage is incidental to the provision of the service or part of the backup processes that restores service in the event of a failure. ISPs are prohibited from knowingly divulging the contents of any communication. There are several exceptions to the law, including allowing an ISP to divulge the contents of a communication to the intended recipient. It would be a shame, wouldn't it, if something prevented you from getting your e-mail and your ISP wasn't allowed to get it to you.

Court orders are also excepted. Finally, if in the process of providing the service, an employee of the ISP inadvertently obtains information that appears to pertain to the commission of a crime, the contents can be disclosed. For any other reason, the government needs a warrant, a court order, or a subpoena to obtain the contents of a transmission.

The rules are pretty stringent for the last 180 days. Less stringent requirements apply for stored communications of more than 180 days ago.

ECPA prohibits the intentional interception of transmissions or the intentional disclosure or use of the contents of transmissions. In this instance, there is no differentiation between government agents and the general public. We do not use the word "transmission" in our explanation because it is during the transmission that the interception is forbidden. When the message is on a disk somewhere, the "stored communications" part of the rule applies. Of course, court orders and/or consent enables the interception.

Also remember that any communication has two parties. If one gives consent, the contents may be disclosed. A last cautionary note is that you may have given your ISP permission to disclose the contents of your messages when you accepted the terms of service provision. We would advise that you reread the terms so that you are familiar with them.

The penalties for violation of ECPA are criminal and include fines and/or imprisonment for up to five years and fines for interception and disclosure and up to one year of imprisonment for violation of the pen register provisions.

In addition, a person whose communications were intercepted can sue. The law provides for civil and punitive damages as well as court costs and attorney's fees. It is with these provisions that the courts are seeing some class action suits which allege that information is collected without notifying the consumer. In particular, companies that provide freeware (programs available without a fee) have used a process that collects information during or following the downloading process. These "spyware" cases seem to be seen as fruitful by litigators.

Additionally, in the 107th Congress, Senator John Edwards of North Carolina has introduced a federal bill (S. 197) that would forbid a program from "calling home" and sending information to its creators or distributors without the knowledge of the person upon whose computer the program resides.

## Electronic Fund Transfer Act

EFTA (15 USC 1693) is the law dealing with the electronic transmission of financial information among financial institutions. It's designed to prevent the misrouting of funds and to make sure that adequate controls are on what money is moving from account to account. So, as with many other laws in this section, it is not primarily intended to be a privacy law, but as part of other conditions, EFTA touches on keeping certain kinds of information private. It requires financial institutions to notify consumers when and which account information is disclosed to third parties. As in other kinds of financial transactions, there are protections for fraud, for misrepresentation, and for theft. It is those protections that are principally addressed with this law. Three parties are informed as part of the transaction: the requestor, the institution currently holding the money, and the destination institution. Other parties should not have information about the transaction.

There are exceptions for notifications. Foreign transfers and normal banking and financial disclosures otherwise required by law must still be made. If the violation of this law is determined to be for commercial advantage, private commercial gain, or for malicious destruction, the violation is punishable by a fine and/or imprisonment of up to one year. If the violation is a subsequent offense, a fine and/or imprisonment of not more than two years is the punishment. If the violation is not for the reasons outlined earlier, the violation is punishable by a fine and/or imprisonment of not more than six months.

## Employee Polygraph Protection Act

This law (29 USC 2001) details a privacy protection that you might not be aware you have—the freedom to refuse a lie detector test requested by any employer or prospective employer engaged in the production or sales of goods. An employer who violates this act may be subject to civil penalties of up to a $10,000 fine. The person whose rights were violated can sue in civil court for damages, lost wages, court costs, and attorney's fees. You can waive your rights but you must give your consent to do so in written form. This law doesn't apply if you work for the government, if you are in the security department, or other similar occupations.

If you decide to take the test, you can disclose the results, of course, after you receive the information from the examiner. The examiner may reveal the results only to you, to your employer, to a person you designate in writing, and to an agent of a court that ordered the test. Your employer can't divulge the results either, except as outlined earlier, or to the government if the information is an admission of criminal conduct.

## Fair Credit Reporting Act (FCRA)

The Fair Credit Reporting Act (15 USC 1681) was passed to address accuracy and privacy (and fairness, of course) in the files of credit bureaus and other consumer reporting agencies. Credit Reporting Agencies (CRAs) are the formal name for organizations such as credit bureaus. Credit bureaus gather information about you and provide it to people who make decisions about your trustworthiness and creditworthiness based on your past behavior. If the behavior attributed to you is not, in fact, your behavior, the system breaks down. Obviously, if the information held about you by these agencies is incorrect, you may be denied employment, a lease, mortgage credit, or other financial services by organizations who base their decisions in part on the financial information provided by the credit bureaus. This is a central problem behind the crime of identity theft. First information about your good past behavior is hijacked and used fraudulently to get credit. That credit is used by the thief to obtain goods and services and then not paid for. Then your credit information is updated to reflect that you didn't pay for goods and services that you did not, in fact, receive. This creates a terrible mess for you, whether or not you end up financially liable for the purchases you didn't make.

The FCRA gives you specific rights, some of which are outlined in the following list. You may also have additional rights under your state's law:

- You can read your file and get a list of who has asked to see it. You can't be charged a fee to check your file if you have had a credit decision go against you, for example, if you were refused credit. You can be charged a fee to see the contents of your file otherwise, unless you are unemployed, on welfare, or you are reporting or clearing a fraud. In those cases, you can have one copy each 12 months.

- You are entitled to the name, address, and phone number of the reporting agency when a decision is made from your file.

- You can dispute the information in your report. The dispute process is designed to protect you during the dispute, to give you written copies of the reports and amendments, and to inform recent requestors of the actions.

- Information older than seven years can't be reported, except for bankruptcy information, which can be reported for ten years.

- Only people with legitimate needs, such as landlords, employers, and insurers, can have access to credit information. You must give your written consent to release the information to your employer, and so on.

- Credit reporting agencies maintain *"Do Not Call"* lists. You can ask that your name be excluded from lists for unsolicited credit and insurance offers. Writing to the agencies is better than calling if you want to keep your name off these lists. If you send a written "Do Not Call" form, your name must be kept off the lists indefinitely. If you inform the agency that you want your name removed from lists via a toll-free number, your name must be kept of the list for two years.

The enforcement of the Fair Credit Reporting Act involves a number of different agencies, based on the type of activity or financial institution. The Federal Trade Commission oversees credit reporting agencies and creditors; the Federal Reserve Board oversees banks; the Office of Thrift Supervisions oversees savings associations and savings banks; the Comptroller of the Currency oversees national banks and branches of foreign banks; the National Credit Union Administration oversees federal credit unions; and the Federal Deposit Insurance Corporation oversees state chartered banks.

Employees of the credit reporting agency who disclose information to an unauthorized person are subject to a fine and/or imprisonment for up to two years. Any person who unlawfully obtains information under false pretenses is subject to the same criminal penalty. Additionally, consumers have the right to sue for damages if an agency fails to comply. The court can award punitive damages as well as attorney fees and court costs.

## Family Education Rights and Privacy Act (1974)

FERPA (20 USC 1232g) sets out requirements designed to protect the privacy of parents and students. You can think of it as the *student privacy policy* statement of each school. The law addresses the rights of parents to see their minor children's records and students of higher education to see their records. It grants the right to challenge and have the records amended. It also grants students privacy, particularly with regard to the release of personally identifying information. The law differs in its treatment of rights to students, depending on the type of educational institution—essentially, a difference granted based on the age of the student involved. Younger students are granted privacy of their records with their parents as advocates. Older students are granted the rights to supervise their own records.

A student at an institution of higher education is allowed the right to decide whether or not his location information should be printed or made available online in student directories. Students are notified of this and the other rights granted to them under this law.

In general, students (or their parents) must consent to the disclosure of material in their records before the information can be shared. Exceptions are allowed for access by personnel of the educational institution (including law enforcement) if the access is for legitimate educational interest. A school may also choose to automatically disclose records to other schools to which the student is applying as long as this practice is part of the privacy notification to the students.

There is no specific penalty for violating FERPA, but a right does exist to file a complaint with the U.S. Department of Education. The Department of Education is permitted to withhold funds as a part of this statute.

# Financial Services Modernization Act/Gramm-Leach-Bliley

Modernization, like beauty, is in the eye of the beholder. Gramm-Leach-Bliley (GLB) (PL 106-102 and incorporated into 12 USC), is a major reworking of the rules governing financial institutions in the United States. Traditionally, Americans have feared the gathering of too much information in one place or too much control lodged in one institution. Laws based on the fear of the harm that could be caused by having a single financial institution grow large enough to control all aspects of a person's or region's finance had kept banks and insurance companies separate. In the 1930's, the United States was in the midst of the Great Depression and many banks had failed. As a result of those failures, the Banking Act of 1933 instituted rules that separated commercial and investment banking and provided for Federal Deposit Insurance. The rules also mandated that banks could not act as brokers in securities or insurance.  The general feeling of the time was that bankers had abused the trust of the people and new rules were needed. Those rules included strict provisions separating securities management (investment banking) and commercial banking.

Economic historians are now more likely to believe that the loss in property value that came with the Depression was more to blame for the bank failures and that our collective fear of large institutions—that local control thing that we feel so strongly about—encouraged small banks, which were undercapitalized and therefore failed quicker than larger institutions would have. It's hard to say because we can't travel backward and replay the sequence with different rules and assumptions. In any case, financial experts successfully argued that larger institutions are not dangerous and the 106th Congress agreed with them.

Gramm-Leach-Bliley provides for new types of bank holding companies that can include merchant banks, insurance companies, and securities companies. This law supports the belief that the economies that come with larger entities make the financial markets more efficient and that the improved financial products and services that result serve consumers well. There are complex rules about percentages of businesses and grandfathered-in non-financial businesses of financial companies and so on. From the perspective of people interested in how information travels, however, the interesting changes come with the information-sharing provisions and privacy rules in Title V of the law.

GLB requires that financial service entities notify consumers of their policies for collecting and sharing *non-public personal information.* Non-public personal information covers any information that is provided to obtain a financial product or service that results from a financial transaction or that is obtained in connection with providing a financial product or service to a consumer.

Consumers must be offered the opportunity to refuse to have their information shared with non-affiliated third parties for marketing purposes. The notification must be given when you open a new account and annually thereafter, with the first notification due to you by June 30, 2001. This means your credit card company can't share your name and address with an insurance company so they can offer you a great deal on a new insurance policy, doesn't it? Well, not precisely. If your credit card company is affiliated (for example, owned by the same holding company that owns the insurance company, or has signed an allowed joint marketing agreement with the insurance company), the information may be shared. The opt-out provision only addresses non-affiliated organizations.

At no time can your account number be shared for marketing purposes. It's part of the non-public information about you that is always protected.

Enforcement of these rules rests with many organizations: the federal banking agencies, the Securities and Exchange Commission, the Treasury Department, and the Federal Trade Commission. Criminal penalties exist for obtaining customer information under false pretenses of fines and imprisonment.

GLB is the minimum standard within the United States. It is federal law. The law explicitly permitted states to enact more stringent rules. A number of laws were proposed and discussed in state legislatures to address financial privacy. Some passed. Others didn't. You can be sure that the discussions will continue.

## Foreign Intelligence Surveillance Act

The Foreign Intelligence Surveillance Act of 1978 (50 USC 1806) is one of many laws that illustrate the concern that we Americans have about intrusive governments spying on us inappropriately. The FISA rules for electronic surveillance require federal agents to request a court order that includes 13 pieces of information. This includes "a certification or certifications by the Assistant to the President for National Security Affairs or an executive branch official or officials designated by the President from among those executive officers employed in the area of national security or defense and appointed by the President with the advice and consent of the Senate" that the information is indeed foreign intelligence information, that the purpose of the surveillance is to obtain that information, and that the information cannot be obtained with normal investigative techniques.

Furthermore, FISA requires that if the capture of the information includes information about a United States citizen, it can only be disclosed if the disclosure meets the minimization requirements and if it's being used in a criminal proceeding. The government is strictly instructed in what it can and cannot present as evidence, in what it can and cannot record, and it must report yearly about the uses of the provisions of this law. The law makes clear that there is great protection for exercising one's rights to freedom of speech and that this exercise should not be confused with being a foreign agent.

These orders are considered by a special court established by FISA and appointed by the Chief Justice. It meets in secret. All its records are secret except for the number of applications for search and surveillance that it grants and denies every year. Since 1979, the court has never denied an original application for surveillance authority.

If a government agent engages in electronic surveillance without the proper authorization or if information gathered that way is disclosed, the penalties can result in a fine of up to $10,000 and/or imprisonment of up to five years.

## Freedom of Information Act

The Freedom of Information Act (5 U.S.C. 552) is a disclosure statute but it has very important exemptions for personal privacy. Our government maintains a lot of records on people. The general rule of FOIA is that the federal executive branch must disclose records. The sixth exemption exempts records the disclosure of which would be "a clearly unwarranted invasion of personal privacy." The seventh exemption, which deals only with law enforcement records, exempts from disclosure records the disclosure of which would be "an unwarranted invasion of personal privacy." There is a huge body of law interpreting these exemptions.

# Health Insurance Portability and Accountability Act (HIPAA)

The privacy portions on the HIPAA rules are especially interesting because they address a potential problem caused by proposing a legislative solution to another problem. The Health Insurance Portability and Accountability Act was passed to make it possible for people to move their health care from one location or physician or hospital to another to make their health insurance portable.

We are all aware that better information allows better decisions to be made. Because good decisions matter so much in medicine, health care workers want the best, most complete information that they can get. Because we directly benefit from good information, we want the healthcare people to gather, store, and find the best information about us that they can.

When information exists, however, it is possible for it to be disclosed. Health information is among the most sensitive of information that can be gathered about us, and we want to be sure that the people who have it are known to us and that they guard it carefully.

Health information privacy has been discussed in Congress since the 1970s. Remember that the Fair Information Principles were outlined then by the Health Education and Welfare Department (the precursor of today's Health and Human Services Department). In 1995, Congress passed a law that required HHS to develop the privacy rules if Congress had not acted by 1998.

The privacy provisions of the Act were developed by Health and Human Services, and after much review and comment, were released by the Clinton Administration just before the Bush Administration took office. Many believed that President Bush would extend the review or roll back the regulations, but he allowed them to take effect, and after April 14, 2001, healthcare entities need to operate under these new privacy rules, although two years are given to get everything implemented.

Each time you visit a doctor, go to a hospital, or visit a health clinic, detailed medical records are made about you. The new information is added to records of previous health visits and together can convey a picture of your physical and mental health. If you carry health insurance, the records of your visit and your treatment are sent to the insurance company for payment. Your doctor or hospital may employ an outside firm to do their billing. If so, information about what you should be charged is sent to the billing company for processing.

Information about your treatment may go to the government if you have a disease that is being tracked. So, statistical information may be sent to federal and state agencies. (Many jurisdictions have laws about reporting child abuse, gunshot wounds, or some other condition that requires notification to an outside agency. These requirements are not changed by these privacy rules.)

The new rules require that you must be told what information in your records is shared and with whom. You now have an explicit right to see and access your own records and to have a list of non-routine disclosures of your information. (A routine disclosure would be to your insurance company, so they could pay.) You can ask that your records be changed if you feel they are incorrect. You must give consent before information can be released—and that consent may be made a condition of treatment.

When you do give consent for another to receive information from your records, the information that is shared must be the minimum necessary to accomplish the task. This means that the billing service doesn't necessarily have access to all your records, just the part that allows a proper bill to be constructed for you. Consents are required for use or disclosure of protected healthcare information to carry out treatment, payment, and healthcare operations.

Certain kinds of information are particularly sensitive and require more than consent to disclose. They require *authorization*. Authorizations are specific written permissions that are more exacting. These types of permissions are likely to be required for research related treatments, where it is necessary that part of the research for information about you, your condition, and your reaction to the treatment be shared.

Marketing and fund-raising requests are considered to be part of healthcare operations. This means that if you have a specific condition, your health maintenance organization can build a list of people with that condition and share the list with a third party who has a medicine you might want to try. It also means that your local hospital where you have received treatment can have a fund-raising arm contact you to ask for a donation. Both of these contacts require that you signed the consent form.

The HIPAA privacy rules are enforced by the Department of Health and Human Services' Office of Civil Rights. If you feel your health information has been inappropriately disclosed, you may file a complaint with the office.

## Health Research Data Statutes

Each year the Secretary of Health and Human Services is required by Congress to prepare a report on healthcare costs and financing, healthcare resources, the utilization of healthcare resources, and the health of the "nations' people." "Such report shall include a description and analysis, by age, sex, income, and geographic area, of the statistics collected...."

The health research data statutes (42 USC 242 m(b)) require that no information gathered to make this report may be released if it identifies a specific person or institution unless that person or institution has provided written consent to the disclosure.

## Identity Theft Statute

This act (18 USC 1028) makes it a crime to possess false identification or to gather, use, or sell personal information under false pretenses.

The specific actions prohibited include

- Showing an identifying document that is false
- Transferring a document that is false
- Using a false identification document to defraud the United States
- Making or possessing something that will produce false documents

The criminal penalties vary, becoming higher if the false papers are used in the commission of a crime, and can be as high as imprisonment for up to 25 years.

## Mail Privacy Statute

The law (39 USC 3623) provides that no sealed letter "of domestic origin shall be opened except under authority of a search warrant authorized by law, or by an officer or employee of the Postal Service for the sole purpose of determining an address at which the letter can be delivered, or pursuant to the authorization of the addressee."

It will be interesting to see if this law gets applied to electronic mail. What constitutes a "sealed" letter? And who is considered a postal service employee? Pat wrote an interesting paper long ago that addresses the ethics of being a Net postmaster. People who work on electronic mail systems frequently look at mangled e-mail to see if it can be sent on to its intended recipient. Generally, those people have seen themselves in the role of "postal service" employee. As far as we know, the law has not been tested with regard to electronic messages. Pat's article can be found at `http://www.funet.fi/pub/unix/mail/Postmaster.ethics`.

## Paperwork Reduction Act of 1980

This law (44 USC 1801) forbids government agencies from gathering information that is already gathered by another agency. Additionally, the Office of Management and Budget can forbid the collection of data if it finds the agency doesn't really need the information. Each form that asks for information must say why the information is being collected and how it is used. Information must be labeled as to whether or not it must be supplied to receive some service or whether you may choose not to give the information. You probably have seen the notices on the forms and wondered how the form could have been related to paperwork reduction. Now you know that the rule is about trying to make sure that paperwork is reduced by not asking for more information than is necessary to produce the desired result.

## Public Officer Disclosure Statute

This statute (18 USC 1905) forbids an officer or employee of the government from disclosing confidential information gained in the execution of employment to anyone other than permitted by law. The criminal penalty is a fine and/or imprisonment of up to one year and termination of employment.

## Privacy Act of 1974

The Privacy Act of 1974 (5 USC 552a) is the seminal privacy law in the United States. We say this because it was the work behind this law, following the work in preparing the 1973 HEW report "Records, Computers, and the Rights of Citizens" that led to not only this law, but to much more because these were the first articulations of the Fair Information Practices. Those same practices were later used by the Organization for Economic Cooperation and Development (OECD) in 1980 and used as a basis for discussion and action.

This law addresses government records and disclosure, not those of businesses or private parties. Federal agencies are prohibited from disclosing information about people except for their publicly announced purposes. They are also required to collect only the minimum amount of information necessary to do the assigned task. Agencies who ask for information about you must tell you why they are asking for it (purpose of collection), by what authority they are asking, what the information is used for, and what happens if you refuse to give the information. You must be provided access to the records about you, and you may challenge the contents. In addition, agencies must keep accurate records about the disclosures that are made: to whom, when, why such disclosure was made; and the records must be kept for a least five years or the life of the record. If corrections are made to information that has been shared, the corrections must be passed on as well.

A particularly important part of the law requires that everyone who is involved in the collection and maintenance of records about persons be trained in the rules about disclosures. Agencies must also establish appropriate safeguards to ensure the security and confidentiality of the information.

The Privacy Act provides for both criminal and civil penalties if information is disclosed when it shouldn't have been. On the criminal side, it is a misdemeanor for a government agent to willfully disclose information or to willfully maintain records without adequate notification. The punishment is a fine of up to $5,000. If an agent knowingly and willfully requests or obtains information under false pretenses, the punishment is also a fine of up to $5,000.

If you believe that an agency has failed to comply with the statute and that failure has had an adverse affect on you, you may sue the agency for actual damages sustained. Should you prove your case, you would be entitled to damage recovery of no less than $1,000 and attorney fees and court costs. Generally, the type of activity anticipated by this part of the law is the failure of an agency to appropriately review and amend a record at your request. You can also sue to gain access to your records if the access is denied by the agency.

## Right to Financial Privacy Act

This act, originally passed in 1978 (12 USC 3401), controls how Federal agencies have access to your financial records. The agency must notify you why they want access and enable you to challenge the request in court, or they must obtain an administrative subpoena. No agency may share financial information about you with another agency unless the records are relevant to law enforcement activity. Your financial institution may not release your records without your approval unless the agency provides written documentation that the request meets the provisions of this law. Your financial institution is not, however, forbidden from telling an agency that your records contain something that is relevant to a criminal investigation; that is, your bank can suggest that law enforcement ask properly.

You may sue the agency that violated this law. If the agency obtained or disclosed information from your financial records, you may be awarded $100 as well as actual damages. Punitive damages are allowed for willful or intentional violations, as are attorney's fees and court costs. There are no criminal penalties.

# Tax Reform Act of 1976

This law (26 USC 6103) limits the sharing of tax return information among the various Federal agencies. It provides for the general confidentiality of tax returns. No officer or employee of the United States, any state, any local child support agency, or any local agency that has access to your tax return information can disclose your return or information about your return. This includes the amount of tax, your refund, your estimated tax due, or any other information you may have included in your return.

There is an extensive list of people who may, usually with your permission, have access to your return, generally to provide you some service or assistance. This enables your spouse or your tax preparer or the executor of your estate to conduct tax business on your behalf. In special cases, the Secretary of the Treasury may be asked for specific return information to respond to committees of Congress. If this happens, the committees see the information only in closed session. The President of the United States may ask the Secretary for your tax return information. This action may be taken if you are being considered for an executive appointment.

Although we wouldn't suggest that reading the United States Code is an entertaining way to spend your time, it is true that reading this particular act can conjure up excellent plots for murder mysteries. It tells you when the Secretary of the Treasury can disclose information from tax returns in conjunction with an emergency need to find someone or as part of a criminal investigation or some other interesting exception—not something one would expect in the Internal Revenue Code.

## Telephone Consumer Privacy Protection Act (1991)

This law (47 USC 227) is the "Do Not Call" list-enabling statute. Congress found that although telemarketing can be a good thing, it can also be invasive. This law forbids automatic telephone dialing systems from being used in unsolicited advertisement or solicitations. The FCC ruled that telephone companies maintain lists of people who do not want to be called. If you request to be added to the "Do Not Call" list, you should not receive more telephone calls from that entity.

The law provides that if you receive more than one call within a 12-month period by or on behalf of the same entity in violation of these regulations, you may sue for injunctive relief and recover actual losses or receive up to $500 in actual damages for each violation, whichever is greater, or both such actions (if permitted by state law).

Because there are many lists and many sources for such lists, we recommend that you contact The Direct Marketing Association's Telephone Preference Service at http://www.the-dma.org/consumers/offtelephonelist.html. You can register with them online. There is a small fee for immediate registration and no fee for registration by mail. The Web site says the following:

> *"When you register with TPS, your name, address and telephone number are placed on a do-not-call file. This "delete file" is updated four times a year—January, April, July, and October—and made available to telephone marketing companies who choose to use it. Your name remains on file for five years. DMA members are required to use it!"*

The DMA's Web page also provides helpful assistance in removing your name from mailing lists (the kind that comes delivered by the postman) and from e-mailing lists. Members of the DMA are required to use the "Do Not" lists to maintain their membership in the association.

# Video Privacy Protection Act (1988)

This law (18 USC 2710) protects the buyers and renters of videotapes from the disclosure of their names and addresses and the subject matter of the purchases. Information can be disclosed to the customer, to the customer's representative with written permission, to law enforcement with a warrant, grand jury subpoena, or court order. Information can also be disclosed with a court order in a civil proceeding as long as "a compelling need" has been demonstrated for information that can be obtained no other way, the customer has been informed, and the customer has been given the opportunity to contest the disclosure.

Additionally, names, addresses, and the subject matter may be disclosed to a marketing organization if the customer has been given the opportunity to prohibit the information transfer.

Customers whose information has been inappropriately disclosed can sue for actual damages, punitive damages, attorney's fees, and court costs. The court may also determine other preliminary and equitable relief.

This is the law that resulted from the high feelings around the confirmation debate of Robert Bork in his nomination to the Supreme Court. A reporter from Washington, D.C.'s *City Paper* obtained Mr. Bork's video rental records, in an attempt to relate his video-viewing habits to his possible decisions in court cases. The results of the invasion of Mr. Bork's private viewing habits were probably not germane to his not being confirmed. However, the publication of the list did cause sufficient debate to get this law passed.

# The Wiretap Law

Wire and electronic communications interception (18 USC 2511) is not allowed in the United States unless you are a law enforcement officer and have an authorizing court order. This law also enables you to conjure up very entertaining stories while working your way through it.

People who work for communications providers, the Federal Communications Commission, or representatives of landlords or employers can disclose what they learn in the regular course of their duties as long as the interception was incidental to their regular tasks. You can imagine some telephone maintenance worker overhearing something criminal. Or picture a secretary in a large firm capturing a discussion of nefarious deeds on some sort of dictation equipment. The possibilities are intriguing.

It is important to remember that most conversations have two parties, and one of the parties may have granted the right to be recorded or intercepted. This is the source of the "wearing a wire" stories where the law enforcement agent is recording a conversation between herself and a presumed criminal and manages to get the target to incriminate himself. This would most likely be legal as the agent has given permission. If, however, the agent didn't grant permission, the material gained could not be disclosed. Of course, it would be important for the taping to take place in Puerto Rico, the District of Columbia, or some other federal location because interception and recording of communications might be against the law in some states.

Our attorney advisor points out that a federal surveillance properly authorized by federal agents under federal law will *always* be lawful and admissible no matter what the state law is, by virtue of the Supremacy Clause. Federal law would govern in the 50 states. Because we are discussing federal law, the agent must have been federal. Too bad. There went another wonderful story idea.

Violations of this law are subject to injunctive relief and a mandatory fine of not less than $500 for each violation is prescribed for subsequent violations.

## What Is the Law within the Several States?

State laws vary widely. They derive from vastly different traditions and recognize the immensely different cultures that come together to form the United States. California, with which we are more familiar simply because we both live there, has many laws derived from Spanish law rather than English. Maryland has laws that more specifically come from the tradition of the Catholic Church. New England states have laws that codify the beliefs of their Puritan founders. Because we usually live in only one state at a time, Americans aren't really familiar with the differences among the state laws. Pretty much we believe that whatever we think the law is where we are is the law everywhere. Those of us who have lived in different states *know* that this isn't true, but that doesn't really stop us all from assuming a standard regime based on what we think we know.

These differences also reflect the tension we maintain between federalism and confederation. Americans are conflicted in what we think about our governments and how we want them to work. We want our government to simultaneously stay out of our way and provide maximum efficient services. We want local control, but our own personal values *should* be the ones that everyone shares and the laws based on them should be enforced centrally. Jurisdictions also compete with one another for residents and businesses by having different laws. You can begin to see why our systems look very strange to people who are used to other ways of doing things. The checks and balances provided between the executive, the legislative, and the judicial branches of government are complicated by the fact that we also have local district, municipality, county, and state governments whose organization frequently parallels the divisions in our federal government. In addition, we have representative government and not all of us agree, so you get confusing and conflicting methods of solving problems.

## Identity Theft Laws Illustrate the Different Approaches to Law

For example, Table 13.1 lists some specific laws that address identity theft as of June 2001. Some laws are very specific. For example, in Illinois, Financial Identity Theft law defines a misdemeanor and four classes of felonies based on the value of the financial theft. The following is the exact wording of the Illinois law:

> *"A person commits the offense of financial identity theft when he or she knowingly uses any personal identifying information or personal identification document of another person to fraudulently obtain credit, money, goods, services, or other property in the name of the other person."*

The Illinois law classifies a financial theft as "aggravated" if the victim is older than 60 years or disabled. This means the classes are redefined so that the misdemeanor becomes a Class 4 felony and so forth. The penalties are higher as the Class 4 felony becomes a Class 3 and so on. If the perpetrator has a previous identify theft conviction, the charge becomes aggravated identity theft automatically.

Nevada divides identity theft law into two parts: rules for what happens if you obtain and use the documents of someone and rules for what happens if you possess, transfer, or sell documents or personally identifying information that can be used for financial gain. The first type of incident is a Class E felony. The second, more severe, is a Class C felony.

Florida takes a third approach. It classifies possessing or intending to fraudulently use personal information without the person's consent as a third degree felony. Florida adds a misdemeanor of using someone's personal information without their consent to harass the person.

Many of the laws listed in Table 13.1 are available online so that you can read them yourself and think about how they might apply to you. It's also interesting to speculate about the historical reasons for the differences in the laws.

## TABLE 13.1    STATE LAWS RELATED TO IDENTITY THEFT

| | |
|---|---|
| Alaska* | 2000 Alaska Sess. Laws 65 |
| Arizona | Ariz. Rev. Stat. § 13-2008 |
| Arkansas | Ark. Code Ann. § 5-37-227 |
| California | Cal. Penal Code § 530.5 |
| Colorado* | 2000 Colo. Legis. Serv. ch. 159 (May 19, 2000) |
| Connecticut | 1999 Conn. Acts 99 |
| Delaware* | 72 Del. Laws 297 (2000) |
| Florida | Fla. Stat. Ann. § 817.568 |
| Georgia | Ga. Code Ann. § § 16-9-121 |
| Idaho | Idaho Code § 18-3126 |
| Illinois | 720 ILCS 5/16G |
| Indiana | Ind.Code 35-43-5-4 (2000) |
| Iowa | Iowa Code § 715A.8 |
| Kansas | Kan. Stat. Ann. § 21-4108 |
| Kentucky | Ky. Rev. Stat. Ann. § 160, ch. 514 [PDF only] |
| Louisiana | La. Rev. Stat. Ann. § 67.16 |
| Maine | Me. Rev. Stat. Ann. tit. 17-A, § 354-2A |
| Maryland | Md. Ann. Code art. 27, § 231 |
| Massachusetts | Mass. Gen. Laws ch. 266, § 37E |
| Michigan | MCL 750.219e; MCL  750.219f |
| Minnesota | Minn. Stat. Ann. §  609.527 |
| Mississippi | Miss. Code Ann. § 97-19-85 |
| Missouri | Mo. Rev. Stat. § 570.223 |

## TABLE 13.1   CONTINUED

| | |
|---|---|
| Nevada | Nev. Rev. State. § 205.465 |
| New Hampshire | N.H. Rev. Stat. Ann. § 638:26 |
| New Jersey | N.J. Stat. Ann. § 2C:21-17 |
| North Carolina | N.C. Gen. Stat. § 14-113.20 |
| North Dakota | N.D.C.C. § 12.1-23-11 |
| Ohio | Ohio Rev. Code Ann. 2913.49 |
| Oklahoma | Okla. Stat. tit. 21, § 1533.1 |
| Oregon | Or. Rev. Stat. § 165.800 |
| Pennsylvania* | Pa. Cons. Stat. Ann. § 4120 |
| Rhode Island | R.I. Gen. Laws § 11-49.1-1 |
| South Carolina | S.C. Code Ann. § 16-13-500, 501 |
| South Dakota | S.D. Codified Laws § 22-30A-3.1. |
| Tennessee | TCA 39-14-150 |
| Texas | Tex. Penal Code § 32.51 |
| Utah | Utah Code Ann. § 76-6-1101-1104 |
| Virginia | VA. Code Ann. § 18.2-186.3 |
| Washington | Wash. Rev. Code § 9.35.020 |
| West Virginia | W. Va. Code § 61-3-54 |
| Wisconsin | Wis. Stat. § 943.201 |
| Wyoming | Wyo. Stat. Ann. § 6-3-901 |

*(Source: http://www.consumer.gov/idtheft/statelaw.htm. Current as of June 2001.)*

Where specific identity theft laws do not exist, the practices may be prohibited under other state laws. States marked with * do not currently have their law available online

# Types of Privacy and Security Laws Found in the States

Several types of laws already in existence affect the treatment of information about individuals. Some of those are quite broad, like California's constitutionally protected Right of Privacy. Others are quite specific.

Many of the laws are concerned with the protection of records gathered by the states themselves:

- **Tax return laws** generally prohibit any disclosure of information gathered on state tax returns.

- **Criminal justice system laws** generally have requirements about who can access particular forms of data gathered about you in conjunction with a law enforcement activity. This means that not all information is automatically public, but, of course, some may be. You are familiar with the "Police blotter" reports in your local newspaper, for example. These laws also generally require that information gathered about you in law enforcement activities be accessible to you, so that you can amend the information or correct it if it is wrong. The disposition of the case is usually required to be recorded, and most states require reporting law enforcement information in promptly standard formats. Some states, such as California, require that police blotter information becomes protected when it is no longer current.

- **School records laws** generally allow students and their parents to inspect school records and to challenge them if they are inaccurate or incomplete. Schools are limited in their ability to disclose information to third parties. This is why you must ask to have your transcripts forwarded when another educational institution requires them.

- **General fair information laws** limit the data that a government can collect and keep. These laws usually allow you to inspect the data and challenge it if you believe it inaccurate. State governments may be restricted in their ability to disclose information to third parties.

- **Election laws** may limit the disclosure of voter registration data, making it available to candidates for election mailings, but not to a marketing organization to sell other products.

- **Motor vehicle registration laws** may limit the disclosure of vehicle registration, identification card, and/or drivers license data to authorized personnel.

The following are other laws that affect how other people are allowed to gather information about you:

- **Medical records laws** allow you to see your records. Restrictions are usually placed on who has access to the records and to whom the records can be disclosed, particularly with regard to mental health records.

- **Genetic records laws** have additional specific restrictions placed upon them. Such records may only be used for therapeutic or diagnostic reasons.

- **Insurance records laws** require that insurers disclose their own information practices to applicants and to policyholders. Applicants must be notified when information about them is gathered, and the notification must include whether or not the information is required solely for marketing or research. Individuals who are denied insurance are able to learn the specific reasons and to see the information that caused the denial. The consent of the individual is required before personal information may be disclosed. Genetic records may not be used to determine eligibility for insurance.

- **Banking records laws** forbid financial institutions from disclosing information about a customer without legal process or consent. Additionally, banks are encouraged to send you your financial transaction records by making the banks responsible for any errors until the customer is informed of the transaction. This is part of the Uniform Commercial Code.

- **Credit reporting laws** forbid the collection of information about race, religion, or sex and restrict the disclosure of credit information.

- **Employment laws** forbid the collection of race, sex, color, religion, national origin, and so on from applicants. All information gathered about you must be available to you. Polygraph (lie detector) tests as a condition of employment are restricted.

- **Junk fax laws** restrict the sending of unsolicited fax advertisements.

- **Telemarketing laws** may restrict the use of recorded messages in marketing calls. They may also establish state do-not-call lists, which must be respected by marketers.

- **Video and cable laws** restrict the disclosure of information about viewing habits and purchases.

- **Journalism shield laws** enable journalists to keep their sources private. This helps whistleblowers and others who might be discriminated against for talking to the media.

- **Legal proceeding limitation laws** help keep personal information about people out of court records by limiting the types of information that can be disclosed by people in the counseling professions, such as clergy or therapists, or who may have other personal information about you, such as accountants. The idea is to allow relevant and only relevant information into the court.

- **Public records acts** are laws that detail when, and under what conditions, government-held information about us may be released. Similar to the Federal Freedom of Information Act (FOIA), these laws contain exemptions from the rules for disclosure that are intended to protect privacy.

Other types of laws that protect your privacy that we've missed probably exist. The important thing for you to remember is that many laws can help you keep your personal information in only the places where it needs to be. You can do simple research on your own now, because many states have their bodies of law online and searchable. However, if you believe you have a specific problem or disagreement with an agency, an employer, or a business, we do encourage you to seek qualified legal counsel. Having a general idea of the law might help you determine who you want to work with, but it is not a substitute for good legal representation.

# If We've Got All These Laws, Why Would We Need More? (The Regulatory Climate: 2001)

Here we are again at divided opinion. Some people think we have plenty of federal laws addressing digital privacy and security needs. Their stance is that what is needed is fair and efficient enforcement of the laws we already have. These are generally (but not always) people from the business community or people who believe that fewer regulations are better than more. Others think that additional laws are necessary. These are generally the privacy and consumer advocate community and people who believe that more regulations are better than fewer. As usual, both arguments have valid points.

The Information Technology Association of America, a trade association that addresses the needs of information technology companies like computer manufacturers, telecommunications companies, Internet service providers, and companies that provide professional services developed a list of challenges that privacy laws must address. This list is like a checklist of points to be considered in developing new laws. The challenges would need to be addressed no matter what jurisdiction (within the United States) the law is intended for. Mark Uncapher, ITAA's Vice President and General Counsel, intended the list of problems to provoke thoughtful consideration of a law's attributes. ITAA's interest is in making sure that information technology is well placed should a law be passed:

- **Notice**—If notice is required by the law, are there required parts of the notice? Is specific placement of a notice with relation to a Web page or online service screen required? What conditions must be met for the notice to be deemed adequate? Who decides whether the notice is adequate? Are there roles for specific agencies, like the Federal Trade Commission or the California Bureau of Consumer Affairs? If a service provider used a privacy notice technology like P3P, would that qualify as adequate notice?

- **Consent**—Will specific requirements need to be met to provide consumers with a consent mechanism? Must a consumer explicitly agree to the use of information? Can implied consent be used? Will technologies like P3P be considered adequate to assist consumers and businesses with consent regimes?

- **Security**—Are there specific requirements for protecting acquired information? Is a security statement required as part of the notice requirement? Are specific practices required or encouraged? Is specific training required on the part of people who are handling the data?

- **Access**—Must the consumer be able to obtain a copy of the information gathered? Must the mechanism work using a specific technology? Will a data correction mechanism be required if the consumer believes the information to be inaccurate? Will specific requirements for authentication be made? What kinds of notification will be required to explain the processes to consumers? What kinds of training and certification will be required of businesses that gather and process personal information?

- **Scope of law**—Assuming that the law addresses the gathering of personal information, does it apply to both online and offline gathering? One of the points made by online businesses is that they believe they are being unfairly singled out for doing the same thing that offline businesses do. Does the new law coordinate with existing law? Sometimes it is easier to get a new law passed than it is to research and understand what the current law provides. This leads to conflicting laws and confusing practice for consumers, the concerned businesses, and law enforcement. Will the proposed standard apply to government data collection as well? Businesses want to make certain that their practices are not unfairly held to standards that government can ignore. Will the law apply equally to large and small business? Is there any consideration for the fact that large businesses are trying to coordinate their practices across the law of multiple jurisdictions or for the fact that small business may not have the same resource as large ones? Will the law apply also to not-for-profit organizations and educational institutions?

- **Preemption**—If the law preempts the laws of other jurisdictions, how broad a preemption is specified? If a U.S. Federal law preempts state law, will there be a role for the State Attorneys General? A usual role for the Attorneys General is the enforcement of consumer protection laws.

- **Third-party information use**— Will transfer of information to another entity require specific notification? If a third party releases personal information, what is the liability of the business?

- **Enforcement**—Who enforces the law, the Federal Trade Commission or The States Attorneys General, or both? Are civil damages allowed? If they are allowed, are they specifically set in law (including the capping of damages)? Are only actual damages allowed or are punitive damages included? Will class action lawsuits be included as remedy? Are criminal penalties involved?

You can see that a lot of questions need to be addressed. The complexity of the issue means that there continues to be a number of different approaches to solving the privacy dilemma in law.

## Who Are the Federal Agency Players?

As of mid-2001, the most active agency in consumer privacy protection is the Federal Trade Commission. The FTC has taken the lead in keeping privacy promises because of its consumer protection role in general and its legislated role in developing and enforcing the rules that protect children online. The Commerce Department negotiated the Safe Harbor

Agreement between the United States and the European Community that enables transfers of information about people into the United States under certain strict conditions. The Department of State, The Department of Justice, and the United States Trade Representative have interests in enforcing current laws and in using the influence of the U.S. Government to build a consensus around business and legal practices that protect privacy for everyone. The Department of Health and Human Services has a special relationship to privacy because its staff developed the HIPPA privacy regulations that affect how medical information is disclosed to other people. The Department of the Treasury has an important role in protecting the personal financial data that comes to it through the Internet Revenue Service. All the agencies are responsible for keeping the information that they gather secure and that the data is not disclosed to people who don't need it.

## Laws Around the World

Our approaches in the United States are not those of the rest of the world, of course. The biggest difference between U.S. law and the law of other countries is the fact that in the United States, law is introduced in response to a specific incident or fear, rather than to address a condition that has not yet happened. The European approach of setting the framework first (top-down approach) is really foreign to the American way of life. We don't build the rules first. The Europeans do. It's a difference so basic that it makes it difficult to even talk to one another about the issue.

In the United States, we fear big government. In Europe, the government is central to all activities and the fear is of big business. Clearly, those statements are oversimplifications, but the differences in attitudes that the statements illustrate are fundamental to our cultures.

The European top-down approach to law led to the European Union Data Directive, but the ideas about privacy came from the United States. In 1973, the fair information principles, upon which much privacy law is based, were first discussed in the context of discussions of health information and privacy by the U.S. Health, Education and Welfare Department. Those principles were cited by the OECD (Organization for Economic Cooperation and Development at http://www.oecd.org, a treaty organization) in refining and promulgating what we now commonly see as those principles.

## The EU Directive

In English at `http://europa.eu.int/eur-lex/en/lif/dat/1995/en_395L0046` `.html`, 95/46/EC is the explicit set of rules concerning the protection of data about individual persons who reside in the European Community. It instructs the individual countries that make up the EU on the content of the laws they must enact concerning the collection, storage, processing, or transfer of the data. The laws were to be enacted by October 1998, but not all the countries were able to meet the deadline.

One significant difference between the EU and the United States in how we see information is that information appearing on a business card would not be considered personally identifying in the U.S. We think of that type of information as "okay for others to know." We hand out business cards and fill out forms at trade shows expecting that the information is going to be added to a database of people interested in a category of products or a contact list for an individual representing another company. In Europe, information on a business card is considered personally identifying.

Of particular interest to American companies was the requirement that data about EU citizens could not be transferred to a country that did not have "adequate" data protection rules. Because the United States does not have a single rule, but rather a lot of them, and it does not have a single office or officer dedicated to protection of data about people, the United States was not considered to have adequate rules. To make sure that international trade didn't come to a halt, or that U.S. multi-national companies wouldn't be able to move information about their employees or customers into the United States for processing, the Department of Commerce negotiated an agreement. The Safe Harbor agreement allows the data to be moved across the U.S. border under certain specific conditions.

## The Safe Harbor

Subscribers to this agreement certify that they provide notice, choice, access, security, data integrity, and onward transfer guarantees that are similar to EU law. They register annually with the Department of Commerce. Companies participating are considered "adequate" and data may be transferred to these companies. The Data Protection officers in each EU country either automatically grant or waive prior approval for each data transfer. Claims brought against the companies by EU citizens generally are heard in U.S. courts. Current information about the Safe Harbor can be found at `http://www.export.gov/safeharbor`, as shown in Figure 13.1.

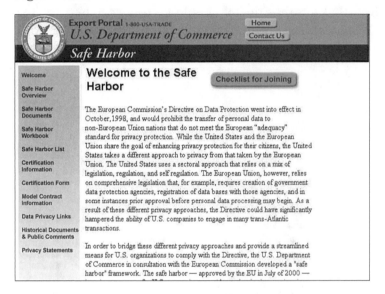

**FIGURE 13.1**

*The Department of Commerce's Safe Harbor Web site.*

The companies who participate must either self-certify or belong to an organization that certifies the accuracy of their statements. Their privacy policies must contain a statement that they belong to the Safe Harbor. The Department of Commerce maintains a list that everyone can use to make sure that the data transfers to the United States from the EU are presumed to be legal. The current Safe Harbor list may be found at the Department of Commerce site at `http://web.ita.doc.gov/safeharbor/` `shlist.nsf/webPages/safe%20harbor%20list!OpenDocument&Start=1`.

In the following sections we've included some more specific information about some of the countries within the EU because the differences are almost as interesting as the similarities.

## Germany

As of June 2001, a German law that implements the EU directive does not exist. The Berlin data protection people operate this Web site. The initial page (available in both German and English) is at `http://www.daten-schutz-berlin.de`, as shown in Figure 13.2. There are three other laws, however, that address how it should be treated. They are Teleservices Data Protection Act/Teledienstedatenschutzgesetze (TDDS), The Media Services State Treaty, and The Federal Data Protection Act.

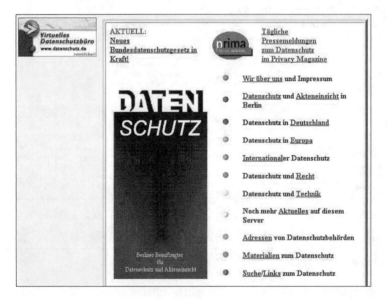

**FIGURE 13.2**

*The Berlin Data Protection Web page.*

An interesting aspect of German law is that it requires any provider of services on the Internet to offer anonymizing or pseudonymizing services if it is technically feasible to do so.

Personal data may be collected, processed, and used by information society service providers only if specifically permitted by legal provision or with the consent of the data subject and only if it is necessary for performing information society services. Use for other purposes is only possible if permitted by another legal provision or if the user has given his consent.

Data subjects must be informed of the type, scope, place and purpose of the collection, processing and use of personal data, and the user's right to withdraw permission at any time prior to the beginning of the collection. The *data subject* is the subject of the data, or the person whose information is collected.

## United Kingdom

The relevant law in the United Kingdom is The Data Protection Act of 1998 (for more information go to http://www.hmso.gov.uk/acts/acts1998/ 19980029.htm). This is the UK implementation of the EU Data Protection Directive: 95/46/EC. It also applies to relevant accessible paper records such as school records, and so on. The Act is enforced by the Office of the Information Commissioner, formerly the Office of the Data Protection Commissioner, whose Web page (as of June 2001) is shown in Figure 13.3.

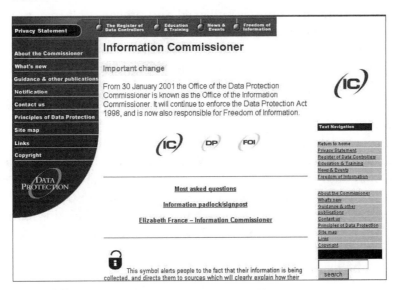

**FIGURE 13.3**

*The UK Office of the Information Commissioner.*

UK law is among those that distinguishes between personal data and sensitive data. This law sets rules for processing (defined as any collection or use of data) of personal information that must be treated *fairly* according to the stated principles of notice, choice, access, security, and so on. It applies to all data about identifiable *living* individuals. The UK Data Protection Act makes specific provision for sensitive personal data. Sensitive data include racial or ethnic origin, political opinions, religious or other beliefs, trade union membership, health, sex life, criminal proceedings, or convictions. Sensitive data must have explicit consent for processing, be required by law for employment purposes, be required for a legal proceeding, or be required to protect the vital interests of the data subject or another person. Otherwise, it may not be processed. Data may only be processed if necessary and shall not be kept longer than is necessary for the purpose.

## Spain

In Spanish, the Agencia De Protección De Datos is at `http://www.agenciaprotecciondatos.org`; Law 15.1999 of 13 Dec 1999 on Protection of Personal Data is the Spanish implementation of the EU Directive.

Personal data may only be collected and processed if they are adequate, relevant, and not excessive in relation to the defined, explicit and legitimate purposes for which they are collected. Unambiguous consent is required for legitimacy of processing. Consent to process sensitive data must be expressly given in writing.

## France

In French, Commission Nationale de l'Informatique et des Libertés is at `http://www.cnil.fr`; the relevant French statute is the Law of January 6, 1978 on data processing, data files, and individual liberties. French law has not yet been aligned with Directive 95/46. The Commission has an excellent piece demonstrating what a server can find out about you without your knowledge. The English version of the demonstration is at `http://www.cnil.fr/traces/index.htm`. Figure 13.4 shows the "detective" searching for information about you.

Sensitive data (racial origin, political, religious or philosophical opinions, trade union affiliation, or sexual morals) cannot be processed without prior consent. Unfair data collection is prohibited. Processing must be adequate, relevant, and not excessive in relation to the purposes for which the data are collected. Data may not be stored longer than necessary. Each data processing file must be declared to CNIL for private individuals and companies or authorized by a ministerial decree for public sector. There are additional specific regulations on health, criminal offences, and defense.

**FIGURE 13.4**

*The English language information demonstration from CNIL.*

## Italy

The Italians have the Law of 31 Dec 1996.

Italian data subjects have the right of access and the right to knowledge of logic of the processing involved. Data must be processed fairly and lawfully; collected for specific, explicit, and legitimate purposes and processed in a way compatible with these purposes. The data must be adequate, relevant, and not excessive; accurate and up-to-date. Data may only be kept in a form where data subjects can be identified no longer than necessary.

Private data collection generally requires consent; public sector data processing (collection and processing by a governmental body) does not require consent.

## Portugal

In Portuguese, Comissão Nacional De Protecção De Dados is at `http://www.cnpd.pt`; Portugal's law is Law 67/98.

Portuguese law also distinguishes between personal and sensitive data. It generally follows the data protection laws of other EU countries. It includes a right "not to be subject to automated individual decisions." This particular provision is found in Article 13. This law also applies to video surveillance.

For the Portuguese, processing is defined as "any operation or set of operations which is performed upon personal data, whether wholly or partly by automatic means, such as collection, recording, organization, storage, adaptation or alteration, retrieval, consultation, use, disclosure by transmission, dissemination or otherwise making available, alignment or combination, blocking, erasure or destruction."

## What About Countries Outside the EU?

The European Union only has 15 countries. That leaves roughly 200 countries and many of them have privacy laws. The laws are similar to the ones we've discussed before.

### Australia

For example, Australia has a privacy commissioner and passed a privacy law in 1998 with amendments in 2001. See the Commissioner's Web site at http://www.privacy.gov.au and shown in Figure 13.5. The law originally dealt with the government's gathering and use of information about people. Rules that include businesses were added with the latest amendments.

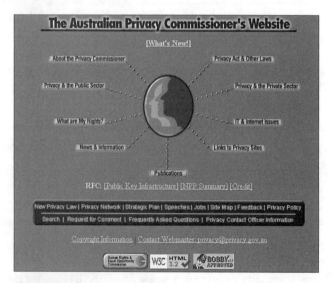

**FIGURE 13.5**

*The Australian Privacy Commissioner's Web site.*

## Hong Kong

While not precisely a country, Hong Kong has a commissioner for Personal Data. The commissioner's English language Web site is at `http://www.pco.org.hk`. The commissioner is responsible for enforcing the privacy ordinance, a law since 1996, which restricts the usage of information that can be used to identify a living person and gives subjects the right to review the data, enable it to be collected, and ensure it is correct.

## Canada

Canada has approached matters concerning individual privacy with an interesting blend of ideas from Europe and from the United States. Like the United States, Canada's Constitution bestows no explicit right to individual privacy. Also, like the United States, their courts have held that the Constitution does grant protections from unreasonable search and seizure. Unlike the United States, Canada has a Privacy Commissioner. The Commissioner's Web page is at `http://www.privcom.gc.ca/` and shown in Figure 13.6. The legislature devoted much discussion to privacy matters during 2000 and considered a Charter of Privacy Rights. That has not yet passed, but the Personal Information Protection and Electronic Documents Act did become law on January 1, 2001.

**FIGURE 13.6**

*The Canadian Privacy Commissioner's Web site.*

This law, also known as Bill C-6 (see `http://www.parl.gc.ca/36/2/parlbus/chambus/house/bills/government/C-6/C-6_3/C-6_cover-E.html`), begins a more stringent privacy regime in Canada. It is initially applied to the collection, use, and disclosure of personal information by companies that are federally regulated within Canada. Those are the financial services, telecommunications, broadcast media, and air transportation industries. Application of the law to health information begins in January 2002. The application of the law to other industries will begin in 2004.

The first trans-border data flow that will be affected is personal information made available for a fee by businesses located in Canada. Those types of transfers will now be subject to the act's 10 fair information practices after the information leaves Canada. This means that the subjects must have consented to the data collection; the uses of the data must be limited to those specified in the consent; access to the collected data must have been provided; and the subject has the right to amend the data that is inaccurate or incomplete.

It would seem this law meets the EU standard for adequacy, so data could be transferred out of the EU to Canada. By the way, the Canadian law specifically exempts information concerning your business title, business address, and business telephone number from the list of personally identifying information.

## Mexico

In June 2000, Mexico's new e-Commerce law took effect. It provides for new rights for consumers who use electronic services including a measure that requires businesses to respect the consumer's desire to not receive commercial solicitations. Information provided by consumers must be respected, treated confidentially, and not transferred to a third party without the expressed consent of the consumer or a legal requirement by a governmental body. Security of the information must be technically maintained and a notification of how the security is maintained must be made to the consumer before the transactions take place.

## A Comprehensive Survey of International Privacy Laws

David Banisar, who is a senior fellow at EPIC and the Deputy Director of Privacy International, provides a comprehensive survey called "Privacy and Human Rights 2000, an International Survey of Privacy Laws." You can find this work online at http://www.privacyinternational. org/survey. You can also buy a printed copy of the report there and see the surveys from 1998 and 1999.

# What About Laws that Don't Exist Yet?

The sections that preceded this one briefly discussed some laws that relate to privacy and security, digital or not. Legislatures, however, meet for the purpose of passing laws, or at least discussing and debating passing new laws.

In the United States, we all learn the path a bill takes between introduction and enactment. The exact path differs from state to state. Some states have legislatures that meet for a fixed period of time every two years. Some states have full-time legislatures. All but one, Nebraska, have two houses through which a bill must pass before being signed by the governor and becoming law. The federal bill process is the one with which we are most familiar because we have been taken through it time and again.

The process seems pretty simple, as we attempt to illustrate in Figure 13.7. Someone has a great idea and composes some legislative language. The language is refined and introduced and becomes a bill. The bill is sent to an appropriate committee where it is debated in committee and hearings are held. If it passes from committee, it returns to the "floor" of the house in which it was introduced where it may be debated again. If it passes, roughly the same process must be undertaken in the other legislative house, until bills pass both houses. If they differ, a conference committee is held to try to match up the differences and produce a coherent bill. If successful, the bills are returned, voted on again, and sent to the President for signature and enactment.

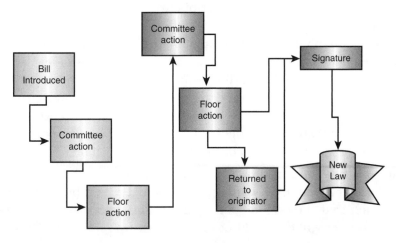

**FIGURE 13.7**

*How a bill becomes a law.*

In practice, things don't usually go that smoothly.

First, a bill needs a *champion*. A champion is a legislator with sufficient political clout to shepherd the bill through the legislative process. The first task is to get the bill assigned to an appropriate committee. Bills die quickly and quietly if they are not assigned to a committee interested or empowered to take up the issue that the bill addresses. Or they may die if there is a fight over which committee will hear the bill. Parliamentary maneuvering can be death for legislation.

After the bill moves to committee, the champion will need to make sure that the bill is heard within the committee. If the chair or the minority leadership of the committee or subcommittee to which it is assigned doesn't want to hear the bill, it is difficult to get the attention of the committee. Many bills need to be considered and if leadership isn't behind the bill, it will languish among many other good ideas that don't get heard.

When a bill is on a committee hearing agenda, the fun really begins. That's when advocates become really active; trying to get the bill heard or ignored, trying to firm up or loosen the language, and trying to get their particular point of view recognized and represented during a hearing. The staff of the legislators on the committee talk about the bill with interested people. The committee staff itself also discuss the bill with interested people. A hearing is scheduled, people testify, the committee members ask questions, and then direct their staff to improve a portion of the bill.

Hearings are public and transcripts are usually made available following the hearing. The transcripts will contain the formal written testimony (which probably didn't get completely presented in the hearing because of time constraints) and the remarks of the legislators and any questions and answers that followed the remarks and the testimony. Frequently, transcripts of committee proceedings will quickly be available on the committee's Web site. Many committees are now presenting their hearings via live Web-cast. Some hearings are broadcast on one of the C-SPAN broadcast networks or on the C-SPAN Web site.

After hearings are held, a committee session is held in which the bill is worked on to make its wording final. Sometimes a bill will be amended so much that the original is tossed out and a completely new bill with a new number will come out of these "mark-up" sessions. These, too, are public and many people who care about the outcome of the bill's language will be present to hear the debate. If the bill is approved by the committee, a report is written describing why the committee has recommended passage. The report gives its name to the process, which is called *reporting out of committee*.

The bill then comes to the floor for debate. Members rise to recommend or oppose the bill's passage. Sometimes rules about the bill's consideration are specified. The bill could be amended during floor debate. Each amendment must be voted on. The bill could be returned to the committee for reconsideration. It could be passed or defeated.

If the bill is passed, it goes to the Senate for consideration along similar lines. Again, a bill is assigned to a committee, heard, marked up, reported out, debated in the full legislature, and passed or defeated. It remains important that a champion be identified if the bill is to have any chance of passage.

If the Senate version is passed with different wording than the House bill, it must be returned to the House for concurrence before it can go to the President for signature.

Sometimes, the same or similar bills are introduced into the House and the Senate at the same time. When this happens, discussion and debate can happen at roughly the same time in both houses and the bill should take less elapsed time to completion.

# Be Your Own Advocate

The job of the advocate is to, (ahem) advocate. Advocacy is the act of representing a point of view. An advocate will be more successful, of course, if the points of view are presented clearly, with good documentation, representing a clear constituency, and some sort of positive message. It doesn't really help if you just say "no" without any alternatives.

Many different kinds of successful advocates are in Washington. When people disagree with the points the advocates are making, the advocates get termed *special interests*. However, all interests are equally special, and most members of the House and Senate are willing to discuss matters of interest to their constituents, but they can't read minds. We have frequently overheard someone decrying the fact that "those idiots in Washington" are doing something with which the speaker disagrees.

However, if you ask, the speakers haven't written, called, e-mailed, or in any way conveyed an opinion on the matter to the Congressperson or Senator who represents them. This is not only unfair to the representatives, but it doesn't get the desired result. Contact your Congress or state legislature people when you have an opinion, so they know what you think. We've found the following list of hints to be helpful in making advocacy visits.

### HOW TO MAKE A SUCCESSFUL ADVOCACY VISIT

Politicians and their staff are more than willing to listen to

- A constituent
- An employer in their constituency
- A representative of an industry that has concerns

You should

- If possible, visit in person accompanying an executive who represents your constituency—your company, your organization, or your group
- Identify yourself and describe your group
- State your concern concisely
- Remember the "Call to Action"—tell them what you want them to do
- Leave behind a one-page description of the problem/action and contact and group info

The whole visit shouldn't take more than 10 or 15 minutes.

It is not necessary to be a large contributor to gain access to a member of Congress or to talk with appropriate committee or legislative staff. Obviously, people who are large contributors are more likely to be well known, but you really only need to have a clearly stated point of view and ask to be heard. The people who work for you in Congress want to know what you think. On the United States House of Representatives Web site, (http://www.house.gov) for example, there is an area on the home page, shown in Figure 13.8, that helps you do just that.

**Write Your Representative**

Constituents may identify and/or contact their elected
Member to the U.S. House of Representatives.

**FIGURE 13.8**

*The House Web pages helps you communicate with your congressperson.*

# Privacy and Security Legislation in Congress

Legislation concerning digital privacy and security matters that are not
matters of national security are usually assigned to the Senate Judiciary
Committee or the Senate Committee on Commerce, Science, and
Transportation. The current Chairman of the Judiciary Committee (as of
June 2001) is Senator Patrick Leahy of Vermont. The ranking member is
Senator Orrin Hatch of Utah. Mr. Hatch and Mr. Leahy switched roles
when Senator Jeffords of Vermont chose to leave the Republican Party
and become an independent. The Chairman of the Committee generally
termed the Senate Commerce Committee is Senator Fritz Hollings of
South Carolina. The ranking member is Senator John McCain of Arizona.
Again, Mr. Hollings and Mr. McCain switched roles when Mr. Jeffords
changed his party affiliation.

If you want to find the bills currently introduced in the 107th Congress
dealing with the Internet and privacy, point your browser to
`http://thomas.loc.gov`, which is the Web site for the Thomas system in the
Library of Congress (see Figure 13.9).

Enter the phrase "Internet privacy" into the search window for
word/phrase. The result shows you the current bills in progress and
indicates their status. The Thomas system can include multiple versions
of bills, if the bills are reported from committee with different wording
than the original, for example. When you select a bill from the result set
and display it, the words "Internet" and "privacy" are highlighted on the
display screen, so you can see why a particular bill was included in your
result set. An example of a status report is shown in Figure 13.10.

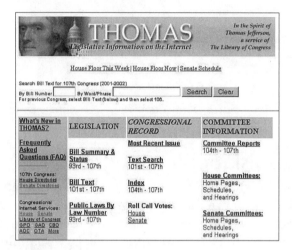

**FIGURE 13.9**

*The Thomas system.*

```
http://thomas.loc.gov/cgi-bin/bdquery/z?d107:HR00237.@@@L&summ2=m&

Bill Summary & Status for the 107th Congress


NEW SEARCH | HOME | HELP


H.R.237
Sponsor: Rep Eshoo, Anna G. (introduced 1/20/2001)
Latest Major Action: 2/14/2001 Referred to House subcommittee
Title: To protect the privacy of consumers who use the Internet.

              Jump to: Titles, Status, Committees, Related Bill Details, Amendments

TITLE(S): (italics indicate a title for a portion of a bill)

  • SHORT TITLE(S) AS INTRODUCED:
    Consumer Internet Privacy Enhancement Act
  • OFFICIAL TITLE AS INTRODUCED:
    To protect the privacy of consumers who use the Internet.


STATUS: (color indicates Senate actions)

1/20/2001:
    Referred to the House Committee on Energy and Commerce.

  2/14/2001:
        Referred to the Subcommittee on Commerce, Trade and Consumer Protection.
```

**FIGURE 13.10**

*A status report from the Thomas system.*

The Thomas system includes a bill status report so that you can determine the exact status of a particular bill. Status includes the name of the legislator who introduced the bill, the introduction date, the date of the latest action, and a description of the action itself. If the bill has been referred to committee, the status report includes the name of the committee as well as any action that may have taken place.

The following sidebars list the various Senate committees that hear and debate legislation, and the various topics they cover. As you can see from these sidebars, Internet or privacy issues may span several committees, which is probably the cause of some of the redundant bills and other confusion in the U.S. legislature.

## THE SENATE COMMITTEE ON THE JUDICIARY

The Senate Committee on the Judiciary is referred all proposed legislation, messages, petitions, memorials, and other matters relating to the following subjects:

- Apportionment of Representatives
- Bankruptcy, mutiny, espionage, and counterfeiting
- Civil liberties
- Constitutional amendments
- Federal courts and judges
- Government information
- Holidays and celebrations
- Immigration and naturalization
- Interstate compacts generally
- Judicial proceedings, civil and criminal, generally
- Local courts in the territories and possessions
- Measures relating to claims against the United States
- National penitentiaries
- Patent Office
- Patents, copyrights, and trademarks
- Protection of trade and commerce against unlawful restraints and monopolies
- Revision and codification of the statutes of the United States
- State and territorial boundary lines

*(Source: Senate Rules, XXV, Standing Committees)*

## THE SENATE COMMITTEE ON COMMERCE

The Committee on Commerce, Science, and Transportation is referred all proposed legislation, messages, petitions, memorials, and other matters relating to the following subjects:

- Coast Guard
- Coastal zone management
- Communications
- Highway safety
- Inland waterways, except construction
- Interstate commerce
- Marine and ocean navigation, safety, and transportation, including navigational aspects of deepwater ports
- Marine fisheries
- Merchant marine and navigation
- Nonmilitary aeronautical and space sciences
- Oceans, weather, and atmospheric activities
- Panama Canal and interoceanic canals generally
- Regulation of consumer products and services, including testing related to toxic substances, other than pesticides, and except for credit, financial services, and housing
- Regulation of interstate common carriers, including railroads, buses, trucks, vessels, pipelines, and civil aviation
- Science, engineering, and technology research and development and policy
- Sports
- Standards and measurement
- Transportation
- Transportation and commerce aspects of Outer Continental Shelf lands
- Such committee shall also study and review, on a comprehensive basis, all matters relating to science and technology, oceans policy, transportation, communications, and consumer affairs, and report thereon from time to time

*(Source: Senate Rules, XXV, Standing Committees)*

---

You can see by comparing the lists of items that the committees are empowered to consider, that there can be conflict when it comes to assigning privacy and security legislation to a committee. The Commerce people argue that the matters are under their purview because communications and interstate commerce are dealt with in this committee. The Judiciary people argue that bankruptcy, counterfeiting, compacts concerning interstate commerce, and civil liberties issues are the purview of that committee and that these matters affect and are affected by digital privacy and security. Of course, both committee members are correct and therefore, some bills are assigned to one committee, some to another, and occasionally bills get assigned to both.

Similarly in the House, bills are referred either to House Commerce or to House Judiciary. The Commerce Committee has a specific subcommittee on Telecommunications and the Internet, chaired by Representative Fred Upton of Michigan. Representative Edward Markey of Massachusetts is the ranking member on the subcommittee. The full committee is chaired by Representative Billy Tauzin of Louisiana and the ranking member is Representative John Dingell of Michigan. Representative James Sensenbrenner of Wisconsin is chair of the House Judiciary Committee. The ranking member is Representative John Conyers of Michigan.

The chair and the ranking member of the committees are the senior elected officials on the committee. If there is a Democratic majority, as in the Senate at the moment, the chair of the committee is a Democrat and the ranking member is a Republican. If there is a Republican majority, as in the House of Representatives, the chair is a Republican and the ranking member is a Democrat. The membership of the committee is usually proportional to the split among the party membership in the Congress. In the 107th Congress in session in 2001, the House has a greater number of Republican members and that is reflected in the committee memberships. The Senate is more nearly even and that is reflected also.

Each Senator or Representative has a staff of assistants. They include schedulers, public relations people, people who work in constituent relations, and legislative directors and assistants. The legislative people prepare legislation or discussion arguments and debate points for their bosses. They work with advocates to hear points of view and summarize and report those meetings to their bosses. Each committee also has staff that includes legislative and legal counsel. There are counsel for the majority and counsel for the minority. The committee counsel are usually the people who seek out people to testify at hearings. Each of these people has input into legislation.

When you want to make sure your point of view is heard on a particular piece of introduced legislation, you need to figure out who is the bill's champion. It is important to understand what problem the bill is intended to solve and why the champion believes this bill is the appropriate solution. You can't talk to anybody about the bill with any authority until you understand that point. After you have found what committee the bill is assigned to, you need to determine whether the majority counsel or the minority counsel is more likely to agree with your point of view. Although you can talk to either side on a bill, you obviously get more mileage from presenting points to the side more likely to help you make those points to the committee at large.

After you have found your natural allies, make an appointment and follow the rules for successful advocacy calls.

The following list of U.S. House of Representative committees is intended, like the Senate lists, to help you find the right place to go to make sure your input is heard on issues you care about.

## THE HOUSE JUDICIARY COMMITTEE

The House Judiciary Committee is referred all proposed legislation, messages, petitions, memorials, and other matters relating to the following subjects:

- The judiciary and judicial proceedings, civil and criminal
- Administrative practice and procedure
- Apportionment of Representatives
- Bankruptcy, mutiny, espionage, and counterfeiting
- Civil liberties
- Constitutional amendments
- Federal courts and judges, and local courts in the Territories and possessions
- Immigration and naturalization
- Interstate compacts, generally
- Claims against the United States
- Meetings of Congress; attendance of Members, Delegates, and the Resident Commissioner; and their acceptance of incompatible offices
- National penitentiaries
- Patents, the Patent and Trademark Office, copyrights, and trademarks
- Presidential succession

- Protection of trade and commerce against unlawful restraints and monopolies
- Revision and codification of the Statutes of the United States
- State and territorial boundary lines
- Subversive activities affecting the internal security of the United States

*(Source: House Rules, X, Organization of Committees)*

---

## THE HOUSE COMMITTEE ON ENERGY AND COMMERCE

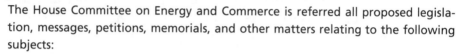

The House Committee on Energy and Commerce is referred all proposed legislation, messages, petitions, memorials, and other matters relating to the following subjects:

- Biomedical research and development
- Consumer affairs and consumer protection
- Health and health facilities (except health care supported by payroll deductions)
- Interstate energy compacts
- Interstate and foreign commerce, generally
- Exploration, production, storage, supply, marketing, pricing, and regulation of energy resources, including all fossil fuels, solar energy, and other unconventional or renewable energy resources
- Conservation of energy resources
- Energy information, generally
- The generation and marketing of power (except by federally chartered or Federal regional power marketing authorities); reliability and interstate transmission of, and ratemaking for, all power; and siting of generation facilities (except the installation of interconnections between Government waterpower projects)
- General management of the Department of Energy and management and all functions of the Federal Energy Regulatory Commission
- National energy policy, generally
- Public health and quarantine
- Regulation of the domestic nuclear energy industry, including regulation of research and development of reactors and nuclear regulatory research
- Regulation of interstate and foreign communications

- Travel and tourism
- The committee shall have the same jurisdiction with respect to regulation of nuclear facilities and of use of nuclear energy as it has with respect to regulation of non-nuclear facilities and of use of non-nuclear energy

*(Source: House Rules, X, Organization of Committees)*

Most states have similar committees. You can ask your state representative for help in figuring out what committees are hearing a bill that you are concerned about. The same sorts of legislative activities take place in most state legislatures as take place in Washington, D.C. A champion is pushing a bill. Seek that person out and make your ideas heard.

# Do I Need to Go to the Capitol Myself?

Advocating on behalf of your point of view is not difficult, but it does usually require that you be in Washington, D.C. or your state capitol. You can write to your legislative representatives, send them e-mail, or send them faxes, but there's nothing quite like a personal visit to illustrate that you are concerned.

If it isn't easy for you to get to Washington, D.C., or it is difficult to figure out when a visit would be the most effective in terms of the bill's life cycle, you can find help that is already there. That's what advocacy groups or individual lobbyists do.

The privacy and security advocates generally break down into the following groups:

- Representing the point of view of businesses who want to use digital media for marketing
- Representing the technology companies that provide "carriage" or transport or that provide software and services used by either the consumer or the marketing companies
- Interested in protecting consumers
- Interested in protecting civil liberties
- Specifically interested in protecting young consumers and their parents

The advocates include trade associations or ad hoc groups of like-minded organizations; companies themselves or lobbyists employed to represent them; consumer protection organizations; and civil liberties organizations.

Trade associations are membership organizations where the companies share the expenses of running the organization. Generally, association dues are based on the size of a company measured by the company's revenue. This gives a small company an opportunity to participate in activities that would normally be available only to much larger organizations. Most trade associations welcome new members.

Ad hoc groups are formed to address specific issues. They, too, share their group's expenses among their members. Some organizations are closed to general membership. Others welcome new members.

The two large consumer groups that are listed here are membership organizations that seek support from individual consumers. If you are not yet a member, they would be happy to have you join.

The civil liberties and privacy advocacy organizations seek support from both organizational and individual members. Memberships and contributions are welcome.

The next sidebar, a column written by Molly Ivins about federal legislative efforts concerning privacy and medical records, shows how advocacy organizations can be helped by supportive press.

## YOUR MEDICAL RECORDS FOR SALE IN WASHINGTON

DON'T YOU JUST love it when they put out the "For Sale" signs at the Capitol and the White House?

Just two weeks before new federal rules to protect the privacy of medical records are due to go into effect, the health-care industry is lobbying the Bush administration to delay, weaken or kill the regulations.

Insurance companies, HMOs and employers all claim that the new regs will impose "costly burdens;" that means they will affect profits.

Congress, which asked the Department of Health and Human Services to draw up the regs in the first place, is threatening to get back into it because, really, the only people who want privacy are the people. And what do we matter?

These are the first comprehensive federal standards for medical records, and they were considered a rare victory for consumers. Except now the industry is out to gut them.

The new standards would require that health-care providers obtain written consent from patients for the use or disclosure of information in their medical records. Quite a concept: You should have full say over who gets to see information about everything from your hernia to your face lift to the time you had that embarrassing medical problem.

Now let's see how much your privacy is worth to this administration compared to the combined contributions of those lobbying to shelve or at least weaken the new rules.

An added festive note in the same old story is that both parties are going flat-out to collect soft money unusually early in the election cycle because they're afraid that Sens. John McCain and Russ Feingold might actually succeed in outlawing it.

This strikes such terror in the hearts of party money people that they are out fund-raising frantically against the evil day. And here's a nice, big interest group that wants something now.

The new privacy regs would:

Allow all Americans to review and copy their medical records, and change them if they find errors.

Require health care providers to state their privacy policies in writing. Patients will also have to consent to any disclosure of information related to treatment, payment and health-care operations.

Allow patients to request that their health-care information not be disclosed. Doctors may choose to override the request if they have compelling reason.

Prevent employers from receiving medical information that could be used in employment decisions.

Require law enforcement to follow legal process to access patient information.

U.S. News & World Report suggested one consequence of the current system, under which medical information is sold to telemarketers so they can make profits off your medical problems: You get a call from a telemarketer in the middle of dinner. It's a pitch for the latest morning sickness medication for pregnant women—but the call is for your 16-year-old daughter.

Meanwhile, how nice it is to see the new social tone in Washington. The American Enterprise Institute held a big do honoring Justice Clarence Thomas with an award given to those who improve government policy and social welfare.

No comment is needed.

Thomas repeatedly told the crowd he has been "subjected to intimidation" because of his conservative views: "Today, no one can honestly be surprised by the venomous attacks unleashed on anyone who disagrees with conventional views."

As a lifelong Texas liberal, I'd have to say he's exactly right, though Texas liberals try to be a little merrier about it. We find that it helps.

My favorite new group is the populist billionaires: Warren Buffett, George Soros and Bill Gates' daddy have all come out against repeal of the estate tax, joined by several Rockefellers and all manner of immensely rich white people. What a great country.

Buffett sensibly points out, "Without an estate tax, you in effect will have an aristocracy of wealth, which means you pass down the ability to command the resources of the nation based on heredity rather than merit."

Buffett said it would "be a terrible mistake, the equivalent of choosing the 2020 Olympic team by picking the eldest sons of the Gold Medal winners in the 2000 Olympics."

These are my kind of billionaires! Think we should invite 'em over for burgers? Do they like Pearl beer and white-trash dip?

*© Copyright 2001 Molly Ivins. Ms. Ivins is a columnist for the Fort Worth Star-Telegram, and this column was originally published Tuesday, February 20, 2001. Used with permission of Ms. Ivins and POM Associates.*

# Trade Association Advocates

The largest trade association representing marketing companies is The Direct Marketing Association, found on the Web at `http://www.the-dma.org`. The DMA promotes legislation that encourages people to go into business and discourages legislation that would add barriers to the process of buying and selling.

Members of the DMA include the household name brand catalog merchants as well as smaller, newer merchants. Because merchants don't really want to waste time or money by sending you materials you don't want to get—after all, it only irritates you—a special feature of the DMA is their "Do Not Send" or "Do Not Call" lists. The Web site tells you how to have your name or the names of family members removed from their mailing lists.

The Internet Advertising Bureau, on the Web at `http://www.iab.net`, specifically addresses the issues of effective advertising on the Internet. Its members include the major advertising networks that operate on the Internet.

Several associations represent software development businesses, the Internet services businesses, and so on. They include:

- **The Information Technology Association of America (ITAA)** is on the Web at http://www.itaa.org. ITAA represents information technology companies who build, develop, and maintain information systems. The members include very large companies like IBM and AT&T as well as very small information companies of whom you have not yet heard. ITAA has a specific division within the organization whose members build and transmit digital products and services.

- **The Software and Information Services Association (SIIA)** is on the Web at http://www.siia.net. SIIA's members are companies that develop software and services that either produce networked services or provide the services themselves. The organization is a result of a merger of the Software Publishers Association and the Information Industry Association, so the association addresses the interests of the traditional as well as the online publishing community. SIIA's members include Oracle and McGraw- Hill as well as smaller publishers of educational or gaming materials. Figure 13.11 shows the SIIA's 2000 Trends Report (successful work done to illustrate industry's moved to new areas).

**FIGURE 13.11**

*The SIIA's Trends Report Web site.*

- **The Information Technology Industry Council (ITI)** is on the Web at http://www.itic.org. ITI also represents companies that provide information technology products and services with an emphasis on maintaining a free market. Among its members are 3Com, Cisco, and Amazon.com, as well as IBM, Hewlett Packard, and Intel. ITI's work on Internet Privacy can be found at http://www.itic.org/sections/Privacy.html.

- **The Internet Alliance** is on the Web at http://www.internetalliance.org. The Internet Alliance grew out of the interactive services groups. Its members came originally from the online services—not Internet service providers, but organizations like America Online and CompuServe—who served individual members. The Alliance's specialty has been addressing the needs of companies serving the consumer Internet, rather than people who sell to other businesses. America Online has long been a significant member.

- **The Commercial Internet eXchange Association (CIX)** is on the Web at http://www.cix.org. CIX was formed as a trade association to represent the needs of Internet service providers who were in the commercial arena as opposed to the academic networking arena. Now 10 years old, CIX's formation was shocking to people who were used to using the academic and government subsidized network that had been available at that time. Over time CIX became a worldwide association that addressed network providers' issues such as making sure that network providers are not required to monitor their users. Typical CIX members include UUNet and Genuity.

Some ad hoc groups represent businesses that are concerned about additional regulatory barriers to conducting business and also want to address issues of consumer trust. They include:

- **The Online Privacy Alliance (OPA)** is on the Web at http://www.privacyalliance.org. OPA is a very large group of companies and associations interested in watching privacy legislation development in the U.S. Congress. It has funded research and additional studies done by some of its members are available on the OPA Web site. Long a champion of self-regulatory measures, the OPA works hard to disseminate information about how to provide privacy policies that truly describe what the Web site is doing. Members of this group include most of the trade associations listed previously and individual companies such as American Express and Microsoft.

- **The Privacy Leadership Initiative (PLI)** is on the Web at `http://www.understandingprivacy.org`. The PLI is an ad hoc group whose mission is to educate and raise the confidence of the general public in digital media with relationship to privacy. Its Web site contains information about laws and studies that concern digital privacy. Its members include Ford Motor Company, IBM, Chubb Insurance, and other important companies. The PLI provides an interesting and educational Web site, shown in Figure 13.12.

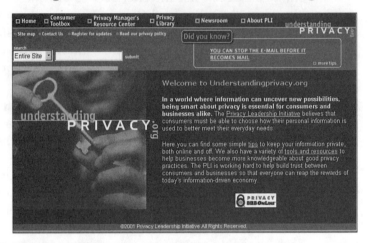

**FIGURE 13.12**

*The Web site for the Privacy Leadership Initiative.*

- **Americans for Computer Privacy (ACP)** is on the Web at `http://www.acp.org`. ACP's interest is a bit different from the other organizations listed here. It is particularly concerned with the ability of the government to dictate what kind of computers and software are eligible for export to other countries. ACP's mission has been to make sure that Congress understands that blocking exports doesn't block terrorism.

## Consumer Protection Advocates

Many consumer protection advocacy organizations have spoken out on matters concerning digital privacy and trust. They include:

- **The Consumers Union**, on the Web at `http://www.consumersunion.org`.

- **The National Consumers League**, on the Web at `http://www.nclnet.org` and with a special emphasis on combating fraud at `http://www.fraud.org`. NCL's Web site is shown in Figure 13.13.

**FIGURE 13.13**

*The National Consumers League Web site.*

- **Center for Media Education**, on the Web at `http://www.cme.org`.
- **The Consumer Project on Technology**, founded by Ralph Nader, on the Web at `http://www.cptech.org`.

## Civil Liberties Organizations

The role of the civil liberty and privacy advocacy groups is sufficiently large that we cover them separately in Chapter 14, "Canaries in the Coal Mine."

Another group of advocates who have worked on legislative issues in the privacy and security arena are the civil liberties organizations. These groups strive to maintain the rights of individuals in the face of growing technology. They include:

- **The Electronic Freedom Foundation (EFF)**, on the Web at `http://www.eff.org`.
- **The Center for Democracy and Technology (CDT)**, on the Web at `http://www.cdt.org`.
- **The American Civil Liberties Union (ACLU)**, on the Web at `http://www.aclu.org`.

## Privacy Advocacy Groups

Finally, the groups specifically founded to address issues of privacy include

- **Privacy International**, on the Web at http://www.privacyinternational.org.
- **Electronic Privacy Information Center (EPIC)**, on the Web at http://www.epic.org.
- **Privacy Rights Clearinghouse**, on the Web at http://www.privacyrights.org.

With this wide range of organizations, it seems likely that you can find at least one that would welcome your participation and reflect and represent your point of view.

# Other Influences on Legislation

The legislative process works formally as we have outlined previously: introduction of bill, committee processing, floor debate and vote, and so on. What isn't as clear from the flow is the time scale involved. It's normally quite long. A bill may be introduced in one Congress, be discussed and die or be resurrected in a later Congress, be debated again and, perhaps, pass. A Congress is a two-year period. It's defined by the elections to the House of Representatives. Two Congresses are in each Presidential term.

With the long time periods involved, there are many opportunities for discussion and deliberation. There are many sources of information that feed informally into the process in addition to those of the formal committee processes.

The two most easily seen sources of additional information available to a Congress are the Congressional Caucuses and the Washington think tanks. *Think tank* is a term used to describe the research organizations, sponsored by a wide variety of organizations, spanning the political spectrum. These groups prepare studies that are used as background to the Congressional deliberations.

A *caucus* is a group united to debate and decide on policy, usually limited to membership. Congressional caucuses are, naturally, limited to members of Congress. Besides the ones discussed here, there are formal caucuses of the political parties: the Democratic Caucus and the Republican Caucus; the Congressional Black Caucus; and the Congressional Hispanic Caucus. The caucuses may have formal activities and supporting organizations.

## The Internet Caucus

The Congressional Internet Caucus is a bipartisan group of more than 150 members in the 107th Congress. It was formed in 1996 by former Congressman Rick White, a Republican who represented the 1st District of Washington State; Senator Patrick Leahy, D-VT; Representative Rick Boucher, D-VA; and Senator Conrad Burns, R-MT. Since its early days, it has grown into a force for education about the potential of the Internet. It has a significant advisory committee of industry, nonprofit, and public interest groups that help the caucus put on programs intended to educate the members and their staffs, the public, and the press about specific items of interest concerning Internet legislation.

The advisory committee maintains a Web site at `http://www.netcaucus.org`, shown in Figure 13.14.

There you can find current information about the membership of the caucus and the policy matters on which emphasis is being placed this term. Naturally, digital privacy and security are among the most discussed matters, and the caucus has prepared an extensive briefing book on the subject. You can read the briefing book on the Web at `http://www.netcaucus.org/books/privacy2001/` and you can watch a RealPlayer video of the caucus program on Internet privacy at `http://www.netcaucus.org/events/2001/privacy/`.

Membership in the advisory committee is open and additional information can be found at The Internet Education Foundation on the Web at `http://www.neted.org`.

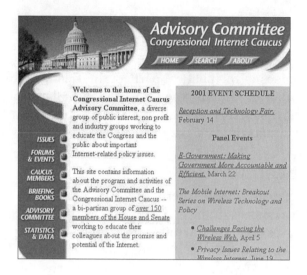

**FIGURE 13.14**

*The Internet Caucus Advisory Committee Web site.*

## The Privacy Caucus

The Congressional Privacy Caucus was formed in 2001 to educate members of Congress on matters of individual privacy and to provide a forum for discussion about privacy as well as being legislative advocates for individual privacy. The forum is not restricted to digital or online privacy and stemmed from concerns on the part of Senator Richard Shelby, R-AL, that the Financial Services Modernization Act (Gramm, Leach, Bliley) did not provide sufficient privacy protection. Mr. Shelby is joined by his fellow co-chairs: Rep. Edward Markey, D-MA; Sen. Richard Bryan, D-NV; and Rep. Joe Barton, R-TX.

## Think Tanks and Research Institutes

Many research institutions formally or informally supply studies to Congressional staff, the public, and the press. Some of these studies begin with the idea of influencing the way legislation is developed. The research may be undertaken at the request of a Congressional committee, a government agency, a political party, or a private citizen. Realizing that not all studies are impartial is important. In looking at the studies, it's important to understand who requested the study, how was it funded, and on what assumptions the researchers and writers based their work. With those thoughts in mind, you can find lots of interesting work being done on privacy matters.

Dr. Alan Westin of Privacy and American Business, a report and information service, has the longest track record in privacy research. He is professor emeritus at Columbia University and he began his work in 1959. His 1967 book, *Privacy and Freedom*, remains one of the important works in the arena. Privacy and American Business itself holds meetings that train Chief Privacy Officers, holds an annual conference, and performs annual surveys. P&AB is on the Web at `http://www.pandab.org`. Their Web site is shown in Figure 13.15.

**FIGURE 13.15**

*The Privacy and American Business Web site.*

The Georgetown Internet Privacy Policy Study by Dr. Mary Culnan, at the time on the faculty of the business school there. The study is on the Web at `http://www.msb.georgetown.edu/faculty/culnanm/gippshome.html`. Dr. Culnan performed the first privacy policy study at the request of the Federal Trade Commission in 1999. The objective of the study was to determine the extent to which American business was presenting its privacy policies on the Net so that consumers could determine for themselves what the companies were doing. It was a follow-up study to one performed by the staff of the Federal Trade Commission in 1998. Dr. Culnan is now on the faculty of Bentley College, but maintains a research interest in privacy.

Several think tanks that more inclined to support free market or less regulatory models. They include

- **The Progress and Freedom Foundation (PFF)**, which has an e-Commerce initiative. For specific publications on commerce issues, go to http://www.pff.org/pff_publications.htm#ecommerce.

- **The Cato Institute**, a nonpartisan research institute with interest in expanding the policy debate, yet including the principles of limited government, individual liberty, and peace. Their writings on privacy and technology can be found at http://www.cato.org/tech/privacy.html.

- **The Pacific Research Institute for Public Policy** contains a Center for Freedom and Technology, which wants to protect the free flow of information on the Internet and opposes policies that would hinder its progress. Sonia Arrison has written several articles on the Internet and privacy. You can find them at http://www.pacificresearch.org/, choosing policy, technology.

The more liberal policy community is ably represented, too, by

- **The Brookings Institute**, a research institution with an emphasis on publishing the results of the research. In the Brookings Review, 2001 issue, Michael O'Neil writes on "The Cybercrime Dilemma: Is It Possible to Guarantee Both Security and Privacy." In the same issue, a group of authors write "Whom to Protect—and How: The Government, the Public and the Internet Revolution." The first article can be found at  http://www.brook.edu/pub/review/winter2001/oneil.htm. The second can be found at http://www.brook.edu/pub/review/winter2001/blendon.htm.

- **The Center for Public Integrity**, a Congressional watch-dog organization, has published "Nothing Sacred: The Politics of Privacy," which asserts that Congress has listened more to business than to top consumer protection advocates. The study released in 1998 is available at http://www.publicintegrity.org/nothing_sacred.html.

- **The Progressive Policy Institute**, the research arm of the moderate Democrats known as New Democrats—see also the New Democrats Online Web page at http://www.ndol.org—has done a lot of work on technology policy. Shane Ham and Rob Atkinson's work on Internet privacy issues called "Online Privacy and a Free Internet" can be found at http://www.ppionline.org/ppi_ci.cfm?knlgAreaID=107&subsecID=123&contentID=3251.

The most important part of all this information is for you to understand that on legislative issues, many people are working to make a wide variety of views available for debate. You can investigate the issues online and arm yourself with points to support your views or to refute the views of others. Your legislators want to hear what you think. It's your responsibility to tell them.

# 14

# CANARIES IN THE COAL MINE

For hundreds of years, before sensitive monitoring devices were invented, miners descended into the earth to dig up treasures and ores. Deep beneath the surface of the earth lay dangers, not the least of which being no air or noxious gases. Some genius miner realized that small birds were more sensitive to air quality than people, and so miners started carrying small caged birds into the mines with them. If the canary keeled over—well, it wasn't good.

Advocacy organizations are our canaries, our social canaries. Because of their special interest in a topic, they are especially sensitive to how changes in law, regulation, or even custom can affect that issue. Luckily, they sing out instead of keeling over if they perceive danger. Some are considered politically left. Others are considered politically right. They are usually non-profit and have staff members who are subject matter experts, legal experts, public relations experts, or all of the above. They are supported by people and institutions who agree with them and they work to bring their message to all via the media, conferences, and venues like congressional hearings.

Advocacy organizations present new ideas and try to help us understand the background and conclusions they draw from thinking through those new ideas.

In this chapter, we try to describe for you some of the important "canaries" that work in the privacy sphere. These groups are the ones whose representatives you see quoted in the press, the experts whose testimony is sought for legislative hearings, and the authors of important white papers you should consider. These groups include ones we, the authors, have supported, as well as ones we've argued against. The descriptions are our own viewpoints. And the list is by no means complete. New groups come into being all the time. That's good in terms of new voices contributing to the debate. However, for the purpose capturing the full range of voices accurately, it's bad. No printed matter can do more than take a snapshot of some players at some point in time.

The work of each of these groups is worthy of your thoughtful consideration. When you've finished reading about these groups and looking through their sites, we urge you to support the ones that most closely match your own ideas. The strength of the Internet is its ability to reach many who could not ordinarily be reached by small organizations with small budgets. If you learn, and tell your friends, and they learn, the electorate is more informed. In a democracy we think that's good, even if you don't necessarily agree with the ideas.

## The ACLU: The Granddaddy of Canaries

The American Civil Liberties Union is the advocacy organization that is associated with support of unpopular causes. Formed in 1920 during a time of extreme isolationism in the United States, the ACLU first defended the rights of newcomers to the United States to stay and speak out. Politically radical immigrants were being harassed and deported. The ACLU stepped forward to defend the rights of these people to speak out against war, for trade-unionism, and for other positions that were definitely anti-establishment at that time

The ACLU was the supporting organization that hired Clarence Darrow to argue the famous Scopes trial in Tennessee in which a biology teacher was tried for ignoring the ban on teaching evolution. The 1925 trial was famous for the quality of oratory on both sides, with William Jennings

Bryan arguing the state's case. we frequently forget that Mr. Darrow lost the case because we now protect the ability of teachers to teach evolution. *Inherit the Wind,* the 1960 screen gem starring Spencer Tracy and Frederic March in the thinly disguised parts of Darrow and Bryan, quoted extensively from the transcripts of the trial itself. Like many other significant arguments of policy and passion, the right of teachers to teach evolution has been challenged again and again.

The ACLU has been involved in many other cases defending our freedoms. They brought cases trying to stop censorship of various kinds and cases supporting academic freedom. The 1950s found it defending the rights of teachers, particularly university professors and other state employees, to refuse to sign "loyalty oaths" that stated they didn't belong to subversive organizations. It is hard to recapture the fervor of the belief that Communism was so inherently evil that even discussion about it must be stopped now that the Cold War is over and the tension between the Communist and non-Communist bloc nations is much lessened. Taking a longer, civil libertarian point of view, the ACLU stood firm in its belief that protecting liberty for all of us was the only way to "win" the war of ideas. The ACLU also defended the rights of everyone to get an education. They argued school desegregation cases and also supported the rights of reproductive choice by litigating *Roe versus Wade.*

In a landmark Internet case, the ACLU was a leader in the coalition that helped strike down the Communications Decency Act, an attempt by the US Congress to ban certain kinds of speech on the Internet.

The ACLU is a law-making organization. Not in the sense that they necessarily write law for the legislative process. But in the sense that a lot of law is not legislated, but litigated; the law becomes understood from the rulings that judges make in individual cases. This is *precedent law,* and *precedents* (court decisions that have been made in the past) are an extremely important part of a judge's decisions in trials. Each judge interprets the law according to the way it is written, the legislative history, which accompanies it through the legislative process, and the way other judges have interpreted the law or a similar law. *Legislative history,* by the way, is the explanatory materials and debate transcripts that show what the legislative body was trying to achieve with a new law. These bits are important because no matter how carefully the language is written, someone interprets it in a manner that wasn't intended.

Legislative histories show judges and attorneys what the legislators intended.

The ACLU has its headquarters in New York City and an office in Washington, D.C., which has expertise in U.S. Government agencies and processes. In addition, the ACLU is a dispersed organization. It has offices around the country, staffed with attorneys who are experts in that locality and who can help people whose freedom is being constrained.

The ACLU's current privacy campaign is one intended to equip each of us to cope in these days of increasing data collection. This is *Defend Your Data*. The ACLU encourages you to be informed, to stay informed (remember things do change all the time), and to support the ACLU in its attempts to reach others. Figure 14.1 illustrates the first page of this campaign.

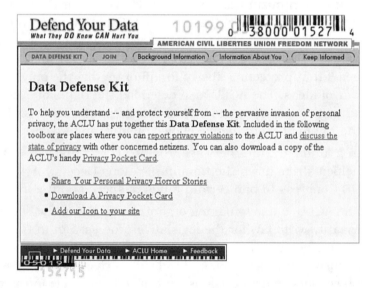

**FIGURE 14.1**

*The start of the ACLU Defend Your Data online campaign.*

You can use the ACLU site to track legislation, to sign up for the newsletter, and to contribute to the cause. You can also, of course, tell your friends.

**NOTE** The American Civil Liberties Union is on the Web at `http://www.aclu.org` and their specific privacy related pages start at `http://www.aclu.org/issues/privacy/hmprivacy.html`.

# CDT: Washington-based Songs

The Center for Democracy and Technology is a Washington, D.C., organization. It isn't the oldest advocacy group. It certainly isn't the biggest advocacy group. And CDT is unusual in that it works *with* government agencies and legislators to achieve its goals. CDT is also funded by donations from industry and industry foundations which makes it vulnerable to charges of being industry-run or industry-apologists. Its pragmatic policies of "compromise to achieve good" make it vulnerable to charges of selling-out, but CDT is very effective at maintaining its core principles and acting with them in mind at all times. CDT works with legislators on controversial legislation. For example, CDT offered opinions on the rework of S. 2448, a computer-crime bill introduced in the 106th Congress by Senators Hatch, Leahy, and Schumer. Other organizations prefer not to comment on legislation in progress, but CDT believes a "seat at the table" enables advocacy of civil liberties positions that might not otherwise be heard.

Work on CDT's mission is guided by the following principles (reprinted with permission):

1. **Unique Nature of the Internet**: The open, decentralized, user-controlled, and shared resource nature of the Internet creates unprecedented opportunities for enhancing democracy and civil liberties. A fundamental goal of our work is seeking public policy solutions that preserve these unique qualities and thereby maximize the democratizing potential of the Internet.

2. **Freedom of Expression**: The Center for Democracy and Technology champions the right of individuals to communicate, publish, and obtain an unprecedented array of information on the Internet. Governmental censorship and other threats to the free flow of information are opposed. As an effective alternative to government controls, individuals believe that a diversity of technology tools can empower families and individuals on the Internet to communicate freely and make choices about the information they receive.

3. **Privacy**: CDT is working for individual privacy on the Internet. Maintaining privacy and freedom of association on the Internet requires the development of public policies and technology tools that give people the ability to take control of their personal information online and make informed, meaningful choices about the collection, use and disclosure of personal information.

4. **Surveillance**: CDT challenges invasive government policies. CDT is working for strong privacy protections against surveillance on the Internet. The content of communications, stored information, and transactional data deserve strong legal protection against unreasonable government search and seizure. Protections against government searches should extend to the network, as well as to the home. CDT advocates for stronger legal standards controlling government surveillance to keep pace with the growing exposure of personal information in communications media.

5. **Access**: CDT is working to foster widely-available, affordable access to the Internet. Broad access to and use of the Internet enables greater citizen participation in democracy, promotes a diversity of views, and enhances civil society. We work for public policy solutions that maximize, in a just and equitable fashion, the unique openness and accessibility of the Internet and preserve its vision as it evolves with ever more powerful broadband technologies.

6. **Democratic Participation**: CDT is pioneering the use of the Internet to enhance citizen participation in the democratic process, and to ensure the voice of Internet users is heard in critical public policy debates about the Internet. CDT believes that the Internet provides unique and effective means of promoting democracy and of facilitating grassroots organizing and public education. We support using the Internet to afford citizens the immediate, broad access to government information necessary to the full practice of democracy.

All advocacy groups depend heavily on the expertise and skills of their members. CDT is no exception to that. Jerry Berman, a founder and the head of the organization, bears the scars of many battles fought to preserve individual and group civil liberties. Starting at UC Berkeley during the days of the Free Speech Movement, Mr. Berman spoke, litigated, started new organizations, and generally "carried on" on free speech and privacy issues. At CDT he has an expert team that focuses on the legal policy issues of free speech, data privacy, government surveillance, cryptography, and international technology issues. The CDT team has both legal and technical expertise and writes and speaks extensively. Its activities attract experts in litigation and technology.

CDT, such as the ACLU and EFF, also sends advocacy experts out to extend their network of caring activists. People who used to work with CDT have gone on to form Web campaign companies and to lead law clinics at prestigious law schools.

CDT believes strongly in education on important policy matters, so much so that it formed the Internet Education Foundation to educate both law and policymakers about Internet issues and to educate the general public, too. On the policymaker front, the IEF supports the Internet Caucus, a bi-partisan group of Senators and Representatives who reach out to other members of Congress. The Caucus and its 150-organization advisory panel, also headed by Jerry Berman, sponsors talks, panels, and demonstrations of technology and ideas.

---

**NOTE**     See the IEF on the Web at www.neted.org.

---

The Internet Education Foundation is also the organizer of two Web sites, GetNetWise, which helps consumers get more information about protecting children in the online environment, and GetPrivacyWise, which helps consumers understand how to protect their personal information. The GetPrivacyWise effort could have been discussed in this book, but it's still under development as of writing this chapter.

The people at CDT work with lawmakers to insert civil liberties concepts into new law and to remove concepts that would endanger the liberties of the individual. CDT's willingness to discuss legislation and to work to improve it is a point that people either love or hate. In fact, it's the point on which CDT was formed, after a severe philosophical disagreement within the Electronic Frontier Foundation (EFF) group. (The EFF is discussed later in this chapter.) Some advocates within EFF believe that working with legislators is the same as dancing with the devil—you cannot, but are hopelessly compromised if you work with advocates representing industry or government agencies. Berman, on the other hand, is a firm believer in sitting at the table and trying to make things better before the bill becomes law.

This doesn't mean they don't go to court to take legal action when bad laws get passed. CDT was a driving force behind the *ALA (American Library Association) versus Reno* case that was joined to the *ACLU versus Reno* case that overturned the Communications Decency Act.

**NOTE**
> Glee worked with the *ALA versus Reno* team as a member of a plaintiff organization. NETCOM On-Line Communications Services, at that time a commercial Internet service provider and also Glee's employer, was one of the organizations that sued the then United States Attorney General Janet Reno to obtain an expedited review of that law. She is very proud to have her work cited in the final Supreme Court ruling.)

CDT was one of the earliest organizations to use the interactivity possible in the Internet for education about privacy matters. They commissioned a little browser test program in which you "clicked here" and the information that your browser presented to the Web world was shown to you. You can try it yourself. The Snoop Test is at `http://snoop.cdt.org`. You can find even more browser test programs at the CDT Privacy Resource library Web site that lists these tools. That page is at `http://www.cdt.org/resourcelibrary/Privacy/Tools/Browser_Test/`.

The Snoop page is interesting and kind of charming. And it does list vulnerabilities and some of the things you can do about them. However, the browser test really only addresses one small part of digital privacy. So, CDT designed a funny privacy quiz, one that would make you think through privacy matters as they might affect you, if you happen to have friends who would surreptitiously record your conversations. Try the quiz for yourself at `http://www.cdt.org/privacy/quiz/`. What you know and what you don't know surprises you. Figure 14.2 shows the fun graphic at the beginning of the quiz.

**NOTE**
> The Center for Democracy and Technology is on the Web at `http://www.cdt.org` and its specific privacy pages begin at `http://www.cdt.org/privacy/`.

**FIGURE 14.2**

*The start of CDT's Privacy Quiz.*

## CPSR: Folk Songs of Freedom

In the last third of the twentieth century, technology became more important to our society. In fact, it began to permeate society. Before this time, technology was left up to "rocket scientists" and the like. It wasn't the business of ordinary people, and unlike today, technology wasn't really part of everyone's lives.

A group of doctors worried about the consequences of nuclear war got together to begin educating others about the physical dangers inherent in the use nuclear weapons. They formed an organization called Physicians for Social Responsibility (PSR). They worked to promote healing and seeking truth. They are firmly against behavior that would endanger all people and sought to extend their knowledge to people who, perhaps, hadn't really considered that polluting the earth with nuclear fall-out would be detrimental to other than "the enemy". PSR stands for telling it like it is, no matter how unpopular or unwanted the facts might be.

Computer Professionals for Social Responsibility came from the same sort of background. Technical people observe and build on the good ideas of others. They saw that they could reach out to teach and inform the general public.

The first big campaign came on the Star Wars defense (then called the Strategic Defense Initiative) during the presidency of Ronald Reagan. CPSR worked hard to demonstrate that computers were not as reliable as would be necessary to have an effective SDI program. The most important part of the campaign was demonstrating a well-reasoned analysis, showing why the SDI program would not be effective. CPSR left the impassioned arguments of right or wrong to others.

The military is not the only place that computers came to be used, of course, and as more and more parts of society used more and more computers, the emphasis of the group spread to encompass all the intersections of technology and society. Privacy and its erosion was an obvious area of concern.

In the late-1980s CPSR started a Washington, D.C., effort to address the technology and civil liberties efforts on behalf of the technical community because other groups lacked the necessary expertise. That group eventually spun out from CPSR and became EPIC. We discuss this later in the chapter.

CPSR's lasting contribution to the discussions of computing and society came from their initial sponsorship of the Annual Computers Freedom and Privacy Conferences. Now an official conference of the Association for Computing Machinery (ACM), CFP holds its twelfth annual conference in San Francisco in March 2002. Information about that conference can be found on the Web at `http://www.cfp2002.org`. Figure 14.3 shows the CFP 2002 logo with the privacy key and the Golden Gate Bridge. Transcripts and videos of previous conferences, as well as announcements about future ones, can be found at `http://www.cfp.org`.

**FIGURE 14.3**

*The logo of CFP 2002.*

CPSR has long been a place where advocates and activists can work together to inform both the general public and decision makers, again with the emphasis on analytical presentations. Anyway, among the effective advocates who participated in the CPSR community are Karen Coyle and Audrie Krause. Ms. Coyle is a systems analyst who writes frequently on the subject of freedom of information, personal liberty, and libraries in the United States. You can find her work at `http://www.kcoyle.net` as well as among the writings on the CPSR Web site. Ms. Kraus is an activist who runs NetAction (on the Web at `http://www.netaction.org`) where you can learn from her and her team. See the part of the NetAction site called The Virtual Activist, an excellent training course on how you can use the features of the Internet to support your cause.

**NOTE**    Computer Professionals for Social Responsibility (CPSR) is on the Web at `http://www.cpsr.org` and its specific privacy pages can be found at `http://www.cpsr.org/program/privacy/privacy.html`.

The following article was written by Junkbusters' President and advocate Jason Catlett; a somewhat different version first appeared in December 1999 on CBS Marketwatch.

## SIX SILLY EXCUSES FOR POSTPONING PRIVACY RIGHTS

The United States has historically—until about 25 years ago—led the world in privacy rights. From measures responding to specific technologies such as the telephone, the VCR and cable TV, to legislation in the 1970's establishing privacy rights for individuals against the Federal government and credit reporting agencies. But since then the US has lagged other developed countries in establishing privacy rights applying to non-governmental organizations—largely due to the lobbying of these companies. Their arguments against privacy rights are often silly excuses for stopping the damage to privacy done by companies that mistreat personal information.

Is accepting a commercial surveillance society the price we have to pay? Of course not.

Is allowing corporations to damage our society and our freedoms a tenet of the American way? No, not for a country that values liberty over convenience. Such struggles are a part of our history, from Boston's rebellion against the British East India Company's tea monopoly, through the slavery of the 19th century cotton industry, to the sweatshops of New York and the early dark satanic assembly lines of Detroit. Today we enjoy tea, T-shirts and the Taurus with little cause for guilt, because socially corrosive practices have been mitigated by laws, regulation, and individual rights.

The loss of privacy is not the necessary price of post-industrial prosperity, any more than pollution was the price of industrial prosperity. Although it took time to muster the political will to stop toxins being routinely dumped into our lakes and rivers, today no sane person would advocate self-regulation by chemical companies as sufficient for environmental protection.

But Internet industry lobbyists ask us to continue to believe in an equally preposterous policy for privacy. Americans want their privacy back, but present law doesn't give them the legal rights they need to protect their own privacy interests. Thirty years ago, the Fair Credit Reporting Act articulated some of those basic rights: that a person should be able to see and correct personal information about him or her, that it be limited to relevant and timely information, and that its use be restricted to purpose for which is was collected. But this law applies only to companies that sell credit reports. These principles of "fair information practice" should apply by law to all entities, governmental and corporate. That's the only way we'll have any privacy in the 21st century.

Most people believe they should have certain rights to control the commercial use of information about them. Privacy is not an absolute right—it must be carefully balanced against the right to free speech for example—but it is a fundamental human right. During the debate we hear several familiar excuses from those who oppose legislation guaranteeing such rights.

The silliness of their excuses can be quickly seen by applying them to comparable questions such as civil rights and the environment.

Excuse: "The federal government is a prime violator of privacy, therefore the federal government shouldn't legislate on privacy."

As silly as saying: The Department of Defense (or the IRS or the FBI) have done a lot of bad things, therefore the government shouldn't be involved in laws about murder or property rights.

Privacy legislation should create rights for individuals, not huge governmental agencies. The Telephone Consumer Protection Act of 1991 took exactly this approach: give individuals the right to sue for $500 any marketer who calls them at 3am.

Excuse: "Market forces and media scrutiny are enough to force companies to respect privacy. Privacy will become a competitive weapon."

As silly as saying: "Market forces will stop companies polluting. Vigilant reporters will expose and stop abuses by the telemarketing industry. Class action suits and "seals of approval" make consumer product safety laws unnecessary. Safety will become a competitive weapon in the airline industry. The FAA isn't needed because passengers won't fly on airlines that frequently crash their planes."

Economists use the name "negative externality" for a downside that isn't accounted for in the market, and know it can't fix them alone.

Excuse: "Privacy legislation would be bad for the economy."

As silly as: "The emancipation of slaves would be bad for the economy" or: "Regulation would ruin the consumer credit business." The credit bureaus tried this line 30 years ago, were overruled, and were proved 100% wrong. It's also as silly as saying that creating an Environmental Protection Agency would ruin the chemical business or the oil business.

On the contrary, surveys now routinely show that the number one factor limiting growth in ecommerce is that people fear they have no recourse if their personal information is misused. Consumer confidence from legally guaranteed rights will grow the market, not shrink it. The $50 limit on credit card liability didn't destroy the industry, it enabled it.

Excuse: "The Internet is international, so there's no point having privacy laws." As silly as: "The Internet is international, so there's no point having copyright laws (or patent laws or taxation laws)."

Wrong.

Companies have sought and obtained strong protection against copyright infringement. Consumers should have strong protection against privacy violation.

Excuse: "Technology is too difficult for the government to understand. They can't get it right."

As silly as: "Technology is too complex to be understood by the US Patent Office, or the Pentagon, or the President, or the people of the United States." Such technocratic arrogance is deeply offensive to the democratic values of this country. It's also directly contradicted by recent experience: the Federal Trade Commission's 100-page rule for the Children's Online Privacy Protection Act of 1998 was widely praised by privacy advocates and trade groups alike.

Excuse: "It's already too late to save privacy. There's already so much data about us we have lost all hope of control forever."

As silly as: "The environment is already too damaged by pollution." The Great Lakes got cleaner this decade.

We can get privacy back within a decade or two.

But because of technology, privacy no longer happens as an accidental byproduct of the obscurity of manual records. In the next century we're not going to get much privacy unless we have privacy rights, and that requires a law. We've got to get this right, or we will have let a fundamental liberty lapse. Who says we can't afford privacy?

That's like saying we can't afford freedom.

# EFF: Western Songs

What do activists want? They want you involved. As mentioned earlier in this chapter, the Internet makes an excellent information sharing and recruiting mechanism. One of the most effective, as well as one of the oldest organizations that wants you involved is EFF. It urges your support of its efforts to preserve civil liberties in the digital world.

The Electronic Frontier Foundation (not the Electronic *Freedom* Foundation, even though that might have been a good name) is a non-Washington, D.C. organization. In 1994, a crisis of organizational philosophy split the organization and the philosophical heart (and the name) moved West to San Francisco. The folks led by Jerry Berman and Deirdre Mulligan stayed in Washington to fight from within as CDT (discussed earlier in the chapter). EFF moved out to be closer to more people who were building and experimenting with the medium itself. Although the split was hard, the individual Internet user benefited because over time, two strong organizations stood where only one stood before.

In 1990, the EFF came together over a judicial case involving the seizure of computers by the Secret Service and the reading by government agents of e-mail stored on the computers. The Steve Jackson Games case became an important first step in determining that e-mail deserves protections. Without this case, you would not have the protections that require warrants to be issued before our government can read e-mail. Now you (and the government) accept that responsible procedures are to be followed when seeking information stored on a computer. The EFF, through their litigation, made those procedures possible.

The EFF has been particularly effective in fighting censorship involved in cryptography export. The Bernstein case is referred to in Chapter 11, "How to Secure Your Internet Transactions," where Cindy Cohn, one of the litigators on that case, and now a permanent member of the EFF legal team, speaks about the status of encryption law in the United States. Additionally, EFF is fighting through the Digital Millennium Copyright law, working on a case where a professor was threatened about his research on copy protection, and on the cases of people who posted code to break the DVD copy protection mechanisms. EFF is challenging the law, which requires filters to be placed on Internet-connected computers in libraries and schools that receive federal funding. It's arguing domain name cases in trademark law, and exploring the legal ramifications of new peer to peer technologies.

So, EFF fights in courts to preserve our freedoms. And they fight online to help you see what those freedoms are, how you are vulnerable, and how you can protect yourself. Their newsletter and Web site remain a primary source of information of which you need to stay informed. Visit their site, seek out the newsletter, and see if EFF is for you.

 **NOTE**   The Electronic Freedom Foundation (EFF) is on the Web at http://www.eff.org and the introduction to their Privacy Now! Campaign is at http://www.eff.org/privnow/.

# EPIC: Strong Songs

Electronic Privacy Information Center (EPIC) is one organization's name that you find over and over again when you seek information about digital privacy. The EPIC team, based in Washington D.C., is frequently invited to testify before Congress, to present before conferences, and is widely quoted in the general and trade press. The EPIC Board and their Advisory Board include some of the important contributors to technology and law, a list of distinguished thinkers about digital freedoms.

Like EFF, EPIC maintains a strong presence in the courts, litigating matters about privacy and censorship. And like CDT, you find them on hearing panels in both the House and the Senate. The EPIC Web site keeps those interested fully informed, and if you prefer, you can receive the EPIC newsletter that summarizes important points and delivers them to your e-mail box.

EPIC also publishes very important books called Sourcebooks. In the privacy area, the *Privacy Law Sourcebook*, is just what it sounds like. This book is a single, comprehensive place to look up the law as it is written and enforced in the United States and abroad. Text of the more important laws and directives are included. Another book available from EPIC is *Privacy and Human Rights.* This book is a compendium of law and recent events in the more digitally developed countries. With each entry found under the name of the country, the book is extremely informative about the newer data protection laws that are being enacted. The EPIC Web site's bookstore features current editions of these important books, and also, for those of you interested in historical perspective, previous versions.

Last, but by no means least, EPIC publishes a list of tools that enable you to achieve better privacy yourself. Figure 14.4 shows the first part of this list.

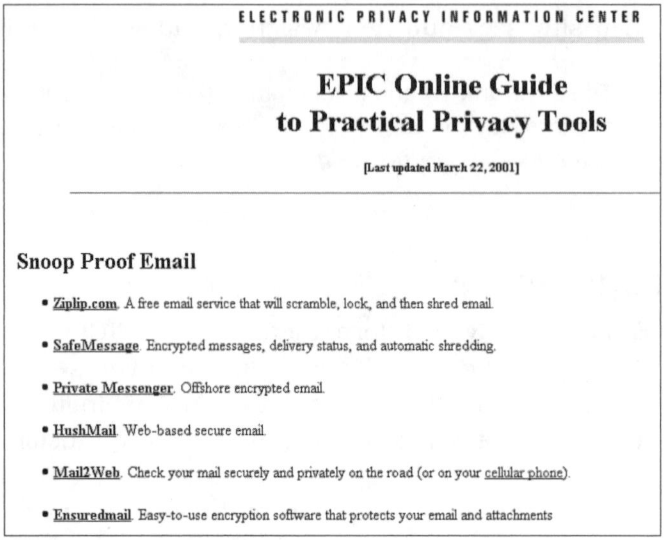

> **ELECTRONIC PRIVACY INFORMATION CENTER**
>
> **EPIC Online Guide
> to Practical Privacy Tools**
>
> [Last updated March 22, 2001]
>
> ---
>
> **Snoop Proof Email**
>
> - **Ziplip.com**. A free email service that will scramble, lock, and then shred email.
> - **SafeMessage**. Encrypted messages, delivery status, and automatic shredding.
> - **Private Messenger**. Offshore encrypted email.
> - **HushMail**. Web-based secure email.
> - **Mail2Web**. Check your mail securely and privately on the road (or on your cellular phone).
> - **Ensuredmail**. Easy-to-use encryption software that protects your email and attachments

**FIGURE 14.4**

*The beginning of the Privacy Tools list from EPIC.*

**NOTE** Electronic Privacy Information Center (EPIC) is on the Web at http://www.epic.org.

# Privacy International: Songs from the Old Country

EPIC's across the pond partner is Privacy International. Based in the United Kingdom, Privacy International (PI) participates in the privacy protection battle from a strong background in English and European laws.

Beginning in 1990, PI has specialized in government surveillance cases and was one of the more articulate voices speaking out against the Regulatory and Investigative Powers Act, an English law that permits much wider government surveillance with much less oversight that was previously possible.

Privacy International monitors compliance of organizations with the European Data Directive and the EU/US Safe Harbor. And each year during the Computers, Freedom, and Privacy Conference, PI announces its Big Brother Awards, not intended to be complimentary. Figure 14.5 shows the boot stomping on the head statue that represents the award. You can see the winners of the United States awards at `http://www.privacyinternational.org/bigbrother/us2001/`.

**FIGURE 14.5**

*Privacy International's Big Brother Award.*

**NOTE**   Privacy International is on the Web at `http://www.privacyinternational.org`.

## Privacy.org: A Duet

Together EPIC and Privacy International operate a service at `http://www.privacy.org`. Here they publish daily news and maintain an excellent list of news resources. This site is a good place for a 'quick fix' on the current status of privacy matters and recent privacy news around the world.

**NOTE**   Privacy.org is on the Web at `http://www.privacy.org`.

# Global Internet Liberty Campaign: Songs Around the World

The Global Internet Liberty Campaign is a coalition of organizations. Formed at an international meeting of the Internet Society (also known as ISOC, see `http://www.isoc.org`). The members of the coalition include the American Civil Liberties Union, the Center for Democracy and Technology, the Electronic Privacy Information Center, the Electronic Frontier Foundation, the Internet Society, NetAction, Privacy International, the Association des Utilisateurs d'Internet, and many others. As you can see, the organizations on this list, and those discussed in this chapter, do compete for your support, but also work together for the important principles shared by all.

The Global Internet Liberty Campaign principles are

- Prohibiting prior censorship of online communication.
- Requiring that laws restricting the content of online speech distinguish between the liability of content providers and the liability of data carriers.
- Insisting that online free expression not be restricted by indirect means such as excessively restrictive governmental or private controls over computer hardware or software, telecommunications infrastructure, or other essential components of the Internet.
- Including citizens in the Global Information Infrastructure (GII) development process from countries that are currently unstable economically, have insufficient infrastructure, or lack sophisticated technology.
- Prohibiting discrimination on the basis of race, color, sex, language, religion, political or other opinion, national or social origin, property, birth, or other status.
- Ensuring that personal information generated on the GII for one purpose is not used for an unrelated purpose or disclosed without the person's informed consent and enabling individuals to review personal information on the Internet and to correct inaccurate information.
- Enabling online users to encrypt their communications and information without restriction.

Many of the civil liberty advocacy organizations (and advocates who work on behalf of business and industry as well) continue to participate in discussion of the Council of Europe's Cybercrime treaty. The GILC has been at the forefront of the campaign to preserve individuals from unwanted and unnecessary surveillance. The idea that Internet Service Providers are forced, under the terms of this treaty and the implementing legislation of the European countries participating, to cooperate with government agencies to track the activities of individual subscribers is feared.

The GILC has urged that the protections built into the laws of individual nations be carried forward into this treaty. Civil liberty advocates fear that the treaty becomes the default law, providing everyone with less privacy.

**NOTE**     The Global Internet Liberty Campaign is on the Web at http://www.gilc.org.

# Global Internet Policy Initiative: International Songs of Liberty

Another international group concerned with policy, including the intersection of interests of security, privacy, and criminal behavior is the Global Internet Policy Initiative. With offices worldwide, GIPI is

- Defining and promoting legal and regulatory reforms that fosters Internet development.
- Hiring full-time Internet policy experts on the ground.
- Establishing working groups with Internet industry, government, and nonprofits.
- Educating policy-makers on the uniquely decentralized, open, and market-driven nature of the Internet.
- Reviewing and commenting upon legislative proposals.

GIPI is hosted in the United States by the Center for Democracy and Technology, and Jim Dempsey, CDT's Deputy Director, also serves as GIPI's Policy Director. GIPI is a joint effort by CDT and Internews, an organization that supports open media worldwide. You can find out more about Internews at http://www.internews.org. GIPI serves as a resource to local stakeholders in the Internet policy development process. The project's goal is to promote transparency and predictability in business regulation; competition, privatization, open networks, and universal service in terms of telecomm policy; and market-driven solutions, user-control, and human rights protection in terms of government control. The key people in GIPI are the country coordinators who help local stakeholders to develop the capacity to promote sound policies supporting an open Internet.

**NOTE** The Global Internet Policy initiative is on the Web at http://www.gipiproject.org and its specific privacy pages are at http://www.gipiproject.org/privavy/.

## Junkbusters: Catchy Jingles

Junkbusters is our favorite advocacy company. That's right, company. They are in it for the money. This is not a typical approach, but it's certainly an idea worth trying, especially in a country that prefers entrepreneurs.

Entrepeneur in residence at Junkbusters is Jason Catlett. Catlett's credentials are unusual in the advocacy community in that he's a technologist who practices what he preaches rather than an attorney representing others. He certainly does represent others, and he does it from a basis of understanding the databases and the data mining techniques that can be used. In fact, he's an expert in that. He's frequently called upon to testify and make presentations about data mining and other potentially privacy invasive techniques. Because he's really good at using catchy phrases to attract your attention and get his point across, he's frequently quoted, too.

Simple, straightforward communications presented in a simple, straightforward manner, that's Junkbusters. You can use tools to remove yourself from mailing lists, postal lists, and so on. You can download forms, and with good instructions to follow. Junkbusters helps you get rid of stuff you categorize as junk.

The most interesting aspect of the Junkbuster program is the Junkbusters Declaration, which tallies your preferences regarding postal and telephone solicitations. Presented as a Web form, it enables you to capture your preferences and either publish them on the Web yourself or have Junkbusters pass along your preferences to the participating mailers and callers. Look at it carefully and think about filling it out for yourself. You find it at `http://www.junkbusters.com/ht/en/jdu.html`.

**NOTE** Junkbusters is on the Web at `http://www.junkbusters.com`.

# Privacy Rights Clearinghouse: Teaching Songs

Another source for sound, practical advice is the Privacy Rights Clearinghouse. These San Diego, California, based advocates have prepared a number of very important, very easy to understand Fact Sheets that help you understand your rights and what actions you can take to be safe and sure consumers of services, to be secure shoppers, and to protect our children.

Topics covered by the Fact Sheets include

- How to put an end to harassing phone calls
- How private is my credit report
- From Cradle to Grave, Government Records and Your Privacy
- Employment Background Checks: A Jobseeker's Guide
- Anti-Spam resources: Halting the Junk e-mail Juggernaut

Perhaps the most important information that Privacy Rights Clearinghouse provides is the information about how to cope with Identity Theft. Their work is mentioned in Chapter 12, "What Can I Do if My Privacy is Compromised?"

Privacy Rights Clearinghouse has been among the best sources of information about the practices of financial institutions in everyone's struggle to comply with the privacy notices now required by U.S. law. Tina Friery and Beth Givens have written extensively on these notices, pointing out the practices that legal notices don't necessarily serve the consumer well. Their opinion piece on the notices can be found at `http://www.privacyrights.org/ar/GLB-CodeOpEd.htm`. This is well worth reading for the explanations of common terms used in the notices that might be misinterpreted by consumers.

Finally, you can call or e-mail them for help. Privacy Rights Clearinghouse operates a hotline for consumers to report privacy abuses and request information on ways to protect their privacy. Call (619) 298-3396 or e-mail them at prc@privacyrights.org.

 **NOTE**     Privacy Rights Clearinghouse is on the Web at http://www.privacyrights.org.

## Singing Along Together

If you've used the URLs to look at the Web sites of the advocacy groups mentioned in this chapter, note that they all ask for your support. Battling on behalf of individual rights and freedoms is not inexpensive. Court costs are high. Web sites are less expensive (in some cases) than print or broadcast advertisements, but they are not free. Money is always an issue. Some of these groups can accept individual contributions. Others can't. If you agree with them, you should see if you can help. Support them with your money or your time. And reach out and educate others.

# 15

# SELF-REGULATION AND PRIVACY

The United States has the most 'do it yourself' culture in the world. Americans pride themselves in their ability to tackle almost any task without extra help. We hate to call in the plumber. And stores such as Home Depot have based entire business plans on our ability to convince ourselves that we can, indeed, completely remodel the bathroom over the weekend.

## What Self-Regulation Is and How It Works

Self-regulation is the development and enforcement of rules within a community that protects the community from being ruled by outsiders. Self-regulation is more complicated, of course, than a single home improvement project, no matter how complex the project. The self-regulators must be strong enough to deter wrong-doers and yet reach out to newcomers to encourage them to learn and obey the rules. Probably the most difficult part of this idea is coming up with rules that the group can agree upon.

Self-regulation is like a group of children playing hide and seek or some other neighborhood or schoolyard game. They all agree on the rules and if someone cheats, they've already decided that the cheater is excluded from the game, doing a distasteful task that helps the group, or taking some other punishment that the group agrees matches the crime.

Meaningful self-regulation involves

- Gathering a group of like-minded companies
- Defining best practices that the group shares
- Sharing information about the practices widely so that both participants and customers know about them
- Determining if and how the practices of the individual companies are monitored to make sure the rules are being followed
- Figuring out how to penalize the companies who aren't playing by the rules

Why would anyone want to specifically organize a self-regulatory activity? One reason is to avoid direct government regulation of that activity. Not only do Americans culturally fear large government, but also the costs in terms of taxation that such a regime incurs. Regulatory programs are expensive and most people don't want to pay for them. In addition, people are not necessarily happy with the programs we have now: the ones, for example, that regulate the broadcast media or the banking industry. Some think the regulators interfere too much and others believe they don't interfere enough. We all agree they are expensive.

Self-regulation is not free, of course. It requires training and audits and checks and balances. However, it is usually less expensive than the sort of compliance mechanisms and associated staff required to address issues of compliance. Licensing mechanisms require dollar and human resource management on the part of both the government and the licensees.

As a body, Americans don't trust governments to do the right thing. This primary American cultural value is exemplified by the Boston Tea Party. Early Bostonians objected to paying a tax for tea which they believe unfair. At the same time, Americans want governments to govern, to provide civic services, and to do it without raising taxes. Generally, Americans have believed that less government is better than more.

Accepting a self-regulatory regime, as the Clinton Administration's *Framework for Electronic Commerce*, released July 1, 1997, proposed, "Let the private sector lead."

## EXCERPT FROM "A FRAMEWORK FOR ELECTRONIC COMMERCE"

### 5. PRIVACY

Americans treasure privacy, linking it to our concept of personal freedom and well-being. Unfortunately, the GII's (Global Information Infrastructure) great promise—that it facilitates the collection, re-use, and instantaneous transmission of information —can, if not managed carefully, diminish personal privacy. It is essential, therefore, to assure personal privacy in the networked environment if people are to feel comfortable doing business.

At the same time, fundamental and cherished principles like the First Amendment, which is an important hallmark of American democracy, protect the free flow of information. Commerce on the GII will thrive only if the privacy rights of individuals are balanced with the benefits associated with the free flow of information.

In June of 1995, the Privacy Working Group of the United States government Information Infrastructure Task Force (IITF) issued a report entitled, PRIVACY AND THE NATIONAL INFORMATION INFRASTRUCTURE: Principles for Providing and Using Personal Information. The report recommends a set of principles (the "Privacy Principles") to govern the collection, processing, storage, and re-use of personal data in the information age.

These Privacy Principles, which build on the Organization for Economic Cooperation and Development's GUIDELINES GOVERNING THE PROTECTION OF PRIVACY AND TRANSBORDER DATA FLOW OF PERSONAL DATA and incorporate principles of fair information practices, rest on the fundamental precepts of awareness and choice:

- Data-gatherers should inform consumers what information they are collecting, and how they intend to use such data; and

- Data-gatherers should provide consumers with a meaningful way to limit use and re-use of personal information.

Disclosure by data-gatherers is designed to stimulate market resolution of privacy concerns by empowering individuals to obtain relevant knowledge about why information is being collected, what the information will be used for, what steps will be taken to protect that information, the consequences of providing or withholding information, and any rights of redress that they may have. Such disclosure will enable consumers to make better judgments about the levels of privacy available and their willingness to participate.

In addition, the Privacy Principles identify three values to govern the way in which personal information is acquired, disclosed and used online—information privacy, information integrity, and information quality. First, an individual's reasonable expectation of privacy regarding access to and use of, his or her personal information should be assured. Second, personal information should not be improperly altered or destroyed. And, third, personal information should be accurate, timely, complete, and relevant for the purposes for which it is provided and used.

Under these principles, consumers are entitled to redress if they are harmed by improper use or disclosure of personal information or if decisions are based on inaccurate, outdated, incomplete, or irrelevant personal information.

In April, 1997, the Information Policy Committee of the IITF issued a draft paper entitled "Options for Promoting Privacy on the National Information Infrastructure". The paper surveys information practices in the United States and solicits public comment on the best way to implement the Privacy Principles. The IITF goal is to find a way to balance the competing values of personal privacy and the free flow of information in a digital democratic society.

Meanwhile, other federal agencies have studied privacy issues in the context of specific industry sectors. In October 1995, for example, the National Telecommunications and Information Administration (NTIA) issued a report entitled Privacy and the NII: Safeguarding Telecommunications-Related Personal Information. It explores the application of the Privacy Principles in the context of telecommunications and online services and advocates a voluntary framework based on notice and consent. On January 6, 1997, the FTC issued a staff report entitled Public Workshop on Consumer Privacy on the Global Information Infrastructure. The report, which focuses on the direct marketing and advertising industries, concludes that notice, choice, security, and access are recognized as necessary elements of fair information practices online. In June of 1997, the FTC held four days of hearings on technology tools and industry self-regulation regimes designed to enhance personal privacy on the Internet.

The Administration supports private sector efforts now underway to implement meaningful, consumer-friendly, self-regulatory privacy regimes. These include mechanisms for facilitating awareness and the exercise of choice online, evaluating private sector adoption of and adherence to fair information practices, and dispute resolution.

The Administration also anticipates that technology will offer solutions to many privacy concerns in the online environment, including the appropriate use of anonymity. If privacy concerns are not addressed by industry through self-regulation and technology, the Administration will face increasing pressure to play a more direct role in safeguarding consumer choice regarding privacy online.

The Administration is particularly concerned about the use of information gathered from children, who may lack the cognitive ability to recognize and appreciate privacy concerns. Parents should be able to choose whether or not personally identifiable information is collected from or about their children. We urge industry, consumer, and child-advocacy groups working together to use a mix of technology, self-regulation, and education to provide solutions to the particular dangers arising in this area and to facilitate parental choice. This problem warrants prompt attention. Otherwise, government action may be required.

Privacy concerns are being raised in many countries around the world, and some countries have enacted laws, implemented industry self-regulation, or instituted administrative solutions designed to safeguard their citizens' privacy. Disparate policies could emerge that might disrupt transborder data flows. For example, the European Union (EU) has adopted a Directive that prohibits the transfer of personal data to countries that, in its view, do not extend adequate privacy protection to EU citizens.

To ensure that differing privacy policies around the world do not impede the flow of data on the Internet, the United States will engage its key trading partners in discussions to build support for industry-developed solutions to privacy problems and for market driven mechanisms to assure customer satisfaction about how private data is handled.

The United States will continue policy discussions with the EU nations and the European Commission to increase understanding about the U.S. approach to privacy and to assure that the criteria they use for evaluating adequacy are sufficiently flexible to accommodate our approach. These discussions are led by the Department of Commerce, through NTIA, and the State Department, and include the Executive Office of the President, the Treasury Department, the Federal Trade Commission (FTC) and other relevant federal agencies. NTIA is also working with the private sector to assess the impact that the implementation of the EU Directive could have on the United States.

The United States also will enter into a dialogue with trading partners on these issues through existing bilateral fora as well as through regional fora such as the Asia Pacific Economic Cooperation (APEC) forum, the Summit of the Americas, the North American Free Trade Agreement (NAFTA), and the Inter-American Telecommunications Commission (CITEL) of the Organization of American States, and broader multilateral organizations.

The Administration considers data protection critically important. We believe that private efforts of industry working in cooperation with consumer groups are preferable to government regulation, but if effective privacy protection cannot be provided in this way, we will reevaluate this policy.

---

Reading these words nearly four years after they were published is interesting; seeing how much and how little has changed in the privacy dialog.

## SELF-REGULATION IS HERE TO STAY [OR, REFORMERS, DON'T HOLD YOUR BREATH]

Many privacy fans say it's only a matter of time before corporate America falls in line with the rest of the developed world and accepts governmental regulation of online privacy like that in Europe and Canada. I think it will take a whole lot of time.

The arguments for a new law do sound good. Public unhappiness is high and rising: every serious opinion poll now shows huge majorities are worried about online privacy. An issue that was third-tier just a few years ago is now up there with education and the environment on the short list of Americans' most pressing concerns. My favorite is the Pew Research Center's poll last year finding that 71% of Internet users think the owners of a company violating its own privacy policy should go to jail, be fined, or have their site shut down.

The European Community's new Data Protection Directive prohibits the export to us of personal data from the 15 member countries unless American data protection is "adequate." This would be legally presumed if our companies would only join the "Safe Harbor" arrangement negotiated by the Clinton administration, but most of them have not. Canada's new law C-6 is phasing in requirements not unlike the EU's, and the Japanese are considering a similar bill.

The bottom line is threatened. In February 2000, in a still-rising market, DoubleClick lost 24% of its market value in 18 days over a privacy scandal involving its merger with Abacus Direct. Recently Amazon.com and its subsidiary Alexa Internet barely escaped FTC punishment for misleading users with its privacy policies, and then only because they had to settle a civil suit for big bucks. RealNetworks and others have suffered from revelations that their software secretly lifted marketing data off users' hard drives, and even Microsoft and Intel have been hit with scandals over built-in universal identifiers. The numerous class actions drag on. The Direct Marketing Association has a study saying 64% of aborted online transactions are abandoned because of security and privacy concerns. Research groups put the annual sales lost due to privacy reservations at up to twelve billion dollars.

One would think our companies would reconsider. One would be wrong. The industry's view is, after all, very American: from the beginning we have mostly regulated privacy only as affected by the government. The Fourth Amendment's prohibition of unreasonable searches and seizures applies only to government actors. The Senate version of the Privacy Act of 1974 originally covered the private sector but was amended in the House to cover government alone. Examples are legion.

Philosophy aside, business does not trust Congress to do an adequate or even competent job of writing an online privacy bill. After a quarter of a century watching Congress' dismal failed efforts to pass a medical records privacy bill, leading to the HIPAA regulations, this is not surprising, or even off the mark.

The new administration makes regulation easier to resist for another four and maybe eight years. The free market mantra is heard everywhere. United States House Minority Leader Dick Gephardt just reversed his longstanding position in favor of privacy legislation and said he's for self-regulation now. A newly appointed FTC commissioner recently said in public that a lot of this concern about privacy is "hysterical." It's safe to assume the high-water mark of FTC enforcement has come and gone.

The EC and the others will surely be unhappy, but in the near term there is not much they can do about it. They need commerce too. If the vast majority of American multinationals ignore the Safe Harbor compromise and hold out for individual contracts they can live with, they will get some contracts. There will be lots of loud sectoral and individual disputes, but no one is sawing through the transatlantic cables anytime soon.

Only two things could change this. One is what corporate privacy people darkly call a "privacy *Exxon Valdez*," a disaster so awful that Congress could not help but act. They are working hard to prevent that. The other is the rising rebellion among the states in passing various strict and inconsistent online privacy laws. It may come to be in the interest of industry to seek out Congressional intervention, in the name of uniformity, which will also expressly pre-empt the states from enforcing any rules more strict than the ones Congress enacts. There is stalemate now because industry opposes any bill without pre-emption, while Congress at the moment does not have the will or the votes to pre-empt the states.

Absent developments on those fronts it's going to be more of the same, except that companies meanwhile will improve and advertise their policies and learn better how to sell privacy itself. We should never underestimate the capacity of our system to absorb and co-opt criticism and subversion and then market it back to us. It happens all the time.

*—Chuck Marson, 07/03/01*

## Looking for Self-Regulatory Information

At the beginning of this chapter, we smilingly used Home Depot's presence in the "do it yourself" market to illustrate our point about the American interest in doing things ourselves.. Home Depot also participates in one kind of Internet self-regulation. At the bottom of their home page, the BBBOnLine Reliability Program seal is displayed (see Figure 15.1). One thing to look for on a merchant or information provider's Web site is some sort of seal indicating membership in a program or trade association. Usually the seal is linked to the Web site of the organization so you can see what the organization stands for.

**FIGURE 15.1**

*The Home Depot Web site with BBBOnLine Reliability Program Seal.*

Look for the standards that each member is held to and the principles upon which the organization is founded. Also, see what reporting mechanisms are available and ask yourself the following questions:

Can you complain to the organization if you feel a member has not lived up to their pledge?

- What is the complaint process?
- What recourse do you have for appeal?

- What are the consequences to the information or service provider if they don't abide by the rules?
- Who is checking on the checkers?
- How do you find out more about the program?

With the information from the self-regulatory program, you can check with the Federal Trade Commission by searching the Commission's Web site at `http://www.ftc.gov`. The Commission faithfully reports any investigations or actions that it has undertaken. Search the commission's Web site using the name of the information or service provider, and then with the name of the self-regulatory organization.

As a consumer, you should decide if you agree with the principles and if you believe that the organization stands by its words. After you decide the self-regulatory organization is trustworthy, search the organization's Web site to see if it publishes information about actions it has taken against wrong-doers or if it makes awards to companies that do especially well. See if the company you are thinking of using is on any of these lists.

When your company passes these "external" checks, you are ready to read the privacy policy and decide whether you have the match of interest and comfort called trust.

# Privacy Policies

The American Heritage Dictionary defines policy as:

> *"A plan or course of action, as of a government, political party, or business, intended to influence and determine decisions, actions, and other matters."*

A company's privacy policy is a description of the actions taken by the company with respect to data gathered about persons and a promise made to the reader that the statement is accurate and true. Because so much has been written about the fair information principles (including in previous chapters of this book), you should have a pretty good idea of what would go into a privacy policy. A well-written policy describes clearly and concisely what kind of data is gathered, how it is stored, how it is protected, and whether (and under what conditions) the data is transferred on to another company.

In additional to this descriptive notice, a policy describes whether you can review the information gathered about you, how you would go about doing that, and perhaps how to correct any information that you believe is in error.

Ideally, the policy is simply stated, easy to find, and makes it especially easy for the reader to determine whether the Web site is trustworthy. The Online Privacy Alliance, an ad hoc group of companies and associations organized to grow an environment of trust and protection, has a list of requirements for privacy polices.

## THE ONLINE PRIVACY ALLIANCE GUIDELINES FOR ONLINE PRIVACY POLICIES

Upon joining the Online Privacy Alliance, each member organization agrees that its policies for protecting individually identifiable information in an online or electronic commerce environment will address at least the following elements, with customization and enhancement as appropriate to its own business or industry sector.

1. Adoption and Implementation of a Privacy Policy. An organization engaged in online activities or electronic commerce has a responsibility to adopt and implement a policy for protecting the privacy of individually identifiable information. Organizations should also take steps that foster the adoption and implementation of effective online privacy policies by the organizations with which they interact; e.g., by sharing best practices with business partners.

2. Notice and Disclosure. An organization's privacy policy must be easy to find, read and understand. The policy must be available prior to or at the time that individually identifiable information is collected or requested. The policy must state clearly: what information is being collected; the use of that information; possible third party distribution of that information; the choices available to an individual regarding collection, use and distribution of the collected information; a statement of the organization's commitment to data security; and what steps the organization takes to ensure data quality and access.

   The policy should disclose the consequences, if any, of an individual's refusal to provide information. The policy should also include a clear statement of what accountability mechanism the organization uses, including how to contact the organization.

3. Choice/Consent. Individuals must be given the opportunity to exercise choice regarding how individually identifiable information collected from them online may be used when such use is unrelated to the purpose for which the information was collected. At a minimum, individuals should be given the opportunity to opt out of such use.

   Additionally, in the vast majority of circumstances, where the third party distribution of individually identifiable information occurs, collected online from the individual, unrelated to the purpose for which it was collected, the individual should be given the opportunity to opt out.

   Consent for such use or third party distribution may also be obtained through technological tools or opt-in.

4. Data Security. Organizations creating, maintaining, using or disseminating individually identifiable information should take appropriate measures to assure its reliability and should take reasonable precautions to protect it from loss, misuse or alteration. They should take reasonable steps to assure that third parties to which they transfer such information are aware of these security practices, and that the third parties also take reasonable precautions to protect any transferred information.

5. Data Quality and Access. Organizations creating, maintaining, using or disseminating individually identifiable information should take reasonable steps to assure that the data are accurate, complete and timely for the purposes for which they are to be used. Organizations should establish appropriate processes or mechanisms so that inaccuracies in material individually identifiable information, such as account or contact information, may be corrected. These processes and mechanisms should be simple and easy to use, and provide assurance that inaccuracies have been corrected. Other procedures to assure data quality may include use of reliable sources and collection methods, reasonable and appropriate consumer access and correction, and protections against accidental or unauthorized alteration.

---

The simple part seems to be the hardest for everyone to live up to. That part has caused considerable comment among those who believe that companies purposefully write their policies in obscure language to make it hard to hold them to their promises.

Readers don't understand why policies have to be so complicated. Many companies didn't think it would be so hard, either. However, remember those policies are promises to the reader. When a company promises something, they need to make sure it's really true.

## Promise Her Anything, But...

This phrase was the beginning of a famous advertising slogan in the mid-20th century. The thrust of the campaign was that you could promise your loved one many things, but the named perfume would always be welcome.

We always thought the campaign was silly. Of course, everyone remembered the slogan, which was certainly one advertising objective. But why would anyone think that giving anything other than what was promised was acceptable? We all know many relationships that come to grief because what was promised was not delivered.

In privacy policies, you just can't do that. When you don't get it right, you are in big trouble. Either the organization your company joined in a self-regulatory effort penalizes you or, if you are in the United States, your mis-statement is called 'deceptive advertising' and the Federal Trade Commission takes action against you.

The fear of Commission action leads to two different kinds of behavior on the part of companies, neither of which is desirable. The first is to not provide a privacy policy at all. The people who do this rationalize that if it isn't there and you didn't promise anything, you can't get into trouble when you screw up. The second kind of behavior is to have a policy which describes everything very, very completely in a way that makes someone's lawyer happy. Attorneys are hired to protect the company, not to make policies easy to read and understand. Attorneys are very conservative when it comes to protecting their clients. They usually find another qualifying phrase to add to a description to protect against another possibly bad circumstance. This leads to a policy with many complex paragraphs.

Then there's just the descriptive part—the part that should be easiest. Let's say you are operating a small business as many people do and have a simple Web site that sold pinwheels in various colors. The Web site has only seven pages:

- An introductory page
- A page where a viewer can choose the pinwheel she wants
- A shopping cart function that lists the pinwheels selected by the shopper
- A page that gathers shipping information

- A page for payment
- An "about us/contact information" page that says who you are
- A privacy policy page

What could be more straightforward? You are not gathering e-mail addresses for future mailings. You aren't building a mailing list for a paper mail order catalog. However, the information you are gathering does identify someone and could help someone else locate that person.

This means you need to be careful with the information you gather.

Let's think. How are you managing the payment process? If you are using a credit card processing operation, you need to transfer enough information about the financial transaction to the processor so that you can get paid. If you are not handling your own packaging and mailing, you need to transfer the ordering and shipping information to the fulfillment operation so that the customer receives the right order. Do you have good contracts with the payment processing and fulfillment people that protects your customer's information? If your subcontractors screw up, what is your liability?

If you don't store the order, fulfillment, and payment information, how do you handle any question that comes up about the transaction?

Because you now understand that you need to store the information, are you making sure that the transaction information is secure? Can your customer review her records? How does the customer ask to do that? How do you make sure the customer, and that customer only, gets to see that transaction record?

Did you make sure that the privacy policy pointed out that if the customer doesn't give you a shipping address, you can not send the pinwheel they want? This is certainly a consequence of not providing information. You are withholding the product if they don't give you the information you need. That's a statement that doesn't look good in the privacy policy.

What happens to the transaction information if you sell your business? What happens to the transaction information if you cease to operate your business?

Because in this example, you have not chosen to support your Web site with additional revenue provided by advertising, you don't have to worry about putting anything in your policy about that. However, remember that if you change your mind and make a contractual arrangement with an advertiser or an advertising network, you need to amend your privacy policy to include the information for your users.

All these not so simple things need to be covered in a good privacy policy. Now think about what kind of policy needs to be written to cover all the bases and effectively protect your company. Does that same policy also protect your customer?

## What Privacy Policies Mean

Whether you are the provider of the product or service or the consumer, the privacy policy is a promise, a legally bound promise, which the organization that gathers information processes and stores the information exactly as they say.

Notice that nowhere in the earlier discussion of the contents of a well-prepared privacy policy did we specify what 'good' information choices you should make if you are the person making the policies. We didn't say that we think that selling or trading information about people is a bad thing. We didn't say that you shouldn't maintain a mailing list and send your customers information about new products.

We didn't say anything about those things earlier because they are choices everyone must make on their own, whether you are the provider or the consumer.

In general, as consumers we are not comfortable with the idea of people selling information about us. However, we shop both online and through paper catalogs. We know that the number of catalogs we see grows when we make purchases. We also know that the catalog merchants cannot survive without customers, and if the merchants don't survive, then we don't have catalogs when we need them. Our feelings about who we trust with our information are very subjective. That is why you need to carefully check and read the information handling policies of the Web sites and catalogs you do business with. Then you can make your own choices.

## How You Can Check a Privacy Policy

Okay, you've found the policy, decided you know what it means, and you've decided you want a little more information. You'd like to check out the policy to see if it's true. How can you do that?

You're going to do the digital equivalent of 'asking around'. Actually, that's always a good thing to do: ask your friends, neighbors, and colleagues if they've heard anything good or bad about a particular information, product, or service provider. Word of mouth is always a good way to check.

Word of mouth checking can be done online, too. We here in the United States are used to checking out products with various organizations. The Consumers' Union (CU), for example, has long been a trusted, respected, unbiased source of information about appliances, automobiles, and products like audio equipment. CU publishes a monthly magazine, *Consumer Reports,* consulted by many seeking good information. CU also maintains an online site that combines information for no charge and a subscription service. The free information includes information regarding product safety. This is an excellent place to see if that pinwheel we are thinking of buying at the example site mentioned earlier, has a significant safety problem. You can find the CU Web site at `http://www.consumersunion.org/`.

Another source of product recall information is The Learning Network's Family Education site. Look under, K-12, Family Education, parent, Raising Kids, and Health and Safety to find a product recall page. Or you can try going there directly by typing the URL `http://familyeducation.com/topic/front/0,1156,1-8306,00.html` into your Web browser. The Family Education folks provide the ability to sign up for an e-mail newsletter that delivers alerts to your e-mail box. Remember however, that The Learning Network people need to store your e-mail address. Otherwise, you don't receive the newsletter.

Besides these exemplary product sites, businesses do have other reputable rating services, such as BizRate (`http://www.bizrate.com`). It gives the consumer an opportunity to report on how they were treated by a business. The illustration in Figure 15.2 is the display of ratings for Coldwater Creek, a catalog and online merchant. Notice that BizRate asks consumers themselves for the information and in the Coldwater Creek example, more than 25,000 people had filled in the online survey since 1999. By the way, this store has excellent word of mouth.

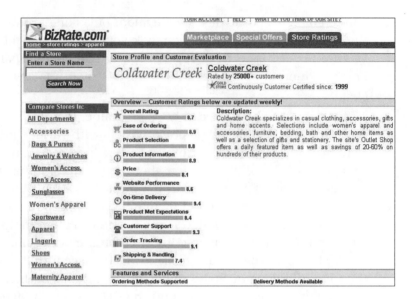

**FIGURE 15.2**

*The BizRate rating screen for Coldwater Creek.*

A similar rating service is ePublicEye-WebWatchdog (http://www.Webwatchdog.com). This site specializes in consumer ratings of small, boutique style Web sites. Shown in Figure 15.3, the first is a listing for sellers of flowers. You can see that one of the symbols—the cloud with an X through it—which are intended to quickly describe a merchant is a privacy policy symbol which indicates whether a merchant shares information with a third party.

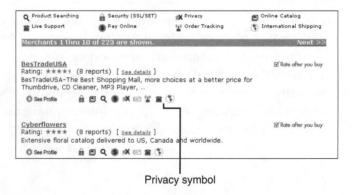

**FIGURE 15.3**

*First listing in WebWatchdog's flower ratings.*

If you haven't already done so, check the organization's trade association or self-regulatory body memberships. Usually you can find those listed at either the bottom of the home page, on the About us page, or on a page which describes terms and conditions of the services provided. You should really read the terms of service, too, rather than just clicking yes.

Gomez Advisors (`http://www.gomez.com`) takes another approach: certification. Gomez.com also provides informative scorecard rankings for Web services. For example, online mortgages have a lot of good players, but which ones are best? In fact, which is the best for me (not everyone needs the same services from a mortgage provider)?. In Figure 15.4 the certification criteria used for mortgage services providers is shown. In Figure 15.5, the services are ranked. Interestingly enough, however, Gomez Advisors do not directly address privacy as an issue in consumer confidence.

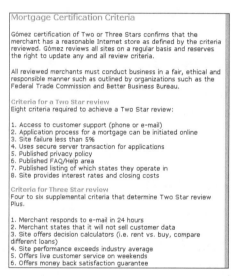

**FIGURE 15.4**

*Gomez.com's Mortgage Service Certification Criteria.*

Because the online marketplace is still relatively new, new online privacy organizations and new rules are developing over time. Predicting where these might come from is hard. However, using a good online search service or portal, or checking with one of the privacy advocacy organizations listed in Chapter 14, helps you keep up to date.

**FIGURE 15.5**

*Gomez.com's Mortgage Scorecard.*

# Today's Self-Regulatory Leaders

Many groups seek to regulate themselves. More online privacy groups are developed as time goes by. In this section we discuss several of the older groups with stronger track records. These groups have contributed significantly to the policy discussions on digital privacy.

## The Online Privacy Alliance (OPA)

The Online Privacy Alliance (OPA) is mentioned throughout this book. OPA was formed solely to "foster on online environment that respects consumer privacy." This is an ad hoc group whose membership ranges from very small net-based organizations to very large companies that are not exclusively associated with the online world. It has some simple principles intended to encourage the development of sound privacy practices and to build an understanding of self-regulatory environments. Effective enforcement of self-regulation has always been at the top of the list of OPA concerns.

**NOTE**    Glee actively participated in this group during her tenure at both NETCOM and Privada.

We cited the OPA's Privacy Policy Guidelines in a sidebar earlier in this chapter.

# The Individual Reference Services Group (IRSG)

The Individual Reference Services Group (IRSG), found on the Web at http://www.irsg.org, is a group of companies that provide access to information about individuals; primarily for verifying individual identities, locating individuals, and preventing fraud. In 1997, as a result of privacy concerns regarding how these companies obtained, used, and sold information, the IRSG worked with the Federal Trade Commission to develop a set of principles that are backed by audits and government enforcement. The IRSG companies promise to

- Acquire information only from reputable sources
- Apply strict safeguards to restrict the distribution of non-public information
- Educate the public about the database services of IRSG companies
- Provide guidance to individuals on how to obtain publicly available information about themselves
- Not distribute information like Social Security Numbers and Dates of Birth to public, commercial and professional markets
- Submit to annual compliance audits by qualified independent auditors or assurance organizations

PriceWaterhouseCoopers, the independent auditing, assurance, and business advisory firm, developed measurement criteria based upon these principles. The criteria are used to audit the information practices of the group's members for inclusion in the annual compliance report. You can read the criteria at http://www.irsg.org/html/criteria.htm.

IRSG companies do not sell directly to consumers, but they do include the 3 major credit assurance and reporting organizations, so these companies are an important part of the online marketplace.

# The Direct Marketing Association (DMA)

The Direct Marketing Association (DMA) , found on the Web at http://www.the-dma.org, is the oldest and largest trade association for users and suppliers in the direct, database, and interactive marketing field. The DMA has developed the 'Privacy Promise' to assure consumers that DMA members respect the wishes of consumers. To display the DMA logo, the member promises to

- Provide customers with notice of their ability to opt out of information rental, sale, or exchange with other marketers
- Honor requests not to share personal information with other marketers
- Honor requests not to receive future mail, telephone, or other solicitations
- Use the DMA's national preference services to remove their names from mail, telephone, or e-mail lists

DMA members must also adhere to a range of other ethical business practices administered by DMA and backed by a peer review program for enforcement. Membership in DMA is valuable and a member that does not keep the promises risks loss of membership.

## The Internet Advertising Bureau (IAB)

The Internet Advertising Bureau (IAB) , found on the Web at http://www.iab.net, is another trade association. Its members are the advertisers, the agencies, public relations, consulting, research, and media companies who make up the larger group known as the Internet advertising profession. IAB activities include "evaluating and recommending standards and practices, fielding research to document the effectiveness of the online medium and educating the advertising industry about the use of online and digital advertising."

The IAB has two projects that are of particular interest in self-regulatory matters: the independent Wireless Advertising Association and the IAB Chief Privacy Officer Council.

One work product of the Wireless Advertising Association is a set of guidelines for privacy practice for wireless advertising.

The IAB's Chief Privacy Officer Council is organized to support CPO's in their effort to educate others in their own organizations and externally about the importance of privacy, the availability of consumer privacy solutions, and "the most effective means" for adopting those solutions.

Additionally, the IAB has commissioned PriceWaterhouseCoopers to formulate practices that are incorporated into the group's privacy guidelines. Those guidelines are the minimum acceptable standard to which members are held.

# The Network Advertising Initiative (NAI)

Like the IRSG, The Network Advertising Initiative (NAI) grew out of well-expressed concerns about how advertising networks could gain information about Web users without the users knowing about it. Their Web site can be found at http://www.networkadvertising.org.

Advertising networks are companies that manage advertising for Web sites by maintaining a catalog of available advertisements and serving them to Web sites on request. In many cases, users aren't really aware that different parts of a Web page came from different Web sites. The technology underlying the Web enables images, for example, to come from one Web server and text to come from another. The advertising community understood that this ability would enable an interesting application: the serving of ads from one location to a number of different Web sites. For ad purchasers, this was an advantage because you can buy ads on a lot of different sites while working with a small number of vendors. In addition, better reporting would be possible in a simpler manner. How many users saw which ads on which Web sites? How many of those ads were selected (clicked-through) to another site for more information? All this would be available from a single vendor. For Web sites, ad networks were advantageous, too. A Web site could negotiate with a single vendor for a number of different kinds of advertisements. All in all, an advertising network seemed like good thing.

About the same time, it occurred to advertisers that it would be possible to get better (more desirable) responses from viewers if it was possible to show them an advertisement that piqued their own interests. The problem with that idea was that it would be difficult to tell what a particular viewer's preferences were. Sometimes, it wouldn't be too difficult. You could probably assume that if someone were looking at a Yahoo! page on the National Football League that the viewer was interested in American professional football. You could probably assume that if someone were looking at an online magazine about home decorating that they might be interested in house paint. However, that would require the advertiser to know all the Web sites, figure out which ones were going to be most appropriate for the ad in question, and so on. It would definitely be easier to use an advertising network.

Advertising networks could probably figure out how not to show the viewer the same ad over and over again, using the viewer's IP address, for instance. That conquered one problem. But what about showing the advertisement for house paint to the football fan? That wouldn't be quite as effective. So, advertising networks started tracking a viewer's path through the Internet. In general, it is possible for a Web site to track the URL of the site from which the viewer came (referring URL), the track through their own Web site, and the URL that follows. However, if an advertising network placed a cookie file on a viewer's computer and read the cookie back each time the viewer was served an ad, it would be possible to know each site visited by a particular computer on a particular ad network. And it would be possible to correlate clicks on a particular kind of ad with the cookie stored on a particular computer and make assumptions based on those actions. For example, if an advertiser was running an ad for disposable diapers and you clicked on that ad to get more information, it would be reasonable to assume you were the parent of a young child and that more ads intended for parents of young children should be served to you.

These relatively innocent plans to serve pertinent ads grew like kudzu (a particularly healthy and fast-growing vine that can grow to take over huge acreage). Privacy advocates began to worry aloud about the wisdom of this practice. Then, DoubleClick, one of the major advertising networks, lit a fire that became a conflagration. DoubleClick offered to buy a data base of consumers and their profiles and announced that it would merge the data gathered online from their advertising network with the consumer profiles of offline behavior. The merger of the data would enable information, such as name and address, to be attached to information that previously didn't contain that specific type of identifying information. This was not desired by consumers who felt their privacy would be invaded beyond what it already is.

Thus we come to the Network Advertising Initiative. DoubleClick and the other NAI companies began meeting with officials at the Federal Trade Commission to come up with a plan that addressed privacy concerns of consumers and yet didn't put them out of business. The NAI privacy principles are the result of those meetings.

The Online Privacy Alliance's member guidelines suggest to Web sites that explicit mention of network advertising membership is included in privacy polices of Web sites, that a complete list of the advertising networks used by a site be available to the user online, and that a method for opting-out of data collection be provided. The popular online portal Yahoo! has a privacy policy that provides an excellent illustration of this guideline. Look at `http://privacy.yahoo.com/privacy/us/adservers/details.html`.

Enforcement of the NAI principles is done by a third party: Arthur Andersen, LLP. The Andersen team has created a Web site called NAI Self-Regulatory Principles Compliance Program at `http://www.andersencompliance.com` to list the companies that comply with the principles and to manage the complaint process.

## NAI SELF-REGULATORY PRINCIPLES

Governing Online Preference Marketing (OPM)

- **Sensitive Personally Identifiable Data**—Network advertisers shall not use personally identifiable information about sensitive medical or financial data, sexual behavior or sexual orientation, nor social security numbers, for OPM.

- **Non-Personally Identifiable OPM**—Network advertisers, when entering into a contract with publisher customers for services which include OPM, shall require that their customers: (1) post a privacy policy that clearly and conspicuously discloses (a) the customer's use of the network advertiser services for OPM; (b) the type of information that may be collected by the network advertiser; and (c) the consumer's ability to choose not to participate; and (2) provide a clear and conspicuous link to the Non-PII Opt-Out Page of the NAI gateway educational site (or, if only one network advertiser services the Web site, to a screen at the site of the network advertiser that has on the screen either the ability to opt-out or a hyperlink to the ability to opt-out) .

- **Merger of PII with Previously Collected Non-PII**—Network advertisers or organizations acting on their behalf will not merge previously collected Non-PII with PII for OPM without the consumer's prior affirmative consent ("opt-in") to any such merger. Network advertisers will collect PII for OPM purposes only from the sites of publisher customers with which they have contractual relationships.

- **Merger of PII with Prospective Non-PII**—Network advertisers will not merge PII with Non-PII collected on a going forward basis (i.e., after the user provides PII) for OPM unless the consumer has been afforded robust notice and choice about such merger before it occurs.

- **Robust Notice**—The notice must be at the time and place of collection of the PII and must disclose: (a) that the PII is shared with a network advertiser for purposes of OPM; (b) the type of information that may be collected and linked by the network advertiser; (c) the consequent loss or partial loss of anonymity to the advertising company of future Web usage; and (d) the ability of the consumer to choose not to participate.

For this category of merger, all such opt-out notices in the screen presented to the user shall be substantially similar in clarity and prominence to the sample notices provided.

- **NAI Gateway Educational Site**—NAI will establish an NAI site that will provide users with information about the privacy practices of NAI companies, as well as the ability readily to opt-out for each NAI company, at a single Web location.

- **Contractual Enforcement**—If network advertisers know or have reason to know that a publisher customer is in breach of the specified contractual requirements for customer compliance, the network advertiser will make reasonable efforts to enforce the contract.

- **Access to PII**—Network advertisers shall provide consumers with reasonable access to PII and other information that is associated with PII retained by the network advertiser for OPM purposes.

- **Enforcement**—The NAI principles themselves are an enforceable document under existing FTC authority. The NAI agrees to establish a third-party enforcement program that will govern compliance with the NAI principles, including the possibility of referrals to the Federal Trade Commission. The NAI believes that these principles will not only safeguard the privacy of online users but increase their trust and confidence in e-commerce as well.

*(Source: http://www.networkadvertising.org/aboutnai_principles.asp)*

## Seal Organizations

In 1994, when we wrote a book about using the Internet, we said that a truly wonderful thing about the net was that almost anyone could be an information provider. Wasn't it fabulous, we said, that small agricultural co-operatives in rural New Mexico could make their sheepskin products available to the whole world in a relatively easy manner.

Yes, it was. And it still is.

But...

The low barriers to entry also made it possible for confidence—artists trying to get your money easily, junior high schools students testing what they can get away with, and genuinely bad folks to set up a service that looks pretty much like a real one. That's a big problem. Lack of trust and confidence in information both received and given remain high on the list for people who do not want to use the Internet. (See in particular the excellent studies done by the Pew Internet and American Life project at `http://www.pewinternet.org`.)

So, how can you tell who to trust? Seal programs try to provide that answer.

Several organizations provide certification and monitoring services to assure customers that the promises that companies make are being kept. These organizations are committed to making sure that individual consumers have control of their own information. They have rules, audits, and enforcement programs so that you know by the appearance of the seal that this Web site has passed some checks and that you can trust it and that if they betray your trust, you have recourse.

**NOTE**    Seal programs do not usually dictate the exact actions that their members may take when processing information about people. Membership does not necessarily mean, for example, that a company does not transfer information to other companies. Membership does mean that companies must disclose what they do. A seal on a Web site means the organization abides by the program rules. You still need to understand the rules and the relevant privacy policy.

# TRUSTe

The TRUSTe program was the first of the privacy seal programs. It grew out of the Electronic Frontier Foundation (discussed in Chapter 14) to be a separate method of ensuring that individual privacy is protected in the digital environment. Open disclosure of privacy practice is the central principle of the TRUSTe program. Each potential member participates in a rigorous application process that includes complete walk-throughs of a Web site by TRUSTe staff and a Web developer. The TRUSTe trustmark is awarded if the practices are as stated. TRUSTe seeds the databases of its trustmark holders with false names to trace inappropriate release of information. TRUSTe's privacy principles include:

- Adoption and implementation of a privacy policy
- Notice and disclosure of information collection and use practices
- Choice and consent options that give users the opportunity to exercise control over their information
- Access measures to protect the security and accuracy of personally identifiable information
- Revocation of the seal and referral to the appropriate federal authorities for any trustmark holder that fails to comply with the policies.

For example, PayPal, an instant and secure payment service available to everyone on the Web, is a member of TRUSTe. PayPal accepts Visa and MasterCard credit cards and is insured by Traveler's Insurance. All these logos appear on the bottom of the PayPal home page at `http://www.pay-pal.com`, as shown in Figure 15.6.

**FIGURE 15.6**

*Truste, Visa, MasterCard, and Traveler's Insurance logos from the PayPal Web site.*

Clicking the TRUSTe trustmark on a Web site opens the site's privacy policy complete with an additional TRUSTe mark on it as shown in Figure 15.7. This mark is a link to the validation page on the TRUSTe Web site shown in Figure 15.8. This means that the business cannot 'spoof' the trustmark or lie about the validation process. Each business must pass the application and validation process to display the trustmark and to link to the validation page.

In general, the kinds of companies that are more interested in the TRUSTe program would be those who haven't yet grown a significant brand name on the Internet. As TRUSTe provides an audit as a trusted third party, the company would not have to wait to join until it was well-known. Membership in TRUSTe would help grow the necessary trust.

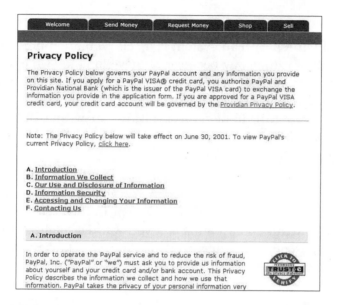

**FIGURE 15.7**

*The PayPal Privacy Policy.*

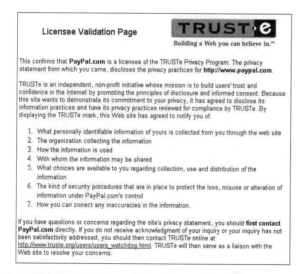

**FIGURE 15.8**

*The PayPal Validation Page on the TRUSTe Web site.*

# BBBOnLine

The Better Business Bureau system is a self-regulation program. Most of us don't think of it that way because we have long known of our ability as a consumer to 'check out' a business or a charity by consulting the BBB. If we had a dispute with a BBB member business, we could use the facilities of the BBB to help resolve it. We knew that BBB members have high principles, are trained to advertise fairly, and are committed to making a good marketplace for all.

The BBB system is online at `http://www.bbb.org`. The system is global in that you can search for a business from anywhere you happen to be, yet local because records on businesses are kept in their local communities by their local bureaus. For instance, if you wanted to check the records of Responsible Roofing in Redwood City, California (a very good roofer, by the way), you would enter the name and location on the BBB system search page at `http://search.bbb.org/national/search.html` and find that information about Redwood City is kept at the BBB of Santa Clara Valley. The national site refers you to the local site at `http://www.bbbsilicon.org`. We can use the link to visit the site, enter the business name, and, Voila! We have a report.

BBB pays particular attention to the use of advertising and making sure that member's advertising is both true and accurate. On the local level, BBB organizations monitor the advertising of their members to make sure that the BBB principles are upheld and that any local, state, or federal laws are not being broken. If you believe that a local advertisement is illegal or untrue, you can complain to your local bureau.

The BBB has two review efforts that address national advertising campaigns: the National Advertising Review Board and the Children's Advertising Review Unit. As you can guess from the name, CARU addresses issues of relating to advertising directed to children. For the same reasons that people feel children should be protected by laws such as COPPA in their Internet lives, people feel children should be protected from misleading broadcast and print advertising. Complaints about national advertising—or advertising being tested for national campaigns—can be directed to the BBB units. The advertising is reviewed. If it is found untruthful, breaking a law, or not meeting guidelines for children's advertising, the advertiser is given a chance to amend or withdraw the offending ad. If the advertiser refuses, the matter is passed on to the appropriate law enforcement agency and releases information to the press.

BBBOnLine grew out of the Council of Better Business Bureaus. It has two seal programs for online businesses: the BBBOnLine Reliability Program and the BBBOnLine Privacy Program. Figure 15.9 shows the seal that you see on BBBOnLine member Web sites.

**FIGURE 15.9**

*The BBBOnLine Privacy Seal.*

BBBOnLine's policy requires that personal information, such as name, postal address, and e-mail address or telephone number, remain private and confidential. Personal information must be stored in a secure location, accessible only to designated staff, and may only be used for the purpose intended. BBBOnLine verifies, monitors, and views its program members and provides dispute resolution and enforcement mechanism as shown in their process illustration in Figure 15.10. You can see that the BBB has specific roles as does the merchant/service provider.

One of the stricter areas of the BBBOnLine's privacy program are the provisions concerning sharing information with other organizations. BBBOnLine requires the following (as paraphrased from the BBBOnLine Web site):

- Agents or contractors who have access to personally identifiable information or prospect information must honor the organization's privacy and security policies, hold such information in confidence, and not use such information for any purpose other than to carry out the services they are performing for the organization.

- Information about prospective customers may not be shared with any outside party or corporate affiliates operating under a different privacy notice when such parties may use prospect information for their own or subsequent parties' marketing.

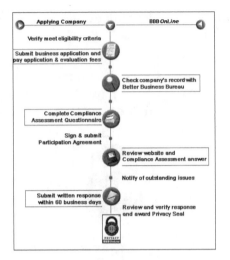

**FIGURE 15.10**

*The Process to receive a BBBOnLine Seal.*

- On transfer of personally identifiable information or information about prospective customers to outside parties or corporate affiliates that use a different privacy notice, processes must be in place to try to ensure that such parties will take reasonable precautions to similarly protect the information as with the original notice.

- Sharing sensitive information with outside parties or corporate affiliates with different privacy notices can be done only when expressly or affirmatively opted-in by the individual.

- Exceptions to these rules can include processing of information required by law, medical diagnosis, or some vital interest of the person.

You have likely noticed the similarities between these rules and the rules for information sharing in the European Union data directive.

BBBOnLine has also implemented a Kids Seal Program directed to the requirements of the COPPA law (see more about this in Chapters 4 and 13). Figure 15.11 shows the Seal that appears on sites directed to children under 13 who are members of the BBBOnLine Privacy Program and have met the additional requirements of the Kids program. These requirements are based on the COPPA act itself, the Online Privacy

Alliance requirements (explained earlier in this chapter), and those developed from the Better Business Bureaus Children's Advertising Review Unit (CARU).

**FIGURE 15.11**

*The seal of BBBOnLine's Kids Privacy Program.*

An important component of any self-regulatory program is notification when something goes wrong. The BBBOnLine program makes that relatively easy with an online complaint form, shown in Figure 15.12.

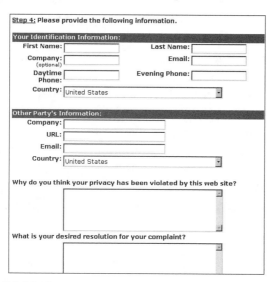

**FIGURE 15.12**

*The BBBOnLine OnLine complaint form.*

## PriceWaterhouseCoopers' CPA WebTrust and Better Web

Most people in the United States, and probably around the world, are aware of the consulting and accounting organization called PriceWaterhouseCoopers or, familiarly, PWC. The group's name is one synonymous with trusted financial, privacy, and security audits; validation tests; and reporting on the best practices of business worldwide.

As management consultants, PWC noted that businesses faced substantial risks if they were unprepared to protect the privacy of personal data gathered in the course of ordinary business, and began advising businesses on intelligent information processing early. PWC advised that consumers want to be able to trust the organizations with whom they interact and businesses could add to their own value by understand that and participating in Seal programs and privacy audits.

Naturally, PWC is not precisely a disinterested party in privacy space. You may have seen their television ads talking about hackers. If you haven't, and would like to do so, the ad is accessible from the PWC Web site at `http://www.pricewaterhousecoopers.com/images/gx/eng/main/campaigns/hacker30.rm`. You need RealPlayer to download and play the commercial on your computer. Because it is video, the file is very large.

PWC has a vigorous practice in helping firms meet privacy requirements such as the U.S./EU Safe Harbor terms, in improved operational procedures and in training privacy officers. As mentioned earlier, PWC performs the audits behind the Internet Advertising Bureau's privacy pledge. PWC has joined forces with Watchfire (on the Web at `http://www.watchfire.com`) to develop Watchfire WebCPO, a "powerful privacy management solution that provides ongoing automated monitoring, analysis, reporting, and alerting of your Web site."

So, with the emphasis on business why should consumers be aware of PWC and their privacy work? Because they worked to create two different seal programs as well.

The first program is CPA WebTrust, found on the Web at `http://www.cpawebtrust.org`. Built in conjunction with the American Institute of Certified Public Accountants (AICPA), WebTrust is a program that certifies that a business has met the international standards developed by the program, has posted its business policies, and has been audited for compliance by a specifically trained public accounting firm.

Accountants have long been respected, neutral parties who are trusted to accurately report what they see. PWC and the accountant's organization have used those already respected professionals to advantage. The AICPA Web site, shown in Figure 15.13, carries the WebTrust seal. When you see the WebTrust seal on a member site, you may also see the logo of the accounting firm that provided the verification. For example, on the Verisign site, shown in Figure 15.14, you can see that the firm that performed the audit was KPMG.

**FIGURE 15.13**

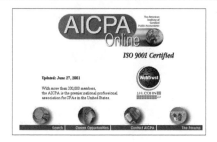

*The AICPA Web site with the WebTrust Seal.*

**FIGURE 15.14**

*The WebTrust certificate on the Verisign Web site.*

The second program is the PWC BetterWeb program, on the Web at `http://www.pwcbetterweb.com`. This program emphasizes the sharing of information between businesses and consumers so that the consumer is aware of sales practices, procedures for dispute resolution, and the privacy and security practices in the business's information handling. The thesis of the program is one that we philosophically agree with: if you know what you are dealing with, you can decide for yourself if you want to continue.

How do businesses choose the seal program that fits their needs? Well, some use more than one. Look at the Privacy policy on the GTE (now Verizon) Web site, for example, at `http://www.gte.com/privacy.html` and shown in Figure 15.15. Verizon was formed by the merger of BellAtlantic and GTE and the merged company lives by the privacy policies of all the companies. The company is a TRUSTe licensee, participates in the BBBOnLine Reliability Program, and it is also a member of BetterWeb.

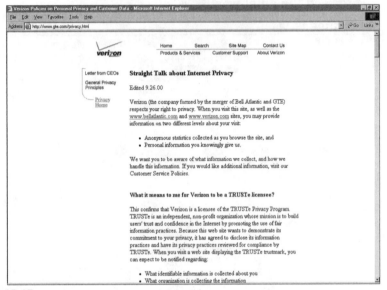

**FIGURE 15.15**

*Part of The GTE/Verizon Privacy Policy Page.*

The eLoan Web site, on the Web at `http://www.eloan.com`, takes a similar stance as shown Figure 15.16. This site belongs to both the PriceWaterhouseCoopers' programs, BetterWeb and WebTrust, and also participates in the BBBOnLine Privacy Program.

Each of the Seal programs has something slightly different to offer. Both of these companies (eLoan and Verizon) felt best about choosing more than one program. The third party validation process should make it easier for you to determine if you want to do business with Verizon online.

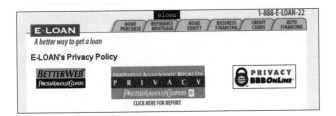

**FIGURE 15.16**

*Part of The eLoan Privacy Policy Page.*

# Wrapping It Up and Sealing It for You

Should you trust a seal? The answer is yes, *if and only if* you have checked to see what and who the seal represents. We could invent a seal tomorrow and give it out to all and sundry. That might be entertaining, but it wouldn't be a good seal program. Remember the important points about effective self-regulation:

- Get like-minded folks
- Share best practices widely
- Make sure the rules are being followed
- Penalize those who aren't playing by the rules

You need to check that someone is watching and report those who are not playing by the rules. When you all participate, you create a good community that works.

# PART V

## PRIVACY AND THE FUTURE

*I think Amazon is the preeminent pioneer in building a new way of doing commerce: personalized, database-driven commerce, where the big value is not in the purchase fulfillment, but in knowing as much about a customer base of 10 or 20 million people as a corner store used to know about a customer base of a few hundred.*

*In today's mass-merchandising world, that's largely gone; Amazon is trying to use computer technology to re-establish it. They are probably on release 2.0 of what they are doing. They've been criticized for some of their experiments, but 20 million people keep going back, which is a very good sign that what they are doing is working.*

Andy Grove
Intel's co-founder and chairman
Wired Magazine, June 2001
http://www.wired.com/wired/archive/9.06/
intel_pr.html

# INTERNET VOTING: DON'T TRY THIS AT HOME...YET

Good elections, at least in the United States, depend on four things:

- **Authenticated, eligible, enfranchised voters**—Usually achieved by voter registration and enabling everyone who is eligible and able to do so to vote

- **Anonymity of the ballot**—So that no one knows which candidate we supported

- **Auditability of the election**—A process for checking that the reported counts were accurate

- **Accountability of the process**—Guarantees that votes were not purchased or sold, that dead people did not vote, that the tallying process was accurate, that all the votes were counted, and that the appropriate checks and balances were present in the election itself

All this needs to be achieved with a safe and secure ballot box (or its electronic equivalent). Additionally, of course, we'd like those accurate results quickly, and those of us in the more western time zones would like to make sure that our votes are relevant in national elections. We are not fond of the news media "calling" the elections before our polling places close.

It's the combination of points one and two in the previous bulleted list that make elections interesting within the context of a book on digital privacy. Would it be possible to provide an authenticated voter and yet provide for the anonymity of the ballot itself?

# How We Do It Now

Voting in the United States is generally managed at the county level. Managed, in this sense, means that county organizations select the voting mechanism; pay for it; prepare it for each election; put it away in storage after; arrange for staffing of polling places; manage tabulation and reporting; and so on. The county also pays for the technology. Counties are divided into zones called *precincts* and each precinct has a certain number of people residing within it who may vote there. Voting is tied to residency, not to property ownership, original place of birth, or other possible methods of enfranchisement. Each county decides for itself what method of voting it uses. The five methods used are paper ballot, voting machine, punch card ballot, scanned ballot, and electronic device.

Each method has its problems. Paper ballots, for example, can be miscounted because the marking isn't clearly in one box or another. Paper ballots and punch card ballots can be "lost" or "misplaced." Punch card ballots can be mispunched or not fully punched. Some punch card ballots may not be counted because they stuck to another ballot. Some electronic devices don't register all the votes. Some marked ballots can't be scanned properly.

The CalTech/MIT Voting Project prepared an excellent, clear report in February 2001 that outlines the various methods and their reliability, compared across four presidential elections. The report (and, according to the team, any updates as new information becomes available) is at http://www.vote.caltech.edu/Reports/report1.pdf. In general, the percentage of error for each technology has been acceptable. Although most of us believed (until the 2000 Presidential election) that elections were fair, that voting was accessible to all who wanted to vote, and that all ballots cast were actually counted.

There have always been problems with elections. Some people vote twice. Some people don't vote in every contest on the ballot. Sometimes the ballots get lost. Sometimes they are marked in error. Sometimes they can't be counted, either by machine or by people. The problems with the various kinds of methods used for voting in the United States have been known by experts who study elections for some time.

The foundation paper on voting methodologies and their problems was done by Roy G. Saltman of the National Bureau of Standards (now NIST) in 1988. You can find the text of it at `http://www.itl.nist.gov/lab/specpubs/500-158.htm`. It's entitled "Accuracy, Integrity, and Security in Computerized Vote-Tallying." Perhaps the most interesting thing is that few, if any, of Mr. Saltman's recommendations for improving elections have been followed.

# Should We Change?

The 2000 Presidential election, particularly the fuss about the ballots in Florida, caused a lot of people to ask again, isn't there a better way? Variations of the statement, "if we can put a man on the moon" or "if we can build a space station, why can't we do a better job of counting our votes?" were found in Letters to the Editor, were voiced on radio talk shows and in Web chat rooms and newsgroups, and were discussed in gathering places around the country.

With the improvements in technology, particularly the expansion of access to the Internet, it was inevitable that people would begin discussing the technology as a way of solving certain problems with elections. The problems most frequently mentioned were low voter turnout and access to elections for those who have trouble physically getting to the polls. In other words, issues of convenience and admission. Additionally, many people assume that counting by computer is more precise, provides quicker results, and is less prone to fraud. Computer tabulation would avoid hand tabulations, misreading optical scanners, or dimpled chad debates. Finally (as is frequently done in discussions of new uses for technologies), there is some promise of saving money using technology. If fair elections were possible without quite so many people and logistical challenges involved in transporting and setting up and counting ballots, it would be less expensive to run the elections and that would be a good thing.

California's Secretary of State, Bill Jones, convened a year 2000 task force to investigate those assertions. Their report can be found at http://www.ss.ca.gov/executive/ivote/.

A quick summary of the report is that although Internet voting may well enable some voters additional access, it may deprive others of that same access and also produce additional technological threats to the security, integrity, and secrecy of the ballots. Electoral access for those with equipment at home or work would increase, but that same access would most likely decrease for those who are not wealthy or interested in purchasing the technology. Use of the open, commercial Internet would present additional challenges. Security is a primary concern. Denial of service attacks, for example, could make it impossible for some to vote. The task force recommended a gradual introduction of the process, where people would come to polling places to use electronic and networked voting mechanisms, allowing the technology to be tested and proven before voting "anytime, anywhere" is enabled.

At the request of the Clinton Administration, the Internet Policy Institute and the National Science Foundation convened a National Workshop on Internet Voting in October of 2000. The report from that workshop, published at http://www.netvoting.org, endorses Internet voting, taking into account special considerations for security, privacy, authentication, access, impact on democracy, and the cost/benefits. The report sees Internet voting as a logical extension of Internet applications in commerce and government. However, like the report from California, the National Science Foundation's press release announcing the release of the report urges caution:

> *"Trials should proceed in which Internet terminals are used at traditional polling places, but remote voting from home or the workplace is not viable in the near future. ...[A] committee of experts calls for further research into complex security and reliability obstacles that for now impede the Internet's use in public elections."*

> **(Source:** http://www.nsf.gov/od/lpa/news/press/ 01/pr0118.htm**)**

The release concludes by citing the following three broad areas for further research, which NSF helps fund through its existing Digital Government program:

- The economics, design, certification, and policies of poll site Internet voting
- The technical factors of security, encryption, and authentication of using kiosks and remote voting
- The political science issues of how poll site and remote Internet voting would affect participation, the character of elections, and democracy itself

The Digital Government program is under the Computer and Information Science and Engineering directorate at NSF. This is the same directorate that brought us the NSFNET project that led to today's Internet.

An earlier cautionary note comes from the People for Internet Responsibility (PFIR), who have a prepared statement that warns of the risks inherent in rushing in where perhaps voters, if not angels, should fear to tread. You can find it at `http://www.pfir.org/statements/voting`.

PFIR was formed by concerned scientists such as computer scientist Peter Neumann of SRI International. In 1993, Mr. Neumann published the "Security Criteria for Electronic Voting," a paper still of great interest and help in thinking through the issues. You can find it at `http://www.csl.sri.com/users/neumann/ncs93.html`.

The thrust of that paper is that it is difficult to develop a complete system (the definition of *system* here is the one that includes all the parts of a system, including the people needed to make it work) that would meet the standards Neumann outlines. Unfortunately, like with the problems raised in the Saltman paper in 1988, not all that much has changed in the election process since the paper was written. Significant research on voting methodologies, though, has been done by Rebecca Mercuri, a computer scientist at Bryn Mawr and by Lorrie Faith Cranor, a computer scientist currently with AT&T Labs.

Ms. Mercuri is most definite in her opposition to fully automatic or Internet-based systems for elections. She prefers systems that provide an "indisputable paper ballot" as being the only kind in which the voter can see whether the ballot cast is the ballot intended. For example, those of us who use paper ballots can see that the checkmark is in the right box. If our ballot is one where we punch out a chad, we can *see* that the right hole is punched (even if we have to take it out of the envelope to check). With electronic systems, we can only see our screen—we cannot verify that the information stored in the database on the other end matches our intentions. As Ms. Mercuri says, "Fully electronic systems do not provide any way that the voter can truly verify that the ballot cast corresponds to that being recorded, transmitted, or tabulated."

Ms. Mercuri's summary statement can be found at `http://mainline.brynmawr.edu/~rmercuri/notable/RMstatement.html`.

Ms. Mercuri and Mr. Neumann have worked together on a short statement entitled "System Integrity Revisited" published in Communications of the Association for Computing Machinery, 44, 1, Janurary 2001 and available at `http://mainline.brynmawr.edu/~rmercuri/notable/Papers/Integrisk.html`.

This statement is a call to action directed to computer scientists, urging their participation in the reviewing systems that are proposed for elections. It is not enough, they argue, to sit back and criticize. Active participation is necessary to improve our processes.

Ms. Cranor, another researcher who has participated in many of the election study panels cited, maintains an excellent list of links regarding research on electronic voting. You can find those links at `http://lorrie.cranor.org/voting/hotlist.html`.

Ms. Cranor's prime research interest today is privacy, rather than voting, and she has done significant work in chairing the P3P specifications working group.

The list of respected researchers who have written on this issue goes on. An additional one is the paper by Deborah Phillips and David Jefferson of the Voting Integrity Project. You can find it on the Web at `http://www.voting-integrity.org/text/2000/internetsafe.shtml`.

It, too, does not recommend remote voting using the Internet. Phillips and Jefferson are particularly concerned that the shifting of the responsibility for the integrity of voting systems is being made from election officials and vendors to *voters* and vendors, making it easier for fraud to be effected and hard for it to be detected. They also point out the changes in voter registration brought about by the National Voter Registration Act, which made it easier to register, also made it harder for election officials to know whether people are registered in more than one place. This is because there is no particularly good way to make sure that people registering in a new location become unregistered (disregistered?) in the old one. The law says that inactive voters remain on the list of eligible voters until they do not vote in two general federal elections. Because lists of inactive voters are obtainable, they become a potential source of fraudulent votes: One could claim to be an inactive voter and take part in an election more than once. Phillips and Jefferson don't quite say, but surely imply, that more dead people will be voting.

# Where We Might Go

In voting, as in other parts of our lives, technology is a two-edged sword.

Cryptographic means can be used to help with voter authentication. We need to watch carefully to make certain that laws passed to keep cryptographic tools out of the hands of criminals and terrorists do not prevent their use for elections (and electronic commerce). A digital signature for each registered voter would provide assurance that the voter was entitled to vote, and that the voter cast only one ballot. However, careful implementation would be needed to make sure that those who are not technically savvy would be either prevented from voting by lack of ability to use the tools or by using them incorrectly. It is important not to exclude training and to remember that good ergonomic design will be important. One solution could issue digital certificates at the time of online voter registration. Then, however, it would be necessary to ensure that the signatures were not too easy to lose, damage, or misplace, that they could not be sold or bargained away, and that they would be available to the correct voter at the time of the election. The registration process would require continued vigilance to make sure that each eligible person got one and only one digital signature, that the person who requested and received the digital signature existed and is a citizen (no dead people voting), and that there was a secure and fair process to cope when the citizen had trouble or misplaced the digital signature. As now, it is important to prevent systematic disenfranchisement.

The second issue considered for technological assistance is anonymity. How is it possible to both know the voter is entitled to vote and yet keep the ballot secret? Again, we think of cryptography. A cryptographic key could be used to sign the ballot, maintaining voter ballot secrecy. Locking a ballot would be similar to drawing the curtains in a voting booth. Yet again we need to guard against laws restricting strong encryption because they may create a barrier.

A continued problem is auditability. The electronic equivalent of the lever-based voting machines have this as their most significant drawback. There is no way to reconstruct the ballots of each voter. These Direct Recording (DRE) machines accrue the tabulations to a storage device (internal or networked) and only the sums are available. Going backward from the sums to the ballots is not possible. Some have suggested printed receipts as a solution to this problem. However, others fear that this will encourage the selling of votes: It would be possible to receive monies on showing a receipt that "proved" you voted for Candidate X. Michael Shamos in his 1993 paper for the Computers Freedom and Privacy conference, on the Web at `http://www.cpsr.org/conferences/cfp93/shamos.html`, points this out quite well.

However, he also argues that no balloting system is actually auditable. He contends that ballots are easily forged, particularly punched card ballots. Shamos believes that

> *"What auditing an election really means is verifying that the software was working correctly, that no unauthorized acts or steps occurred during the election (such as resetting the counters to zero) and maintaining intermediate records so that votes will not be lost in case of an equipment or power failure. Auditing does not, and cannot, mean the ability to rebuild each individual ballot after the polls have closed."*

We discussed the experts' serious doubts about the security of an online voting system. Vote manipulation and thrill-seeking hackers could disrupt the system. The thrill of hacking into a system that carries election results of national significance may be awfully tempting to a hacker or a desperate and unscrupulous candidate. Smartcards may prove too expensive to generally deploy to all voters, so lack of appropriate protection technology may be a significant problem.

The secret ballot is strongly valued in our democracy. Our ability to vote without intimidation and fear is based on our ability to mark a ballot without others knowing what we did. As earlier chapters in this book have shown, the Internet as it is in 2001 does not really protect your privacy. It is possible to track users through Web bugs, cookies, and so on. Today we fear that encryption methods used to verify voting eligibility could be broken to reveal voter identity and votes cast. The voting system itself may be vulnerable to hacking. Who has access to the voting system, what methods are in place to maintain privacy, and what backup system is there to verify integrity of the system? If the voting system fails, is it possible to identify voters, whether or not they voted, if they possess some sort of valid receipt? Clearly, additional technological protections will need to be developed before remote Internet voting will enable a truly secret ballot.

A final complication is providing a system that upholds availability and fairness. Today not everyone has easily available online access. Many public places provide access, but shared access (even if provided as a civic benefit as is done in many public libraries) presents separate problems unless the election is held at designated locations with a system designed to be used by multiple voters. There are issues of literacy and training. Not all that are eligible to vote are sufficiently comfortable with technology and others may be unable to see a display screen. Thus, it would see that a system of offline voting must be maintained with an equal level of integrity. Whatever kind of system is developed, the level of privacy afforded to online voters must maintain the same level of anonymity as we are used to in offline elections.

# How Might We Get There?

One very interesting effort is the Internet Voting Technology Alliance (IVTA). IVTA (`http://www.ivta.org`) was founded in February, 2000.

IVTA is a group of experts and companies working on the public development and open peer review of standards to be used in Internet voting. Of course, this group is well aware of the research we've cited in this chapter. Its membership includes government, nonprofit, and private sector representatives. The primary goal of the Alliance is to ensure a high level of quality and integrity in the resources and information provided, to foster public confidence in Internet voting:

> *"As defined in its mission statement, the IVTA affords companies, individuals and government sectors with a way to provide and request input in a unified environment with public peer review, while preserving the independence of each participant. The alliance is dedicated to serving the public by acting as an information center, discussion forum, voluntary standards setting body and Web publisher focused on technological issues of Internet voting."*

It will be interesting to watch the group and see if the open standards approach will work as well in solving the problems identified in Internet voting as the Internet Engineering Task Force (IETF—http://www.ietf.org) has done with solving the problems involved in improving internet-working.

We've cited the California task force. Other states are working on Internet voting studies, workshops, and proposals, too. Minnesota's report—"Click and Vote: Citizenship on the Internet," released June 18, 2001—is available from the Minnesota Planning department at http://www.mnplan.state.mn.us/Report.html?Id=1241.

In 1998, David M. Elliot, then Assistant Director of Elections for the State of Washington's Department of Elections, published a white paper on Internet voting. It's available from the Secretary of State at http://www.secstate.wa.gov/elections/evoting_paper.asp.

Washington is currently defending its support of vote by mail programs that have been very effective in rural Washington. Many of the same criticisms of Internet voting are used to critique mail balloting. Sam Reed and Bill Bradbury, respectively the Secretaries of State of Washington and Oregon, have published a rebuttal to those criticisms at http://www.secstate.wa.gov/news/misc/nytimes_20010827.asp.

In these two Western states, everyone may vote by mail. The practice is widely approved. Their experience has confirmed that voter turnout is much greater and it is generally felt that people appreciate more time to mark their ballots, particularly because we in the west tend to have more ballot propositions than are common in other parts of the country. The secretaries believe that signature verification that can be used in vote-by-mail (and cannot be legally used at poll sites) improves the authentication process and makes the election less prone to voter fraud.

The key to electronic voting is the assurance of privacy and security. Any suggestion or hint that electronic systems could be corrupted or manipulated will quickly erode the confidence and acceptance of the public in such technologies.

So, where does that leave us? Some elections don't present the same magnitude of problems as we have outlined here. In elections that are not required to process the ballots of so many people on the same day, the general importance of the election makes it less likely to attract fraud. Some of those are private elections: corporate ballots, shareholder voting, union elections, elections in student organizations, and so on. In these elections the level of privacy required is not quite so high, not because the elections are not important to those participating, but because the likelihood of fraud is less because they are not as important to so many others. These elections, though, provide a good test-bed for electronic and Internet voting systems. Conversely, an effective system for public elections could roll over to private elections and ensure the anonymity afforded by privacy safeguards.

Interested enough now to explore the issue on your own? The following are some companies in the election business in 2001. Visit their Web sites, read their white papers, and decide for yourself. If your local election people begin to explore new ways of voting, you'll be able to help them reach appropriate decisions:

- **VoteHere**—http://www.votehere.net
- **Election.com**—http://www.election.com
- **eSlate (electronic voting system)**—http://www.internetvoting.com
- **Safevote**—http://www.safevote.com

# Toward Improved Elections for All

The "butterfly ballots" of Florida have much to answer for. They spawned many jokes and a feeling that perhaps things are not as they should be. On the other hand, they focused the awareness of a nation to problems to which researchers have been trying to call our attention for many years. That's probably good. Now, more informed people are working toward good solutions. In a democracy, the ability to trust that elections are valid and that those in office were, in fact, elected fairly, is very important. Perhaps with new attention, we'll be able to design new voting systems that preserve our privacy and the integrity of the elections and improve the electoral process.

# 17

# WHERE ARE WE GOING?

Clearly, none of us has a crystal ball. We didn't expect to find ourselves in the world we live in after September 11, 2001. That world gives us more decisions and more responsibility than before, especially in the area of privacy.

In the wake of the terrorist attacks on the Pentagon and the World Trade Center, everyone is looking for ways to make life safer, and with more assurance. Legislators, being accustomed to making laws and regulations, are looking for rules that will prevent dangerous situations, such as hijackings, from occurring. Civil libertarians, who are no less moved by the deaths and carnage than legislators and rule-makers, worry that the rules and restrictions will be more dangerous in the long run than the physical danger we want to eliminate today. Privacy is one of the rights that can go by the wayside in this kind of climate, and we as individuals need to stay aware of the debates and of the consequences of the choices we make.

As authors, we don't pretend to be able to tell the future. However, some people are very good at looking at the big picture. We talked to a lot of those folks, read many people's prognostications, and developed some trends and indications that we can presume will continue.

While we've put sidebar essays in many of the other chapters, more are in this section. These authors are people whose opinions we respect, and who have important things to say to you about the future.

We can see clear tendencies in four areas: people and their behaviors, marketing and corporate practices, technologies, and the legislative and regulatory climate.

# Your Behavior Can Make a Big Difference

If the majority of people don't care about their privacy, the rest of the debate is moot. The advocates will still try to get the message across (for a while; nobody funds a losing battle forever) and a few privacy-aware individuals will work to keep their own privacy protected. However, universal privacy protections will be nonexistent because no one believes they are necessary.

At this point, while surveys say that concern about privacy is rising, it's clear that the levels of concern don't match the behaviors online.

In March 2001, a Business Week/Harris Poll reported that over 35% of those polled were uncomfortable at the thought of being profiled, and that 82% were nervous about records of their online activities being merged with personally identifiable information, such as "your income, driver's license, credit data, and medical status." Yet at the same time, a survey released by the Pew Internet and American Life project says that 29% of online users are using the Internet more than they did in 2000. Seventeen percent are using the Internet less, and among the reasons they list, not one is concern for personal privacy.

Internet users who are spending less time online cited the following reasons in a Pew Institute study:

- 19% say they are not as interested in the things they used to do on the Internet.
- 16% say they don't have time or are too busy.
- 11% say they no longer need to use the Internet for work or school.
- 11% say they didn't find it useful or worthwhile.
- 8% say they no longer have access or have less access than before.
- 5% say the Internet is too slow or took them too long to find information.

- 4% say they spend less time online because they can do things online more quickly than before.
- 1% say they have a faster Internet connection.
- 21% cited some other reason, such as the loss of a free Internet connection, a medical reason that makes it harder to use the Internet, or a problem with their computer or Internet provider.

*(Source: Pew Internet Project, July 16, 2001,*
`http://www.pewinternet.org/index.asp)`

In March 2000, a clear majority of those polled by Business Week/Harris (57%) favored some sort of laws regulating how personal information is collected and used. A similar poll in June 2001, conducted by the Gallup organization, found that 66% of Internet users think that the government should pass laws protecting privacy.

At the same time, an April 2001 Pew study found that Americans were more worried about Internet security issues than the year before. The results:

- 87% of Americans say they are concerned about credit card theft online.
- 82% are concerned about how organized terrorists can wreak havoc with Internet tools.
- 80% fear that the Internet can be used to commit wide-scale fraud.
- 78% fear hackers getting access to government computer networks.
- 76% fear hackers getting access to business networks.
- 70% are anxious about criminals or pranksters sending out computer viruses that alter or wipe out personal computer files.

*(Source: Pew Internet and American Life study, released April 2, 2001.)*

Most people, including those surveyed, don't realize that security is the enabler of privacy protections. Yet, another 2001 Gallup study shows that of the people who believe that more laws are needed to protect privacy, over half of those surveyed believe that the government can't be trusted to do the right thing when armed with laws pertaining to security technology (Gallup, June 2001).

## Convenience Is the Death of Privacy

In the privacy debate, the greatest tension is between people's desire to retain their privacy and their desire to get a benefit. Most observers believe that the majority of online users generally tip the balance in favor of their benefit, and that this behavior will continue. Mark Waks, a technologist in Boston, says:

> *"The greatest threat to privacy in the near future is Convenience. The concern isn't people who are going to surveil your life covertly, without your knowledge or assent—a few horror stories will probably produce reasonable laws against that. The truly serious problem is the people who pay you to give away your privacy. I'm talking about the stupid, mundane stuff here. The little discount card that gives you discounts at the supermarket if you use it every time you shop. The password-enablers built into the Web browsers. Stuff like that. Combine that with serious data-mining capability, and you get truly impressive profiles of individuals. And nothing illicit is required: people are giving their privacy away for free, because they haven't yet considered that it may have value."*

Waks isn't alone—of the 30 individuals who responded to our *ad hoc* survey, all but four mentioned convenience as a key factor in the threat to personal privacy.

Convenience has been mentioned as the root of many evils in American society—many Web pages for family and child health directly cite the TV remote control as a major contributor to obesity in teenagers. (For an example, see Idaho State University's Early Childhood Information Clearinghouse at `http://www2.state.id.us/dhw/hwgd_www/ecic/AP/television.htm`.) Riding lawnmowers and golf carts, supermarkets, catalog shopping, and a dozen other ways that life has been made more convenient have been linked to social ills. In the case of the TV remote, parents can get control of the situation by wrestling the handset away from their teen and setting a good example of diet and exercise. With personal information, it's not so easy. In fact, some futurists believe that once information is released, it can never be recaptured.

# Opening Pandora's Box

Like trying to recapture the pain and suffering released from the box in the legend of Pandora, many privacy advocates believe that it's too late to really preserve ownership of personal information. Network design engineer Chet Johnson described it this way: "The information has been released to the wild to replicate forever." It's almost impossible to track down all the places your information has been shared and get the holders to give it up. Just as an example, think about all the catalogs that deluge most households in September and October, just before the Christmas shopping season starts. Until a few years ago, it was very common for catalog companies to sell mailing lists on a regular basis. They also commonly had forms that invited you to send them the names of 5 or 10 friends who might be interested in their catalog or products. If you filled in the form, you frequently got a discount, but the company also got 5 or 10 more validated addresses for their databases. Validated addresses are a valuable commodity for resale, too.

Now, because of the rise in concern over personal privacy, most catalog companies have a way (either a phone number or address) for you to get off their list. Almost all have a check box so you can tell them not to share your name with others. This is just one way the privacy movement is affecting offline practices, too.

Privacy advocates work hard to educate the average person about protecting their personal information *before* they become online users, but many of them also want to stop the potential cascade of invasion that happens as more and more databases and corporations are linked together.

There were many papers written that talked about the dangers of the AOL/Time Warner merger. Most of them talked about the problems that would ensue if most Internet users' news and other information were to be funneled through the same pipeline. Table 17.1 looks at some other potential issues of aggregating information in mergers and partnerships.

### TABLE 17.1 POTENTIAL INFORMATION AGGREGATION IN MERGERS AND PARTNERSHIPS

| Business | Merged or Partnered with | Information Potentially Pooled |
|---|---|---|
| Major Western Bank | Major Southern Bank | Credit records, ATM, and bank card records (including all purchases made on those cards); personal information for loan applications; business and partnership information; Social Security Numbers; drivers' license numbers; addresses; family members and co-signers; marriage, birth, death, and divorce chronologies; records of withdrawals and deposits; check payees; and so on. |
| Pharmaceutical Company | Physicians' Specialty ISP (services include multimedia conferencing and health care, site hosting, remote database and records management) | Patient records; patient test results (delivered via online mechanism to patient), doctor billing records; insurance profiles and claims; prescription records; Web site clickstream data; subscriber profiles (both health professionals and their patients); drug testing records; side effect testing; health profiles; credit card information; Social Security Numbers; addresses; employment information and history; experimental drug subject records; and so on. |

**TABLE 17.1     CONTINUED**

| Business | Merged or Partnered with | Information Potentially Pooled |
|---|---|---|
| Entertainment Electronics Firm (owns movie theatres, recording labels, and media playing and recording equipment) | Online music and video store (owned by a magazine publishing company) | All Web site purchase records, including credit card info, purchase history; clickstream data; addresses; friends to whom purchases have been sent; browsing history; e-mail addresses of friends to whom samples or pages have been sent; theatre schedule mailing list members; discount card holders; fan club members; magazine subscribers; equipment warranty information (and all those profile questions on the bottom of the warranty cards); and so on. |

# In an Attention Economy Your Information Is More Valuable

For the last dozen or so years, information technology professionals have been discussing the "digital economy," in which information was the major commodity and the old industries, including the rising service industry, would be less important. In the late 90s, a discussion arose about the "attention economy," in which having (and holding) the attention of individuals was the most valuable.

Michael H. Goldhaber described the attention economy in a conference paper in 1997:

> "If the Web and the Net can be viewed as spaces in which we will increasingly live our lives, the economic laws we will live under have to be natural to this new space. These laws turn out to be quite different from what the old economics teaches, or what rubrics such as "the information age" suggest. What counts most is what is most scarce now, namely attention. The attention economy brings with it its own kind of wealth, its own class divisions—stars vs. fans—and its own forms of property, all of which make it

*incompatible with the industrial-money-market based economy it bids fair to replace. Success will come to those who best accommodate to this new reality."*

**(Source: Michael H. Goldhaber, 1997,**
`http://www.well.com/user/mgoldh/natecnet.html`**)**

We referred to this in Chapter 2, "What *Is* Privacy in a Digital World?," as part of Seth Grodin's definition of privacy. Grodin also says that "The Internet is the greatest direct marketing medium ever invented." According to Grodin, in an era of increasing demand on your attention, companies that match your needs the most closely—those who have you profiled the most accurately—will capture and keep your attention and get your business. This benefits everyone—people who want the product, or information, get it and those who don't, get less junk mail competing for their attention. The two ideas—the attention economy and your personal information as a valuable commodity—come together here.

*If* individuals have preserved control of their own personal information— that information that makes up a profile on them—then they can barter (or even sell) that information in return for quality delivery of goods and services that are tailored to them. Sigal Louchheim, a data-mining specialist, sees the time coming when people suddenly realize that their information has value:

> *"What I see as the influential catalyst is when monetary value will be placed on people's information. Once people realize that what they have is of value (their own privacy, their private information, personal preferences, etc.), the awareness to these issues will escalate dramatically. That will bring about many of the changes you listed below: legislation and standards will need to be established, the social climate will change in ways that are hard to predict: will people be unwilling to share very basic facts that are now taken for granted? Will people be unwilling to divulge their names, ages, addresses, favorite color, favorite TV show, gender, signature, etc. etc. etc.?"*

It makes a lot of sense that personal information is valuable. If it wasn't, these companies wouldn't be investing in technology to capture it and build profiles about their customers. It remains to be seen, of course, whether individuals—even armed with laws to help them protect their information assets—can or even *will* do something about it.

## DATA MINING: FINDING THE PATTERN OF NEEDLES IN THE HAYSTACK

Just what *is* data mining? The Webopedia defines it this way:

*A hot buzzword for a class of database applications that look for hidden patterns in a group of data. For example, data mining software can help retail companies find customers with common interests. The term is commonly misused to describe software that presents data in new ways. True data mining software doesn't just change the presentation, but actually discovers previously unknown relationships among the data.*

*(Source:* `http://webopedia.internet.com/`
`TERM/d/data_mining.html`*)*

Some people feel that definitions like this one, which describe the patterns and juxtapositions as "hidden," imply that somehow the data miner has hunted up some secret knowledge. In truth, the patterns are there—and for years, analysts have found these kinds of patterns with grueling hand analysis. That kind of analysis would take years with some of the massive databases now in existence—for example, some government housing administration databases now have more than 10 million entries.

Data mining software simply allows the same kind of analysis to take place in an automated—and faster—fashion on these immense databases. Analysts still have to define the problem in such a way that it can be answered and formulate the questions.

The Direct Marketing Association, those folks whose livelihood depends on being able to accurately profile and target customers, say this about data mining:

*Data Mining, by its simplest definition, automates the detection of relevant patterns in a database. For example, a pattern might indicate that married males with children are twice as likely to drive a particular sports car than married males with no children. If you are a marketing manager for an auto manufacturer, this somewhat surprising pattern might be quite valuable. However, Data Mining is not magic. For many years, statisticians have manually "mined" databases looking for statistically significant patterns. Today, Data Mining uses well-established statistical and machine learning techniques to build models that predict customer behavior. The technology enhances the procedure by automating the mining process, integrating it with commercial data warehouses, and presenting it in a relevant way for business users.*

*(Source: Kurt Thearling, Direct Marketing Magazine,*
*February 1999,* `http://www3.shore.net/~kht/text/`
`integration/integration.htm`*)*

Thearling goes on to describe how Data Mining helps answer business questions.

"Data Mining helps marketing professionals improve their understanding of customer behavior. In turn, this better understanding allows them to target marketing campaigns more accurately and to align campaigns more closely with the needs, wants and attitudes of customers and prospects.

"If the necessary information exists in a database, the Data Mining process can model virtually any customer activity. The key is to find patterns relevant to current business problems.

"Typical questions that Data Mining answers include:

- Which customers are most likely to drop their cell-phone service?
- What is the probability that a customer will purchase at least $100 worth of merchandise from a particular mail-order catalog?
- Which prospects are most likely to respond to a particular offer?"

From this description of how data mining works, it's easy to see why gathering as much information as possible about individuals, their preferences, habits, and circumstances is a very valuable process for companies. In a tight economy making sales and keeping customers is critical to the continued existence of a company. Getting that information on customers will be more and more important. As a result, individual information will be more and more valuable. And, let's not forget the benefits we as individuals receive: products and services that really meet our needs, formulated as a result of analyzing our wants, problems, and circumstances.

Privacy advocate Jason Catlett, who wrote a sidebar in Chapter 14, "Canaries in the Coal Mine," is one of the world's leading experts on data mining. It's one of the reasons he's so very effective, and can see where certain practices and regulations will lead.

(For some really fascinating papers on how data mining is used in many professions, type the words *data mining definition* into your favorite Web search engine.)

## Experts Will Need to Give Up Some of Their Privacy

In the new world of data mining that we've been talking about, another commodity will be expertise. Information technology planners are talking about staffing with e-lancers, specialists who can be recruited short- or long-term from any locale to work virtually with teams in any location.

Sources of information that can be trusted and which are kept up-to-the minute will be exceptionally valuable to those individuals and those companies. So will the individuals who generate the information (or who provide solutions to problems). Dave Hartley, formerly a city manager in a major midwestern city and now a knowledge and information management specialist, says that those experts will pay a privacy penalty for marketing their skills and information:

> *"[New] applications are looking for experts. If you want to be an expert, sell your expertise, etc. you will need to pay the privacy price for being such. Here is the analogy. When I was a public person (elected or appointed) I lost nearly all rights to privacy due to the weight of the first amendment (freedom of speech and expression). ...The Internet is a public place where we are all becoming public persons. We freely express our views and others may express their views. When we want to be seen (as an expert for whatever value) we have crossed over into the public person category. Said another way you can't have it both ways. Privacy and exposure?"*

Others see the privacy equation a little differently. Tim Casey sees the price of privacy as not lack of exposure but the removal of our uniqueness. Once again we draw lines, where the privacy line is the demarcation between ourselves and society.

## WHY MAINTAINING PRIVACY IS MORE IMPORTANT NOW THAN EVER

So many things changed on September 11, for both individuals and our communities. There have been many discussions on how we shouldn't allow those events to change us, but they have already done so. Before the attacks, tragic events affecting a single individual were notable and important. Now, our scale of tragedy has changed dramatically. We were brutally ambushed with those horrifying images of thousands of our family and friends and neighbors being murdered. We cannot escape them and now we will forever measure our losses against what we saw that day.

One of the most visible changes is that our sense of security is gone, possibly forever. We feel the need to find and destroy not just this particular group of attackers but anyone and anything that threatens our security, our lives, our piece of mind. To facilitate that search there are now many people willing to surrender to the government their personal privacy in exchange for a greater perception of security. They are willing to trade their privacy to keep the horrors of September 11 from ever returning. But in this time of cataclysmic change, it is crucial that we keep the foundation of our society intact, the respect for each individual that privacy ensures.

Privacy comes from deciding for yourself who can know the details of your life that you believe make you a unique individual. Since each of us decides what is unique about ourselves, our individual sense of privacy establishes the line between ourselves and others, and more importantly, between ourselves and society. It is an intimate, entirely personal thing, a feeling of personal dignity and worth that comes from the right to decide what is public and what is just for our own knowing. Privacy is an inalienable human right, every bit as valuable to individual liberty as the freedom of expression.

Protecting your privacy is difficult in a large society because your privacy is not as important to others as is their own. Others will treat your privacy in an off-hand way, or worse. Corporations and governments argue that finding and holding private information about an individual is perfectly harmless, as long the information is used in a way somehow beneficial to society at large. However, this assumes these groups will remain completely trustworthy forever, and in reality, the malice and neglect inherent in large organizations will always eventually expose us to personal damage.

Beyond the misuse of personal data, however, is a much more fundamental truth about the harm from an invasion of privacy: The very act of taking my private information injures me, *even if nothing is done with the information.* Taking personal information about me without my permission ignores my personal choices. It usurps my control over my own life. Put another way, an invasion of privacy is akin to the most dehumanizing of crimes, rape. Physically they are different, but the underlying premise is the same—someone forces themselves on you uninvited and treats the intimate aspects of your person with contempt, as valueless. Anything that happens or doesn't happen afterward does not mitigate the injury, because your dignity, your individuality, has already been destroyed, and in most cases you cannot ever get that dignity back.

Just as a society without free expression fosters tyranny, so does one without privacy. Without privacy none of us can maintain our uniqueness, and then all individual lives become devalued. A society without privacy has no respect for the lives of its citizens, much less their civil treatment, because people without privacy have lost their uniqueness, and are reduced to non-human, interchangeable objects. People then become objects that can be easily and dispassionately moved, substituted, or even eliminated as needed for the greater good, with no need to feel concern about anyone's "feelings."

And the definition of "terrorist" is someone who sees no value in any human life whatsoever.

The respect of privacy is the most powerful way of measuring the respect and value a society has for an individual. If in our grief and rage our search for the guilty drives us to broadly invade the privacy of our citizens, no matter how important or benign that may seem, then we have lost what differentiates us from the terrorists. Losing privacy, even voluntarily, means losing our personal value, our liberties and our way of life. We need to reenforce privacy, not destroy it, to make us strong enough to withstand the changes of the coming years.

The memories and emotions of that day of change will always be with us, and it may take many generations before they become less frightening. Beyond the difficulty of dealing with the emotions of these changes, however, is the real danger in the way we act on them. We must not inflict the terrorists' same brutality on ourselves in the name of justice. If we allow those memories to overwhelm our ability to respect every single individual, then we have become like them. When we begin to value individuals as little as the terrorists do, then the terrorists truly have won.

*—Timothy Casey*

## Healthy Skepticism Lags Behind the Law

Previously we discussed how more than 90% of Americans did not return the privacy preference forms from our financial institutions. In fact, Computer World reported on August 13, 2001, that it's even worse than we thought:

> *"Despite the clamor for new privacy laws, the public doesn't seem overly concerned, if the response to Gramm-Leach-Bliley's opt-out options is any indication. The returns are incomplete, but financial services companies have thus far received a piddling 0.5% to 0.75% response rate from customers demanding that all of their data be kept under wraps, according to Arabella Hallawell, a Gartner analyst."*

**(Source: Mark Hall, *The Politics of Privacy*, Computer World,** `http://www.computerworld.com/cwi/story/` `0,1199,NAV47_ST062937,00.html`**)**

That means that most U.S. citizens do not understand what the banks mean to do with their information, are not aware of the consequences, or don't care. A database security expert says that this lethargic attitude could be predicted by the way our country has responded to the decline of air quality or the rise in urban crime:

> "The cat is out of the bag...and my guess is that pragmatic Americans everywhere will make outraged sounds and then will simply accept the loss the same way they accept the loss of their ability to see the stars at night or have their kids walk to school."

Others believe that people didn't respond because we despair that our privacy is already gone. So much new technology is available to be used that we feel helpless before such an onslaught.

## Creation of Virtual Personas

In Chapter 10,"The Least You Should Do to Guard Your Privacy When Online," we suggested creating several profiles to be used on your online explorations. This creation of virtual *personas* is something that is being discussed in the privacy field as a way to shield personal information from online services, while not sacrificing complete control of your information. Dave Schroeder, Chief Technology Officer for an information technology company, sees software to manage multiple online personalities as a coming trend:

> *"My idea is the creation of virtual personae that will represent various facets of our personality and our buying profiles that we can share with vendors, thereby keeping the various spheres of our lives more separate and more private. For example: I'm the Chief Technology Officer of a company. I'm a developer, a designer, an author, an amateur historian and social scientist, a cook, a songwriter, a performer, a father, a travel enthusiast, and a member of the SCA [a medieval re-creation group]. By creating "virtual personaes" for each of these facets of my personality I could subscribe to relevant services or information feeds and buy various products, all without necessarily threatening my"core" personal privacy. It would be great to have software to help me manage multiple personaes."*

You can do this today, to some extent, with Microsoft's Internet Explorer and Netscape Communicator. Several companies have marketed products or services to do this. One of these companies is digitalme, which lets you create different "business cards" for different needs, and also offers a tracking service to help you remember to whom you gave what info. Figure 17.1 shows the digitalme information site.

**FIGURE 17.1**

*The digitalme meCard.*

You can find out how to get a digital identity from this company at
`http://www.digitalme.com/`.

One advantage of the digitalme plan is that your address book, the master list of your personas, is online, so you can get to it from anywhere you sign on, at home, at work, or an Internet Café. Figure 17.2 shows digitalme's explanation of their online address book.

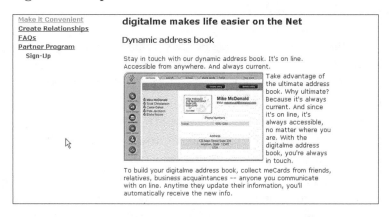

**FIGURE 17.2**

*The digitalme's online address book.*

Unfortunately, there used to be a lot more companies that offered either identity management services or proxy services. Many of them have gone out of business—perhaps a case of being ahead of demand. For the most current list, check the WebVeil site: `http://webveil.com/matrix.html`.

 **NOTE**     Have we told you about Privacy.net's analysis of what is actually going out of your machine when you hit a Web page? Try connecting to `http://www.privacy.net/analyze/` and see what's what.

## Corporate and Marketing Practices

Generally, only two potential bad guys are in any privacy violation scenario—the government or Big Business. Business has the power to affect us in many ways—because not only are we all consumers, but many of us also have employers. These are the two aspects of how businesses will operate in the future that we will explore.

Businesses are not unaware of the value of your information. As we've detailed above, that information is more and more valuable to them, too, as it helps them develop you and retain you as a customer. This is not evil: This is good business. Steve Larsen, vice president marketing for Net Perceptions, Inc., a company that develops personalization software, says, "You have to put customers at the center of your business, which means that serving them is even more important than getting new customers." (Source: Office.com, May 2000, `http://www.office.com/global/0,2724,285-17561,FF.html`) Market forces, if nothing else, impel businesses to be better than their competitors at meeting your needs.

This is the root of the self-regulation discussion in Chapter 15, "Self-Regulation and Privacy." If you only patronize companies who handle your information in ways that you approve of, you will influence others to handle data more appropriately, too.

In fact, many Libertarians, among them the Libertarian think tank The Cato Foundation, believe that there should be no regulation of privacy, and only market forces. They believe that if people ignore companies, both online and off, that treat their information without respect, then companies will be forced to change their practices or go out of business.

# More Bang for Your Info

Earlier we discussed Seth Grodin's idea that businesses *not* sending you things you don't want is as valuable as them sending you things you *do* want. Today, according to John F. Goodman on Office.com's online Web newsletter, customers are

> *"...no longer just a 'target.'" He says that the customer is now "becoming an active participant in e-commerce. And that fact has implications for the way all business, including manufacturing, is done. 'Personalization' is the new buzzword for this smarter business model. It really means integrating the customer's needs and wants into the entire network of company operations, from supply and production to order generation, sales and support. This process ultimately creates a relationship that mutually benefits the business and the customer. ...Now, largely through the Internet and software technology, customers are becoming collaborators with businesses in creating value. C. K. Prahalad et al of the University of Michigan Business School report that personalization is creating a consumer-centric world, 'giving consumers the ability to actively and dynamically reconfigure the products and services they consume.'"*

> **(Source: 4 May 2000,**
> `http://www.office.com/global/0,2724,285-17561,FF.html`**)**

The Andy Grove quote at the beginning of the section highlights why this model is powerful for both business and consumer. We want the intimacy and complete customer service that we had with small neighborhood businesses, but we also want the variety of goods, competitive pricing, and fast response of large concerns. J.G. Sandom has called personalization the "future of one-to-one marketing." Web-based electronic commerce has the potential to bring two-way relationships to our fingertips. In return, we bring unprecedented brand loyalty to companies that serve us well. In the August 21 issue of Newmedia.com, Daniel Muggeo says "online branding carries with it even greater potential than offline branding, mainly because the Web is a user-driven environment that fosters a unique, two-way relationship with the consumer. With the Web, customers can experience a brand hands-on, even before the normal purchase cycle is complete (think about researching an automobile that you've never owned before). The interactive nature of the Web produces greater opportunities—and greater challenges—for those looking to successfully brand online."

In early 2000, ActivMedia Research did a study on brand loyalty and repeat visitors to online stores, especially clothing vendors. The study reports that 40 percent of online buyers who shopped for clothing during 1999 had been catalog or in-person customers of the same clothing vendor *offline* in 1998. "Most are loyal, repeat customers interested in product look-and-feel, branding, functionality and vendor accessibility, selection, price, convenience, service and reliability," the study states. And then comes the real payoff. "Loyal customers are willing to pay premium prices, ignore competitive pitches, transfer a greater share of market activity online, and cost less to service and support than new customers," ActivMedia says.

That kind of payoff, coupled with the fact that retaining customers costs less than finding new ones, will increasingly drive companies to develop better profiles on its customers. And consumers will let them.

| **NOTE** | For a fascinating story on how casinos use customer tracking and personalization to build brand loyalty, see "Casinos Hit Jackpot With Customer Data," `http://www.computerworld.com/storyba/0,4125,NAV47_STO61799,00.html`. |
|---|---|

Many privacy experts already believe that consumers will barter their personal information for better service or a better deal. Jim Sleezer, a corporate privacy compliance manager, says, "I think the average person is willing to sell some of their privacy in exchange for a 3% savings on an item." Most online selling experiences prove him correct. Experience also shows that we, as consumers, like the benefits we get. We like having forms filled in for us for shipping and billing information. We like having an address book at the online store for folks we send Christmas or birthday presents to every year, especially if we can point, click, and ship to those on the other side of the country. We like not having to type our credit card information every time we shop. We like one-click or Express buy buttons. We also like being able to shop from our offices and homes instead of having to make time in our day to go out, either to the store or the post office.

Ernst and Young reported just before Christmas 2000 that Australians and Americans were increasingly turning to the Web for shopping. In Australia, online shoppers planned to conduct 17% of total Christmas shopping online, compared to only 7% last year.

The survey found that about 1 in 10 of all online shoppers would use half or more of their Christmas holiday budget on the Internet to avoid crowds and save time. Ernst & Young said Australia's rate of growth for online shopping was only slightly behind that of the United States. Online consumers in the United States were estimated to make 29% of their total holiday purchases over the Internet this year compared to 16% last year. (Source: I.T. online magazine, `http://www.it.mycareer.com.au/breaking/20001218/A7064-2000Dec18.html`)

BizRate.com's survey at the same time showed that those online purchases came to over 1 billion (yes, "B") dollars a week between Thanksgiving 2000 and Christmas day. A Sacramento radio survey in August 2001 found that of the 2,400 people who responded, well over half planned to shop online rather than fight crowds at the mall in 2001. That's a big benefit to online business, as well as to consumers' feet and patience. We can only assume that as long as online businesses keep meeting—and exceeding—their customers' expectations, consumers will continue this rising trend of shopping online.

## More Data, More Success, Bigger Targets

Of course, with all that data warehoused, companies are going to have to make sure they don't lose the customer's trust by exposing all that data. One of the risks they must anticipate and counter is that of being hacked, or getting a virus and exposing everything. A database security expert told us that

> "CodeRed II highlighted for me the distinction between privacy "policy" and privacy "reality." [Hundreds of thousands] of back-doored servers, including my doctor's, my financial advisor's, my insurance agent, my local police department, and my own home PC...means, de facto, that privacy no longer exists in the United States. Maybe this isn't literally true yet, but in principle, it's inevitable. The expertise does not exist outside Fortune 500 America to do anything about this threat, and none of us are going to ask our service providers to certify their security."

CodeRed, and CodeRed II, of course, is the extremely virulent network worm that hit the world's Internet servers in the summer of 2001. For a complete technical description of how CodeRed works, see the Symantec

Virus Dictionary at `http://www.symantec.com/avcenter/venc/data/` `codered.worm.html` or The Network Associates Virus dictionary at `http://www.mcafee.com` under "anti-virus."

Briefly, CodeRed only affected Microsoft Index Server 2.0 and the Windows 2000 Indexing service on computers running Microsoft Windows NT 4.0 and Windows 2000 that run IIS 4.0 and 5.0 Web servers. Symantec says that the worm "sends its code as an HTTP (WWW) request. The HTTP request exploits a known buffer-overflow vulnerability (a memory management problem), which allows the worm to run on your computer. The malicious code is not saved as a file, but is inserted into and then run directly from memory. Once run, the worm checks for the file C:\Notworm. If this file exists, the worm does not run and the thread goes into an infinite sleep state. If the file C:\Notworm does not exist, new threads are created. If the date is before the 20th of the month, the next 99 threads attempt to exploit more computers by targeting random IP addresses. To avoid looping back to infect the source computer, the worm will not make HTTP requests to the IP addresses `127.*.*.*`. (Essentially, your generic local Internet address.)

CodeRed defaced Web sites, corrupted data, and prevented legitimate access to the servers. It also opened a "back door" for future intrusions. Moreover, it impacted productivity for hundreds of thousands of workers. Many corporate networks shut down entirely for up to four days, e-mail was corrupted or shut down within and between companies, and even individual users were impacted. For example, on Pat's home computer, which sees 15–20 various attacks a day (only slightly above normal for a DSL subscriber in Northern California) her home firewall recorded 2,356 HTTP port probes in 90 hours in mid-August. Glee's dial up, at something under 56K, had 88 hits in a single hour, which is 10–15 times more than she usually sees in a day. Sometimes these attacks came so hard and fast that regular Internet traffic—e-mail out and Web sites loading in—couldn't move. In effect, this was a Denial of Service attack as well as an attempt to propagate a virulent worm.

CodeRed wasn't even a targeted attack; it created targets by random number generation. You can bet that big companies, with very prominent brands and databases of customer and supplier information, are targets for hackers every day. Their IT departments must boost their security measures and make policy and procedures to minimize the risk to this data.

One such effort in the United States is the IT ISAC (Information Technology Information Sharing and Analysis Center). According to *Information Security Magazine,* this is a "collaborative effort among fifteen high-tech giants to exchange information...on cyber threats and vulnerabilities to help ward off cracker attacks. The FBI will also participate, providing and receiving confidential information through the Information Technology Information Sharing and Analysis Center (IT-ISAC) to facilitate better protection of the nation's computer infrastructure....Infosec companies included in the IT-ISAC include Entrust Technologies, RSA Security, Symantec and VeriSign. Other participants include AT&T, HP, EDS, Computer Associates, Intel, KPMG, Titan Systems and Veridian." This is how it will work: When one of the member companies gets attacked, they will send a notice to the ISAC Network Operations Center (NOC). The NOC will examine the information and relay technical specifications to other members via e-mail, fax or telephone. The target of the attack will remain anonymous. (Source: `http://www.infosecuritymag.com/digest/2001/01-18-01.shtml#1a`).

The financial, insurance, and automotive industries have had ISACs for some time. This will be the first time such an arrangement has been tried to help protect the nation's critical Internet infrastructure. We will surely see more companies becoming members of such associations in the future.

We will also see a trend where insurers rate the "InfoSec preparedness" of companies alongside their auditing practices and other risk management techniques. Since the summer of 2000, insurer Lloyd's of London has been offering "hacker insurance" against loss of revenue and valuable data due to network security breaches. Lloyd's has partnered with Counterpane, an Internet security firm, to support this service for their customers. Other insurers have similar policies. Many companies are signing up, because insurance of this kind protects not only them, but their customers and helps prevent lawsuits if a successful attack causes a customer business loss.

This is not a paranoid fantasy. Online music seller CDUniverse was threatened with a massive lawsuit after allegedly losing 300,000 of its customers' credit card numbers to a Russian cracker in December 2000.

Financial companies are already under government mandate to beef up their security measures to protect their clients' personal and financial information. As more and more companies work to make the transition to "e-Corporations," we will see this improved security across most industries, with or without government mandate. It's just good business. Better security means better protection of *your* data. Better data protection means more trust for the company, which in the long run contributes to a healthy bottom line.

## More Privacy Teams in Businesses

As a part of this focus, more and more companies are creating privacy teams. Frequently this team is headed by a Chief Privacy Officer (CPO). *Computerworld* described the trend this way:

> *"The sudden interest in appointing chief privacy officers (CPO) stems as much from fear as it does from the desire to protect customers. The CPO movement is young: About 50 to 75 companies have created such positions in the past several months, according to Alan Westin, a business privacy expert who in July started the Association of Corporate Privacy Officers (ACPO) in Hackensack, N.J.*

> *Many more CPOs are expected to be hired as a result of the growing corporate angst over whether Congress will pass strict privacy laws that may hamper business. The Federal Trade Commission (FTC) has already suggested that corporate self-regulation isn't working.*

> *But having a CPO is fast becoming a checklist item to help companies ward off government regulation and to reassure customers that their privacy will be protected, says Jonathan Gaw, an analyst at International Data Corp. in San Mateo, Calif."*

> **(Source: Computerworld, November 2000** `http://www.`
> `computerworld.com/cwi/story/0,1199,NAV47_ST053899,00.html`**)**

IBM, which has a CPO, also has a privacy executive to handle European issues. They advise other companies to also create a privacy office to manage corporate compliance with privacy regulations globally. ZDNet-UK reports that IBM warns that such a move is critical to retaining customer trust. "Our research has shown that about 12 million people stopped buying online because of privacy concerns so it becomes a make-or-break issue for e-commerce," said Armgard von Reden, IBM's European privacy officer. "Only 10% felt that Web companies would handle their data adequately and according to data privacy laws. It affects advertising, your brand and your bottom line so if I were a Web company I would have very good compliance." (Source: ZDNet-UK `http://news.zdnet.co.uk/story/0,,s2085587,00.html`)

The job description for a Chief Privacy Officer is interesting. So few items are listed as duties yet there is so much scope of responsibility. Just think about how important each of these tasks are. Now imagine how you would try to handle these tasks for your bank? How different would that be from the same tasks at the company that makes the cat food you buy?

## JOB DESCRIPTION FOR A CPO

The job description varies but, according to the Association for Corporate Privacy Officers, general duties include the following:

- Training employees about privacy.
- Comparing the company's privacy policies with potential risks and then figuring out whether or not and how to fill gaps.
- Managing a customer-privacy dispute and verification process.
- Informing senior executives on how the company deals with privacy issues.

*(Source: `http://www.pandab.org/`)*

Many corporate privacy teams find themselves developing corporate data-handling policies and cleaning up from previous years' business practices. For example, companies with separate product divisions may have as many as 100 separate marketing databases. Data analysts in the past have felt free to mine other divisions' information looking for other potential contacts and customers. Under the current laws and regulations, this may no longer be a legitimate way to do business. Privacy teams have to figure out what the right business practice should be, and then work to get those business practices adopted. For so long those customer databases, as we described before, have been a marketer's chief asset, sometimes getting the fact that the world has changed into actual business reality is not a simple task.

That doesn't even begin to talk about the task of figuring out the right set of business practices for employee privacy.

## THE FUTURE OF PRIVACY: THE LITTLE THINGS WILL ADD UP

Imagine that for every day of your life, you kept notes on little scraps of paper for everyone you met, everyone you talked to on the phone, all the e-mail and paper mail that you got, every purchase that you made, every time you moved from place to place, and every time a key opened a lock. At the end of the day you'd collect those little scraps of paper and meticulously jot them down in your daily calendar blotter, occasionally getting a name misspelled or a face misremembered, but mostly having things right.

Do this for 50 years of your life, day in, day out, accumulating your own personal dossier of where you were in the world. Lose a page or two here and there, sometimes a whole week or month (the ink spilled and ran one day, leaking onto November and making it mostly unreadable).

Imagine that this is the normal way of living, and that every person keeps their own filing system on who they all see and talk to and instant message, with each in their own different way with their own quirky logic and categories and their own idiosyncratic retrieval schemes should they ever need to see anything again. And people being people, they gossip among each other, telling stories about who they saw 15 years ago and what they were wearing and the clothes they bought then and whether they paid cash check or charge. (And if the check bounced.)

Some of these "people" are corporate people, big and small corporate organizations like Wal-Mart or Safeway or MasterCard or the State of New Jersey Turnpike. They have exceptional memories for detail (Do you like skim milk, or 1%, or 2%? Blue jeans or khakis? Do you drive too fast on the turnpike? When?) and when they make mistakes, like confusing you with someone else, they have a hard time admitting their mistakes or correcting them.

In the future—which, after the events of September 11, might unfortunately already be here—many people will have a very long memory of what you were up to on any given moment of any given day, and that memory will be shared imperfectly with every other organization that might ever want to deal with you. And some of those memories will be wrong.

The face-imaging system at every airport, which helps the new security guard (and the National Guard) know your name and whether you're a regular at the airport or a stranger new in town, also alerts security if you match the profile of a terrorist. The probability of an erroneous match is small but nonetheless possible, and people with faces that look unusual to the computer system need to travel by private car, because it's nearly impossible to get out of the system once you're in.

The DNA scans done routinely for newborns at some maternity hospitals, which can help a new nurse (hired from the nursing school day-labor pool) know whether a newborn baby needs special care for a rare condition, also allow law enforcement to attempt to match these scans against DNA samples in evidence in the course of their criminal investigations. The probability of erroneous matches again is small but always possible. Falsely marked individuals should have been born at home in the locales where that is not illegal.

The friendly voice from the dashboard of your new car that helps you out when you're lost and alerts the authorities when your airbag goes off also knows where you've been and how fast you've been going to get there. Your insurance rates are lower, though there is always, again, that nagging probability that when the system thinks you were going unauthorized off-road joyriding it was really just a new bit of freeway that hadn't made it into their database. That's not all that bad except that you drive that stretch of new highway on your commute, so it will be an expensive year for insurance—they'll figure it out eventually, you hope.

The future of privacy is full of these little errors and omissions creeping into our lives and making us pay attention to the mistakes that far-away and unfeeling organizations make all the time. It's the story of the failure of complex systems to do what would seem to be a simple thing because no one can possibly anticipate the consequences of minor errors to cause major problems. As computers and networks grow ever larger in our lives, it will take more and more precise attention to detail to make sure that privacy is not eroded drip by drip by the steady pattern of typos and blunders. Our work is cut out for us.

—*Edward Vielmetti*

---

# Will Your Employer Become Big Brother?

This is an area where regulation, practice, and custom interact in murky and uncertain ways. In the United States, for a long time, employers have been prohibited from asking certain kinds of questions during the hiring process, but have kept massive amounts of data on their employees after hiring. The corporate culture is so used to having—and using—that information that changes will be hard to implement. The issues of employee privacy revolve around two areas: monitoring of employee activity and treatment of employee data.

We'll discuss employee monitoring first.

## Are They Looking over Your Shoulder?

It's a generally accepted business rule that stuff you do at the employer's site should conform to the employer's rules of appropriate conduct. This includes not hitting on your subordinates and not operating a business out of your employer's mailroom. For folks in the service industries, especially customer care call centers, some routine monitoring is part of the job. We've all heard the recorded announcement, "This call may be monitored to assure quality of service" as we wait on hold to speak to a real human. Call center operators and agents know that just about everything they do is monitored and recorded: how long they take to resolve a call; how long they are idle between calls (which sometimes also means how long they take finishing paperwork for a call); how long they take on breaks and lunch; how many *upsells* they make (those "extras" you can get just for ordering *right now!);* and how many errors they make in collecting and recording data. Manufacturing line workers know that they are watched—sometimes with video recording equipment—for both quality and performance reasons. No sleeping on the job, taking too long in the bathroom, or sticking empty bottles in a door cavity of a new car.

For white-collar workers, however, the situation is usually not so clear-cut. They know that there are business rules, and that they differ from company to company. "Appropriate personal use of business phones" is allowed at some companies and strictly prohibited at others. Using the company photocopier is a perk at some places. Every copy is logged and charged for at others. When computers—and computer networks—arrived on the scene, appropriate use policies were developed. In general, most companies decided that the computer and the network were like desks, lockers, and phones. If you could have personal material in your locker or desk, you could put a reasonable amount of personal stuff on your hard drive. If you could use the phone for personal reasons, you could use the network (including e-mail or Web access) for a reasonable amount of personal use. If you weren't allowed to use your desk, locker, or phone for non-company activities, you couldn't use the computer for them, either.

In general, in the mainframe days, monitoring and control of resources was pretty easy. You could get reports on user activity on an hourly, weekly, or monthly basis. You could restrict the games directory until non-work hours. However, with the rise of internal networks (intranets) the job got harder.

Some companies manage compliance by managing performance. Who cares if Harry is doing a lot of e-mail with his sister as long as he gets his work done on time and his customers and co-workers are happy with his interaction with them? Or, if Sally's use of the network to download pornographic pictures is slowing data transfer for the finance people, it can be dealt with on a "misuse of company resources" basis.

However, other companies manage compliance with their policies by monitoring employee's computer activities. AP reported in July 2001 that more than a third of U.S. workers with Internet access have their e-mail messages and Web surfing regularly monitored by their employers, according to a new study by the Workplace Surveillance Project of the Privacy Foundation, a research group based at the University of Denver. According to the AP report, Andrew Schulman, the study's chief researcher, attributes the prevalence of workplace surveillance to its ease and low cost—an average of $5.25 per monitored employee each year using commercial software packages.

The news in the past few years has been full of reports of employee firings due to inappropriate Internet use. In 2000 The Dow Chemical Co. fired 50 workers and disciplined another 200 for e-mailing pornography and violent images from company computers. Previously, Xerox Corp. fired 40 workers for spending work time at porn and shopping sites. GE had a similar incident, and several state governments have pink-slipped employees for collecting pornographic images. Even the Armed Services have had instances where servicemen or officers have been disciplined for an infraction of the moral code while using government-issued computers.

Although many cases have been resolved in favor of the employer, saying that employers have some rights to monitor use of their equipment, Schulman said companies sometimes go too far. Frequently, warnings to employees about computer use monitoring are deep inside employee handbooks or physically posted on an obscure bulletin board. The Privacy Foundation study estimates that 14 million employees are under continuous surveillance using commercially available software. According to NielsenNetRatings, the total online work force in the United States is about 40 million.

Still other companies use keystroke monitoring programs that catch every character typed in by an employee. In fact, the FBI used a keystroke capturing hardware device to gather evidence in one of its cases.

E-mail is frequently monitored using keyword filtering. If certain keywords (obscenities, titles of family members such as aunt or brother, names of genitalia, either formal or slang, graphics formats in attachments, and so on) are spotted, a copy of the message is slotted for further examination.

This is a slippery problem for employers. Resources cost money. Wasted time and loss of productivity cuts company profits and may cause raises to be deferred or layoffs to occur. Yet increasingly courts and regulations claim that employees have a "reasonable expectation" of privacy while at work, and monitoring can be defined in so many ways. Is the network management software that helps the engineers keep the network humming along, and which samples packets and records traffic origins and destinations monitoring? Is the remote management software that your IT department uses to deliver new virus signatures, program upgrades, and operating system patches monitoring because it does an inventory of what's on your machine? In differing circumstances, the answer might be either yes *or* no, and be the right answer for some situations.

We will see more network and routine workday monitoring in the next few years, and also more instances of firings, discipline, and the court challenges to them. Especially in a tight economy when IT budgets are being slashed to the bone and every network packet becomes a measurable and scarce resource, this issue is going to remain a hot one.

## Who Owns Your HR File?

We predict that this is going to be an even hotter potato in the coming years than routine monitoring. Global companies are going to have to face it soon because the European Union has employee data protection regulations. If a company does business in Europe and moves European employee data across country borders—say to a central HR database in England or Brazil or the United States—then their employee data handling practices come under the jurisdiction of the European law. That law states that employee data must be handled with the same kinds of fair information practices that consumer data is subject to. That means, if you remember, Notice, Choice, Access, and Security. In Europe they also require data minimalization—you may not collect and retain anything more than you need for the task at hand.

Violation of the EU Data Protection Laws can mean loss of the right to do business in *any* EU signatory country. For many transnational corporations, that's a big risk to their future profitability. So companies are scrambling to find ways to stay in compliance.

Some companies are responding by changing their integrated HR management plans by *not* shipping that info out of the countries where the employees live. Some others are modifying their business practices so that their general policy complies with the stringent EU requirements. Modifying your business practice requires some cultural change, as we mentioned above. U.S. HR managers are so used to having vast personnel files—and to limiting employee access to those files—that even the notion of employees having a right to data privacy is foreign to them. Letting employees have some say in how that data is handled may seem even more unnatural.

Currently, U.S. companies may adopt the provisions in a Safe Harbor agreement negotiated by the U.S. Department of Commerce (http://www.export.gov/safeharbor/) with European officials.

The Safe Harbor provisions cover both consumer and employee data practices. Companies can sign up for either or both. In February 2001, Hewlett-Packard (HP) announced that it was adopting both parts of the agreement. As of that time, HP was the largest company to do so, and one of the few to adopt the employee provisions. Barbara Lawler, HP's Corporate Privacy Officer, said the Safe Harbor provisions would apply to all of its data transactions from now on. Many privacy advocates see the Safe Harbor rules as a way to help raise privacy standards in the United States in addition to its main goal of providing a self-regulatory framework for companies doing business in Europe.

Employees are pushing for more privacy protection, too. In many companies, corporate IDs are no longer based on Social Security numbers or other government sponsored IDs because of employee demand. Some corporate insurance plans will issue non-SSN member IDs to covered employees and dependants. Other issues under debate are restricted access to employee databases, drug testing results, background investigation results, internal Web site personalization, and biometric profiles.

Even with HP and similar large multinational companies such as Microsoft, CitiBank, and Intel leading the way, employee data privacy issues are going to provide stormy sailing in the U.S. for some time to come. Between the cultural issues and the cost of compliance, the struggle will be an interesting one.

# Technology Helps and Hurts

All through this book we've talked about technology and its effect on privacy—either to aid in the collection of information or protect against inappropriate use. In this section we discuss some potential changes in technology—either privacy enhancing (PET) or privacy threatening.

In general, we're in a transition period for technology. Laws are changing. Security products (VPNs, firewalls, antivirus software, and digital certificates) are maturing and becoming more useful, but technology designed specifically with privacy protection in mind is still in the early stages. Technology for capturing data, storing it, and analyzing it is maturing at a faster rate than PET.

Companies founded on privacy protection products are foundering, which will probably lead to a decided lack of innovation in privacy-enhancing products. Companies such as Microsoft, which developed the Passport Wallet and the operating system XP, both of which offer significant improvements in the user online experience, are also plagued by security issues. Privacy advocates, suspicious of Microsoft's motives in the bigger picture, see these security holes as significant threats to user privacy.

So there may not be too many great leaps forward in privacy protection technology. Dave Schroeder, the CTO in our *ad hoc* polling group, says that he foresees "no major improvements, just greater availability and more idiot-proofing. Personal firewalls will be standard for broadband home connections. Smarter VPNs will be available for businesses."

Chet Johnson, the network expert, is even more cynical. He says, "The most significant privacy enhancing technology (and most threatening) is personal vigilance (or lack thereof). Short of going back to kerosene lamps and wood stoves, data can and will be developed about your personal choices. Someone, somewhere, will map this data back to names, addresses, and government identification numbers."

Let's look at where the interaction between technology and privacy may go.

## More Kinds of Information Will Be in Play

Currently, what constitutes *personally identifiable information* is defined loosely as information that would enable someone to locate your name, address, Social Security number, phone number, and so on. However, what happens as technology improves in medical research? The recent decision by the Bush administration to enable limited stem cell research, and the debate over who owns which lines (think "families") of cell types points up that genetic identity may become an issue in privacy. Hong Li, a senior security architect who works with Pat, sent e-mail suggesting this after watching a documentary. "I saw a piece of TV news the other day about hospitals and medical research institutes owning/sharing patients' gene information (for all the "good causes" of course: e.g., finding cures to certain diseases)," she wrote. "In the future this type of information might become a major part of 'personal information'."

Many companies—and state motor vehicle departments—now routinely record and categorize biometric information. Some of this is being developed as methods for better authentication and identification of individuals. However, some companies have collected the data during routing photographic badge issuance without notice to employees, to use for testing new systems.

## Better Tracking Online

Marketers, working to improve that user experience and user relationship, are working on ways to improve how you and your activities are tracked. Some recent examples are illustrative of where the industry may go.

A Web company, Predictive Networks, Inc. of Boston, has developed software to track every site user's visit. The software builds a *digital silhouette*, a profile of the user based on those visits. Predictive says that the silhouettes are "anonymous, predictive models of user preferences and affinities." (Source: `http://www.predictivenetworks.com/internet.htm`)

If someone were to visit a sewing site or a fashion design site, Predictive's profile model might immediately send that person fabric, embroidery, and sewing machine ads in pop-up windows. According to their Web site, the data analysis mechanism and digital silhouettes encompass over 140 demographic and content "affinity" categories. The digital silhouette demographics consist of six major categories (gender, age, income, education, occupation, and race), which are further broken down into subcategories. The content affinities consist of over 90 subcategories (golf, music, software, and so on). Predictive has similar products for interactive TV and wireless devices.

New York-based DigitalConvergence invented a cat-shaped scanner and distributed more than 1 million free scanners through Radio Shack and to readers of *Forbes* and *Wired* magazines. Figure 17.3 shows the CueCat devices. The CueCat (Keystroke Automation Technology) optical reader is a free hand-held device, attached to the computer, about the size of a mouse. The concept is pretty cool. Bill Pettit of the *Umbrella Computing Journal* says, "Imagine being able to use your television, radio, newspapers, magazines, catalogs, books, compact discs, even a soda can, to transfer you instantly to specific Web pages on your computer. It eliminates all the frustrating searches and sifting that comes with trying to locate information about a specific item." (Source: `http://www.exis.net/umbrella/0012/med0012.htm`)

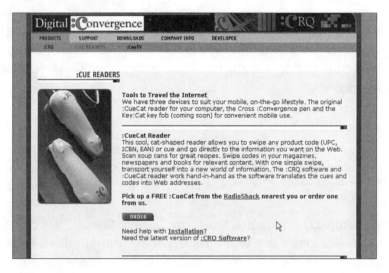

**FIGURE 17.3**

*The CueCat from Digital Convergence.*

DigitalConvergence's Web site describes the "cues" that its Cats read this way:

> *"Cues are our own proprietary slant code or even a specific audio tone. Our technology also reads product codes like UPC, ISBN or EAN symbols found on products like books, CDs, or tapes, and UPC codes from just about anything in your kitchen pantry. Our print cues consist of a series of thin, slanted bars and spaces that, when swiped, link your computer browser to a specific Web page."*

**(Source:** `http://www.crq.com/ master_templ.cfm?view=products`**)**

By using a CueCat linked to a computer, you can swipe bar codes (or cues) on any advertisements or editorial to be transported to the related Web sites. To use the device, you must go to the DigitalConvergence Web site and register some personal information, including name, e-mail address, gender, age range, and ZIP code. This information is then linked to a unique identifier within the CueCat and sent to servers at DigitalConvergence each time a bar code is scanned. While the company has an extensive privacy policy, a security breach at their Web site in September 2000 exposed about 140,000 consumers' names, e-mail addresses, and ZIP codes. This problem alerted may privacy advocates and new members of the potential risk to their information.

The CueCat is an interesting development in bridging the gap between the physical world and cyberspace. Another similar device was the eMarker, a gadget to help you remember or identify songs you hear on the radio.

eMarker was a key fob device that works with a preset list of radio stations on your Web browser. Figure 17.4 shows the eMarker key fob. According to the Web site at `http://www.emarker.com`, "pressing the button on the eMarker creates a timestamp." The service was permanently closed at the end of September 2001. Their Web site explains:

*"eMarker's device and services have been well received by those who used it and a good deal of excitement was successfully created in the market. However, under the current economic conditions, eMarker was not able to generate a reasonable return on investment to maintain its operation. It was only after thorough evaluation, that we needed to make a business decision that we discontinue the operation."*

**FIGURE 17.4**

*The eMarker fob device.*

When you inserted the eMarker into its cradle, it automatically connected to the Web site. Your eMarks were uploaded to your personalized account. eMarker.com then displayed playlist information from your preset stations. You were able to choose from a list of over 1,100 radio stations across the country." Figure 17.5 shows preselected stations that you would have been listening to.

On September 30, 2001, eMarker closed its services. Although this particular service failed in an economic downturn, it seems likely that other ideas that make easier connections between users and services (and record the connections for later processing) will be developed.

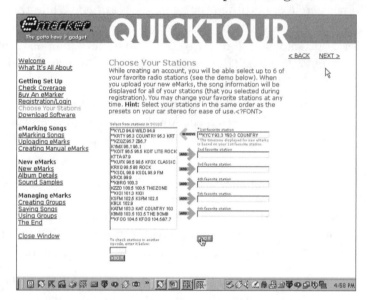

**FIGURE 17.5**

*Preselecting participating radio stations.*

eMarker was a Sony company, and their privacy policy made it clear that Sony will use the information submitted for their marketing and analysis purposes. In part, it said:

> *"Data collected during your visit to eMarker.com is used for internal review and may be used to improve or customize the Website content or layout and/or notify consumers about updates to our Websites.*
> *The information may be shared with other Sony organizations and/or third parties if we think it appropriate to do so, e.g., for marketing purposes."*

If you don't want to enable this, but do want the service, you have two choices. eMarker suggests that you use privacy shielding software on your browser. NetSkulker's suggestion (http://www.netskulker.com) is to fib on the registration. This is another instance when using a separate identity created for this purpose is a good practice.

While the eMarker was basically a timeclock that recorded the time the song was played (and you remember which station), the only privacy risk we could see was that your registration could be linked to your song preferences (and maybe whether you're listening to the radio when you're supposed to be working). However, because the database of available stations was so limited, it seemed unlikely to be a significant risk. And in the long run, market forces prevailed—not enough people used the service to keep it in business.

Expect to see many similar sorts of devices and services to bridge the gap between the physical and the electronic. Most will require that you at least register, and then your actions will be tracked somehow. If you want to take advantage of the service, check these things at the least:

- Do they have a privacy policy? Does it seem to offer you sufficient protection for your information?
- How does the system work? Where does the information go, how is it transported, and who can see it?
- Are they storing PII, or demographic data? And how can you tell?

## You May Never Really Be Alone

We've discussed the rise in video surveillance, the inclusion in cell phones and other wireless devices of GPS and other tracking technology, and all the ways in which someone can find out what you're doing even when you're not online.

In discussions concerning this topic, several folks mentioned David Brin's book *The Transparent Society.* In it, Brin looks at current trends and threats to privacy and goes in a rather different direction than other authors. Brin agrees that there may be no way to hold back the tide of public observation and inevitable loss of privacy—at least outside of our own homes. Too many of our transactions are already monitored, and cameras used to observe and reduce crime in public areas have been successful. Some proponents are even discussing recording sound. The use of these cameras to enable facial recognition software is clearly rising. However, Brin's idea is that by sharing all the information all the time—sort of a cyberspace, 24/7, 156 channel reality show—there will be no way for police, government, or even big business to use the information to harm us. If the information is already public, why bother to hide it?

Self-described anarchist-anachronist-economist David Friedman, in his essay *Privacy and Technology*, says that if Brin's future comes to pass, "physical privacy in realspace will vanish. One implication is that individuals will protect their informational privacy in the same ways in which people in primitive societies without physical privacy protect it, by adopting patterns of speech and behavior that reveal as little as possible of what they actually believe and intend." In other words, Friedman believes that our public encounters will be more ritualized and less likely to express feelings, preferences, or personality. He also postulates that for Brin's future to come true, "the technology of surveillance is going to outrun the technology of physical privacy, that the bugs will beat the scanners, that the video mosquitoes will not fall victim to automated dragonflies. While he may be correct, it is hard to predict in advance how the balance will turn out. We might end up in a world where legal surveillance is cheap and easy, illegal surveillance difficult, giving us the choice of how much privacy we will have." (Source: *Social Philosophy & Policy* 17:186-212, 2000, http://www.daviddfriedman.com/).

British society may give some help on evaluating Friedman's and Brin's theories. An official British government program provides closed-circuit television surveillance in many municipalities. As we've seen, in London's Newham Borough, the system even includes facial recognition scanning. Prime Minister Tony Blair has made "livability" one of his key themes, including helping make the streets safer and people more confident in their environment. Evidence that the crime reduction is necessary is provided by a 2001 Mori survey of deprived neighborhoods where the British environmental regeneration charity Groundwork had been active. This showed that 55% of the areas' residents felt too scared to go outdoors. The collapse of community feeling and civic involvement in those neighborhoods was further called out by the finding that 90% of those surveyed could not say who their local councilor was.

According to a story in *New Start* magazine, Fall 2001, "Mr. Blair gathered under the livability umbrella such familiar initiatives as the neighborhood warden scheme, the extension of the closed circuit TV camera program, and measures to tackle anti-social behavior. The new power of local councils to promote economic, social, and environmental well-being also fits in with the thinking, as does the neighborhood renewal strategy's emphasis on raising public service standards to improve life in deprived neighborhoods."

The British government recently allotted £70 million (pounds sterling) to help local councils install or upgrade their TV surveillance equipment. City planners know that the technology diverts crime to areas not covered by the cameras. A Scottish Centre for Criminology report on CCTV in Airdre was unable to rule out displacement as a factor, although various studies in other countries indicate that burglars and other criminals will travel long distances to commit crimes. Discussing the justification for establishing a surveillance system of 16 cameras in Manchester, Gordon Conquest, chairman of the city center subcommittee of Manchester Council, candidly admitted, "No crackdown on crime does more than displace it, and that's the best we can do at the moment."

The programs are reported to be very popular with citizens because crime in central areas has been significantly reduced. The *Barnsley Chronicle* in the UK reported on the installation of a closed-circuit TV system in Platts Common Industrial Estate (what Americans would call an office or industrial park). In the story, Richard Cooper, managing director of Wybone, one of the tenants in the park, said: "The lads on the factory floor who leave their cars in the car park are happier now that their vehicles are covered by security cameras."

The practice of surveillance will continue to expand in Britain. The *Local Policing Plan for the West Midlands (2001/2002)* describes how CCTV is viewed as an essential part of their policing efforts:

> "The anti-robbery operation includes high-visibility police patrols, a clampdown on the rise of mobile phone robberies from young people and officers being visible to the community and reassuring them with crime-prevention advice and their presence. In connection with local authorities we use closed circuit TV with high-visibility policing to put off robbers and protect the people who are vulnerable."

> **(*Source:* `http://www.west-midlands.police.uk /literature/policing_plan/`)**

Privacy International has a fact sheet on British use of CCTV that points out the privacy risks of such practices. It reports

*"In the past decade, the use of CCTV has grown to unprecedented levels. In Britain between 150 and 300 million pounds (225—450 million dollars) per year is now spent on a surveillance industry involving an estimated 300,000 cameras. Most British towns and cities are moving to CCTV surveillance of public areas, housing estates [subdivisions], car parks and public facilities. Growth in the market is estimated at fifteen to twenty per cent annually."*

**(*Source:* `http://www.privacyinternational.org/`**
`issues/cctv/cctv_faq.html`**)**

They also point out some of the less obvious uses to which CCTV is being put in Britain, and to Americans it sounds like a very scary list indeed:

*"Originally installed to deter burglary, assault and car theft, in practice most camera systems have been used to combat 'anti-social behavior', including many such minor offenses as littering, urinating in public, traffic violations, obstruction, drunkenness, and evading meters in town parking lots. They have also been widely used to intervene in other 'undesirable' behavior such as underage smoking and a variety of public order transgressions. Other innovative uses are constantly being discovered. When combined with observation of body language, the cameras are particularly effective in detecting people using marijuana and other substances. These systems are used increasingly to police public morals and public order. According to a glossy UK Home Office promotional booklet, "CCTV: Looking out for you," the technology can be a solution for such problems as vandalism, drug use, drunkenness, racial harassment, sexual harassment, loitering and disorderly behavior."*

**[Ibid.]**

The Privacy International essay points out that a British Home Office study shows that not all citizens are delighted with the growing practice. In fact, 7 out of 10 people felt that local government and private companies should not make the decision to install such systems. Almost 40% felt the cameras could be used for other purposes than "the public good." Perhaps the most important conclusion in the Home Office study was that when issues about CCTV were raised and discussed in public groups, unconditional support fell in most areas. To the privacy-minded, of course, this points up the fact that this kind of public surveillance needs to have civilian input and controls.

The practice of installing CCTV is growing in the United States, as well, although not as fast as in Britain. The cultural differences have slowed acceptance here in the past, but immediately after September 11, 2001, our attitudes about a great many security issues seem to be changing, but we can expect to see it grow, nonetheless.

On September 17, 2001, Oakland International Airport in California announced it will become the first airport in the country to use face-recognition technology. The Oakland Airport will use a system that captures the contours of a traveler's eye sockets and the curvatures of her nose on film, then compares the images to a law enforcement database.

In the following sidebar, technologist and security analyst Ross Stapleton-Gray talks about his concerns with the growing use of surveillance and the problems their inaccuracies will cause.

## ANTI-SENSOR TECHNOLOGIES AND TACTICS: A FUTURE OF FALSE POSITIVES?

[The following essay was written two months prior to the events of September 11, 2001. Rather than amending it, it is preserved here as a benchmark of how things stood then. The underlying issue remains the same—the intensity may have been raised a few notches.]

The growth in application of surveillance systems suggests that we might see a rosy future as well for anti-sensor technologies and tactics, i.e., simple, perhaps low-tech, attacks to disable, frustrate or spoof sensors, for all sorts of ill.

In the immediate wake of the 1996 TWA 800 crash, since determined to be the result of aircraft system failure and not a terrorist attack, the U.S. Congress enacted legislation to significantly tighten airport security, providing the FAA billions to upgrade and enhance airports' abilities to detect potential threats.

And now airports are on a hair trigger. In an August 1999 incident at Chicago's O'Hare, one of the busiest airports in the world, a passenger bolted through a security checkpoint at the United terminal, and lost himself in the crowd. Because it couldn't be determined that the man wasn't a bomb-toting terrorist (rather than the most likely scenario, a self-important jerk), all of the travelers in two concourses were evacuated (approximately 6,000 people), and any flights which the man might have boarded were cancelled—in all, some 69 flights, with many other arriving and departing flights delayed.

Imagine now that all of the country's airports have deployed bomb-sniffing devices, on the alert for a spectrum of chemical signatures. And now imagine anyone wishing to disrupt the U.S. transportation grid arming themselves with that most ominous of weapons, a spray bottle of relatively harmless chemicals, smelling, to the "nose" of the sniffers, like something far worse.

There have already been numerous incidents where facilities were evacuated after envelopes or packages alleged to contain anthrax were discovered—media hype of the threats of chemical and biological terrorism has made disrupting work at a government agency, abortion clinic, or other political target as easy as tossing an envelope full of flour into the mail (a decidedly low-tech "denial of service" attack).

The fundamental problem is the asymmetry of the effort required to detect actual threats, versus the ability to spoof them. For the terrorist, or more peaceable political activist, whose goal is as much attention to their political agenda as anything else, it doesn't much matter whether O'Hare is shut down for the holiday travel weekend by a bomb, or by a teenage kid paid fifty bucks to surreptitiously shpritz a cart-full of luggage with chemicals. (Though if you really do need to use a bomb, you can start by causing enough false alarms"—"the airport alarm system that cried wolf"—to the point that they shut the system off out of frustration. )

Increasing application of automation in general compounds the problem: the same automation that allows systems to be tweaked toward greater efficiency, e.g., in routing more traffic in the crowded central city, can be "monkeywrenched" to far greater disaster, when a few failures produce a denser gridlock.

If nothing else, the above is an endorsement of keeping some humans in the loop, and a caution against relying too much on IT and surveillance to solve all our problems. We certainly can't expect to detect every threat—and probably ought not to believe everything we do see.

*[Nothing in the above is belied by the events of 9/11; in a post-9/11 world of more sensors, and looking over the shoulder against terrorist threats, anti-sensor stunts are likely to be all the more disruptive and will remain cheap to perform. Notwithstanding the 9/11 hijackings, the airports were on a hair trigger, just looking for the wrong threat signatures—we'll add dozens more things to worry about, providing dozens of new ways to create false and paralyzing threats.]*

*—Ross Stapleton-Gray*

## Encryption Becomes *De Rigueur*

We've talked about encryption in other parts of the book. As you remember, the use of encryption/decryption is as old as the art of communication. In wartime, a cipher, often incorrectly called a "code," can be employed to keep the enemy from obtaining the contents of transmissions. (Technically, a code is a means of representing a signal without the intent of keeping it secret; examples are Morse code and ASCII.) Simple ciphers include the substitution of letters for numbers, the rotation of letters in the alphabet, and the "scrambling" of voice signals by inverting the sideband frequencies. More complex ciphers work according to sophisticated computer algorithms that rearrange the data bits in digital signals.

To easily recover the contents of an encrypted signal, the correct decryption key is required. The key is an algorithm that "undoes" the work of the encryption algorithm. Alternatively, a computer can be used in an attempt to "break" the cipher. The more complex the encryption algorithm, the more difficult it becomes to eavesdrop on the communications without access to the key.

In secure eCommerce, the encoding of confidential information in preparation of transmission is a critical step in protecting your privacy and information.

Strong encryption alone does not guarantee protection against all threats. What it does do is make getting to the information so difficult that the attacker may not be able to decode it while the information is still valuable. For example, some password encryption schemes are theoretically able to protect a password for up to six months (that is, statistics show that it would take at least six months for a person running a very powerful computer to break, or decrypt, it). Coupled with a security policy requiring users to change passwords every five months, strong encryption has a very good chance of being able to protect your passwords.

Data warehousing manager David Schlesinger talked to us about the way the pursuit of privacy has changed in the last 100 years. Our grandparents would go out in an open field or out on the lake to have a conversation not overheard by others. Schlesinger likens encryption to that remote location, and sees the extension of encryption into many Internet services as necessary to protect individual privacy:

> *"The desire to eliminate encryption is a tricky issue. Yes, the bad guys can use it to chat. Just like they used codes and the public mail for the last 100 years. But encryption is the only way for people who cannot find that open field to chat in private. Hushmail is such a service, and Phil Zimmerman*

*[developer of PGP encryption software] is one of the managers. They are sell-ing privacy. They even keep the information on their servers encrypted and only the user has the key. If they give the data to the courts, they will give it in its encrypted form. A number of secure e-mail services are developing that go further. Much information can be gained from traffic analysis. Even encrypted messages have value. The time of the transmission, the person who received it, and who they sent messages to after that are all information. The Mixmaster technique offers a multi-packet system to both send and retrieve information. The Cult of the Dead Cow unveiled their own system during this last Defcon. There is a lot of work being done to protect not only privacy but also identity."*

**David Schlesinger**

We see two distinct areas where encryption will change in the next few years. The first is the inclusion of strong encryption in more applications and network devices. The second is in the development of new, stronger encryption standards.

## Wrapped Up from Beginning to End

Just as it is now standard for Web-based stores to use SSL encryption to protect your transactions, more and more services will offer this protec-tion. As more of our personal life management goes online—insurance claim filing, employee benefits, and online banking—the need to encrypt those transactions becomes more evident. For a long time Webmasters and systems administrators avoided putting SSL on any page that didn't absolutely need it (such as credit card numbers and so on) because of the load that running the encryption put on the server. SSL would seri-ously slow down a site's performance, causing user dissatisfaction and loss of customer base. However, specialized SSL accelerator chips and CPUs with more horsepower are making that concern less important, and it will be in the best interest of both customers and corporations to encrypt information transmission as well as financial information. Given the choice of a financial planning service that uses SSL to protect invest-ment advice and one that doesn't, many savvy Internet users will choose the one that offers them the most protection.

As more and more transactions happen outside of traditional protected intranets, companies are insisting that those transactions have protection when they go out onto the public infrastructure. This will require applications to either encrypt packets before they send them out, use something like SSL, use a virtual private network to provide an encrypted tunnel to the server, or perhaps to use encrypting network interface cards to talk between machines. All of these solutions are possible, and none of them is the right answer in every case. IT planners are keeping all of these in their toolkit of solutions to have flexible answers to complex business problems. We will see more of these solutions in both our work and personal lives in the coming years.

We'll also see information delivery systems where content is delivered in an encrypted wrapper, keyed to a digital certificate or other individual credentials. Digital books, contracts, movies, and nearly any other form of content where the delivery mechanism is over the networks will likely come this way.

## Build a Stronger Wrapper

In the past three years, many encryption schemes have been broken using more powerful computers and the combination of many computers on the Internet working together. DES and digital wireless encryption are two examples. For that reason, the U.S. Government decided to sponsor a competition to come up with a new public encryption standard that would defeat attempts to crack it. Both governments and private interests care about having strong encryption.

The new encryption standard would be called AES, or Advanced Encryption Standard, and would be specified for use by U.S. Government organizations to protect sensitive information. Members of the cryptography community also anticipate that commercial users outside of the government and outside of the United States will use the new standard voluntarily. Developers of the standard will not receive royalties or financial rewards for the winning algorithm.

The National Institute of Standards and Technology, in developing the competition, required that proposed algorithms must implement a symmetric block cipher, with a block size of 128 bits, and key sizes of at least 128, 192, and 256 bits. They want an algorithm whose security is at least as good as Triple-DES, but with enhancements in efficiency. What this technical language means is that the new standard must be at least as strong as the best older standards, and it must also offer flexibility in the strength of encryption available. That is accomplished with varying key sizes—in general, the longer the key size, the stronger the encryption and the longer it takes to break it.

> **NOTE**
>
> For an excellent paper on new encryption standards, and in particular the AES standard, see the SANS security institute's discussion at `http://www.sans.org/infosecFAQ/encryption/rijndael.htm`.

## Airtight Authentication and Authorization Technology

One of the aspects of keeping information private is the ability to enable access only to folks with a real need to know. To make a system like this work, you need a strong way to verify that the person asking for permission is really the person authorized for access. Let's briefly look at authentication technology available today.

> **NOTE**
>
> Remember, *authentication* is a mechanism that verifies your identity—that you are who you claim to be. Authentication relies on presentation of two of the three following items: something you know (a PIN, for example), something you are (your picture, voiceprint, or retina scan), and something you carry (a SmartCard or ID).
>
> *Authorization* is a process that grants you access, or privileges, based on characteristics or *attributes* of the authenticated identity. For example, a bar will check your ID against your face. If you have the attribute of being over 21, you can come in and drink. At work, your badge may be color-coded, granting you access to areas or materials because of your job description.

## Are You Who You Say You Are?

Four major methods can be reasonably used for identifying and authorizing access to material across the Net. Those methods are, generally, ID and password, biometric, digital certificates, and proxies. Each has its own benefits and drawbacks.

## ID and Password

IDs and passwords are acceptable for access to material that does not need to be protected with high assurance. However, they are the most common form of authentication in use on the Web. Many Web browsers will even store your passwords for you in a cookie. They are, we discussed, vulnerable to cracking, theft, and other attacks. In addition, humans don't use passwords effectively because of differences in ability to remember passwords and IDs. There is also general unwillingness to use security processes (such as frequent changes or one-time passwords) that make IDs and passwords more effective.

## Biometrics

Biometric technologies offer some interesting advantages for identification and the creation of credentials that can be linked with a high degree of assurance to a given human being. Most biometric identification systems have problems because the measured characteristic (voice pitch and timbre, for example) can change substantially from morning to evening. Fingerprints and iris geometry are two biometric techniques that have excellent accuracy records.

## Digital Certificate

Digital certificates have the advantage over biometrics in that they are not based on characteristics that can change rapidly. They can be issued in a cryptographically secure fashion so that they are less vulnerable to cracking than other forms of credentials. However, certificates in isolation, separate from a security or authorization process, offer little advantage over any of the other forms of authorization and credentialing.

## Proxies

We include proxies in this list because they can be configured to prevent access from a specific client to a given range of hosts. Families, schools, and businesses find the use of proxies, or screening software, of value in preventing access to inappropriate material.

## Security Process

Credentials can only be used to make a security decision (access or not) in context of an appropriate security process. For example, look at the process you go through when you check a driver's license for identification. When you check a person's driver's license, you're doing a biometric test (face versus picture). That involves taking a sample (of the face), reading in the template (picture), and doing a comparison. You do all three of those steps inside your own body—presumably an environment you have some assurance has not been compromised. When we do this sort of credential checking over the Net, we must rely on some other entity—a card reader, a biometric device, or a keyboard—which is not under our control. The computer that the user wants to access must rely on another entity to take the sample or take in the credentials. It can compare the presented credentials against the records in its access database, but the process is as weak as the element that takes the sample—and in the case of a computer in someone's house or school or library, that element is weak and untrustworthy.

Carl Ellison, well-known expert in digital certificates and authentication systems, tells this story to illustrate the problems in trusting a remote system. "Suppose your local liquor store did delivery and took orders over the phone. If a teenager called up to place an order, imagine this dialogue between the teen and the clerk. 'Is your birthday before 1980? Super! Do you have a driver's license with a picture? Good! Now, go in the bathroom and look in the mirror. Does the face in the mirror match the picture on the license? Great! What do you want to buy?' Trusting a computer you don't control is like trusting that teenager to identify himself."

## What Will Come Next?

This is a tough question. Smartcards, digital certificates, biometrics, and many other mechanisms for authenticating users have been discussed in the past. Some have even been given semi-magical status—assurance that once this method arrives, all our authentication woes will be solved. However, with all these methods the issuing, verifying, managing, and revoking logistics are proving to be beyond our current capabilities for anything like a large-scale implementation.

Within a couple of years we expect that these problems will be solved. In fact, American Express is offering a special online credit card with a computer chip in it—a smartcard—for use on and off the Internet. Figure 17.6 shows the American Express site with details about their Blue card.

The card comes with a card reader that you can hook into your computer or laptop, eliminating the need to find a special terminal or card reader. This looks like a likely trend, at least for credit cards and other methods of payment.

**FIGURE 17.6**

*American Express's Blue card with a smart chip.*

But what about anonymous access, or at least access where your identity is shielded? One privacy compliance manager at a Fortune 500 company makes this prediction:

> *"There will be many calls for non-identifiable authentication and access mechanisms, but it will be more in the 3–4 year range before these are readily available and implemented on a large scale. Real availability of such capabilities will be dependent on the large SW companies (e.g. Microsoft, Oracle, Peoplesoft, SAP, I2, Siebel) and the logistics service providers (e.g. UPS, FedEx, Ingram, credit card verifiers) incorporating anonymous capabilities into their solutions. I loosely use the word 'anonymous,' as I think the same sort of needs/goals can be obtained by these major suppliers adopting robust authentication & access mechanisms."*

We talk more about anonymity in Chapter 18. Besides the proxies and personas we've already mentioned, we don't know of any truly anonymous access solutions. We will see a rise in the use of single use credit card numbers and stored value cards, but the driver for that will likely be the ability to manage money, not anonymity.

## P3P and Other PETs are Slow to Get Going

As we discussed before in Chapter 5, "Online Disclosures and That Barn Door," and Chapter 10, "The Least You Should Do to Guard Your Privacy When Online," Privacy Enhancing Technologies (PETs) are being proposed and developed across the information industry. P3P, or Platform for Privacy Preferences, is a standard that will enable users' Web browsers to automatically understand Web sites' privacy practices.

How will it work? By using the ability to embed metacharacters (which can loosely be described as indexing or management codes) in documents, Web owners will be able to encode their privacy policies in their Web site. Users will need to configure their browsers with their privacy preferences, so that P3P-enabled browsers can read the codes and decide automatically how to respond. For instance, if the site is an e-commerce site and its privacy policies meet the user's defined preferences, the browser can automatically provide shipping info. If the site is requesting demographic info, the browser will know to provide it anonymously.

The W3C (World Wide Web Consortium) P3P Syntax, Harmonization, and Protocol Working Groups developed the P3P specification. The teams included W3C member organizations and experts in the field of Web privacy. P3P is based on W3C specifications that have already been established, including HTTP, XML, and Resource Description Framework (RDF).

However, as one of our technologists commented,

> "P3P 1.0 will be very slow to get off the ground, as it's a chicken & egg issue (i.e., do you first add P3P to client to drive site adoption, or first enable sites so P3P-client will add value)."

The P3P specification has been under attack by privacy experts and technologists for several different reasons. Some claim it misrepresents the trust situation on the Web; some feel that it is designed to make it easy to collect information from users, not harder. The jury is still out on this one. As of December 2000, there were less than 100 Web sites enabled for P3P. Some advocates object. For an excellent summary of the objections, see privacy activist and technologist Karen Coyle's work at `http://www.kcoyle.net/p3p.html`.

For more information, see the W3C site at `http://www.w3.org/P3P/`. The Center for Democracy and Technology (CDT) has an analysis at `http://www.cdt.org/privacy/pet/p3pprivacy.shtml`.

# Legislation and Regulation

*Resolution of the contemporary and future privacy concerns will take more than the collective will of society. True there are new forces coming into prominence, new technologies for widespread communication and quick organization of positions and groups—the facsimile machine and electronic mail among others. In the end, though, law is almost certainly essential; getting the attention of the political process is always hard but there is homework to be done first. Privacy as a social phenomenon, driven so hard by technology and the exploitation of information, must be understood and its intricacy structured. Until that can be done, we are likely to be taking potshots at problems and consequences that may not be the central problems in the big picture.*

**(Source: Willis H. Ware, Rand Corporation, July 2001,**
`http://www.southernct.edu/organizations/rccs/`
`resources/research/comp_and_priv/ware/intro.html)`

Just as there is tension in humans between preserving privacy and receiving some benefit like a discount on a purchase, there is tension between the desire to protect rights by building a legal infrastructure, and the desire to minimize government restriction and regulation, which is seen as an intrusion. Predictably, different governments have responded differently. In the United States, regulation has been narrowly focused on specific business sectors or affected audiences. In Europe and Australia, the governments have adopted privacy principles and have then developed rules that require compliance to those principles. We will continue to see both the tension and differences in regulatory styles.

## More Countries Will Adopt EU-Style Regulations

We can expect to see privacy legislation in Asia, Latin America, and Eastern Europe. Australia has adopted wide-reaching privacy laws, including Privacy Principles concerning government and subcontractor handling of personal data, children's privacy, and so on. (For fact sheets, see `http://www.law.gov.au/privacy/`.)

Most of these countries likely will follow the EU model—generic privacy rights, as opposed to U.S.-style regulations sharply divided by business sector. Because most of these new laws will be modeled after existing legislation, we can expect to see some *de facto* harmonization of laws. Such harmonization will help to enable international expansion of self-regulatory programs. Whether that growth is done by new seal organizations arising in separate countries, or by cross-licensing of seals, like BBBOnline's agreement with JIPDEC, remains to be seen.

## The United States Remains a Puzzle

Putting the pieces of the United States privacy regulation together is much like working a picture puzzle. Small clusters come together, and then larger bits. Even after quite a bit of work there are still holes in the picture. Not everyone will agree where a specific piece fits.

There is debate among technologists, policy wonks, soccer moms, and street corner politicians whether the Federal Government will manage to create a unified framework into which these puzzle pieces will fit, or whether the states will create a crazy-quilt of regulations. If the states beat the Federal Government to the punch, each enacting their own, slightly differing laws, those laws will then have to be harmonized. If no such harmonization occurs, interstate commerce via the Internet in the United States will be extremely difficult.

One area of U.S. regulation that will affect privacy is the movement to require corporations who do business on the Net to meet a minimum set of security standards and practices. Companies who do not have adequate security systems, and who get hit by a crippling attack, could be liable not only for their only damages, but the damages (and loss of business) of their business partners and key customers. For example, imagine that a company who makes baseballs gets hacked by a hacker who happens to be a rabid baseball fan. He orders 100,000 baseballs to be sent to his hometown team's biggest rivals, with the payment money automatically debited from the rival's account. Because their bank account is now empty, the rivals have trouble traveling to their next game, and get a huge shipment of baseballs, maybe delivered to the coach's home. The baseball company could be liable for the bounced check charges, fines for missing a game, shipping, and any other damages the rivals incurred.

This is a silly scenario, and we know that. However, more serious ones could happen. Imagine, if you will, that a hacker breaks into the machine that controls the mixing of sausage on a major meatpacking company's assembly line. Those machines regulate everything from how much fat is mixed into the formula to how much contamination is acceptable. (Don't ever read the nutrition and ingredients statements on Vienna-style sausages if you want to eat them comfortably again.) What if the hacker changes the formula, so that instead of harmless bulk carbohydrates (oatmeal or bran) as filler, the hoppers are filled with some other product that's available in meatpacking plants, like hair or ground hooves?

A lot of debate exists as to whether something like this will be regulated by law, or *de facto* regulated by insurance companies adopting liability requirements. Either way, coupled with the rise in hacker attacks, viruses, threats of cyber-terrorism, and nationalist industrial espionage, companies will be working to improve their security.

And, as we said, security is the enabler of privacy protection.

## VOLUNTARY GOVERNMENT?

On a mailing list I read, a thread started in 1994 about "voluntary government"— government that required the people's assent to govern. A side thread of that was about how the USA was supposed to be that sort of government, but had gotten seriously off-track in some very dangerous ways. As is the nature of such things, it became a discussion of how we're all doomed to live in a police state.

One respondent, trying to restore what he thought was balance to this onslaught of doom-saying, said:

*I notice tons of fear and loathing, and this feeling of 1984 is upon us, etc. I seriously wonder who is trying to create a repressive government. Clinton cannot pass a simple crime bill, much less become Big Brother. Congress has to do tons of head butting to vote for a pay raise, much less turn the US into a totalitarian society*

My response to him:

*It isn't that anyone is trying to create a repressive government—it's that we already have one that people are blindly accepting, and it's getting worse.*

*Think about all the areas in which government already prescribes the boundaries of your life. Forget assault weapons or gang abatement tactics: think about what clothes you may wear, or whether; what it's legal for you to smoke, or swallow; who you may love or marry; what you may sell to persons under a certain age.*

*Control extends into areas so simple, and so longstanding, that people have forgotten that they're being controlled. Parking meters: why should it cost $20* *to forget to pay two minutes' rent on a curb, when you can park all day at that same curb for $6? Traffic lights: why is it illegal for pedestrians to cross the street against a red light, even when there's no cross traffic? Mostly, these laws were intended to promote safety and efficiency; but their interpretation is based not on those principles, but on simple obedience to authority. And if you don't obey, and fail to pay the fine, and refuse to submit to the authorities for your failure, this escalating disobedience will get you treated very much like a murderer. All this, for crossing a street without permission?*

*For that matter (still thinking about roads), "yield" signs, or even uncontrolled intersections, used to be very common in California—we trusted drivers to do the right thing on the road. Nowadays, they're very scarce, and "stop" signs appear at every street corner. And speed bumps...don't get me started on speed bumps! I don't think drivers have gotten more stupid; so what happened?*

*Then, of course, there are glaring examples of large-scale misuse of power: forfeiture laws, which the police have turned into revenue generators. "Reasonable suspicion" in the case of large prizes has been shown to mean, "we want your property." And at that, all the chemicals that are generally cited in this "official" theft of property used to be legal. LSD, for example, was outlawed only in 1966, and MDMA (Ecstasy) in 1984. Heroin used to be advertised on posters side-by-side with aspirin.*

*Personally, I don't care nearly so much about where we're going as a society, as I do about where we are; and I would like to find a means of going back to where we were in many areas.*

[An editorial note: looking backward from the lofty vantage point of 2001, my thoughts in 1994 seem in many respects almost hopelessly optimistic and naive. Yes, the USA was prosecuting Phillip Zimmermann (which prosecution was later dropped) because someone else posted a copy of his encryption software where furriners could see it and copy it; but we hadn't got to the point of arresting a foreign citizen, at the request of one of our corporations, for having written software that was perfectly legal in his own country. We hadn't yet caused the police of a foreign country to threaten to arrest one of their own citizens because he wouldn't reveal the name of an anonymous subscriber to his remailing service, whom a religious group (the Scientologists) claimed had posted their copyrighted material without their permission. We didn't have the Digital Millennium Copyright Act, or laws against owning lewd pictures of people who *appear to be* less than 18—not who *are*, mind you, just who *look* like they might be. We weren't yet to the point of throwing people in jail for making factual statements about illegal drugs.

As cynical as I thought I was, things became a lot worse than I thought they would, a lot faster than I would have believed. We hadn't…quite…gotten to the point of having more people in our prisons, and a larger percentage of our people in prisons, than any other civilized nation, including South Africa—and a staggering proportion of them imprisoned for acts that had not even been crimes 40 years ago, all done in the name of "protecting" us. Now I wonder how far it's going to go, how far it *can* go before something breaks. I simultaneously despair of and fear for my country and my people, and I reflect on the words of John F. Kennedy: "Those who make peaceful revolution impossible will make violent revolution inevitable." And in no small part, I also remember Albert Einstein saying, "It has become appallingly clear that our technology has surpassed our humanity." ]

*—Nitnorth*

## Posting a Policy Won't Be Enough

These days, posting a policy and complying with it is enough to get most of the seal organization's approval. This means, of course, that if you say up front that you're going to sell people's information to anyone with the money, and send lots of paper junk mail to boot, anyone who doesn't opt out has little recourse besides choosing to do business with another or waging a public opinion campaign. One of our futurists believes that a major public outcry will happen. He also believes that the backlash will hit the seal organizations, not the companies themselves:

> *"Though P3P won't change the landscape significantly, I think it will further draw attention to the fact that the US-based approach of pushing for clear notice means some companies are doing ugly things—all legally, so long as they tell you about it. It will further shock people to learn that you can get a privacy seal, so long as you have clear notice (even if the notice says, "you have zero privacy on this site"). There will be some [mess-up] highlighting this shortcoming, which will cause one or both of the major privacy seal orgs to raise the floor above just giving notice."*

For the privacy seal organizations to be able to do this, and make it stick, consumers will have to adopt a personal discipline that we haven't seen in the United States, ever. Not even the two largest consumer boycotts ever, table grapes and baby formula, produced more than about 15% of households actually boycotting the products. If the seal organizations are to have the clout that they need, consumers will need to make tough decisions between convenience (and potentially brand loyalty) and protecting their information.

## Citizens Want Protection, but Distrust the Government

In the United States, there is support for the idea of law enforcement being able to use new capabilities, such as intercepting criminal's e-mail or doing keystroke monitoring of their systems. According to a Pew Internet Project study, 54% of Americans approve of the FBI monitoring e-mail, phone calls, and paper mail. However, the U.S. public is skeptical about this, too. While more than half support more technical capability for law enforcement, less than one in three say they trust the government to do the right thing most of the time or all of the time. That figure is down from 41% in 1988. As in many other areas, the majority of Americans want a law to protect them. Sixty-two percent of Americans say new laws should be written to make sure that ordinary citizens' privacy is protected from government agencies. (Source: Pew Internet and American Life study, released April 2, 2001.)

Perhaps their fears aren't too misplaced. At the moment, it seems as though the government is being successful in its attempts to get and retain information on individual activities. In August 2001, the Massachusetts Turnpike Authority has turned over Fast Lane records to the courts for use in criminal prosecution, and the judge in the case refused to allow the MTA to notify the suspect that his records were being investigated. New York has used its E-ZPass system in "dozens" of prosecutions, according to a story in the *Boston Globe* on August 22. (Source: http://www.globe.com/dailyglobe2/225/business/MTA_gives_court_toll_use_data+.shtml.)

In May, the BBC reported that the Council of the European Union, the body that negotiates the treaties that the EU agrees to, proposed a plan that, among other things, would record and archive phone and Internet traffic data for at least seven years. (Source: http://news.bbc.co.uk/hi/english/sci/tech/newsid_1334000/1334371.stm.)

Existing provisions permit data to be retained for the length of the billing period (up to 90 days). While privacy activists around the world have protested the plan, which includes a number of restrictions that seem to be anti-business, this is just one of several instances where massive record retention for government use has been proposed. There's no sign that such legislation will stop being written, as governments struggle to balance those tensions between government management and personal liberty.

## PRIVACY REGULATION: CAN WE BEAR THE COST?

Who could ever oppose Internet privacy? We're told that being let alone, as Justice Louis Brandeis famously described it, is a fundamental human right that should be enshrined in law as surely as freedom of expression and freedom of religion are. Privacy is, after all, already part of the UN's Universal Declaration of Human Rights and immortalized in countless Supreme Court decisions.

It's also, some groups inform us, under attack. In a letter sent to Congress in April, 2001, the Electronic Privacy Information Center spoke of much of the privacy community when complaining that "Internet users today still have no legal protection against the surreptitious collection of personal information and tracking of their activities online."

That dark warning neatly summarizes the current thinking in Washington, where detailed discussions of the best way to regulate how corporations compile and use personal information occupy countless lobbyist hours and encourage regulatory enthusiasts to constantly up their demands. Currently there are few regulations that govern how U.S. Web sites collect, store, and use information. This could change soon: The U.S. Congress has convened dozens of hearings on the topic, and most observers expect some kind of legislation to be enacted this year.

As proof of a problem, politicians cite polls saying that Americans are worried about privacy. One survey found that 81 percent of Net users are concerned about threats to privacy online. In another, 72.2 percent of Americans polled said there should be new "Internet privacy laws."

One problem with such polls, though, is that talking abstractly about privacy is a pointless exercise. If you ask would-be car buyers if they value low prices, you'll likely get general agreement. But if you broaden your query to include safety, fuel efficiency, performance and reliability, you'll likely hear that those options easily justify a higher sticker price.

So it is with privacy. The polls do not explain the downside of regulations. Imposing Draconian new rules on marketing and information sharing would raise costs to consumers, particularly the less affluent who rely more on free or low-cost services supported by advertising. By hurting startups that would otherwise rent physical or electronic mailing lists, regulation hands established firms an unfair advantage.

A study by Robert Hahn of the American Enterprise Institute includes some telling figures. Hahn estimated how many companies would be regulated by draft legislation, then surveyed consulting companies to learn how much it would cost for an average Web site to comply with the rules. Depending on the assumptions used in the estimates, Hahn concluded the total cost ranges between $9 billion and $36 billion. If Hahn's estimates are anywhere near correct, that means marginal tech companies will be required to lay off workers, or in some cases, be driven to bankruptcy.

Another problem is that the polls are internally inconsistent. One Business Week survey says that 57 percent of Americans hope the federal government will pass federal privacy laws for the Internet. But a Jupiter Consumer survey reports that only 14 percent of consumers say that new laws will make them more likely to trust Web sites.

Don't get me wrong. It's natural to be a little nervous about privacy. But nobody—except the government—can force you against your will to hand over your personal information online. If you don't feel comfortable giving information to a Web site, you have plenty of other options: Don't type it in. Don't go there any more. Sign up with a service like anonymizer.com. Or lie.

Much of the current debate revolves around what should be the default standard for online data collection: opt-in or opt-out? Should businesses be able to collect and use information by default unless users object by clicking a box on a Web site? Under an opt-out standard, the data you provide to a company is theirs to use unless you say otherwise. Under opt-in, the data is to be kept completely private unless you give your permission. Defaults are important, after all: Some research suggests that when it comes to privacy, only 10 percent of users will alter their privacy profile when given a chance.

Economist Ronald Coase won his Nobel prize for an insight that's relevant here. Simply put, if transaction costs are zero, then any initial definition of rights leads to an efficient outcome. But if transaction costs are not zero, then the initial allocation of rights under the law—in this case, opt-in vs. opt-out—can make a big difference.

If an opt-out standard gives companies rights by default to information they collect, then businesses likely will crop up to educate consumers, rate dot com firms, or allow privacy-cautious Internet users to shield their identities. But if an opt-in standard is the default, then it's more likely that firms will err on the side of caution and retard innovation. It might seem that if Internet privacy remains unregulated then consumers will suffer. But if consumers do care about privacy, Web sites will have an incentive to offer options that consumers prefer. And there will be an incentive for third parties to provide information about privacy policies.

With the exception of sites targeted at young children, which are regulated, the current market resembles the market for traditional publications: Consumers are able to rely on non-governmental rating and reputation systems to steer them toward desirable destinations. Just as the Michelin Guide reviews restaurants and kosher seals certify foodstuffs, so do these systems rate privacy. TRUSTe, BBBOnLine, and WebTrust offer "privacy seals" to Web sites so consumers can take their business to only companies they trust. TRUSTe claims it has 2,000 member companies, including many high-profile sites, and BBBOnLine has awarded its Privacy Seal to over 500 Web sites.

To earn a TRUSTe seal, for instance, firms sign a contract that requires the site to prominently disclose how it collects, uses, and distributes personally identifiable information about its users. The cost ranges between $300 and $7,000 a year, depending on the company's size, and participating companies can display a bright green TRUSTe logo.

Add to that an overwhelming number of sites that are now taking a kind of full-disclosure approach to privacy by saying exactly what they'll do with personal data they collect. Even though Europe has strict regulations in the area, the free-market approach of the U.S.—which requires firms to respond to market demand—seems more effective. A January 2001 report from Consumers International, a global association of over 260 pro-regulation groups, concludes that "despite tight EU regulation, sites within the EU are no better at telling users how they use their data than sites based in the U.S. Indeed, some of the best privacy policies were found on U.S. sites."

That's one more reason why, in a free society, government regulation should be a last resort. Economists generally agree that the government should step in only when the free market has a glaringly obvious problem. They even have a term for this: market failure.

But when it comes to privacy, so-called market failures are typically federal bureaucrats or privacy advocates disagreeing with choices consumers have made. By and large, the bulk of consumers do not care as much about online privacy as they claim in polls. Web sites without privacy policies have received thousands of e-mail addresses typed in by people hoping to get daily or weekly updates on topics they care about.

Arguments for government heavy-handedness aren't supported by either theory or experience. Much-reviled "privacy intrusions" by corporations generally are far from the enemy of the consumer. In many cases, they are essential to providing the zero-cost content Internet users prefer. Compiling personal information lets businesses become more efficient and produce only products that people want. It reduces waste—who really wants to get tons of glossy catalogs about topics they care nothing about? It also helps in customization, as anyone who uses my.yahoo.com knows.

Don Boudreaux, president of the Foundation for Economic Education, likens customization to a good tailor. "Wealthy people get custom shirts, custom-made shoes, and a lot of custom-made items. They take your measurements and keep your name on file," he says. "What this new technology is doing is making it easier for merchants to give the same benefits of customization that were only available to the wealthy before."

Government collection of information is a different matter. When the Feds step in, consumers don't have a choice—they get a one-size-fits-all rule. Government plans like the creation of an air traveler profiling system, the FBI's Carnivore surveillance system, and the trend toward larger and more intrusive government databases should give any thoughtful person cause for concern. But entirely appropriate worries about government data collection should not be used as an excuse to rush to regulate the private sector.

*—Declan McCullagh*

---

# Taking the Single Step

*"The longest part of the journey is said to be the passing of the gate."*

**Marcus Terentius Varro (116 BC—27 BC), On Agriculture**

As we said at the start of this chapter, our crystal balls are out for servicing, so we can only hope to point out the road signs for this journey. At this point in our journey, we are armed with healthy skepticism and more information about what's possible. Given those, we can make some broad speculation about the general state of privacy in the coming years.

In some ways, the general need for watchfulness has not changed in the last fifteen years. In fact, the stakes may be significantly higher now. As evidence, we submit these two signature lines from e-mails, one from 1984 and one from 2001:

1984:

Never send anything in e-mail that you don't want posted on the cafeteria bulletin board.

2001:

> Never send anything in an e-mail that you don't want to see reprinted in *The New York Times*.

## Will There Be a "Privacy Chernobyl"?

Jacques Surveyer wrote in *Canada Computes* in December, 2000 that many privacy experts fear that only such a catastrophe will speed the development of privacy-protecting security technology. He said:

> *"Likewise the confidential, private personal data obtained during e-commerce and other Web transactions may now become available to the highest bidder given that quite a number of consumer Web companies have gone belly up with their only asset being their database of customer information. Even healthy Web companies, such as Amazon.com, eager to avoid the financial plight of failing business-to-consumer (B2C) dot-coms, have quietly reversed privacy policies and will now be selling gathered customer information to third parties. In the industry, there is the haunting fear of the all but certain "privacy Chernobyl."*

Many insiders were surprised that Amazon's announcement did not precipitate a broader crisis. Here are some of the trigger events that might produce an Internet privacy disaster:

- Bankrupt consumer Internet sites sells customer list to many and any bidders.
- "Free software" downloaded from the Web makes itself non-removable, scours the PC for all program and data assets, and reports this plus all Web and program usage, yet fails to tell users except in fine print of user agreement that this is the bargain. Actuate has already done this. Others are close.
- Spammers continue to generate unrequested e-mail at a 30% per year growth rate.
- E-mail spam scripts contain extremely malicious "buried" virus that flattens every PC that responds to e-mail.
- Internet sites do user profiling, tracking all of a Web user's actions and exchange the info without users' permission.
- Metrics firms would link user cookie info with on-site click activity without getting user permission.

(*Source:* http://www.canadacomputes.com/v3/story/1,1017,5002,00.html)

Perhaps even worse than the fear of privacy meltdown is the bleak vision that many technologists have, that we are already under the avalanche and can't get free. CTO Dave Schroeder predicts:

> *"More highly publicized cases of very high-profile corporations getting maliciously hacked and exposing wide arrays of private information will lead to an increased focus on security and privacy by extension. The emphasis on making money from Web-based initiatives will not decline, so corporations will continue to share private data broadly."*

In January 1999 Sun Microsystems CEO Scott McNealy told a group of reporters and analysts that privacy was a lost cause. "You have zero privacy anyway." Nonetheless, many of us working in the privacy field feel that some privacy battles haven't been fought yet. In the United States, we have begun to protect the privacy of children under 13, with the intent of shielding that very vulnerable group from the worst of abuses. The Graham-Leach-Bliley Act was another major step forward in reforming the business practices of financial institutions, including how they handle personal data. The EU Data protection directives will set a standard that other countries will have to scramble to match. While it's true that getting the attention of a mule frequently requires the application of a very large 2×4, we hope that it will not need a "Privacy Chernobyl" to get the attention of consumers in time to protect the privacy they still have.

## Some See the Need for Privacy Shrinking

Futurist Travis Charbeneau wrote in January 2001 that the need for privacy is shrinking because a more open social climate has eliminated the need to hide many things. He may have a point: *Newsweek* magazine, in its August 6, 2001 issue on homosexuality and the Boy Scouts, reported on a Gallup poll that shows the majority of Americans consider homosexuality "an acceptable alternative lifestyle." In part, his essay says:

> *The essential question respecting the current assault on privacy is, can trends for greater tolerance, combined with vigilant legislative constraints protecting traditional privacy rights, outstrip technology's fast-growing power to invade and harm? Relatedly, we are also questioning the structure of some institutions.*
>
> *With DNA profiling, for example, we gain a growing ability to predict who will get what diseases. But this presents a real privacy danger only in America,*

*where the first order of our health care system is not to care for health, but to eliminate profit risks. Do we sweat bullets trying to keep insurers from finding out who is and is not a risk? Or do we follow the rest of the industrialized world in obtaining a system that unconditionally protects everyone?*

*Do Swedes predisposed to arthritis worry that some prospective employer will find out about it? In this case the enlightenment required applies not to any irrational social stigma respecting health, but to irrational social contracts. The need for privacy can be obviated in some cases by institutional reform.*

*Elsewhere, government needs to act quickly and decisively to keep privacy legislation and court decisions up to speed. At the user end, wonderfully secure encryption software and anonymity procedures are already available for e-mail, newsgroup postings; Web browsing. These protections need to be made more widespread and user-friendly. Perhaps foremost, however, continued progress towards a more human-friendly society will do more than anything else to guarantee privacy where it's really needed.*

*A simultaneously more open and open-minded society enables us to shrink our respective privacy spheres. A smaller, more manageable privacy sphere, safeguarding only those issues that remain genuinely sensitive, means more certain protection irrespective of technological advance.*

**(Source:** `http://www.itmweb.com/f010501.htm`**)**

# Eternal Vigilance Is the Price of Liberty

Privacy advocates and civil libertarians see the next few years as one of the most challenging to the privacy of individuals in the last decades. Many fear "two steps forward, three steps back" repercussions in the wake of the destruction of the World Trade Center, the attack on the Pentagon, and the counter-attacks in Afghanistan. They worry that the civil liberty ground that has been hard-won in the last 20 years will be wiped out in the emotional response to these events.

Perhaps the best lesson we can learn from considering privacy and its future issues comes from network designer Chet Johnson, who muses that this issue has been with us even before the invention of intrusive technologies:

*On the other hand...In my old neighborhood, there were always a couple of people that sat on their front porch and watched everything that happened on the street. Everyone was the subject of this intense data harvesting activity.*

*The compiled information would then be carefully analyzed and disseminated throughout the community. Every social gathering was an opportunity for downloading of information regarding everything from new purchases to "adult rendezvous." A shameless effort to collect and disseminate potentially quite exploitative data. It was not necessarily the act, but the interpolation of the data that could be damaging.*

*Ultimately, this bred an instinct for personal discretion. If one must engage in untoward behavior, one should keep in mind that others are watching. I suppose that brings us back full circle. Perhaps there has never been any assurance of privacy. As I said before, the most significant privacy enhancing technology is personal vigilance.*

# CAN YOU REALLY BE ANONYMOUS?

In a phrase: probably not. Electrons and paper-work are forever.

Too much ties together what we do and where we are to who we are. This is true whether we are in cyberspace or in real space. Each of us is tied to our nation by citizenship, to our name, to our parentage and ethnicity, and to our birth-date on paper via birth and hospital certificates from the time we are born. According to the United States Passport rules:

> *"A birth certificate must include your given name and surname, date and place of birth, date the birth record was filed, and seal or other certifica-tion of the official custodian of such records."*

Soon after we are born, some of us even acquire baptismal certificates or similar documents, associating us with a particular religion.

We begin early in our well-documented society. Just look at our document-oriented lives.

To enter elementary school the following is needed: proofs of age, guardianship, residency and immunization are required. To play youth soccer, baseball, or softball, and so on the following is needed: proofs of age, guardianship, medical approval, waiver of responsibility are required. To enter college or university the following is needed: proof of citizenship is required. Proof of residency and immunization also may be required. To marry the following is needed: both parties must provide proofs of identity and age, and, in some states, absence of certain disease.

To drive, you must obtain a driver's license. To obtain a driver's license proof of identity, citizenship, and age, are required. Some places have surprisingly extensive documentation rules. For example, the following are the rules for obtaining a new driver's license if you move to New Jersey:

## STATE OF NEW JERSEY, MOTOR VEHICLE SERVICES: PROOFS OF AGE AND IDENTITY

All NJ driver license applicants must present proofs of age, identity and that their presence in this country is authorized under federal law. MVS may recheck your proofs at anytime during the licensing process. MVS will accept current out-of-state driver licenses and New Jersey driver licenses if expired less than three years for the permit issuance and road test waiver, but you must produce one of the proofs below to obtain a NJ driver license.

Your U.S. Birth certificate in English (or a certified copy) is your primary proof of age and identity. Proofs of identity must verify that your presence in the U.S. is authorized under federal law. Other proofs are acceptable only in situations where the birth certificate or a certified copy is no longer available. To be valid, all proofs (e.g., birth certificate, copy of a birth certificate, marriage certificate) that you present must be the original or a certified copy and have the required state or municipal seal.

Proofs of identity that do not include a birth date must be accompanied by another proof of age. If your surname is different from the one on your primary proof of age and identity, you must document the name change with certified adoption, marriage or divorce papers, or a name change court order before MVS can complete the transaction. Name changes through divorce must be part of the divorce decree and/or contain an addendum signed by the hearing judge.

The following proofs are listed in descending order of importance:

- Original U.S. civil birth certificate in English or a U.S. Department of State birth certificate with U.S. Consulate Seal
- Certified copy of U.S. birth certificate
- Active or expired U.S. Passport or valid foreign passport (with current, acceptable I-94 visa)
- Valid U.S. alien registration card or valid work authorization card, combined with a Social Security card, or a U.S. certificate of naturalization
- U.S. citizenship papers
- U.S. Military I.D. Card (active duty only, no dependent cards), or Military discharge papers (DD-214)
- U.S. adoption papers with proof of legal presence in the U.S.
- Original legal name change papers, civil marriage or divorce documents or certified copy of same with proof of legal presence in the U.S.
- Any other document issued by the U.S. that establishes the applicant's proof of identity and date of birth, and verifies that the applicant's presence in the U.S. is authorized under federal laws.

*(Source: http://www.state.nj.us/mvs/testing.htm#Proofs)*

---

To travel across national borders, a passport is required. To obtain one, you need proof of citizenship, which is a certified birth certificate or previous passport.

# Work Qualifications Need Records, Too

To work you need proof of identity, citizenship, social security number, and if you are a minor, proof of age and permission to work are required. To obtain licenses to conduct a business is some jurisdictions you need proof of citizenship. Figure 18.1 shows a checklist for starting a business in Maryland. Notice that you have to register the business, register the business name, obtain tax forms, ascertain what licenses apply, and so on.

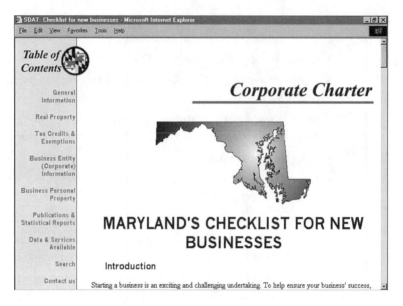

**FIGURE 18.1**

*The State of Maryland's New Business Checklist.*

To work in certain professions, you must be licensed. Those professions include doctors, nurses, pharmacists, manicurists, hair-stylists, barbers, general contractors, electricians, plumbers, accountants, architects, interior designers, engineers, morticians and funeral directors, real estate agents and brokers, mental health professionals, chiropractors, dentists and dental hygienists, dieticians and nutritionists, dispensing opticians, optometrists, alarm installers, home inspectors, real estate appraisers, nursing home administrators, radio and TV technicians, airline pilots, boat pilots, surveyors and mappers, respiratory therapists, auctioneers, veterinarians, and bus and truck drivers.

In California, the Contractors State License Board offers specialty licenses in the following fields: air conditioning, boiler, hot water heating and steam fitting, building moving and demolition, cabinet and mill work, carpentry, concrete, construction zone traffic control, drywall, earthwork and paving, electrical (general), electrical signs, elevator installation, fencing, fire protection, flooring and floor covering, general manufactured housing, glazing, insulation and acoustical, landscaping, lathing and plastering, limited specialty, low voltage systems, masonry, metal roofing, ornamental metals, painting and decorating, parking and high-way improvement, pipeline, plastering, plumbing, refrigeration, roofing, sanitation system, sheet metal, solar, steel, reinforcing, steel, structural, swimming pool, tile (ceramic & mosaic), warm-air heating, ventilating and, water conditioning, welding, well-drilling (water). Amazing, isn't it?

If you are over 16 or so in most states, to hunt or fish requires a license. In general, residents pay lower fees than non-residents. This in turn requires proof of residency.

We award benefits to those who are "Senior Citizens." Although the definition of seniors may vary, the requirement for proof of age does not.

Not only are our persons documented, but much around us is documented also. Our residences and the buildings in which we work and shop are recorded by a local jurisdiction, taxed when a new owner takes possession, and again each year. If we make improvements to them, we need to get permit approval and pay a fee. Our automobiles are registered and taxed. The pumps where we get gasoline for our vehicles are inspected and licensed. Hotels, motels, and restaurants are all inspected and licensed. Elevators are inspected.

# Can You Avoid A Paper Trail?

Avoiding being documented is very difficult.

Let's contrast that with England approximately 500 years ago:

> *"Jenny asked if historians knew whether births were recorded in mediaeval times. I can only speak for England, but I can state categorically that until the reign of Henry VIII (if I remember correctly, in about 1537, after the dissolution of the monasteries) there was no systematic recording of births, marriages or deaths at all. Henry ordered that each parish keep records of these in a register, but at first this was erratic at best and most parishes don't have anything like a complete set until Elizabeth's reign—and even then there are subsequent gaps, due no doubt to incompetence, loss, fire, war or rats!*

> *"In mediaeval times they obviously didn't attach as much importance to birth-days etc as we do. There are fascinating series of records known as 'proofs of age'. Basically when an heir came of age and inherited, it was important to know the actual date when he would come into his inheritance. Because*

*there were no records or birth certificates (and this applied right up the social scale, often the actual dates of birth of royal children have to be guessed by historians because they weren't recorded at the time) people who could remember the heir being born had to swear as to the date before someone in authority. I can't recall the exact details of these affidavits (and there are hundreds) but the dates were generally pinned down along the lines of 'The year before King X's death, on such and such a saint's day', or 'I remember the date because it was during the great storm just after Christmas and that was the year following the drought'. Not only were days and months of birth not generally known, but quite often people wouldn't know exactly how old they were either.*

*I have no idea what the situation was on the Continent, but that's what it was like in England."*

**(Pamela Belle, author, reprinted with permission from a mailing list conversation about personal documentation.)**

In these times, it was only important to determine who you were, and how old you were, if it were a matter of transferring property held in the monarch's name. Property belonged to the monarch. When the holder died, the property returned to the monarch and was given again, usually to the heir. If you weren't one of these people, chances were that your existence would not have been recorded at all.

Many people in England in the 1500's really were anonymous—at least as far as officialdom was concerned. It does seem likely that their parents, friends, and children all knew who they were. Imagining a life in which no one would ever record your passage is hard. However, at that time, few people were literate, so recording and subsequent reading of the records would have required learning that was not readily available to the general populace.

In contrast today, we strongly believe in literacy. We support school systems with our taxes and rail at them if they produce graduates who are unable to function effectively in our society. Neither of us would recommend returning to a non-literate world. Not only do we write, but we both derive way too much pleasure from reading to even contemplate such a thing!

Obviously, even without being more than casually interested in history, as the circle in which people operated became widerit was more necessary to distinguish between Tom the baker in the village by the mill, and

Tom the money lender in the large house by the ocean. That's where "last names" came from in many languages; in conversation, you could tell the difference between Tom Baker and Tom d'Mer. That would be just for normal interaction among human beings.

As more requirements were put on governments to provide more services, it's clear that keeping track of all people, not just those who owned real property, became more important. To get levies of soldiers to fight for wars, rulers required some idea of how many men could come from what area. To levy money to support those same wars, taxation required better accounting of what resources were where. Governments were trying to account for people long before King Henry VIII. The Biblical New Testament story of Jesus begins with a Roman census—Jesus' parents returning to the city of Joseph's birth to be counted. Clearly, it's been hard to hide from one's government for at least 2000 years. We know less about the older Asian cultural customs because they aren't part of our own cultural tradition, but it seems likely, given the organization and literacy of the administrative class in both China and Japan, that counting people for military and taxation purposes would have been important as well.

As more people owned property, the property laws changed—or perhaps, vice versa. From our vantage point as people who are not legal historians, it's hard to tell which was the chicken and which the egg. Recording of property transactions became important. People needed to prove that they owned things. And legal proof demanded absolute identification as a particular person. We don't think real property ownership has ever been anonymous. Someone has always been able to connect the property to the person. People who lived in the neighborhood always knew who owned what property. As records began being kept in known places, people from further away could consult the records to determine who owned the property.

# The Urge to Make Lists

Something is very human about counting, categorizing, and naming things. We all do it, implicitly or explicitly, like when we list things to buy at the grocery store. Sometimes we record the list; other times we don't. We are taught early in our schooling to make lists of tasks to be accomplished, gifts we'd like to get, spelling words to learn. We usually learn pretty early, too, that committing some things to paper can be hurtful or embarrassing, either to ourselves or others. As girls, we learned this getting caught passing notes about dreamed-for boyfriends in 5th grade. Nothing is quite like having the teacher read your private note aloud in class to teach you about secrecy—not to mention the wisdom of putting potentially embarrassing things on paper.

On the other hand, we can also understand, and usually sympathize with, the need of law enforcement to trace the behavior of criminals. In the wake of the Pentagon and World Trade Center attacks, many people see more clearly than before the benefits to law enforcement of being able to track and trace behavior. Without the massive data collection and retention that is part of our modern society, global authorities would not have been track down the involved parties as quickly as they did.

We worry, however, about the widespread and massive collection of data that is available for law enforcement to synthesize. The agents can obtain hotel/motel records, airline records, purchase records from stores, credit card records, driver's license and car registration records, banking records, and information from the commercial database providers in addition to the records available under subpoena from telephone and Internet providers. The FBI's digital wiretap ability and their controversial Carnivore program, which processes traffic logs from Internet Service Providers give them more and more access to the activities of ordinary, non-criminal citizens. Because we don't necessarily know if information about us has been included, we can't know if it is accurate, and we certainly aren't able to control its further dissemination. Information gathered without controls isn't a good thing.

## Does the Pattern Add Up Correctly?

In the wake the events of September 11, 2001, some of our illusions of our anonymity in the world were abruptly shattered. Since that time, the problems with the collation and analysis of widely collected data have been graphically illustrated. In the weeks following the attacks, hundreds of people were arrested or detained for questioning. Many were Arab-Americans, like Dr. Al-Badr Al-Hazmi of San Antonio, Texas. Al-Hazmi, a radiologist, was held for 12 days before being cleared of suspicion and released, because the collection of information about him, even though it was purely coincidental, added up to a pattern that made the FBI suspicious. On October 4, 2001, NPR[1] reported that the records showed these facts about Dr. Al-Hazmi, who is a medical student studying before going back to Saudi Arabia to practice medicine.

- His last name, Al-Hazmi, is the same as two of the suspected terrorists, Nawaf Alhazmi and Salem Alhazmi.

- He received several phone calls in Oct. 1999 from a man named Abdullah bin Laden.

- He and three other people with Arab surnames had plane tickets to fly to San Diego on September 22, and they made the reservations online via Travelocity.com.

- He made several trips to Boston, Washington DC, and New York in 2000 and 2001, as evidenced by credit card records and receipts found in his home.

- He transferred $10,000 to a friend, also Arab-American, in Houston several months before he arrived in the United States in 1997.

On investigation, these other facts came to light[2]—but not before Dr. Al-Hazmi spent 12 days in jail.

- The name *Al-Hazmi* is as common in Saudi Arabia as the surnames *Jones*, *Wong*, or *Sanchez* is in the United States.

- The name *bin Laden* is similarly common. Dr. Al-Hazmi had exchanged about five phone calls with the man, who works for the World Assembly of Muslim Youth two years earlier, trying to obtain books and videotapes about Islamic teachings for the Islamic Center of San Antonio. He has not spoken with bin Laden since.

- The doctor and his family (his wife and their two children) were scheduled to go to San Diego on September 22 for a one-month special residency before his board exams.

- A meal receipt from the National Mall in Washington, D.C. was evidence of a trip in May, when he was there studying at the Armed Forces Institute of Pathology for six weeks.

- Travelocity is one of the most popular airline reservations services on the Internet.

- The money was sent in advance of the family's arrival, and was spent on furniture from a San Antonio store and to purchase a car. (And the credit card receipts for those were available to the FBI, too.)

It's clear from the statements of the doctor during the investigation and after his release that he had no idea of the trail of activities that he was leaving as he went about his innocent, everyday activities. The pattern of events and behaviors that brought Dr. Al-Hazmi to the attention of the authorities is a very clear example of the potential to make invalid assumptions about individuals, based on the picture presented by patterns in collected records. Before the terrorist attacks of 2001, no one had combined all these disparate records in just this way, looking for the whole picture of someone's life. The illusion of relative anonymity held for most people.

In the weeks and months ahead we will wrestle with the ethical balance between the need to protect ourselves and the need not to pre-judge people. We (and our legislators and regulators) need to make sure we keep that balance in mind as we seek to put mechanisms in place for security, lest we do greater damage to our liberty than the terrorists can.

## The Urge to Not Be Noticed

Something in each of us wants to be anonymous. We are not necessarily trying to hide, just not to flaunt our actions before the world or to feel that everything we do is known by others. Walking through a public place like a shopping mall shouldn't require us to identify ourselves. There is no authentication or authorization necessary to window shop. Similarly, we don't need to identify ourselves if we pay cash using legal currency. However, we give up the right to remain anonymous if we vandalize the shopping mall or provide counterfeit currency for our purchases. Then, those of us who didn't vandalize or pass bad money want the authorities to have reasonable tools to search for and find the miscreants.

Unfortunately, as we noted in earlier chapters, with newer technologies, it's getting easier to do "preventative" surveilance in public places. Cameras record the activities of more and more of us doing more and more things. Public safety authorities argue that it's more efficient to record everyone's activities so that should there be a bad action, the bad actor can more easily be found and brought to trial.

As long as the recorded data is not processed and no one attempts to connect the actions in the recording and the identities of the people in it, the people on the recording remain anonymous. However, as soon as someone processes the data, at least some of the people in the recording are identified. Some links between the recorded persons and their identities can be made.

A similar situation exists in cyberspace. All transactions are recorded, because the people who operate networks use the transaction record (or "log") as part of their diagnostics for possible problem solving. The transactions are recorded on the initiating user's device, on the carrier's devices, and on the receiving devices. Most transaction recordings are transitory, disappearing after a few days. If a bad action occurs, a logical connection can be made among the receiving devices through the carrier, to the initial connected device. Logs can make the connection between the device that received the action and the device that initiated it. It isn't always possible to determine who committed the action ("who was at the keyboard?"), but likely assumptions are made, based on evidence on the computer used. So a message might be found on your computer. It might be found on some other specific computer to which you sent it. The message might be discoverable in the computers of the carriers providing the message service. You cannot assume that your messages aren't discoverable, even if you take steps to hide the transmission or hide your identity within the transmission itself.

In the connected world today so many messages are going to so many places through so many computers, tracing a single message, or tracking a single specific person is not usually worth the cost or the aggravation except to law enforcement personnel. Furthermore, as we have mentioned, the surveillance technology isn't necessarily always accurate. Technology's accuracy will improve, though, so we aren't able to count on aggravation and inaccuracy as inhibitors to processing massive amounts of data to provide profiles of a specific person's activities. In the meantime, massive amounts of collected data continue to accumulate, waiting to be processed. Collected data seldom gets thrown away. If nothing else, it provides trend information to people willing to purchase the results.

Financial transactions are especially traceable. Regulations require that monetary transactions be recorded and saved for a predetermined length of time. Almost all those rules are intended to protect the consumer so that you can get your money back for defective merchandise or protest a charge on your account that you did not make, for example. Money can almost always be traced, whether it's transferred via smart card, credit card, electronic funds transfer, or hand-written check. Someone knows that you have moved money from your account to someone else's, even if it's through a third party system. Living an all cash life is difficult.

Just as we have taught our children to watch where they are going and to be wary of strangers, we've tried to teach them similar tactics to use in cyberspace. In this book, we share what we've learned and what we've tried to teach them with you. Most of the time, everything is fine. To be and remain safe online, you need to understand what information about yourself exists and control, to the extent you can, its distribution. We hope we have shown you some ways in this book that enable you to choose what you show through the digital curtain.

*Glee Harrah Cady*

*Pat McGregor*

*October 2001*

[1] All Things Considered, "Detained, Questioned, and Released", http://search.npr.org/cf/cmn/cmnpd01fm.cfm?PrgDate=10/04/2001&PrgID=2

[2] Seattle Post-Intelligencer, "Innocent Muslim doctor tells of arrest, two-week ordeal", http://seattlep-i.nwsource.com/national/40917_doctor01.shtml

# GLOSSARY

These are our definitions and reflect our understanding of standard definitions of these terms available in dictionaries and other glossaries. You might want to look up these terms for yourselves in other sources. Here are some other sources: WhatIs.com, TrustE, GeoTrust, KidPrivacy.Org, Jason Eric Staijich and Duke University's Computer Science online projects list, and the American Bar Association. Here is a list of the people who read the glossary to help us make sure that we wrote things that would make sense: Carrollynn Brown, Tim Casey, Rob Gratchner, Hong Li, Sigal Louchheim, John Stracke, and Elton and Caitlin Wildermuth.

Throughout this glossary, any terms appearing in definitions that are themselves defined elsewhere in the glossary are indicated with *italics*.

**Access control**   Process of limiting Web site, network, or information access to authorized users, usually by means of security safeguards that detect and prevent unauthorized access. Portions of Web sites or information in databases can be classified into different levels and users are granted privileges to view those levels for which they are authorized. The use of user names and passwords or smart cards with PINs for specific sites or areas of sites are examples of access control.

**Active Server Pages (ASP)**    A proprietary technology from the Microsoft Corporation. They are a specification for Web pages that are created dynamically when the user clicks a link. Depending on what information is known about the user (either through fields that have been filled in or cookies that have been set), different information is displayed to the user. ASP uses ActiveX scripting, usually Visual Basic script or JavaScript. The acronym ASP can also refer to *Applications Service Provider*, a name used to describe companies that provide computing or networking application services for other businesses.

**ActiveX**    ActiveX Controls from Microsoft are a method of running programs, called scripts, either on the server or on the user's Windows-based computer, as a response to accessing a Web site. Because ActiveX scripts can be run on the user's computer, they can be easily used by those with malicious intent to deliver viruses, hostile programs, or simply to acquire information that has been stored on your computer, such as your e-mail address, information about your Internet connection, what kind of machine or programs you are using, and so on. An ActiveX control, unlike a Java applet, has no limitations on what it can do, so it has much greater privacy implications.

**Aggregate information**    Web sites may collect information from users, and combine data from many users. This information is useful, but is not necessarily *personally identifiable* to you. Information from your use of the site is gathered together with information from other users to the same site and used to describe user behavior. Frequently the information collected and aggregated may include information about referring Web sites, next page destinations, and so on. Aggregated information is the sum of information from visitors to a site, not information about specific users.

**Anonymous**    Something that is not named or identified. In Internet terms, a method of accessing a site or establishing a connection to a server where the user is not identified. The word may also describe the display of data where the subject of the information is identified neither by name nor by implication.

**Antivirus software**    Software programs that detect, cleanse, and erase harmful virus files on a computer, Web server, or network by comparing files to a known pattern, sometimes called a "signature" that matches known viruses. Unchecked, virus files can unintentionally be forwarded to others, including trading partners. Because new viruses regularly emerge, and consequently new virus signatures are understood. antivirus software should be updated frequently to remain effective.

**Applet**   An applet is a little application. Prior to the World Wide Web, the built-in writing and drawing programs that came with Windows were sometimes called "applets." On the Web, an applet is a small program written using Java, JavaScript, or ActiveX that can be sent along with a Web page to a user. Java applets can perform interactive animations, immediate calculations, or other simple tasks without having to send a user request back to the server. Applets can also carry hostile code, so some users prefer not to let them run on their machines.

**Application Service Provider (ASP)**   An Internet-based applications and services host or outsourcer, such as a business-to-business auction site or electronic catalog. An ASP provides comprehensive services to fill a market need.

**Authentication**   Process where a person or a computer establishes that they are who they claim to be. For example, when you identify yourself to your financial institution with your mother's maiden name, you are authenticating yourself. Two sources at minimum are required for authentication—something you are, something you know, or something you carry.

**Authorization**   The process of determining which operations an *authenticated* user can perform.

**Back-end systems**   Systems that handle a company's internal processing and computing tasks, such as inventory, receivables, and order processing. The term is used to describe those systems that the customer never sees directly.

**Bandwidth**   The information-carrying capacity of a network connection. Usually measured in bits per second (bps); a typical modem line carries 56,000 bits per second (56kbps), a typical large Web site has a T3 line, with 45 million bps (45Mbps), while a few ultra-high-end trunk lines carry up to 6 billion bps (6Gbps).

**Biometric**   Authentication systems which work by measuring some aspect of the user's body; the best-known examples are fingerprints or retinal scans.

**Broadband**    High-bandwidth. Generally, a broadband Internet connection for the home is at least 384Kbps. Related terms are wideband (a synonym), baseband (a one-channel band), and narrowband (sometimes meaning just wide enough to carry voice, or simply "not broadband," and sometimes meaning specifically between 50cps and 64Kbps).

**Browser**    Also called a Web browser. A program that enables you to search and or navigate through Web sites or "browse" parts of the Internet, especially the World Wide Web. Examples: Netscape Navigator and Microsoft Internet Explorer.

**Bulletin board**    A public area online where you can post a message for everyone else to read. If you post a message to a bulletin board, in nearly all cases, other member participants are able to contact you by e-mail because the e-mail address from which you are posting is included in the message.

**Business-to-business (B2B)**    Indicates commerce conducted from one business to another business entity, as opposed to business-to-consumer (B2C) transactions where a business sells directly to a consumer.

**Catalog aggregators**    eCommerce super sites that list items for sale by multiple companies. Often, these listings are organized by type of merchandise, not by vendor.

**Certificate**    A computer-based record documenting that a particular *public key* belongs to an identified person or company.

**Certificate authority**    Manages security credentials for Web sites and other online transmissions. Certificate Authorities are sometimes abbreviated as "CA."

**Certificate Revocation List (CRL)**    A list of certificates that have been revoked by the issuing certification authority. Each certification authority maintains a CRL that includes revoked certificates issued by that authority.

**Channel enablers**    Web sites that list products from multiple companies, driving eCommerce traffic to company-owned sites rather than handling the transactions themselves, like a catalog in which the products come from different vendors.

**Chat**    A function that enables a group of people to communicate simultaneously by typing messages to one another online. Typically, everyone participating in the chat sees your message as soon as you send it.

Designated chat areas are often referred to as "chat rooms," and any individual or group of individuals you respond to in the room may be able to contact you by e-mail because your e-mail address may be included in your posting.

**Churn**    Turnover. In business, it may mean either the cycle of acquiring new customers to replace lost customers, or the rate at which employees leave and are replaced by new ones.

**Clickstream data**    The data about what pages you have viewed, how long you looked at a page, what links you went to afterward, and from what page you arrived at a specific Web page. This data helps a Web designer or customizer figure out how to make the site more attractive to you.

**Common Gateway Interface (CGI)**    A standard that describes how information is transferred to external programs from a Web HTTP server. External programs are called "gateways" because they open up an outside world of information to the server.

**Computer fraud**    Computer-related crimes involving deliberate misrepresentation, alteration, or disclosure of data to obtain something of value, usually for monetary gain.

**Cookie**    Pieces of text placed in a file or files on your computer's hard drive by a Web site you've visited. Some cookies (called "persistent cookies") may be used to identify you the next time you access the site by storing your password for you. Others may store information about the contents of your shopping cart. Cookies cannot identify an individual user specifically unless the cookie data is attached to personally identifiable information collected some other way, such as via an online registration form. Cookie data may include such information as a credit card number, the particular size or weight of a part ordered, or a password.

**COPA**    Child Online Protection Act.

**COPPA**    Children's Online Privacy Protection Act.

**Credit card number**    A Credit card number is the 12-digit number on the front of your credit card that identifies your account. Credit cards are one of the easiest means of making a purchase on the Internet. This number can be used to make a long distance phone call or to order a new ski-jacket online. Remember that credit cards are stolen easier off line than online, via purchase receipts in your trash or by malicious clerks, waiters, and salespeople. However, if an insecure connection is used to transmit credit card information or if poor security is practiced by the Web site, your credit card information could be given to someone other than the merchant you intended.

**Critical mass**    In Internet commerce, an amount or level of *B2B* transactions between companies or vertical or horizontal marketplaces that serve to maximize technical and commercial efficiencies. Without critical mass, the B2B market or trading group is not able to stay in business long, because there won't be enough money to support all the partners. Otherwise, it means a large enough grouping to produce a particular result, a critical mass of snow is required to make a snowman, for example.

**Cryptography**    The use of codes to scramble or convert information into a format that can be read only by those who have the "key" which unscrambles it. Common examples include the simple substitution of numbers or letters for other numbers or letters. For example, changing all occurrences of the letter e to the number 5, the letter f to the number 6, and so on.

**Customer segment**    A group of prospects or customers who are selected from a database based on characteristics they possess or exhibit. For example, parents of children under 12 who own mini-vans might be a customer segment.

**Data confidentiality**    Security, policies, and practices, which ensure that data collected by or offered to a Web site is held in confidence.

**Data mining**    A database application that looks for patterns in data to build statistically relevant conclusions. In medical research, data mining is used in clinical trials to study courses of treatment. In marketing, data mining is used to build profiles of consumer behavior to present items for purchase that are likely to please the eye or meet a suspected need or desire. Data mining techniques enable programmers to collate and extract meaningful data from the *data warehouse*; data mining software enables data warehouse users to see as much detail or summarization as they need to support decision-making.

**Data warehouse**    A repository for as much relevant business data as possible in the hope that somehow a meaningful picture will emerge. Although traditional databases primarily store current operational data, data warehouses consolidate data from multiple operational and external sources to attain an accurate, consolidated view of customers and the business.

**Date/time stamp**    The attachment of a block of text showing the date and/or time that some action takes place. Date and time stamps are used in computer logs, transaction records, and in the use of digital certificates to record the time of a particular event.

**Denial of service attack**    A network-based attack that prevents the legitimate owners of a computing or networking resource from using it. This may be by flooding a site with gibberish messages, blocking the incoming connections, or several other methods of preventing access. Denial of service attacks are the simplest form of hacker attack and one of the hardest to defend against.

**Digital signature**    A digital code that uniquely identifies the sender. Digital signatures can be attached to electronic purchase orders, contracts, e-mail, and so on. They were awarded legal status in the United States in July 2000.

**Digital Subscriber Lines (DSL)**    A technology for sending large amounts of data over the same lines used for local phones. DSL is a relatively low-cost way of providing broadband connections, but it does have some technical complications (including limitations on how far away from the phone switch a subscriber can be), which means not everybody can use it.

**Digital wallets**    Electronic commerce software that holds confidential information in hidden form, often used in conjunction with electronic payment methods.

**Disintermediation**    The process that occurs when a business removes intermediaries, such as brokers, distributors, and agents, and replaces the channel with a direct sale to customers. Common examples in the Internet marketplace are sites operated directly by manufacturers, such as Godiva Chocolates. Sites like Amazon.com replace one intermediary (your local bookstore) with another, Internet-based one.

**Domain name**    The company, individual, or organization "name" you use to access a Web site, for example, truste.org, pacbell.net, nytimes.com, or house.gov.

**Due diligence**    Exercising judgment, care, prudence, and activities that a person is reasonably expected to perform under particular circumstances, usually when transacting business; "looking before leaping."

**Dynamic Call**   An online catalog where prices are continuously updated, sometimes in direct response to market price-points.

**ECPA (Electronic Communications Privacy Act)**   A federal statute that prohibits a third party from intercepting or disclosing electronic communications. The Act applies to both government employees and private citizens, and it imposes both criminal and civil penalties for violation.

**Electronic Commerce Modeling Language (ECML)**   Proposed guidelines for Web merchants that enable digital wallets from multiple vendors to automate the exchange of information between buyers and merchants. More information is available on the ECML.org Alliance Web site.

**Electronic Data Interchange (EDI)**   A method of exchanging business transaction information across a computer network. It was developed many years before the rise of the World Wide Web and was frequently used among manufacturers who provide goods and services for the U.S. Government.

**Electronic Funds Transfer (EFT)**   The paperless, often automatic, exchange of money between entities, such as between two banks, or between buyer and seller. The use of a credit card to purchase goods is an example of an electronic funds transfer, as is moving money from your savings to your checking at an ATM station. In banking terms, EFT describes the transaction that "wires" money from one bank to another.

**Electronic mail**   Commonly referred to as e-mail, this form of communication enables you to send messages and files from your computer through an online service or the Internet to one or more e-mail addresses.

**E-mail address**   The computer version of a postal address. Like a postal address, it contains information about who the e-mail recipient is and the domain (q.v.) where he or she "resides" on the Internet.

**E-mail Spoofing**   Practice of sending an e-mail that has a forged sender address, generally to disguise the actual sender or to create mischief for a business.

**Encryption**   The conversion of data into a form, called a "ciphertext," that cannot be easily understood by unauthorized people. Decryption, however, is the process of converting encrypted data back into its original form so it can be understood.

**Enrollment**   Sometimes referred to as "entitlement," the process of registering a person at a Web site or company and determining what characteristics the person possesses. Those characteristics, or roles, assist in figuring out what the person can be *authorized* to access.

**eXtensible Markup Language (XML)**   A specification for documents enabling designers to create formatting commands that enable the definition, transmission, validation, and interpretation of data between applications and between organizations.

**Extranet**   A computer network that has been selectively opened to limited audiences, such as a company's suppliers, customers, employees, or strategic allies, via the Internet, often using a Web-type interface. Digital encryption, password access, or both generally secure Extranets.

**Fair Credit Billing Act (FCBA)**   A U.S. law that protects credit card users from excessive damages from from fraud or misuse.

**Fair Information Practices**   The collective term for the principles developed by the 1972 Advisory Committee on Health Education and Welfare Automated Data Systems.

1. There must be no personal data record-keeping systems whose very existence is secret.

2. There must be a way for a person to find out what information about the person is in a record and how it is used.

3. There must be a way for a person to prevent information about the person that was obtained for one purpose from being used or made available for other purposes without the person's consent.

4. There must be a way for a person to correct or amend a record of identifiable information about the person.

5. Any organization creating, maintaining, using, or disseminating records of identifiable personal data must assure the reliability of the data for their intended use and must take precautions to prevent misuses of the data.

Since 1972 many organizations have reviewed and built on the principles, so the number of practices vary from list to list. Some notable lists are those developed by the Organization for Economic Cooperation and Development (OCED) and by the United States Federal Trade Commission.

**File Transfer Protocol (FTP)**   A software protocol used to transfer files from a remote host over a network to another computer; also used as a command to execute the file transfer. Many systems support "anonymous FTP," which lets you access a remote host without having to provide your password or user ID on the receiving system.

**File Transfers**   The copying of electronic files to another computer, including via Electronic Data Interchange (EDI) and Virtual Private Networks (VPN), over the Internet or a network of two or more computers.

**Firewall**   A combination of specialized hardware and software designed to keep unauthorized users from accessing information within a computer network.

**GPS (Global Positioning System)**   A worldwide radio navigation system formed from a constellation of 24 satellites and their ground stations. GPS uses these "man-made stars" as reference points to calculate positions accurate to a matter of meters.

**Handshaking**   A dialog between two entities, such as your computer and that of the eCommerce Web site to which you are connecting.

**Hubs**   Web sites that make it easy for trading partners to exchange data necessary to negotiate and complete eCommerce transactions.

**HyperText Transfer Protocol (HTTP)**   The protocol used to transmit and receive all data over the World Wide Web. When you type a URL into your browser, you're actually sending an HTTP request to a Web server for a page of information (that's why URLs all begin with "http://"). HTTP/1.1, the latest version, adds refinements to make it work more efficiently with TCP/IP.

**Insecure**   An insecure connection or protocol is one in which it is possible for a third party to intercept or overhear an exchange between two parties. Phone systems are insecure because wiretaps still occur and can overhear the conversation of two parties. Wireless communications, unless using strong encryption as in Blackberry two-way pagers, are insecure. Computer networks that have not implemented security measures are insecure and thus the transmission of data through a network can be overheard. Steps can be taken to ensure secure communications.

**Intelligent Transportation Systems (ITS)**   Automated roadway or toll way systems that use radio or radar technology to track cars on the highway.

**Internet**   A worldwide system of interconnected computer networks, whose use is not controlled by any single government agency or central authority.

**Internet access provider**   See *Internet service provider*.

**Internet service provider (ISP)**   Also called an Internet access provider. A company that provides direct access to the Internet for individuals, companies, and institutions. Unlike commercial online service providers, ISPs usually do not provide their own content, but may offer e-mail capability, browser software, and direct links to sites on the World Wide Web.

**Intranet**   A local area network or a company network limited to a specific population (like employees of a corporation) that may or may not be connected to the larger Internet.

**Java**   A programming language expressly designed for use in the distributed environment of the Internet. It was designed to have the "look and feel" of the C++ language, but it is simpler to use than C++ and enforces an object-oriented programming model (unlike C++, which can be programmed as if it were C, a structural language). Java can be used to create complete applications that may run on a single computer or be distributed among servers and clients in a network. It can also be used to build a small application module or applet for use as part of a Web page. Applets make it possible for a Web page user to interact with the page. Java is designed to work within a restricted area, or "sandbox," in a computer's virtual environment. This is supposed to ensure that an instruction cannot contain the address of data storage in another application or in the operating system itself, either of which would cause the program and perhaps the operating system itself to terminate or "crash." The sandbox is also designed to keep the Java program from getting at personal information stored outside itself.

**JavaScript**   An interpreted programming or script language from Netscape. In general, script languages are easier and faster to code in than the more structured and compiler languages, such as C and C++. Script languages generally take longer to process than compiled languages, but are very useful for shorter programs. JavaScript is used in Web site development to do such things as:

- Automatically change a formatted date on a Web page
- Cause a linked-to page to appear in a popup window
- Cause text or a graphic image to change during a mouse rollover

JavaScript uses some of the same ideas found in Java, the compiled object-oriented programming language derived from C++. JavaScript code can be imbedded in HTML pages and interpreted by the Web browser (or client). JavaScript can also be run at the server as in Microsoft's Active Server Pages (ASP) before the page is sent to the requestor. Both Microsoft and Netscape browsers support JavaScript, but sometimes in slightly different ways.

**Metrics**     A numeric measure of data that is used to evaluate entities or people. For example, the operator who answers your call at customer service is evaluated by the number of calls per week he or she handles.

**Micropayment**     A small-funds eCommerce transaction, ranging from amounts smaller than a penny to a few dollars.

**Modem**     A word made up from its function, **MO**dulate/**DEM**odulate. A device, usually within your computer, but sometimes attached externally, which translates communications signals from your computer onto a telecommunications link, such as a telephone line. Modems used on regular telephone lines "modulate" (translate) the computer's signals, which are digital, into an analog signal that can be carried on regular phone lines. Modems on other communication lines, such as cable, ISDN, or DSL, modulate the digital signal directly into your computer. Because all electrical lines are analog, all computer devices that send signals over electrical lines have to use a digital encoding to put those signals onto the analog medium. Some digital encodings are simpler than others, and the modem's job is to translate to a simpler encoding; for example, an external modem translates from the complex V.90 encoding used for 56k modems to the simple string-of-bits encoding used on serial lines.

**Network security**     The protection of networks and their services from unauthorized modification, destruction, or disclosure to or by unauthorized third parties.

**Newsgroup**     Topic groupings for articles and information posted by readers of that group. If you post a message to a newsgroup, other participants of the group are most likely able to contact you because your e-mail address is usually included in your posting.

**Non-repudiable Receipts**     Complete, accurate, and undeniable records of an event or interaction.

**Non-secure**     Refers to content, a Web site, or a transaction that is not protected from third-party interference.

**Online service**    A proprietary, commercial network that provides a variety of information and other services to its subscribers. Commercial online services typically provide their own content, forums (for example, chat rooms and bulletin boards), e-mail capability, and information available only to their subscribers.

**Opt-in**    A description of consumer choice in which you agree to the specified use of information that you provide, for example, you supply your e-mail address to receive a newsletter, but not to have your e-mail address transferred to another site.

**Opt-out**    A description of consumer choice in which you provide information to obtain some benefit and you restrict the use of that information by answering usage questions posed by the site—for example, you provide your shipping address for a product and check a box on the shipping form that requests that no additional information is sent to you.

**Packets**    In an online context, pieces of a message, each containing the destination address and the data necessary to recombine the packets when received at the destination, that enable the participants to conduct a communication or a transaction. Think of it this way: If you cut a letter into pieces and put each piece in a numbered envelope addressed to the person you were sending the letter to, each envelope and its content would be one packet.

**Password**    A private, unique series of letters and/or numbers that you create and must use to gain access to an online service or the Internet, specific data available online, or to make modifications to restricted-access software (for example, parental control software).

**Payment Gateway**    A party, such as a credit card processing service, that provides an interface between the computer systems of an eCommerce merchant, the merchant's bank, and the purchaser's bank.

**PDA**    Personal Digital Assistant (for example, PalmPilots, Newtons, and so on). A small, handheld computer, capable of accepting input that the user writes on-screen with a stylus, that's designed to provide all the tools an individual would need for day-to-day organization. This would include an appointment calendar, an address book, a notepad, and a fax modem.

**Personal Information, Personally identifiable information (PII)**    In the United States, full name, home address, e-mail address, telephone number, or other information that would enable someone to identify or contact an identified person. Also considered personal information are hobbies, interests, or information collected through *cookies* or other types of tracking mechanisms when they are tied to individually identifiable information.

**PGP**   Pretty Good Privacy, written by Phil Zimmerman, was the first publicly available military-grade, public-key cryptography program. It provided an easy and simple interface to creating public and private key pairs. Zimmerman's program was "encryption for the masses" and enabled anyone to download the software and use it to establish communication. His company, PGP, was bought by the software company Network Associates.

**PKI (Public Key Infrastructure)**   Enables users to securely and privately exchange data using a public and a private cryptographic key pair that is obtained and shared through a trusted authority.

**Portal**   A Web site that offers a collection of links to other Web-accessed services or products. Portals frequently offer personalization services to assist users in finding information and using the portal more effectively.

**Privacy**   With Web content (including eCommerce), the ability to control the collection, storage, sharing, security, and dissemination of confidential personal and company information gathered internally or from other sources.

**Privacy certification**   Seal from any of several independent entities that assess a company's online privacy statements based on a set of industry guidelines established by the Online Privacy Alliance, the United States Federal Trade Commission (FTC), or other authorities. Seals do not ensure that confidential information is not sold, shared, licensed, or leased, but that the company's practices match what they have stated in their policies.

**Privacy Policy**   A statement from the Web site operator or online service outlining what information it collects, how that information is used, who might be given the information, and how to contact the Web site operator. In the United States, a link to the privacy policy must be prominently displayed on the home page of the Web site and on any other area where personal information can be collected from children. It is a formal disclosure. Commercial Web sites in the United States can be penalized by the Federal Trade Commission if they do not abide by their stated policies.

**Privacy seal**   Some Web sites have icons that look like privacy policy seals of approval. However, this does not mean that the privacy policy has received official approval from the Federal Trade Commission (FTC). As yet, the FTC has not authorized any privacy seal programs. Officially authorized privacy seal programs are part of the FTC's "safe harbor" program. Parents need to remember that just because a Web site displays a privacy seal does not guarantee its compliance with *COPPA*.

**Private/public key cryptography**   A dual-key encryption system used when confidential information, such as a bid, offer, or credit card number, is sent over the Internet. The information is encrypted with a "public key" data field by the recipient's system and uses a secret digital code or "private key" to decipher the encrypted information.

**Profile**   Data that accurately portrays the significant features of a personal or business entity, especially the data that leads to building online trust.

**Public key cryptography**   Public key cryptography is more sophisticated than single key cryptography. It enables a user to distribute freely a key that enables other users to send encoded messages that only he can read. The public key is used for encryption and the private key is used for decryption. Anyone trying to intercept the message en route would find that it is gibberish.  Public key cryptography places into the hands of individuals a level of security that was formerly available only to the top levels of government security agencies.

**Registration authority**   Verifies the identity of a requestor before a certificate authority grants a digital certificate. Sometimes abbreviated as "RA."

**Repository**   A digital "place" for storing and retrieving certificates or other data.

**Risk analysis**   In security, the process of identifying security risks, determining their magnitude, and identifying areas needing safeguards. Risk analysis is a part of risk management. Synonymous with risk assessment.

**RSA**   A public key algorithm developed by RSA Data Security, Inc. It can be used to generate digital signatures, encrypt messages, and provide private/public key management encryption.

**Scoring**   A practice that uses a model to predict future behavior. The score assigned to each individual in a database indicates that person's likelihood of exhibiting a particular customer behavior. Scoring on the fly or dynamic scoring is the ability to score an already-defined customer segment within a campaign-management tool. Rather than scoring an entire database, dynamic scoring works with only the required customer subsets, and only when needed. In credit fraud, scoring is used to restrict the online ordering of certain items during certain times with certain e-mail addresses or ZIP codes.

**Scrip[t] kiddies**   Generally, scrip kiddies are new hackers who are relatively unskilled. They do not create hacking programs on their own, but download attack programs (called "scrips") from various sites on the Net. These scrips come with instructions on how to run the scrip against millions of machines. There are thousands of scrip-kiddies out there, so if you have an always-on connection (cable-modem, DSL, or you leave your modem connection on all day), you can expect about one of these scans per day. During the CodeRed infestation, many systems that normally got one or two scans a day got hundreds. (For more information, see `http://www.sans.org/infosecFAQ/hackers/monkeys.htm`).

**Seal**   A digital confirmation that content is secure and/or authentic.

**Secure**   A secure connection is one in which information can be exchanged between two or more parties without significant fear of an untrusted third-party interception. Data and communications that are protected from interference, tampering, and viewing by unintended third parties. This is especially important when transferring critical data such as financial information, pass codes, or military information to name a few. Steps can be taken to ensure secure communication.

**Secure communication protocol**   Secure communication protocols are methods of communication in which information cannot be intercepted by an untrusted third party. SSL, S/MIME, and Digital Certificates are some examples.

**Secure Electronic Transaction Protocol (SET)**   A protocol developed jointly by Visa and MasterCard that enables secure credit card transactions over the Internet.

**Secure Sockets Layer (SSL)**   SSL is the Internet standard for layering communication between two parties and using public key encryption techniques to ensure a secure communication. It is a protocol for transmitting private documents via the Internet, including confidential user information such as credit card numbers. The Netscape company first developed SSL.

**Server wallet**   An application in which an eCommerce purchaser's credit card and certificate information is stored on a server at the user's financial institution.

**Single-key cryptography**   Enables a user to encrypt a message and submit to another user only if he uses a pre-arranged key that both parties agreed on. Once the data is encrypted it can only be decrypted by using the secret key. This enables the information to be transferred confidently across a network without worrying about third-party interception. Also called "secret-key cryptography", or "symmetric cryptography" (as opposed to asymmetric cryptography, which is *public key*).

**Site authentication**   The practice of verifying that the Web site being viewed is really the Web site that the user intends to use, and not a site that is "hijacked" or altered by a third party.

**Smart update**   Notifies the user of an available upgrade for an online application, ensuring that the most up-to-date version of the application is available for use. The additional information is transmitted with sufficient knowledge of the user's environment that only the necessary data is sent and, should the transmission be interrupted, it may be able to continue where it was stopped.

**Social Security Number**   A U.S. Government-issued identity number, which is used for tax and other government purposes. You should not give this number out lightly. Other countries have similar government-issued IDs.

**Spam**   Also called "junk e-mail." Unsolicited, unwanted e-mail usually sent by people who want you to buy things.

**Steganography**   (pronounced STEHG-uh-NAH-gruhf-ee, from Greek steganos, or "covered," and graphie, or "writing") The hiding of a secret message within an ordinary message and the extraction of it at its destination. Steganography takes cryptography a step further by hiding an encrypted message so that no one suspects it exists. Ideally, anyone scanning your data fails to know it contains encrypted data.

In modern digital steganography, data is first encrypted by the usual means and then inserted, using a special algorithm, into redundant (that is, provided but unneeded) data that is part of a particular file format such as a JPEG image. Think of all the bits that represent the same color pixel repeated in a row. By applying the encrypted data to this redundant data in some random or nonconspicuous way, the result is data that appears to have the "noise" patterns of regular, nonencrypted data. A trademark or other identifying symbol hidden in software code is sometimes known as a watermark.

After September 11, 2001, Osama Bin Laden's terrorist network has been rumored to be using steganography to transmit information via pornographic images.

**Stickiness**   Refers to Web sites' abilities to have visitors "stick around," rather than just look and leave. It's a measurement of desirability. Buyers who get partially through a purchase process, such as adding items to a shopping cart (in *B2C*) or negotiating (in *B2B*), but do not complete potential transactions give the eCommerce site a 'problem with stickiness.' Many eCommerce sites attempt to boost 'stickiness' with value-added services, such as news about the products or industries, or by providing B2B trust services.

**Third parties**   In an Internet context, anyone who is not part of the Web site or online service, such as advertising and marketing companies. Information collected from children on the Web can be sold or given to third parties to help them target children to buy particular products, watch specific TV shows, listen to certain CDs, all based on a child's interests.

**Trading partner**   In an Internet context, either the purchaser or seller of online goods, services, or rights.

**Transponder**   A radio or radar set that upon receiving a designated signal emits a radio signal of its own and that is used especially for the detection, identification, and location of objects.

**Trojan Horse**   A seemingly useful program that contains malicious code. When a user downloads and runs the Trojan Horse, it attacks the user's computer or sometimes other computers. Trojans are distinct from a virus (a piece of malicious code that embeds itself into other programs) and a worm (a standalone program which spreads on its own, instead of fooling the user into running it). Script kiddies often use Trojan Horses that get spread widely and are run by many users; they don't attack those users' computers, but instead await instructions from the script kiddies. When the instructions come, the Trojan Horses simultaneously connect the computer the script kiddies actually want to attack. This is known as a distributed denial of service attack.

**TRUSTe**   An independent, non-profit privacy initiative dedicated to building users' trust and confidence on the Internet by ensuring online privacy with a third-party "seal" (http://www.truste.org).

**Trusted computing base**   The complete set of protection mechanisms within a computer system, including hardware, firmware, and software, responsible for enforcing a security policy.

**Trustmark**   An online seal awarded by TRUSTe to Web sites that agree to post their privacy practices openly via privacy statements, as well as adhere to enforcement procedures that ensure that their privacy promises are met. When you click on the TRUSTe trustmark, you're taken directly to the privacy statement of the licensed Web site.

**Uniform Resource Locator (URL)**   Global address for resources on the World Wide Web. http://www.nuit.org is a URL. URLs look strange and complex because they were designed originally to be read by computers, not people. They take the format "<protocol>://<locator>"—in the example above, "http" is the Web protocol, and www.nuit.org is the machine name.

**Verifiable parental consent**   Any reasonable effort (taking into consideration available technology) to ensure that a parent of a child receives notice of the operator's personal information collection, use, and disclosure practices. Most important, verifiable parental consent means that a Web site or online service must have a parent's authorization before collecting, using, and disclosing a child's personal information.

**Virtual Private Network (VPN)**   Although some vendors and service providers might disagree, in common usage a virtual private network is a group of two or more computer systems, typically connected to a private network (a network built and maintained by an organization solely for its own use) with limited public-network access, that communicates "securely" over a public network. VPNs may exist between an individual machine and a private network (client-to-server) or a remote LAN and a private network (server-to-server). Security features differ from product to product, but most security experts agree that VPNs include encryption, strong authentication of remote users or hosts, and mechanisms for hiding or masking information about the private network topology from potential attackers on the public network.

**Virus**   A file or program maliciously planted in your computer that can damage files and disrupt your system.

**Virus engine**    Software that searches your computer to find and neutralize viruses.

**Virus Signature**    Patterns the Virus Engine compares files and programs against to see if they are viruses.

**Warez**    Warez (generally pronounced as though spelled "wares," although some pronounce it like the city of "Juarez") is a term used by software "pirates" to describe software that has been stripped of its copy protection and made available on the Internet for downloading. People who create warez sites sometimes call them "warez sitez" and use "z" in other pluralizations. Some warez sites include freeware and shareware that is legally downloadable.

**Web browser**    See *browser*.

**Web site**    A collection of "pages" or files on the World Wide Web that are linked together and maintained by a company, organization, or individual. Anyone with a Web site is a content provider or a publisher. Most Web sites are organized under one domain, such as ftc.gov (the Federal Trade Commission).

**Webmaster**    Typically, an individual or an individual within a company or organization assigned with the task of updating and maintaining an individual Web site. The Webmaster's e-mail address is often listed on the Web site as the contact person for queries and questions related specifically to the site's content and/or format.

**World Wide Web**    A part of the Internet that links text, sound, and images in the form of Web pages and sites.

# EXPANDED PRIVACY CHECKLIST

This is a more detailed list of questions you should think about when you go to a Web site that wants information from you. The answers to these questions will help you decide how much, or how little, information to share, and what the benefit is to you. While this checklist is primarily intended for use with online sites, it is equally useful when dealing with paper questionnaires, telephone surveys, and other ways information is gathered.

## Personally Identifiable Information

What Information am I being asked to give?

- Name
- Street address
- ZIP+Four code in the United States
- Social Security Number or other government issued identification number
- Fingerprint, retinal scan, iris print, voiceprint, or other biometric information
- Phone number
- Credit card number
- Medical history or information
- Photograph of myself

- Driver license number
- Passport number

What demographic data is being gathered?

- Age
- Gender
- Racial self-description
- Marital status
- Employment status
- Occupation
- Job function
- Children, how many, and their ages
- Pets and their type
- What kind of car, bicycle, or truck I own
- The town I live in (and/or my ZIP code, as long as I don't include the +4 extension)
- Yearly income for me, my spouse, and/or my household
- What kind of books or magazines interest me
- What kind of activities I enjoy
- Will this demographic data be linked to the PII above?

# Notice

- Does this site have a privacy policy?
- Does the privacy policy or instruction for the site tell me how they will use my information?
- Does it tell me what my options are if I do not give them my information?
- Will my information be shared with anyone else?
- If so, under what circumstances, and what use will that third party make of my info?
- Will my information be kept forever, or will it be discarded at some point?

# Choice

- Do I have a choice about sharing my information?
- Look for opt-in or opt-out boxes. Read what the checked box says carefully.
- Does the privacy policy or instruction for the site tell me what will happen if I do *not* share my information?
- Does the privacy policy tell me how to communicate with the site owners if I change my mind?

# Access

- Does the privacy policy or instruction tell me how to see what information is being held about me?
- Does the policy tell me how to make changes to that information?

# Security

- Does this site have a page explaining how they protect my information?
- If I am filling out a form with personally identifiable information, does SSL or other security protect that page? (Is the key or lock symbol glowing or dark, or is the lock icon open or closed?)
- If I type in a password, do the letters appear visibly, or are they replaced with asterisks (*) or other symbols (better)?
- When I display my profile or billing information, is my entire credit card number printed out, or just the last four or five digits (better)?
- Do I have to re-enter my billing information every time, or is it stored away?
- If it's stored, how do I access it to change it?
- Can I find other people's billing info?
- If I forget my password, how do I get back in?
- Do I have to make up a new account?
- Does the site display my password to me when I type in my ID (not very secure) or does the site send it to me at the e-mail I first registered with (much safer)?

- Does the site ask for a hint to help me remember my password?
- When I answer the hint, does it display my password (less secure) on screen or e-mail it to me (more secure)?
- If I forget my password and have to have it re-issued, does the site set a temporary password which is good only for one use?

# What Am I Revealing about Myself?

If I have a Web site, I should reveal items about myself and my family deliberately, and consider whether I am giving away info I don't want to have floating around out there. For example, if I have e-mail addresses on my Web site, a SPAM harvester has probably lifted them by now. And so on....

If I have a Web site, what information can be lifted from it?

- My name?
- My spouse and/or children's names?
- My home address?
- My phone number?
- My e-mail address?
- Pictures of myself or my children?
- Details of My work life, schedule, and so on?

If I have a profile on a public site, such as Amazon.com, Yahoo, or HotMail, what does it say about me?

- My name?
- My spouse and/or children's names?
- My home address?
- My phone number?
- My e-mail address?
- Pictures of myself or my children?
- Do I have a calendar listing my vacation dates, and so on?

# LIST OF PRIVACY BILLS IN THE STATES IN 2001

In Chapter 13, "Privacy and the Law: 2001," we discussed laws and proposed legislation that speak to digital privacy issues. This appendix lists the legislation that was proposed, and to some extent acted on, during the 2001 legislative season. Table C.1 was prepared for the Internet State Coalition and is used with the permission of Emily Hackett, their director. Figure C.1 is a map that shows the privacy legislative action in the various states.

The Internet Alliance (IA), through its state and law enforcement programs, is the leading consumer Internet industry association at the state level. The IA's mission is to build the consumer confidence and trust necessary for the Internet to become the leading global marketing medium of this century. Leading members of the Internet Alliance include: @once, 24/7 Media, Computer Internet Exchange Association, eBay, America Online/Time Warner, IBM, Juno, Netcentives, and Yuroka.

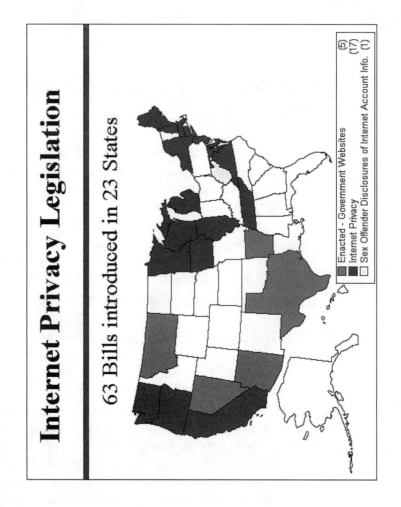

**FIGURE C.1**

**TABLE C.1    INTERNET STATE COALITION—INTERNET PRIVACY BILLS INTRODUCED IN 2001**

| State/Bill# | Category | Summary | Sponsor | Status | Bill Text |
|---|---|---|---|---|---|
| AR HB 2403 | State Government | An act to amend Arkansas code 25-4-110(c) to require state agencies to develop policies regarding the use of the internet. | Files | 04/05/2001Enacted | http://www.arkleg.state.ar.us/ftproot/acts/2001/htm/act1287.pdf |
| AZ HB 2043 | State Government | State web sites; privacy statement (NOW: state | Hatch-Miller | 04/30/2001 Enacted Chapter: 269 Chaptered Version: Senate Engrossed Version | http://www.azleg.state.az.us/legtext/45leg/1r/bills/hb2043s.htm web sites; privacy) |
| AZ HB 2320 | State Government Web Site | State web sites; access; privacy | Voss | Died in House Committee | http://www.azleg.state.az.us/legtext/45leg/1r/bills/hb2320p.htm |
| AZ HB 2429 | State Government Security | Information systems security information; confidentiality | Foster | Died in House Committee | http://www.azleg.state.az.us/legtext/45leg/1r/bills/hb2429p.htm |
| CA SB 0763 | | Title Bill: Personal Privacy Protection Act of 2001, with unspecified provisions | Murray | 3/12/01 In Rules Committee | http://www.leginfo.ca.gov/pub/bill/sen/sb_0751-0800/sb_763_bill_20010223_introduced.html |

## TABLE C.1   CONTINUED

| State/Bill# | Category | Summary | Sponsor | Status | Bill Text |
|---|---|---|---|---|---|
| CT SB 1239 | State Government | An act concerning internet privacy. | Energy and Technology Committee | Died on Foot of House Calendar | `http://www.cga.state.ct.us/2001/cbs/S/SB-1239.htm` |
| IA HSB 0058 | Web Site Registration (voluntary) | This bill relates to disclosure of certain information by persons engaged in selling or leasing goods or services via the internet. | | | `http://www.legis.state.ia.us/GA/79GA/Legislation/HSB/00000/HSB00058/Current.html` |
| IA SSB 1035 | Web Site Registration (voluntary) | This bill relates to disclosure of certain information by persons engaged in selling or leasing goods or services via the internet. | | | `http://www.legis.state.ia.us/GA/79GA/Legislation/SSB/01000/SSB01035/Current.html` |
| IL HR 0263 | State Government | Auditor Gen-Audit Agency Web Sites | Lang | 05/25/2001 H Resolution Adopted As Amended 118-000-000 | `http://www.legis.state.il.us/legisnet/legisnet92/hrgroups/hr/920HR0263LV.html` |
| MA SB 0113 | ISP Opt-In | Relative to on-line privacy | Senator Charles E. Shannon | Public Hearing date Apr 18 am at 10:30 in Room A-2 | `http://www.state.ma.us/legis/bills/st00113.htm` |
| MA SB 0904 | ISP | Petition relative to issuance of subpoenas for records of providers of electronic communication services. | Stanley, Harriett | 12/21/2000 S Senate concurred -SJ 2138 | `http://www.state.ma.us/legis/bills/st00904.htm?Gabillnum=SB00904` |

**TABLE C.1   CONTINUED**

| State/Bill# | Category | Summary | Sponsor | Status | Bill Text |
|---|---|---|---|---|---|
| MA SB 1790 | State Government/Business/Web Site Privacy Policy | Relative to privacy on the Internet. | Lynch | 01/03/01 S Referred to the committee on Senate Science and Technology | Http://www.state.ma.us/legis/bills/st01790.htm |
| MA SB 1798 | State Government/Business/Opt-Out | For legislation to protect individuals' identifying information during Internet transactions. | Senator David P. Magnani | 01/03/2001 S Referred to the committee on Senate Science and Technology | Http://www.state.ma.us/legis/bills/st01798.htm |
| MA SB 1799 | State Government/Business/Opt-Out | For legislation to protect consumers' identifying information during electronic commerce transactions. | Senator David P. Magnani | 01/03/2001 S Referred to the committee on Senate Science and Technology | Http://www.state.ma.us/legis/bills/st01799.htm |
| MA SB 1801 | Opt-Out | Relative to consumer internet service provider privacy. | Magnani | 1/3/01S referred to committee on Senate Science and Technology | Http://www.state.ma.us/legis/bills/st01801.htm |
| MA SB 1806 | Access / Study | Establishing the Massachusetts Internet Technology Commission | Panagio-takos... | 1/3/01S referred to committee on Senate Science and Technology | Http://www.state.ma.us/legis/bills/st01806.htm |
| MD SB 0219 | Opt-Out | Maryland Internet Privacy Act | Ferguson... | 03/05/2001 S Unfavorable Report by Finance; Died | http://mlis.state.md.us/2001rs/bills/sb/sb0219f.rtf |

**TABLE C.1  CONTINUED**

| State/Bill# | Category | Summary | Sponsor | Status | Bill Text |
|---|---|---|---|---|---|
| ME LD 1227 | Business | An Act to Provide for the Disclosure of Company Information and Appointment of a Registered Agent in Maine by Persons or Business Entities Selling or Leasing Goods or Services via the Internet | Saxl | 05/02/2001 Pursuant to Joint Rule 310.3 Placed in the Legislative Files (DEAD) | http://janus.state.me.us/legis/bills/billdocs/LD122701.doc |
| MI HB 4680 | ISP | To regulate internet service providers and certain internet users; to provide certain rights of privacy associated with the use of the internet | Bogardus | 05/01/2001 HJ 34 P. 509 referred to Committee on Commerce | http://198.109.122.10/pdf/house.bills.intro/2001-2002/4680hhhh.pdf?GAbillnum=HB4680 |
| MN HF 1283 | Business | Internet sales and leases regulated, and domain names and agents for service of process information disclosure provided | Seagren | Carried over to 2002, House Civil Law | http://www.revisor.leg.state.mn.us/cgi-bin/bldbill.pl?bill=H1283.1&session=ls82 |
| MN SF 1108 | Business | Internet Sales and leases regulation: providing for the disclosure of information relating to the ownership of domain names an agents for service of process. | Scheid | Carried over to 2002, in Senate Judiciary | http://www.revisor.leg.state.mn.us/cgi-bin/bldbill.pl?bill=S1108.0&session=ls82 |
| MT HB 0281 | State Government Web Site | Governmental internet information privacy act | M. Lindeen | 04/10/2001 Enacted | http://data.opi.state.mt.us/bills/2001/BillHtml/HB0281.htm |
| MT LC 0969 | No bill text | Facilitate e-commerce in insurance and securities | By request of State Auditor | Died in drafting process | |

**TABLE C.1    CONTINUED**

| State/Bill# | Category | Summary | Sponsor | Status | Bill Text |
|---|---|---|---|---|---|
| NH HB 0104 | ISP Disclosure | Relative to internet service dial-up providers. | Marshall E Quandt | Formerly LSR 65, referred to Science, Technology and Energy | http://gencourt.state. nh.us/legislation/ 2001/hb0104.html |
| NH HB 0314 | State Government | Relative to administrative rules governing privacy. | Dickinson | 04/12/2001 H Retained in House Executive Departments & Administration Committee | http://gencourt.state. nh.us/legislation/2001/ hb0314.html?GAbillnum =hb0314 |
| NH HB 0620 | Business/Web Site Privacy Policy | Relative to the sale or lease of goods or services to residents of this state via the internet. | Belanger | 2/13/01 Introduced, in House Commerce Committe | http://gencourt.state. nh.us/legislation/2001/ HB0619.html |
| NJ AB 0591 | State Government/ Business/Web Site Privacy Policy | Online Privacy Protection Act | Buono, Barbara | 01/11/00-Referred To Assembly Telecommunications and Utilities Committee | http://www.njleg.state. nj.us/2000/Bills/a1000/ 591_i1.htm |
| NJ AB 0592 | Children | Children's Privacy Online | Buono, Barbara/ Geist, George F. | 6/15/00 to Senate Education | http://www.njleg.state. nj.us/2000/Bills/a1000/ 592_i1.htm |
| NJ AB 0593 | Children | Children's Online Privacy Act | Buono, Barbara/ Geist, George F. | 01/11/00-To Assembly Telecom and Utilities | http://www.njleg.state. nj.us/2000/Bills/a1000/ 593_i1.htm |

## TABLE C.1 CONTINUED

| State/Bill# | Category | Summary | Sponsor | Status | Bill Text |
|---|---|---|---|---|---|
| NJ AB 1250 | Children | Privacy: Children's Privacy | Cottrell, Melvin/ Malone, Joseph R. | 01/11/00-To Assembly Senior Issues and Community Services Committee | http://www.njleg.state. nj.us/2000/Bills/a1500/ 1250 |
| NJ AB 2944 | ISP Disclosure | Clarifies authority of municipal court to issue subpoena directing release of certain information concerning subscriber of electronic communication or remote computing services. | Zisa | 11/09/2000 Introduced And Referred To Assembly Judiciary Committee | http://www.njleg.state. nj.us/2000/Bills/a3000/ 2944_i1.htm |
| NJ ACR 0125 | | Memorializes Congress to enact laws protecting individual privacy in cyberspace. | Blee | Sep-25-2000 Introduced And Referred To Assembly Tele- communications and Utilities Committee | http://www.njleg.state. nj.us/2000/Bills/acr/ 125_i1.htm |
| NJ ACR 125 | General/Website/ Opt out | Memorializes Congress to enact laws protecting individual privacy in cyberspace. Identical to SCR 94 | Blee | Introduced And Referred To Assembly Tele- communications and Utilities Committee | ftp://www.njleg.state. nj.us/20002001/ACR/ 125_I1.HTM |
| NJ AJR 0052 | General/Opt out | Urges Congress to enact statutes to enhance privacy in cyberspace. | Russo | 10/12/2000 Introduced And Referred To Assembly Tele- communications and Utilities Committee | http://www.njleg.state. nj.us/2000/Bills/ajr/ 52_i1.htm |

**TABLE C.1** **CONTINUED**

| State/Bill# | Category | Summary | Sponsor | Status | Bill Text |
|---|---|---|---|---|---|
| NJ AR 0145 | | Memorializes Congress to enact legislation requiring Federal Trade Commission to promulgate regulations protecting individuals' privacy on the Internet | Geist | Oct-12-2000 Introduced And Referred To Assembly Tele-communications and Utilities Committee | http://www.njleg.state. nj.us/2000/Bills/ar/ 145_i1.htm |
| NJ SCR 0094 | General/Website/ Opt out | Memorializes Congress to enact laws protecting individual privacy in cyberspace. Identical to HCR 125 | Sinagra | 12/14/2000 Introduced And Referred To Senate Judiciary Committee | ftp://www.njleg.state. nj.us/20002001/SCR/ 94_I1.HTM |
| NV AB 0060 | State Government Web Site | Requires public body to post additional notice of its meetings on its Internet website, if any. | Beers | 06/08/2001 Approved by the Governor. Chapter 484. Effective July 1, 2001. | http://www.leg.state. nv.us/71st/bills/AB/ AB60_R3.html |
| NV SB 0048 | State Government/ Business/Cookie | BDR 259: Prohibits various acts related to Internet, networks, computers and electronic mail. | Judiciary | Approved by Governor; Chapt. 274; effective October 1, 2001 | http://www.leg.state. nv.us/71st/bills/SB/ SB48_R1.html |
| NV SB 0551 | ISP's | BDR 442: Makes various changes concerning computers, technology, Internet and crimes against children. | Judiciary | 06/14/2001 Chapter 560. Effective June 13, 2001 | http://www.leg.state. nv.us/71st/bills/SB/ SB551_R2.html |

## TABLE C.1  CONTINUED

| State/Bill# | Category | Summary | Sponsor | Status | Bill Text |
|---|---|---|---|---|---|
| NY AB 2358 | State Government | Enacts the Internet Privacy Policy Act | Sweeney | 05/30/2001 Referred To Rules | http://assembly.state.ny.us/leg/?bn=A02358&days=3 |
| NY AB 5789 | Business/Web Site Privacy Policy | Enacts New York State Internet Privacy Law to which operators of websites may voluntarily be subject; limits disclosure of personal information to those submitting | Stringer | 04/18/2001 reported referred to codes | http://assembly.state.ny.us/leg/?bn=A05789&days=3 |
| NY AB 6191 | ISP/Business | Regulates the dissemination of personal information acquired by a provider of on-line computer services | Ortiz | 03/05/2001 referred to consumer affairs and protection | http://assembly.state.ny.us/leg/?bn=A06191 |
| NY AB 8329 ny.us/leg/?bn=A08329&sh=t | ISP/Business Opt-In | Provides for the protection of users of Internet websites from the misuse of information regarding such users obtained by operators of commercial Internet websites | Rules Comm; Pheffer | 04/03/2001 referred to Consumer Affairs and Protection | http://assembly.state.ny.us/leg/? |
| NY AB 8456 | Business/Opt In | Provides that it shall be unlawful to sell or lease any consumer's electronic mail address without affirmative consent of consumer | RULES COM Pheffer | 05/08/2001 reported referred to codes | http://assembly.state.ny.us/leg/?bn=A08456&days=3 |
| NY SB 4353 | Voluntary | Enacts New York State Internet Privacy Law to which operators of websites may voluntarily be subject; limits disclosure of personal information to those submitting | Hannon | 4/11/01 referred to Consumer Protections | http://assembly.state.ny.us/leg/?bn=S04353&sh=t |

**TABLE C.1 CONTINUED**

| State/Bill# | Category | Summary | Sponsor | Status | Bill Text |
|---|---|---|---|---|---|
| NY SB 4402 | Business/Opt-In | Requires on-line internet profilers to first gain consent from the information subject before compiling personal information with respect thereto | Connor | 04/12/2001 Referred To Consumer Protection | http://assembly.state.ny.us/leg/?bn=S04402&days=0 |
| NY SB 4624 | State Government | Enacts the Internet Privacy Policy Act: provides protective measures for customers of state agencies vis a vis internet and web site information applicable to them | Hannon | 06/15/2001 amend (t) and recommit to Energy and Telecommunications Print Number 4624a | http://assembly.state.ny.us/leg/?bn=S04624&days=0 |
| NY SB 4760 | State Government | Enacts the "Internet privacy policy act" prohibiting state agencies from disclosing personal information on subscribers to state interactive computer services | Hannon | 06/11/2001 Passed Senate; Delivered to Assembly and referred to governmental operations | http://assembly.state.ny.us/leg/?bn=S04760&days=3 |
| OR HB 3077 | | Relating to computer software. Prohibits person from placing in another person's computer any software that transmits information about use of computer. | Barnhart | 4/24/01 Avancing E-Government Committee Held public hearing | http://www.leg.state.or.us/01reg/measures/hb3000.dir/hb3077.intro.html |

**TABLE C.1   CONTINUED**

| State/Bill# | Category | Summary | Sponsor | Status | Bill Text |
|---|---|---|---|---|---|
| OR HB 3157 | State Government | Requires Economic and Community Development Department to create credentials system for confirming identity of parties in Internet-based transactions | Committee on Advancing E-Government (at the request of Oregon Internet Commission) | 3-8(H) First reading. Referred to Speaker's desk | http://www.leg.state.or.us/01reg/measures/hb3100.dir/hb3157.intro.html |
| OR SB 0727 | State Government | Creates joint interim task force to study and make recommendations about Oregon Internet identification badge system to enhance security of electronic commerce by identifying, credentialing and rating persons conducting electronic commerce | Deckert | In Senate Business, Labor, and Economic Development | http://www.leg.state.or.us/01reg/measures/sb0700.dir/sb0727.intro.html |
| TN HB 1001 | Business/Opt-In | An Act to enact the Tennessee Internet Personal Information Privacy Act of 2001. | *Bowers | 04/24/2001 Action Def. in s/c Civil Procedure and Practice of JUD to 1/8/02 | http://www.legislature.state.tn.us/bills/currentga/BILL/HB1001.pdf? GABillNum=HB1001 |
| TN SB 1466 | Business/Opt-In | An Act to enact the Tennessee Internet Personal Information Privacy Act of 2001. | *Dixon | 4/24/01 Assigned to Gen. Sub of C.L&A Comm | http://www.legislature.state.tn.us/bills/currentga/BILL/SB1466.pdf? GABillNum=SB1466 |

**TABLE C.1    CONTINUED**

| State/Bill# | Category | Summary | Sponsor | Status | Bill Text |
|---|---|---|---|---|---|
| TX HB 1922 | State Government | Relating to state government privacy policy. | McCall \| Wolens | 06/15/2001 E Signed by the Governor | http://www.capitol. state.tx.us/ cgi-bin/db2www/tlo/ billhist/billhist.d2w/ report?LEG=77&SESS= R&CHAMBER=H&BILLTYPE= B&BILLSUFFIX=01922 |
| TX HB 2589 | State Government | Relating to the required posting of information on a state agency's Internet site and to the security, confidentiality, and management of certain information. | Hochberg | 06/11/2001 E Effective on 9/1/01 | http://www.capitol. state.tx.us/ cgi-bin/db2www/tlo/ billhist/billhist. d2w/report?LEG= 77&SESS=R&CHAMBER =H&BILLTYPE= B&BILLSUFFIX=02589 |
| TX HB 3209 | State Government | Relating to the management of state agency information resources technologies | Turner | Sent to Governor | http://www. capitol.state.tx.us/ cgi-bin/tlo/ textframe.cmd? LEG=77&SESS= R&CHAMBER=H&BILLTYPE= B&BILLSUFFIX= 03207&VERSION=1&TYPE=B |
| TX SB 0866 | State Government Web Site | Relating to the creation of a Texas Privacy Act and addressing the ways in which the information practices of state and local governmental entities affect personal privacy. | Nelson | Died in House State Affairs | http://www.capitol. state.tx.us/cgi-bin/ tlo/textframe.cmd? LEG=77&SESS=R&CHAMBER= S&BILLTYPE= B&BILLSUFFIX= 00866&VERSION=3&TYPE=B |

**TABLE C.1   CONTINUED**

| State/Bill# | Category | Summary | Sponsor | Status | Bill Text |
|---|---|---|---|---|---|
| TX SB 0867 | Study | Relating to the creation, operation, and duties of a joint interim task force to study various issues affecting personal privacy. | Nelson | Died in House State Affairs | http://www.capitol.state.tx.us/cgi-bin/db2www/tlo/billhist/billhist.d2w/report?LEG=77&SESS=R&CHAMBER=S&BILLTYPE=B&BILLSUFFIX=00867 |
| TX SB 0918 | ISP Disclosure | The attorney general may issue a subpoena to an electronic communications service for business records that disclose information about customers | Shapiro | Died in Senate Criminal Justice | http://www.capitol.state.tx.us/cgi-bin/db2www/tlo/billhist/billhist.d2w/report?LEG=77&SESS=R&CHAMBER=S&BILLTYPE=B&BILLSUFFIX=00918 |
| VA HB 2382 | Web Site Privacy Policy/Opt-Out/Cookie | Internet Privacy Protection Act; created. | Rhodes (all patrons) ...notes | Died in the House | http://leg1.state.va.us/cgi-bin/legp504.exe?011+ful+HB2382 |
| WA HB 1053 | State Government | Protecting privacy in the use of governmental information services: internet services operated by state. | Romero | 04/25/2001 By resolution, reintroduced and retained in present status. | http://www.leg.wa.gov/pub/billinfo/2001-02/house/1050-1074/1053.pdf |
| WI AB 0176 | State Government | Collection of personally identifiable information by certain state entities from Internet sites. | Powers | 03/22/2001 S. Read first time and referred to committee on Privacy, Electronic Commerce and Financial Institutions ... 135 | http://www.legis.state.wi.us/2001/data/AB-176.pdf |

**TABLE C.1   CONTINUED**

| State/Bill# | Category | Summary | Sponsor | Status | Bill Text |
|---|---|---|---|---|---|
| WV HB 2409 | Sex Offenders | Crimes—Sexual Offenses: requiring registrants to provide information about their internet accounts and screen names | Staton | Enacted 4/14/01; Chapter 266, Acts, 2001 | `ftp://129.71.161.247/` `ftp-house01/` `HB2401-2450/` `hb2409%20enr.wpd` |

# OUR CO-CONSPIRATORS

Many folks have helped with this book. Many of them provided the essays that we have included as sidebars in the book. We were striving for balance, and so we brought you many voices that were different from our own. We invited our friends to describe themselves so that you can understand more of why we included them, and how to find out more about them.

**Martin E. Abrams** leads the Center for Information Policy Leadership at Hunton & Williams and shapes digital-age global privacy concepts by providing thought leadership for companies, consumer leaders and policy makers. As Senior Policy Advisor to Hunton & Williams' Privacy and Information Management Practice, Mr. Abrams provides clients with total solution strategic business consulting on all aspects of information policy, security, privacy, and intellectual property. He advises chief privacy officers and other senior executives with the development of values-oriented global information management strategies for customer, consumer and employee information. He has expertise with corporate values development, industry best practices, and he works closely with firm attorneys to develop and implement comprehensive compliance programs for financial privacy regulations, the EU Data Protection Directive and Safe Harbor requirements, and the Fair Credit Reporting Act.

Mr. Abrams actively participates in national and international forums on privacy policy. He serves as an advisor to the Privacy Leadership Initiative Executive Committee, and he is active in the Online Privacy Alliance. He has previously served in leadership roles on the Information Industry Association's Public Policy & Government Relations Council, the U.S. Internet Alliance, Individual Reference Services Group, Coalition on Sensible Public Records Access, Better Business Bureau Online Privacy Steering Committee, Florida State Task Force on Technology and Privacy, Direct Marketing Association Privacy Committee, Associated Credit Bureaus Privacy Committee, Privacy and American Business Privacy Task Force, the Coalition of Services Trans Border Data Flow Task Force, and he chaired the Intelligent Highways and Vehicles Systems of America Privacy Committee. Mr. Abrams is a frequent speaker on privacy and information policy topics.

Prior to joining Hunton & Williams, Mr. Abrams served as Vice President of Information Policy and Privacy at Experian, where he led the company's global fair information practices programs and developed the values approach to privacy.

*Martin Abrams*

**Pamela Belle** lives near Devizes, Wiltshire in the United Kingdom, with her husband Steve, sons Hugh and Patrick, plus four Burmese cats, thirteen chickens and an overweight Labrador called Maddie. She has written thirteen novels, historical, fantasy and modern, and is currently working on a book set in London at the time of the Jacobite Rebellion in 1715.

**Jo Beverley** was born and raised in England, and has a degree in English history from Keele University in Staffordshire. She and her husband emigrated to Canada, where they now live. They have two sons.

Though she started to write as a child, it was only in the 80s that she began to think that it was something ordinary people can do, and after a talk at a local library, she settled to seriously writing her first historical romance.

She is the author of twenty-two romance novels and many novellas, which have brought her many awards, including five RITA awards from the Romance Writers of America and awards from Romantic Times including two Career Achievement awards. She is a member of the RWA Honor Roll and the RWA Hall of Fame for Regency romance, and her 2000 Georgian novel, *Devilish*, won the RITA for Long Historical Romance. The award was presented at a gala event in New Orleans as part of the 2001 RWA annual conference in July.

*Jo Beverley*

**Timothy Casey** has spent most of his 20-year professional career designing secure communications systems, in both government and commercial applications. Most recently this involved architecting a system to enable security and privacy features in circuits manufactured by Intel Corp.

A life-long Libertarian, Timothy unquestionably believes that "freedom will end...with the closing of a file drawer." Since trust is the foundation for privacy, he has ensured that the designs of his systems guard against the possibility of being used clandestinely for snooping or surveillance. He also works vigilantly to limit the erosion of privacy rights, both personal and community, and campaigns actively against politicians and local sheriffs who believe that personal dignities, such as privacy and free speech, are subordinate to government convenience.

Timothy lives with his wife and two young daughters in the deserts near Phoenix, Arizona. Until recently he designed government and commercial security systems for several major high-tech companies. In addition to enjoying the outdoors with his family and debating privacy issues with his homeowner's association, Timothy helps small nonprofit organizations handle their technology and privacy problems. He is also a founder and Co-Director of The `FundClass` (`http://www.fundraiser-software.com/fundclass.html`), a free on-line school that teaches the concepts of nonprofit fundraising to those who are new to the field.

**Jason Catlett** is President and founder of Junkbusters Corp. A computer scientist with a Ph.D. in data mining, Dr. Catlett is arguably the nation's leading expert on the interplay between technology, marketing, and privacy.

Dr. Catlett is frequently quoted in major newspapers, magazines, and trade journals. He has appeared on *60 Minutes* and many times on leading national television networks including MSNBC, C-SPAN, Fox, and CNN. He has testified on privacy issues before the U.S. Senate, the House of Representatives, Federal Trade Commission, the Department of Commerce, and the National Governors' Association. He is a frequent speaker at international conferences.

Dr. Catlett's Ph.D. was in Computer Science, which he taught for several years at the University of Sydney, including courses on technology and privacy. In 1992 he moved to AT&T Bell Laboratories in Murray Hill, NJ, where he continued work on "data mining" of large databases. He has served as an external examiner of Ph.D. candidates at Rutgers University, on the Editorial Board of the journal Machine Learning, and as a visiting scholar at the department of Computer Science at Columbia University. In addition to many academic publications, he has also contributed articles to trades such as *Privacy Journal* and the direct marketing trade newspaper *DM News*. And yes, he still gets annoyed by the occasional telemarketing call. He also enjoys face-to-face discussion at conferences; a list of his upcoming speaking appearances is available at http://www.junkbusters.com/forum.html. He welcomes your (non-bulk) e-mail at catlett@junkbusters.com.

*Jason Catlett*

**Emilio (Milo) W. Cividanes** is a partner in the Electronic Commerce and Privacy practice group of the Washington, D.C. office of Piper Marbury Rudnick & Wolfe, LLP Mr. Cividanes has long been involved with issues of personal privacy, dating back to his tenure as counsel to the Technology and the Law Subcommittee of the U.S. Senate Judiciary Committee in 1987-88. Mr. Cividanes was educated at University of Pennsylvania Law School (J.D., 1983, Comment Editor of the Law Review) and at Haverford College (B.A., 1979).

Mr. Cividanes has lectured in the United States and abroad on privacy, computer law, and related issues. He also co-authored the chapter on privacy in *Internet and Online Law* (Law Journal Press). Mr. Cividanes serves as an adjunct professor at Georgetown University Law Center and as a member of the faculty of the U.S. Court of Appeals for the District of Columbia Circuit's annual program on appellate advocacy.

Mr. Cividanes has represented clients in the principal federal privacy rulemaking proceedings of recent years, including the proceedings pertaining to the Children's Online Privacy Protection Act (COPPA), the financial privacy provisions of the Gramm-Leach-Bliley Act, the Department of Health and Human Services's health privacy rules, and the Department of Commerce's (DOC) Safe Harbor Program for compliance with the European Union's Data Protection Directive.

Mr. Cividanes lobbies on privacy matters in the U.S. Congress and advises clients on the development of privacy policies and on compliance with existing privacy laws and self-regulatory programs. For example, he helped draft the compliance questionnaire for the BBB*OnLine* Privacy Seal Program of the Council of Better Business Bureaus and the Direct Marketing Association's self-regulatory guidelines governing the use of health information. In addition, he advised the country's major entertainment companies on compliance with COPPA. He also has advised clients on compliance with the DOC Safe Harbor program.

In addition, Mr. Cividanes litigates privacy cases, and has been part of the legal teams that represented GeoCities in the first Internet privacy enforcement case brought by the Federal Trade Commission, challenged the GLBA privacy regulations in federal court, and defended Time Warner Cable in several class action suits filed under the subscriber privacy provisions of the Cable Act.

**Judi Clark**, a NetAction Advisory Board Member, has been riding the curl of the Internet wave for more than 12 years. During that time, she has explained, instructed, illustrated, documented, written copy, set context, and provided perspectives for a wide variety of businesses, schools, and clients. Ms. Clark's essay for NetAction forms the basis of Chapter 6, "Broadband: Always On, Always Connected, Always Exposed," which we use with NetAction's permission.

**Cindy Cohn** is the Legal Director for the Electronic Frontier Foundation. Ms. Cohn first became involved with the EFF more than 6 years ago, when the EFF asked her to serve as the lead attorney in Bernstein versus the Department of Justice, the successful federal court challenge to the U.S. export restrictions on cryptography. That case was the first to rule that source code was protected expression and subject to protection under the First Amendment. The case was one of the major catalysts for decision by the U.S. government in January, 2000, to dramatically loosen its restrictions on the export of encryption software.

As Legal Director, Ms. Cohn is responsible for overseeing the EFF's overall legal strategy. Currently, that includes defending the rights of anonymous online speakers, the rights of those subjected to broad subpoenas and court orders concerning online speech, and the challenge to the First

Amendment presented by recent changes in intellectual property law. This includes barriers to scientific research fair use and reverse engineering of digital media such as DVDs and electronically distributed music.

Ms. Cohn is a graduate of the University of Michigan Law School. She did her undergraduate studies at the University of Iowa and the London School of Economics. For 10 years prior to joining the EFF, she was a civil litigator in private practice handling Internet-related cases, including domain name disputes, suits arising from unsolicited commercial e-mail (also known as SPAM), and challenges to government efforts to gather information from Internet Service Providers about their customers. Before starting private practice, she worked for a year at the United Nations Centre for Human Rights in Geneva Switzerland. In 1997, as a result of her work on the Bernstein case, Ms. Cohn was named as one of the "Lawyers of the Year" by California Lawyer magazine.

*Cindy Cohn*

**Carl Ellison** enjoys variety in professional life. He was a pioneer of ARPA network work (as budding network architect and then chief of system programming at Utah-10 when it became node #4 on the ARPANet). Mr. Ellison has been a researcher in many areas: digital signal processing, time sharing scheduling, real-time systems, data flow hardware and software, real-time 3D computer graphics hardware and software, fault tolerant system architecture, and computer security. Most recently, he is associated with the SPKI effort (http://world.std.com/~cme/html/spki.html). At present, Carl is a Senior Security Architect with Intel Corporation.

Mr. Ellison was one of many voices engaged against the government in the days of the Clipper chip, as a pre-publication reviewer of Dorothy Denning's ACM article in late 1992 that presaged the Clipper and Carnivore projects and as a vocal opponent of Clipper when it was announced in 1993. Carl coined the term GAK (Government Access to Keys) to counteract the spread of euphemisms such as Key Escrow that tried to make an unacceptable intrusion palatable.

Mr. Ellison has been preaching since about 1991 that public keys are perfectly good identifiers, and needn't be bound to names (or, worse, national ID numbers) to be effective. It is only in the last few years that a darker side of that practice has received his attention: that if public keys are good identifiers, we don't need to bind them to names. That binding would permit unprecedented invasions of privacy by data aggregation. Any authentication method permits that aggregation, if we use it in too many places. On the other hand, authentication is costly to establish and sometimes we need to offer aggregated data to get some desired access. Needless to say, this area does not admit to simple solutions.

*Carl Ellison*

**Angela Gunn** is ethics columnist for *Yahoo! Internet Life* and a regularly published writer on technology, politics, and culture. At the start of the commercial Internet boom she co-founded two publications, Web Week and ZD (later Yahoo!) Internet Life; she has since made a full recovery. A native of Nebraska, she currently divides her time between New York and Seattle and her attention between an upcoming book on writers' habits and the Cosmic Baseball Association (www.cosmicbaseball.com). An irregularly updated collection of her writings is available at www.agunn.com.

**Molly Ivins** is a nationally syndicated political columnist, who remains cheerful despite Texas politics. She emphasizes the more hilarious aspects of both state and national government, and consequently never has to write fiction.

Ms. Ivins is from Houston, Texas. She graduated from Smith College in 1966, and then from Columbia University's School of Journalism and studied for a year at the Institute of Political Sciences in Paris.

Her first newspaper job was as the Complaint Department of the *Houston Chronicle*. She rapidly worked her way up to the position of sewer editor, where she wrote a number of gripping articles about street closings. She went on to the *Minneapolis Tribune* and was the first woman police reporter in that city. In the late 1960's, she was assigned to a beat called "Movements for Social Change," covering angry blacks, radical students, uppity women, and a motley assortment of other misfits and trouble-makers.

Ms. Ivins returned to Texas as co-editor of the Texas Observer, a sprightly, muckraking publication devoted to coverage of Texas politics and social issues. She roamed the state in search of truth, justice, and good stories. In 1976, Ms. Ivins joined the New York Times, first as a political reporter in New York City and Albany: she was later named Rocky Mountain Bureau Chief, chiefly because there was no one else in the bureau. For three years she covered nine mountain states by herself and was often tired.

In 1982, she returned to Texas as a columnist for the late Dallas Times-Herald, and after its lamented demise, spent the next nine years with the Fort Worth Star-Telegram. She became an independent journalist in 2001 and also in that year won the William Allen White Award from the University of Kansas, the Smith Medal from Smith College, and was elected to the National Academy of Arts and Sciences.

Her freelance work has appeared in Esquire, Harper's, Atlantic, the Nation, and many less-worthy publications when she desperately needed the money; the most memorable was something called *Playgirl*. She is also known for her essays on the Lehrer News Hour and National Public Radio, as well as four best-selling books, the most recent being, "SHRUB; the Short But Happy Political Life of George W. Bush."

Ms. Ivins is active in the journalism network of Amnesty International and supports the Reporters Committee for Freedom of the Press, the

American Civil Liberties Union, and often writes about First Amendment issues. She donates a speech every month to the First Amendment.

She became one of the world's leading authorities on George W. Bush entirely by accident. She has known him since they were in high school and as Sir Edmond Hillary said of Mount Everest—he was there. Bush is a *lot* less interesting than Everest, however. She counts as her highest honors that the Minneapolis police force named its mascot pig after her and that she was once banned from the campus of Texas A&M.

*Molly Ivins*

**Tess Koleczek** was a pioneer in Internet privacy as the data protection specialist at Netscape Communications Corporation, where she developed, implemented, and maintained Netscape's privacy policy and Web site compliance practices. She also performed a public policy role at trade associations such as USCIB and the Online Privacy Alliance representing Internet industry concerns on privacy and data protection relative to the U.S. Government requests for industry self-regulation and the EU Directive on Transborder Data Flows. She was also on the Board of Advisors for TRUSTe in Cupertino, CA.

As an associate attorney at Gray Cary Ware & Freidenrich in Palo Alto, CA, as private privacy consultant, and in her role with Zero-Knowledge Systems, a Montreal technology solutions developer, Ms. Koleczek has worked extensively for a variety e-commerce, network infrastructure, and wireless/telecommunications clients on the development of corporate policies and integrating privacy-related legislation, regulations, and practices across engineering, marketing, and business development departments.

Ms. Koleczek has a B.A. in Political Science from the College of St. Catherine in St. Paul, MN and a J.D. in Intellectual Property from Franklin Pierce Law Center in Concord, NH. She is also a frequent author and speaker on Cyber Rights.

**Chuck Marson** is a California lawyer who practiced and sometimes lobbied for 30 years. These days he writes, speaks, and consults about privacy, the Internet, politics, and government.

Mr. Marson has been outside counsel for Netscape Communications Corporation, Director of the California Internet Industry Alliance, a member of the Public Policy Committee of the Interactive Services Association, a partner in a Montgomery Street law firm, a Stanford Law professor, and an ACLU lawyer.

He lives and works in San Francisco.

**Declan McCullagh** is the Washington bureau chief for Wired News. He lives and works in Washington DC. An award-winning journalist, Mr. McCullagh writes and speaks frequently about technology and politics. Before taking his current job, he has been a reporter for Time Digital Daily, The Netly News, and Time Magazine, as well as a correspondent for HotWired.

He has written the *washington dot com* column for George magazine, a technology column for UPI, a column for Business 2.0 magazine, and occasionally contributes to publications such as Slate, The New Republic, and the Wall Street Journal. He's written for everything from Playboy magazine to Communications of the ACM.

Mr. McCullagh has been writing about the Internet since 1990. He was the first Internet reporter to join the National Press Club; he participated in the first White House dot com press pool; and was one of the first online reporters to receive credentials from the press gallery of the U.S. Congress.

He also wrote the first article to report that in the 2000 U.S. presidential election, the race had suddenly changed from a seemingly certain George W. Bush win to a tossup with a margin of as little as a few hundred votes. CNET radio says Mr. McCullagh "might go down in history as having some of the first accurate reports that Bush's lead had dwindled." He was also the first journalist to question former Vice President Gore's claim to have created the Internet and broke the story that U.S. District Judge Thomas Jackson ruled that Microsoft violated antitrust laws.

Mr. McCullagh moderates Politech, a well-known mailing list looking broadly at politics and technology that he founded in 1994. He has been a visiting faculty member at George Mason University's Institute for Humane Studies and is a founding editor of cluebot.com, a technology and politics news site. He was also the first journalist to be sent a sub-poena for linking to information (in an article) that was allegedly illegal to distribute, and intervened in the landmark DVD/DeCSS lawsuit asking the court to open proceedings to reporters.

He currently amuses himself with analog photography (including the self-portrait below). His photographs have appeared in the programs or publications of the Australian Broadcasting Corporation, the Canadian Broadcasting Corporation, Silicon Alley Reporter, Premiere magazine, and Ziff Davis' Interactive Week. In addition to tinkering with his classic NeXT cube at home, Mr. McCullagh programs in C and Perl, and maintains a Linux server that supports about seven Web sites, some with a MySQL backend. The mccullagh.org photo database is his own design. You can reach him at declan@well.com and his Web site is at http://www.mccullagh.org.

*Declan McCullagh*

**Ron Plesser** is a graduate of George Washington University with a degree in English Literature and Law. In 1972, Mr. Plesser joined the Center for Study of Responsive Law and was primarily responsible for litigation and legislative activities concerning the Freedom of Information Act. In 1975, Mr. Plesser served as General Counsel to the U.S. Privacy Protection

Study Commission. Currently he is a partner with the law firm of Piper Marbury Rudnick & Wolfe, LLP in Washington, D.C. Mr. Plesser is past-Chair of the Individual Rights and Responsibilities Section of the American Bar Association. He has been an adjunct professor of law at George Washington University (1982-1986). He also was Deputy Director of the Science, Space, and Technology Cluster of the 1992 Clinton-Gore Transition.

Mr. Plesser specializes in issues that concern international communications, Internet law, legislative matters, telecommunications, privacy, data base companies, publishers, information and software providers and users, marketers, and other companies affected by the emergence of new information technologies. This includes matters of wireless and terrestrial communications issues. His clients include trade associations and individual companies represented before the United States Congress, federal agencies, and all federal and state courts. Mr. Plesser has also represented clients in world regulatory organizations.

*Ron Plesser*

**Jerzy Rub** has a real job at Intel where he leads a team that sometimes aids in setting up and running secure systems and at other times hacking those systems to see just how vulnerable they are. In his past he worked with some three-letter organizations and discovered that working in information security is both challenging and fun, and that privacy depends on security. Mr. Rub is a graduate of the University of Michigan and has CISSP certification. He lives with his wife, cat, and various water creatures that visit their pond near Portland, OR.

**John Stracke** has been using the Internet since 1990, and writing Internet software since 1993. He is currently Chief Scientist of eCal

Corp., a Philadelphia-based maker of event-driven collaborative infrastructure. He likes the usability of Macs, but prefers Linux for its stability and general geekly power.

**Ross Stapleton-Gray**, Ph.D., is a technology and policy consultant, and co-founder of Sandstorm Enterprises, a security software company headquartered in Boston, MA. He was formerly an intelligence analyst and planning officer with the Central Intelligence Agency and Intelligence Community Management Staff. You can reach Ross at amicus@well.com

**Brad Templeton** was founder and publisher at ClariNet Communications Corp., the #1 internet-based electronic newspaper publisher, until selling it to Newsedge Corporation in 1997. ClariNet gathers information from a variety of sources including major newswires such as UPI and the AP and edits it into a constantly updated package that is sent to subscriber's computers over the Internet, to be read on their own machines. He has been active in the computer network community since 1979, participated in the building and growth of USENET from its earliest days—including being one of the first to set up an international link—and in 1987 he founded and edited a special USENET conference devoted to comedy. This newsgroup, named "rec.humor.funny" became the most widely read computerized conference in the world, demonstrating the popularity and marketability of edited information. It now also exists on the Web at www.netfunny.com.

Mr. Templeton was the first employee of Personal Software/Visicorp, the first major microcomputer applications software company. He is also the author of a dozen packaged microcomputer software products, including VisiPlot for the IBM-PC, the compressor in Stuffit—the world's most widely used Macintosh application, various games, popular tools and utilities for Commodore computers, special Pascal and Basic programming environments (ALICE) designed for education, an add-in spreadsheet compiler (3-2-1 Blastoff) for Lotus 1-2-3 (picked by PC World as one of the top software products of 1987), and various network related software tools.

In 1993, Mr. Templeton also published a CD-ROM containing the largest anthology of current fiction made to date. ClariNet's experiment in electronic books gathered all the material nominated for Science Fiction's top awards in one place, in time for award voters to use it as a resource. Via ClariNet, he was a plaintiff in the case to get the U.S. Communications

Decency Act successfully overturned in the Supreme Court. He also serves on the board of the directors of the Electronic Frontier Foundation, the leading civil rights advocacy group for cyberspace. He currently is on the advisory boards of Topica, Inc. and Troba, two Internet startups. He is chairman of the board of directors of the Electronic Frontier Foundation and a longtime writer on cyberspace issues.

Mr. Templeton also does fine-art panoramic landscape photography.

He was born in 1960, grew up near Toronto and now lives in Silicon Valley in California. He holds a Bachelor of Mathematics degree from the University of Waterloo. More information can be found at `www.templetons.com/brad/`.

*Brad Templeton*

**Ed Vielmetti** is the founder of The Vacuum Group, a loose-knit collection of people all over the world who share a common interest in the intersection of social and computer networks. Mr. Vielmetti has been contributing to the development of the Internet since 1985, working in companies ranging from the tiniest basement-based unfounded startup to networking giant Cisco Systems. He is a graduate of the University of Michigan and lives in Ann Arbor, MI.

**Elton Wildermuth** (also called Nitnorth) is a curmudgeon-in-training who wants to be either H. L. Mencken or Dorothy Parker when he grows up. If he grows up. He's also a pathological defender of people's inalienable right to be who they are, even if it offends their neighbors or their government, and agrees with Robert Anton Wilson that government's primary job should be to tell people to stay out of other people's business. Oh, and when he's not busy pontificating, he runs a rock band. You can find many more of his opinions on nearly everything at http://www.nuit.org, the band's Web site.

# PRIVACY-RELATED WEB SITES

This is a list of a few sites that are worth visiting again and again. These pages are well-made or "centrally located" (in the topical sense) and therefore are usually current and always inform-ative on digital privacy.

## Personal Web Sites

The following Web sites are maintained by indi-viduals.

## Phil Agre

http://dlis.gseis.ucla.edu/people/pagre/

Phil Agre is a communications instructor at UCLA, and a prominent writer on privacy. The site provides links to his important publications. You may, in particular, want to investigate the links referring to the book he edited with Marc Rotenberg from EPIC: *Technology and Privacy: the new landscape.* He also includes links to his writings on effective action on the Internet and annotated syllabi and notes from his classes.

## Peter Swire

http://www.osu.edu/units/law/swire1/pspriv.htm

Peter Swire is a law professor at Ohio State University and the person charged with the privacy watch during the Clinton Administration. Besides the official archives of his work, he maintains this personal page concerning online privacy.

His site contains papers and presentations on various privacy legislation and regulation, including Safe Harbor, Financial Privacy, and legal analysis which will be helpful for businesses.

# Organizational Sites

The following Web sites are maintained by privacy organizations.

## The Federal Trade Commission Privacy Site

http://www.ftc.gov/privacy/

This site has latest word on what the commission is doing to protect individual privacy online. You alos find a linkto a special KIDZ Privacy site which the FTC provides for families to better understand privacy. (http://www.ftc.gov/bcp/conline/edcams/kidzprivacy/index.html).

## BBBOnline

http://www.bbbonline.org

BBBOnLine's mission is to promote trust and confidence on the Internet through the BBBOnLine Reliability and BBBOnLine Privacy programs. BBBOnline is a seal program, and this site provides the online filing of complaints about seal holders. There are also many tips for consumers about safe online shopping.

## The Center for Democracy and Technology (CDT)

http://www.cdt.org/privacy

This site includes an issues overview, a resource library, a comprehensive privacy guide, legislative proposals, analysis of privacy surveys, and an extensive section on reading and writing privacy policies.

# Cyber Angels

http://www.cyberangels.com

This is an all-volunteer organization that helps combat child pornography, cyberstalking, and other crimes, particularly crimes related to children. The site also enables the reporting of cyber crimes.

# The Electronic Frontier Foundation (EFF)

http://www.eff.org/privnow

This site is home to the Privacy Now! Campaign and reports extensively on digital privacy and news about potential and perceived threats to civil liberties. You can also sign up for their alerts newsletter.

# The Electronic Privacy Information Center (EPIC)

http://www.epic.org

The Electronic Privacy Information Center is the policy arm formed from the Computer Professionals for Social Responsibility Group. This site includes EPIC's extensive testimony in Congress on privacy matters, the Privacy Law sourcebook, and the Privacy and Human Rights assessment documents.

# Junkbusters

http://www.junkbusters.com

This site has the current and good information about blocking spam as well as the latest news about digital privacy. The easy to use financial privacy opt-out letters may be a great help to you.

# The Privacy Foundation

http://www.privacyfoundation.org

The Privacy Foundation is the source of advisories and reports and programs like Bugnosis that can help you use technology to protect yourself from technology. Look for Richard Smith's Tipsheets.

## Privacy Rights Clearinghouse

http://www.privacyrights.org

This site has the best collection of material on Identity Theft that you find anywhere. Additionally, the clearinghouse has sample letters and an extensive set of Fact Sheets (which we certainly reviewed in writing this book). The site is particularly informative about California consumer law.

## TRUSTe

http://www.truste.org

Visit this seal program's site to report a violation of your privacy by a TRUSTe seal holder. You can also read the summary reports of the organization, to see what kinds of complaints are filed and how they are handled.

## SafeKids

http://www.safekids.com/

Columnist Larry Magid provides this site . SafeKids provides guidelines for both kids and parents and a Family Contract for Online Safety. Take the quiz and find out how you do.

# Technology Sites

The following Web sites are useful for keeping up with computer technology news and trends.

## CNET

http://cnet.search.com

A privacy word search at this site makes this a good place to track new privacy technologies. See in particular "How to protect online privacy" at http://home.cnet.com/internet/0-3761-7-2426162.html.

## ZDNET

http://www.zdnet.com

At this site you find links to products for sale, products for download in addition to reviews, and news articles.

# Index

# Q-R